The Classic 1000 Pasta and Rice Recipes

Carolyn Humphries

foulsham
LONDON • NEW YORK • TORONTO • SYDNEY

foulsham

The Publishing House
Bennetts Close, Cippenham, Berks SL1 5AP

ISBN 0-572-02300-6

Printed by Creative Print & Design Wales, Ebbw Vale

C O N T E N T S

Everyday Eating made more exciting

		QUANTITY	AMOUNT
New Classic 1000 Recipes	0-572-02575-0	£5.99	
Classic 1000 Chinese	0-572-02849-0	£6.99	
Classic 1000 Indian	0-572-02807-5	£6.99	
Classic 1000 Italian	0-572-02848-2	£6.99	
Classic 1000 Pasta & Rice	0-572-02300-6	£5.99	
Classic 1000 Vegetarian	0-572-02808-3	£6.99	
Classic 1000 Quick and Easy	0-572-02330-8	£5.99	
Classic 1000 Cake & Bake	0-572-02803-2	£6.99	
Classic 1000 Calorie-counted Recipes	0-572-02405-3	£5.99	
Classic 1000 Microwave Recipes	0-572-01945-9	£5.99	
Classic 1000 Dessert Recipes	0-572-02542-4	£5.99	
Classic 1000 Low-Fat Recipes	0-572-02804-0	£6.99	
Classic 1000 Chicken Recipes	0-572-02646-3	£5.99	
Classic 1000 Seafood Recipes	0-572-02696-X	£6.99	
Classic 1000 Beginners' Recipes	0-572-02734-6	£5.99	

*Please allow 75p per book for post & packing in UK
Overseas customers £1 per book.*

*POST & PACKING

TOTAL

Foulsham books are available from local bookshops. Should you have any difficulty obtaining supplies please send Cheque/Eurocheque/Postal Order (£ sterling only) made out to BSBP or debit my credit card:

☐ ACCESS   ☐ VISA   ☐ MASTER CARD   ☐☐☐☐☐☐☐☐☐☐☐☐☐☐☐☐

EXPIRY DATE   SIGNATURE

ALL ORDERS TO:
Foulsham Books, PO Box 29, Douglas, Isle of Man IM99 1BQ
Telephone 01624 836000, Fax 01624 837033, Internet http://www.bookpost.co.uk

NAME

ADDRESS

Please allow 28 days for delivery.
Please tick box if you do not wish to receive any additional information ☐
Prices and availability subject to change without notice.

Introduction

With the cost of potatoes soaring, we are increasingly turning to pasta and rice as our staple foods. They are the perfect vehicles for a multitude of taste-tingling dishes from every corner of the globe – from simple soups and starters to incredible creations of exotic seafood and vegetables, from meaty main courses to delectable desserts, and a vast array of breads and cakes.

This book is full of tantalising ideas from all over the world. There are also tips on the different types of pasta and rice and the best ways to cook them and even a chapter on using up the left-overs.

With *The Classic 1000 Pasta and Rice Dishes* to hand, you'll be able to create authentic classic specialities and many exciting new dishes quickly and easily.

Pasta Fact File

Varieties

There are over six hundred different pasta shapes made in Italy alone, in a variety of colours and flavours: the standard pale creamy-coloured durum wheat; the more golden egg pasta; the popular green spinach; the rustic wholewheat; the glorious orangey sun-dried tomato; the black mushroom; the speckled olive-flavoured; and many more. Then there is the exciting variety of noodles from the Far East and the flat noodles of German-speaking countries. It would be impossible to list every one in this book, but here are some you are most likely to use:

Strands – long threads of pasta in different thicknesses:
Capelli d'angelo or *Capellini:* 'angel hair'- the thinnest of all
Fusilli: 'fuses'- thick spiral spaghetti (also available in short pieces)
Spaghetti: probably the best known of all pastas. It is long, thin and straight
Spaghettini: 'little spaghetti' – a thinner version of spaghetti
Vermicelli: 'little worms' – thin spaghetti often sold in round bundles

Tubes – these are some of the most common of the many shapes and sizes of tubes:
Bucatini: long macaroni, like spaghetti but thicker and hollow
Cannelloni: short fat tubes, for stuffing
Ditali: short-cut macaroni
Penne: quill-shaped tubes
Rigatoni: ribbed tubes
Tubetti: short elbow-shaped macaroni
Zite: wide short-cut macaroni

Shapes – there is a superb variety of shapes to choose from, including:
Conchiglie: conch-shaped shells
Farfalle: 'butterflies'

Lumachi: snail-shaped shells
Maltagliati: 'badly cut' pasta. Make from fresh pasta (page 8)
Maruzze: shells of varying sizes
Rotelli or *spiralli:* spirals
Ruote: 'wheels'
Twistetti: twists

Ribbon Noodles – flat pasta cut into varying widths, sometimes with a rippled edge:
Fettuccine: flat ribbons about 5 mm/$^1/_4$ in wide
Fettuccelli: narrow fettuccine
Fettucci: flat ribbons about 1 cm/$^1/_2$ in wide
Linguini: very narrow ribbons, like flattened spaghetti
Mafalde: wide ribbons with a rippled edge
Pappardelle: wide ribbons about 2 cm/$^3/_4$ in wide
Tagliatelle: similar to fettuccine but slightly wider
Tagliarini: narrow tagliatelle

Stuffed Shapes and Dumplings
Agnolotti: small, filled half-moons
Cappelletti: 'little hats'

Gnocchi: Italian dumplings made with flour, semolina or potato
Ravioli: stuffed cushions
Tortellini: small crescent shapes with joined ends
Dim sum: bite-sized Chinese dumplings
Noque: pasta dumplings from the Alsace. Further south they are known as *nockerln*
Wontons: the oriental equivalent to ravioli but with lighter dough

Chinese Noodles

Egg noodles: wiggly strands in various thicknesses, sold in square-shaped nests
Wheat noodles: sold in square-shaped nests or as long spaghetti-like strands
Rice noodles or sticks: white strands
Rice vermicelli: very thin white threads
Arrowroot vermicelli: sold in pure white bundles
Cellophane or pea starch noodles: transparent thin strands
Chow mein noodles: yellow fried noodles

Japanese Noodles

Harusame: like cellophane noodles
Soba: thin brownish noodles made with buckwheat flour
Somen: fine white noodles, like vermicelli
Udon: more filling wheat flour noodles

9

Quick Fresh Pasta

You can mix the dough by hand, working the flour into the eggs then kneading until smooth, but it takes longer!

Serves 4

3 eggs
275 g/10 oz/2 1/2 cups strong (bread)
  flour
Flour for dusting

Break the eggs into a food processor and run the machine for 30 seconds. Add the flour and blend for a further 30 seconds or until the mixture forms a soft but not sticky dough. Turn out on to a floured board and knead until the dough is smooth and elastic, adding a little more flour if it becomes sticky. Wrap in a polythene bag and allow to rest for 30 minutes. On a large floured surface roll out and stretch the dough, rolling away from you and giving the dough a quarter turn every so often until it is almost thin enough to see through. For shapes, cut now (see below); for tagliatelle, cover with a cloth and leave for 15 minutes before cutting.

To Shape

Cannelloni and **Lasagne:** cut the rolled dough into oblongs 10 ×· 12.5 cm/4 × 5 in. Boil in lightly salted water for 1 minute then place in a bowl of cold water with 5 ml/1 tsp of oil added. Drain on a damp cloth when ready to use.

Farfalle: cut the rolled dough into 5 cm/2 in squares with a fluted pastry wheel. Pinch the squares together diagonally across the middle to form butterflies or bows.

Maltagliati: cut the rolled dough into small triangles about the size of a thumb nail. Used mainly in soups.

Pappardelle: cut the rolled dough with a plain or fluted cutter into strips 2 cm/³/₄ in wide.

Ravioli: cut the dough in half and roll out each half to a similar sized square or rectangle. Put teaspoonfuls of the chosen filling at regular intervals in rows across one sheet of the dough. Brush all round and between the filling with water. Lay the second sheet on top and press down gently between each pile of filling. Use a fluted pastry wheel to cut between the filling down the length and then across the width to form little cushions of filled pasta.

Tagliatelle: roll up the rested sheet of pasta like a Swiss (jelly) roll. Cut into slices about 5 mm/¹/₄ in thick. Unroll and drape on a clean cloth over the back of a chair (or a clothes-horse) while you cut the rest.

Note: If you are a pasta fanatic, you could buy a pasta machine to roll and cut the dough into professional-looking shapes. The best ones, in my opinion, are chrome-plated with stainless steel rollers.

To Cook

Allow 100 g/4 oz/1 cup of pasta per person. Bring a large pan of lightly salted water to the boil. Add 15 ml/1 tbsp of olive oil or a knob of butter and the pasta and cook for about 4 minutes until *al dente* – just tender but not soggy. Drain and use as required.

To Microwave

For 4 people, put 225 g/8 oz/2 cups of pasta (break spaghetti types into thirds for even cooking) into a large microwave-safe bowl. Add 600 ml/1 pt/2¹/₂ cups of boiling water, 5 ml/1 tsp of salt and 10 ml/2 tsp of olive oil. Cook uncovered for 6-7¹/₂ minutes on full power, stirring gently four times. Cover and leave to stand for 5 minutes until the pasta swells and absorbs most of the water. Drain and use as required.

Note: The times given are for a 650 watt

oven; reduce slightly for a higher output oven, increase for a lower one.

Dried Pasta

To Cook

Follow the packet directions, allowing 50-100 g/2-4 oz of pasta per person, according to appetites. Add 15 ml/1 tbsp of olive oil or butter to the boiling water to prevent it boiling over.

To Microwave

For 4 people, put 225 g/8 oz/2 cups of pasta (break spaghetti types into thirds for even cooking) into a large microwave-safe bowl. Add 900 ml/1½ pts/3¾ cups of boiling water, 5 ml/1 tsp of salt and 10 ml/2 tsp of olive oil. Cook uncovered for 12-15 minutes on full power, stirring gently four times. Cover and leave to stand for 6-8 minutes until the pasta swells and absorbs most of the water. Drain and use as required.

Note: The times given are for a 650 watt oven; reduce slightly for a higher output oven, increase for a lower one.

Rice Fact File

Rice is the staple food of over a third of the world's population. There are many varieties, with different flavours and cooking properties, so it is important to use the right sort of rice for the type of dish you are cooking. As a rough guide, for savoury dishes, allow 25 g/1 oz/2 tbsp of uncooked brown rice per portion and up to 50 g /2 oz/¹/₄ cup of uncooked other varietes per portion. For puddings, see individual recipes.

Brown rice: this is available in short-, medium- and long-grain varieties. It is brown because it has not been polished to remove the outer bran. All rice is good for you but brown rice is higher in B vitamins and fibre than white varieties. It also takes longer to cook and benefits from being soaked first. The long and medium grains can be used as a vegetable or as a basis for pilaf or salad. Short grains make excellent, nutty-textured puddings.
To cook: allow only 25-40 g/1-1¹/₂ oz/2-3 tbsp of uncooked long- or medium-grain brown rice per portion. Boil in plenty of salted water for 40-45 minutes until just tender. Drain well. The texture will be chewier than that of white rice and it is more filling. For puddings, see individual recipes.

Patna (long-grain) rice: the long milky-white grains when cooked properly should remain fluffy and separate with a slight resistance when squeezed between the thumb and forefinger. Ideal as a vegetable, for pilaf, salad, stuffings and all 'dry' rice dishes.
To cook: boil in plenty of salted water for 10-15 minutes or according to the packet directions. Drain, rinse with boiling water and drain again. Or cook as for basmati rice.

American long-grain rice: milky-white thin grains, four or five times longer than they are wide. Of consistent quality, use for any savoury dishes.
To cook: as for patna rice.

Easy-cook rice: also known as 'pre-fluffed' or par-boiled rice. Usually American varieties of white or brown rice, the long grains have been steam-treated which helps retain the nutrients and hardens the grains so they are less likely to overcook.
To cook: follow packet directions.

Basmati rice: greyish in colour, basmati has an excellent flavour and texture for all savoury dishes. It is used extensively in Indian cookery. It should be picked over to remove any bits of husk and grit then rinsed well under running water to remove excess starch before cooking.
To cook: Put 1 part rice to 3 parts cold water with a little salt added in a pan with a tight-fitting lid. Bring to the boil. Turn down the heat as low as possible. Cover (use foil under the lid if it isn't very tight-fitting) and leave for 12-15 minutes. Uncover and fluff up with a fork.

Thai fragrant rice: another rice with a wonderful flavour and texture. Whiter than basmati, it is served plain boiled at the cen-

mati, then cook as for patna rice. (It can be cooked as for basmati but, if the rice is fairly old and dry, it will need more water. Follow directions on the packet.)

Carolina rice: Bright, shiny-white, angular long-grain variety. Good for all savoury dishes.
To cook: as for patna rice, but it may take a few minutes longer as the grains are harder.

Java rice: long, flat, almost transparent grains. Suitable for all savoury dishes.
To cook: as for patna rice but cook for up to 20 minutes.

Italian (risotto) rice: Arborio and Piedmontese are probably the most common. Its short, round grains can absorb a great deal of liquid over a fairly long period without becoming too soft. This produces the grainy but 'creamy' result expected of good risottos, paellas and jambalayas. Its flavour also sets it apart from other short-grain varieties.
To cook: see individual recipes.

Short-grain (pudding) rice: short, fat grains with a chalky-white colour. The grains are softer than long-grain varieties so swell and stick together as they cook.

Spanish bomba rice: hard, round grains – the ultimate for paella because the grains remain more separate than risotto rice when cooked.
To cook: as for risotto rice.

Wild rice: the grains range from dark brown to black. Wild rice is actually an aquatic grass related to the rice family. It has a distinctive nutty flavour and is more expensive than rice. You can now buy it as a long-grain and wild rice mix, which makes an ideal accompaniment to many dishes and excellent for stuffings.
To cook: bring to the boil in salted water. Drain, then simmer in just enough boiling water to cover for about 30 minutes or until just beginning to split.

Ground rice: ground from polished grains of rice. It can be cooked with milk and flavourings for a smooth dessert or added to biscuits to improve their texture.

Flaked rice: usually cooked in milk and sugar or honey for a pudding.

Rice flour: white or brown rice ground to a fine powder. It can be used as a thickener or binder instead of flour. Particularly useful for sauces to be frozen as it does not separate on thawing.

Notes on the Recipes

- When following a recipe use either metric, imperial or American measures, never a combination.
- All spoon measures are level.
- All eggs are size 3 unless otherwise stated.
- Always wash, dry and peel, if necessary, fresh produce before using.
- Fresh herbs are used in the recipe unless dried are specified.
- All cooking times are approximate and should be used as a guide only.
- Every recipe suggests a suitable quantity of rice or pasta. In any dish that requires it being boiled in an unspecified amount of water, you can increase or decrease the quantity according to appetite. But if changing the quantity in a recipe with a specified amount of cooking liquid, such as a risotto, you must alter the liquid content too or it will not cook correctly.
- Many of the recipes do not contain meat or fish so are suitable for vegetarians. But make sure the cheese you use is also suitable; in supermarkets they are usually clearly marked.

Soups

The addition of rice or pasta to soups can often make them substantial enough for a main meal, perhaps served with a bowl of grated cheese to sprinkle over and hunks of warm crusty bread. They also add interesting texture and flavour and their starch content can help to thicken the liquid. If using rice or pasta for a garnish in clear soups, add it ready-cooked just before serving to prevent the mixture going cloudy.

Cypriot Fish Soup with Egg and Lemon

Serves 6

450 g/1 lb any inexpensive white fish fillet
Fish or chicken stock
2 onions, quartered
20 ml/4 tsp olive oil
6 courgettes (zucchini), chopped
6 carrots, chopped
4 celery sticks, chopped
½ bunch of parsley, chopped
Salt and freshly ground black pepper
Ground cinnamon
90 ml/6 tbsp long-grain rice
Juice of 2 small lemons
2 eggs

Place the fish in a pan with enough stock to just cover. Add the onions, bring to the boil, reduce the heat, cover and simmer until the fish is tender. Lift out the fish with a draining spoon. Add the olive oil, vegetables, parsley and a little salt, pepper and cinnamon to the stock. Simmer until the vegetables are tender. Purée the fish, vegetables and stock and return to the saucepan. Meanwhile, simmer the rice in twice its weight of chicken stock until tender. Add to the purée and heat through.

Beat the lemon juice and eggs together. Add a ladleful of soup to the egg mixture and whisk well. Pour this mixture back into the soup and stir. Do not allow to boil. Ladle into soup bowls and serve hot.

Avgolemono

Serves 6

900 ml/1½ pts/3¾ cups lamb or chicken stock, preferably fresh
50 g/2 oz/¼ cup long-grain rice
2 eggs
Juice of 1 lemon
15 ml/1 tbsp water
Salt and white pepper
Chopped parsley

Put the stock and rice in a pan. Bring to the boil, reduce the heat and simmer gently for 10-12 minutes until the rice is tender. Break the eggs into a bowl. Whisk in the lemon juice and water. Add a ladleful of the hot stock and whisk in. Whisk in a further 2 ladlefuls. Remove the stock from the heat. Stir the egg mixture into the pan. Season to taste. Serve straight away, garnished with the parsley.

Meatballs in Greek Broth

Serves 4

175 g/6 oz/1¹/₂ cups minced (ground) lamb
100 g/4 oz/¹/₂ cup long-grain rice
1 size 5 egg, beaten
10 ml/2 tsp chopped mint
Salt and freshly ground black pepper
A little plain (all-purpose) flour
1.2 litres/2 pts/5 cups chicken stock
2 eggs
Juice of 1 large lemon

Mix the meat with the rice, size 5 egg, mint and a little salt and pepper. Shape into small balls and roll in the flour. Bring the stock to the boil, drop in the meatballs and simmer gently for 15 minutes. Beat the eggs and lemon juice together in a large soup tureen. Gradually strain the chicken stock into the egg mixture, whisking all the time. Add the meatballs and serve straight away.

Rice Soup with Asparagus

Serves 4

1.5 litres/2¹/₂ pts/6 cups chicken stock
15g/¹/₂ oz/1 tbsp unsalted (sweet) butter
175 g/6 oz/³/₄ cup arborio or other risotto rice
8 asparagus spears, trimmed and chopped
Salt

Bring the stock and butter to the boil in a large saucepan. Add the rice and aspara-gus, reduce the heat and simmer over a moderate heat for 15-20 minutes or until the rice is just cooked but still has texture. Season with salt, if necessary, and serve straight away.

Italian Rice and Spinach Soup

Serves 4

275 g/10 oz/1 carton frozen chopped spinach, thawed
1.2 litres/2 pts/5 cups chicken or vegetable stock
15 g/¹/₂ oz/1 tbsp unsalted (sweet) butter
100 g/4 oz/¹/₂ cup arborio or other risotto rice
Salt and freshly ground black pepper
Freshly grated Parmesan cheese

Place the spinach in a pan with the stock and butter. Bring to the boil. Add the rice, reduce the heat and simmer for 15-20 minutes until the rice is just tender. Season to taste, ladle into soup bowls and serve with the Parmesan cheese.

Minted Rice and Pea Soup

Serves 4
1.2 litres/2 pts/5 cups chicken stock
25 g/1 oz/2 tbsp unsalted (sweet) butter
100 g/4 oz/¹/₂ cup arborio or other risotto rice
225 g/8 oz/2 cups petits pois
15 ml/1 tbsp plain (all-purpose) flour
Salt and freshly ground black pepper
15 ml/1 tbsp chopped fresh mint or 5 ml/1 tsp dried mint

Put the stock and half the butter in a large pan. Bring to the boil. Add the rice and peas and simmer gently for 15 minutes. Meanwhile, mash the remaining butter with the flour. Whisk a piece at a time into the bubbling soup until thickened. Season to taste and add the mint. Simmer for 5 minutes then serve.

Tomato and Basil Soup

Serves 4
3 beef tomatoes, skinned and chopped
1.2 litres/2 pts/5 cups chicken stock
10 ml/2 tsp tomato purée (paste)
15 g/¹/₂ oz/1 tbsp unsalted (sweet) butter
100 g/4 oz/¹/₂ cup arborio or other risotto rice
4 basil leaves, chopped
Salt and freshly ground black pepper

Put the tomatoes in a pan with the stock, tomato purée and butter. Bring to the boil. Add the rice, reduce the heat and simmer for 15-20 minutes until the rice is just tender but still has texture. Stir in the basil and season to taste. Serve straight away.

Italian Milk Rice Soup

Serves 4
1.5 litres/2¹/₂ pts/6 cups milk
100 g/4 oz/¹/₂ cup arborio or other risotto rice
15 g/¹/₂ oz/1 tbsp unsalted (sweet) butter
Salt

Bring the milk to the boil. Add the rice and simmer gently for 15-20 minutes until the rice is just tender. Stir in the butter and season with salt.

Tuscan Chicken Liver Soup

Serves 6
200 g/7 oz/1³/₄ cups chicken livers, trimmed and chopped
15 g/¹/₂ oz/1 tbsp unsalted (sweet) butter
1.75 litres/3 pts/7¹/₂ cups chicken stock
225 g/8 oz/1 cup arborio or other risotto rice
Salt and freshly ground black pepper
30 ml/2 tbsp chopped parsley
Freshly grated Parmesan cheese

Fry (sauté) the chicken livers in the butter for about 2-3 minutes until pink and almost firm. Put the stock in a large saucepan and bring to the boil. Add the rice, reduce the heat and simmer for 12 minutes. Add the chicken livers and their juice and continue to cook for 4 minutes. Season to taste and stir in the parsley. Ladle into soup bowls and sprinkle with the Parmesan cheese before serving.

Hot and Sour Soup with Rice

Serves 4

225 g/8 oz/4 cups button
  mushrooms, sliced
30 ml/2 tbsp soy sauce
10 ml/2 tsp chopped coriander
  (cilantro)
1 bunch of spring onions (scallions),
  chopped
100 g/4 oz/1 cup baby sweetcorn
  (corn), thinly sliced
75 ml/5 tbsp white wine vinegar
Salt and freshly ground black
  pepper
1.2 litres /2 pts/5 cups chicken stock
175 g/6 oz/ 1¹/₂ cups cooked chicken
  or turkey, shredded
50 g/2 oz/¹/₂ cup cooked long-grain
  rice

Place all the ingredients except the chicken or turkey and rice in a saucepan. Bring to the boil and simmer for 10 minutes. Add the meat and rice and simmer for a further 5 minutes. Serve hot.

Sherried Turkey and Rice Soup

Serves 4

1 turkey carcass
1.75 litres/3 pts/7¹/₂ cups water
1 bouquet garni sachet
2 onions
2 whole cloves
1 carrot, chopped
50 g/2 oz/¹/₄ cup long-grain rice
Few drops of gravy browning
15 ml/1 tbsp cornflour (cornstarch)
45 ml/3 tbsp medium dry sherry
Salt and freshly ground black pepper

Pick any meat off the carcass, finely chop and reserve. Break up the carcass and place in a large saucepan with the water and bouquet garni sachet. Stud the onions with the cloves and add to the pan with the carrot. Bring to the boil, skim the surface, reduce the heat, cover and simmer gently for 2 hours (or cook in a pressure cooker for 40 minutes with just enough water to cover the bones). Strain and return the stock to the rinsed-out saucepan. Add the rice and chopped turkey meat, bring to the boil and simmer for 15 minutes or until the rice is tender. Stir in the gravy browning. Blend the cornflour with the sherry and stir into the soup. Bring to the boil and cook for 1 minute, stirring. Season to taste and serve hot.

Old English Stilton Soup

Serves 4

15 g/¹/₂ oz/1 tbsp butter
15 ml/1 tbsp oil
1 onion, finely chopped
1 English eating (dessert) apple,
* finely chopped*
600 ml/1 pt/2¹/₂ cups vegetable or
* chicken stock*
100 g/4 oz Stilton cheese, crumbled
15 ml/1 tbsp Madeira
150 ml/¹/₄ pt/²/₃ cup single (light)
* cream*
Salt and freshly ground black
* pepper*
100 g/4 oz/1 cup cooked long-grain
* rice*
Snipped chives

Melt the butter with the oil in a saucepan. Add the onion and apple, cover and cook gently, stirring occasionally, for 2 minutes until softened but not browned. Add the stock, bring to the boil, reduce the heat and simmer for 10 minutes. Cool slightly then place in a blender or food processor with the Stilton and run the machine until smooth. Return to the saucepan and stir in the Madeira and cream. Season to taste, add the rice and heat through but do not boil. Garnish with the chives before serving.

Hortosouppa (Cyprus vegetable soup)

Serves 6

350 g/12 oz carrots, chopped
2 courgettes (zucchini), chopped
2 potatoes, diced
2 celery sticks, chopped
1 bay leaf
1.2 litres /2 pts/5 cups chicken or
* vegetable stock*
Salt and freshly ground black
* pepper*
1 piece cinnamon stick
15 ml/1 tbsp tomato purée (paste)
50 g/2 oz/¹/₄ cup long-grain rice
15 ml/1 tbsp olive oil
15 ml/1 tbsp lemon juice

Put all the prepared vegetables in a pan with the bay leaf, stock, a little salt and pepper and the cinnamon stick. Bring to the boil, reduce the heat, cover and simmer for 10 minutes. Add the tomato purée and rice and simmer for a further 10-15 minutes or until the rice and vegetables are really tender. Remove the bay leaf and cinnamon stick. Taste and add olive oil, lemon juice and a little more salt and pepper to taste.

Floating Island Soup

Serves 4

4 large onions, roughly chopped
40 g/1¹/₂ oz/3 tbsp butter
900 ml/1¹/₂ pts/3³/₄ cups beef stock
50 g/2 oz/¹/₄ cup long-grain rice
Salt and freshly ground black pepper
15 ml/1 tbsp cornflour (cornstarch)
15 ml/1 tbsp water
4 slices French bread, toasted
100 g/4 oz Gruyère (Swiss) cheese,
* grated*

Fry (sauté) the onions gently in the butter for 5 minutes, stirring until soft, then turn up the heat and fry for a further 4 minutes or so until the onions are golden brown, stirring all the time. Add the stock, rice and a little salt and pepper, bring to the boil, cover and simmer gently for 20 minutes. Blend the cornflour with the water. Stir into the soup and cook for 1 minute, stirring. Ladle into four flameproof soup bowls. Top each with a piece of toasted French bread and cover with the cheese. Place until a hot grill (broiler) until the cheese melts and bubbles. Serve straight away.

Louvana
(Fasting soup)

Serves 6

450 g/1 lb/2²/₃ cups yellow split peas,
* soaked*
2 onions, sliced
15 ml/1 tbsp olive oil
2 potatoes, diced
100 g/4 oz/¹/₂ cup long-grain rice
Juice of 2 lemons
Salt
Olive oil, for drizzling
Black olives
Sesame seed bread

Drain the peas. Place in a large saucepan with enough water to cover. Bring to the boil and simmer for about 1 hour until tender, adding boiling water as the mixture dries. Fry (sauté) the onions in the oil for 2 minutes, stirring. Add the potatoes and fry, stirring for 5 minutes until golden. Add this mixture to the peas with the rice and more water, simmer for 10-15 minutes. When tender, purée in a blender or food processor, adding more water to thin slightly (the soup should be very thick). Add lemon juice and salt to taste. Ladle into bowls and drizzle with olive oil. Serve with olives and lots of sesame seed bread.

Sherried Carrot and Orange Soup

Serves 6

2 large oranges
450 g/1 lb carrots, sliced
1 onion, sliced
25 g/1 oz/2 tbsp butter
900 ml/1¹/₂ pts/3³/₄ cups vegetable
* stock*
1 bay leaf
Salt and freshly ground white
* pepper*
30 ml/2 tbsp medium dry sherry
50 g/2 oz/¹/₂ cup cooked brown rice
A little crème fraîche

Thinly pare the rind off half of an orange. Cut into thin strips and boil in a little water for 2 minutes then drain and rinse with cold water. Grate the rind off the other half and reserve. Squeeze the juice from both oranges and reserve. In a saucepan, fry (sauté) the carrots and onion gently in the butter for 2 minutes, stirring. Add the stock, bay leaf, a little salt and pepper, the grated orange rind and the juice. Bring to the boil, reduce the heat, cover and simmer for about 25 minutes or until the carrots are really tender. Discard the bay leaf then purée the mixture in a blender or processor. Stir in the sherry and rice. Reheat or chill, ladle into soup bowls and serve garnished with a spoonful of crème fraîche and the strips of orange rind.

Heartwarming Haddock Soup

Serves 4

1 large onion, finely chopped
25 g/1 oz/2 tbsp butter
400 g/14 oz/1 large can chopped
* tomatoes*
300 ml/¹/₂ pt/1¹/₄ cups milk
150 ml/¹/₄ pt/²/₃ cup fish stock
15 ml/1 tbsp chopped thyme
50 g/2 oz/¹/₄ cup long-grain rice
100 g/4 oz broccoli, cut into tiny
* florets*
350 g/12 oz haddock fillet, skinned
* and diced*
Salt and freshly ground black
* pepper*
Croûtons (cubes of bread fried in oil
* or butter until golden)*

Fry (sauté) the onion in the butter in a saucepan for 2 minutes until softened but not browned. Add the tomatoes, milk, stock, thyme and rice. Bring to the boil, reduce the heat, cover and simmer for 10 minutes. Stir, add the broccoli and simmer for 3 minutes. Add the fish and a little salt and pepper and cook for a further 3-5 minutes or until the fish is tender but still holds its shape. Taste and re-season if necessary. Ladle into soup bowls and garnish with the croûtons before serving.

Eastern Saffron Soup

Serves 6

2 onions, thinly sliced
15 g/¹/₂ oz/1 tbsp butter
2 potatoes, thinly sliced
600 ml/1 pt/2¹/₂ cups chicken stock
45 ml/3 tbsp dried milk powder
(non-fat dry milk)
Salt and freshly ground white
pepper
2.5 ml/¹/₂ tsp powdered saffron
A pinch of ground turmeric
225 g/8 oz/2 cups cooked chicken,
cut into small strips
50 g/2 oz/¹/₂ cup cooked basmati or
fragrant Thai rice
300 ml/¹/₂ pt/1¹/₄ cups crème fraîche
6 thin slices of lemon
Chopped parsley

Gently fry (sauté) the onions in the butter for 2 minutes, stirring until softened but not browned. Add the potatoes and stock. Bring to the boil, cover and simmer for about 5 minutes until tender. Purée in a blender or food processor and return to the rinsed-out pan. Stir in the milk powder and season with salt and pepper and the saffron and turmeric. Stir well. Add the chicken and rice and heat through for 2-3 minutes. Stir in the crème fraîche and heat through again. Taste and re-season if necessary. Ladle into warm bowls and garnish each with a slice of lemon and a little parsley.

Almond Cream Soup

Serves 6

100 g/4 oz/1 cup ground almonds
1.2 litres/2 pts/5 cups hot chicken
stock
Salt and freshly ground white
pepper
50 g/2 oz/¹/₄ cup long-grain rice
150 ml/¹/₄ pt/²/₃ cup double (heavy)
cream
2 egg yolks

Put the almonds in a saucepan. Add about 300 ml/¹/₂ pt/1¹/₄ cups of the hot stock, whisking all the time until the mixture is smooth. Blend in the remaining stock and a little salt and pepper. Bring to the boil, reduce the heat and simmer for 30 minutes. Add the rice for the last 10 minutes of the cooking time. In a bowl, whisk the cream and egg yolks together. Whisk in a ladleful of the hot soup. Return this mixture to the saucepan and heat through, stirring but do NOT allow to boil. Serve straight away without garnish.

Brittany Mussel Bisque

Serves 4

1 kg/2¼ lb fresh mussels
600 ml/1 pt/2½ cups water
300 ml/½ pt/1¼ cups dry cider
2 celery sticks, finely chopped
1 onion, finely chopped
1 bunch of parsley, chopped
Salt and freshly ground black
*   pepper*
50 g/2 oz/¼ cup long-grain rice
1 large tomato, skinned, seeded and
*   finely chopped*
10 ml/2 tsp lemon juice

Scrub the mussels, discarding any that are damaged or open and won't close when sharply tapped. Remove the beards. Put into a large pan with the water, cider, celery, onion and half the parsley. Season and bring to the boil. Cover and cook for 2 minutes. Remove the mussels with a draining spoon and discard any that have not opened. Take the mussels out of their shells and reserve. Meanwhile add the rice and tomato to the cooking liquid, bring to the boil and cook for 10 minutes or until the rice is tender. Stir in the lemon juice and mussels and reheat. Taste and re-season if necessary. Serve in soup bowls, garnished with the remaining parsley.

Madras Mulligatawny Soup

Serves 4-6

1 eating (dessert) apple, chopped
2 carrots, chopped
2 onions, chopped
30 ml/2 tbsp oil
15 ml/1 tbsp Madras curry powder
25 g/1 oz/2 tbsp plain (all-purpose)
*   flour*
1.2 litres/2 pts/5 cups lamb stock
15 ml/1 tbsp mango chutney,
*   chopped if necessary*
15 ml/1 tbsp tomato purée (paste)
40 g/1½ oz/¼ cup sultanas (golden
*   raisins)*
Salt and freshly ground black
*   pepper*
50 g/2 oz/½ cup cooked basmati rice
15 ml/1 tbsp chopped coriander
*   (cilantro)*
15 ml/1 tbsp lemon juice
4-6 lemon slices

Fry (sauté) the apple, carrots and onions in the oil for 2 minutes, stirring. Stir in the curry powder and flour and cook for 1 minute. Gradually blend in the stock and bring to the boil, stirring. Stir in the chutney, tomato purée and sultanas and season to taste. Cover and simmer gently for 45 minutes. Purée in a blender or processor and return to the pan. Stir in the rice, coriander and lemon juice and reheat. Ladle into bowls and garnish each with a slice of lemon.

Minestra alla Milanese

Serves 6-8

30 ml/2 tbsp olive oil
1 small garlic clove, crushed
1 onion, finely chopped
2 celery sticks, chopped
2 tomatoes, skinned, seeded and
  chopped
1 large potato, finely diced
1 large carrot, finely diced
2 courgettes (zucchini), chopped
100 g/4 oz French (green) beans, cut
  into short lengths
100 g/4 oz/1 cup frozen peas
45 ml/3 tbsp chopped parsley
425 g/15 oz/1 large can black-eyed
  beans, drained
2.25 litres/4 pts/10 cups vegetable
  stock
Salt and freshly ground black
  pepper
175 g/6 oz/1¹/₂ cups arborio or other
  risotto rice
100 g/4 oz green cabbage, shredded
Freshly grated Parmesan cheese

Heat the oil in a large pan. Add the garlic, onion, celery, tomatoes, potato, carrot and courgettes and fry (sauté), stirring for 3 minutes. Add the remaining ingredients except the rice, cabbage and cheese. Bring to the boil, reduce the heat, cover and simmer for 1 hour. Add the rice and cabbage, bring to the boil again, reduce the heat and simmer for 15-20 minutes. Taste and re-season if necessary. Ladle into soup bowls and serve with the Parmesan cheese.

Cooling Cucumber Soup with Wild Rice

Serves 6

50 g/2 oz/¹/₄ cup butter
1 onion, finely chopped
1 cucumber, diced
25 g/1 oz/¹/₄ cup plain (all-purpose)
  flour
900 ml/1¹/₂ pts/3³/₄ cups chicken
  stock
300 ml/¹/₂ pt/1¹/₄ cups milk
Salt and freshly ground black
  pepper
150 ml/¹/₄ pt/²/₃ cup soured (dairy
  sour) cream
25 g/1 oz/¹/₄ cup cooked wild rice
Snipped chives

Melt the butter in a saucepan. Add the onion and cucumber. Toss lightly then cover and cook gently for 10 minutes, shaking the pan occasionally. Stir in the flour and cook for 1 minute. Blend in the stock, bring to the boil, reduce the heat and simmer gently for 15 minutes. Purée in a blender or processor, then stir in the milk and season to taste. Leave to cool, then chill. Just before serving, stir half the soured cream into the soup. Ladle into soup bowls and garnish each with a swirl of soured cream, a spoonful of wild rice and a sprinkling of chives.

Minted Pea and Yoghurt Soup

Serves 4
50 g/2 oz/¹/₄ cup butter
Bunch of spring onions (scallions), chopped
450 g/1 lb/4 cups frozen peas
5 ml/1 tsp dried mint
150 ml/¹/₄ pt/²/₃ cup plain yoghurt
300 ml/¹/₂ pt/1¹/₄ cups water or cold vegetable stock
100 g/4 oz/1 cup cooked long-grain rice
Salt and freshly ground black pepper

Melt the butter in a saucepan. Add the spring onions and cook gently, stirring for 2 minutes. Add the peas and mint, cover and cook for about 10-15 minutes, stirring occasionally, until the peas are tender. Cool slightly, then purée in a blender or food processor with the yoghurt and a little of the water or stock. Stir in the remaining liquid and the cooked rice. Season to taste and chill until ready to serve.

Glistening Tomato Soup with Fragrant Rice

Serves 4
550 g/20 oz/1 large can tomato juice
30 ml/2 tbsp tomato purée (paste)
3 whole cloves
1 lemon slice
300 ml/¹/₂ pt/1¹/₄ cups chicken stock
1 bay leaf
¹/₄ onion
6 whole black peppercorns
Salt
75 g/3 oz/³/₄ cup cooked Thai fragrant rice
1 tomato, thinly sliced
A few snipped chives

Put the tomato juice in a saucepan and stir in the tomato purée. Add the cloves, lemon slice, stock, bay leaf, onion, peppercorns and a good pinch of salt. Bring to the boil, reduce the heat and simmer for 5 minutes. Strain and return to the pan. Stir in the rice and heat through. Ladle into warm bowls and float a slice of tomato on each. Top with a few chives.

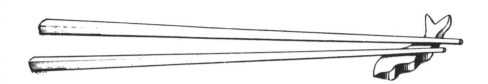

Curried Apple and Parsnip Soup

Serves 4-5

25 g/1 oz/2 tbsp butter
1 onion, chopped
1 parsnip, finely diced
2 eating (dessert) apples, chopped
5 ml/1 tsp curry paste
450 ml/³/₄ pt/2 cups vegetable stock
150 ml/¹/₄ pt/²/₃ cup single (light) cream
50 g/2 oz/¹/₂ cup cooked long-grain rice
Salt and freshly ground black pepper
Snipped chives

Melt the butter in a saucepan. Add the onion and parsnip and fry (sauté), stirring for 3 minutes. Stir in the apple and cook for 2 minutes. Stir in the curry paste and the stock. Bring to the boil, reduce the heat, cover and simmer gently for 8 minutes until the parsnips are tender. Purée in a blender or food processor. Return to the pan. Stir in the cream and rice and season to taste. Heat through but do not boil. Serve garnished with the chives.

Curried Carrot Soup

Serves 4

Prepare as for Curried Apple and Parsnip Soup but substitute 4 large carrots for the parsnip and apples.

Greek Vegetable Soup with Halloumi

Serves 6

1 onion, chopped
1 courgette (zucchini), chopped
1 carrot, chopped
1 small aubergine (eggplant), chopped
25 g/1 oz/2 tbsp butter
50 g/2 oz/¹/₄ cup long-grain rice
1.2 litres/2 pts/5 cups chicken stock
2.5 ml/¹/₂ tsp dried oregano
1 egg yolk
300 ml/¹/₂ pt/1¹/₄ cups Greek-style plain yoghurt
6 thin slices Halloumi cheese
A little olive oil
15 ml/1 tbsp chopped mint
10 ml/2 tsp grated lemon rind

Fry (sauté) the prepared vegetables in the butter for 2 minutes, stirring. Stir in the rice and cook for 1 minute. Add the stock and oregano. Bring to the boil, reduce the heat, cover and simmer for 20 minutes until the vegetables and rice are really tender. Whisk the egg yolk and yoghurt together. Remove the pan from the heat. Add a ladleful of the hot soup stock to the yoghurt mixture. Stir well, then stir back into the saucepan. Meanwhile, lay the Halloumi slices on a grill (broiler) rack. Brush with the oil and grill (broil) quickly until turning golden. Ladle the soup into warm bowls. Top each with a slice of Halloumi and sprinkle with the mint and lemon rind. Serve immediately.

Swedish Tomato and Dill Cucumber Soup

Serves 6

1 onion, finely chopped
1 small garlic clove, crushed
30 ml/2 tbsp sunflower oil
300 ml/¹/₂ pt/1¹/₄ cups chicken stock
400 g/14 oz/1 large can tomatoes
15 ml/1 tbsp tomato purée (paste)
Salt and freshly ground black
  pepper
15 ml/1 tbsp chopped dill (dill weed)
15 ml/1 tbsp mayonnaise
45 ml/3 tbsp plain yoghurt
50 g/2 oz/¹/₂ cup cooked long-grain
  rice
2 large dill pickled cucumbers (dill
  pickles)

Fry (sauté) the onion and garlic in the oil for 2 minutes, stirring. Add the stock, tomatoes, tomato purée and a little salt and pepper. Bring to the boil, reduce the heat and simmer for 10 minutes. Cool slightly then purée with 10 ml/2 tsp of the dill in a blender or food processor. Leave until cold then whisk in the mayonnaise and yoghurt. Stir in the rice. Cut off 6 slices of pickled cucumber for garnish. Finely chop the remainder and stir into the soup. Taste and re-season, if necessary. Chill until ready to serve, garnished with the cucumber slices and the remaining dill.

Creamy Country Vegetable with Rice Soup

Serves 6

1 onion, finely chopped
2 large potatoes, diced
50 g/2 oz/¹/₄ cup butter
450 g/1 lb/4 cups frozen mixed
  country vegetables
450 ml/³/₄ pt/2 cups vegetable stock
l bouquet garni sachet
Salt and freshly ground black
  pepper
450 ml/³/₄ pt/2 cups milk
50 g/2 oz/¹/₂ cup cooked long-grain
  rice
150 ml/¹/₄ pt/²/₃ cup single (light)
  cream

Fry (sauté) the onion and potato in the butter for 2 minutes, stirring in a large saucepan. Add the remaining ingredients except the rice and cream. Bring to the boil, reduce the heat, cover and simmer gently for 20 minutes. Discard the bouquet garni. Purée in a blender or food processor and return to the rinsed-out pan. Add the rice and half the cream and heat through. Taste and re-season if necessary. Ladle into warm bowls and garnish each with a swirl of the remaining cream.

Country Chicken and Vegetable Soup

Serves 6

Prepare as for Creamy Country Vegetable with Rice Soup but use chicken instead of vegetable stock, reduce the amount of vegetables to 225 g/8 oz/2 cups and add 175 g/6 oz/1¹/₂ cups cooked, diced chicken and 50 g/2 oz/1 cup of sliced mushrooms.

Peter Piper Soup

Serves 6

25 g/1 oz/2 tbsp butter
8 streaky bacon rashers (slices),
  rinded and diced
2 onions, finely chopped
75 g/3 oz/¹/₃ cup long-grain rice
1.2 litres/2 pts/5 cups chicken stock
6 tomatoes, skinned, seeded and
  diced
1 small green (bell) pepper, thinly
  sliced
1 small red (bell) pepper, thinly
  sliced into rings
1 small yellow (bell) pepper, thinly
  sliced into rings
5ml/1 tsp pickled pink peppercorns,
  crushed
Salt and freshly ground black
  pepper

Melt the butter in a saucepan. Add the
bacon and onions and fry (sauté) for 3 minutes, stirring. Add the rice and fry for a further 1 minute, stirring. Stir in the stock,
bring to the boil, reduce the heat and simmer for 20 minutes. Add the remaining
ingredients and simmer for 5 minutes.

Chicken Corn and Noodle Soup

Serves 4

600 ml/1 pt/2¹/₂ cups chicken stock
85 g/3¹/₂ oz/1 small packet chicken-
  flavoured instant noodles
100 g/4 oz/1 cup cooked chicken,
  chopped
200 g/7 oz/1 small can sweetcorn
  (corn)
30 ml/2 tbsp dry sherry

Put the stock in a pan and bring to the boil.
Crush the noodles and add to the pan
(reserve the flavour sachet). Stir in the
chicken, corn and sherry and simmer for 4
minutes, stirring. Add the flavour sachet to
taste and serve hot.

Dutch Peanut and Corn Chowder

Serves 6

25 g/1 oz/2 tbsp butter
1 bunch of spring onions (scallions),
  finely chopped
45 ml/3 tbsp smooth peanut butter
25 g/1 oz/2 tbsp light brown sugar
300 ml/¹/₂ pt/1¹/₄ cups milk
450 ml/³/₄ pt/2 cups vegetable stock
200 g/7 oz/1 small can sweetcorn
  (corn)
50 g/2 oz/¹/₂ cup cooked long-grain
  rice
225 g/8 oz Edam cheese, grated
A pinch of cayenne
Salt and freshly ground black
  pepper
Chopped parsley

Melt the butter in a saucepan. Add the
spring onions and fry (sauté) for 3 minutes,
stirring. Remove from the heat and stir in
the peanut butter, sugar and milk. Heat
gently, stirring until smooth. Blend in the
stock and corn with its juice. Bring to the
boil, stirring, reduce the heat and simmer
for 5 minutes. Stir in the rice and cheese
until melted. Add a pinch of cayenne and
salt and pepper to taste. Ladle into warm
bowls and garnish with the parsley.

Chilled Spiced Plum Soup

Serves 4-6

*430 g/15¹/₂ oz/1 large can red plums,
drained, reserving the syrup*
150 ml/¹/₄ pt/²/₃ cup water
*50 g/2 oz/¹/₄ cup caster (superfine)
sugar*
2.5 ml/¹/₂ tsp mixed (apple pie) spice
A pinch of ground cinnamon
*Salt and freshly ground black
pepper*
150 ml/¹/₄ pt/²/₃ cup red wine
15 ml/1 tbsp cornflour (cornstarch)
Grated rind and juice of 1 orange
30 ml/2 tbsp long-grain rice
150 ml/¹/₄ pt/²/₃ cup crème fraîche
A little grated nutmeg

Remove the stones (pits) from the plums. Place the pulp in a saucepan with the syrup, water, sugar, mixed spice, cinnamon and a pinch of salt and pepper. Bring to the boil, reduce the heat and simmer for 5 minutes. Blend the wine and cornflour together and stir into the soup with the orange rind and juice. Bring to the boil and simmer for 2 minutes, stirring. Purée in a blender or food processor. Turn into a bowl, add the rice and chill. Ladle into bowls and garnish each with a swirl of crème fraîche and a dusting of nutmeg before serving.

Golden Lemon Plum Soup

Serves 4-6

Prepare as for Chilled Spiced Plum Soup but use a can of golden plums instead. Use a German white wine instead of red and the grated rind and juice of a lemon instead of an orange. Reserve a little of the lemon rind to sprinkle on top instead of the nutmeg.

Tomato and Yoghurt Refresher

Serves 6

400 g/14 oz/1 large can tomatoes
30 ml/2 tbsp tomato purée (paste)
5 cm/2 in piece cucumber
2 spring onions (scallions), chopped
1 red (bell) pepper, chopped
15 ml/1 tbsp Worcestershire sauce
A few drops of Tabasco sauce
*150 ml/¹/₄ pt/²/₃ cup thick Greek-style
plain yoghurt*
A little milk
*50 g/2 oz/¹/₂ cup cooked long-grain
rice*
*Salt and freshly ground black
pepper*
A few snipped chives

Put the tomatoes in a blender or food processor. Add the tomato purée. Cut off 6 thin slices of cucumber for garnish, roughly chop the remainder and add to the tomatoes with the spring onions, red pepper, Worcestershire and Tabasco sauces. Purée until smooth. Blend in the yoghurt and thin with a little milk if necessary. Stir in the rice and season if necessary. Ladle into soup bowls and garnish each with a slice of cucumber and a few chives.

Caribbean Chicken with Coconut Soup

Serves 4

4 spring onions (scallions), chopped
1 garlic clove, crushed
30 ml/2 tbsp oil
5 ml/1 tsp ground turmeric
300 ml/¹/₂ pt/1¹/₄ cups canned
   coconut milk
900 ml/1¹/₂ pts/3³/₄ cups chicken
   stock
50 g/2 oz spaghetti, broken into
   small pieces
1 lemon slice
100 g/4 oz/1 cup cooked chicken,
   diced
Salt and freshly ground black
   pepper
A few coriander (cilantro) leaves

Fry (sauté) the spring onions and garlic in the oil for 2 minutes, stirring until softened but not browned. Add the turmeric, coconut milk, stock, spaghetti and lemon slice. Bring to the boil, reduce the heat, cover and simmer gently for 10 minutes. Discard the lemon, stir in the chicken and season. Heat through for 2 minutes. Ladle into warm bowls and garnish each with a coriander leaf.

Chilli Winter Warmer

Serves 4

100 g/4 oz/1 cup minced (ground)
   lamb or beef
2 onions, finely chopped
2 carrots, finely chopped
2.5 ml/¹/₂ tsp chilli powder
15 ml/1 tbsp tomato purée (paste)
900 ml/1¹/₂ pts/3³/₄ cups beef stock
5 ml/1 tsp yeast extract
100 g/4 oz/1 cup soup pasta shapes
15 ml/1 tbsp cornflour (cornstarch)
30 ml/2 tbsp water
Chopped parsley

Put the meat, onions and carrots in a large saucepan and cook, stirring, until the grains of meat are brown and separate. Stir in the chilli powder, tomato purée, stock and yeast extract. Bring to the boil, reduce the heat and simmer for 20 minutes, stirring occasionally. Add the pasta and cook for a further 10 minutes. Blend the cornflour with the water. Stir into the soup and cook, stirring, for 1 minute. Serve hot, garnished with the parsley.

Rich Kidney Carbonnade Soup

Serves 4
25 g/1 oz/2 tbsp butter
1 onion, finely chopped
1 parsnip, finely chopped
225 g/8 oz pig's kidneys, skinned,
  cored and finely chopped
300 ml/¹/₂ pt/1¹/₄ cups brown ale
750 ml/1¹/₄ pts/3 cups beef stock
1 bouquet garni sachet
Salt and freshly ground black
  pepper
100 g/4 oz/1 cup conchiglietti or
  other soup pasta
15 ml/1 tbsp plain (all-purpose) flour
30 ml/2 tbsp water

Heat the butter in a large saucepan. Add the onion and parsnip and fry (sauté), stirring for 2 minutes. Add the kidney and toss quickly for 30 seconds. Add the brown ale, stock and bouquet garni sachet and season with salt and pepper. Bring to the boil, reduce the heat, cover and simmer gently for 1 hour. Add the pasta for the last 10 minutes. Blend the flour with the water until smooth and stir into the soup. Bring to the boil, stirring for 2 minutes until thickened. Remove the bouquet garni. Taste and re-season if necessary.

Harira Soup for Ramadan

Serves 4
45 ml/3 tbsp plain (all-purpose) flour
120 ml/4 fl oz/¹/₂ cup water
50 g/2 oz/¹/₃ cup chick peas
  (garbanzos)
50 g/2 oz/¹/₃ cup brown lentils
15 g/¹/₂ oz/1 tbsp butter
100 g/4 oz lamb, diced
1 large onion, chopped
A pinch of saffron powder
15 ml/1 tbsp paprika
Salt and freshly ground black
  pepper
400 g/14 oz/1 large can chopped
  tomatoes
30 ml/2 tbsp chopped parsley
30 ml/2 tbsp chopped coriander
  (cilantro)
750 ml/1¹/₄ pts/3 cups lamb stock
45 ml/3 tbsp vermicelli, broken into
  small pieces
Lemon slices

Mix the flour and water together and leave to stand overnight. Put the chick peas and lentils in a bowl of water and leave to soak overnight. Melt the butter in a large pan. Add the meat and onion and fry (sauté) until brown. Add the drained chick peas and lentils, the saffron, paprika, a little salt and pepper, the tomatoes, herbs and stock. Bring to the boil, reduce the heat, cover and simmer gently for 2 hours. Stir in the vermicelli and flour and water for the last 20 minutes of cooking. Ladle into warm soup bowls and garnish with lemon slices.

Minestrone

Serves 6

1 small onion, grated
15 ml/1 tbsp oil
1 small parsnip, grated
1/4 small cabbage, shredded
50 g/2 oz/1/2 cup frozen peas
25 g/1 oz/1/4 cup quick-cook short-
cut macaroni
400 g/14 oz/1 large can chopped
tomatoes
430 g/15 1/2 oz/1 large can cannellini
beans, drained
1 vegetable stock cube
2.5 ml/1/2 tsp dried oregano
Salt and freshly ground black
pepper
Grated Parmesan cheese

Fry (sauté) the onion in the oil in a large
pan for 1 minute, stirring. Add the remaining ingredients except the Parmesan
cheese. Fill the tomato can with water
twice and add to the pan. Bring to the boil,
reduce the heat and simmer for 10 minutes
or until the vegetables and pasta are tender.
Taste and re-season if necessary. Serve the
Parmesan cheese separately for sprinkling.

Soupe au Pistou

Serves 4-6

1 large onion, chopped
90 ml/6 tbsp olive oil
400 g/14 oz/1 large can chopped
tomatoes
450 g/1 lb French (green) beans, cut
into short lengths
2 courgettes (zucchini), finely diced
2 potatoes, finely diced
900 ml/1 1/2 pts/3 3/4 cups vegetable
stock
Salt and freshly ground black
pepper
430 g/15 1/2 oz/1 large can haricot
(navy) beans, drained
45 ml/3 tbsp vermicelli, broken into
small pieces
3 garlic cloves, chopped
75 g/3 oz/3/4 cup grated Parmesan
cheese
12 large basil leaves

Fry (sauté) the onion in 45 ml/3 tbsp of the
oil in a large saucepan for 3 minutes until
softened but not browned. Add the tomatoes, bring to the boil and simmer for 5
minutes. Add the prepared vegetables,
stock and a little salt and pepper. Bring to
the boil again and simmer for 10 minutes.
Add the beans and vermicelli and simmer
for a further 10 minutes. Meanwhile, make
the pistou. Purée the garlic, Parmesan
cheese and basil in a blender or processor.
Scrape down the sides then add the oil in a
thin stream with the machine running all
the time until the mixture forms a glistening paste. Alternatively, pound in a pestle
and mortar, then stir in the oil a drop at a
time. Just before serving the soup, stir in
the pistou.

Smoked Haddock and Butter Bean Chowder

Serves 4-6
4 streaky bacon rashers (slices),
finely diced
1 onion, finely chopped
600 ml/1 pt/2¹/₂ cups chicken stock
50 g/2 oz/¹/₂ cup short-cut macaroni
225 g/8 oz smoked haddock fillet
450 ml/³/₄ pt/2 cups milk
200 g/7 oz/1 small can butter beans,
drained
Salt and freshly ground black
pepper
150 ml/¹/₄ pt/²/₃ cup single (light)
cream
Chopped parsley

Fry (sauté) the bacon in a large saucepan until the fat runs, stirring. Add the onion and fry for 2 minutes. Add the stock and pasta, bring to the boil, reduce the heat and simmer for 15 minutes. Meanwhile, poach the fish in the milk for 5 minutes or until it flakes easily with a fork. Remove the skin, flake the fish and add it to the soup with the cooking milk. Stir in the butter beans and a little salt and pepper. Bring to the boil, reduce the heat and simmer for a further 5 minutes. Remove from the heat. Stir in the cream and serve straight away, garnished with the parsley.

Creamy Mushroom Bisque

Serves 6
50 g/2 oz/¹/₄ cup butter
2 onions, chopped
350 g/12 oz/6 cups button
mushrooms, quartered
5 ml/1 tsp dried tarragon
15 ml/1 tbsp paprika
1.5 ml/¹/₄ tsp cayenne
Salt and freshly ground black
pepper
600 ml/1 pt/2¹/₂ cups vegetable stock
5 ml/1 tsp yeast extract
150 ml/¹/₄ pt/²/₃ cup crème fraîche
100 g/4 oz/1 cup cooked maltagliati

Melt the butter in a large saucepan. Add the onion and cook, stirring for 2 minutes. Add the mushrooms, tarragon, paprika, cayenne and a little salt and pepper. Cover and cook over a gentle heat for 5 minutes, stirring occasionally. Add the stock and yeast extract. Bring to the boil, reduce the heat, cover and simmer gently for 5 minutes. Purée in a blender or processor and return to the pan. Stir in the crème fraîche, taste and re-season if necessary. Stir in the maltagliati. Heat through and serve straight away.

Macaroni Cheese and Celery Soup

Serves 4-6

1 large potato, finely diced
1 large onion, finely chopped
1 large carrot, finely diced
2 celery sticks, finely chopped
600 ml/1 pt/2¹/₂ cups chicken stock
50 g/2 oz/¹/₂ cup short-cut macaroni
100 g/4 oz Cheddar cheese, grated
150 ml/¹/₄ pt/²/₃ cup single (light)
  cream
Salt and freshly ground white
  pepper
A little milk
Chopped celery leaves

Put all the prepared vegetables in a pan with the stock and macaroni. Bring to the boil, reduce the heat, part-cover and simmer for 20 minutes. Stir in the cheese and cream. Season to taste and thin, if liked, with a little milk. Heat through but do not boil. Ladle into warm soup bowls and garnish with a few chopped celery leaves.

Golden Peasant Soup

Serves 6

1 onion, finely chopped
1 garlic clove, crushed
25 g/1 oz/2 tbsp butter
1 large potato, finely diced
2 celery sticks, finely chopped
1 yellow (bell) pepper, finely diced
1 large carrot, finely diced
1.5 litres/2¹/₂ pts/6 cups beef stock
2.5 ml/¹/₂ tsp turmeric
50 g/2 oz/¹/₂ cup lumachi or other
  small pasta shapes
430 g/15 oz/1 large can chick peas
  (garbanzos), drained
100 g/4 oz streaky bacon rashers
  (slices), finely diced
Salt and freshly ground black
  pepper
Grated Cheddar cheese

Fry (sauté) the onion and garlic in the butter for 2 minutes until softened but not browned. Add the remaining prepared vegetables and fry, stirring for 1 minute. Add the stock, turmeric and pasta. Bring to the boil and simmer for 10 minutes. Stir in the chick peas and bacon and simmer for a further 10 minutes. Season to taste and serve the Cheddar cheese separately for sprinkling over.

Oriental Spinach and Egg Noodle Soup

Serves 6

1.5 litres/2¹/₂ pts/6 cups chicken stock
225 g/8 oz Chinese egg noodles
225 g/8 oz/2 cups cooked chicken, diced
Soy sauce
Freshly ground black pepper
30 ml/2 tbsp oil
225 g/8 oz/1 cup frozen leaf spinach, thawed
50 g/2 oz/1 cup button mushrooms, sliced

Heat the stock in a large saucepan. Add the noodles and simmer gently until cooked (4-10 minutes depending on the make). Add the chicken and soy sauce and pepper to taste. Heat the oil in a frying pan (skillet). Add the spinach and toss over a high heat for 2 minutes. Stir into the soup, add the mushrooms and simmer for 5 minutes. Serve hot.

Sweetcorn and Pasta Chowder

Serves 4-6

2 rashers (slices) bacon
50 g/2 oz/¹/₂ cup conchiglietti or other soup pasta
600 ml/1 pt/2¹/₂ cups milk
475 g/1 lb 1 oz/1 large can creamed sweetcorn (corn)
75 g/3 oz/¹/₃ cup curd (smooth cottage) cheese
2.5 ml/¹/₂ tsp grated nutmeg
Salt and freshly ground black pepper
Chopped parsley

Grill (broil) or dry-fry (sauté) the bacon until crisp then chop or crumble into small pieces and reserve. Simmer the pasta in the milk for about 5 minutes until tender. Stir in the remaining ingredients except the parsley and heat through. Ladle into soup bowls and garnish with the bacon and parsley.

Pancit Molo
(Wontons in Garlic Soup)

Serves 6

*50 g/2 oz/¹/₂ cup peeled prawns
(shrimp), chopped*
*50 g/2 oz/¹/₂ cup minced (ground)
pork*
50 g/2 oz/¹/₂ cup chicken, chopped
5 ml/1 tsp soy sauce
*1 bunch of spring onions (scallions),
chopped*
¹/₂ garlic bulb, crushed
Salt
*100 g/4 oz/1 cup plain (all-purpose)
flour, sifted*
2 eggs, beaten
15 ml/1 tbsp corn oil
1 onion, finely chopped
*1.75 litres/3 pts/7¹/₂ cups chicken
stock*

Mix the prawns with the pork, chicken, soy sauce, half the spring onions, 1 of the garlic cloves and a pinch of salt. Put the flour in a separate bowl, add the eggs and work with the fingers into a dough. Add a little cold water if necessary to form a soft but not sticky dough. Knead gently on a lightly floured surface and roll out thinly. Cut into 7.5 cm/3 in triangles. Divide half the prawn and meat mixture among the triangles. Dampen the edges with water. Fold in the two side points and roll up. Heat the oil in a large saucepan or wok. Fry (sauté) the remaining garlic and the chopped onion until lightly golden. Add the remaining filling and fry, stirring, for 3 minutes. Add the chicken stock and season to taste with salt. Bring to the boil, drop in the dumplings, cover and simmer for about 15 minutes. Sprinkle the remaining spring onion into the pot just before serving in warm soup bowls.

Quick Tomato and Lentil
Soup with Spaghetti

Serves 4-6

*50 g/2 oz/1 cup cooked chopped
spaghetti*
425 g/15 oz/1 large can lentil soup
*300 ml/¹/₂ pt/1¹/₄ cups passata (sieved
tomatoes)*
30 ml/2 tbsp medium dry sherry
*120 ml/4 fl oz/¹/₂ cup single (light)
cream*
Snipped chives

Mix all the ingredients except the cream and chives in a saucepan. Heat through, stirring. Ladle into warm soup bowls and garnish each with a large swirl of cream and some snipped chives.

Hungarian Chowder

Serves 6

1 small boned breast of lamb
4 potatoes, diced
2 carrots, diced
2 onions, finely chopped
1 green (bell) pepper, diced
1 garlic clove, crushed
15 ml/1 tbsp oil
15 ml/1 tbsp paprika
400 g/14 oz/1 large can chopped
tomatoes
15 ml/1 tbsp tomato purée (paste)
Salt and freshly ground black
pepper
1.2 litres/2 pts/5 cups chicken or
lamb stock
50 g/2 oz/¹/₂ cup short-cut macaroni
15 ml/1 tbsp plain (all-purpose) flour
30 ml/2 tbsp water
Chopped parsley

Discard as much fat as possible from the lamb and cut the meat into small pieces. Fry (sauté) the meat, the prepared vegetables and the garlic in the oil, stirring for 3 minutes. Add the paprika and fry for 1 minute. Stir in the tomatoes, purée, a little salt and pepper and the stock. Bring to the boil, reduce the heat, cover and simmer gently for 40 minutes. Add the macaroni and cook for a further 10 minutes. Blend the flour with the water, stir into the soup, bring to the boil and cook for 2 minutes, stirring. Taste and re-season if necessary, garnish with the parsley and serve.

Italian-style Consommé

Serves 4

40 g/1¹/₂ oz/¹/₃ cup soup pasta shapes
298 g/10¹/₂ oz/ 1 small can
condensed beef consommé
30 ml/2 tbsp port
Grated Parmesan cheese

Cook the pasta in boiling water until tender. Drain and rinse with hot water. Empty the consommé into a saucepan. Add water as directed, the pasta and port. Heat through until piping hot. Serve with the Parmesan cheese sprinkled over.

Griessnockerlsuppe

Serves 6

25 g/1 oz/2 tbsp butter
1 egg, beaten
Salt
75 g/3 oz/¹/₂ cup semolina (cream of
wheat)
15 ml/1 tbsp cold water
2 × 298 g/2 × 10¹/₂ oz/2 small cans
condensed beef consommé

Beat the butter in a bowl to soften. Beat in the egg, salt and semolina to form a dough. Beat in the water to soften if necessary. Drop spoonfuls of the mixture into a large pan of boiling salted water and simmer until they rise to the surface. Remove with a draining spoon. Meanwhile make up the consommé with water according to can directions. Heat through. Ladle into warm soup bowls and add the dumplings. Serve hot.

Leberknödelsuppe

Serves 6

25 g/1 oz/2 tbsp butter
1 small onion, finely chopped
1 garlic clove, crushed
30 ml/2 tbsp chopped parsley
5 ml/1 tsp caraway seeds
100 g/4 oz/1 cup lambs' liver, minced
  (ground) or very finely chopped
Salt and freshly ground black
  pepper
2 soft bread rolls
1 egg, beaten
A little plain (all-purpose) flour
3 beef stock cubes
900 ml/1¹/₂ pts/3³/₄ cups boiling water
5 ml/1 tsp Worcestershire sauce

Melt the butter in a saucepan. Add the onion and garlic and fry (sauté) for 2 minutes, stirring until softened and lightly browned. Stir in half the parsley, the caraway seeds, liver and a little salt and pepper. Remove from the heat. Soak the bread rolls in water then squeeze out all the moisture and mash into the liver mixture. Work in the beaten egg to form a dough. Leave to stand for 10 minutes. Using well-floured hands, shape the dough into small dumplings, adding a little flour to the mixture if too wet. Drop into a large pan of boiling, lightly salted water and cook for 10-12 minutes. Remove from the pan with a draining spoon and discard the water. Dissolve the stock cubes in the measured boiling water in a pan with the Worcestershire sauce. Bring to the boil. Pour into a soup tureen and add the dumplings. Sprinkle with the remaining parsley and serve hot.

Roman-style Fish Soup

Serves 4

45 ml/3 tbsp olive oil
1 onion, finely chopped
1 carrot, chopped
1 celery stick, chopped
1 garlic clove, crushed
400 g/14 oz/1 large can chopped
  tomatoes
15 ml/1 tbsp tomato purée (paste)
1 sun-dried tomato, chopped
45 ml/3 tbsp chopped parsley
5 ml/1 tsp dried oregano
1 bay leaf
225 g/8 oz halibut fillet, skinned and
  diced
10 ml/2 tsp anchovy essence
  (extract)
100 g/4 oz/1 cup conchiglietti
Salt and freshly ground black
  pepper
100 g/4 oz/1 cup peeled prawns
  (shrimp)

Heat the oil in a large pan. Add the prepared vegetables and fry (sauté) for 3 minutes until slightly softened but not browned. Add the tomatoes, tomato purée, sun-dried tomato, half the parsley, the oregano and bay leaf. Bring to the boil and simmer for 5 minutes. Add the fish, anchovy essence and pasta. Simmer for a further 10 minutes. Season to taste, stir in the prawns and heat through for 2 minutes. Serve garnished with the remaining parsley.

Sherried Chicken Liver Soup

Serves 6
1 onion, finely chopped
1 garlic clove, crushed
25 g/1 oz/2 tbsp butter
200 g/7 oz/1³/₄ cups chicken livers,
   finely chopped
225 g/8 oz/2 cups frozen peas
1.2 litres/2 pts/5 cups chicken stock
50 g/2 oz/¹/₂ cup conchiglietti
30 ml/2 tbsp dry sherry
Salt and freshly ground black
   pepper
5 ml/1 tsp chopped sage
15 ml/1 tbsp chopped parsley

Fry (sauté) the onion and garlic in the butter for 2 minutes, stirring. Add the chicken livers and cook for a further 2 minutes, stirring. Add the remaining ingredients except the parsley. Bring to the boil, reduce the heat and simmer for 10-12 minutes until the pasta is tender. Serve sprinkled with the parsley.

Creamy Cheese Tomato and Basil Soup

Serves 6
1 onion, chopped
1 garlic clove, chopped
40 g/1¹/₂ oz/3 tbsp butter
400 g/14 oz/1 large can chopped
   tomatoes
30 ml/2 tbsp tomato purée (paste)
1.2 litres/2 pts/5 cups vegetable
   stock
5 ml/1 tsp caster (superfine) sugar
Salt and freshly ground black
   pepper
50 g/2 oz/¹/₂ cup vermicelli, broken
   into short lengths
85 g/3¹/₂ oz/scant ¹/₂ cup cream
   cheese
10 ml/2 tsp chopped basil
30 ml/2 tbsp single (light) cream
6 small basil leaves

Fry (sauté) the onion and garlic in the butter for 2 minutes until softened but not browned. Add the tomatoes, purée, stock, sugar and a little salt and pepper. Bring to the boil, reduce the heat, cover and simmer gently for 20 minutes. Add the vermicelli and cook for a further 5-8 minutes until tender. Stir in the cheese until melted, add the chopped basil and leave to stand for 1 minute. Ladle into warm bowls, add a swirl of cream to each and top with a basil leaf.

Cress Soup with Ditallini

Serves 6
25 g/1 oz/2 tbsp butter
8 spring onions (scallions), finely chopped
1 bunch of watercress, finely chopped
1 box of mustard and cress
1.2 litres/2 pts/5 cups chicken stock
Good pinch of grated nutmeg
Salt and freshly ground black pepper
75 g/3 oz/³/₄ cup ditallini or other soup pasta
1 hard-boiled (hard-cooked) egg, finely chopped

Melt the butter in a saucepan. Add the spring onions and fry (sauté) for 2 minutes, stirring. Add the watercress and mustard and cress and cook, stirring, for 1 minute. Add the stock, nutmeg, a little salt and a good grinding of pepper. Bring to the boil, reduce the heat, cover and simmer for 20 minutes. Add the ditallini and cook for a further 5-8 minutes or until tender. Taste and re-season if necessary. Ladle into warm bowls and sprinkle with the egg.

Spinach Pasta Soup

Serves 4
Prepare as for Cress Soup with Ditallini but substitute 350 g/12 oz/3 cups spinach for the watercress and mustard and cress.

Bacon and Mushroom Chowder

Serves 4
25 g/1 oz/2 tbsp butter
1 onion, finely chopped
6 lightly smoked streaky bacon rashers (slices), rinded and chopped
1 garlic clove, crushed
100 g/4 oz/2 cups button mushrooms, chopped
15 ml/1 tbsp plain (all-purpose) flour
600 ml/1 pt/2¹/₂ cups chicken stock
300 ml/¹/₂ pt/1¹/₄ cups milk
Salt and freshly ground black pepper
50 g/2 oz/¹/₂ cup short-cut macaroni
15 ml/1 tbsp chopped parsley
50 g/2 oz strong Cheddar cheese, grated

Melt the butter in a saucepan. Add the onion, bacon and garlic and fry (sauté) gently, stirring for 2 minutes. Add the mushrooms and cook gently for 1 minute. Stir in the flour and cook for 1 minute. Gradually blend in the stock, bring to the boil and simmer for 2 minutes. Stir in the milk, a little salt and pepper and the macaroni. Bring to the boil again, reduce the heat, part-cover and simmer gently for 20 minutes, stirring occasionally. Add the parsley. Taste and re-season. Ladle into warm bowls and serve sprinkled with the cheese.

Bacon and Corn Chowder

Serves 4

Prepare as for Bacon and Mushroom Chowder but substitute 200 g/7 oz/1 small can of sweetcorn (corn) for the mushrooms.

Italian White Bean Soup

Serves 4-6

45 ml/3 tbsp olive oil
1 onion, chopped
1 celery stick, chopped
1 carrot, chopped
1 garlic clove, chopped
100 g/4 oz pancetta or streaky
bacon, chopped
425 g/15 oz/1 large can cannellini
beans, drained
750 ml/1¼ pts/3 cups beef stock
5 ml/1 tsp dried thyme
30 ml/2 tbsp chopped parsley
50 g/2 oz/½ cup conchiglietti
Salt and freshly ground black
pepper
30 ml/2 tbsp grated Parmesan
cheese

Heat the oil in a large pan. Add the onion, celery, carrot, garlic and pancetta and fry (sauté) over a gentle heat for 10 minutes, stirring until very soft but not brown. Add the remaining ingredients except the cheese. Bring to the boil, part-cover and simmer gently for 10 minutes. Taste and re-season if necessary. Ladle into bowls and sprinkle with the Parmesan before serving.

Main-meal Meatball and Vegetable Soup

Serves 4

1.2 litres/2 pts/5 cups vegetable
stock
1 carrot, diced
1 celery stick, chopped
100 g/4 oz tiny cauliflower florets
400 g/14 oz/1 large can chopped
tomatoes
15 ml/1 tbsp tomato purée (paste)
45 ml/3 tbsp red wine
225 g/8 oz/2 cups minced (ground)
veal
50 g/2 oz/1 cup sage and onion
stuffing mix
25 g/1 oz/¼ cup grated Parmesan
cheese
Salt and freshly ground black
pepper
1 egg, beaten
15 ml/1 tbsp olive oil
100 g/4 oz/1 cup stellini or other
soup pasta

Bring the stock to the boil in a large saucepan. Add the prepared vegetables, the chopped tomatoes, purée and wine. Cover and simmer gently for 10 minutes. Meanwhile, mix the meat with the stuffing, cheese and a little salt and pepper. Add the egg to bind. Shape into small balls. Heat the oil in a frying pan (skillet) and fry (sauté) the balls until browned all over. Drain on kitchen paper. Add to the soup with the pasta. Simmer for 10 minutes.

Olive and Pasta Potage

Serves 6

25 g/1 oz/2 tbsp butter
1 onion, finely chopped
2 celery sticks, finely chopped
1 carrot, finely chopped
2 potatoes, finely chopped
750 ml/1¼ pts/3 cups chicken stock
100 g/4 oz/⅔ cup stuffed olives,
   finely sliced
1 bay leaf
50 g/2 oz/½ cup soup pasta shapes
Freshly ground black pepper
75 g/3 oz Emmental (Swiss) cheese,
   grated
6 slices French bread, toasted

Melt the butter in a saucepan. Add the
onion, celery, carrot and potato and fry
(sauté), stirring for 2 minutes. Add the
stock, olives, bay leaf and pasta. Bring to
the boil, reduce the heat and simmer gently
for 12-15 minutes until the vegetables and
pasta are really tender. Season to taste and
ladle into flameproof bowls. Pile the
cheese on the toasted bread. Float a piece
on each bowl and flash under the grill
(broiler) until the cheese melts and bubbles. Serve straight away.

Hong Kong Chowder

Serves 6

1 litre/1¾ pts/4¼ cups chicken stock
200 g/7 oz/1 small can sweetcorn
   (corn)
5 ml/1 tsp grated fresh root ginger
30 ml/2 tbsp dry sherry
30 ml/2 tbsp light soy sauce
2 spring onions (scallions), finely
   chopped
2 × 200 g/2 × 7 oz/2 small cans
   crabmeat
85 g/3½ oz/1 packet chicken-flavour
   instant noodles

Put all the ingredients in a large saucepan.
Bring to the boil and simmer for 4 minutes,
stirring. Serve hot.

Prawn Chowder

Serves 6

Prepare as for Hong Kong Chowder but
substitute 225 g/8 oz/2 cups peeled prawns
(shrimp) for the crabmeat.

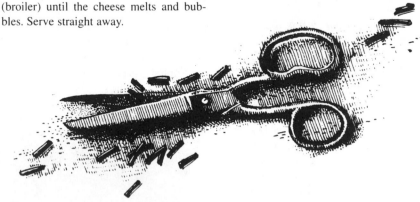

Oriental Pork and Noodle Soup

Serves 4-6

100 g/4 oz pork fillet, cut into small,
very thin strips
5 ml/1 tsp cornflour (cornstarch)
2.5 ml/¹/₂ tsp ground ginger
30 ml/2 tbsp soy sauce
15 ml/1 tbsp sesame oil
225 g/8 oz carrots, thinly sliced
2 spring onions (scallions), sliced
1.2 litres/2 pts/5 cups chicken stock
50 g/2 oz/¹/₂ slab Chinese egg
noodles
Salt and freshly ground black
pepper

Toss the pork in the cornflour and ginger.
Sprinkle with the soy sauce and sesame oil
and toss. Leave to marinate for 15 minutes.
Meanwhile, cook the carrots and spring
onions in the stock for 5 minutes. Add the
pork with its marinade and the noodles and
simmer for 10 minutes, stirring occasionally. Season to taste and serve hot.

Oriental Chicken Noodle Soup

Serves 4

Prepare as for Oriental Pork and Noodle
Soup but substitute 1 boneless chicken
breast for the pork fillet and add a 2.5 cm/
1 in piece of cucumber, coarsely grated,
just before serving.

Sumptuous Starters

The following all make wonderful appetizers before a light main course, and are also delicious served for lunch or supper in their own right.

Rice in Black Butter

Serves 6

350 g/12 oz/1¹/₂ cups arborio or
  other risotto rice
40 g/1¹/₂ oz/3 tbsp unsalted (sweet)
  butter
30 ml/2 tbsp grated Parmesan
  cheese
Salt and freshly ground black pepper

Cook the rice in plenty of boiling salted water for about 18 minutes until just tender. Drain well. Melt the butter in a heavy pan until turning golden (do not let it burn). Add the rice and toss well until coated. Stir in the cheese and season well to taste. Serve hot.

Buttery Rice with Sage

Serves 6

350 g/12 oz/1¹/₂ cups arborio or
  other risotto rice
40 g/1¹/₂ oz/3 tbsp unsalted (sweet)
  butter
10 sage leaves, chopped
Freshly ground black pepper
50 g/2 oz/¹/₂ cup grated Parmesan
  cheese

Cook the rice in plenty of boiling salted water for 18 minutes. Drain well and turn into a warm serving dish. Heat the butter until foamy, stir in the sage and cook until the butter is golden brown. Drizzle all over the rice and add a good grinding of pepper. Serve the cheese separately.

Baked Garlicky Rice

Serves 6

40 g/1¹/₂ oz/3 tbsp unsalted (sweet)
  butter
3 garlic cloves, crushed
450 g/1 lb/2 cups arborio or other
  risotto rice
1.2 litres/2 pts/5 cups beef or
  chicken stock
Salt and freshly ground black
  pepper
Lettuce leaves
Lemon wedges

Heat two-thirds of the butter in a flame-proof casserole (Dutch oven). Add the garlic and fry (sauté) until lightly browned. Stir in the rice and cook for 1 minute. Add the stock and bring to the boil. Stir in the remaining butter, cover and transfer to the oven. Bake at 180°C/350°F/gas mark 4 for 20 minutes or until the rice is just tender and has absorbed the liquid. Serve straight from the dish with the lettuce leaves and lemon wedges.

Ham and Pineapple Cocktail

Serves 6

75 g/3 oz/¹/₃ cup long-grain rice
50 g/2 oz/¹/₂ cup frozen peas
30 ml/2 tbsp olive oil
10 ml/2 tsp lemon juice
5 ml/1 tsp soy sauce
2 spring onions (scallions), finely chopped
213 g/7¹/₂ oz/1 small can ham, diced, discarding jelly
225 g/8 oz/1 small can pineapple chunks in natural juice, drained, reserving juice
30 ml/2 tbsp mayonnaise
12 stoned (pitted) black olives

Cook the rice in plenty of boiling salted water for 10 minutes until just tender. Add the peas half-way through cooking. Drain, rinse with cold water and drain again. Mix the oil, lemon juice, soy sauce and spring onions together. Add to the rice, toss well and divide between 6 small serving plates. Mix the ham and pineapple together with the mayonnaise. Slice 6 of the olives and fold in. Thin the mixture with a little of the pineapple juice if necessary. Pile on to the rice and garnish each with an olive.

All-American Appetizer

Serves 6

175 g/6 oz/³/₄ cup long-grain rice
2 canned pimientos, chopped
2 green chillies, seeded and chopped
3 eggs, beaten
75 ml/5 tbsp milk
Salt and freshly ground black pepper
50 g/2 oz Cheddar cheese, grated
15 ml/1 tbsp snipped chives

Cook the rice in plenty of boiling salted water for 15 minutes until tender. Drain and rinse with hot water. Drain again. Mix with the pimientos and chillies and spread in a greased 20 cm/8 in square, shallow baking tin (pan). Beat the eggs with the milk and a little salt and pepper. Pour over and sprinkle with the cheese. Top with the chives. Bake at 180°C/350°F/gas mark 4 for 35 minutes or until golden brown and set. Serve cut into small squares.

Creamy Ham and Mushroom Risotto

Serves 6

50 g/2 oz/1 cup dried porcini mushrooms
25 g/1 oz/2 tbsp unsalted (sweet) butter
30 ml/2 tbsp olive oil
1 small onion, finely chopped
450 g/1 lb/2 cups arborio or other risotto rice
1.2 litres/2 pts/5 cups hot chicken stock
Salt and freshly ground black pepper
100 g/4 oz/1 cup cooked ham, diced
120 ml/4 fl oz/¹/₂ cup single (light) cream
Chopped parsley
100 g/4 oz/1 cup freshly grated Parmesan cheese

Soak the mushrooms in hot water for 1 hour. Drain and wash thoroughly under running water. Pat dry on kitchen paper, then slice. Heat the butter and oil in a large flameproof casserole (Dutch oven) and fry (sauté) the onion for 2 minutes. Add the rice and cook for 1 minute, stirring. Add 2 ladlefuls of the stock and simmer until it is absorbed. Continue this way until the rice is just tender. Season to taste. Stir in the ham and cream. Spoon on to small warmed plates, sprinkle with the parsley and cheese and serve hot.

Risotto with Melon and Prosciutto

Serves 6

l ripe honeydew melon
75 g/3 oz/¹/₃ cup unsalted (sweet) butter
1 small onion, finely chopped
450 g/1 lb/2 cups arborio or other risotto rice
375 ml/13 fl oz/1¹/₂ cups dry white wine
900 ml/1¹/₂ pts/3³/₄ cups hot chicken stock
250 ml/8 fl oz/1 cup single (light) cream
100 g/4 oz thinly sliced prosciutto
Salt and freshly ground black pepper
Parsley sprigs
100 g/4 oz/1 cup freshly grated Parmesan cheese

Halve the melon, remove the seeds and cut away the skin. Dice the flesh and purée briefly in a blender or food processor. Heat the butter in a large flameproof casserole (Dutch oven). Add the onion and fry (sauté) for 2 minutes. Stir in the rice and cook for 1 minute. Add half the wine and simmer until it is absorbed. Repeat with the rest of the wine. Then add about 250 ml/8 fl oz/1 cup of the stock and simmer until it is absorbed. Repeat until the rice is just tender and creamy, about 15-20 minutes. Quickly stir in the melon, cream and ham. Season to taste. Spoon on to warmed plates, garnish with parsley sprigs and serve the cheese separately.

Polish Stuffed Cabbage Leaves

Serves 4 or 8

8 large cabbage leaves
175 g/6 oz/1¼ cups minced (ground) beef
50 g/2 oz/¼ cup long-grain rice
Salt and freshly ground black pepper
30 ml/2 tbsp tomato purée (paste)
15 ml/1 tbsp chopped parsley
1 garlic clove, crushed
Beef stock
4 bacon rashers (slices), rinded
Gravy browning

Remove the thick central cores from the cabbage leaves. Plunge in boiling water for 3 minutes. Drain, rinse with cold water and drain again. Mix well together the mince, rice, some salt and pepper, the tomato purée, parsley and garlic. Shape into 8 small rolls and place one on each cabbage leaf. Fold in the sides and roll up not too tightly. Pack in a single layer in a flameproof casserole (Dutch oven). Pour on enough beef stock to just cover. Bring to the boil, cover with a lid, reduce the heat and simmer gently for 1½ hours. Meanwhile, grill (broil) or dry-fry the bacon until crisp. Crumble into small pieces. When cooked, transfer the cabbage rolls to a warm serving dish. If necessary, boil the stock rapidly until syrupy and add a few drops of gravy browning. Spoon over the cabbage and top with the bacon.

Dolmades

Serves 6

450 g/1 lb vine leaves
250 ml/8 fl oz/1 cup olive oil
2 large onions, chopped
225 g/8 oz/1 cup long-grain rice
30 ml/2 tbsp pine nuts
120 ml/4 fl oz/½ cup passata (sieved tomatoes)
250 ml/8 fl oz/1 cup chicken stock
15 ml/1 tbsp chopped mint
15 ml/1 tbsp chopped parsley
10 ml/2 tsp ground allspice
Salt and freshly ground black pepper
15 ml/1 tbsp granulated sugar
Juice of 2 lemons
250 ml/8 fl oz/1 cup water
Lemon wedges

Rinse the vine leaves then boil in salted water for 2-3 minutes. Drain, rinse with cold water, drain again and pat dry on kitchen paper. Heat the oil in a saucepan. Add the onions and cook over a gentle heat for 5 minutes. Add the rice and pine nuts and continue cooking gently for 15 minutes, stirring occasionally. Add the passata, stock, herbs and allspice. Season with salt and pepper and add half the sugar and half the lemon juice. Simmer for 5 minutes. Cool slightly. Lay a vine leaf shiny-side down on a board. Remove the stem. Place a small amount of the filling near the stem end. Fold in the sides then roll up and place in a saucepan. Continue until all the vine leaves are stuffed, packing them tightly in the pan in two or three layers. Boil the remaining lemon juice, sugar and water together until the sugar dissolves. Pour over the vine leaves, bring to the boil, reduce the heat, cover and simmer for 1¼ hours. Cool, then chill overnight in the pan. Serve chilled, garnished with the lemon wedges.

Sogan Dolma

Serves 6-8

16 smallish onions
450 g/1 lb/4 cups minced (ground)
    beef
225 g/8 oz/1 cup long-grain rice
Salt and freshly ground black pepper
2.5 ml/^{1}/$_2$ tsp dried mixed herbs
450 ml/^{3}/$_4$ pt/2 cups passata (sieved
    tomatoes)
120 ml/4 fl oz/^{1}/$_2$ cup beef stock
3 lemons

Peel the onions and cut out the cores at the root ends. Make a slit from top to bottom on one side of the onion. Cook in boiling water for 5 minutes. Drain, rinse with cold water and drain again. Carefully separate the onions into layers. Mix the minced beef with the rice, a little salt and pepper and the herbs. Press a small amount into each onion 'shell'. Place in a single layer in a roasting tin (pan). Blend the passata with the stock and pour over. Cover with foil and bake at 180°C/350°F/gas mark 4 for about 40 minutes until the onions are tender and the meat is cooked. Squeeze the juice of one of the lemons and drizzle all over. Serve hot with the remaining lemons cut into wedges.

Jalopeno John

Serves 6

15 g/^{1}/$_2$ oz/1 tbsp butter
4 beef or turkey breakfast slices or
    streaky bacon rashers (slices),
    diced
1 onion, finely chopped
100 g/4 oz/^{1}/$_2$ cup long-grain rice
Boiling water
425 g/15 oz/1 large can black-eyed
    beans, drained
Salt and freshly ground black
    pepper
1 jalopeno pepper, seeded and
    chopped
Corn chips
Ready-prepared tomato salsa

Melt the butter in a large frying pan (skillet). Add the meat and onion and fry (sauté) for 3-4 minutes. Add the rice and cook for 1 minute. Just cover with boiling water, bring to the boil, reduce the heat and simmer for 10-15 minutes until the rice is tender, topping up with boiling water if necessary. Stir in the beans, a good seasoning of salt and pepper and the jalopeno pepper. Toss gently. Spoon on to plates and serve with the corn chips and tomato salsa.

Grilled Aubergine with Peanut Sauce and Wild Rice

Serves 4

100 g/4 oz/¹⁄₂ cup wild rice
1 large aubergine (eggplant), sliced
45 ml/3 tbsp olive oil
Salt and freshly ground black pepper
1 garlic clove, crushed
150 ml/¹⁄₄ pt/²⁄₃ cup water
75 ml/5 tbsp smooth peanut butter
30 ml/2 tbsp soy sauce
Few drops of Tabasco sauce
5 ml/1 tsp grated fresh root ginger
2.5 ml/¹⁄₂ tsp cayenne
1 red (bell) pepper, chopped

Cook the rice according to the packet directions and drain. Meanwhile, place the aubergine slices on a grill (broiler) rack. Brush with half the oil and season with salt and pepper. Grill (broil) until golden, turn over, brush again with oil and season lightly. Grill until cooked through. Put all the remaining ingredients except the red pepper in a small pan and heat through, stirring, for 2 minutes. Arrange the aubergine slices on a bed of rice, top each slice with a little peanut sauce and scatter the red pepper over.

Ceviche with Baby Corn Rice

Serves 6

450 g/1 lb firm white fish fillet, skinned and cubed
1 onion, sliced into rings
1 green (bell) pepper, diced
1 green chilli, seeded and chopped
Salt and freshly ground black pepper
75 ml/5 tbsp fresh lime or lemon juice
15 ml/1 tbsp chopped parsley
175 g/6 oz/³⁄₄ cup long-grain rice
6 baby corn cobs, cut into quarters
Cayenne

Put the fish in a shallow dish. Add the onion, green pepper and chilli. Season with salt and pepper and drizzle over the lime or lemon juice and add the parsley. Toss lightly and leave to stand for 2 hours or until the fish turns pure white (as if cooked). Meanwhile, cook the rice in plenty of boiling, salted water for 10 minutes or until tender. Add the corn cobs for the last 3 minutes of cooking. Drain, rinse with cold water and drain again. Spoon in a small pile at the side of 6 serving plates. Dust with the cayenne. Spoon the ceviche beside the rice and serve cold.

Cloud Nine

Serves 4-6

225 g/8 oz/1 cup arborio or other
* risotto rice*
4 canned anchovy fillets, drained
* and finely chopped*
185 g/6¹/₂ oz/1 small can tuna,
* drained*
75 ml/5 tbsp olive oil
50 g/2 oz/¹/₂ cup chopped parsley
Freshly ground black pepper
Parsley sprigs

Boil the rice in plenty of salted water for 15-20 minutes until just tender but still with some texture. Drain, rinse with cold water and drain again. Put the anchovies, tuna, oil, chopped parsley and some pepper in a small saucepan and simmer for 10 minutes until well blended, stirring frequently. Spoon the cool rice on to small serving plates. Spoon the hot sauce over, add a good grinding of pepper and garnish with the parsley sprigs.

Huevos a la Cubana

Serves 4

175 g/6 oz/³/₄ cup long-grain rice
1 onion, finely chopped
1 small garlic clove, crushed
60 ml/4 tbsp olive oil
2 bananas, cut into thick chunks
4 eggs

Cook the rice in plenty of boiling salted water for 10 minutes or until tender. Drain. Meanwhile, fry (sauté) the onion and garlic in 15 ml/1 tbsp of the oil until soft and brown. Remove from the pan with a draining spoon and keep warm. Add a further 15 ml/1 tbsp of the oil to the pan and fry the bananas until just cooked but still

holding their shape. Add to the onion. In a clean frying pan (skillet) heat the remaining oil and fry the eggs until set. Pile the rice on 4 warm plates. Slide an egg on top of each and garnish with the fried onion and garlic and the bananas.

Cooling Stuffed Peaches

Serves 4

50 g/2 oz/¹/₂ cup cooked long-grain
* rice*
175 g/6 oz/³/₄ cup cottage cheese
2 celery sticks, chopped
¹/₂ small red (bell) pepper, finely
* chopped*
4 spring onions (scallions), finely
* chopped*
Juice of ¹/₂ lemon
30 ml/2 tbsp mayonnaise
15 ml/1 tbsp sultanas (golden
* raisins)*
Salt and freshly ground black
* pepper*
8 canned peach halves, drained
Lollo rosso leaves

Mix the rice with all the ingredients except the peaches and salad leaves. Stir gently then pile the mixture on to the peach halves. Arrange on a bed of lollo rosso leaves and chill until ready to serve.

Spiced Stuffed Pears

Serves 4

Prepare as for Cooling Stuffed Peaches but substitute canned pear halves for the peaches and add a green chilli, seeded and chopped, to the stuffing.

Avocado Ambrosia

Serves 4

2 ripe avocados, halved and stoned (pitted)
5 ml/1 tsp lemon juice
50 g/2 oz/¹/₂ cup cooked long-grain rice
30 ml/2 tbsp mayonnaise
1 red eating (dessert) apple, finely chopped with skin on
100 g/4 oz/1 cup cooked ham, finely diced
200 g/7 oz/1 small can Mexican sweetcorn (corn with bell peppers)

Scoop out the avocado flesh into a bowl. Mash well with the lemon juice. Add the remaining ingredients and mix thoroughly. Pile back into the avocado shells and serve straight away.

Sesame Avocado with Pink Grapefruit

Serves 4

2 small avocados, peeled, stoned (pitted) and sliced
Lemon juice
1 pink grapefruit, peeled and cut into segments
15 ml/1 tbsp chopped mint
100 g/4 oz/1 cup cooked long-grain rice
15 ml/1 tbsp sunflower oil
15 ml/1 tbsp sesame oil
A pinch of caster (superfine) sugar
Salt and freshly ground black pepper
Lettuce leaves
Toasted sesame seeds

Toss the avocado slices in lemon juice to prevent browning. Halve the grapefruit segments. Mix together in a bowl with the mint and rice. Whisk the oils with the sugar and a little salt and pepper. Whisk in 5 ml/1 tsp lemon juice. Add to the salad and toss gently. Pile on to a bed of lettuce and sprinkle with the sesame seeds before serving.

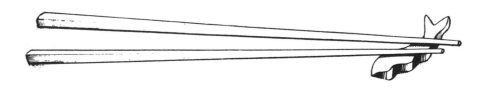

Tuna Mousse-stuffed Lemons

Serves 6

6 large lemons
185 g/6¹/₂ oz/1 small can tuna, drained
5 ml/1 tsp Dijon mustard
45 ml/3 tbsp mayonnaise
1.5 ml/¹/₄ tsp cayenne
Salt and freshly ground black pepper
15 ml/1 tbsp snipped chives
50 g/2 oz/¹/₂ cup cooked long-grain rice
1 egg white
45 ml/3 tbsp whipping cream
¹/₂ cucumber, thinly sliced

Trim one end of the lemons so they stand up. Scoop out the lemon flesh. Discard any pith and membranes and chop the flesh. Place in a bowl and mix in the tuna, mustard, mayonnaise, cayenne, a little salt and pepper, the chives and rice. Whisk the egg white until stiff, then the cream until peaking. Fold the cream, then the egg white into the fish mixture. Pile the mixture up in the lemons and chill for 2 hours. Serve on saucers, surrounded by the cucumber slices.

Hollywood Stuffed Tomatoes

Serves 6

50 g/2 oz/¹/₄ cup brown rice
6 beefsteak tomatoes
200 g/7 oz/1 packet low-fat soft cheese
A little single (light) cream
10 ready-to-eat stoned (pitted) prunes, chopped
30 ml/2 tbsp snipped chives
Freshly ground black pepper
6 pecan halves

Cook the rice according to the packet directions (or see page 12). Drain, rinse with cold water and drain again. Meanwhile, cut a slice off the top of each tomato, scoop out the seeds and discard. Wipe dry with kitchen paper. Mash the cheese with a little cream, the prunes and the chives. Work in the rice and add a little more cream to soften if necessary. Season with pepper. Pile into the tomatoes and top each with a pecan half. Chill before serving.

Devilled Stuffed Eggs

Serves 4

175 g/6 oz/³/₄ cup long-grain rice
30 ml/2 tbsp olive oil
10 ml/2 tsp lemon juice
Salt and freshly ground black
pepper
15 ml/1 tbsp pumpkin seeds
4 hard-boiled (hard-cooked) eggs
200 g/7 oz/1 packet low-fat soft
cheese
Anchovy essence (extract)
45 ml/3 tbsp Worcestershire sauce
30 ml/2 tbsp tomato ketchup
(catsup)
15 ml/1 tbsp tomato chilli relish
2.5 ml/¹/₂ tsp made mustard
30 ml/2 tbsp mayonnaise
4 anchovy fillets, split lengthways
Parsley sprigs

Cook the rice in plenty of boiling, salted water until tender. Drain, rinse with cold water and drain again. Place in a bowl. Add the oil, lemon juice, a little salt, lots of pepper and the pumpkin seeds. Toss well and spoon on to individual serving plates. Halve the eggs lengthways and scoop out the yolks. Mash with the cheese and anchovy essence to taste. Season lightly. Spoon back into the whites and place on the rice. Blend together the remaining ingredients except the anchovies and parsley. Thin with a little lemon juice if liked. Spoon over the eggs and garnish each with half an anchovy rolled into a curl and a small parsley sprig.

Cornish Stuffed Eggs

Serves 4

4 hard-boiled (hard-cooked) eggs
120 g/5 oz/1 small can pilchards in
tomato sauce
10 ml/2 tsp snipped chives
25 g/1 oz/¹/₄ cup cooked long-grain
rice
15 ml/1 tbsp salad cream
15 ml/1 tbsp single (light) cream
A pinch of cayenne
Shredded lettuce
Parsley sprigs

Halve the eggs lengthways. Scoop the yolks into a bowl and mash with the pilchards (discarding the bones, if preferred). Add the chives, rice, salad cream, single cream and a pinch of cayenne. Mix well, then pile back into the egg halves. Serve on a bed of lettuce, garnished with parsley sprigs.

Portuguese Stuffed Eggs

Serves 4

Prepare as for Cornish Stuffed Eggs but substitite sardines in oil, drained, for the pilchards and add 10 ml/2 tsp horseradish cream to the mixture.

Tortellini in Black Butter

Serves 6

*250 g/9 oz/1 packet tortellini with 3
   cheeses*
*175 g/6 oz/³/₄ cup unsalted (sweet)
   butter*
3 garlic cloves, halved
*175 g/6 oz/1¹/₂ cups grated Parmesan
   cheese*
*Salt and freshly ground black
   pepper*
Chopped parsley

Cook the pasta according to the packet
directions, drain and return to the
saucepan. Meanwhile, melt the butter in a
frying pan (skillet). Add the garlic and fry
(sauté) until the garlic is golden and the
butter nut-brown. Remove and discard the
garlic. Pour the butter over the pasta with
half the cheese, a little salt and pepper and
half the parsley. Toss well over a gentle
heat then serve immediately, garnished
with the remaining parsley and the rest of
the cheese handed separately.

Eggs Italian-style

Serves 4

175 g/6 oz green tagliatelle (verdi)
Knob of butter
*4 large tomatoes, skinned, seeded
   and chopped*
A few torn fresh basil leaves
2 eggs
*150 ml/¹/₄ pt/²/₃ cup single (light)
   cream*
*Salt and freshly ground black
   pepper*

Cook the pasta according to the packet
directions. Drain and toss with the butter.
Divide between 6 individual ovenproof
dishes. Spoon the tomatoes over and scatter with the basil leaves. Beat the eggs and
cream together with a little salt and pepper.
Spoon over the tomatoes. Cover each dish
with foil and bake at 160°C/325°F/gas
mark 3 for 30 minutes or until the egg is
set. Serve hot.

Prawn and Avocado Cream

Serves 6

175 g/6 oz/1¹/₂ cups twistetti
3 large or 6 small ripe avocados
75 ml/5 tbsp chicken stock
150 ml/¹/₄ pt/²/₃ cup whipped cream
Lemon juice
Tabasco sauce
*100 g/4 oz/1 cup peeled prawns
   (shrimp)*
Shredded lettuce
Cayenne

Cook the pasta according to the packet
directions. Drain, rinse with cold water and
drain again. Halve the avocados and scoop
out the flesh, discarding the stones (pits).
Place in a blender or food processor and
blend until smooth. Blend in the stock.
Fold in the cream and spike with the lemon
juice and Tabasco. Fold in the prawns.
Place the lettuce in individual bowls or
plates. Top with the pasta, then spoon over
the sauce. Garnish with cayenne.

Japanese Crab Stick Ravioli with Lime Sauce

Serves 4

100 g/4 oz/1 cup strong plain (bread)
flour
1 size 1 egg
Pinch of salt
15 ml/1 tbsp olive oil
5 ml/1 tsp sesame oil (or extra olive
oil)
30 ml/2 tbsp semolina (cream of
wheat)
175 g/6 oz crab sticks, chopped
45 ml/3 tbsp single (light) cream
Salt and freshly ground black
pepper
1 size 4 egg, beaten
200 ml/7 fl oz/scant 1 cup vegetable
stock
A few drops of anchovy essence
(extract)
3 kaffir lime leaves (or pared rind of
1/2 lime)
2.5 ml/1/2 tsp dried lemon grass
5 ml/1 tsp grated fresh root ginger
15 ml/1 tbsp soy sauce
15 ml/1 tbsp cornflour (cornstarch)
30 ml/2 tbsp water

Put the flour, egg, salt, oils and semolina in a food processor and run the machine to form a firm dough. Alternatively, work all the ingredients together by hand. Knead on a lightly floured surface until smooth and elastic. Wrap in a plastic bag and leave to rest for 30 minutes. Mix together the crab sticks, cream and a little salt and pepper. Roll out the dough thinly and cut into 16 rounds using a 6 cm/2 1/2 in cutter. Place the crab filling in the centre of 8 of the circles. Brush the edges with beaten egg and place the other 8 circles on top. Press the edges well together and crimp between finger and thumb to seal. Put the stock, anchovy essence, lime, lemon grass, ginger and soy sauce in a saucepan. Bring to the boil and simmer for 5 minutes. Blend the cornflour with the water, stir into the sauce and simmer for a 2 minutes. Meanwhile, drop the ravioli into a pan of boiling salted water and cook for 5 minutes until just tender. Drain. Place 2 ravioli on each of 4 warm serving plates. Strain the sauce over and serve.

Crisp Fried Noodles

Serves 4

225 g/8 oz/4 cups cooked ribbon
noodles, cut into short lengths
Oil for deep frying
Coarse sea salt
Black and green olives
Gherkins (cornichons)
Radishes

Make sure the pasta is completely dry and that the strands are separate. Heat the oil to 190°C/375°F or until a cube of day-old bread browns in 30 seconds. Deep-fry the noodles in small batches in a wire basket until crisp and golden brown. Drain on kitchen paper then toss in the salt. Arrange the olives, gherkins and radishes in small piles or in little dishes on individual serving plates or bowls. Add a pile of crispy noodles to each plate and eat with the fingers.

Note: Other pasta shapes can be deep fried. They also make a good garnish for oriental dishes and soups.

Little Souffléed Sardines

Serves 4

2 × 100 g/2 × 4 oz/2 small cans sild
   sardines in tomato sauce
298 g/10^{1}/$_2$ oz/1 can condensed celery
   soup
2 eggs, separated
175 g/6 oz/3 cups cooked conchiglie
30 ml/2 tbsp grated Parmesan
   cheese
Salt and freshly ground black
   pepper

Lay the fish in 4 individual ovenproof
dishes, each about 12 cm/5 in diameter (or
1 larger soufflé dish). Whisk the soup with
the egg yolks. Stir in the pasta with the
Parmesan. Season lightly. Whisk the egg
whites until stiff and fold into the mixture
with a metal spoon. Pile on top of the fish
and bake at 190°C/375°F/gas mark 5 for
about 25 minutes or until well risen and
golden on top. Serve straight away.

Tuna-stuffed Cucumber

Serves 6

1 large straight cucumber
Lettuce leaves
1 red (bell) pepper, cut into thin
   rings
185 g/6^{1}/$_2$ oz/1 small can tuna,
   drained
Grated rind and juice of 1 lime
15 ml/1 tbsp mayonnaise
100 g/4 oz/2 cups cooked wholewheat
   zite or other pasta shapes
Salt and freshly ground black
   pepper
Lime twists

Cut channels down the length of the
cucumber all round with a cannelling tool

or a small sharp knife. Cut into 6 equal
lengths. Scoop out and discard the seeds
and place the cucumber on a bed of lettuce
leaves on individual plates. Finely chop
half the pepper and mix with the tuna, lime
rind and juice, mayonnaise and pasta. Toss
lightly but thoroughly, adding salt and pepper to taste. Pile into the cucumber pieces
and garnish with the reserved pepper rings
and lime twists.

Tuna Baked Custard

Serves 4

75 g/3 oz/^{3}/$_4$ cup soup pasta
100 g/4 oz/1 cup frozen mixed
   vegetables
185 g/6^{1}/$_2$ oz/1 small can tuna,
   drained
2 eggs
300 ml/^{1}/$_2$ pt/1^{1}/$_4$ cups milk
2.5 ml/^{1}/$_2$ tsp dried mixed herbs
Salt and freshly ground black
   pepper
Parsley sprigs

Cook the pasta and mixed vegetables in
plenty of boiling salted water for 5 minutes. Drain. Mix with the tuna and divide
between 4 individual ovenproof dishes.
Beat the eggs and milk together with the
herbs and some salt and pepper. Pour over
the tuna. Stand the dishes in 2.5 cm/1 in of
hot water in a baking tin (pan). Bake at
190°C/375°F/gas mark 5 for about 30 minutes until set. Serve hot, garnished with the
parsley.

Peruvian Ocopa

Serves 6

1 small onion, chopped
2 garlic cloves, crushed
Corn oil
2 green chillies, seeded and chopped
175 g/6 oz/1¹/₂ cups walnut halves
6 salted wholewheat digestive
  biscuits (Graham crackers)
6 plain sweet biscuits (cookies)
225 g/8 oz/1 cup cottage cheese
Milk, if necessary
15 ml/1 tbsp chopped coriander
  (cilantro)
Lettuce leaves
225 g/8 oz cooked penne or rigatoni,
  or sliced boiled potatoes
2 hard-boiled (hard-cooked) eggs,
  cut into wedges
6 black olives

Fry (sauté) the onion and garlic in 15 ml/
1 tbsp of the oil until a rich golden brown.
Place in a blender or food processor with
the chillies and add enough oil to just
cover the blades. Add the nuts, biscuits,
cottage cheese and coriander and purée
until smooth. Add a little milk if too stiff.
Pile on to the lettuce leaves on 6 plates.
Arrange a little of the cold pasta around
each and garnish with wedges of egg and a
black olive.

Seafood and Fennel Tagliatelle

Serves 6

350 g/12 oz multicoloured tagliatelle
45 ml/3 tbsp olive oil
1 fennel bulb, finely chopped,
  reserving the green fronds
8 spring onions (scallions), chopped
30 ml/2 tbsp white wine
225 g/8 oz/2 cups frozen seafood
  cocktail, just thawed
Salt and freshly ground black
  pepper
Lemon twists

Cook the pasta according to the packet
directions. Drain. Meanwhile, heat the oil
in a saucepan. Add the chopped fennel and
spring onions and cook, stirring, for 3 minutes. Cover with a lid and cook gently for
5 minutes until softened. Add the wine and
the seafood. Bring to the boil, reduce the
heat and cook gently, stirring until hot
through, for about 3 minutes. Season to
taste with salt and pepper. Toss with the
tagliatelle and garnish with the lemon
twists and the reserved fennel fronds.

Vermicelli Tarragonna

Serves 4

100 g/4 oz/1½ cup butter, softened
30 ml/2 tbsp chopped tarragon
1 garlic clove, crushed
Freshly ground black pepper
225 g/8 oz vermicelli
Olive oil
Thin slivers of fresh Parmesan

Mash the butter with the tarragon, garlic and a good grinding of pepper until well blended. Shape into a roll on a sheet of greaseproof (waxed) paper or clingfilm (plastic wrap). Roll up and chill until required. Cook the pasta according to the packet directions. Drain well. *Either* unwrap the tarragon butter and cut into thin slices, toss the vermicelli in a little olive oil then pile on to plates and dot all over with the tarragon butter and garnish with the Parmesan, *or* roughly cut up the butter, add to the vermicelli and toss over a gentle heat until melted, pile on to warm plates and drizzle with olive oil then top with the Parmesan cheese.

Note: the butter mixture is also good spread on slices of French bread, reshaped into a loaf, wrapped in foil and baked in a moderate oven for about 20 minutes.

Bagna Cauda Con Spaghetti

Serves 4-6

225-350 g/8-12 oz wholewheat spaghetti
75 ml/5 tbsp walnut oil
75 ml/5 tbsp olive oil
3 garlic cloves, finely chopped
50 g/2 oz/1 small can anchovies, drained and chopped
25 g/1 oz/2 tbsp unsalted (sweet) butter
1 tomato, seeded and finely chopped
45 ml/3 tbsp double (heavy) cream (optional)

Cook the spaghetti according to the packet directions. Drain and return to the saucepan. Meanwhile, heat the oils in a saucepan. Add the garlic and fry (sauté) until golden. Reduce the heat, add the anchovies and cook gently, stirring until they have 'melted' into the oil. Stir in the butter until melted. Add the tomato and cream, if using, and heat through. Taste and add salt if necessary. Add to the cooked spaghetti. Toss well and serve piping hot.

Aromatic Angel Hair

Serves 4-6
225 g/8 oz capellini
200 ml/7 fl oz/scant 1 cup olive oil
4 garlic cloves, chopped
25 ml/1¹/₂ tbsp grated fresh root
  ginger
Freshly grated Parmesan cheese

Cook the pasta according to the packet directions. Drain. Heat the oil in a saucepan. Add the garlic and ginger and cook for 2-3 minutes until lightly golden. Remove from the heat. Pile the pasta on warm plates and drizzle over the fragrant oil. Serve with lots of Parmesan cheese.

Tapenade-dressed Linguini

Serves 4-6
250 ml/8 fl oz/1 cup olive oil
225 g/8 oz/1¹/₃ cups stoned (pitted)
  black olives
225 g/8 oz/1¹/₃ cups stoned (pitted)
  green olives
3 garlic cloves
2 × 50 g/2 × 2 oz/2 small cans
  anchovies, drained
75g/3 oz/³/₄ cup chopped parsley
45 ml/3 tbsp lemon juice
Freshly ground black pepper
350 g/12 oz linguini
Thin slivers of fresh Parmesan
  cheese

Put all the ingredients except the linguini and Parmesan in a food processor or blender. Run the machine until a smooth paste is formed. Stop the machine and scrape down the sides from time to time. Cook the pasta according to the packet directions. Drain and return to the saucepan. Add the tapenade. Toss well over a gentle heat and serve garnished with thin slivers of Parmesan cheese.

Curried Conchiglie, Melon and Prawn Cocktail

Serves 6
100 g/4 oz/1 cup conchiglie
150 ml/¹/₄ pt/²/₃ cup mayonnaise
45 ml/3 tbsp crème fraîche
10 ml/2 tsp curry paste
225 g/8 oz/2 cups peeled prawns
  (shrimp)
¹/₂ honeydew melon, diced or scooped
  into balls
2 celery sticks, sliced
Salt and freshly ground black
  pepper
Shredded lettuce
Lemon wedges

Cook the pasta according to the packet directions. Drain, rinse with cold water and drain again. Meanwhile, mix the mayonnaise with the crème fraîche and curry paste. Add the prawns, melon and celery to the pasta and season with salt and pepper. Spoon on to the lettuce in 6 wine goblets. Spoon the curry sauce over and serve garnished with a lemon wedge on the side of each glass.

Japanese-style Dipped Noodles

Serves 4-6

450 ml/³/₄ pt/2 cups dashi (Japanese seaweed and fish stock), or water and 2 fish stock cubes
45 ml/3 tbsp mirim (Japanese rice wine), or dry sherry
45 ml/3 tbsp soy sauce
225 g/8 oz dried bonito (fish) flakes, or anchovy essence to taste
Japanese soba or somen noodles, or Chinese egg noodles

Place all the ingredients except the noodles in a saucepan. Bring slowly to the boil. Reduce the heat and simmer gently for 10 minutes. If using the fish flakes, strain through a sieve (strainer) lined with muslin (cheesecloth). Pour into 4 or 6 individual bowls. Meanwhile, cook the noodles according to the packet directions (or cook them in advance and serve cold). Serve for dipping in the bowls of sauce.

Spaghetti with Pesto

Serves 4

14 large basil leaves
2 garlic cloves, chopped
5 ml/1 tsp coarse sea salt
15 ml/1 tbsp toasted pine nuts
30 ml/2 tbsp freshly grated Parmesan cheese
45 ml/3 tbsp olive oil
Freshly ground black pepper
225 g/8 oz spaghetti
Flakes of butter
Extra Parmesan cheese

Place the basil leaves in a blender or food processor with the garlic and salt and run the machine until they form a purée, or pound in a pestle and mortar. Add the nuts and measured cheese and blend until smooth, scraping the mixture from the sides as necessary, or pound in the mortar. Gradually add the oil a drop at a time until the mixture becomes a thick green sauce. Add a good grinding of pepper. Meanwhile, cook the spaghetti according to the packet directions. Drain and return to the saucepan. Add the pesto and toss over a gentle heat until glistening. Serve dotted with the butter and Parmesan cheese.

Spinach and Cashew Nut Glory

Serves 4-6

225 g/8 oz young spinach, washed thoroughly and drained
100 g/4 oz/1 cup grated Pecorino cheese
100 g/4 oz/1 cup unsalted cashew nuts
2 garlic cloves, crushed
30 ml/2 tbsp lemon juice
250 ml/8 fl oz/1 cup olive oil
Salt and freshly ground black pepper
A little hot water
350 g/12 oz wholewheat spaghetti

Chop the spinach in a blender or food processor. Add the cheese, nuts, garlic and lemon juice and run the machine until well blended. Add the olive oil in a thin stream with the machine running all the time until a smooth paste is formed. Season lightly. If too thick, add a little hot water. Meanwhile, cook the spaghetti according to the packet directions. Drain and return to the saucepan. Add the paste to the cooked spaghetti and toss well over a gentle heat until the paste has melted. Serve straight away.

Sun-kissed Tagliarini

Serves 4

285 g/10¹/₂ oz/1 small jar sun-dried tomatoes, drained, reserving the oil
Olive oil
100 g/4 oz/1 cup grated Parmesan cheese
50 g/2 oz/¹/₂ cup chopped mixed nuts
50 g/2 oz/¹/₂ cup chopped parsley
2 garlic cloves
225 g/8 oz tagliarini

Put the tomatoes in a blender or food processor. Make up the reserved tomato oil to 300 ml/¹/₂ pt/1¹/₄ cups with olive oil. Add the oil to the blender with the remaining ingredients except the pasta. Run the machine until the mixture forms a smooth paste, stopping the machine and scraping down the sides from time to time. If the paste is a too thick, add a little hot water. Cook the pasta according to the packet directions. Drain and return to the saucepan. Add the paste and heat gently, tossing until every strand is coated. Serve straight away.

Kitchen Garden Spaghettini

Serves 4

100 g/4 oz/¹/₂ cup butter
50 g/2 oz/¹/₂ cup ground almonds
20 ml/4 tsp grated Parmesan cheese
45 ml/3 tbsp chopped parsley
10 ml/2 tsp chopped sage
Salt and freshly ground black pepper
225 g/8 oz spaghettini
Crumbled Wensleydale cheese
Toasted flaked almonds

Mash the butter with the ground almonds. Work in the Parmesan cheese and the herbs and season well. Cook the spaghettini according to the packet directions. Drain and return to the saucepan. Add the herb paste and toss over a gentle heat until melted and the sauce coats every strand. Serve garnished with the Wensleydale cheese and the flaked almonds.

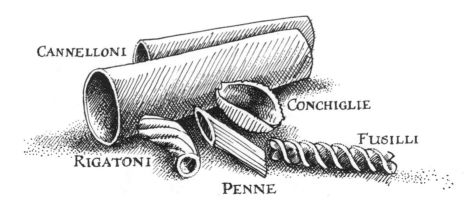

CANNELLONI
CONCHIGLIE
FUSILLI
RIGATONI
PENNE

Spaghetti with Attitude

Serves 4-6

3 garlic cloves
50 ml/2 fl oz/3¹/₂ tbsp olive oil
30 ml/2 tbsp sun-dried tomato oil
25 g/1 oz/¹/₄ cup grated Parmesan
cheese
8 basil leaves
200 g/7 oz/1³/₄ cups sun-dried
tomatoes
Freshly ground black pepper
225-350 g/8-12 oz spaghetti,
preferably fresh
Thin shavings of fresh Parmesan
cheese
A few extra torn basil leaves

Put the garlic in a blender or processor and chop. Add the olive and tomato oils and run the machine until well blended. Add the grated cheese and blend briefly again. Add the 8 basil leaves and the tomatoes and run the machine until roughly chopped but not a smooth paste. Season with lots of black pepper. Cook the spaghetti according to the packet directions. Drain and return to the saucepan. Add the tomato mixture and toss over a gentle heat. Pile on to plates and serve with the Parmesan shavings and torn basil leaves scattered over.

Fusilli Fantastico

Serves 4-6

400 g/14 oz/1 large can pimientos,
drained
2 garlic cloves
300 ml/¹/₂ pt/1¹/₄ cups olive oil
75 g/3 oz/¹/₂ cup stuffed olives
50 g/2 oz/¹/₂ cup grated Parmesan
cheese
50 g/2 oz/¹/₂ cup chopped parsley
30 ml/2 tbsp lemon juice
Salt and freshly ground black
pepper
350 g/12 oz fusilli
A little grated Mozzarella cheese

Put all the ingredients except the salt and pepper, pasta and Mozzarella in a food processor or blender. Run the machine until the mixture forms a paste. Stop the machine and scrape down the sides from time to time. Taste and season with a little salt and lots of black pepper. Cook the fusilli according to the packet directions. Drain and return to the saucepan. Add the paste and toss over a gentle heat until bathed in the rich sauce. Serve topped with the Mozzarella.

Melon and Salami Antipasto

Serves 6

100 g/4 oz/1 cup conchiglie
45 ml/3 tbsp olive oil
15 ml/1 tbsp white wine vinegar
A pinch each of salt and freshly
    ground black pepper
A pinch of caster (superfine) sugar
2.5 ml/¹/₂ tsp dried oregano
2.5 ml/¹/₂ tsp Dijon mustard
1 small cantaloupe melon, seeded
    and chopped
50 ml/2 oz/¹/₂ cup coarsely chopped
    pecans
45 ml/3 tbsp raisins
Lettuce leaves
120 g/5 oz/1 small can sild sardines,
    drained
12 salami slices

Cook the pasta according to the packet directions. Drain, rinse with cold water and drain again. Whisk the oil, vinegar, seasoning, sugar, oregano and mustard together in a bowl. Add the pasta, melon, nuts and raisins and toss lightly. Pile on to a bed of lettuce and arrange the sardines and salami in rolls or cornets around the edge.

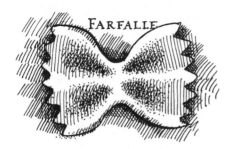
FARFALLE

Kipper Pâté Rolls

Serves 6

6 lasagne sheets
450 g/1 lb/2 packets boil-in-the-bag
    kipper fillets
200 g/7 oz/1 packet low-fat soft
    cheese
Juice of ¹/₂ lemon
Cayenne
Freshly ground black pepper
Mixed salad leaves
150 ml/¹/₄ pt/²/₃ cup soured (dairy
    sour) cream
Tomato and lemon wedges

Drop the lasagne sheets one after the other into a pan of boiling, lightly salted water. Cook for about 10 minutes until tender. Drain, rinse with cold water then lay over the side of the colander so they don't stick together. Meanwhile, cook the kipper fillets according to the packet directions. Drain and remove the skins. When cool, mash well with the cheese and add the lemon juice, cayenne and black pepper to taste. Spread over the lasagne sheets and roll up. Place on individual plates on a bed of mixed leaves, spoon a little soured cream over, sprinkle with a little more cayenne and garnish with the tomato and lemon wedges.

Smoked Salmon Rolls

Serves 6

Prepare as for Kipper Pâté Rolls but substitute finely chopped smoked salmon pieces for the kippers. Garnish with a small spoonful of Danish lumpfish roe on top of the soured cream.

Smoked Trout with Horseradish Rolls

Serves 6

Prepare as for Kipper Pâté Rolls but substitute smoked trout fillets for the kippers and poach in water for 10 minutes to cook. Add 15 ml/1 tbsp horseradish cream and omit the cayenne in the seasoning. Sprinkle with snipped chives instead of cayenne.

Garlicky Smoked Mackerel Rolls

Serves 6

Prepare as for Kipper Pâté Rolls but substitute 85 g/3^1/$_2$ oz/scant ^{1}/$_2$ cup garlic and herb soft cheese for half the low-fat plain soft cheese and add 15 ml/1 tbsp chopped parsley. Garnish with more parsley on top of the soured cream.

Huevos Verdi

Serves 4

175 g/6 oz green tagliatelle (verdi)
15 ml/1 tbsp olive oil
Salt and freshly ground black
  pepper
450 g/1 lb/4 cups frozen peas
25 g/1 oz/2 tbsp unsalted (sweet)
  butter
30 ml/2 tbsp crème fraîche
15 ml/1 tbsp chopped mint
4 eggs
Mint sprigs

Cook the pasta according to the packet directions. Drain, rinse with boiling water and drain again. Add the olive oil and a little salt and pepper. Toss and divide between 4 individual warm bowls. Meanwhile, purée the peas, butter, crème fraîche, chopped mint and a little salt and pepper in a blender or food processor. Turn into a saucepan and heat through gently, stirring until piping hot and smooth. Meanwhile, soft-boil (soft-cook) the eggs for 4 minutes. Carefully remove the shells under cold water. Push an egg gently into each pile of pasta and spoon the sauce over. Garnish with the mint sprigs and serve straight away.

Avocado-dressed Pasta

Serves 6

225 g/8 oz/2 cups multicoloured
  conchiglie
15 ml/1 tbsp olive oil
Salt and freshly ground black
  pepper
1 large ripe avocado, halved and
  stoned (pitted)
15 ml/1 tbsp lemon juice
1 small garlic clove, crushed
2.5 ml/^{1}/$_2$ tsp caster (superfine) sugar
150 ml/^{1}/$_4$ pt/^{2}/$_3$ cup crème fraîche
4 spring onions (scallions), chopped
2 celery sticks, finely chopped
15 ml/1 tbsp chopped parsley

Cook the pasta according to the packet directions. Drain, rinse with cold water and drain again. Toss in the olive oil and a little salt and pepper. Spoon on to 6 individual shallow dishes. Meanwhile, scoop out the avocado flesh into a food processor or blender. Add the lemon juice, garlic, sugar and crème fraîche. Run the machine until smooth. Season to taste. Spoon over the pasta and sprinkle with the spring onions, celery and parsley.

Strawberry and Melon Cooler

Serves 6
100 g/4 oz/1 cup red conchiglie (al
    pomodoro)
1 small ripe honeydew melon
100 g/4 oz strawberries, sliced
5 cm/2 in piece cucumber, diced
Grated rind and juice of 1 lime
A little caster (superfine) sugar
    (optional)
15 ml/1 tbsp sunflower oil
Freshly ground black pepper
15 ml/1 tbsp chopped mint
Mint sprigs

Cook the pasta according to the packet
directions. Drain, rinse with cold water and
drain again. Mix with all the remaining
ingredients except the mint sprigs. Toss
gently and chill for 2 hours to allow the
flavours to develop. Spoon into large wine
goblets and garnish each with a sprig of mint.

Creamy Tarragon Mushrooms on Noodles

Serves 4-6
225 g/8 oz mixed green and white
    tagliatelle (paglia e fieno)
15 ml/1 tbsp olive oil
Salt and freshly ground black pepper
450 g/1 lb/4 cups baby button
    mushrooms
30 ml/2 tbsp water
Squeeze of lemon juice
150 ml/¼ pt/⅔ cup soured (dairy
    sour) cream
30 ml/2 tbsp mayonnaise
15 ml/1 tbsp chopped tarragon
10 ml/2 tsp chopped parsley
A few tarragon sprigs

Cook the pasta according to the packet
directions. Drain, rinse with cold water and
drain again. Toss in the oil with a little salt
and pepper and pile on to individual serving plates. Meanwhile, cook the mushrooms in the water and lemon juice either
in a saucepan or in a bowl in the
microwave. Drain, reserving the liquid,
and leave to cool. Mix the soured cream
with the mayonnaise, chopped tarragon,
parsley and a little salt and pepper. Fold in
the mushrooms and thin the mixture with a
little of the mushroom liquid if necessary.
Spoon on to the cold pasta and garnish
with the sprigs of tarragon. Chill until
ready to serve.

Tuna-stuffed Tomatoes

Serves 4
50 g/2 oz/½ cup conchiglietti or
    other soup pasta
8 large ripe tomatoes
2 spring onions (scallions), chopped
90 g/3½ oz/1 small can tuna,
    drained
200 g/7 oz/1 small can pimientos,
    drained and chopped
45 ml/3 tbsp mayonnaise
15 ml/1 tbsp curried fruit chutney
30 ml/2 tbsp plain yoghurt
Salt and freshly ground black pepper

Cook the pasta in plenty of boiling salted
water for about 6-8 minutes until just
tender. Drain, rinse with cold water and
drain again. Cut off and reserve the tops of
the tomatoes, scoop out the seeds and discard. Drain upside-down on kitchen paper.
Mix the pasta with the spring onions, tuna
and pimientos. Blend the mayonnaise with
the chutney, yoghurt and a little salt and
pepper and fold in. Pile back into the
tomato shells and replace the 'lids'. Chill
until ready to serve.

Salmon-stuffed Tomatoes

Serves 4

Prepare as for Tuna-stuffed Tomatoes but substitute red salmon for the tuna and use cucumber relish instead of curried fruit chutney.

Stuffed Tomatoes with Pesto

Serves 6-8

6 or 8 large tomatoes
3 garlic cloves
16 basil leaves
25 g/1 oz/¼ cup ground almonds
120 ml/4 fl oz/½ cup olive oil
50 g/2 oz/½ cup grated Parmesan cheese
225 g/8 oz spaghettini, broken into thirds
Salt and freshly ground black pepper

Cut the tops off the tomatoes. Scoop out the seeds and drain upside down on kitchen paper. Put the garlic, basil and almonds in a food processor. Run the machine briefly to blend, then add the oil in a thin stream. Finally blend in the Parmesan. Cook the pasta according to the packet directions. Drain and return to the saucepan. Add the pesto and toss until well coated in the paste. Season to taste. Spoon into the tomatoes and place in a baking tin (pan). Bake at 200°C/400°F/gas mark 6 for 15 minutes until hot through but the tomatoes still hold their shape.

Aromatic Spaghetti Parcels

Serves 6

15 ml/1 tbsp olive oil
2 garlic cloves, crushed
1 small onion, finely chopped
2 × 400 g/2 × 14 oz/2 large cans chopped tomatoes
100 g/4 oz/1 cup sun-dried tomatoes in oil, drained and chopped
30 ml/2 tbsp sun-dried tomato oil
60 ml/4 tbsp red wine
Salt and freshly ground black pepper
350 g/12 oz spaghetti
Chopped basil
6 × 30 cm/12 in squares double-thickness non-stick baking parchment

Heat the oil in a pan. Add the garlic and onion and fry (sauté) for 2 minutes. Add the two types of tomatoes, the tomato oil, wine and a little salt and pepper. Bring to the boil, reduce the heat and simmer for 20 minutes until thick and pulpy. Meanwhile, cook the spaghetti according to the packet directions. Drain, add to the sauce and toss well. Divide the mixture between one half of each of the 6 squares of double-thickness baking parchment. Sprinkle each portion with chopped basil. Fold over, then roll and crimp the edges to seal all round. Place on a baking sheet and bake at 190°C/375°F/gas mark 5 for 15 minutes until piping hot and fragrant. Transfer to serving plates and let each guest open their own parcel to enjoy the full aroma.

Linguini with Hot Chilli Oil

Serves 6
350g/12 oz linguini
375 ml/13 fl oz/1¹/₂ cups olive oil
6 garlic cloves, chopped
2 thin green chillies, seeded and chopped
1 red jalopeno pepper, seeded and chopped
Freshly ground black pepper
Grated Parmesan cheese

Cook the linguini according to the packet directions. Drain and return to the pan. Heat the oil in a frying pan (skillet). Add the garlic and the green and red chillies and fry (sauté) for 2 minutes. Pour immediately over the pasta, add a good grinding of black pepper and toss well. Serve straight away with the Parmesan cheese and lots of crusty bread.

Peppered Fettuccine with Chicory

Serves 6
350 g/12 oz fettuccine
1 head chicory (Belgian endive)
2 tomatoes, seeded and chopped
15 ml/1 tbsp chopped basil
225 g/8 oz/1 cup unsalted (sweet) butter
175 g/6 oz/1¹/₂ cups grated Pecorino cheese
45 ml/3 tbsp coarsely crushed black peppercorns

Cook the fettuccine according to the packet directions, drain and return to the saucepan. Cut a cone-shaped core out of the base of the chicory. Shred the leaves and mix with the tomatoes and basil. Melt the butter. Pour over the fettuccine and add the cheese and peppercorns. Toss thoroughly over a gentle heat, pile on to serving plates and top each with a spoonful of the chicory and tomato mixture.

Meaty Meals for Every Occasion

This chapter is broken down into Beef and Veal, Pork, Lamb and Poultry and Game recipes.

Turkish Beef and Rice Pot

Serves 4-5

12 button (pearl) onions
30 ml/2 tbsp olive oil
1 aubergine (eggplant), cubed
450 g/1 lb/4 cups minced (ground) beef
400 g/14 oz/1 large can tomatoes
150 ml/¹/₄ pt/²/₃ cup red wine
175 g/6 oz/³/₄ cup long-grain rice
450 ml/³/₄ pt/2 cups beef stock
15 ml/1 tbsp tomato purée (paste)
5 ml/1 tsp ground cinnamon
Salt and freshly ground black pepper
150 ml/¹/₄ pt/²/₃ cup Greek-style plain yoghurt

Fry (sauté) the onions in the oil in a flameproof casserole (Dutch oven), stirring for about 5 minutes until turning golden. Remove from the pan with a draining spoon. Add the aubergine and fry until golden, stirring. Remove from the pan. Add the beef and fry, stirring, until browned and all the grains are separate. Stir in the remaining ingredients except the yoghurt. Return the onions and aubergine to the pan. Bring to the boil. Cover and place in the oven at 190°C/375°F/gas mark 5 for about 1¹/₂ hours until the rice is tender and the liquid has been absorbed. Taste and re-season if necessary. Spoon the yoghurt over and return to the oven for 5 minutes.

Chilli Beef with Rice

Serves 4

4 rashers (slices) streaky bacon, diced
2 onions, finely chopped
1 red (bell) pepper, chopped
450 g/1 lb top rump steak, cubed
Seasoned flour
Olive oil
10 ml/2 tsp chilli powder
10 ml/2 tsp ground cumin
10 ml/2 tsp cumin seeds
2.5 ml/¹/₂ tsp dried oregano
400 g/14 oz/1 large can chopped tomatoes
425 g/15¹/₂ oz/1 large can red kidney beans, drained
300 ml/¹/₂ pt/1¹/₄ cups beef stock
Salt and freshly ground black pepper
225 g/8 oz/1 cup long-grain rice
1 pickled chilli, finely chopped

Dry-fry the bacon in a large pan until the fat runs. Add the onion and pepper and fry (sauté) for 2 minutes. Remove from the pan. Toss the meat in the seasoned flour and brown a little at a time in the pan, adding olive oil as necessary. Return the onion mixture to the pan and add the spices and oregano. Fry, stirring for 1 minute. Add the tomatoes, beans and stock, bring to the boil, reduce the heat, cover and simmer gently for about 45 minutes to 1 hour or until the meat is tender. Season to taste. Meanwhile, cook the rice in plenty of boiling, salted water for about 10-12 minutes until just tender. Drain, rinse with boiling water and drain again. Stir in the pickled chilli. Pile the rice on to warm serving dishes. Top with the meat mixture and serve hot.

Greek Stuffed Tomatoes

Serves 4 as a main course or 8 as a starter

8 large beef tomatoes
Sugar
Salt
750 g/1¹/₂ lb/6 cups minced (ground) lamb
120 ml/4 fl oz/¹/₂ cup olive oil
75 g/3 oz/¹/₃ cup long-grain rice
30 ml/2 tbsp chopped parsley
2 eggs, beaten
75 g/3 oz Cheddar cheese, grated
150 ml/¹/₄ pt/²/₃ cup water

Cut a slice off the round end of each tomato. Scoop out the centre and reserve. Sprinkle the inside with sugar and salt. Fry (sauté) the meat in half the oil until browned and all the grains are separate. Add a little of the tomato pulp, the rice, half the parsley and a little salt. Cook gently, stirring until almost dry. Stir in the eggs and cheese. Spoon into the tomatoes and pack in a shallow ovenproof dish. Pour the remaining oil around and add the reserved tomato pulp. Pour on the water, cover with foil and bake at 180°C/350°F/gas mark 4 for about 1 hour until the rice is tender and the tomatoes are bathed in thick sauce.

Holishkes

Serves 4-6

1 white cabbage
1 onion, finely chopped
50 g/2 oz/¹/₄ cup butter
50 g/2 oz/¹/₄ cup long-grain rice
120 ml/4 fl oz/¹/₂ cup chicken stock
450 g/1 lb/4 cups lean minced (ground) beef
Salt and freshly ground black pepper
175 g/6 oz/³/₄ cup tomato purée (paste)
300 ml/¹/₂ pt/1¹/₄ cups water
60 ml/4 tbsp light brown sugar
Juice of 1 large lemon

Plunge the whole cabbage in boiling water for 3 minutes. Drain and rinse with cold water. Carefully remove 12 leaves (store the remaining cabbage in the fridge to use for another meal). Cook the onion in the butter for 2 minutes until softened but not browned. Stir in the rice and cook for 2 minutes. Add the stock and simmer until the rice has absorbed it. Stir in the meat and season well. Divide the filling among the cabbage leaves. Fold in the sides then roll up to form parcels. Pack into a large casserole (Dutch oven). Blend the tomato purée with the water, sugar and lemon juice. Add salt and pepper to taste. Pour over the cabbage rolls. Cover and cook in the oven at 150°C/300°F/gas mark 2 for 2 hours. Remove the lid, turn the oven up to 190°C/375°F/gas mark 5 and cook for a further 20 minutes or until lightly browned on top.

Picnic Pie

Serves 6

Oil for greasing
350 g/12 oz/3 cups wholemeal flour
A good pinch of salt
175 g/6 oz/³/₄ cup margarine
75 ml/5 tbsp approx. cold water
1 bunch of spring onions (scallions),
    chopped
25 g/1 oz/2 tbsp butter
340 g/12 oz/1 large can corned beef
30 ml/2 tbsp tomato relish
100 g/4 oz/1 cup cooked long-grain
    rice
Salt and freshly ground black
    pepper
3 hard-boiled (hard-cooked) eggs
A little plain (all-purpose) flour
Beaten egg to glaze

Line a 900 g/2 lb loaf tin (pan) with a double thickness of foil, folding down the edges
over the rim. Lightly grease with the oil.
Mix the flour and salt in a bowl. Add the
margarine, cut into small pieces, and rub in
with the fingertips until the mixture resembles fine breadcrumbs. Mix with enough
water to form a firm dough. Knead gently
on a lightly floured surface. Cut off about a
quarter of the dough and reserve for a lid.
Roll out the remaining dough and use to
line the prepared tin, easing it gently into
the corners. Fry (sauté) the spring onions
in the butter for 2 minutes to soften. Mash
the corned beef, work in the tomato relish,
the rice and the fried onion. Season lightly.
Press half this mixture into the pastry-lined
tin. Dust the eggs with flour and place in a
row down the centre of the tin. Top with
the remaining beef mixture, pressing down
well. Roll out the remaining pastry to a
rectangle for a lid. Brush the edges with a
little of the beaten egg and press into posi-
tion. Crimp the edges between finger and
thumb and make a hole in the centre to
allow the steam to escape. Make leaves out
of any pastry trimmings and use to decorate the top. Brush the surface with beaten
egg. Bake at 200°C/400°F/gas mark 6 for
20 minutes then reduce the heat to
180°C/350°F/gas mark 4 and continue
cooking for a further 1 hour. Cover the top
with foil if over-browning. Leave to cool
in the tin for 30 minutes, then carefully lift
out using the foil, and cool on a wire rack.
Chill until ready to serve, cut into slices.

Beef Madras with Cinnamon Rice

Serves 4-6

2 onions, chopped
2 garlic cloves, crushed
75 ml/5 tbsp groundnut (peanut) oil
30 ml/2 tbsp Madras curry powder
1.2 litres/2 pts/5 cups beef stock
30 ml/2 tbsp tomato purée (paste)
30 ml/2 tbsp lemon juice
2 bay leaves
15 ml/1 tbsp light brown sugar
750 g/1¹/₂ lb lean braising steak, cut
    into chunks
Salt and freshly ground black
    pepper
225 g/8 oz/1 cup basmati rice
5 cm/2 in piece cinnamon stick
5 ml/1 tsp ground turmeric

Fry (sauté) the onion and garlic in half the oil for 2 minutes. Stir in the curry powder and fry for 1 minute. Stir in the stock, tomato purée and lemon juice. Add the bay leaves and sugar and bring to the boil. Reduce the heat, cover and simmer for 20 minutes. Meanwhile, brown the meat in the remaining oil in a separate pan. Strain the curry sauce over the meat and season well to taste. Bring to the boil, reduce the heat, cover and simmer gently for 1½ hours or until the meat is really tender. Meanwhile, cook the rice by the absorption method, adding the cinnamon, turmeric and a little salt to the rice. Fluff up when cooked and remove the cinnamon stick before serving with the curry.

Keema Pulao

Serves 6

*100 g/4 oz/⅓ cup brown lentils,
  soaked*
450 g/1 lb/2 cups basmati rice
2 bay leaves
2 large potatoes, sliced
10 ml/2 tsp ground turmeric
30 ml/2 tbsp boiling water
60 ml/4 tbsp groundnut (peanut) oil
4 onions, thinly sliced
*225 g/8 oz/2 cups minced (ground)
  beef or lamb*
10 ml/2 tsp grated fresh root ginger
1 garlic clove, crushed
1 red chilli, seeded and chopped
2 small pieces cinnamon stick
3 cardamom pods, split
1 whole clove
150 ml/¼ pt/⅔ cup plain yoghurt

Cook the lentils in plenty of boiling water for about 1 hour until tender. Drain if necessary. Cook the rice in plenty of boiling salted water with the bay leaves for 10 minutes or until just tender, drain and dis-card the bay leaves. Place the potatoes in a bowl. Blend the turmeric with the boiling water and stir half the mixture into the potatoes. Leave to soak. Heat half of the oil in a pan and fry (sauté) the onions until golden brown. Transfer a quarter of the onions to a saucepan. Add the minced meat and all the spices. Cover with water, bring to the boil and simmer, stirring occasionally, until all the water has evaporated. Meanwhile, drain the potatoes and pat dry on kitchen paper. Fry in the remaining oil until golden. Put half the cooked rice in the base of a large, greased casserole (Dutch oven). Spread the meat over, then all the cooked lentils. Blend the remaining onions with the yoghurt and a little salt and pepper. Spoon over, then top with the potatoes and then the remaining rice. Drizzle the remaining turmeric liquid over. Cover tightly and cook in the oven at 160°C/325°F/gas mark 3 for about 45 minutes or until the potatoes are tender.

71

Roast Veal with Orange and Walnuts

Serves 6

100 g/4 oz/1¹/₂ cup long-grain rice
1.5 ml/¹/₄ tsp saffron powder
750 ml/1¹/₄ pts/3 cups veal or chicken stock
50 g/2 oz/¹/₄ cup butter
100 g/4 oz streaky bacon rashers (slices), rinded and diced
1 bunch of watercress, chopped
75 g/3 oz/³/₄ cup chopped walnuts
Grated rind and juice of 1 orange
Salt and freshly ground black pepper
1 egg, beaten
1.5 kg/3 lb boned veal shoulder
150 ml/¹/₄ pt/²/₃ cup pure orange juice
15 ml/1 tbsp orange liqueur

Cook the rice with the saffron in 450 ml/³/₄ pt/2 cups of the stock for 15 minutes until really tender. Meanwhile, melt half the butter in a frying pan (skillet). Add the bacon and fry (sauté) for 2-3 minutes until crisp, stirring. Add to the cooked rice with the watercress, walnuts, orange rind and a little salt and pepper. Mix with the beaten egg to bind. With a sharp knife, open the cavities in the meat where the bones were to make pockets for the stuffing. Spread the stuffing evenly in the pockets then roll up and tie securely with string. Brown the joint quickly in the remaining butter in a roasting tin (pan). Pour half of the remaining stock and half the orange juice around. Roast in the oven at 180°C/350°F/gas mark 4 for 1¹/₂ hours, basting from time to time. Transfer to a carving dish and keep warm. Stir the remaining stock and orange juice and the orange liqueur into the meat residue in the roasting tin. Bring to the boil, stirring and scraping. Boil rapidly until reduced by half. Taste and season if necessary. Strain into a gravy boat and serve with the meat, thickly sliced.

Rice with Kidneys in Chianti

Serves 4

350 g/12 oz veal or lambs' kidneys
Red wine vinegar
350 g/12 oz/1¹/₂ cups arborio or other risotto rice
15g/¹/₂ oz/1 tbsp unsalted (sweet) butter
30 ml/2 tbsp olive oil
100 g/4 oz/1 cup chopped parsley
120 ml/4 fl oz/¹/₂ cup Chianti Classico
Salt and freshly ground black pepper

Wash the kidneys under cold running water. Skin, snip out the cores with scissors and slice thinly. Place in a dish and cover with red wine vinegar. Chill for 2 hours. Cook the rice in plenty of boiling salted water for 18 minutes. Drain thoroughly. Meanwhile, heat the butter with half the oil in a frying pan (skillet). Drain the kidneys and fry (sauté) for 3 minutes until browned, stirring all the time. Stir in the parsley and wine and simmer for 1-2 minutes until the kidneys are tender. Season to taste. Pile the rice on to a hot serving dish. Add the remaining olive oil and toss gently. Spoon the kidneys over the rice and serve immediately.

Osso Buco con Risotto Milanese

Serves 6

1.1 kg/2¹/₂ lb shin of veal, sawn into 2.5 cm/1 in thick slices
Seasoned flour
50 g/2 oz/¹/₄ cup unsalted (sweet) butter
2 large carrots, chopped
2 onions, chopped
3 celery sticks, chopped
3 garlic cloves, finely chopped
300 ml/¹/₂ pt/1¹/₄ cups dry white wine
300 ml/¹/₂ pt/1¹/₄ cups veal or chicken stock
400 g/14 oz/1 large can tomatoes
Salt and freshly ground black pepper
5 ml/1 tsp caster (superfine) sugar
2 rosemary sprigs
Risotto alla Milanese (page 229)
45 ml/3 tbsp chopped parsley
Finely grated rind of 2 lemons

Wipe the meat and remove any bone chips. Dust with the flour. Melt the butter in a large flameproof casserole (Dutch oven). Add the meat and brown quickly. Carefully remove from the pan, taking care not to dislodge the marrow. Add the carrots, onions, celery and a third of the garlic and fry (sauté) for 2 minutes, stirring. Carefully return to meat to the pan. Pour the wine and stock around and add the tomatoes. Season well and add the sugar and rosemary sprigs. Bring to the boil, cover, reduce the heat and simmer very gently for 1¹/₂ hours until the meat is tender. Meanwhile, prepare the Risotto Milanese. Carefully transfer the meat to warm serving plates. Spoon the sauce over. Mix the parsley with the lemon rind and the remaining garlic. Sprinkle over the Osso Buco and serve with the Risotto Milanese.

Risotto alla Genovese

Serves 4

60 ml/4 tbsp olive oil
1 small onion, finely chopped
60 ml/4 tbsp chopped parsley
225 g/8 oz/2 cups minced (ground) veal
450 g/1 lb/2 cups arborio or other risotto rice
1.2 litres/2 pts/5 cups hot veal or chicken stock
50 g/2 oz/¹/₂ cup grated Parmesan cheese
Salt

Heat the oil in a flameproof casserole (Dutch oven). Add the onion, parsley and veal and fry (sauté), stirring for about 4 minutes until the onion is lightly golden and the grains of meat are brown and separate. Add the rice and cook for 1 minute. Add 2 ladlefuls of the stock and simmer, stirring until it is absorbed. Repeat the process until the rice is just tender and creamy (about 15-20 minutes). Remove from the heat, stir in the cheese and season with salt. Serve hot.

Baked Bean Chilli with Cheesey Rice

Serves 4

350 g/12 oz/3 cups minced (ground) beef
1 onion, finely chopped
1 garlic clove, crushed
2.5 ml/¹/₂ tsp chilli powder
2.5 ml/¹/₂ tsp ground cumin
2.5 ml/¹/₂ tsp dried oregano
300 ml/¹/₂ pt/1¹/₄ cups passata (sieved tomatoes)
15 ml/1 tbsp tomato purée (paste)
150 ml/¹/₄ pt/²/₃ cup beef stock
400 g/14 oz/1 large can baked beans in tomato sauce
Salt and freshly ground black pepper
225 g/8 oz/1 cup long-grain rice
25 g/1 oz/¹/₄ cup grated Parmesan cheese
100 g/4 oz Cheddar cheese, grated

Put the beef in a saucepan with the onion and garlic. Cook, stirring, until the meat is brown and all the grains are separate. Stir in the spices and oregano and cook for 1 minute. Stir in the passata, tomato purée, stock and baked beans. Bring to the boil, reduce the heat and simmer gently for 30 minutes, stirring occasionally. Season to taste. Meanwhile, cook the rice in plenty of boiling salted water until just tender. Drain, rinse with boiling water and drain again. Stir in the Parmesan. Spoon into a flameproof dish. Cover completely with the Cheddar cheese and flash under a hot grill (broiler) until the cheese melts and bubbles. Serve hot with the chilli.

Spicy Beef and Rice Flan

Serves 4

225 g/8 oz/1 cup long-grain rice
2 eggs, beaten
100 g/4 oz Emmental (Swiss) cheese, grated
100 g/4 oz Mozzarella cheese, grated
1 onion, finely chopped
450 g/1 lb/4 cups minced (ground) beef
1 garlic clove, crushed
30 ml/2 tbsp tomato purée (paste)
150 ml/¹/₄ pt/²/₃ cup passata (sieved tomatoes)
1 red chilli, seeded and chopped
2.5 ml/¹/₂ tsp dried oregano
Salt and freshly ground black pepper
3 tomatoes, sliced
A few black olives

Cook the rice in plenty of boiling salted water until tender. Drain, rinse with cold water and drain again thoroughly. Mix in the eggs and half the cheeses. Press into the base and sides of a large 25 cm/10 in flan dish (pie pan). Bake in the oven at 230°C/450°F/gas mark 8 for 12-15 minutes until set and golden. Meanwhile, cook the onion, meat and garlic in a saucepan, stirring until all the grains of meat are brown and separate. Stir in the tomato purée, passata, chilli and oregano and simmer until thick, stirring occasionally, for about 6 minutes. Season to taste. Spoon into the cooked flan. Arrange the tomato slices on top and sprinkle with the remaining cheese. Return to the oven at the same temperature and cook for a further 10-15 minutes or until the top is bubbling and golden. Serve hot, garnished with the olives.

Dry Beef Curry with Spiced Rice

Serves 4

30 ml/2 tbsp sunflower oil
2 onions, sliced
1 green (bell) pepper, diced
1.5 ml/¼ tsp chilli powder
2.5 ml/½ tsp ground cumin
2.5 ml/½ tsp ground coriander
(cilantro)
1.5 cml/¼ tsp ground cinnamon
30 ml/2 tbsp garam masala
450 g/1 lb/4 cups minced (ground)
beef
Salt and freshly ground black
pepper
225 g/8 oz/1 cup basmati rice
25 g/1 oz/2 tbsp unsalted (sweet)
butter
Chopped coriander (cilantro)
Plain yoghurt

Heat the oil in a large pan. Add the onions and pepper and fry (sauté) for 3 minutes, stirring. Add the chilli, cumin, coriander, cinnamon and 10 ml/2 tsp of the garam masala and fry for 1 minute. Stir in the beef and fry until all the grains are brown and separate. Season to taste. Cover with foil or a lid and cook very gently for 15 minutes, stirring occasionally. Meanwhile, wash the rice well, then cook in boiling salted water until tender. Drain and return to the pan. Add the remaining garam masala, the butter and the coriander and toss well. Serve with the meat spooned on top and a spoonful of yoghurt.

Spicy Beef Roll

Serves 4-6

750 g/1½ lb/6 cups minced (ground)
beef
75 g/3 oz/¾ cup cooked long-grain
rice
15 ml/1 tbsp plain (all-purpose) flour
2.5 ml/½ tsp chilli powder
5 ml/1 tsp dry mustard
1 onion, grated
30 ml/2 tbsp chopped coriander
(cilantro)
Salt and freshly ground black
pepper
2 eggs, beaten
Butter for greasing
50 g/2 oz/1 cup breadcrumbs
100 g/4 oz Cheddar cheese, grated

Mix the beef with the rice, flour, chilli, mustard, onion, half the coriander and a little salt and pepper. Mix with enough egg to bind. Butter a large square of foil, covering a baking sheet. Dust liberally with the breadcrumbs. Press the meat out on the foil to a square about 1 cm/½ in thick. Chill for 30 minutes. Sprinkle the cheese over, then roll up, using the foil to help. Carefully wrap the roll in the foil, sealing the ends. Bake in the oven on the baking sheet for 1 hour at 180°C/350°F/gas mark 4. Cool for 5 minutes, then cut into thick slices and sprinkle with the remaining coriander to garnish.

Simple Beef and Vegetable Rice-pot

Serves 4

30 ml/2 tbsp sunflower oil
225 g/8 oz/1 cup long-grain rice
450 g/1 lb/4 cups minced (ground)
  beef
1 onion, finely chopped
2 carrots, diced
100 g/4 oz green beans, cut into
  short lengths
200 g/7 oz/1 small can pimientos,
  chopped
100 g/4 oz/2 cups button
  mushrooms, sliced
1 packet country vegetable soup mix
900 ml/1¹/₂ pts/3³/₄ cups water
5 ml/1 tsp yeast extract
Grated Cheddar cheese

Heat the oil in a large saucepan. Add the rice and cook for 1 minute. Add the beef, onion and carrots and fry (sauté), stirring until the grains of meat are brown and separate. Stir in the remaining ingredients except the cheese. Bring to the boil, reduce the heat, cover and simmer gently for 15-20 minutes until the rice is tender and has absorbed all the liquid. Sprinkle with the cheese and serve hot.

Beef and Noodle Stir-fry

Serves 4

100 g/4 oz quick-cooking Chinese
  egg noodles
225 g/8 oz fillet steak, cut into thin
  strips
30 ml/2 tbsp oil
1 onion, sliced
1 carrot, cut into matchsticks
2 celery sticks, cut into matchsticks
1 red (bell) pepper, cut into
  matchsticks
50 g/2 oz mushrooms, sliced
¹/₄ cucumber, cut into matchsticks
30 ml/2 tbsp dry sherry
30 ml/2 tbsp soy sauce
15 ml/1 tbsp clear honey
5 ml/1 tsp ground ginger
Salt and freshly ground black
  pepper

Cook the noodles according to the packet directions. Drain. Stir-fry (sauté) the steak in the oil for 2 minutes. Add the onion, carrot and celery and continue stir-frying for a further 3 minutes. Add the pepper, mushrooms and cucumber and stir-fry for 2 minutes. Add the noodles and the remaining ingredients and toss well over a gentle heat until hot through. Serve straight away.

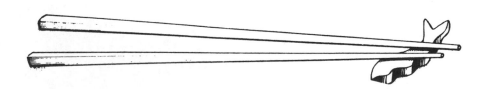

Asian Jap Chi

Serves 4

4 shiitake mushrooms
150 ml/¼ pt/⅔ cup warm water
100 g/4 oz spinach
30 ml/2 tbsp groundnut (peanut) oil
1 carrot, sliced
1 onion, sliced
100 g/4 oz beef flank, sliced very
 thinly and cut into strips
Salt and freshly ground black
 pepper
2.5 ml/½ tsp monosodium glutamate
 (optional)
100 g/4 oz/1 cup cellophane noodles
15 ml/1 tbsp snipped chives
1 garlic clove, crushed
15 ml/1 tbsp soy sauce
5 ml/1 tsp toasted sesame seeds
2.5 ml/½ tsp sesame oil

Soak the mushrooms in the warm water for
15 minutes. Drain, discard the stems and
shred the caps. Wash the spinach well in
several changes of water. Place in a
saucepan and cook without extra water for
3 minutes. Drain and shred. Heat the oil in
a wok or large frying pan (skillet). Add the
carrot, onion and mushrooms and stir-fry
(sauté) for 2 minutes. Add the beef and
stir-fry for 3 minutes. Season with salt and
pepper and the MSG, if using. Soak the
noodles in boiling water for 5 minutes.
Drain and add to the pan with the spinach
and remaining ingredients. Toss over a
gentle heat until piping hot, then serve.

Spaghetti with Meatballs Bake

Serves 6

750 g/1½ lb/6 cups minced (ground)
 beef
40 g/1½ oz/¾ cup breadcrumbs
1 onion, finely chopped
5 ml/1 tsp dried mixed herbs
30 ml/2 tbsp milk
1 egg, beaten
Tabasco sauce
Salt and freshly ground black pepper
50 g/2 oz/¼ cup butter
400 g/14 oz/1 large can chopped
 tomatoes
30 ml/2 tbsp tomato purée (paste)
1 garlic clove, crushed
350 g/12 oz spaghetti
225 g/8 oz/1 cup cottage cheese with
 chives
150 ml/¼ pt/⅔ cup plain yoghurt

Mix the meat with the breadcrumbs, onion,
half the herbs, the milk, egg, a few drops of
Tabasco and a little salt and pepper. Shape
into small balls. Melt half the butter in a
large frying pan (skillet) and fry (sauté) the
balls all over until browned. Remove from
the pan with a draining spoon and drain on
kitchen paper. Meanwhile, blend the tomatoes with the tomato purée, the garlic and
the remaining herbs. Cook the spaghetti
according to the packet directions. Drain.
Place the cooked pasta in a lightly buttered
casserole (Dutch oven). Arrange the meatballs over and then spoon over the tomato
sauce. Mix the cottage cheese and yoghurt
together and pour over. Dot with the
remaining butter. Cover with a lid and
bake at 180°C/350°F/gas mark 4 for about
30 minutes or until bubbling and turning
golden at the edges.

Pasta Grill

Serves 4
225 g/8 oz/2 cups penne or rotelli
1 onion, chopped
1 garlic clove, crushed
225 g/8 oz/2 cups minced (ground) beef
400 g/14 oz/1 large can chopped tomatoes
2.5 ml/¹/₂ tsp dried mixed herbs
Salt and freshly ground black pepper
75 g/3 oz Cheddar cheese, grated

Cook the pasta according to the packet directions. Drain. Meanwhile fry (sauté) the onion, garlic and beef in a pan, stirring until all the grains of meat are brown and separate. Add the tomatoes, herbs and a little salt and pepper. Bring to the boil, reduce the heat and simmer for 10 minutes until the sauce is thickened and rich. Stir in the cooked pasta. Turn into a 1.5 litre/2¹/₂ pts/6 cups flameproof dish. Sprinkle with the cheese and place under a hot grill (broiler) until the cheese is melted and golden brown. Serve straight away.

Canny Pasta Supper

Serves 4
225 g/8 oz/2 cups rotelli
425 g/15 oz/1 large can minced steak with onions
5 ml/1 tsp dried mixed herbs
50 g/2 oz Cheddar cheese, grated
3 tomatoes, sliced

Cook the pasta according to the packet directions, drain. Return to the saucepan and stir in the can of mince and the herbs. Heat through, stirring until piping hot. Turn into a flameproof dish. Top with the cheese and place the tomato slices round the edge. Place under a hot grill (broiler) for about 4 minutes until golden and bubbling.

Spaghetti with Hamburger Sauce

Serves 4
30 ml/2 tbsp olive oil
1 large onion, finely chopped
1 green (bell) pepper, diced
1 garlic clove, crushed
100 g/4 oz mushrooms, chopped
400 g/14 oz/1 large can chopped tomatoes
30 ml/2 tbsp tomato purée (paste)
5 ml/1 tsp sugar
5 ml/1 tsp dried oregano
Salt and freshly ground black pepper
450 g/1 lb hamburgers (4 large or 8 small)
350 g/12 oz spaghetti

Heat the oil in a saucepan. Add the onion, pepper and garlic and fry (sauté) for 4 minutes until soft and lightly golden. Stir in the mushrooms and fry for 1 minute. Add the tomatoes, tomato purée, sugar, oregano and a little salt and pepper. Bring to the boil, reduce the heat and simmer for 10 minutes until pulpy. Meanwhile, grill (broil) the hamburgers until browned and cooked through on both sides. Cook the spaghetti in boiling, salted water until tender. Drain. Pile on to a serving dish. Lay the hamburgers on top and spoon the sauce over.

Everyday Spaghetti Bolognese

Serves 4

350 g/12 oz/3 cups minced (ground)
  beef or lamb
1 onion, chopped
1 garlic clove, crushed
400 g/14 oz/1 large can chopped
  tomatoes
15 ml/1 tbsp tomato purée (paste)
Salt and freshly ground black
  pepper
5 ml/1 tsp dried oregano
A pinch of caster (superfine) sugar
350 g/12 oz spaghetti
Grated Parmesan cheese

Put the meat, onion and garlic in a saucepan. Cook, stirring, until the grains of meat are brown and separate. Add the remaining ingredients except the spaghetti and Parmesan cheese. Stir well. Bring to the boil, reduce the heat, half-cover and simmer gently for 15-20 minutes until a rich sauce has formed. Stir gently from time to time. Meanwhile, cook the spaghetti according to the packet directions. Drain and pile on to serving plates. Spoon the sauce over and top with lots of Parmesan cheese.

Lasagne Bolognese

Serves 4

1 quantity Everyday Bolognese
6-8 sheets no-need-to-precook
  lasagne
1 quantity cheese sauce (see Basic
  Macaroni Cheese page 296)
A little grated Parmesan cheese

Put a spoonful of the meat mixture in the base of a fairly shallow ovenproof dish. Top with a layer of lasagne sheets, breaking them to fit the dish. Add half the remaining meat, more lasagne, the rest of the meat, then a final layer of lasagne. Top with the cheese sauce and sprinkle with Parmesan. Bake at 190°C/375°F/gas mark 5 for 35 minutes until cooked through and golden brown, or microwave for about 15 minutes or until the lasagne feels tender when a knife is inserted through the centre. Then place under a hot grill (broiler) to brown the top.

Ragu alla Bolognese Con Tagliatelle

Serves 4-6

45 ml/3 tbsp olive oil
1 onion, finely chopped
2 garlic cloves, crushed
1 carrot, finely chopped
1 celery stick, finely chopped
450 g/1 lb/4 cups minced (ground)
  beef
3 streaky bacon rashers (slices),
  rinded and diced
3 ripe beef tomatoes, skinned,
  seeded and chopped
150 ml/¹/₄ pt/²/₃ cup beef stock
1 wineglass red wine
1 thick slice lemon
1 bay leaf
Salt and freshly ground black
  pepper
30 ml/2 tbsp double (heavy) cream
  (optional)
350 g/12 oz tagliatelle
A little olive oil
Freshly grated Parmesan cheese

Heat the olive oil in a large saucepan and fry (sauté) the onion, garlic, carrot and celery for 3 minutes until softened but not browned. Add the beef and bacon and fry, stirring, until browned and the grains of meat are separate. Add the tomatoes, stock, wine, lemon slice and the bay leaf. Season with salt and pepper and bring to the boil, stirring. Reduce the heat and simmer as gently as possible uncovered for about 2 hours until the sauce is well reduced and thick, topping up with a little more wine or stock as necessary. (Alternatively, cook in a slo-cooker for 5-6 hours). Discard the lemon slice and bay leaf. Taste and re-season if necessary. Stir in the cream, if using. Cook the tagliatelle according to the packet directions. Drain and toss in a little olive oil. Pile on to serving plates, top with the ragu and serve plenty of Parmesan separately to sprinkle over.

Ranchers' Rotelli

Serves 4

1 onion, sliced
1 green (bell) pepper, sliced
15 g/¹/₂ oz/1 tbsp butter
350 g/12 oz/3 cups minced (ground)
  beef
25 g/1 oz/¹/₄ cup plain (all-purpose)
  flour
250 ml/8 fl oz/1 cup passata (sieved
  tomatoes)
150 ml/¹/₄ pt/²/₃ cup beef stock
Salt and freshly ground black
  pepper
50 g/2 oz/1 cup button mushrooms,
  sliced
225 g/8 oz/2 cups rotelli
100 g/4 oz Gruyère (Swiss) cheese,
  grated

Fry (sauté) the onion and pepper in the butter for 3 minutes until soft and slightly golden. Add the meat and cook, stirring, until all the grains are brown and separate. Stir in the flour and cook for 1 minute. Add the passata and stock. Season well and bring to the boil, stirring. Reduce the heat and simmer for 10 minutes. Stir in the mushrooms and cook for a further 2 minutes. Meanwhile, cook the rotelli according to the packet directions. Drain. Arrange the pasta around the edge of a large flameproof dish. Spoon the meat mixture into the centre. Sprinkle the pasta liberally with the cheese and flash under a hot grill (broiler) until the cheese melts. Serve straight away.

Lasagne Verdi Al Forno

Serves 6

50g/2 oz/¹/₄ cup butter
50 g/2 oz/¹/₂ cup fat ham, finely diced
1 small onion, finely chopped
1 carrot, finely diced
50 g/2 oz/¹/₂ cup button mushrooms,
  thinly sliced
225 g/8 oz/2 cups minced (ground)
  beef
100 g/4 oz/1 cup chicken livers,
  finely chopped
15 ml/1 tbsp tomato purée (paste)
150 ml/¹/₄ pt/²/₃ cup dry white wine
300 ml/¹/₂ pt/1¹/₄ cups beef stock
5 ml/1 tsp caster (superfine) sugar
Salt and freshly ground black
  pepper
450 ml/³/₄ pt/2 cups milk
25 g/1 oz/¹/₄ cup plain (all-purpose)
  flour
1 bay leaf
8 sheets no-need-to-precook green
  lasagne (verdi)
50 g/2 oz/¹/₂ cup grated Parmesan
  cheese

Melt a quarter of the butter in large saucepan. Fry (sauté) the ham, onion and carrot for 3 minutes. Add the mushrooms and cook for 1 minute. Add the beef and chicken livers and cook, stirring, until brown and all the grains are separate. Stir in the tomato purée, wine, stock, sugar and a little salt and pepper. Bring to the boil, reduce the heat and simmer gently for 30 minutes until a rich sauce is formed, stirring occasionally. Meanwhile, blend the milk with the flour in a saucepan. Add 25 g/1 oz/2 tbsp of the remaining butter and the bay leaf. Bring to the boil and cook for 2 minutes, stirring all the time until thickened. Season to taste. Discard the bay leaf. Put a thin layer of the meat mixture in the base of a large shallow ovenproof dish, greased with the remaining butter. Top with a layer of white sauce, then a layer of lasagne sheets. Repeat the layers until all the ingredients are used, finishing with a layer of white sauce. Sprinkle the top with Parmesan and bake in the oven at 190°C/375°F/gas mark 5 for 40 minutes until cooked through and golden brown.

Manti
(Turkish Ravioli)

Serves 4-6

350 g/12 oz/3 cups plain (all-
*   purpose) flour*
100 ml/3¹/₂ fl oz/6¹/₂ tbsp water
1 egg
1 egg yolk
15 ml/1 tbsp salt
225 g/8 oz/2 cups minced (ground)
*   beef or lamb*
1 onion, grated
Salt and freshly ground black
*   pepper*
5 ml/1 tsp dried oregano
450 ml/³/₄ pt/2 cups plain yoghurt
4 garlic cloves, crushed
100 g/4 oz/¹/₂ cup butter
450 ml/³/₄ pt/2 cups passata (sieved
*   tomatoes)*

Put the flour in a bowl. Make a well in the centre and add the water, the egg beaten with the egg yolk, and the salt. Gradually work the mixture into a dough, then knead gently until smooth. Wrap in cling film (plastic wrap) and leave to stand for at least 30 minutes. Cut the dough in half. Roll out one half on a lightly floured surface to as thin a square as possible. Keep the other half covered. Mix the meat with the onion, a little salt and pepper and the oregano. Cut the dough into 4 cm/1¹/₂ in squares. Put a tiny bit of filling on each. Dampen the edges and fold over to form a triangle. Press the edges well together to seal. Place on a floured baking sheet. Repeat with the remaining dough. Drop a few at a time into a large pan of boiling water and cook until they rise to the surface. Remove with a draining spoon and keep warm in a large serving dish while cooking the remainder. Mix the yoghurt and garlic together. Melt the butter, stir in the passata and boil until the mixture thickens. When all the ravioli is cooked, spoon the garlic yoghurt and then the hot tomato sauce over and serve straight away.

Tortellini alla Rustica

Serves 4-6

450 g/1 lb meat-filled tortellini
1 onion, finely chopped
1 garlic clove, crushed
30 ml/2 tbsp olive oil
400 g/14 oz/1 large can chopped
*   tomatoes*
15 ml/1 tbsp tomato purée (paste)
Salt and freshly ground black
*   pepper*
2.5 ml/¹/₂ tsp dried oregano
1 quantity cheese sauce (see Basic
*   Macaroni Cheese page 296)*
50 g/2 oz/¹/₂ cup grated Pecorino
*   cheese*

Cook the tortellini according to the packet directions and drain. Meanwhile, fry (sauté) the onion and garlic in the oil for 2 minutes. Add the tomatoes, tomato purée, a little salt and pepper and the oregano. Bring to the boil, reduce the heat and simmer for 6-8 minutes until pulpy. Stir in the cooked pasta. Turn into a flameproof dish. Spoon the cheese sauce over and top with the Pecorino. Place under a hot grill (broiler) to brown. Serve straight away.

Beef Stroganoff with Noodles

Serves 4
225 g/8 oz fillet steak
65 g/2¹/₂ oz/scant ¹/₃ cup butter
2 onions, thinly sliced
100 g/4 oz/2 cups button
    mushrooms, sliced
Salt and freshly ground black
    pepper
15 ml/1 tbsp brandy
150 ml/¹/₄ pt/²/₃ cup soured (dairy
    sour) cream
225 g/8 oz ribbon noodles
Chopped parsley

Cut the steak into thin strips about 2.5 cm/1 in long. Heat 25 g/1 oz/2 tbsp of the butter in a large frying pan (skillet). Add the onions and fry (sauté) for 2-3 minutes until softened and lightly golden. Add the mushrooms and continue cooking, stirring, for 2-3 minutes until cooked through. Remove from the pan and reserve. Heat 25 g/1 oz/2 tbsp of the remaining butter and add the beef. Season well with salt and pepper and fry, stirring, for about 3 minutes until just cooked through. Add the brandy, ignite and shake the pan until the flames subside. Return the onions and mushrooms to the pan with any cooking juices. Stir in the cream and heat through. Cook the noodles according to the packet directions. Drain, add the remaining butter and toss well. Pile on to serving plates, spoon the stroganoff on top and sprinkle with the parsley.

Spaghetti with Rich Steak Sauce

Serves 4-6
2 onions, finely chopped
25 g/1 oz/2 tbsp dripping or lard
    (shortening)
450 g/1 lb lean top rump steak,
    minced (ground)
450 ml/³/₄ pt/2 cups beef stock
A little gravy salt or browning
Salt and freshly ground black
    pepper
Plain (all-purpose) flour
350 g/12 oz spaghetti
Warmed passata (sieved tomatoes)
    or tomato ketchup (catsup)
Chopped parsley

Fry (sauté) the onion in the dripping until softened and lightly golden. Add the steak and fry, stirring, until browned and the grains are separate. Add the stock, a little gravy salt or browning and seasoning to taste. Half-cover and simmer very gently for 1 hour until really tender (or cook in a pressure cooker for 20 minutes or a slo-cooker for up to 6 hours). Blend the flour with a little water until smooth. Stir into the meat and bring to the boil. Simmer, stirring, for 2 minutes. Taste and re-season if necessary. Meanwhile, cook the spaghetti according to the packet directions. Drain. Pile on to a hot serving dish, spoon the meat sauce over and drizzle with a little warmed passata or some tomato ketchup and sprinkle with the parsley.

Veal Escalopes with Artichokes and Buttered Noodles

Serves 4

4 large or 8 small veal escalopes
Seasoned flour
100 g/4 oz/¹/₂ cup unsalted (sweet)
butter
15 ml/1 tbsp finely chopped onion
400 g/14 oz/1 large can artichoke
bottoms, drained and quartered
120 ml/4 fl oz/¹/₂ cup dry vermouth
300 ml/¹/₂ pt/1¹/₄ cups chicken stock
Grated rind and juice of 1 lemon
150 ml/¹/₄ pt/²/₃ cup crème fraîche
Salt and freshly ground black pepper
350 g/12 oz tagliatelle
30 ml/2 tbsp chopped parsley

Beat the escalopes with a mallet or the end of a rolling pin to flatten if necessary. Dust with the seasoned flour. Melt half the butter in a large frying pan (skillet) and fry (sauté) the meat on both sides until golden. Pile on one side of the pan. Add the onion and cook, stirring, for 1 minute. Spread the escalopes out again. Add the artichoke bottoms. Pour on the vermouth and enough stock to cover the meat. Add the lemon juice, bring to the boil, reduce the heat, cover and simmer for 20 minutes until the veal is tender. Push the meat to one side again. Stir in the crème fraîche, spread the meat out again and simmer until the sauce is thickened. Season to taste. Meanwhile, cook the tagliatelle according to the packet directions. Drain and return to the saucepan. Add the remaining butter, the parsley and a good grinding of black pepper. Toss gently and pile on to a warmed serving plate. Top with the veal and the sauce, sprinkle with the lemon rind and serve hot.

American-style Spaghetti with Meatballs

Serves 4

450 g/1 lb/4 cups minced (ground)
beef
25 g/1 oz/¹/₂ cup parsley and thyme
stuffing mix
1 garlic clove, crushed
30 ml/2 tbsp grated Parmesan
cheese
30 ml/2 tbsp plain (all-purpose) flour
30 ml/2 tbsp groundnut (peanut) oil
40 g/1 lb/1 large jar of red and green
pepper sauce
350g/12 oz spaghetti
Chopped parsley

Mix the meat with the stuffing, garlic and cheese. Shape into small balls and toss in the flour. Heat the oil in a large frying pan (skillet) and fry (sauté) the meatballs until browned all over. Drain off any excess oil. Stir in the pepper sauce, cover and simmer gently for 20 minutes, stirring gently occasionally. Meanwhile, cook the spaghetti according to the packet directions. Drain. Pile on to serving plates and top with the meatballs. Sprinkle with the parsley before serving.

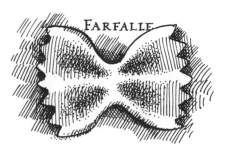

FARFALLE

Meatball Casserole

Serves 4
450 g/1 lb/4 cups minced (ground)
beef or lamb
50 g/2 oz/1 cup breadcrumbs
1 small onion, grated
1 carrot, grated
Salt and freshly ground black
pepper
1 egg, beaten
30 ml/2 tbsp oil
100 g/4 oz/1 cup rigatoni
1 large onion, finely chopped
100 g/4 oz mushrooms, sliced
15 ml/1 tbsp plain (all-purpose) flour
300 ml/¹/₂ pt/1¹/₄ cups beef or lamb
stock
30 ml/2 tbsp tomato purée (paste)
2.5 ml/¹/₂ tsp dried oregano

Mix the meat with the breadcrumbs, grated onion and carrot. Season well, then mix with the egg to bind. Shape into 16 balls. Brown on all sides in the hot oil. Remove from the pan with a draining spoon. Drain on kitchen paper. Meanwhile, cook the pasta according to the packet directions. Drain and place in a casserole (Dutch oven). Arrange the meatballs on top. Fry (sauté) the chopped onion and mushrooms, stirring, in the meatball pan for 2 minutes. Stir in the flour and cook for 1 minute. Remove from the heat and blend in the stock and tomato purée. Bring to the boil, stirring. Pour over the meatballs. Sprinkle with the oregano and a little salt and pepper. Cover and cook in the oven at 180°C/350°F/gas mark 4 for 30 minutes.

Big Bite Bucatini

Serves 6
60 ml/4 tbsp olive oil
2 garlic cloves, crushed
1 onion, quartered
1 green (bell) pepper, cut into
chunks
225 g/8 oz peperoni, cut into thick
slices
225 g/8 oz/2 cups minced (ground)
beef
2 × 400 g/2 × 14 oz/2 large cans
chopped tomatoes
2 courgettes (zucchini), cut into
thick slices
2 large carrots, cut into thick slices
100 g/4 oz/²/₃ cup stoned (pitted)
black olives
5 ml/1 tsp dried oregano
10 ml/2 tsp caster (superfine) sugar
10 ml/2 tsp tomato purée (paste)
Salt and freshly ground black
pepper
450g/1 lb bucatini

Heat the oil in a large pan. Add the garlic, onion and green pepper and fry (sauté) for 3 minutes, stirring. Add the sausage and beef, broken into chunks. Fry until the chunks are brown, but do not break up in the usual way. Add all the remaining ingredients except the pasta. Simmer for 20 minutes, stirring occasionally, until thick and the vegetables are tender. Meanwhile, cook the bucatini according to the packet directions. Drain. Pile on to serving plates and serve the sauce spooned over.

Steak with Pink Peppercorns and Poppy Seed Noodles

Serves 4

4 fillet steaks
15 ml/1 tbsp pickled pink
   peppercorns, coarsely crushed
225 g/8 oz any ribbon noodles
50 g/2 oz/¼ cup unsalted (sweet)
   butter
15 ml/1 tbsp poppy seeds
15 ml/1 tbsp olive oil
30 ml/2 tbsp brandy
15 ml/1 tbsp lemon juice
60 ml/4 tbsp double (heavy) cream
Salt and freshly ground black
   pepper
Chopped parsley

Trim the steaks if necessary. Press the peppercorns into the surfaces, cover and leave at room temperature for 30 minutes. Cook the pasta according to the packet directions. Drain, return to the pan. Add half the butter, toss and sprinkle on the poppy seeds. Toss again and keep warm. Melt the remaining butter with the oil in a frying pan (skillet). Add the steaks and fry (sauté) on each side until well browned and cooked as you like (about 3-5 minutes on each side). Transfer to warm serving plates. Add the brandy, ignite and shake the pan until the flames subside. Stir in the lemon juice and cream, heat through and season with salt and pepper. Spoon over the steaks. Spoon the noodles on the side and garnish with the parsley.

Steak with Creamy Spring Vegetable Pasta

Serves 6

750 ml/1¼ pts/3 cups beef stock
2 garlic cloves, crushed
750 ml/1¼ pts/3 cups double (heavy)
   cream
350 g/12 oz spaghettini
750 g/1½ lb fillet steak, cut into 6
   slices
40 g/1½ oz/3 tbsp unsalted (sweet)
   butter, melted
Salt and freshly ground black
   pepper
100 g/4 oz mangetout (snow peas),
   topped and tailed
2 courgettes (zucchini), thinly sliced
   diagonally
1 carrot, thinly sliced diagonally
1 red (bell) pepper, cut into
   diamonds
1 bunch of spring onions (scallions),
   cut into diagonal pieces
Parsley sprigs

Put the stock and garlic in a saucepan. Bring to the boil and boil rapidly for 10 minutes or until reduced by half. Add the cream and continue to boil for about 10 minutes until thick and reduced. Cook the pasta according to the packet directions. Drain. Brush the steaks with the butter and season lightly. Grill (broil) for 4-5 minutes on each side until slightly pink in the centre (longer for well-done). When cooked on one side, add the prepared vegetables to the cream and continue to cook for 3-4 minutes until almost tender but still 'nutty'. Pile the pasta on to warm plates. Spoon the sauce over. Slice the steaks in diagonal slices and arrange attractively on top or to one side. Garnish each with a parsley sprig.

Steak and Broccoli Stir-fry with Soy Noodles

Serves 4

225 g/8 oz rump steak, cut into thin
  strips
5 ml/1 tsp salt
5 ml/1 tsp light brown sugar
5 ml/1 tsp sherry vinegar
15 ml/1 tbsp cornflour (cornstarch)
225 g/8 oz any short ribbon noodles
60 ml/4 tbsp groundnut (peanut) oil
1 small green (bell) pepper, cut into
  thin strips
225 g/8 oz broccoli, cut into tiny
  florets
4 spring onions (scallions), cut into
  diagonal slices
100 g/4 oz/2 cups button
  mushrooms, sliced
45 ml/3 tbsp soy sauce

Put the steak in a shallow dish. Add half
the salt, the sugar, sherry vinegar and cornflour, toss and leave to stand for 30 minutes. Cook the noodles according to the
packet directions. Drain and return to the
saucepan. Meanwhile, heat half the oil in a
large frying pan (skillet) or wok. Add the
pepper and broccoli and stir-fry for 5 minutes. Remove from the pan with a draining
spoon. Heat the remaining oil and stir-fry
the steak and marinade for 1 minute. Add
the spring onions and mushrooms and continue frying for 1 minute. Return the broccoli to the pan, add half the soy sauce and
the remaining salt and toss well. Add the
remaining soy sauce to the noodles, toss
and pile into bowls. Top with the stir-fry
and serve straight away.

Buttery Veal Rolls with Fennel Noodles

Serves 4

175 g/6 oz/³/₄ cup butter
30 ml/2 tbsp chopped parsley
10 ml/2 tsp chopped thyme
1 garlic clove, crushed
Grated rind and juice of ¹/₂ lemon
Salt and freshly ground black
  pepper
4 veal escalopes
20 g/³/₄ oz/3 tbsp plain (all-purpose)
  flour
300 ml/¹/₂ pt/1¹/₄ cups chicken stock
225 g/8 oz pappardelle
10 ml/2 tsp fennel seeds
150 ml/¹/₄ pt/²/₃ cup crème fraîche

Mash 100 g/4 oz/¹/₂ cup of the butter with
the herbs, garlic, lemon and a little salt and
pepper. Beat the veal out thinly with a
meat mallet or with the end of a rolling pin.
Spread the butter mixture over and roll up.
Secure with wooden cocktail sticks (toothpicks). Melt 15 g/¹/₂ oz/1 tbsp of the
remaining butter in a large frying pan (skillet). Add the veal and brown on all sides.
Remove from the pan. Add the flour and
cook for 1 minute. Blend in the stock,
bring to the boil and simmer, stirring, for 2
minutes. Return the meat to the pan, cover
and simmer gently for 20 minutes.
Meanwhile, cook the pasta according to
the packet directions and drain. Melt the
remaining butter in the pasta pan. Add the
fennel seeds and fry until they sizzle. Add
the pasta, toss and turn on to a serving
dish. Lift out the veal rolls, discard the
cocktail sticks and arrange on the pasta.
Stir the crème fraîche into the cooking liquid. Taste and re-season. Heat through and
pour over the veal. Serve straight away.

French-style Creamy Veal

Serves 4-6

40 g/1¹/₂ oz/3 tbsp unsalted (sweet) butter
1 large onion, finely chopped
450 g/1 lb/4 cups minced (ground) veal
450 ml/³/₄ pt/2 cups crème fraîche
30 ml/2 tbsp tomato purée (paste)
15 ml/1 tbsp chopped tarragon
15 ml/1 tbsp lemon juice
5 ml/1 tsp caster (superfine) sugar
Salt and freshly ground black pepper
350 g/12 oz red tagliatelle (al pomodoro)
A few tarragon sprigs

Melt the butter and fry (sauté) the onion for 3 minutes until soft but not brown. Add the veal and fry, stirring until all the grains of meat are separate. Stir in the remaining ingredients except the pasta and tarragon sprigs. Simmer, stirring occasionally, for 10-15 minutes. Meanwhile, cook the pasta according to the packet directions. Drain. Pile on to serving plates. Taste and re-season the sauce if necessary. Spoon over the pasta and garnish with the tarragon sprigs.

Delicate Dinner for Two

Serves 2

25 g/1 oz/2 tbsp unsalted (sweet) butter
15 ml/1 tbsp sunflower oil
1 shallot, finely chopped
175 g/6 oz thin veal escalopes
50 g/2 oz oyster mushrooms, chopped, stems discarded
85 ml/3 fl oz/5¹/₂ tbsp dry white wine
250 ml/8 fl oz/1 cup crème fraîche
Salt and freshly ground black pepper
175 g/6 oz capellini
15 ml/1 tbsp chopped flat-leaf parsley
Grated rind of 1 lemon

Melt the butter with the oil and fry (sauté) the shallot, stirring for 2 minutes. Add the veal and fry until browned on both sides for about 3 minutes. Remove the veal with a draining spoon. Add the mushrooms and fry for 2 minutes. Remove from the pan with a draining spoon. Add the wine and simmer for about 8 minutes until reduced by over half. Stir in the cream and add the veal and mushrooms. Simmer gently for 5 minutes. Season with salt and pepper. Meanwhile, cook the capellini according to the packet directions. Pile on to serving plates and top with the veal and its sauce. Sprinkle with the parsley and lemon rind and serve hot.

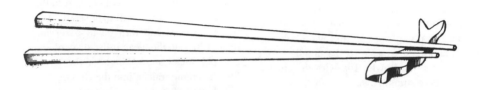

Bratwurst with Noodles

Serves 4

4 veal bratwursts
45 ml/3 tbsp unsalted (sweet) butter
45 ml/3 tbsp sunflower oil
750 ml/1¼ pts/3 cups soured (dairy sour) cream
350 g/12 oz ribbon noodles
30 ml/2 tbsp German mustard
15 ml/1 tbsp chopped sage
Salt and freshly ground black pepper
2 onions, separated into rings

Place the sausages in a pan of water. Bring to the boil and drain. Dry on kitchen paper. Melt two-thirds of the butter in a large pan with 15 ml/1 tbsp of the oil. Add the bratwursts and fry until golden on all sides. Remove from the pan with a draining spoon. Add the cream and boil, scraping up the meat residue, for about 10 minutes until it is thick and reduced by half. Meanwhile, cook the pasta according to the packet directions. Drain, toss in the remaining butter and keep warm. Add the mustard, sage and a little salt and pepper to the cream. Heat through, stirring. Thickly slice the bratwursts and add to the sauce. Heat through for 2 minutes. Meanwhile, fry (sauté) the onion rings in the remaining oil until golden. Drain on kitchen paper. Pile the noodles on to serving plates. Top with the sauce and garnish with the onion rings.

Nasi Goreng

Serves 4

350 g/12 oz/1½ cups long-grain rice
1 large onion, quartered
2 garlic cloves
1 green chilli, seeded
4 canned anchovy fillets
75 ml/5 tbsp sunflower oil
225 g/8 oz pork fillet, cubed
15 ml/1 tbsp soy sauce
4 eggs

Cook the rice in plenty of boiling salted water for 10 minutes or until just tender. Drain, rinse with cold water and drain again. Purée the onion, garlic, chilli and anchovies with 60 ml/4 tbsp of the oil in a blender or processor. Spoon into a large frying pan (skillet) and fry (sauté) for 30 seconds. Add the pork and fry for 5-10 minutes until the meat is cooked through. Add the rice and continue to cook, stirring, until the rice is hot through and glistening. Stir in the soy sauce. Fry the eggs in the remaining oil. Pile the Nasi Goreng on to warm serving plates and top each portion with a fried egg.

Roast Pork Michaelangelo

Serves 6
1 small onion, finely chopped
1 garlic clove, crushed
1 celery stick, finely chopped
25 g/1 oz/2 tbsp butter
1 cooking (tart) apple, finely chopped
50 g/2 oz/¹/₂ cup ground almonds
50 g/2 oz/1 cup cooked soup pasta shapes
15 g/1 tbsp chopped parsley
2.5 ml/¹/₂ tsp dried summer savory
10 ml/2 tsp lemon juice
5 ml/1 tsp light brown sugar
Salt and freshly ground black pepper
1.5 kg/3 lb boned pork shoulder
Olive oil
15 ml/1 tbsp cornflour (cornstarch)
300 ml/¹/₂ pt/1¹/₄ cups medium-sweet cider

Fry (sauté) the onion, garlic and celery in the butter for 2 minutes. Stir in the apple and cook for 1-2 minutes until softened. Remove from the heat and stir in the almonds, pasta, herbs, lemon juice, sugar and a little salt and pepper. Mix well. Make sure the rind of the pork is well scored. Open out flat and spread the stuffing over the meat side. Roll up and secure with string at regular intervals. Place on a rack in a roasting tin (pan). Rub the rind well with olive oil, then rub in some salt. Roast at 220°C/425°F/gas mark 7 for 30 minutes, then reduce the heat to 190°C/375°F/gas mark 5 and continue cooking for 1¹/₂ hours or until the crackling is golden and crisp and the juices run clear when the joint is pricked with a skewer. Transfer to a carving dish and spoon off all but 30 ml/2 tbsp of the fat in the tin. Dust the pan juices with the cornflour and stir in well. Gradually blend in the cider. Bring to the boil, stirring all the time and scraping up any meat residue. Season to taste and strain into a sauceboat. Carve the meat into thick slices and serve with the gravy and vegetables.

West Country Pork-a-leekie

Serves 4
175 g/6 oz/³/₄ cup brown rice
450 g/1 lb pork fillet, cut into thin strips
15 ml/1 tbsp olive oil
4 leeks, sliced
1 garlic clove, crushed
150 ml/¹/₄ pt/²/₃ cup medium-sweet cider
Salt and freshly ground black pepper
2 eating (dessert) apples, sliced
25 g/1 oz/2 tbsp butter
150 ml/¹/₄ pt/²/₃ cup crème fraîche

Cook the rice according to the packet directions (or see page 12). Meanwhile, fry (sauté) the pork in the oil for 3-4 minutes until lightly browned. Add the leeks and garlic, cover and cook gently for 5 minutes, stirring occasionally. Add the cider and some salt and pepper, bring to the boil, reduce the heat, cover and simmer gently for 15 minutes. Meanwhile fry the apple slices in the butter until golden on both sides but still holding their shape. Add to the drained rice and keep warm. Stir the crème fraîche into the leek and pork. Heat through. Make a nest of the rice and apple on 4 warm serving plates. Spoon the pork and leek mixture into the centre and serve straight away.

Quick Saveloy Pilaf

Serves 4

225 g/8 oz/1 cup basmati rice
225 g/8 oz/2 cups frozen diced mixed
* vegetables*
25 g/1 oz/2 tbsp butter
2 onions, finely chopped
10 ml/2 tsp paprika
2.5 ml/¹/₂ tsp dried thyme
350 g/12 oz saveloys, sliced
Salt and freshly ground black
* pepper*

Cook the rice in plenty of boiling lightly salted water for 10 minutes. Add the vegetables for the last 5 minutes of cooking time. Drain, rinse with boiling water and drain again. Meanwhile, melt the butter in a large frying pan (skillet). Add the onion and fry (sauté), stirring, for about 4 minutes until lightly golden. Stir in the paprika, thyme and saveloys. Heat through for 2 minutes, stirring. Add the rice and vegetable mixture, season to taste and cook, stirring until piping hot.

Barbecued Bangers with Rice

Serves 4

225 g/8 oz/1 cup long-grain rice
425 g/15 oz/1 large can red kidney
* beans, drained*
30 ml/2 tbsp chopped parsley
Salt and freshly ground black
* pepper*
2.5 ml/¹/₂ tsp grated nutmeg
450 g/1 lb chipolata sausages
15 g/¹/₂ oz/1 tbsp butter
15 ml/1 tbsp lemon juice
15 ml/1 tbsp red wine vinegar
30 ml/2 tbsp tomato purée (paste)
15 ml/1 tbsp brown table sauce
30 ml/2 tbsp golden (light corn)
* syrup*

Cook the rice in plenty of boiling salted water in a non-stick saucepan for 10 minutes or until tender. Drain and return to the pan. Stir in the beans, parsley, a little salt and pepper and the nutmeg. Cover and heat very gently, stirring until hot. Meanwhile dry-fry the sausages in a large frying pan (skillet) for about 10 minutes until cooked through and brown all over. Remove from the pan. Stir in the butter until melted, then blend in the remaining ingredients. Return the sausages to the pan and spoon the glaze over. Cook for about 3 minutes until stickily coated. Pile the rice mixture on to serving plates and top with the sausages. Serve hot.

Peasant-style Risotto

Serves 4

30 ml/2 tbsp olive oil
1 onion, finely chopped
1 carrot, finely chopped
1 celery stick, finely chopped
1 salsiccia (sweet Italian sausage),
  cut into bite-sized pieces
450 g/1 lb/2 cups arborio or other
  risotto rice
1.2 litres/2 pts/5 cups hot beef or
  chicken stock
15 g/¹/₂ oz/1 tbsp unsalted (sweet)
  butter
100 g/4 oz/1 cup grated Parmesan
  cheese

Heat the oil in a large flameproof casserole (Dutch oven). Add the onion, carrot, celery and sausage and fry (sauté) for 2 minutes. Add the rice and cook, stirring for 1 minute. Add 250 ml/8 fl oz/1 cup of the stock. Simmer, stirring, until the liquid is absorbed. Repeat until the rice is just tender and creamy, about 15-20 minutes. Remove from the heat and stir in the butter and cheese. Serve straight away.

Spiced Sausage Rice with Olives

Serves 4

2 red (bell) peppers, cut into thin
  strips
250 ml/8 fl oz/1 cup dry white wine
1.5 ml/¹/₄ tsp saffron powder
15 ml/1 tbsp tomato purée (paste)
60 ml/4 tbsp olive oil
15g/¹/₂ oz/1 tbsp unsalted (sweet)
  butter
1 onion, finely chopped
1 red chilli, seeded and chopped
450 g/1 lb/2 cups arborio or other
  risotto rice
2 hot-spiced Italian sausages (about
  100g/4 oz each), thickly sliced
20 stoned (pitted) black olives,
  quartered
Salt and freshly ground black
  pepper
1.2 litres/2 pts/5 cups chicken or
  beef stock

Put the peppers on a baking sheet and roast in the oven at 180°C/350°F/gas mark 4 for about 12 minutes until tender. Mix the wine with the saffron and tomato purée. Heat the oil and butter in a flameproof casserole (Dutch oven). Add the onion and chilli and fry (sauté) for 2 minutes. Add the rice and cook, stirring, for 1 minute. Stir in the sausages and olives and blend in the wine mixture. Simmer until the wine has evaporated, then season well and stir in the stock. Cover and simmer for about 15 minutes or until the rice is just tender. Spoon on to a large warm serving plate. Scatter the peppers and olives over and serve straight away.

Risotto con Salsiccia

Serves 4
30 ml/2 tbsp olive oil
25 g/1 oz/2 tbsp unsalted (sweet)
   butter
1 small onion, finely chopped
350 g/12 oz salsiccia (sweet Italian
   sausage), cut into bite-sized pieces
450 g/1 lb/2 cups arborio or other
   risotto rice
1.2 litres/2 pts/5 cups hot beef stock
Salt and freshly ground black
   pepper

Heat the oil and butter in a flameproof casserole (Dutch oven) and fry (sauté) the onion and sausage for 3 minutes, stirring. Stir in the rice and cook for 1 minute. Add 250 ml/8 fl oz/1 cup of the stock and simmer, stirring, until it is absorbed. Repeat until the rice is just tender, about 15-20 minutes. Season to taste and serve very hot.

Italian Sausage Rice

Serves 4
20 g/³/₄ oz/1¹/₂ tbsp butter
250 g/9 oz salsiccia (sweet Italian
   sausage), cut into chunks
350 g/12 oz/1¹/₂ cups arborio or
   other risotto rice
100 g/4 oz/1 cup grated Parmesan
   cheese
Salt and freshly ground black
   pepper

Melt the butter in a frying pan (skillet) and fry (sauté) the sausage for about 15 minutes over a gentle heat until cooked through. Meanwhile, cook the rice in plenty of boiling salted water for about 18 minutes until just tender. Drain and return to the saucepan. Stir in the sausages and the cooking juices. Add the cheese and season to taste. Toss and serve straight away.

Knock-up Jambalaya

Serves 4
225 g/8 oz/1 cup long-grain rice
15 ml/1 tbsp dried onion flakes
15 ml/1 tbsp dried green (bell)
   pepper flakes
15 ml/1 tbsp chopped parsley
2.5 ml/¹/₂ tsp dried snipped chives
1.5 ml/¹/₄ tsp garlic granules
Salt and freshly ground black
   pepper
250 ml/8 fl oz/1 cup passata (sieved
   tomatoes)
450 ml/³/₄ pt/2 cups chicken stock
425 g/15 oz/1 large can frankfurters,
   drained and cut into chunks

Mix all the ingredients except the frankfurters in a large frying pan (skillet). Bring to the boil, reduce the heat, cover, and simmer gently for 20 minutes. Add the frankfurters and cook gently until hot through and the rice is tender and has absorbed all the liquid. Serve straight from the pan.

93

Dutch Pork Roll

Serves 6

750 g/1¹/₂ lb/6 cups minced (ground)
 pork
1 onion, finely chopped
1 garlic clove, crushed
225 g/8 oz/2 cups cooked long-grain
 rice
30 ml/2 tbsp chopped parsley
5 ml/1 tsp chopped sage
15 ml/1 tbsp Worcestershire sauce
3 eggs
225 g/8 oz Edam cheese, finely diced
225 g/8 oz puff pastry (paste)

Mix the pork with the onion, garlic, rice, parsley, sage and Worcestershire sauce in a large bowl. Beat 2 of the eggs together and add to the mixture. Mix well to bind. Press half the mixture into a greased 900 g/2 lb loaf tin (pan). Top with the cheese. Press the remaining pork on top. Cover with foil and place in a roasting tin (pan) containing 2.5 cm/1 in boiling water. Bake at 190°C/375°F/gas mark 5 for 1¹/₄ hours. Drain off the liquid in the tin and reserve to make gravy. Roll out the pastry to a rectangle about 30 × 20 cm/12 × 8 in. Turn the meat loaf out on to the centre of the pastry. Beat the remaining egg and use to brush the edges of the pastry. Fold over the meat loaf and seal well together. Transfer, sealed side down, on to a dampened baking sheet. Use any pastry trimmings to make leaves. Place on top and brush all over with beaten egg to glaze. Make 2 slits in the top to allow steam to escape. Bake at 230°C/450°F/gas mark 8 for about 20 minutes until puffy and golden brown. Serve cut in thick slices with gravy made from the meat juices.

Cheesey Porkers

Serves 4

225 g/8 oz/2 cups minced (ground)
 pork
225 g/8 oz/2 cups pork sausagemeat
75 g/3 oz/³/₄ cup cooked long-grain
 rice
5 ml/1 tsp dried mixed herbs
5 ml/1 tsp onion powder
5 ml/1 tsp Dijon mustard
Salt and freshly ground black
 pepper
4 slices processed Cheddar cheese
15 ml/1 tbsp oil
4 finger rolls
Tomato ketchup (catsup)

Mash the pork with the sausagemeat and work in the rice, herbs, onion powder, mustard and a little salt and pepper. Shape into 8 flat fingers. Cut the cheese slices into thirds. Lay three strips on top of each other and place on 4 of the fingers. Top with the remaining fingers and mould the meat around to encase the cheese completely. Heat the oil in a large frying pan (skillet). Fry (sauté) the fingers for about 5 minutes on each side or until golden and cooked through, turning occasionally. Place in the rolls and serve with ketchup.

Sweet and Sour Pork with Pineapple Rice

Serves 4
15 g/½ oz/1 tbsp butter
4 pork chops
300 g/11 oz/1 small can pineapple chunks, drained, reserving the juice
Apple juice
30 ml/2 tbsp cornflour (cornstarch)
45 ml/3 tbsp light brown sugar
45 ml/3 tbsp redcurrant jelly (clear conserve)
30 ml/2 tbsp soy sauce
45 ml/3 tbsp malt vinegar
225 g/8 oz/1 cup long-grain rice
1 green (bell) pepper, finely chopped

Melt the butter in a large frying pan (skillet). Add the chops and fry (sauté) quickly on both sides to brown. Make the pineapple juice up to 300 ml/½ pt/1¼ cups with apple juice. Place the cornflour in a saucepan and blend in the juice. Add the sugar, redcurrant jelly, soy sauce and vinegar. Bring to the boil and simmer, stirring, for 2 minutes. Pour over the chops and continue cooking for 15-20 minutes until the chops are tender. Meanwhile, cook the rice in plenty of boiling salted water for 10 minutes until just tender. Add the pepper for the last 2 minutes. Drain, rinse with boiling water and drain again. Return to the pan, add the pineapple and heat through. Pile on to a serving dish. Top with the chops and the sauce.

Pork Teryaki with Crispy Greens and Rice

Serves 4
750 g/1½ lb pork fillet, cut into very thin slices
5 ml/1 tsp grated fresh root ginger
1 onion, finely chopped
60 ml/4 tbsp light soy sauce
45 ml/3 tbsp caster (superfine) sugar
45 ml/3 tbsp dry sherry
225 g/8 oz/1 cup Japanese or Thai fragrant rice
450 g/1 lb/4 cups spring greens (spring cabbage), shredded
Oil for deep-frying
Coarse sea salt

Put the pork in a bowl. Add the ginger, onion, soy sauce, sugar and sherry. Toss well, then leave to marinate for 1 hour. Meanwhile, steam or boil the rice in plenty of salted water until just tender. Drain in a colander, cover with a clean cloth and keep warm. Wash and dry the greens on kitchen paper. Place in a frying basket (in two batches if necessary) and deep-fry in hot oil until crisp. Drain on kitchen paper and toss in a little sea salt. Thread the meat on to 4 skewers. Grill (broil) for 3 minutes on each side, basting with the marinade. Serve on the rice with the crispy greens.

Spinach and Liver Stir-fry with Green Rice

Serves 4

450 ml/³/₄ pt/2 cups chicken stock
225 g/8 oz/1 cup long-grain rice
1 bunch of spring onions (scallions),
  finely chopped
350 g/12 oz/3 cups pigs' liver, cut
  into thin strips
30 ml/2 tbsp cornflour (cornstarch)
2.5 ml/¹/₂ tsp Chinese five-spice
  powder
60 ml/4 tbsp sunflower oil
450 g/1 lb/4 cups spinach, shredded
Salt and freshly ground black
  pepper
5 ml/1 tsp grated fresh root ginger
15 ml/1 tbsp soy sauce
15 ml/1 tbsp dry sherry

Bring the stock to the boil in a saucepan.
Add the rice and spring onions. Bring to
the boil, reduce the heat, cover tightly and
cook very gently for 20 minutes.
Meanwhile, toss the liver in the cornflour
and five-spice powder. Heat half the oil in
a large frying pan (skillet) or wok. Add the
spinach and stir-fry for 2 minutes. Season
lightly. Remove from the pan and keep
warm. Heat the remaining oil, add the liver
and toss quickly. Stir in the ginger, soy
sauce and sherry and stir-fry for 3 minutes.
Add the spinach to the rice, toss gently and
pile round the edge of a serving plate.
Spoon the liver mixture in the centre and
serve straight away.

Pork and Apricot Fork Supper

Serves 4

750 g/1¹/₂ lb pork fillet, cubed
25 g/1 oz/¹/₄ cup plain (all-purpose)
  flour
Salt and freshly ground black
  pepper
5 ml/1 tsp paprika
50 g/2 oz/¹/₄ cup butter
15 ml/1 tbsp oil
410 g/14¹/₂ oz/1 large can apricot
  halves in natural juice, drained,
  reserving the juice, and chopped
30 ml/2 tbsp Worcestershire sauce
5 ml/1 tsp soy sauce
30 ml/2 tbsp light brown sugar
10 ml/2 tsp white wine vinegar
10 ml/2 tsp lemon juice
150 ml/¹/₄ pt/²/₃ cup chicken stock
225 g/8 oz/1 cup long-grain rice
15 ml/1 tbsp snipped chives

Toss the pork in the flour seasoned with a
little salt, pepper and the paprika. Melt the
butter in a flameproof casserole (Dutch
oven). Add the meat and fry (sauté) quickly
to brown. Add the remaining ingredients
except the rice and chives to the pan. Bring
to the boil, stirring and scraping any meat
sediment off the base of the pan. Reduce
the heat, cover and simmer gently for 10
minutes or until the meat is tender.
Meanwhile, cook the rice in plenty of boiling salted water for 8 minutes until almost
tender. Drain and add to the casserole.
Cook for a further 10 minutes until the rice
has swelled and absorbed most of the
sauce. Taste and re-season. Serve garnished with the chives.

Clever Ham Casserole

Serves 4-6

350 g/12 oz/1¹/₂ cups long-grain rice
750 ml/1¹/₄ pts/3 cups chicken stock
450g/1 lb/1 large can ham, diced
2 eggs, beaten
298 g/10¹/₂ oz/1 can condensed celery
  soup
120 ml/4 fl oz/¹/₂ cup milk
Freshly ground black pepper
50 g/2 oz/¹/₂ cup frozen peas
2.5 ml/¹/₂ tsp dried mixed herbs
Tomato wedges

Place the rice in a pan. Add the stock, bring to the boil, stirring, cover, reduce the heat and cook gently for 15 minutes or until the rice is tender and has absorbed the liquid. Add the ham, including any jelly, and the remaining ingredients except the tomatoes. Toss over a gentle heat until creamy and piping hot. Garnish with the tomato wedges and serve hot.

Barcelona Rice

Serves 4

8 rashers (slices) streaky bacon,
  diced
1 onion, finely chopped
2 garlic cloves, crushed
1 green (bell) pepper, diced
225 g/8 oz/1 cup long-grain rice
400 g/14 oz/1 large can chopped
  tomatoes
150 ml/¹/₄ pt/²/₃ cup chicken stock
150 ml/¹/₄ pt/²/₃ cup dry white wine
5 ml/1 tsp paprika
Salt and freshly ground black
  pepper

Dry-fry the bacon until the fat runs. Add the onion, garlic and pepper and fry (sauté)

for 3 minutes, stirring. Add the rice and cook for 1 minute, stirring. Add the remaining ingredients, bring to the boil, reduce the heat, cover and simmer gently for 20 minutes or until the rice is tender and has absorbed the liquid. If necessary, boil rapidly for a few minutes to allow any excess liquid to evaporate. Serve piping hot straight from the pan.

Mozzarella-topped Pork Ragout

Serves 4

350 g/12 oz/3 cups minced (ground)
  pork
1 onion, finely chopped
2 garlic cloves, crushed
15 ml/1 tbsp olive oil
150 ml/¹/₄ pt/²/₃ cup white wine
400 g/14 oz/1 large can chopped
  tomatoes
2.5 ml/¹/₂ tsp dried thyme
Salt and freshly ground black
  pepper
350 g/12 oz tagliatelle
60 ml/4 tbsp grated Mozzarella cheese
60 ml/4 tbsp grated Parmesan cheese

Fry (sauté) the meat, onion and garlic in the olive oil, stirring, until browned and all the grains are separate. Add the wine, tomatoes, thyme and a little salt and pepper. Bring to the boil, reduce the heat, part-cover and simmer until nearly all the liquid has evaporated and the sauce is thick. Taste and re-season if necessary. Meanwhile, cook the tagliatelle according to the packet directions. Drain. Add to the cooked meat mixture and toss well. Turn into a flameproof serving dish. Top with the Mozzarella and Parmesan. Place under a hot grill (broiler) until the Mozzarella melts and bubbles. Serve straight away.

Spaghetti al Pomodoro Con Peperoni

Serves 4

Prepare as for Spaghetti Al Pomodoro (textured version, page 257) but add 100 g/4 oz/1 cup of sliced peperoni to the tomato mixture after 15 minutes cooking.

Fegatini Tagliarini

Serves 4

350 g/12 oz pig's liver
2 onions
1 slice of bread
15 ml/1 tbsp chopped sage
1 egg, beaten
Salt and freshly ground black
  pepper
15 ml/1 tbsp olive oil
450 g/1 lb tomatoes, chopped
15 ml/1 tbsp tomato purée (paste)
60 ml/4 tbsp water
2.5 ml/¹/₂ tsp sugar
350 g/12 oz tagliarini
15 g/¹/₂ oz/1 tbsp unsalted (sweet)
  butter

Mince (grind) or process the liver, one of the onions and the bread. Add the sage, egg and a little salt and pepper. Mix well. Chop the remaining onion. Heat the oil in a saucepan and cook the onion for 2 minutes. Add the tomatoes, tomato purée and water. Cover and simmer for about 5 minutes, stirring occasionally, until pulpy. Season to taste and add the sugar. Meanwhile, bring a large pan of water to the boil. Drop tablespoonfuls of the liver mixture into the pan and simmer for about 4 minutes until cooked through. Drain. Add to the tomato sauce and heat through. Meanwhile, cook the tagliarini according to the packet directions. Drain and toss in the butter. Pile the pasta on to serving plates and spoon the fegatini and tomato sauce over.

Chinese Pork Supper

Serves 6

250 g/9 oz/1 packet Chinese quick-
  cook egg noodles
45 ml/3 tbsp sunflower oil
225 g/8 oz pork stir-fry meat
2 carrots, cut into matchsticks
1 green (bell) pepper, cut into strips
225 g/8 oz broccoli, cut into small
  florets
2 celery sticks, cut into matchsticks
1 bunch of spring onions (scallions)
  cut diagonally into 2.5 cm/1 in
  lengths
1 garlic clove, crushed
10 ml/2 tsp grated fresh root ginger
100 g/4 oz/1 cup beansprouts
45 ml/3 tbsp soy sauce
5 ml/1 tsp light brown sugar

Cook the noodles according to the packet directions, drain. Heat the oil in a large frying pan (skillet) or wok. Fry (sauté) the meat for 4 minutes, stirring. Add the carrots, pepper, broccoli, celery and spring onions and fry, stirring, for a further 4 minutes. Add the remaining ingredients and cook, stirring, for 2 minutes. Stir in the noodles and fry for a further 1 minute. Serve straight from the pan.

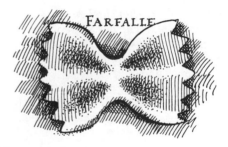
FARFALLE

Parma Ham and Mushroom Ribbons

Serves 4
30 ml/2 tbsp olive oil
100 g/4 oz/2 cups button
  mushrooms, sliced
5 ml/1 tsp yeast extract
100 g/4 oz Parma ham, cut into
  strips
25 g/1 oz/2 tbsp butter
75 ml/5 tbsp crème fraîche
Salt and freshly ground black
  pepper
1.5 ml/¼ tsp grated nutmeg
350 g/12 oz any ribbon noodles
Grated Pecorino cheese

Heat the oil in a small saucepan and add
the mushrooms. Cook gently for 2 minutes
until softened. Stir in the yeast extract,
ham and the butter in small flakes. Heat
gently, stirring until the butter melts. Stir in
the crème fraîche, salt and pepper to taste
and the nutmeg. Heat through for 2 minutes. Meanwhile, cook the noodles according to the packet directions. Drain and
return to the saucepan. Add the ham mixture and toss well over a gentle heat. Pile
on to warm plates and serve with the
Pecorino cheese.

Milanese Spiced Red Pasta

Serves 4
2 red onions, sliced
1 red (bell) pepper, cut into thin
  strips
1 red chilli, seeded and thinly sliced
1 garlic clove, crushed
45 ml/3 tbsp olive oil
400 g/14 oz/1 large can chopped
  tomatoes
15 ml/1 tbsp tomato purée (paste)
45 ml/3 tbsp water
5 ml/1 tsp dried oregano
8 stuffed green olives (optional)
50 g/2 oz Mortadella, diced
50 g/2 oz Milano salami, diced
Salt and freshly ground black
  pepper
350 g/12 oz/3 cups red conchiglie (al
  pomodoro)
Grated Parmesan cheese

Fry (sauté) the onion, pepper, chilli and
garlic in the oil for 3 minutes until softened
but not browned. Add the tomatoes and the
tomato purée blended with the water and
the oregano. Bring to the boil, reduce the
heat and simmer gently for about 10 minutes until pulpy. Add the olives, if using,
and the diced sausages and cook for a further 2 minutes. Season to taste with salt, if
necessary, and plenty of black pepper.
Cook the pasta in plenty of boiling, salted
water according to the packet directions.
Drain and return to the pan. Add the sauce
and toss well. Pile on to hot plates and
serve with the Parmesan cheese.

Middle-Eastern Madness

Serves 4

25 g/1 oz/2 tbsp butter
1 onion, chopped
1 small green (bell) pepper, chopped
2 celery sticks, chopped
1 large carrot, chopped
40 g/1¹/₂ oz/¹/₄ cup raisins
30 ml/2 tbsp tomato purée (paste)
300 ml/¹/₂ pt/1¹/₄ cups chicken or ham stock
175 g/6 oz/1¹/₂ cups cooked ham, diced
25 g/1 oz/¹/₄ cup pine nuts
15 ml/1 tbsp white wine vinegar
10 ml/2 tsp cornflour (cornstarch)
350 g/12 oz bucatini
100 g/4 oz Feta cheese, crumbled

Melt the butter in a large saucepan. Add the onion, pepper, celery and carrot and cook gently, stirring for 5 minutes until softened but not browned. Add the remaining ingredients except the vinegar, cornflour, pasta and Feta. Bring to the boil, reduce the heat and simmer gently for 20 minutes. Blend the vinegar with the cornflour. Stir into the sauce and cook until thickened and clear. Meanwhile, cook the bucatini according to the packet directions. Drain and pile on to serving dishes. Spoon the sauce over and top with the Feta cheese.

Chipolata Cantata

Serves 4

225 g/8 oz/2 cups ruote
450 g/1 lb chipolata sausages
25 g/1 oz/2 tbsp butter
2 onions, sliced
1 green (bell) pepper, sliced
100 g/4 oz/2 cups button mushrooms, sliced
150 ml/¹/₄ pt/²/₃ cup soured (dairy sour) cream
Salt and freshly ground black pepper

Cook the pasta according to the packet directions and drain. Grill (broil) or dry-fry the sausages until golden brown all over and cooked through. Meanwhile, melt the butter in a saucepan. Add the onion and fry (sauté) for 3 minutes until turning golden. Add the pepper and mushrooms and fry until golden and tender. Stir in the cooked pasta, the soured cream and a little salt and pepper. Heat through gently. Cut the sausages into bite-sized pieces and fold through the mixture just before serving.

Smoked Pork and Carrot Bake

Serves 4
225 g/8 oz/2 cups rotelli
45 ml/3 tbsp olive oil
1 bunch of spring onions (scallions),
  chopped
1 smoked pork sausage ring, sliced
200 g/7 oz/1 small can sweetcorn
  (corn)
300 ml/¹/₂ pt/1¹/₄ cups chicken stock
10 ml/2 tsp cornflour (cornstarch)
30 ml/2 tbsp water
Salt and freshly ground black
  pepper
225 g/8 oz carrot, grated
Grated nutmeg

Cook the pasta according to the packet directions and drain. Meanwhile, heat 30 ml/2 tbsp of the oil and fry (sauté) the onions for 3 minutes to soften. Add the sausage, the contents of the can of corn and the stock. Blend the cornflour with the water and stir in. Bring to the boil, stirring until thickened. Season to taste. Turn into a large ovenproof dish. Cook the carrot in boiling water for 3 minutes. Drain, mix with the pasta and spread over the dish. Drizzle with the remaining oil and sprinkle with nutmeg. Cover with foil and bake at 190°C/375°F/gas mark 5 for 20 minutes. Serve hot.

Chorizo with Greens

Serves 4
90 ml/6 tbsp olive oil
2 leeks, sliced
2 garlic cloves, crushed
350 g/12 oz spring greens (spring
  cabbage), shredded
225 g/8 oz chorizo sausage, sliced
45 ml/3 tbsp water
8 stoned (pitted) black olives, sliced
Salt and freshly ground black
  pepper
15 g/¹/₂ oz/1 tbsp butter
350 g/12 oz/3 cups rigatoni
Cayenne
Grated Parmesan cheese

Heat 60 ml/4 tbsp of the oil in a large saucepan. Add the leeks and garlic, cover and cook gently for 5 minutes until soft but not brown. Add the greens and cook, stirring for a few minutes until they begin to 'fall'. Add the sausage and the water. Cover and cook gently for 5 minutes or until soft, stirring occasionally. Add the remaining oil and the olives and season with a little salt and plenty of pepper. Stir in the butter in small flakes. Meanwhile, cook the rigatoni in plenty of boiling, salted water, according to the packet directions. Drain and return to the pan. Add the sauce, toss well and season with cayenne. Pile on to serving plates and sprinkle with the Parmesan cheese.

Wiltshire Penne

Serves 4
350 g/12 oz/3 cups penne
225 g/8 oz/2 cups cooked ham pieces
2 onions, finely chopped
100 g/4 oz/¹/₂ cup butter
Olive oil
100 g/4 oz/1 cup frozen peas
50 g/2 oz/¹/₂ cup grated Parmesan
* cheese*
Salt and freshly ground black
* pepper*

Cook the penne in plenty of boiling, salted water according to the packet directions. Drain and return to the pan. Meanwhile, cut the ham into very small dice, discarding any fat or gristle. Fry (sauté) the onion gently in half the butter and 15 ml/1 tbsp of oil until soft but not brown. Add the ham and peas, cover, reduce the heat and cook gently for 5 minutes, stirring occasionally. Add the remaining butter, the cheese, a very little salt and lots of pepper. Add to the cooked pasta and toss well over a gentle heat. Pile on to serving plates and drizzle a little extra olive oil over.

Macaroni Masterpiece

Serves 4
100 g/4 oz/1 cup short-cut macaroni
4 streaky bacon rashers (slices),
* diced*
100 g/4 oz red Leicester cheese,
* grated*
5 ml/1 tsp Worcestershire sauce
Salt and freshly ground black pepper
25 g/1 oz/2 tbsp butter, melted
15 ml/1 tbsp snipped chives

Cook the macaroni according to the packet directions. Drain and return to the saucepan. Meanwhile dry-fry (sauté) the bacon until crisp and drain on kitchen paper. Add the cheese, Worcestershire sauce, a little salt and plenty of pepper to the macaroni with the butter. Toss well. Pile on to warm serving plates and sprinkle with the bacon and chives before serving.

Basic Chow Mein Supper

Serves 4
45 ml/3 tbsp sunflower oil
8 spring onions (scallions), trimmed
* and cut into 2.5 cm/1 in lengths*
6 streaky bacon rashers (slices),
* rinded and cut into thin strips*
2 celery sticks, cut into matchsticks
100 g/4 oz/2 cups button
* mushrooms, sliced*
200 g/7 oz/1 small can bamboo
* shoots, drained and cut into strips*
45 ml/3 tbsp soy sauce
150 ml/¹/₄ pt/²/₃ cup chicken stock
5 ml/1 tsp cornflour (cornstarch)
15 ml/1 tbsp dry sherry
250 g/9 oz/1 packet quick-cook
* chow mein (or Chinese egg)*
* noodles*

Heat the oil in a large saucepan. Add the spring onions and bacon and fry (sauté), stirring, for 2 minutes. Add the celery and mushrooms and fry for a further 2 minutes, stirring. Add the bamboo shoots, soy sauce and chicken stock. Bring to the boil, half-cover and simmer gently for 5 minutes. Blend the cornflour with the sherry and stir into the sauce. Simmer, stirring for 1 minute. Meanwhile soak or cook the noodles according to the packet directions. Drain. Add to the sauce and toss well for 2 minutes over a gentle heat. Serve hot.

Special Chow Mein Supper

Serves 4-6
1 quantity Basic Chow Mein Supper
100 g/4 oz/1 cup cooked chicken,
* shredded*
100 g/4 oz/1 cup peeled prawns
* (shrimp)*
Prawn crackers

Prepare the Basic Chow Mein Supper and
add the chicken and prawns with the bamboo shoots, soy sauce and stock. Serve
with a large bowl of prawn crackers.

Cheddar Gorgeous Pasta

Serves 4
1 onion, chopped
1 garlic clove, crushed
15 g/¹/₂ oz/1 tbsp butter
8 streaky bacon rashers (slices),
* rinded and diced*
50 g/2 oz/1 cup button mushrooms,
* sliced*
400 g/14 oz/1 large can chopped
* tomatoes*
5 ml/1 tsp dried thyme
15 ml/1 tbsp tomato purée (paste)
1.5 ml/¹/₄ tsp caster (superfine) sugar
Salt and freshly ground black pepper
45 ml/3 tbsp clotted cream
350 g/12 oz/3 cups farfalle or other
* pasta shapes*
100 g/4 oz farmhouse Cheddar
* cheese, grated*

Fry (sauté) the onion and garlic in the butter until softened but not browned. Add the
bacon and mushrooms and fry, stirring, for
2 minutes. Add the remaining ingredients
except the cream, pasta and cheese, bring
to the boil, reduce the heat and simmer for
about 10 minutes until pulpy. Stir in the
cream. Meanwhile, cook the pasta according to the packet directions. Drain. Add to
the sauce, toss well and turn into a flameproof dish. Smother thickly with the cheese
and brown under a hot grill (broiler).

Bacon Dumplings with Sauerkraut

Serves 4
225 g/8 oz unsmoked bacon, rinded
* and finely chopped*
1 bunch of parsley, chopped
400 g/14 oz/3¹/₂ cups plain (all-
* purpose) flour*
A pinch of salt
1 egg, beaten
90 ml/6 tbsp water
1 jar sauerkraut
10 ml/2 tsp caraway seeds

Mix the bacon with all but 15 ml/1 tbsp of
the parsley and shape into small balls.
Cover and chill. Sift the flour and salt into
a pile on a board. Make a well in the centre and add the egg and the remaining parsley. Gradually work the flour into the egg,
adding water as you go until the mixture
forms a dough. Knead gently until smooth
then divide into 3 equal pieces. Roll out
each piece to a thin rectangle. Cut into 10
cm/4 in squares. Place a ball of bacon in
the middle of each, brush the edges with
water and wrap the dough around. Press
well together to seal. Cook in boiling salted water until the dumplings rise to the
surface. Remove from the pan with a
draining spoon. Meanwhile, heat the sauerkraut with the caraway seeds and spoon on
to a warmed serving dish. Pile the
dumplings on top and serve hot.

Salzburg Noodles

Serves 4

1.5 kg/3 lb potatoes, cut into chunks
200 g/7 oz/1³/₄ cups plain (all-purpose) flour
50 g/2 oz/¹/₄ cup butter
100 g/4 oz streaky bacon rashers (slices), finely diced

Boil the potatoes in salted water until tender. Drain and mash well. Beat in the flour to form a dough. Roll out on a lightly floured surface and cut into narrow fingers. Grease a baking tin (pan) liberally with 15 g/¹/₂ oz/1 tbsp of the butter. Lay the strips in the pan and sprinkle with the bacon. Melt the remaining butter and drizzle over. Bake in the oven at 190°C/375°F/gas mark 5 for about 20 minutes until the bacon is sizzling. Serve straight from the tin.

Creamy Pork and Mushroom Twists

Serves 6

750 g/1¹/₂ lb pork fillet, cut into strips
45 ml/3 tbsp plain (all-purpose) flour
50 g/2 oz/¹/₄ cup butter
225 g/8 oz/4 cups button mushrooms, quartered
120 ml/4 fl oz/¹/₂ cup dry cider
150 ml/¹/₄ pt/²/₃ cup pork or chicken stock
150 ml/¹/₄ pt/²/₃ cup soured (dairy sour) cream
1.5 ml/¹/₄ tsp dried sage
Salt and freshly ground black pepper
350 g/12 oz/3 cups rotelli
Chopped parsley

Dust the pork with the flour. Melt half the butter in a flameproof casserole (Dutch oven) and fry (sauté) the pork to brown. Remove from the pan with a draining spoon. Add the remaining butter and cook the mushrooms, stiring for 2-3 minutes. Return the meat to the pan. Add the cider and stock and bring to the boil, stirring. Simmer gently for 10 minutes. Add the cream, sage and a little salt and pepper and stir well. Simmer for a further 5 minutes, stirring occasionally. Taste and re-season if necessary. Meanwhile, cook the rotelli according to the packet directions. Drain and add to the sauce. Toss gently, spoon on to warm plates and garnish with the parsley.

Pork and Carrot Ragout with Orange Noodles

Serves 4

100 g/4 oz/¹/₂ cup unsalted (sweet) butter
4 onions, chopped
15 ml/1 tbsp fennel seeds
450 g/1 lb/4 cups minced (ground) pork
3 carrots, coarsely grated
600 ml/1 pt/2¹/₂ cups pork stock
45 ml/3 tbsp tomato purée (paste)
Salt and freshly ground black pepper
350 g/12 oz ribbon noodles
Grated rind and juice of 2 oranges
Chopped parsley

Melt half the butter in a saucepan. Add the onion and fennel seeds and fry (sauté) for 2-3 minutes. Add the pork and fry, stirring, until the meat is brown and all the grains are separate. Add the carrot and cook for a further 1 minute. Add the stock, bring to the boil, stir in the tomato purée and a little salt and pepper. Simmer, stirring occasionally, for 10-15 minutes. Meanwhile, cook the noodles according to the packet directions. Drain and return to the saucepan. Add the remaining butter, orange rind and juice and toss over a gentle heat until the pasta has absorbed the liquid. Season with a little pepper. Pile on to warm plates and top with the pork ragout. Sprinkle with the parsley and serve.

Crumble-topped Sausage and Noodle Casserole

Serves 4

450 g/1 lb pork sausages
225 g/8 oz pappardelle
100 g/4 oz/¹/₂ cup butter
50 g/2 oz/¹/₂ cup plain (all-purpose) flour
400 g/14 oz/1 large can chopped tomatoes
10 ml/2 tsp Worcestershire sauce
15 ml/1 tbsp tomato purée (paste)
Salt and freshly ground black pepper
120 ml/4 fl oz/¹/₂ cup dry cider
85 g/3¹/₂ oz/1 packet sage and onion stuffing mix
50 g/2 oz/¹/₂ cup grated Parmesan cheese

Put the sausages in an ovenproof serving dish. Bake in the oven at 200°C/400°F/gas mark 6 for about 15 minutes until browned, turning once. Remove from the dish and drain off the fat. Meanwhile, cook the pasta according to the packet directions. Drain and toss in 15 g/¹/₂ oz/1 tbsp of the butter. Place in the base of the ovenproof dish. Lay the sausages on top. Melt 25 g/1 oz/2 tbsp of the remaining butter in a saucepan. Add 25 g/1 oz/¹/₄ cup of the flour and cook for 1 minute. Stir in the tomatoes, Worcestershire sauce, tomato purée, a little salt and pepper and the cider. Bring to the boil, stirring. Spoon over the sausages. Put the stuffing mix in a bowl. Stir in the remaining flour and rub in the remaining butter until crumbly. Stir in the cheese. Spoon over the sauce to cover completely. Return to the oven and cook for about 30 minutes until golden. Serve hot.

Conchiglie Puttanesca

Serves 4

50 ml/2 fl oz/3¹/₂ tbsp olive oil
225 g/8 oz back bacon, rinded and
 diced
6 garlic cloves, chopped
3 green chillies, seeded and chopped
4 red onions, chopped
2 × 400 g/2 × 14 oz/2 large cans
 chopped tomatoes
5 ml/1 tsp dried oregano
5 ml/1 tsp dried basil
5 ml/1 tsp dried thyme
5 ml/1 tsp caster (superfine) sugar
Salt and freshly ground black pepper
350 g/12 oz/3 cups conchiglie

Heat the oil and fry (sauté) the bacon, garlic, chillies and onions for 5 minutes, stirring. Add the tomatoes, herbs, sugar and a little salt and pepper. Simmer for 20 minutes until thick and pulpy. Meanwhile, cook the pasta according to the packet directions. Drain. Add to the sauce, toss well and serve straight away.

Shady Afternoon Spaghetti

Serves 6

450 g/1 lb spaghetti
250 ml/8 fl oz/1 cup olive oil
450 g/1 lb back bacon, rinded and
 diced
2 garlic cloves, chopped
175 g/6 oz/1 cup stoned (pitted)
 green olives, chopped
50 g/2 oz/1 cup button mushrooms,
 chopped
25 g/1 oz/¹/₄ cup chopped parsley
5 ml/1 tsp dried oregano
Salt and freshly ground black pepper

Cook the spaghetti according to the packet directions. Drain and return to the pan. Heat the oil and fry (sauté) the bacon and garlic for 3 minutes, stirring. Add the olives and mushrooms and cook for a further 2 minutes. Stir in the parsley and oregano. Pour over the spaghetti, toss and season to taste. Pile on to serving plates and serve straight away.

Rigatoni with Sweet Smoked Ham and Sage

Serves 4

350 g/12 oz/3 cups rigatoni
60 ml/4 tbsp olive oil
1 onion, finely chopped
2 garlic cloves, crushed
450 g/1 lb/4 cups sweet cured
 smoked ham, diced
2 × 400 g/2 × 14 oz/2 large cans
 chopped tomatoes
30 ml/2 tbsp chopped sage
10 ml/2 tsp clear honey
Salt and freshly ground black
 pepper
50 g/2 oz Bavarian smoked cheese,
 grated

Cook the rigatoni according to the packet directions. Drain. Meanwhile, heat the oil and fry (sauté) the onion and garlic for about 3 minutes until soft but not brown. Add the ham, tomatoes, sage, honey and a little salt and pepper and simmer, stirring occasionally, for 15 minutes. Add to the rigatoni, toss well and pile on to serving plates. Top with the cheese.

Salami and Mozzarella Mafalde

Serves 4

50 g/2 oz/¹/₄ cup unsalted (sweet)
butter
30 ml/2 tbsp olive oil
225 g/8 oz salami, in one piece,
diced
3 garlic cloves, crushed
2 onions, chopped
2 × 400 g/2 × 14 oz/2 large cans
chopped tomatoes
250 ml/8 fl oz/1 cup crème fraîche
5 ml/1 tsp dried oregano
10 ml/2 tsp caster (superfine) sugar
1 bay leaf
2 sun-dried tomatoes, finely chopped
15 ml/1 tbsp sun-dried tomato oil
15 ml/1 tbsp tomato purée (paste)
350 g/12 oz mafalde
450 g/1 lb Mozzarella cheese, diced
Salt and freshly ground black
pepper

Melt the butter with the oil. Add the salami, garlic and onion and fry (sauté) for 3 minutes, stirring. Add all the remaining ingredients except the pasta, Mozzarella and seasoning. Bring to the boil and simmer gently for 15 minutes until thick and pulpy. Meanwhile, cook the pasta according to the packet directions. Drain. Add salt and pepper to taste to the sauce. Pour over the mafalde and toss. Add the cheese and toss gently until melting. Spoon on to serving plates and serve straight away.

Farfalle with Pork and Green Beans

Serves 4

350 g/12 oz/3 cups minced (ground)
pork
1 onion, finely chopped
1 garlic clove, crushed
15 ml/1 tbsp plain (all-purpose) flour
250 ml/8 fl oz/1 cup pork or chicken
stock
120 ml/4 fl oz/¹/₂ cup red wine
30 ml/2 tbsp tomato purée (paste)
15 ml/1 tbsp chopped basil
100 g/4 oz/2 cups button
mushrooms, sliced
225 g/8 oz green beans, cut into
short lengths
Salt and freshly ground black
pepper
350 g/12 oz/3 cups farfalle
Grated Parmesan cheese

Put the pork in a pan with the onion and garlic. Cook gently until the fat runs then fry (sauté), stirring until the meat is brown and all the grains are separate. Add the flour and cook for 1 minute. Stir in all the remaining ingredients except the pasta and cheese. Bring to the boil, stirring, reduce the heat and simmer for 20-30 minutes until the sauce is rich and thick and the beans are tender. Taste and re-season if necessary. Meanwhile, cook the pasta according to the packet directions. Drain. Add to the cooked pork and toss gently. Pile on to serving plates and sprinkle with the Parmesan cheese before serving.

Oriental Minced Pork with Rice Noodles

Serves 6

24 dried shiitake mushrooms
Warm water
60 ml/4 tbsp sunflower oil
4 garlic cloves, crushed
30 ml/2 tbsp grated fresh root ginger
550 g/1¼ lb/5 cups minced (ground)
* pork*
60 ml/4 tbsp sesame seeds
250 ml/8 fl oz/1 cup black bean
* sauce*
60 ml/4 tbsp hot chilli oil
60 ml/4 tbsp rice or white wine
* vinegar*
45 ml/3 tbsp light soy sauce
225 g/8 oz Chinese rice noodles
4 spring onions (scallions), chopped

Soak the mushrooms in the warm water for 15 minutes. Drain, discard the stems and chop the caps. Heat the oil in a large frying pan (skillet) or wok. Add the garlic, ginger, pork, mushrooms and sesame seeds and fry (sauté) until the meat is brown and all the grains are separate. Add the black bean sauce, chilli oil, vinegar and soy sauce and simmer for a further 5 minutes. Cook the rice noodles according to the packet directions. Add to the meat, toss well and serve garnished with the spring onion.

Frankfurter Lunch Special

Serves 4

225 g/8 oz/2 cups farfalle
40 g/1½ oz/3 tbsp butter
½ bunch of spring onions
* (scallions), chopped*
40 g/1½ oz/⅓ cup plain (all-purpose)
* flour*
450 ml/¾ pt/2 cups milk
75 g/6 oz Munster cheese, grated
5 ml/1 tsp German mustard
200 g/7 oz/1 small can sweetcorn
* (corn), drained*
400 g/14 oz/1 can frankfurters,
* drained and cut into short lengths*
Salt and freshly ground black
* pepper*

Cook the pasta according to the packet directions. Drain. Meanwhile, melt the butter in a pan. Stir in the spring onions and fry (sauté) for 2 minutes. Stir in the flour and cook for 1 minute. Gradually blend in the milk, bring to the boil and cook for 2 minutes. Stir in half the cheese, the mustard, sweetcorn, frankfurters and seasoning to taste. Add to the pasta, toss and turn into a flameproof serving dish. Sprinkle with the remaining cheese and brown quickly under a hot grill (broiler).

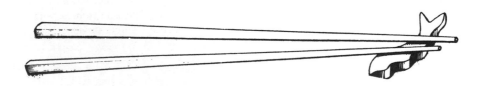

Midweek Stir-fry Special

Serves 4

1 onion, sliced
2 carrots, cut into matchsticks
1 red (bell) pepper, cut into thin strips
1/4 cucumber, cut into matchsticks
1/4 green cabbage, shredded
30 ml/2 tbsp olive oil
175 g/6 oz cooked pork, cut into thin strips
410 g/14 1/2 oz/1 large can beansprouts, drained
2.5 ml/1/2 tsp garlic salt
30 ml/2 tbsp soy sauce
15 ml/1 tbsp dry sherry
5 ml/1 tsp caster (superfine) sugar
Salt and freshly ground black pepper
2.5 ml/1/2 tsp ground ginger
100 g/4 oz/1 cup peeled prawns (shrimp)
2 × 85 g/2 × 3 1/2 oz/2 small packets instant chicken-flavoured noodles

Stir-fry (sauté) the onion, carrot, pepper, cucumber and cabbage in the olive oil for 4 minutes until softened. Add the remaining ingredients except the prawns and noodles and stir-fry for 5 minutes. Add the prawns, cover and cook for 5 minutes. Meanwhile, cook the noodles according to the packet directions. Add to the stir-fry and toss gently until well blended. Serve hot.

Peperami Carbonara

Serves 4

350 g/12 oz spaghetti
1 onion, chopped
60 ml/4 tbsp olive oil
1 garlic clove, crushed
2 peperami sticks, chopped
Salt and freshly ground black pepper
30 ml/2 tbsp chopped parsley
2 eggs
30 ml/2 tbsp milk
Grated Parmesan cheese

Cook the spaghetti according to the packet directions. Drain and return to the pan. Meanwhile, fry (sauté) the onion in the oil for 1 minute. Add the garlic, peperami, a little salt and pepper and the parsley. Cover with a lid and cook gently for 5 minutes. Add to the pasta and toss well. Beat the eggs with the milk. Add to the pan and stir over a gentle heat until creamy and lightly scrambled. Spoon on to serving plates and top with lots of grated Parmesan cheese.

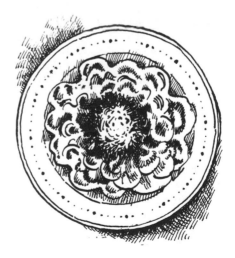

Maklouba
(Middle Eastern
Upside-down Pudding)

Serves 6

450 g/1 lb/2 cups risotto or long-grain rice
900 g/2 lb boned shoulder of lamb, diced
100 g/4 oz/¹/₂ cup butter
60 ml/4 tbsp corn oil
900 g/2 lb cauliflower, cut into florets
Salt and freshly ground black pepper
Ground cinnamon
50 g/2 oz/¹/₂ cup pine nuts
Plain yoghurt

Boil the rice in water for 10 minutes. Drain. Put the lamb in a large saucepan and just cover with boiling water. Cover and simmer for 30 minutes. Meanwhile, melt half the butter with the oil in a large frying pan (skillet). Fry (sauté) the cauliflower until golden brown. Drain the lamb, reserving the cooking liquid. Wash the saucepan and return the meat to the pan. Season well with salt, pepper and cinnamon to taste. Put the cauliflower in a thick layer on top and season again. Put the drained rice on top and spread in an even layer. Pour the lamb cooking water over to 5 mm/¹/₄ in above the rice, topping up with water if necessary. Do not stir. Season again with salt, pepper and a little more cinnamon. Cover and cook fairly gently over a moderate heat until the liquid has been absorbed and the rice is tender. Turn off the heat and leave undisturbed for a further 20 minutes. Invert over a warm serving dish and leave the saucepan in place for a further 15 minutes. Meanwhile fry (sauté) the pine nuts in the remaining butter. Lift off the saucepan, spoon the pine nuts and their butter over and serve warm with yoghurt.

Lamb Biryani

Serves 6

5 onions
4 garlic cloves, chopped
15 ml/1 tbsp grated root ginger
5 ml/1 tsp ground coriander (cilantro)
5 ml/1 tsp ground cumin
1.5 ml/¹/₄ tsp chilli powder
5 ml/1 tsp salt
60 ml/4 tbsp lemon juice
250 ml/8 fl oz/1 cup plain yoghurt
750 g/1¹/₂ lb boned leg or shoulder of lamb, cubed
2 litres/3¹/₂ pts/8¹/₂ cups lamb stock or water
450 g/1 lb/2 cups basmati rice, washed and drained
100 g/4 oz/¹/₂ cup butter
15 ml/1 tbsp saffron powder
45 ml/3 tbsp warm milk
4 bay leaves
6 cardamom pods, split along one side
1 large piece cinnamon stick, broken in half
30 ml/2 tbsp ground almonds

Chop 2 of the onions and, using a pestle and mortar or a bowl and the end of a rolling pin, pound them to a paste with the garlic, ginger, coriander, cumin, chilli, salt and lemon juice. Mix in the yoghurt and lamb and leave to marinate for 2 hours. Transfer to a heavy-based saucepan. Add 250 ml/8 fl oz/1 cup of the stock or water, bring to the boil, reduce the heat, cover and simmer gently for 30 minutes. Remove the lid and boil rapidly, stirring occasionally for a further 30 minutes until the meat is

110

coated in a thick paste. Meanwhile, bring the remaining stock or water to the boil. Add the rice and boil rapidly for 6 minutes to part-cook it. Drain well, reserving the stock. Slice the remaining onions and fry (sauté) in the butter until golden. Remove from the pan with a draining spoon and drain on kitchen paper. Reserve the butter. Soak the saffron in the milk. Put 45 ml/3 tbsp of the reserved stock in a large casserole (Dutch oven). Add half the meat, half the rice and half the onions and top with half the herbs and spices and the almonds. Repeat the layers but keep the remaining onion for garnish. Pour over the saffron milk and drizzle with the reserved butter. Cover with foil, then a tight-fitting lid and cook in the oven at 150°C/300°F/gas mark 2 for 1 hour. Toss together lightly, then serve garnished with the remaining fried onions.

Turkish Lamb and Rice Pot

Serves 4-6

Prepare as for Turkish Beef and Rice Pot (page 68) but substitute minced (ground) lamb for the beef, and sliced courgettes (zucchini) for the aubergine (eggplant).

Quick Eastern Lamb

Serves 4

1 onion, sliced
15 ml/1 tbsp sunflower oil
225 g/8 oz/2 cups cooked lamb, diced
1 garlic clove, crushed
2.5 ml/¹/₂ tsp ground ginger
2.5 ml/¹/₂ tsp ground cumin
2.5 ml/¹/₂ tsp ground coriander (cilantro)
15 ml/1 tbsp turmeric
150 ml/¹/₄ pt/²/₃ cup plain yoghurt
Salt and freshly ground black pepper
350 g/12 oz/1¹/₂ cups basmati rice, washed and drained
30 ml/2 tbsp chopped coriander (cilantro)
30 ml/2 tbsp desiccated (shredded) coconut
15 ml/1 tbsp currants

Fry (sauté) the onion in the oil for 3 minutes until golden brown. Add the lamb, garlic, ginger, cumin, ground coriander, half the turmeric, the yoghurt and a little salt and pepper. Simmer, stirring occasionally, for 20 minutes until the mixture is bathed in a paste (the mixture will curdle during cooking). Meanwhile, cook the rice in plenty of boiling, salted water to which the rest of the turmeric has been added, for 10 minutes or until just tender. Drain well, return to the pan and stir in the chopped coriander. Pile the rice on to a serving dish, top with the lamb mixture and sprinkle with the coconut and currants before serving.

Kofteh Berenji

Serves 4-6

75 g/3 oz/$1^1/_2$ cup yellow split peas,
  soaked
225 g/8 oz/1 cup long-grain rice
2 onions, grated
15 ml/1 tbsp groundnut (peanut) oil
750 g/$1^1/_2$ lb/6 cups minced (ground)
  lamb
15 ml/1 tbsp chopped parsley
15 ml/1 tbsp chopped dill (dill weed)
2.5 ml/$1/_2$ tsp crushed dried rosemary
2 eggs, beaten
Salt and freshly ground black
  pepper
75 g/3 oz/$1^1/_2$ cup ready-to-eat prunes,
  stoned (pitted)
50 g/2 oz/$1/_2$ cup pine nuts
600 ml/1 pt/$2^1/_2$ cups lamb stock
50 g/2 oz/$1/_4$ cup tomato purée
  (paste)
30 ml/2 tbsp malt vinegar
15 ml/1 tbsp granulated sugar

Boil the soaked peas in plenty of water
until tender. Drain. In a separate pan, cook
the rice in plenty of boiling salted water
until just tender. Drain, rinse with cold
water and drain again. Fry (sauté) half the
onion in the oil until lightly golden. Put to
one side. Mix the rice, split peas and
minced meat. Add the herbs and work in
well. Mix in the remaining onion, the eggs
and a little salt and pepper. Knead until
thoroughly mixed. Take large spoonfuls of
the mixture and flatten. Put a prune and a
few pine nuts in the centre of each and
shape the mixture around to form a small
ball. Bring the stock to the boil in a
saucepan. Drop the balls into the stock a
few at a time and cook until they rise to the
surface. Remove with a draining spoon.
Repeat until all the balls are cooked. Stir
the tomato purée into the remaining cooking liquid and add the vinegar and sugar.
Bring to the boil, taste and re-season if
necessary. Return the meatballs to the
sauce and heat through for 5 minutes.

Glazed Stuffed Lamb

Serves 6

4 small breasts of lamb, boned and
  trimmed
Salt and freshly ground black
  pepper
50 g/2 oz/$1/_4$ cup butter
1 small onion, finely chopped
100 g/4 oz mushrooms, finely
  chopped
100 g/4 oz liver sausage
100 g/4 oz/1 cup cooked long-grain
  rice
5 ml/1 tsp dried rosemary
1 size 5 egg, beaten
60 ml/4 tbsp redcurrant jelly (clear
  conserve)
30 ml/2 tbsp plain (all-purpose) flour
600 ml/1 pt/$2^1/_2$ cups lamb stock

Wipe the meat with kitchen paper and season lightly. Melt the butter in a saucepan.
Add the onion and mushrooms and fry
(sauté), stirring for 2 minutes. Mash in the
liver sausage and the rice. Add the rosemary and a little salt and pepper. Mix in the
beaten egg to bind. Sandwich the breasts
of lamb together in pairs with this mixture.
Sew up with a trussing needle and string or
secure all round with skewers. Place in a
roasting tin (pan). Cover with foil or a lid
and roast for 1 hour at 190°C/375°F/gas
mark 5. Half-way through cooking, remove
the cover, brush all over with half the redcurrant jelly and cook uncovered for the
remaining time. Transfer to a warmed
carving dish and keep warm. Spoon off all
but 30 ml/2 tbsp of the fat in the pan. Stir

in the flour and cook for 1 minute. Blend in the stock, bring to the boil and cook for 2 minutes, stirring and scraping up any sediment in the tin. Stir in the remaining redcurrant jelly and season to taste. Strain into a gravy boat. Carve the meat into 6 thick slices, discarding string or skewers. Serve hot with the gravy.

Marinated Lamb on Rice

Serves 6

1 small leg of lamb
15 ml/1 tbsp coarse-grain mustard
10 ml/2 tsp mild chilli seasoning
3 garlic cloves, crushed
60 ml/4 tbsp light brown sugar
300 ml/¹/₂ pt/1¹/₄ cups water
300 ml/¹/₂ pt/1¹/₄ cups pure orange juice
300 ml/¹/₂ pt/1¹/₄ cups rosé wine
15 ml/1 tbsp brandy
225 g/8 oz/1 cup long-grain rice
2 oranges, sliced
Parsley sprigs

Trim off any excess fat from the lamb. Place in a shallow dish. Mix the remaining ingredients except the rice, oranges and parsley. Spoon over the lamb and leave to marinate overnight, turning from time to time. Drain, reserving the marinade. Place the lamb in a roasting tin (pan) and roast at 180°C/350°F/gas mark 4 for about 2 hours or until just cooked (or longer according to taste). Meanwhile, measure 600 ml/1 pt/2¹/₂ cups of the marinade into a flameproof casserole (Dutch oven). Use any remaining marinade to baste the lamb during cooking. Bring the marinade in the casserole to the boil and add the rice. Cover and cook in the oven with the lamb for 45 minutes or until the rice is tender and has absorbed the liquid. Pile the rice on to a serving dish. Carve the lamb into thick slices and serve hot, garnished with the orange slices and parsley.

Middle-Eastern Mashey

Serves 4-6

1 kg/2¹/₄ lb courgettes (zucchini)
225 g/8 oz/1 cup long-grain rice
225 g/8 oz/2 cups minced (ground) lamb
Salt and freshly ground black pepper
1 garlic clove, crushed
30 ml/2 tbsp melted butter
100 g/4 oz/¹/₂ cup tomato purée (paste)
Grated rind of 1 lemon
5 ml/1 tsp dried mint
250 ml/8 fl oz/2 cups vegetable stock

Cut a slice off the top of the length of each courgette and carefully hollow out the insides, using a long-handled teaspoon. Rinse the rice well then mix with the meat and a little salt and pepper, the garlic and the melted butter. Pack loosely into the courgettes, leaving a gap of about 2 cm/³/₄ in at the top of each. Lay in a single layer in a large flameproof casserole (Dutch oven). Blend the tomato purée with the lemon rind, mint and stock. Pour over the courgettes, adding water if necessary to cover them completely. Bring to the boil, reduce the heat, cover and simmer very gently for about 45 minutes until tender and the meat and rice are cooked through. Carefully transfer to a serving dish and serve the cooking juices separately.

Dijon Kidneys with Rice

Serves 4

8 lambs' kidneys, skinned, cored and
    cut into chunks
25 g/1 oz/2 tbsp unsalted (sweet)
    butter
1 small onion, finely chopped
20 ml/4 tsp plain (all-purpose) flour
300 ml/¹/₂ pt/1¹/₄ cups lamb stock
15 ml/1 tbsp Dijon mustard
15 ml/1 tbsp redcurrant jelly (clear
    conserve)
30 ml/2 tbsp double (heavy) cream
15 ml/1 tbsp tawny port
Salt and freshly ground black
    pepper
225 g/8 oz/1 cup long-grain rice
2 carrots, finely diced

Fry (sauté) the kidneys in the butter for 3 minutes, stirring. Remove from the pan with a draining spoon and keep warm. Fry the onion in the same pan for 2 minutes to soften. Stir in the flour, then gradually add the stock and bring to the boil, stirring until thickened. Stir in the mustard and redcurrant jelly and stir until well blended. Then add the cream and port and season with salt and pepper. Return the kidneys to the sauce and cook gently for 2-3 minutes until piping hot. Meanwhile cook the rice with the carrots in plenty of boiling water for about 10 minutes until tender. Drain, rinse with boiling water and drain again. Pile the rice on to warmed serving plates and form into 'nests'. Spoon the kidneys into the centre and serve straight away.

Devilled Kidneys with Coriander Rice

Serves 4

8 lambs' kidneys
100 g/4 oz/¹/₂ cup butter
15 ml/1 tbsp curry paste
1.5 ml/¹/₄ tsp made English mustard
10 ml/2 tsp Worcestershire sauce
2.5 ml/¹/₂ tsp paprika
30 ml/2 tbsp tomato ketchup
    (catsup)
Salt and freshly ground black
    pepper
225 g/8 oz/1 cup long-grain rice
30 ml/2 tbsp chopped coriander
    (cilantro)

Skin, halve and core the kidneys. Open out almost flat and thread on kebab skewers on a grill (broiler) rack. Melt 25 g/1 oz/2 tbsp of the butter and brush all over. Mash the remaining butter with all the remaining ingredients except the rice and coriander. Cook the rice in plenty of boiling, salted water for 10 minutes or until just tender. Drain, rinse with boiling water, drain again and return to the pan. Add the corinader and a good grinding of pepper and toss gently. Meanwhile, grill (broil) the kidneys for 3-4 minutes on each side, brushing occasionally with the melted butter. Place on a warm flameproof serving dish. Spread the spicy butter over and return to the grill until sizzling. Serve with the coriander rice.

Mustard Kidneys with Noodles

Serves 4

*350 g/12 oz tagliatelle or any ribbon
  noodles*
4-6 lambs' kidneys
40 g/1¹/₂ oz/3 tbsp butter
15 ml/1 tbsp olive oil
30 ml/2 tbsp brandy
15 ml/1 tbsp coarse-grain mustard
60 ml/4 tbsp double (heavy) cream
*Salt and freshly ground black
  pepper*
30 ml/2 tbsp snipped chives
30 ml/2 tbsp toasted breadcrumbs

Cook the noodles according to the packet
directions. Drain. Meanwhile, peel off any
skin on the kidneys, then cut in halves.
Snip out the cores with scissors, then snip
the kidneys into small pieces. Heat the butter and oil in a frying pan (skillet). Add the
kidneys and cook, stirring, for 2-3 minutes
until browned and tender. Do not overcook. Add the brandy and ignite. When the
flames die down, add the mustard and
cream and heat through, stirring until well
blended. Season to taste and stir in the
chives. Pile the noodles on warm serving
plates. Top with the kidney mixture and
sprinkle with the breadcrumbs before serving.

Minted Apple Lamb

Serves 4

1 onion, thinly sliced
1 cooking (tart) apple, sliced
15 ml/1 tbsp oil
4 lamb chump chops
20 ml/4 tsp plain (all-purpose) flour
300 ml/¹/₂ pt/1¹/₄ cups cider
*Salt and freshly ground black
  pepper*
30 ml/2 tbsp chopped mint
225 g/8 oz any ribbon noodles
15 g/¹/₂ oz/1 tbsp butter
15ml/1 tbsp currants
A few sprigs of mint

Fry (sauté) the onion and apple in the oil
for 3-4 minutes until softened. Remove
from the pan. Fry the chops for about 10-
15 minutes, turning once, until just cooked
through. Transfer the onion, apple and
chops to a warm dish and keep warm.
Blend the flour with a little of the cider.
Stir in the remainder and add to the juices
in the pan. Season to taste. Add half the
chopped mint, bring to the boil and cook
for 2 minutes, stirring. Spoon over the
lamb. Meanwhile, cook the noodles
according to the packet directions. Drain
and toss in the butter with the remaining
chopped mint and the currants. Serve with
the lamb, garnished with a few mint sprigs.

Lamb Kebabs with Buttered Rice and Feta

Serves 4

350g/12 oz lamb neck fillet, cubed
15 ml/1 tbsp olive oil
10 ml/2 tsp red wine vinegar
5 ml/1 tsp dried oregano
Salt and freshly ground black pepper
¹/₂ green (bell) pepper, cut into 8 pieces
8 button mushrooms
225 g/8 oz/1 cup long-grain rice
15 g/¹/₂ oz/1 tbsp butter
50g/2 oz Feta cheese, crumbled
8 black olives

Put the meat in a bowl. Drizzle over the oil and vinegar and add the oregano and a little salt and pepper. Toss well and leave to marinate for 30 minutes. Thread the meat, pepper and mushrooms alternately on kebab skewers. Grill (broil) for about 10 minutes until golden and cooked through, turning occasionally and brushing with the remaining marinade during cooking. Meanwhile, cook the rice in plenty of boiling water for 10 minutes or until just tender. Drain, rinse with boiling water and drain again. Toss in the butter and pile on a serving dish. Scatter the Feta and olives over and top with the kebabs.

Sheek Kebabs with Cardamom Rice

Serves 4

450 g/1 lb/4 cups minced (ground) lamb
2 onions, finely chopped
l garlic clove, crushed
5 ml/1 tsp grated fresh root ginger
1.5 ml/¹/₄ tsp ground cumin
1.5 ml/¹/₄ tsp ground coriander (cilantro)
1.5 ml/¹/₄ tsp ground cinnamon
Salt and freshly ground black pepper
1 egg, beaten
30 ml/2 tbsp sunflower oil
225 g/8 oz/1 cup basmati rice
6 cardamom pods, split
Coriander (cilantro) sprigs
Lemon wedges

Mix the lamb with half the onion, the garlic, ginger, spices and a little salt and pepper. Add the egg to bind. Shape into 8 sausages. Thread on skewers and brush with half the oil. Grill (broil) for 10 minutes, turning occasionally. Meanwhile, cook the rice in plenty of boiling salted water until just tender. Drain, rinse with boiling water and drain again. Heat the remaining oil in the rinsed-out pan. Add the remaining onion and fry (sauté) until golden. Add the cardamom pods and fry for 1 minute. Stir in the rice and toss well. Pile on to serving plates and top with the kebabs. Garnish with the coriander sprigs and lemon wedges.

Lamb Pilau

Serves 6

750 g/1¹/₂ lb lean lamb, diced
Grated rind and juice of 1 lemon
100 g/4 oz/¹/₂ cup unsalted (sweet)
  butter
225 g/8 oz/1 cup long-grain rice
300 ml/¹/₂ pt/1¹/₄ cups crème fraîche
300 ml/¹/₂ pt/1¹/₄ cups lamb or
  chicken stock
2.5 cm/1 in piece cinnamon stick
5 ml/1 tsp cumin seeds, lightly
  crushed
5 ml/1 tsp fennel seeds, lightly
  crushed
Salt and freshly ground black
  pepper
Chopped parsley

Sprinkle the lamb with the lemon juice. Toss gently and leave to marinate while preparing the rice. Melt half the butter in a large flameproof casserole (Dutch oven). Add the rice and cook gently for 10 minutes, stirring. Do not allow to brown. Stir in the crème fraîche, the stock, spices and a little salt and pepper. Cover and cook in the oven at 180°C/350°F/gas mark 4 for 15 minutes. Meanwhile, fry (sauté) the lamb in the remaining butter until lightly browned. Add to the rice. Cover and return to the oven for a further 30-40 minutes or until the lamb and rice are tender. Remove the lid, stir well and leave to stand for 5 minutes before serving garnished with the grated lemon rind and the parsley.

Lamb and Rice Pie

Serves 4

175 g/6 oz/1¹/₂ cups cold cooked
  lamb, diced
100 g/4 oz/1 cup cooked long-grain
  rice
15 ml/1 tbsp chopped mint
225 g/8 oz/1 cup cottage cheese with
  pineapple
Salt and freshly ground black
  pepper
30 ml/2 tbsp milk
225 g/8 oz puff pastry (paste)
1 egg, beaten

Mix the lamb with the rice, mint, cottage cheese and a little salt and pepper in a pie dish. Add the milk. Dampen the rim of the dish with water. Roll out the pastry and use to cover the pie. Flute the edge, make a hole in the centre to allow steam to escape and make leaves out of pastry trimmings. Brush with the egg to glaze. Bake in the oven at 220°C/425°F/gas mark 7 for 15 minutes then reduce the heat to 180°C/350°F/gas mark 4 and continue cooking for 30 minutes until piping hot and the top is crisp and golden. Cover loosely with foil if over-browning.

117

Minted Lamb Puffs

Serves 4

30 ml/2 tbsp olive oil
1 leek, finely chopped
450 g/1 lb/4 cups minced (ground)
  lamb
15 ml/1 tbsp chopped mint
75 g/3 oz/³/₄ cup cooked long-grain
  rice
10 ml/2 tsp clear honey
2 tomatoes, skinned, seeded and
  chopped
Salt and freshly ground black
  pepper
375 g/13 oz puff pastry (paste)
30 ml/2 tbsp mint jelly (clear
  conserve)
1 egg, beaten

Heat the oil in a pan. Add the leek and fry (sauté) for 3 minutes until soft. Remove from the heat. Add the lamb, mint, rice, honey, tomatoes and a little salt and pepper. Shape into 4 cakes. Grill (broil) until brown on both sides. Roll out the pastry and cut into quarters. Trim to squares. Place a spoonful of mint jelly on each and top with a meat cake. Brush the edges of the pastry with egg and fold over to form parcels. Place, sealed sides down, on a dampened baking sheet. Brush the tops with egg. Make leaves out of trimmings, lay on top and brush again. Bake at 200°C/400°F/gas mark 6 for 25 minutes until the pastry is puffy and golden and the meat is cooked through. Serve hot.

Indian Naan Burgers

Serves 4

50 g/2 oz/¹/₄ cup unsalted (sweet)
  butter
10 ml/2 tsp garam masala
15 ml/1 tbsp Madras curry powder
350 g/12 oz/3 cups minced (ground)
  lamb
100 g/4 oz/1 cup cooked basmati rice
30 ml/2 tbsp plain yoghurt
Salt and freshly ground black
  pepper
1 size 4 egg, beaten
4 pieces naan bread
Shredded lettuce
Chopped tomato
Chopped cucumber
Lemon wedges

Melt half the butter in a pan. Add the garam masala and the curry powder and fry (sauté) for 2 minutes. Remove from the heat and work in the lamb, rice, yoghurt and a little salt and pepper. Stir in the egg and chill for 30 minutes. Shape into 4 oval cakes. Melt the remaining butter and fry the cakes for 3-4 minutes on each side until browned and cooked through. Lift on to pieces of warm naan bread, add the lettuce, tomato and cucumber. Fold over and serve with the lemon wedges.

Crunchy Lamb Fingers

Serves 4

350 g/12 oz/3 cups minced (ground) lamb
100 g/4 oz/1 cup cooked long-grain rice
1 Weetabix, crumbled
1 onion, grated
1 carrot, grated
1 parsnip, grated
Grated rind of 1 lemon
15 ml/1 tbsp Worcestershire sauce
Salt and freshly ground black pepper
2 eggs, beaten
85 g/3¹/₂ oz/1 packet parsley, thyme and lemon stuffing mix
Oil for shallow-frying
Parsley sprigs
Lemon twists

Mix the lamb with the rice, Weetabix, onion, carrot, parsnip and lemon rind. Season with the Worcestershire sauce and some salt and pepper. Mix with about a quarter of the beaten egg to bind. Shape into sausages. Dip in beaten egg then in stuffing mix. Shallow-fry in hot oil for about 5 minutes until crisp, golden and cooked through, turning occasionally. Drain on kitchen paper and serve hot garnished with the parsley and lemon twists.

Devilled Breast of Lamb with Buttered Rice

Serves 4

900 g/2 lb breast of lamb, trimmed and cut into ribs
30 ml/2 tbsp olive oil
3 celery sticks, chopped
1 large onion, chopped
1 carrot, chopped
3 tomatoes, skinned and chopped
10 ml/2 tsp Dijon mustard
10 ml/2 tsp Worcestershire sauce
150 ml/¹/₄ pt/²/₃ cup cider vinegar
15 ml/1 tbsp tomato ketchup (catsup)
150 ml/¹/₄ pt/²/₃ cup lamb stock
225 g/8 oz/1 cup long-grain rice
25 g/1 oz/2 tbsp unsalted (sweet) butter
Paprika

Wipe the lamb and brown in the oil in a flameproof casserole (Dutch oven). Remove with a draining spoon. Add the celery, onion, carrot and tomato and fry (sauté) for 3 minutes, stirring. Stir in the remaining ingredients except the rice, butter and paprika, then return the meat to the pan. Cover and simmer gently for about 1 hour or until the meat is tender, basting with the sauce occasionally. Meanwhile, cook the rice in plenty of boiling salted water until tender. Drain, rinse with boiling water and drain again. Add the butter and toss well. Sprinkle with paprika and serve with the devilled lamb.

Pompeii Hot-pot

Serves 4

225 g/8 oz/2 cups minced (ground)
    lamb
Salt and freshly ground black pepper
30 ml/2 tbsp plain (all-purpose) flour
30 ml/2 tbsp olive oil
2 onions, finely chopped
50 g/2 oz/1 small can anchovies,
    chopped, reserving the oil
400 g/14 oz/1 large can chopped
    tomatoes
15 ml/1 tbsp tomato purée (paste)
2.5 ml/^{1}/$_2$ tsp dried oregano
50 g/2 oz/^{1}/$_2$ cup stoned (pitted)
    black olives, sliced
50 g/2 oz/1 cup button mushrooms,
    sliced
225 g/8 oz fettuccine
50 g/2 oz Cheddar cheese, grated

Season the lamb well with salt and pepper
and shape into 16 small balls. Roll in seasoned flour. Fry (sauté) in the oil in a large
frying pan (skillet) until browned all over.
Drain on kitchen paper and keep warm.
Add the onions to the pan and fry until soft
and lightly brown. Add the anchovies,
tomatoes, tomato purée, oregano, olives
and mushrooms. Bring to the boil, reduce
the heat and simmer gently for 10 minutes
until pulpy. Taste and season if necessary.
Meanwhile, cook the pasta according to
the packet directions. Drain. Place a third
of the noodles in a deep ovenproof dish.
Put half the meatballs in a layer on top and
then spoon on half the sauce. Repeat the
layers and finish with a layer of pasta.
Sprinkle with the cheese and bake at
190°C/375°F/gas mark 5 for 20 minutes or
until the top is bubbling and golden.

Welsh Mountain Pasta Pie

Serves 4-5

2 leeks, sliced
2 carrots, diced
2 turnips, diced
450 g/1 lb lean lamb, diced
1 bouquet garni sachet
600 ml/1 pt/2^1/$_2$ cups lamb or
    chicken stock
40 g/1^1/$_2$ oz/^{1}/$_3$ cup plain (all-purpose)
    flour
45 ml/3 tbsp water
300 ml/^{1}/$_2$ pt/1^1/$_4$ cups single (light)
    cream
30 ml/2 tbsp chopped mint
Salt and freshly ground black pepper
8 sheets no-need-to-precook lasagne
2 eggs, beaten
150 ml/^{1}/$_4$ pt/^{2}/$_3$ cup milk
50 g/2 oz Caerphilly cheese,
    crumbled

Put the leeks, carrots, turnips and lamb in a
saucepan with the bouquet garni and stock.
Bring to the boil, reduce the heat, cover
and simmer gently for about 1 hour or until
the lamb is tender. Blend the flour with the
water and stir into the lamb. Bring to the
boil and cook for 2 minutes, stirring until
thickened. Stir in half the cream, the mint
and seasoning to taste. Put a thin layer of
the meat mixture in the base of a fairly
shallow ovenproof dish. Top with a layer
of lasagne. Put half the meat in the dish,
top with lasagne and then repeat the layers.
Beat the eggs and milk with the remaining
cream. Season with salt and pepper and
pour over. Sprinkle with the cheese. Bake
in the oven at 190°C/375°F/gas mark 5 for
about 40 minutes until the topping is set
and golden and the pasta feels tender when
a knife is inserted through the centre.

Gingered Lamb with Noodles

Serves 4

30 ml/2 tbsp soy sauce
30 ml/2 tbsp dry sherry
15 ml/1 tbsp pineapple or orange juice
2 garlic cloves, crushed
2 cm/³/₄ in piece root ginger, grated
450 g/1 lb lean lamb, diced
225 g/8 oz broccoli, cut into small florets
30 ml/2 tbsp sunflower oil (or half sunflower and half sesame oil)
225 g/8 oz cellophane noodles, soaked
2.5 ml/¹/₂ tsp light brown sugar
Salt and freshly ground black pepper
5 ml/1 tsp sesame seeds

Mix the soy sauce with the sherry, juice, garlic and ginger. Add the lamb, toss well and leave to marinate for 3 hours. Drain, reserving the marinade. Blanch the broccoli in boiling water for 2 minutes. Drain. Heat the oil in a wok or large frying pan (skillet) and fry (sauté) the lamb, stirring for 10 minutes. Add the broccoli and cook, stirring for 2 minutes. Add the marinade and noodles, bring to the boil and cook for 4 minutes, stirring occasionally. Sprinkle with the sugar and season to taste. Scatter the sesame seeds over and serve straight from the pan.

Herby Steamed Lamb Dome

Serves 4-6

175 g/6 oz spaghettini
1 onion, finely chopped
1 garlic clove, crushed
225 g/8 oz/2 cups minced (ground) lamb
300 ml/¹/₂ pt/1¹/₄ cups lamb or chicken stock
60 ml/4 tbsp tomato purée (paste)
5 ml/1 tsp caster (superfine) sugar
85 g/3¹/₂ oz/1 packet parsley, thyme and lemon stuffing mix
5 ml/1 tsp dried rosemary, crushed
2 eggs, beaten
Salt and freshly ground black pepper
300 ml/¹/₂ pt/1¹/₄ cups passata (sieved tomatoes)

Cook the spaghettini according to the packet directions. Drain, rinse with cold water, drain again and chop. Put the onion, garlic and lamb in a saucepan. Cook, stirring, until the meat is brown and all the grains are separate. Stir in the stock, tomato purée and sugar. Bring to the boil. Remove from the heat and stir in the stuffing, rosemary and pasta. Leave to swell for 3 minutes then beat in the eggs and season with salt and pepper. Turn into a greased 1.2 litre/2 pts/5 cups pudding basin and level the surface. Cover with a double thickness of greased foil and steam for 2 hours. Turn out on to a serving dish and serve with hot passata spooned over.

Spaghetti with Spicy Meatballs

Serves 4

450 g/1 lb/4 cups minced (ground) lamb or beef
1 onion, finely chopped
1 garlic clove, crushed
50 g/2 oz/1 cup fresh breadcrumbs
1.5 ml/¹/₄ tsp chilli powder (or more to taste)
1.5 ml/¹/₄ tsp ground coriander (cilantro)
1.5 ml/¹/₄ tsp ground cumin
Salt and freshly ground black pepper
1 size 4 egg, beaten
Oil for shallow-frying
500 ml/17 fl oz/1 jar passata (sieved tomatoes)
5 ml/1 tsp dried oregano
350 g/12 oz spaghetti
Grated Parmesan cheese

Mix the meat, onion, garlic, breadcrumbs, spices and a little salt and pepper thoroughly in a bowl. Add the egg and mix well to bind. Shape into small balls. Fry (sauté) in hot oil for about 3 minutes until golden brown. Drain on kitchen paper. Pour the passata into a saucepan. Add the oregano and meatballs. Simmer for 10 minutes, stirring gently occasionally. Meanwhile, cook the spaghetti according to the packet directions. Drain and pile on to warm serving plates. Spoon the meatballs and sauce over and serve with the Parmesan cheese.

Spaghetti with Italian Meatballs

Serves 4

Use the recipe for Spaghetti with Spicy Meatballs. Omit the spices and add an extra 5 ml/1 tsp dried oregano to the meat mixture instead. Add 8-12 halved, stoned (pitted) black olives to the passata when adding the meatballs.

Lamb Paprikash

Serves 4

2 onions
30 ml/2 tbsp oil
225 g/8 oz lamb or pork fillet, finely diced
15 ml/1 tbsp paprika
190 g/6³/₄ oz/1 small can pimientos, drained and sliced
150 ml/¹/₄ pt/²/₃ cup chicken stock
A pinch of light brown sugar
Salt and white pepper
15 ml/1 tbsp plain (all-purpose) flour
15 ml/1 tbsp water
150 ml/¹/₄ pt/²/₃ cup soured (dairy sour) cream
350 g/12 oz pappardelle
15 g/¹/₂ oz/1 tbsp butter

Chop one of the onions. Heat half the oil in a saucepan and fry (sauté) the onion until soft but not brown. Add the meat and cook, stirring, for 4 minutes. Add the paprika and fry for 1 minute. Add the pimientos and stock. Season with the sugar and a little salt and pepper. Bring to the boil, reduce the heat, half-cover and simmer gently for 15 minutes. Blend the flour with the water and stir into the pan. Cook, stirring, for 2 minutes. Stir in the cream and heat through. Taste and re-season if necessary.

Meanwhile, cook the pappardelle according to the packet directions. Drain, add the butter and toss. Slice the second onion, separate into rings and fry in the remaining oil until crisp and golden. Drain on kitchen paper. Divide the pappardelle among serving plates. Spoon the paprikash sauce over and garnish with the onion rings.

Lamb Goulash

Serves 4

1 onion, chopped
15 ml/1 tbsp oil
400 g/14 oz/1 large can chopped
  tomatoes
15 ml/1 tbsp tomato purée (paste)
2.5 ml/¹/₂ tsp caster (superfine) sugar
150 ml/¹/₄ pt/²/₃ cup chicken or lamb
  stock
15 ml/1 tbsp paprika
225 g/8 oz/2 cups cooked lamb, diced
Salt and freshly ground black
  pepper
50 g/2 oz/¹/₂ cup frozen peas
350 g/12 oz mafalde
150 ml/¹/₄ pt/²/₃ cup soured (dairy
  sour) cream
A few caraway seeds

Fry (sauté) the onion in the oil for 2 minutes until softened slightly but not browned. Add the tomatoes, tomato purée, sugar, stock, paprika, the lamb and a little salt and pepper. Bring to the boil, reduce the heat and simmer gently for about 30 minutes until pulpy and lamb is really tender. Add the peas for the last 5 minutes cooking time. Taste and re-season if necessary. Meanwhile, cook the mafalde according to the packet directions. Drain and spoon on to serving plates. Spoon over the goulash sauce, top with the soured cream and a sprinkling of caraway seeds.

Baked Liver Paprika

Serves 4

350 g/12 oz lambs' liver, cut into
  thin strips
30 ml/2 tbsp plain (all-purpose) flour
Salt and freshly ground black
  pepper
40 g/1¹/₂ oz/3 tbsp butter
1 red onion, chopped
30 ml/2 tbsp paprika
600 ml/1 pt/2¹/₂ cups lamb or beef
  stock
225 g/8 oz/2 cups penne
298g/10¹/₂ oz/1 can condensed
  tomato soup
60 ml/4 tbsp soured (dairy sour)
  cream

Dust the liver with the flour, seasoned with a little salt and pepper. Melt half the butter and fry (sauté) the onion for 2 minutes to soften. Stir in half the paprika and fry for 1 minute. Transfer with a draining spoon to a casserole (Dutch oven). Melt the remaining butter and fry the liver quickly to brown. Transfer to the casserole. Meanwhile, bring the stock to the boil in a saucepan. Add the pasta and cook for 8 minutes until nearly tender. Stir in the soup. Pour over the liver and stir well. Season with a little more salt and pepper. Cover and bake at 180°C/350°F/gas mark 4 for 30 minutes. Serve garnished with the soured cream and a dusting of the remaining paprika.

Mediterranean Lamb Chops

Serves 4

4-8 lamb chops, trimmed
15 ml/1 tbsp oil
Salt and freshly ground black
  pepper
1 onion, chopped
298 g/10¹/₂ oz/1 can condensed
  cream of tomato soup
5 ml/1 tsp dried basil
225 g/8 oz/2 cups tagliatelle
A little olive oil
12 black stoned (pitted) olives, sliced
15 ml/1 tbsp chopped parsley

Fry (sauté) the chops in the oil on each side to brown. Transfer to a shallow casserole (Dutch oven) and season lightly. Add the onion to the pan and fry until lightly golden. Spoon over the chops. Spoon the soup over and sprinkle with the basil. Cover and cook in the oven at 160°C/325°F/gas mark 3 for 1¹/₂ hours. Meanwhile, cook the tagliatelle in plenty of boiling water for 10 minutes or until just tender. Drain and return to the pan. Stir in a little olive oil, the olives and parsley. Pile on to serving plates and top with the chops and their sauce.

Paupiettes with Pasta

Serves 4

8 thin slices lambs' liver
8 thin slices pancetta or streaky
  bacon
Juice of ¹/₂ orange
Salt and freshly ground black
  pepper
A pinch of crushed rosemary
50 g/2 oz/¹/₄ cup butter
15 ml/1 tbsp plain (all-purpose) flour
120 ml/4 fl oz/¹/₂ cup Marsala or
  medium dry sherry
200 g/7 oz/1 small can chopped
  tomatoes
60 ml/4 tbsp chicken stock
350 g/12 oz mafalde
15 ml/1 tbsp olive oil
15 ml/1 tbsp chopped parsley

Trim the liver if necessary. Lay a slice of pancetta on each, folding in the edges to fit the liver if necessary. Sprinkle with the orange juice, a little salt and pepper and the rosemary. Roll up and secure with wooden cocktail sticks (toothpicks). Melt the butter in a large frying pan (skillet). Add the paupiettes and brown all over. Whisk the flour with the Marsala, tomatoes and stock. Pour into the pan. Bring to the boil, stirring gently. Season lightly. Cover with foil or a lid, reduce the heat and simmer gently for 10 minutes. Meanwhile, cook the mafalde according to the packet directions. Drain and return to the pan. Add the olive oil, a good grinding of pepper and the parsley. Toss gently. Pile on to warm serving plates. Top with the paupiettes and sauce and serve hot.

Ligurian Liver

Serves 4–6
30 ml/2 tbsp olive oil
1 onion, sliced
1 garlic clove, crushed
1 green (bell) pepper, sliced into thin
strips
450 g/1 lb lambs' liver, cut into thin
strips
30 ml/2 tbsp plain (all-purpose) flour
400 g/14 oz/1 large can chopped
tomatoes
2.5 ml/¹/₂ tsp dried oregano
75 g/3 oz/¹/₂ cup stoned (pitted)
green olives
15 ml/1 tbsp tomato purée (paste)
Salt and freshly ground black
pepper
175 g/6 oz/1¹/₂ cups conchiglie

Heat the oil in a large frying pan (skillet).
Add the onion, garlic and sliced pepper
and fry (sauté) for 2 minutes, stirring. Toss
the liver in the flour and add to the pan.
Fry, stirring, until browned. Add the
remaining ingredients except the pasta and
simmer gently for 10 minutes. Meanwhile,
cook the pasta according to the packet
directions. Drain and add to the liver.
Simmer for a further 1 minute, then taste
and re-season if necessary. Serve piping
hot.

Creamy Liver with Basil

Serves 4
450 g/1 lb lambs' liver, thinly sliced
and cut into bite-sized pieces
25 g/1 oz/¹/₄ cup plain (all-purpose)
flour
Salt and freshly ground black
pepper
25 g/1 oz/2 tbsp unsalted (sweet)
butter
15 ml/1 tbsp olive oil
2 red onions, sliced
1 garlic clove, crushed
150 ml/¹/₄ pt/²/₃ cup lamb or chicken
stock
15 ml/1 tbsp tomato purée (paste)
1 sun-dried tomato, finely chopped
15 ml/1 tbsp chopped basil
150 ml/¹/₄ pt/²/₃ cup double (heavy)
cream
350 g/12 oz green tagilatelle (verdi)

Toss the liver in the flour seasoned with
salt and pepper. Melt the butter and oil in a
large frying pan (skillet). Add the onion
and garlic and fry (sauté) for 2 minutes.
Add the liver and fry until brown on all
sides. Stir in the stock, tomato purée and
sun-dried tomato. Bring to the boil, reduce
the heat and simmer very gently for 15
minutes. Stir in the basil and cream and
season to taste. Meanwhile, cook the tagliatelle according to the packet directions.
Drain. Pile on to serving plates. Top with
the sauce and serve straight away.

Offally Good Macaroni

Serves 6

350 g/12 oz/3 cups elbow macaroni
25 g/1 oz/2 tbsp butter
1 onion, finely chopped
1 leek, finely chopped
4 lambs' kidneys, skinned and cored and cut into small pieces
200 g/7 oz/1³/₄ cups chicken livers, trimmed and roughly chopped
30 ml/2 tbsp plain (all-purpose) flour
250 ml/8 fl oz/1 cup chicken stock
100 g/4 oz/2 cups button mushrooms, sliced
2.5 ml/¹/₂ tsp dried thyme
120 ml/4 fl oz/¹/₂ cup passata (sieved tomatoes)
15 ml/1 tbsp tomato purée (paste)
150 ml/¹/₄ pt/²/₃ cup dry white wine
Salt and freshly ground black pepper
15 ml/1 tbsp chopped parsley

Cook the macaroni according to the packet directions. Drain. Meanwhile, melt the butter in a large pan. Add the onion and leek and fry (sauté) for 2 minutes, stirring. Add the kidney and liver and fry for 2 minutes, stirring. Stir in the remaining ingredients except the parsley. Bring to the boil, stirring, reduce the heat, cover and simmer gently for 15 minutes. Stir in the macaroni, taste and re-season if necessary. Pile on to serving plates and sprinkle with the parsley.

Andalucian Rice

Serves 4

175 g/6 oz boneless chicken meat, diced
1 small green (bell) pepper, diced
1 small red (bell) pepper, diced
30 ml/2 tbsp olive oil
225 g/8 oz/1 cup bomba, arborio or other risotto rice
600 ml/1 pt/2¹/₂ cups chicken stock
100 g/4 oz/1 cup frozen mixed peas and sweetcorn (corn)
100 g/4 oz/1 cup peeled prawns (shrimp)
Salt and freshly ground black pepper
A few green olives

Fry (sauté) the chicken and peppers in the oil for 4 minutes, stirring. Add the rice and cook for 1 minute, stirring. Pour on the stock, bring to the boil, cover and simmer for 10 minutes. Add the peas and sweetcorn and prawns, re-cover and cook very gently for a further 10 minutes or until the rice is cooked and has absorbed nearly all the liquid. Season to taste and stir lightly. Garnish with the olives before serving.

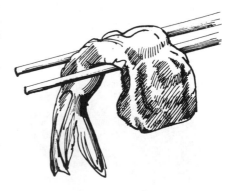

Japanese-style Sesame Chicken

Serves 4

175 g/6 oz/³/₄ cup long-grain rice
50 g/2 oz/¹/₂ cup plain (all-purpose) flour
Salt and freshly ground black pepper
15 ml/1 tbsp sesame seeds
4 boneless chicken breasts, skinned
50 g/2 oz/¹/₄ cup butter
15 ml/1 tbsp sesame oil
300 ml/¹/₂ pt/1¹/₄ cups chicken stock
45 ml/3 tbsp rice wine or dry white wine
2.5 ml/¹/₂ tsp ground coriander (cilantro)
1.5 ml/¹/₄ tsp ground ginger
1.5 ml/¹/₄ tsp chilli powder
300 ml/¹/₂ pt/1¹/₄ cups double (heavy) cream

Cook the rice in plenty of boiling salted water until tender. Drain, rinse with boiling water, drain again and return to the pan. Meanwhile, mix the flour with a little salt and pepper and the sesame seeds. Use to coat the chicken breasts. Melt half the butter with the oil in a large frying pan (skillet). Fry (sauté) the chicken for 3 minutes on each side until golden. Drain off any excess oil in the pan. Add the stock and wine, bring to the boil, reduce the heat, cover and simmer for 10-15 minutes or until the chicken is cooked through. Stir the remaining butter into the cooked rice with a little salt and pepper. Mix the coriander and spices together and sprinkle over. Toss well and heat through, gently. Pile on to a serving dish. Remove the chicken breasts from the cooking liquid and arrange on the rice. Keep warm. Stir the cream into the cooking liquid and simmer, stirring, until slightly thickened. Pour over the chicken and serve straight away.

Iranian Shireen Polow

Serves 6

Thinly pared rind of 2 oranges
225 g/8 oz carrots, cut into matchsticks
75 g/3 oz/³/₄ cup flaked almonds
75 g/3 oz/³/₄ cup shelled pistachio nuts
120 ml/4 fl oz/¹/₂ cup cold water
100 g/4 oz/¹/₂ cup granulated sugar
450 g/1 lb chicken meat, diced
Salt and freshly ground black pepper
5 ml/1 tsp saffron powder
30 ml/2 tbsp boiling water
450 g/1 lb/2 cups long-grain rice
150 ml/¹/₄ pt/²/₃ cup groundnut (peanut) oil
5 ml/1 tsp ground cinnamon
15 ml/1 tbsp melted butter

Cut the orange rind into thin strips and boil in water for 10 minutes. Drain, rinse with cold water and drain again. Place in a pan with the carrots, nuts, the measured cold water and sugar. Bring to the boil and simmer for 3 minutes. Place the chicken in a separate pan with enough water to just cover and add a little salt and pepper. Bring to the boil and simmer for 8 minutes. Dissolve the saffron in the boiling water. Stir half the saffron into the chicken and set aside. Cook the rice in plenty of boiling salted water until just tender. Drain. Pour the oil into a large flameproof casserole (Dutch oven). Put a layer of the nut mixture in the base. Add a layer of chicken and dust with cinnamon. Add a layer of rice. Repeat the layers until all the ingredients are used. Cover and cook over a very gentle heat for 40 minutes. Mix the remaining saffron with the melted butter and drizzle over the surface before serving.

Chicken and Tarragon Risotto

Serves 4
45 ml/3 tbsp olive oil
2 onions, finely chopped
2 garlic cloves, crushed
2 celery sticks, chopped
1 red (bell) pepper, chopped
1 green (bell) pepper, chopped
100 g/4 oz/2 cups button mushrooms, quartered
275 g/10 oz/1¼ cups arborio or other risotto rice
750 ml/1¼ pts/3 cups chicken stock
350 g/12 oz/3 cups cooked chicken, diced
Salt and freshly ground black pepper
Grated rind and juice of ½ small lemon
30 ml/2 tbsp chopped tarragon

Heat the oil in a large frying pan (skillet). Add the onions, garlic and celery and cook, stirring, for 2 minutes. Add the peppers and mushrooms and stir for 1 minute. Add the rice and stir until all the grains are coated in the oil. Stir in the stock, bring to the boil, reduce the heat, cover and cook gently for 15 minutes. Stir, add the chicken, a little salt and pepper, the lemon rind and juice and the tarragon. Re-cover and cook for a further 5 minutes or until the rice has absorbed all the liquid and is tender. Serve hot straight from the pan.

Savoury Chicken Liver Risotto

Serves 4
40 g/1½ oz/¾ cup dried porcini mushrooms
45 ml/3 tbsp olive oil
1 garlic clove
50 g/2 oz/1 small can anchovies, drained and chopped
450 g/1 lb/2 cups arborio or other risotto rice
1.2 litres/2 pts/5 cups hot chicken stock
200 g/7 oz/1¾ cups chicken livers, trimmed and cut into pieces
Freshly ground black pepper

Soak the mushrooms in boiling water for 30 minutes. Drain, rinse thoroughly then cut into bite-sized pieces. Heat the oil in a flameproof casserole (Dutch oven). Add the garlic clove, fry (sauté) until golden then remove and discard. Stir in the mushrooms, anchovies and rice. Cook for 1 minute. Add 250 ml/8 fl oz/1 cup of the stock, bring to the boil and simmer, stirring, until the stock is absorbed. Repeat with 2 more cups of stock. Then add the chicken livers and continue adding the stock until the rice is just tender and creamy (about 15-20 minutes). Serve straight away with a good grinding of black pepper.

Speciality Chicken Risotto

Serves 6
1.1 kg/2½ lb oven-ready chicken
1 large carrot, chopped
1 celery stick, chopped
30 ml/2 tbsp olive oil
1 onion, finely chopped
450 g/1 lb/2 cups arborio or other
 risotto rice
375 ml/13 fl oz/1½ cups dry white
 wine
400 g/14 oz/1 large can chopped
 tomatoes
Salt and freshly ground black
 pepper
100 g/4 oz/1 cup freshly grated
 Parmesan cheese
A few celery leaves

Wipe the chicken inside and out with kitchen paper. Place in a large pot. Cover with water, add the carrot and celery. Bring to the boil, reduce the heat, cover and simmer gently for 1½ hours until the chicken is really tender and falling off the bones. Remove from the stock, cool slightly then take all the meat off the bones, discarding the skin. Dice the meat. Put the bones back in the stock and simmer for a further 1 hour. Strain and leave to cool then skim the surface of any fat. Measure 900 ml/1½ pts/3¾ cups to use for the recipe (the remainder can be frozen). Heat the oil in a large flameproof casserole (Dutch oven). Add the onion and fry (sauté) for 2 minutes. Stir in the rice and cook for 1 minute. Stir in the wine and tomatoes and simmer until the wine is absorbed. Stir in a quarter of the stock and simmer, stirring until it has been absorbed. Repeat the process once more, then add the chicken and the remaining stock and simmer, stirring, until the rice is just tender and has absorbed the liquid. Season to taste and serve hot with the cheese sprinkled over and garnish with the celery leaves.

Syrian Chicken Dome

Serves 6
1.5 kg/3 lb oven-ready chicken, cut
 in portions
10 ml/2 tsp dried onion flakes
2.5 ml/½ tsp allspice
2.5 ml/½ tsp turmeric
Salt and freshly ground black pepper
25 g/1 oz/2 tbsp butter
1.2 litres/2 pts/5 cups boiling water
100 g/4 oz/1 cup frozen peas
450 g/1 lb/2 cups long-grain rice
25 g/1 oz/¼ cup toasted flaked
 almonds

Put the chicken portions in a dish. Sprinkle with the onion flakes, spices and a little salt and pepper and leave to stand for 30 minutes. Melt the butter in a large saucepan or flameproof casserole (Dutch oven). Add the chicken and brown on all sides. Pour over the water, bring to the boil again, cover and simmer for about 20 minutes until the chicken is tender. Remove the chicken with a draining spoon. Add the peas and rice to the cooking liquid. Bring to the boil, reduce the heat, cover and simmer gently for about 20 minutes until the rice is tender and has absorbed the liquid. Top up with a little water if necessary during cooking. Season to taste. Meanwhile, cut all the chicken meat off the bones, discarding the skin. Cut into neat pieces. Grease a large warmed soufflé dish or mould (mold). Sprinkle the nuts over the base then lay the chicken on top. Cover with the hot rice mixture and press down firmly. Leave in a warm place for 3 minutes, then turn out and serve.

Chicken and Mushroom Pilaf

Serves 6

1 large onion, finely chopped
1 garlic clove, crushed
100 g/4 oz/¹/₂ cup unsalted (sweet) butter
350 g/12 oz/1¹/₂ cups long-grain rice
1 litre/1³/₄ pts/4¹/₄ cups chicken stock
225 g/8 oz/4 cups button mushrooms, sliced
2.5 ml/¹/₂ tsp saffron powder
Salt and freshly ground black pepper
225 g/8 oz/2 cups cooked chicken, cut into bite-sized pieces
4 tomatoes, skinned, seeded and chopped

Fry (sauté) the onion and garlic in the butter in a large flameproof casserole (Dutch oven) until soft but not brown. Stir in the rice and cook for 2 minutes until transparent and glistening. Add the stock, mushrooms and saffron. Season with salt and pepper, stir well and bring to the boil. Stir again, cover and transfer to the oven. Cook at 180°C/350°F/gas mark 4 for 40 minutes then stir in the chicken and tomatoes. Return to the oven and cook for about 25 minutes until the rice is cooked and has absorbed all the liquid. Add a little more stock or water when you add the chicken if the rice is already looking dry.

Pot-roast Chicken with Rice

Serves 6

15 ml/1 tbsp olive oil
1 onion, finely chopped
225 g/8 oz/1 cup long-grain rice
1 red (bell) pepper, chopped
100 g/4 oz/2 cups button mushrooms, sliced
30 ml/2 tbsp tomato purée (paste)
600 ml/1 pt/2¹/₂ cups chicken stock
1 bouquet garni sachet
Salt and freshly ground black pepper
1.5 kg/3¹/₂ lb oven-ready chicken
225 g/8 oz/2 cups frozen peas with sweetcorn (corn)

Heat the oil in a large flameproof casserole (Dutch oven). Add the onion and fry (sauté) for 2 minutes until soft but not brown. Add the rice and stir to coat in the oil. Add the pepper and mushrooms. Blend the tomato purée into the stock and stir into the pan. Add the bouquet garni and season with salt and pepper. Wipe the chicken inside and out and place on top of the rice. Sprinkle lightly with salt and pepper. Cover and cook in the oven at 190°C/375°F/gas mark 5 for 1 hour. Stir the peas and sweetcorn into the rice around the chicken, re-cover and cook for a further 15 minutes. Discard the bouquet garni, carve the chicken and serve with the rice.

Indonesian Chicken, Prawn and Egg Rice

Serves 6-8

1 small oven-ready chicken
3 onions
2 whole cloves
1 bay leaf
3 parsley sprigs
6 whole peppercorns
Salt
450 g/1 lb/2 cups basmati rice
45 ml/3 tbsp olive oil
30 ml/2 tbsp peanut butter
5 ml/1 tsp chilli powder
100 g/4 oz/1 cup peeled prawns (shrimp)
100 g/4 oz/1 cup cooked ham, diced
5 ml/1 tsp ground cumin
5 ml/1 tsp ground coriander (cilantro)
1 garlic clove, crushed
A little grated nutmeg
30 ml/2 tbsp toasted cashew nuts
12 cooked unpeeled prawns (shrimp)
2 hard-boiled (hard-cooked) eggs,
  quartered

Wipe the chicken inside and out with kitchen paper. Place in a saucepan. Stud one of the onions with the cloves and add to the pan with the bay leaf, parsley, peppercorns and a little salt. Add enough water to cover the bird. Bring to the boil, reduce the heat, cover and simmer for 1 hour or until the chicken is tender. Leave to cool slightly then lift out the chicken. Strain the stock and return to the pan. Bring to the boil, add the rice and simmer for 10 minutes or until the rice is tender. Drain if necessary and keep warm, covered with a cloth to absorb any remaining moisture. Cut all the chicken off the bones, discarding the skin. Cut into neat pieces. Thinly slice the remaining onions. Heat the oil in a large pan. Add the onions and cook until soft and lightly golden. Stir in the peanut butter and the chilli powder (add less if you don't like food too hot!). Add the peeled prawns, ham, chicken and rice. Continue frying, tossing gently until the rice is lightly golden. Stir in the cumin and coriander, the garlic and a little nutmeg. Toss gently until well blended, then season to taste. Pile on to a hot serving dish. Sprinkle with the cashew nuts and garnish with the unpeeled prawns and eggs.

No-nonsense Piquant Chicken Bake

Serves 4-6

225 g/8 oz/1 cup long-grain rice
600 ml/1 pt/2½ cups hot chicken stock
1 red (bell) pepper, diced
30 ml/2 tbsp chopped parsley
Salt and freshly ground black pepper
25 g/1 oz/2 tbsp butter
10 ml/2 tsp onion salt
10 ml/2 tsp celery salt
10 ml/2 tsp paprika
1 kg/3 lb oven ready chicken, cut
  into 4 or 6 pieces
15 ml/1 tbsp chopped capers
50 g/2 oz/⅓ cup stuffed olives, sliced
10 ml/2 tsp lemon juice

Mix the rice, stock, pepper, parsley and a little salt and pepper together in a large flameproof casserole (Dutch oven). Stir well. Add the butter in small pieces. Blend the onion and celery salt and the paprika together and rub over the chicken. Lay on top of the rice and bring to the boil. Cover and bake in the oven at 180°C/350°F/gas mark 4 for about 45 minutes or until the chicken and rice are tender. Stir the capers, olives and lemon juice into the rice. Taste and re-season if necessary. Leave to stand, covered, for 5 minutes, then serve.

Crispy Chicken and Vegetable Rolls

Makes 24

100 g/4 oz/1 cup shredded Brussels
sprouts
1 onion, finely chopped
2 carrots, grated
100 g/4 oz/1 cup cooked chicken,
finely chopped
50 g/2 oz/¹/₂ cup cooked long-grain
rice
30 ml/2 tbsp soy sauce
5 ml/1 tsp light brown sugar
15 ml/1 tbsp medium dry sherry
A pinch each of ground ginger, salt
and pepper
375 g/13 oz frozen puff pastry
(paste), thawed
A little beaten egg
Oil for deep-frying

Mix the sprouts, onion, carrots, chicken and rice together in a bowl. Add the soy sauce, sugar, sherry, ginger, salt and pepper. Mix well. Roll out the pastry thinly on a floured surface to a rectangle 60 × 40 cm/24 × 16 in. Cut into 10cm/4 in squares. Divide the filling among the centres of the pieces of pastry. Brush the edges with egg. Fold in the two sides then roll up each one in a sausage shape to enclose the filling. Heat the oil to 190°C/375°F or until a cube of day-old bread browns in 30 seconds. Fry the rolls, a few at a time, until crisp and golden brown. Drain on kitchen paper and serve hot.

Washday Rice

Serves 4

350 g/12 oz/1¹/₂ cups long-grain rice
30 ml/2 tbsp olive oil
4 eggs, beaten
100 g/4 oz/1 cup cooked chicken,
diced
5 cm/2 in piece cucumber, chopped
4 spring onions (scallions), chopped
50 g/2 oz/1 cup mushrooms, sliced
15 ml/1 tbsp soy sauce
Salt and freshly ground black
pepper

Cook the rice in plenty of boiling salted water until tender. Drain, rinse with cold water and drain again. Heat half the oil in a frying pan (skillet) and fry (sauté) half the egg until just beginning to set. Stir in the cooked rice, the chicken, cucumber, onions, mushrooms and soy sauce. Cook, stirring until piping hot. Season to taste. Meanwhile, in a separate small frying pan heat the remaining oil and make an omelette, using the remaining beaten egg seasoned with salt and pepper. Pile the rice mixture on to a warmed serving dish, slice the omelette and scatter on top.

Chicken Jambalaya

Serves 6

1 poussin (Cornish hen), cut into 6
   pieces
120 ml/4 fl oz/1½ cup olive oil
1 large red onion, finely chopped
2 garlic cloves, crushed
2 celery sticks, chopped
1 green (bell) pepper, diced
450 g/1 lb/2 cups arborio or other
   risotto rice
225 g/8 oz/2 cups cooked ham, diced
350 g/12 oz/3 cups shelled king
   prawns (jumbo shrimp)
225 g/8 oz/2 cups chorizo sausage,
   thickly sliced
200 g/7 oz/1 small can chopped
   tomatoes
60 ml/4 tbsp tomato purée (paste)
2 sun-dried tomatoes, finely chopped
1 bouquet garni sachet
A pinch of ground cloves
1.5 ml/¼ tsp cayenne
Salt and freshly ground black pepper
1.2 litres/2 pts/5 cups chicken stock
90 ml/6 tbsp dry white wine
Chopped parsley
6 unshelled king prawns (jumbo
   shrimp)
A few black olives

Brown the chicken pieces in half the oil in
a large frying pan (skillet). Remove from
the pan. Heat the remaining oil and fry
(sauté) the onion, garlic, celery and pepper
for 2 minutes until softened but not
browned. Add the rice and stir over a gentle heat for 1 minute. Return the chicken to
the pan with all the remaining ingredients
except the parsley, unshelled prawns and
olives. Bring to the boil, stirring, reduce
the heat, cover and simmer gently for 15-
20 minutes, adding a little more stock or
wine if the rice is becoming too dry. Stir
gently, taste and add a little more seasoning if necessary. Discard the bouquet garni
sachet, garnish with the parsley, the whole
prawns and olives and serve straight away.

Louisiana Jambalaya

Serves 4

4 chicken portions
30 ml/2 tbsp oil
225 g/8 oz/2 cups smoked pork
   sausage, sliced
1 onion, chopped
2 celery sticks, chopped
2 garlic cloves, crushed
1 green (bell) pepper, sliced into
   strips
1 carrot, chopped
750 ml/1¼ pts/3 cups chicken stock
225 g/8 oz/1 cup risotto or
   long-grain rice
10 ml/2 tsp paprika
2 beef tomatoes, skinned, seeded
   and chopped
Tabasco sauce
1 bunch of spring onions (scallions),
   chopped
Salt and freshly ground black pepper

Brown the chicken in the oil. Add the
sausage and fry (sauté) for 3 minutes.
Remove from the pan with a draining
spoon and keep warm. Add the prepared
vegetables and fry for 2-3 minutes, stirring. Return the chicken and sausage to the
pan. Add the stock, cover and simmer gently for 15 minutes. Add the rice, paprika,
tomatoes, a little Tabasco and half the
spring onions. Cover and cook gently for a
further 15 minutes or until the rice is tender and has absorbed the liquid. Taste and
season if necessary. Sprinkle with the
remaining spring onions before serving.

New Orleans Chicken Gumbo

Serves 6

40 g/1¹/₂ oz/3 tbsp butter
15 ml/1 tbsp groundnut (peanut) oil
30 ml/2 tbsp plain (all-purpose) flour
1 litre/1³/₄ pts/4¹/₄ cups chicken stock
2 thick rashers (slices) belly pork, rinded and diced
1 onion, chopped
2 celery sticks, chopped
2 garlic cloves, crushed
450 g/1 lb okra, trimmed and sliced
400 g/14 oz/1 large can chopped tomatoes
225 g/8 oz/2 cups peeled prawns (shrimp)
450 g/1 lb/4 cups cooked chicken, diced
50 g/2 oz/¹/₂ cup frozen peas
Tabasco sauce
Salt and freshly ground black pepper
225 g/8 oz/1 cup long-grain rice

Melt half the butter in a large pan with the oil. Add the flour and stir until lightly browned. Gradually blend in the stock and bring to the boil, stirring. Remove from the heat. In a large separate pan, brown the pork until the fat runs. Stir in the onions, celery and garlic and fry (sauté) for 2 minutes. Add the okra and fry for 5 minutes, stirring. Stir in the tomatoes and simmer for 10-15 minutes. Stir in the slightly thickened stock, bring to the boil, reduce the heat, cover and simmer gently for 1 hour. Add the prawns, chicken and peas and cook for 5 minutes. Season with Tabasco, salt and pepper to taste. Meanwhile, boil the rice in plenty of salted water for about 12 minutes until tender. Drain, rinse with boiling water and drain again. Serve the gumbo in bowls with a spoonful of plain boiled rice on top.

Roast Chicken with Lemon Grass and Rice Stuffing

Serves 6

225 g/8 oz/1 cup wild rice mix
900 ml/1¹/₂ pts/3³/₄ cups chicken stock
1.5 kg/3 lb oven-ready chicken
1 stem lemon grass, finely chopped
1 large eating (dessert) apple, grated
15 ml/1 tbsp chopped spring onion (scallion)
Salt and freshly ground black pepper
A pinch of grated nutmeg
1 egg, beaten
25 g/1 oz/2 tbsp unsalted (sweet) butter, melted
Lemon juice (optional)

Cook the rice in the stock for about 20 minutes or until just tender. Drain off any excess stock and reserve for gravy. To part-bone the chicken, make a slit along the backbone then carefully scrape away each side of the rib cage until it is exposed on both sides. Cut through the joints at the wings and legs, but leave the limbs intact. Lift out the rib cage and backbone. Mix the rice with the lemon grass, apple, spring onion and a little salt and pepper. Stir in the nutmeg and the beaten egg to bind. Pile the stuffing on the chicken where the bones were. Re-shape and sew up or secure with cocktail sticks (toothpicks). Place in a roasting tin (pan). Brush with melted butter and season lightly. Cover with foil. Roast at 190°C/375°F/gas mark 5 for 1¹/₂ hours, removing the foil for the last 30 minutes. Make gravy with any reserved stock and the juices in the roasting tin, adding stock made from the giblets as necessary. Spike with lemon juice if liked.

Honey-roast Stuffed Turkey

Serves 10

4.5 kg/10 lb oven-ready turkey
100 g/4 oz/1 cup cooked brown rice
100 g/4 oz/1 cup streaky bacon
  rashers (slices), rinded and finely
  chopped
198 g/7 oz/1 small can sweetcorn
  (corn), drained
2.5 ml/^{1}/$_2$ tsp dried mixed herbs
Salt and freshly ground black
  pepper
2.5 ml/^{1}/$_2$ tsp grated nutmeg
1 egg, beaten
25 g/1 oz /2 tbsp butter
45 ml/3 tbsp clear honey
15 ml/1 tbsp brandy

Wipe the turkey inside and out with kitchen paper. Mix the rice with the bacon, sweetcorn, herbs, salt and pepper to taste and the nutmeg. Mix with beaten egg to bind. Stuff the neck end of the bird and secure the skin underneath with a skewer. Tuck the wing tips under and place in a roasting tin. Spread the breast with butter then cover with foil, crimping it under the edges of the roasting tin. Roast for 2^1/$_2$ hours at 180°C/350°F/gas mark 4. Remove the foil and drain off any cooking juices into a saucepan. Spoon 30 ml/2 tbsp of the honey over the breast and return to the oven for 15 minutes to glaze. Insert a skewer into the thickest part of the thigh. If the juices run clear, the turkey is cooked. If not, re-cover the breast and return to the oven for a further 10-15 minutes. Make gravy in your normal way (the giblets could be used to make the stock) and add the remaining honey and brandy to it.

Duck with Orange Rice

Serves 6

100 g/4 oz/^{1}/$_2$ cup unsalted (sweet)
  butter
1 onion, finely chopped
3 celery sticks, chopped
Grated rind and juice of 2 large
  oranges
900 ml/1^1/$_2$ pts/3^3/$_4$ cups chicken
  stock
450 g/1 lb/2 cups long-grain rice
Salt and freshly ground black
  pepper
1 bouquet garni sachet
3 large or 6 small duck breasts
Watercress sprigs

Heat 50 g/2 oz/^{1}/$_4$ cup of the butter in a large, heavy-based saucepan. Add the onion and celery and fry (sauté) gently, stirring, for 2 minutes until soft but not brown. Stir in the orange rind, juice and the stock. Bring to the boil. Stir in the rice, add some salt and pepper and the bouquet garni sachet. Bring back to the boil, reduce the heat and simmer gently, stirring occasionally, for about 20 minutes until the rice is cooked and has absorbed all the liquid. Remove the bouquet garni. Meanwhile, season the duck breasts with salt and pepper. Heat the remaining butter in a large frying pan (skillet) and fry (sauté) the duck breasts for about 10 minutes until cooked but still slightly pink in the centre, turning twice. Remove from the pan and leave to rest in a warm place until the rice is cooked. When ready to serve, cut the duck breasts in thick, diagonal slices. Arrange on warm serving plates and spoon any juices over. Put a pile of the orange rice to one side. Garnish with the watercress.

Duck Shoot Rice

Serves 4

2 kg/4¹/₂ lb duck
Salt and freshly ground black
  pepper
75 g/3 oz/¹/₄ cup apricot jam
  (conserve)
75 g/3 oz/¹/₄ cup orange marmalade
30 ml/2 tbsp light brown sugar
Grated rind and juice of 1 lemon
150 ml/¹/₄ pt/²/₃ cup orange juice
225 g/8 oz/1 cup wild rice mix
¹/₂ celeriac (celery root), grated
600 ml/1 pt/2¹/₂ cups water
90 ml/6 tbsp redcurrant jelly (clear
  conserve)
15 ml/1 tbsp Worcestershire sauce
5 ml/1 tsp soy sauce
15 ml/1 tbsp Dijon mustard

Wipe the duck inside and out with kitchen paper. Prick all over with a fork. Place on a rack over a roasting tin and rub with salt and pepper. Roast at 230°C/450°F/gas mark 8 for 15 minutes. Pour off the fat and remove the rack. Mix the jam, marmalade, sugar, lemon rind and juice and 45 ml/3 tbsp of the orange juice together. Spread all over the duck and roast for 15 minutes until a rich, deep brown. Reduce the heat to 180°C/350°F/gas mark 4 and continue cooking for 20 minutes or until the duck is tender. Cut into 4 portions. Meanwhile, cook the rice and celeriac in the water for about 20 minutes or until just tender and the water is absorbed, stirring occasionally. Heat the remaining orange juice with the redcurrant jelly, Worcestershire sauce, soy sauce and mustard until smooth and hot. Pile the rice on to warmed serving plates. Top each with a duck portion and serve hot with the sauce.

Braised Quail in Hock with Seasoned Rice

Serves 6

350 g/12 oz/1¹/₂ cups long-grain rice
6 quail
50 g/2 oz/¹/₄ cup butter
30 ml/2 tbsp olive oil
25 g/1 oz/¹/₄ cup shelled pistachio
  nuts
25 g/1 oz/¹/₄ cup pine nuts
2 red onions, finely chopped
150 ml/¹/₄ pt/²/₃ cup hock
600 ml/1 pt/2¹/₂ cups chicken stock
Grated rind and juice of 1 orange
15 ml/1 tbsp redcurrant jelly (clear
  conserve)
Salt and freshly ground black
  pepper
Chopped parsley

Wash the rice well in several changes of cold water then leave to drain. Wipe the quail inside and out with kitchen paper. Heat half the butter and oil in a large flameproof casserole (Dutch oven) and fry (sauté) the quail on all sides to brown. Remove from the casserole. Add the nuts and fry until turning lightly golden. Remove from the pan and drain on kitchen paper. Add the onion to the casserole and fry until soft and lightly golden. Return the quail to the pan, add the wine and 150 ml/¹/₄ pt/²/₃ cup of the stock, the orange rind and juice, the redcurrant jelly and a little salt and pepper. Bring to the boil, reduce the heat, cover very tightly (with foil first, if necessary, then the lid) and simmer very gently for 30-40 minutes until the quail are tender. Meanwhile, heat the remaining butter and oil in a saucepan. Add the rice and fry for 2 minutes, stirring. Add the remaining stock and a little salt and pepper. Simmer for 15 minutes until the rice is tender, adding more stock or water if necessary. Pile rice on to individual serving plates, top with the quail. Spoon the juices over and garnish with the fried nuts and the parsley.

Risotto con le Quaglie

Serves 4

4 quail
Salt
4 thin slices pancetta or streaky
  bacon
15 ml/1 tbsp olive oil
375 ml/13 fl oz/1½ cups dry white
  wine
25 g/1 oz/2 tbsp unsalted (sweet)
  butter
1 small onion, finely chopped
450 g/1 lb/2 cups arborio or other
  risotto rice
1.2 litres/2 pts/5 cups hot chicken
  stock
Freshly ground black pepper
100 g/4 oz/1 cup freshly grated
  Parmesan cheese
Chopped parsley

Wipe the quail inside and out with kitchen paper. Season with salt and wrap each in a slice of pancetta. Heat the oil in a large frying pan (skillet) and fry (sauté) the quail on all sides for about 15 minutes until brown and almost tender. Add the wine and simmer until it has almost evaporated. Leave in the pan and keep warm. Meanwhile, melt half the butter in a large flameproof casserole (Dutch oven). Add the onion and fry for 2 minutes. Stir in the rice and cook for 1 minute. Add about a quarter of the stock and simmer, stirring, until it has been absorbed. Repeat the process until the rice is just tender (about 15-20 minutes). Remove from the heat, stir in the remaining butter, a little salt and pepper and the

cheese. Quickly pack into a large ring mould (mold) and press down firmly. Invert on to a serving plate and place the quail in the centre. Spoon any cooking juices over and sprinkle with the parsley.

Devilled Chicken Drummers with Paprika Rice

Serves 4

8 chicken drumsticks
75 g/3 oz/⅓ cup butter, softened
Salt and freshly ground black
  pepper
5 ml/1 tsp made mustard
20 ml/4 tsp paprika
1.5 ml/¼ tsp cayenne
5 ml/1 tsp red wine vinegar
225 g/8 oz/1 cup long-grain rice
200 g/7 oz/1 small can pimientos,
  drained and chopped
Chopped parsley

Make several slashes in the thick part of the drumsticks. Lay on foil on a grill (broiler) rack. Mash the butter with a little salt and pepper, the mustard, 5 ml/1 tsp of the paprika, the cayenne and vinegar. Spread half of it over the drumsticks. Grill (broil) under a moderate heat for 10 minutes, turning and basting occasionally. Spread the remaining butter mixture over and continue grilling for a further 10 minutes until well browned, sizzling and cooked through. Meanwhile, cook the rice in plenty of boiling salted water until tender. Drain, rinse with boiling water and drain again. Return to the saucepan. Add the remaining paprika and the pimiento. Toss gently until hot through. Pile on to a serving dish. Top with the drumsticks and sprinkle with the parsley.

Chicken, Rice and Vegetable Wedges

Serves 4

100 g/4 oz/¹½ cup long-grain rice
50 g/2 oz/¹⁄4 cup butter
2 courgettes (zucchini), thinly sliced
100 g/4 oz/2 cups button
  mushrooms, sliced
4 tomatoes, skinned and chopped
100 g/4 oz/1 cup cooked chicken,
  diced
1 chicken stock cube
5 ml/1 tsp Worcestershire sauce
4 eggs, beaten
Salt and freshly ground black
  pepper
15 ml/1 tbsp chopped parsley

Cook the rice in plenty of boiling salted water until tender. Drain. Meanwhile, melt the butter in a large frying pan (skillet). Add the courgettes and mushrooms and fry (sauté) for 4 minutes until soft and golden brown. Stir in the cooked rice, the tomatoes, chicken, crumbled stock cube and Worcestershire sauce. Pour over the eggs, season with salt and pepper, and stir well. Cook over a gentle heat until the base is set and golden brown. Place under a moderate grill (broiler) until the top is golden and the egg is completely set. Sprinkle with the parsley and cut into wedges.

Chicken and Egg Situation!

Serves 4

225 g/8 oz/2 cups minced (ground)
  chicken
50 g/2 oz/¹½ cup cooked long-grain
  rice
1 onion, grated
2.5 ml/¹½ tsp dried tarragon
60 ml/4 tbsp double (heavy) cream
Salt and freshly ground black
  pepper
5 eggs
A little plain (all-purpose) flour
50 g/2 oz/2 cups cornflakes, crushed
30 ml/2 tbsp sunflower oil
25 g/1 oz/2 tbsp butter

Mix the chicken with the rice, onion, tarragon, cream and some salt and pepper. Beat one of the eggs and add a little to the mixture to bind. With floured hands, shape the mixture into 4 cakes. Dip in the rest of the beaten egg then coat in cornflakes. Heat the oil in a frying pan (skillet). Add the chicken patties and fry (sauté) for about 8 minutes until brown on both sides and cooked through. Drain on kitchen paper. Melt the butter and fry the remaining eggs. Slide on top of the patties and serve hot.

Barbecued Chicken with Tomato Rice

Serves 4

4 chicken portions
40 g/1½ oz/3 tbsp butter
225 g/8 oz/1 cup long-grain rice
2 × 400 g/2 × 14 oz/2 large cans chopped tomatoes
Chicken stock
Salt and freshly ground black pepper
1 bay leaf
1 onion, finely chopped
15 ml/1 tbsp clear honey
45 ml/3 tbsp brown table sauce
15 ml/1 tbsp tomato ketchup (catsup)

Wipe the chicken. Place skin side up in a roasting tin (pan). Dot with 15 g/½ oz/1 tbsp of the butter and roast in the oven at 200°C/400°F/gas mark 6 for 20 minutes. As soon as the chicken is cooking, put the rice in an flameproof dish. Make one of the cans of tomatoes up to 600 ml/1 pt/2½ cups with stock. Pour over the rice. Season with salt and pepper and add the bay leaf. Bring to the boil, cover with foil or a lid and transfer to the oven on the shelf below the chicken. Melt the remaining butter in a pan and stir in the remaining ingredients. After the 20 minutes cooking, pour the sauce over the chicken. Check the rice, stir and re-cover. Cook for a further 15-20 minutes, basting occasionally, until the chicken is coated in the sauce and the rice is tender and has absorbed the liquid. Discard the bay leaf. Serve the chicken hot with the rice.

Indonesian Chicken Satay with Fragrant Rice and Chick Peas

Serves 4

450 g/1 lb chicken meat, cubed
30 ml/2 tbsp soy sauce
2 spring onions (scallions), finely chopped
1 garlic clove, crushed
1.5 ml/¼ tsp chilli powder
30 ml/2 tbsp lime juice
225 g/8 oz/1 cup Thai fragrant rice
25 g/1 oz/2 tbsp unsalted (sweet) butter
425 g/15 oz/1 large can chick peas (garbanzos), drained
Coriander (cilantro) leaves

Put the chicken in a dish. Add the soy sauce, spring onions, garlic, chilli and lime juice. Toss well and leave to marinade for at least 1 hour. Thread on soaked wooden skewers and grill (broil) for about 5 minutes, turning and basting frequently, until cooked through. Meanwhile, cook the rice in plenty of boiling salted water until tender, drain and rinse with boiling water. Drain again. Melt the butter in the pan. Add the chick peas and cook gently, stirring, for 3 minutes. Stir in the rice and toss well. Pile on to a serving dish. Top with the chicken, carefully sliding it off the skewers. Scatter a few coriander leaves over and serve.

Chicken Pepper Pot

Serves 4

50 g/2 oz/¹/₄ cup butter
4 chicken portions
600 ml/1 pt/2¹/₂ cups chicken stock
225 g/8 oz/1 cup long-grain rice
1 red (bell) pepper, chopped
1 green (bell) pepper, chopped
1 large onion, chopped
1 garlic clove, crushed
15 ml/1 tbsp tomato purée (paste)
5 ml/1 tsp paprika
5 ml/1 tsp coarsely crushed green
    peppercorns
2.5 ml/¹/₂ tsp dried mixed herbs
Salt
Chopped parsley

Melt the butter in a flameproof casserole
(Dutch oven). Add the chicken and brown
well on all sides. Add half the stock, bring
to the boil, cover and simmer gently for 15
minutes. Add the remaining ingredients
except the parsley and stir well. Cover and
cook gently for a further 15-20 minutes or
until the chicken and rice are tender and all
the liquid has been absorbed. Serve sprinkled with the parsley.

Chicken and Asparagus Plait

Serves 4

375 g/13 oz puff pastry (paste)
298 g/10¹/₂ oz/1 can condensed
    cream of asparagus soup
300 g/11 oz/1 can cut asparagus
    spears, drained
225 g/8 oz/2 cups cooked chicken,
    chopped
100 g/4 oz/1 cup cooked long-grain
    rice
2.5 ml/¹/₂ tsp dried mixed herbs
Freshly ground black pepper
Beaten egg to glaze

Roll out the pastry to a large rectangle.
Mix the soup, asparagus, chicken and rice
together with the herbs and a good grinding of pepper. Spoon down the centre of
the pastry. Make slashes either sides at
1 cm/¹/₂ in intervals down the length. Brush
with egg. Fold over the ends, then wrap the
strips over the filling one at a time from
each side alternately to form a plaited
effect. Carefully transfer to a dampened
baking sheet. Brush with egg and bake at
200°C/400°F/gas mark 6 for about 25-30
minutes until golden brown and piping hot.
Serve hot or cold.

Glazed Chicken Quills

Serves 4

25 g/1 oz/2 tbsp butter, melted
45 ml/3 tbsp clear honey
15 ml/1 tbsp soy sauce
2.5 ml/¹/₂ tsp ground ginger
4 chicken portions
75 ml/5 tbsp dry white wine
Salt and freshly ground black
  pepper
225 g/8 oz/2 cups penne
100 g/4 oz dwarf beans, cut into
  short lengths
2 canned pimiento caps, cut into
  thin strips
30 ml/2 tbsp olive oil

Mix the butter with the honey, soy sauce and ginger. Place the chicken portions in a roasting tin (pan) and brush the glaze over. Turn over so the skin is facing down and brush again. Pour the wine around and season the chicken lightly with salt and pepper. Bake at 220°C/425°F/gas mark 7 for 20 minutes. Turn the chicken over, baste with the juices and any remaining glaze. Return to the oven and cook for a further 15-20 minutes, basting twice. Meanwhile, cook the pasta in plenty of boiling, salted water, according to the packet directions, adding the beans for the last 5 minutes cooking. Drain and return to the pan. Add the pimientos and olive oil and toss lightly over a gentle heat. Pile on to a warm serving dish. Place the chicken on top and keep warm. Boil the juices rapidly in the pan until syrupy. Spoon over the chicken and serve straight away.

Peasant Chicken

Serves 4

4 chicken portions
30 ml/2 tbsp olive oil
25 g/1 oz/2 tbsp butter
Salt and freshly ground black
  pepper
100 g/4 oz button mushrooms
45ml/3 tbsp chopped parsley
2 garlic cloves, chopped
150 ml/¹/₄ pt/²/₃ cup chicken stock
225 g/8 oz/2 cups conchiglie or
  rigatoni

Brown the chicken portions in the oil and butter in a large frying pan (skillet). Season with salt and pepper, cover and cook gently for 20 minutes. Add the mushrooms and cook for 10 minutes. Sprinkle the chicken with the parsley and garlic, cover and cook for 4 minutes. Lift the chicken out of the pan and keep warm. Add the stock to the juices in the pan and boil, stirring, until slightly reduced. Meanwhile, cook the pasta in plenty of boiling, salted water for 10 minutes until just tender, drain. Stir the pasta into the juices in the pan. Top with the chicken and serve straight away.

Chicken with Cashew Nuts and Noodles

Serves 4

100 g/4 oz quick-cook Chinese egg
  noodles
30 ml/2 tbsp oil
225 g/8 oz boneless chicken thighs,
  cut into strips
1 bunch of spring onions (scallions),
  cut into short lengths
1 carrot, grated
275 g/10 oz/2¹/₂ cups bean sprouts
25 g/1 oz/¹/₄ cup cashew nuts
300 ml/¹/₂ pt/1¹/₄ cups chicken stock
15 ml/1 tbsp cornflour (cornstarch)
15 ml/1 tbsp soy sauce

Cook the noodles according to the packet directions. Drain. Heat the oil in a large frying pan (skillet) or wok and fry (sauté) the chicken, spring onions and carrot for 5 minutes, stirring. Add the bean sprouts and cook for a further 3 minutes, stirring. Add the cashew nuts and stock. Blend the cornflour with the soy sauce and stir into the pan. Bring to the boil and cook for 2 minutes, stirring. Stir in the noodles and heat through. Serve piping hot.

Chicken Liver and Hazelnut-stuffed Cannelloni

Serves 4

45 ml/3 tbsp olive oil
1 onion, finely chopped
1 garlic clove, crushed
450 g/1 lb/4 cups chicken livers,
  finely chopped or minced (ground)
5 ml/1 tsp dried oregano
200 g/7 oz/1 small can chopped
  tomatoes
30 ml/2 tbsp tomato purée (paste)
50 g/2 oz/¹/₂ cup hazelnuts, roughly
  chopped
Salt and freshly ground black
  pepper
8 cannelloni tubes
1¹/₂ quantities cheese sauce (see
  Basic Macaroni Cheese page 296)
30 ml/2 tbsp grated Parmesan
  cheese

Heat the oil in a saucepan. Add the onion and garlic and fry (sauté), stirring, for 2 minutes. Add the chicken livers, oregano, tomatoes, tomato purée, nuts and a little salt and pepper. Cook gently for 5 minutes, stirring occasionally. Spoon into a piping bag fitted with a large plain tube (tip). Use to fill the cannelloni tubes. Arrange in a single layer in a greased ovenproof dish. Pour over the cheese sauce and sprinkle with the Parmesan. Bake at 190°C/ 375°F/gas mark 5 for about 35 minutes or until the cannelloni is tender and the top is golden brown.

Chicken and Spinach Lasagne

Serves 6

30 ml/2 tbsp oil
1 large onion, finely chopped
1 garlic clove, crushed
225 g/8 oz chicken meat, diced
200 g/7 oz/1¼ cups chicken livers,
  trimmed and chopped
100 g/4 oz/2 cups button
  mushrooms, sliced
5 ml/1 tsp dried thyme
2.5 ml/½ tsp ground mace
65 g/2½ oz/⅓ cup plain (all-purpose)
  flour
300 ml/½ pt/1¼ cups chicken stock
225 g/8 oz/1 cup frozen chopped
  spinach, thawed
450 ml/¾ pt/2 cups milk
50 g/2 oz/¼ cup butter
50 g/2 oz Fontina cheese, grated
Salt and freshly ground black
  pepper
8 sheets no-need-to-precook lasagne
Grated Pecorino cheese

Heat the oil in a large pan. Add the onion and garlic and fry (sauté) for 2 minutes. Add the chicken and cook, stirring for 4 minutes. Stir in the chicken livers, mushrooms, thyme and mace and cook for 30 seconds. Stir in 15 ml/1 tbsp of the flour and cook for 1 minute. Blend in the stock, bring to the boil, reduce the heat, cover and simmer for 10 minutes. Squeeze out all the moisture from the spinach, stir into the chicken and season to taste. Meanwhile, whisk the milk with the remaining flour in a saucepan. Add the butter and bring to the boil, stirring all the time. Simmer for 2 minutes, stir in the Fontina cheese and season to taste. Spoon a very thin layer of the chicken mixture into a greased 2 litre/3½ pt/8½ cup ovenproof dish. Top with a layer of pasta. Add a layer of half the remaining chicken, then a third of the cheese sauce then a layer of pasta. Add the rest of the chicken, half the remaining cheese sauce and all the remaining pasta. Top with the remaining cheese sauce. Sprinkle with the Pecorino cheese and bake at 180°C/350°F/gas mark 4 for 40 minutes or until the lasagne is tender when a knife is inserted down through the centre.

Sherried Chicken Liver Lasagne

Serves 4

1 large onion, finely chopped
1 garlic clove, crushed
75 g/3 oz/¹/₃ cup butter
100 g/4 oz streaky bacon, rinded and
    diced
200 g/7 oz/1³/₄ cups chicken livers,
    trimmed and chopped
175 g/6 oz/3 cups button
    mushrooms, chopped
450 ml/³/₄ pt/2 cups chicken stock
50 g/2 oz/¹/₂ cup plain (all-purpose)
    flour
45 ml/3 tbsp medium dry sherry
Salt and freshly ground black
    pepper
300 ml/¹/₂ pt/1¹/₄ cups milk
75 g/3 oz Cheddar cheese, grated
6-8 sheets wholewheat no-need-to-
    precook lasagne

Fry (sauté) the onion and garlic in 50 g/2 oz/¹/₄ cup of the butter for 3 minutes until softened· and lightly golden. Stir in the bacon and chicken livers and cook, stirring, for 2 minutes. Stir in the mushrooms and cook for a further 1 minute. Add the stock, bring to the boil, reduce the heat, cover and simmer for 10 minutes. Blend half the flour with the sherry. Stir into the pan and bring to the boil, stirring until thickened. Season to taste. Meanwhile, melt the remaining butter in a saucepan. Stir in the remaining flour and the milk until smooth. Bring to the boil and cook for 2 minutes, stirring all the time until thickened. Season to taste and stir in half the cheese. Put a thin layer of the chicken liver mixture in the base of a large, shallow ovenproof dish. Top with a layer of lasagne. Add half the remaining chicken liver mixture then another layer of lasagne. Repeat the layers. Top with the cheese sauce and sprinkle with the remaining cheese. Bake at 190°C/375°F/gas mark 5 for about 40 minutes or until the pasta is cooked and the top is golden brown.

Piquant Chicken Liver Farfalle

Serves 4

225 g/8 oz/2 cups farfalle
2 onions, finely chopped
25 g/1 oz/2 tbsp butter
15 ml/1 tbsp olive oil
1 wineglass red vermouth
450 g/1 lb/4 cups chicken livers,
    trimmed and chopped
5 ml/1 tsp chopped sage
Salt and freshly ground black
    pepper
Chopped parsley

Cook the pasta according to the packet directions, drain and return to the saucepan. Meanwhile, fry (sauté) the onions in the butter and oil until soft but not brown. Add the vermouth and simmer until reduced by half. Add the chicken livers and sage and cook quickly for about 2-3 minutes until brown but not dry. Season to taste. Add to the farfalle, toss well and sprinkle with the parsley before serving.

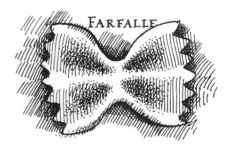
FARFALLE

Maybe Chicken Chow Mein

Serves 4

225 g/8 oz quick-cook chow mein
noodles
225 g/8 oz/2 cups cooked chicken,
cut into strips
425 g/15 oz/1 large can stir-fry
vegetables, drained
1 garlic clove, crushed
30 ml/2 tbsp soy sauce
30 ml/2 tbsp sherry
5 ml/1 tsp ground ginger
15 ml/1 tbsp light brown sugar
25 g/1 oz salted peanuts or cashew
nuts

Cook the noodles according to the packet
directions. Drain. Put all the remaining
ingredients except the nuts in a large pan
or wok and cook, stirring, until piping hot.
Stir in the noodles and cook for 2 minutes
more. Sprinkle with the nuts and serve hot.

Somerset Chicken Bake

Serves 4-5

225 g/8 oz/2 cups rotelli
2 onions, finely sliced
450 g/1 lb cooking (tart) apples,
sliced
75 g/3 oz/¹/₃ cup butter
350 g/12 oz/3 cups chicken stir-fry
meat
300 ml/¹/₂ pt/1¹/₄ cups dry cider
50 g/2 oz/¹/₃ cup raisins
5 ml/1 tsp dried thyme
1 chicken stock cube
10 ml/2 tsp cornflour (cornstarch)
15 ml/1 tbsp water
Salt and freshly ground black pepper

Cook the pasta according to the packet
directions, drain. Meanwhile, fry (sauté)
the onion and half the apples in a third of
the butter until soft and lightly golden.
Remove from the pan with a draining
spoon. Melt half the remaining butter in
the pan. Add the chicken and cook, stirring, for 5 minutes. Stir in the cider,
raisins, thyme and crumbled stock cube
and bring to the boil, stirring. Blend the
cornflour with the water and stir into the
pan. Bring to the boil, stirring until thickened. Return the onion and apple mixture
to the pan and season to taste. Put half the
pasta in an ovenproof dish. Top with half
the chicken mixture then repeat the layers.
Top with a layer of remaining apple slices.
Melt the remaining butter and brush over.
Bake at 180°C/350°F/gas mark 4 for about
25 minutes until piping hot and the apples
on top are tender and lightly golden.

Chicken, Leek and Walnut Vermicelli

Serves 4

2 small leeks, thinly sliced
15 ml/1 tbsp walnut oil
15 ml/1 tbsp olive oil
50 g/2 oz/¹/₂ cup chopped walnuts
2 chicken breast fillets, finely diced
150 ml/¹/₄ pt/²/₃ cup medium dry
white wine
150 ml/¹/₄ pt/²/₃ cup crème fraîche
Salt and freshly ground black
pepper
350 g/12 oz vermicelli
Chopped parsley

Fry (sauté) the leeks in the two oils for 2 minutes until slightly softened. Add the walnuts, cover with a lid, reduce the heat and cook gently for 5 minutes until soft. Add the chicken and wine, re-cover and simmer gently for 10 minutes until the chicken is tender. Stir in the crème fraîche and season to taste. Meanwhile, cook the vermicelli according to the packet directions. Drain and pile on to warm serving plates. Spoon the hot sauce over and garnish with the parsley.

Sweet and Sour Chicken Delight

Serves 4

15 ml/1 tbsp sunflower oil
2 chicken breast fillets, cut into
small thin strips
1 carrot, cut into matchsticks
1 small red (bell) pepper, cut into
thin strips
¹/₄ cucumber, diced
430 g/15¹/₂ oz/1 large can pineapple
pieces
30 ml/2 tbsp tomato purée (paste)
45 ml/3 tbsp soy sauce
2.5 ml/¹/₂ tsp ground ginger
60 ml/4 tbsp malt vinegar
10 ml/2 tsp cornflour (cornstarch)
15 ml/1 tbsp water
250g/9 oz/1 packet Chinese egg
noodles

Heat the oil in a large saucepan. Fry (sauté) the chicken in the oil for 4 minutes until cooked through. Remove from the pan. Add the remaining ingredients except the cornflour, water and noodles. Bring to the boil and boil for 5 minutes. Blend the cornflour with the water and stir into the sauce. Cook, stirring, until thickened and clear. Return the chicken to the sauce and heat through. Meanwhile, cook the noodles according to the packet directions. Drain. Add to the sweet and sour sauce and toss well.

Spaghetti with Turkey and Mushrooms

Serves 4

60 ml/4 tbsp olive oil
175 g/6 oz/1½ cups diced turkey
  meat
1 carrot, finely chopped
1 celery stick, finely chopped
1 garlic clove, crushed
100 g/4 oz mushrooms, sliced
4 tomatoes, chopped
50 g/2 oz/½ cup frozen peas
350 g/12 oz spaghetti
Salt and freshly ground black
  pepper
Grated Parmesan cheese

Heat the oil in a large pan. Add all the ingredients except the spaghetti, seasoning and cheese and fry (sauté), stirring, for 3 minutes. Reduce the heat, cover and cook gently for 10 minutes, stirring occasionally. Meanwhile, cook the spaghetti according to the packet directions. Drain and add to the turkey mixture. Season to taste. Toss lightly and serve hot with the Parmesan cheese.

Turkey Veronica

Serves 4

300 ml/½ pt/1¼ cups chicken stock
1 bay leaf
40 g/1½ oz/3 tbsp butter
225 g/8 oz/2 cups turkey stir-fry
  meat
25 g/1 oz/¼ cup plain (all-purpose)
  flour
5 ml/1 tsp grated lemon rind
150 ml/¼ pt/⅔ cup single (light)
  cream
75 g/3 oz/½ cup seedless (pitless)
  white grapes, halved
Salt and white pepper
350 g/12 oz green tagliatelle (verdi)
Chopped parsley

Put the stock in a pan. Add the bay leaf. Bring to the boil and leave to infuse while preparing the rest of the sauce. Melt the butter in a separate pan. Add the turkey and cook, stirring, for 4-5 minutes until cooked through. Add the flour and cook, stirring, for 1 minute. Discard the bay leaf, then gradually blend the stock into the turkey mixture, stirring all the time. Add the lemon rind. Bring to the boil and cook for 3 minutes, stirring. Stir in the cream, add the grapes and season to taste. Meanwhile, cook the pasta according to the packet directions. Drain and return to the pan. Add the sauce, toss well, pile on to warm plates and garnish with the parsley.

Crunchy Turkey Escalopes with Lemon Noodles

Serves 4

4 turkey breasts
1 size 1 egg, beaten
85 g/3½ oz/1 packet parsley, thyme and lemon stuffing mix
Oil for shallow-frying
225 g/8 oz tagliatelle
Grated rind and juice of 1 lemon
30 ml/2 tbsp chopped parsley
50 g/2 oz/¼ cup butter
Freshly ground black pepper

Place the turkey breasts one at a time in a plastic bag and beat flat with a rolling pin or meat mallet. Dip in the egg then the stuffing mix to coat completely. Fry (sauté) in hot oil on each side for about 5 minutes until golden brown and cooked through. Drain on kitchen paper and keep warm. Meanwhile, cook the pasta according to the packet directions. Drain and return to the saucepan. Add the lemon rind and juice, the parsley and the butter cut into small flakes. Toss gently over heat until the butter has melted. Add a good grinding of pepper, pile on to a serving dish and lay the escalopes on top.

Hunters' Mafalde

Serves 4

4 hare joints
15 ml/1 tbsp olive oil
100 g/4 oz streaky bacon rashers (slices), rinded and diced
1 garlic clove, crushed
1 onion, finely chopped
2 celery sticks, finely chopped
2 carrots, finely chopped
100 g/4 oz mushrooms, chopped
45 ml/3 tbsp plain (all-purpose) flour
120 ml/4 fl oz/½ cup port
450 ml/¾ pt/2 cups beef stock
Salt and freshly ground black pepper
1 bouquet garni sachet
Grated rind and juice of 1 lemon
350 g/12 oz mafalde
Grated Parmesan cheese

Cut all the meat off the hare joints and remove any tendons. Cut into small pieces. Heat the oil in a large pan and fry (sauté) the bacon, garlic, onion, celery and carrot for 5 minutes, stirring until golden brown. Add the hare meat and mushrooms and cook, stirring for 2 minutes. Stir in the flour and cook for 2-3 minutes, stirring until browned. Remove from the heat and blend in the port and stock. Return to the heat and bring to the boil, stirring until thickened. Add salt and pepper to taste and the bouquet garni. Cover, reduce the heat and simmer gently for 1 hour, stirring occasionally. Add the lemon rind, salt and pepper and enough lemon juice to taste. Meanwhile, cook the mafalde according to the packet directions. Spoon into nests in shallow bowls and spoon the hare sauce into the middle. Dust with the Parmesan cheese before serving.

Japanese Chicken Dumplings

Serves 4

225 g/8 oz/2 cups plain (all-purpose) flour
A pinch of salt
120 ml/4 fl oz/¹/² cup warm water
450 g/1 lb Chinese leaves (stem lettuce), diced
225 g/8 oz/2 cups chicken stir-fry meat, very finely chopped
6 spring onions (scallions), finely chopped
2.5 ml/¹/² tsp grated fresh root ginger
Soy sauce
15 ml/1 tbsp dry sherry
15 ml/1 tbsp sesame oil
Hot chilli sauce

Sift the flour and salt into a bowl. Gradually work in the water to form a dough. Knead gently on a lightly floured surface until smooth and elastic and no longer sticky. Cover and leave to rest for 30 minutes. Meanwhile, boil the Chinese leaves in lightly salted water for 3 minutes. Drain and dry on kitchen paper. Mix with the chicken, spring onion, ginger, 15 ml/1 tbsp soy sauce, the sherry and oil. Roll the dough into a long sausage shape. Cut into 50 equal pieces and flatten each, then roll into a 6 cm/2¹/² in circle. Put a small spoonful of filling into the centre of each circle. Dampen the edges, fold over and press well together to seal. Drop into a large pan of boiling water, return to the boil and cook for 5 minutes. Remove from the pan with a draining spoon. Serve with a bowl of soy sauce and a bowl of hot chilli sauce.

Stir-fried Chicken with Angel Hair

Serves 4

45 ml/3 tbsp sunflower oil
1 garlic clove, crushed
1 bunch of spring onions (scallions), cut into diagonal slices
1 green (bell) pepper, cut into thin strips
50 g/2 oz/1 cup button mushrooms, sliced
1 courgette (zucchini), cut into matchsticks
225 g/8 oz/2 cups cooked chicken, shredded
30 ml/2 tbsp soy sauce
225 g/8 oz capellini
15 g/¹/² oz/1 tbsp unsalted (sweet) butter
Salt and freshly ground black pepper
50 g/2 oz/¹/² cup toasted flaked almonds

Heat the oil in a large frying pan or wok. Add the garlic, spring onions and pepper and stir-fry for 3 minutes. Add the mushrooms and courgette and stir-fry for a further 2 minutes. Add the chicken and soy sauce and toss gently for 3 minutes. Meanwhile, cook the pasta according to the packet directions. Drain and add to the pan with the butter. Toss and stir until well combined. Taste and season if necessary. Pile into warm bowls and sprinkle with the almonds before serving.

Chicken and Pasta Parcels

Serves 4
100 g/4 oz/1 cup conchiglie
15 g/¹/₂ oz/1 tbsp butter
2 onion, sliced thinly into rings
2 carrots, thinly sliced
1 courgette (zucchini), thinly sliced
4 tomatoes, quartered
4 chicken portions
5 ml/1 tsp dried oregano
Salt and freshly ground black
  pepper
150 ml/¹/₄ pt/²/₃ cup red wine

Cook the pasta in boiling salted water for 10 minutes. Drain. Butter four large squares of foil. Divide the pasta among the squares. Top with the vegetables then the chicken. Sprinkle with the oregano, salt and pepper. Spoon the wine over. Wrap loosely over the chicken, sealing the edges well. Transfer carefully to a baking sheet. Bake in the oven at 190°C/375°F/gas mark 5 for 45 minutes. Part-open the foil for the last 10 minutes to brown the chicken skin. Serve hot straight from the foil.

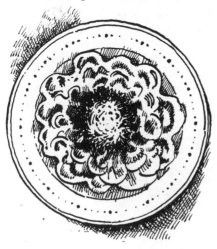

Chicken Ravioli

Serves 6
45 ml/3 tbsp olive oil
15 g/¹/₂ oz/1 tbsp butter
3 garlic cloves, crushed
750 ml/1¹/₄ pts/3 cups passata (sieved
  tomatoes)
45 ml/3 tbsp tomato purée (paste)
5 ml/1 tsp dried basil
5 ml/1 tsp dried rosemary
Salt and freshly ground black
  pepper
100 g/4 oz/1 cup minced (ground)
  pork
175 g/6 oz/1¹/₂ cups cooked chicken,
  chopped
50 g/2 oz/¹/₂ cup cooked ham,
  chopped
30 ml/2 tbsp chopped parsley
3 eggs, beaten
450 g/1 lb/4 cups plain (all-purpose)
  flour
250 ml/8 fl oz/1 cup water

Heat 30 ml/2 tbsp of the oil and the butter in a pan and fry (sauté) 2 of the garlic cloves for 1 minute. Add the passata, tomato purée, basil and rosemary. Season to taste, bring to the boil, cover and simmer gently for 30 minutes, stirring occasionally. Remove the lid after 20 minutes. Meanwhile, brown the pork with the remaining garlic, stirring until all the grains of meat are separate. Remove from the heat and mix with the remaining meats, the parsley and one of the eggs to bind. Chill until ready to use. Sift the flour with a pinch of salt into a large bowl. Make a well in the centre, add the remaining eggs and half the water and mix to form a firm dough, adding more water as necessary. Knead gently on a lightly floured surface. Cut the dough in half. Roll out each to a large, thin square. Place spoonfuls of the filling at regular intervals over one sheet of dough. Brush between each mound of filling with water. Top with the second sheet and press down well between the filling. Cut into squares using a pastry cutter or a sharp knife. Drop into a large pan of boiling, salted water in batches and cook for 4 minutes or until they rise to the surface. Remove with a draining spoon and keep warm while cooking the remainder. Add to the tomato sauce and simmer for 5 minutes. Serve hot.

American-style Chicken Tetrazzini

Serves 4
350g/12 oz spaghetti
25 g/1 oz/2 tbsp unsalted (sweet) butter
1 onion, finely chopped
175 g/8 oz/4 cups button mushrooms, sliced
1/2 celeriac (celery root), grated
1 carrot, grated
15 ml/1 tbsp plain (all-purpose) flour
150 ml/1/4 pt/2/3 cup chicken stock
150 ml/1/4 pt/2/3 cup single (light) cream
225 g/8 oz/2 cups cooked chicken meat, diced
Milk
50 g/2 oz/1/2 cup grated Parmesan cheese
30 ml/2 tbsp flaked almonds
15 ml/1 tbsp chopped parsley

Cook the pasta according to the packet directions. Drain. Meanwhile, melt the butter and cook the onion, mushrooms, celeriac and carrot for 4 minutes, stirring until softened but not browned. Blend in the flour, then the stock and cream. Bring

to the boil and simmer for 2 minutes, stirring. Add the chicken and heat through. Stir in the pasta and thin with a little milk if necessary. Toss over a gentle heat. Pile into a flameproof dish. Sprinkle with the Parmesan, almonds and parsley. Grill (broil) until bubbling and the almonds are toasted.

Sherried Chicken and Ham Spaghettini

Serves 4
50 g/2 oz/1/4 cup butter
40 g/1 1/2 oz/1/3 cup plain (all-purpose) flour
300 ml/1/2 pt/1 1/4 cups chicken stock
300 ml/1/2 pt/1 1/4 cups single (light) cream
30 ml/2 tbsp medium dry sherry
Salt and freshly ground black pepper
50 g/2 oz/1/2 cup cooked peas
100 g/4 oz/1 cup cooked ham, diced
225 g/8 oz/2 cups cooked chicken, diced
350 g/12 oz spaghettini
Grated Parmesan cheese

Melt the butter in a saucepan. Add the flour and cook for 2 minutes. Remove from the heat and blend in the stock, cream and sherry. Bring to the boil and simmer for 2 minutes. Season to taste and add the peas, ham and chicken and cook gently for 5 minutes. Meanwhile, cook the spaghettini according to the packet directions. Drain, rinse with boiling water, drain again. Pile on to a serving dish, spoon the hot sauce over and sprinkle with Parmesan cheese.

Creamy Lemon Chicken Noodles

Serves 4-6

50 g/2 oz/¹/₄ cup unsalted (sweet) butter
1 large onion, finely chopped
3-4 chicken breasts, cut into thin strips
Grated rind and juice of 1 lemon
450 ml/³/₄ pt/2 cups crème fraîche
25 g/1 oz/¹/₄ cup capers, chopped
25 g/1 oz/¹/₄ cup chopped parsley
Salt and freshly ground black pepper
350 g/12 oz any ribbon noodles

Melt the butter and fry (sauté) the onion until soft but not brown. Add the chicken and fry for 3-5 minutes until cooked and lightly golden. Add the lemon rind and juice and cook, scraping up any meat residue until almost evaporated. Stir in the cream and simmer until thickened and reduced by half. Stir in the capers, half the parsley and a little salt and pepper. Meanwhile, cook the pasta according to the packet directions. Drain and pile on to warm plates. Spoon the chicken sauce over and garnish with the remaining parsley.

Turkey Chop Suey with Spicy Noodles

Serves 4

350 g/12 oz/3 cups cooked turkey, diced
298 g/10¹/₂ oz/1 can condensed cream of mushroom soup
45 ml/3 tbsp soy sauce
5 ml/1 tsp grated fresh root ginger
Salt and freshly ground black pepper
1 garlic clove, crushed
30 ml/2 tbsp sunflower oil
1 carrot, grated
1 green (bell) pepper, chopped
2 celery sticks, chopped
5 cm/2 in piece cucumber, grated
100 g/4 oz mushrooms, sliced
10 ml/2 tsp cornflour (cornstarch)
30 ml/2 tbsp dry sherry
225 g/8 oz/2 cups bean sprouts
250 g/9 oz/1 packet Chinese egg noodles
5 ml/1 tsp Chinese five-spice powder
A pinch of grated nutmeg

Mix the turkey with the soup, soy sauce, ginger, a little salt and pepper and the garlic. Heat the oil in a large frying pan (skillet) or wok. Add the carrot, pepper, celery, cucumber and mushrooms and stir-fry for 1 minute. Stir in the turkey mixture and bring to the boil. Blend the cornflour with the sherry and stir into the pan. Add the bean sprouts and cook, stirring, for 5 minutes. Meanwhile, cook the noodles according to the packet directions. Drain and add the Chinese five-spice powder and nutmeg. Toss well, pile into bowls and top with the turkey mixture.

Turkey Olivetto

Serves 4-6

30 ml/2 tbsp olive oil
1 green (bell) pepper, chopped
1 red (bell) pepper, chopped
1 onion, chopped
1 garlic clove, chopped
450 g/1 lb/4 cups minced (ground)
*   turkey*
2 × 400 g/2 × 14 oz/2 large cans
*   chopped tomatoes*
100 g/4 oz/⅔ cup stoned (pitted)
*   black olives, sliced*
30 ml/3 tbsp tomato purée (paste)
10 ml/2 tsp caster (superfine) sugar
Salt and freshly ground black
*   pepper*
30 ml/2 tbsp chopped basil
350 g/12 oz spaghetti flavoured with
*   olives*

Heat the oil and fry (sauté) the peppers, onion and garlic for 3 minutes. Add the turkey and fry, stirring until all the grains of meat are separate. Add the tomatoes, olives, tomato purée, sugar and a little salt and pepper and simmer, stirring occasionally, for 20 minutes. Stir in half the basil. Meanwhile, cook the spaghetti according to the packet directions. Drain. Pile on to serving plates. Spoon the sauce over and garnish with the remaining basil.

153

Fish and Seafood Dishes

Fresh, frozen or canned, just about every kind of fish and other seafood lends itself to rice and pasta dishes.

Riviera Cod and Rice

Serves 4
15 ml/1 tbsp olive oil
1 onion, chopped
2 garlic cloves, crushed
1 red (bell) pepper, sliced
600 ml/1 pt/2¹/₂ cups passata (sieved
  tomatoes)
15 ml/1 tbsp tomato purée (paste)
150 ml/¹/₄ pt/²/₃ cup water
228 g/8 oz/1 cup long-grain rice
Salt and freshly ground black
  pepper
450 g/1 lb cod fillet, skinned and
  cubed
Chopped parsley
A few black olives

Heat the oil in a saucepan. Add the onion, garlic and pepper and fry (sauté) stirring for 2 minutes. Stir in the passata, tomato purée, water, rice and a little salt and pepper. Cover and cook gently, stirring occasionally, for 10 minutes. Add the fish and, if getting dry, a little more water. Season with salt and pepper and cook for a further 5 minutes until all the liquid has been absorbed and the rice and fish are cooked. Serve sprinkled with parsley and olives.

Deep South Fish Stew

Serves 6
225 g/8 oz/1 cup long-grain rice
900 ml/1¹/₂ pts/3 cups fish stock
1 onion, sliced
1 green (bell) pepper, sliced
1 red (bell) pepper, sliced
50 g/2 oz/¹/₄ cup butter
15 ml/1 tbsp plain (all-purpose) flour
1 green chilli, seeded and chopped
400 g/14 oz/1 large can chopped
  tomatoes
100 g/4 oz/1 cup frozen peas
100 g/4 oz green beans, cut into
  short lengths
15 ml/1 tbsp cider vinegar
15 ml/1 tbsp light brown sugar
450 g/1 lb firm white fish (cod,
  haddock etc), skinned and cubed
225 g/8 oz/2 cups peeled prawns
  (shrimp)
30 ml/2 tbsp medium dry sherry
Tabasco sauce

Cook the rice in 600 ml/1 pt/2¹/₂ cups of the stock until tender, about 15 minutes, when the stock should be absorbed. Press into a ring mould (mold) and keep warm. Fry (sauté) the onion and peppers in the butter for 5 minutes until soft. Stir in the flour and gradually blend in the remaining stock. Bring to the boil, stirring until thickened. Add the chilli, tomatoes, peas, beans, vinegar and sugar. Bring to the boil and cook for about 10 minutes until pulpy. Add the fish and cook for 5 minutes. Add the prawns, sherry and Tabasco to taste. Turn the rice out on to a serving dish. Spoon the stew into the centre and any remaining around the edge. Serve hot.

Country Fish Stew

Serves 4
1 onion, thinly sliced
2 carrots, thinly sliced
1 small swede, diced
2 potatoes, diced
1/4 small green cabbage, shredded
25 g/1 oz/2 tbsp butter
400 g/14 oz/1 large can tomatoes
450 ml/³/4 pt/2 cups fish stock
Salt and freshly ground black pepper
100 g/4 oz/¹/2 cup long-grain rice
350 g/12 oz cod or other white fish fillet, skinned and cubed
Chopped parsley

Fry (sauté) the prepared vegetables in the butter in a large flameproof casserole (Dutch oven), stirring for 10 minutes. Add the tomatoes, stock and a little salt and pepper. Bring to the boil and simmer for 10 minutes. Add the rice and fish, cover and simmer for a further 10 minutes, stirring occasionally, until the rice, fish and vegetables are tender. Taste and re-season if necessary. Ladle into bowls and serve garnished with parsley.

Cod Piri Piri

Serves 4
450 g/1 lb cod fillet, skinned and diced
A little plain (all-purpose) flour
Salt and freshly ground black pepper
30 ml/2 tbsp olive oil
1 large onion, chopped
1 green (bell) pepper, finely chopped
1 garlic clove, crushed
6 rashers (slices) streaky bacon, rinded and diced
1 bay leaf
A pinch of ground mace
Milk
225 g/8 oz/1 cup long-grain rice
200 g/7 oz/1 small can chopped tomatoes
Chicken stock

Toss the cod in the flour, seasoned with a little salt and pepper. Fry (sauté) in half the oil for 3 minutes, stirring until lightly golden. Remove from the pan with a draining spoon. Add the remaining oil and fry the onion, pepper and garlic for 3 minutes to soften. Add the bacon and fry for a further minute, stirring. Add the bay leaf and mace and stir in enough milk to form a thick sauce, stirring all the time. Discard the bay leaf. Return the fish to the pan. Season well and bake uncovered at 200°C/400°F/gas mark 6 for about 30 minutes until brown and bubbling. Put the rice in a separate flameproof casserole. Make the tomatoes up to 450 ml/³/4 pt/2 cups with the chicken stock and add to the rice. Bring to the boil. Season lightly, cover and cook in the oven with the fish for 20-30 minutes until tender and the rice has absorbed all the liquid.

South-of-the-Border Casserole

Serves 4

350 g/12 oz/1¹/₂ cups long-grain rice
50 g/2 oz/¹/₄ cup butter
3 celery sticks, chopped
2 onions, chopped
1 small red (bell) pepper, chopped
298 g/10¹/₂ oz/1 can condensed cream of celery soup
150 ml/¹/₄ pt/²/₃ cup milk
450 g/1 lb/4 cups raw king prawns (jumbo shrimp), shelled
30 ml/2 tbsp chopped coriander (cilantro)
Cayenne
Salt and freshly ground black pepper

Cook the rice in plenty of boiling salted water for 10–15 minutes until just tender. Drain, rinse with boiling water and drain again. Meanwhile, melt the butter in a saucepan and fry (sauté) the celery, onions and pepper for 4 minutes until soft and lightly golden. Blend the soup with the milk, add to the pan and bring to the boil. Reduce the heat, add the prawns, cover and simmer gently for 15 minutes. Add the coriander and rice and heat through, stirring. Pile on to warm serving plates, garnish with cayenne and season to taste before serving.

Tangy Monkfish with Saffron Rice

Serves 4

50 g/2 oz/¹/₄ cup unsalted (sweet) butter
1 bunch of spring onions (scallions), chopped
225 g/8 oz/1 cup long-grain rice
600 ml/1 pt/2¹/₂ cups hot fish or chicken stock
2.5 ml/¹/₂ tsp saffron powder
100 g/4 oz/1 cup chopped green beans
450 g/1 lb monkfish, cut into bite-sized pieces
300 ml/¹/₂ pt/1¹/₄ cups milk
2 limes
Salt and freshly ground black pepper
30 ml/2 tbsp cornflour (cornstarch)
300 ml/¹/₂ pt/1¹/₄ cups single (light) cream
Watercress sprigs

Melt 15 g/¹/₂ oz/1 tbsp of the butter in a saucepan. Add the spring onions and fry (sauté) for 2 minutes, stirring. Add the rice and cook for a further 1 minute, stirring. Add the stock and saffron. Bring to the boil and simmer for about 10 minutes or until the rice is tender, adding the beans halfway through cooking. Drain off any excess stock. Press the rice into a lightly greased ring mould (mold), press down well, cover with foil and keep warm. Meanwhile, cook the fish in the milk for 5-10 minutes until just tender. Drain off the milk into a clean saucepan. Grate the rind and squeeze the juice of 1 of the limes. Blend the cornflour with a little water. Stir into the milk and add the cream. Bring to the boil and simmer for 1 minute. Stir in the remaining butter in small flakes, stirring until melted.

Stir in the lime rind and juice and season lightly. Fold in the fish. Turn the rice ring out on to a serving dish. Pile the fish into the centre. Cut the remaining lime in wedges and use to garnish the ring with the sprigs of watercress.

Golden Kedgeree

Serves 4
225 g/8 oz/1 cup long-grain rice
5 ml/1 tsp turmeric
225 g/8 oz smoked cod, haddock or whiting fillet, skinned
3 hard-boiled (hard-cooked) eggs, roughly chopped
45 ml/3 tbsp evaporated milk
Salt and freshly ground white pepper
Grated nutmeg
Chopped parsley

Cook the rice in plenty of lightly salted boiling water to which the turmeric has been added for 10 minutes or until just cooked. Drain and return to the saucepan. Meanwhile, poach the fish in water for 5-10 minutes until it flakes easily with a fork. Drain and break up discarding any bones. Stir the fish into the rice with the remaining ingredients except the parsley. Heat through, stirring gently. Serve garnished with the parsley.

Poached Egg and Mushroom Kedgeree

Serves 4
350 g/12 oz undyed smoked haddock fillet
75 g/3 oz/¹/₃ cup butter
1 onion, sliced
100 g/4 oz/2 cups button mushrooms, sliced
225 g/8 oz/1 cup long-grain rice
1.5 ml/¹/₄ tsp cayenne
Salt and freshly ground black pepper
10 ml/2 tsp lemon juice
300 ml/¹/₂ pt/1¹/₄ cups water
2.5 ml/¹/₂ tsp grated nutmeg
4 eggs
20 ml/4 tsp single (light) cream
Chopped corinader (cilantro)

Skin and dice the fish, discarding any bones. Melt the butter in a large frying pan (skillet) and fry (sauté) the onion for 2 minutes, stirring until lightly softened. Add the mushrooms and fry for a further 2 minutes, stirring. Stir in the rice, fish, seasonings, lemon juice and the water. Bring to the boil, reduce the heat, cover and cook gently for 20 minutes or until the rice has absorbed nearly all the water. Stir in the grated nutmeg. Make 4 wells in the rice mixture. Break an egg into each and top each with 5 ml/1 tsp of cream. Cover and cook gently for 15-25 minutes depending how well-cooked you like your eggs. Sprinkle with the coriander and serve straight from the pan.

Salmon and Dill Kedgeree

Serves 4-6

450 g/1 lb salmon tail fillet
900 ml/1¹/₂ pts/3³/₄ cups water
30 ml/2 tbsp sunflower oil
1 bunch of spring onions (scallions),
    cut in diagonal slices
350 g/12 oz/1¹/₂ cups long-grain rice
4 hard-boiled (hard-cooked) eggs,
    quartered
1 dill pickle, chopped
30 ml/2 tbsp single (light) cream
25 g/1 oz/2 tbsp butter
15 ml/1 tbsp chopped dill (dill weed)
Salt and freshly ground black
    pepper
15 ml/1 tbsp chopped parsley

Cook the fish in the water for 10 minutes or until just tender. Drain, reserving the cooking liquid. Remove the skin and any bones from the fish and break into biggish chunks. Heat the oil in a large pan and fry (sauté) the spring onions for 3 minutes, stirring. Add the rice and cook for 1 minute, stirring. Pour over the fish-cooking liquid, bring to the boil, reduce the heat, cover and simmer for 15-20 minutes or until the rice is cooked and has absorbed all the liquid. Add the fish, eggs, dill pickle, cream, the butter in flakes, the chopped dill, a little salt and a good grinding of pepper. Stir gently then heat through for 3-4 minutes. Sprinkle with the parsley and serve hot.

White Fish Kedgeree

Serves 4

225 g/8 oz white fish fillet
225 g/8 oz/1 cup long-grain rice
3 hard-boiled (hard-cooked) eggs,
    roughly chopped
15 ml/1 tbsp chopped parsley
45 ml/3 tbsp single (light) cream
Salt and freshly ground black
    pepper

Put the fish in a pan with just enough water to cover. Cook gently for 10 minutes until tender. Drain and flake, discarding the skin and any bones. Meanwhile, cook the rice in plenty of boiling salted water for 10 minutes or until just tender. Drain, rinse with boiling water, drain again and return to the pan. Add the eggs and fish to the rice and stir in the parsley and cream. Season to taste, heat through and serve hot.

Cod and Mushroom Soufflé

Serves 4

225 g/8 oz cod fillet
A little oil
100 g/4 oz mushrooms, chopped
25 g/1 oz/2 tbsp butter
25 g/1 oz/^{1}/$_4$ cup plain (all-purpose) flour
150 ml/^{1}/$_4$ pt/^{2}/$_3$ cup milk
2.5 ml/^{1}/$_2$ tsp made mustard
1.5 ml/^{1}/$_4$ tsp dried fennel
Salt and freshly ground black pepper
75 g/3 oz/^{3}/$_4$ cup cooked long-grain rice
3 eggs, separated

Brush the cod with oil and grill (broil) until just tender, turning once. Flake the fish, discarding the skin and any bones. Fry (sauté) the mushrooms in the butter for 2 minutes, stirring. Stir in the flour and cook for 1 minute. Remove from the heat and blend in the milk. Return to the heat, bring to the boil and cook for 2 minutes, stirring until thick. Stir in the mustard, fennel and a little salt and pepper. Stir in the rice and beat in the egg yolks. Stir in the fish. Whisk the egg whites until stiff and fold in with a metal spoon. Pour into a greased 1.2 litre/2 pt/5 cup soufflé dish and bake at 190°C/375°F/gas mark 5 for 35 minutes until risen and golden brown. Serve straight away.

Curried Fish Croquettes

Serves 4

350 g/12 oz white fish fillet
100 g/4 oz/^{1}/$_2$ cup mashed potato
100 g/4 oz/1 cup cooked long-grain rice
1 small onion, grated
10 ml/2 tsp curry powder
10 ml/2 tsp mango chutney
Salt and freshly ground black pepper
1 egg, beaten
25 g/1 oz/^{1}/$_2$ cup breadcrumbs
Oil for deep-frying
Lemon wedges

Put the fish in a pan with enough water to just cover. Cook gently for 10 minutes until tender. Drain, discard the skin and any bones and flake the fish. Mix with the potato, rice, onion, curry powder, chutney and salt and pepper to taste. Shape into 8 small rolls. Coat with the egg then the breadcrumbs. Heat the oil to 190°C/375°F or until a cube of day-old bread browns in 30 seconds. Deep-fry until crisp and golden brown. Drain on kitchen paper and serve garnished with the lemon wedges.

Paella Valencia

Serves 6

1 small chicken, cut into 6 pieces
60 ml/4 tbsp olive oil
1 onion, finely chopped
1 red (bell) pepper, diced
1 green (bell) pepper, diced
350 g/12 oz bomba or risotto rice
450 g/1 lb mussels in their shells,
   scrubbed
Chicken stock
5 ml/1 tsp saffron powder
225 g/8 oz/2 cups tomatoes, skinned,
   seeded and chopped
225 g/8 oz/2 cups frozen peas
Salt and freshly ground black
   pepper
1 bay leaf
1 sprig of marjoram
100 g/4 oz/1 cup chorizo sausage,
   sliced
100 g/4 oz/1 cup peeled prawns
   (shrimp)
400 g/14 oz/1 large can artichoke
   hearts, drained and halved
Lemon wedges
6 unpeeled prawns (shrimp)

Brown the chicken pieces in the oil in a
paella pan or large frying pan (skillet).
Remove from the pan. Fry (sauté) the
onion in the oil until soft and lightly gold-
en. Stir in the peppers and rice and cook,
stirring, for 2 minutes. Return the chicken
to the pan. Add the mussels and enough
chicken stock to cover the ingredients. Stir
in the saffron, tomatoes, peas, a little salt
and pepper and add the bay leaf and marjoram. Bring to the boil, reduce the heat,
cover and simmer gently for 20 minutes or
until the rice is cooked and has absorbed
nearly all the liquid. Add a little more
stock during cooking if necessary. Remove

the mussels, snap off the top shells and
keep the mussels warm in the bottom
shells. Discard the bay leaf and marjoram.
Stir the chorizo, prawns and artichokes
into the rice mixture and heat through.
Return the mussels in their shells to the
paella and garnish with lemon wedges and
the whole prawns before serving.

Quick Party Paella

Serves 4

1 packet savoury vegetable rice
450 ml/³/₄ pt/2 cups boiling water
100 g/4 oz/1 cup cooked chicken,
   diced
250 g/9 oz/1 small can mussels in
   brine, drained
100 g/4 oz/1 cup peeled prawns
   (shrimp)
Chopped parsley

Put the rice in a saucepan with the boiling
water. Stir, cover and simmer for 12 minutes. Add the remaining ingredients except
the parsley, cover and simmer gently for a
further 8 minutes until the liquid has been
absorbed and the rice is tender. Fluff up
with a fork and sprinkle with the parsley
before serving.

Parayemista (Stuffed Squid)

Serves 4

450 g/1 lb baby squid, cleaned
1 onion, finely chopped
120 ml/4 fl oz/¹/₂ cup olive oil
50 g/2 oz/¹/₄ cup long-grain rice
120 ml/4 fl oz/¹/₂ cup tomato juice
Salt and freshly ground pepper
120 ml/4 fl oz/¹/₂ cup dry white wine
5 whole cloves
1 piece cinnamon stick

Chop the tentacles. Fry (sauté) with the onion in a little of the oil for about 3 minutes until the onion is soft but not brown. Stir in the rice and tomato juice. Bring to the boil, reduce the heat and simmer until the rice has absorbed the liquid. Season to taste. Spoon into the squid. Heat the remaining oil in a large flameproof casserole (Dutch oven). Fry the squid gently until turning golden, turning once, carefully. Add the wine, spices and enough water to cover the squid completely. Bring to the boil, reduce the heat, cover with a plate that sits on top of the squid and simmer gently until the squid is tender. Transfer with a draining spoon to a serving dish and boil the liquid rapidly until well reduced and syrupy. Discard the spices and spoon over.

Seafood Risotto

Serves 4

45 ml/3 tbsp olive oil
1 large garlic clove
1 small onion, finely chopped
450 g/1 lb squid, cleaned, sliced and tentacles chopped
1 small octopus, cleaned, sliced and tentacles chopped
225 g/8 oz/2 cups raw, peeled prawns (shrimp)
50 g/2 oz/¹/₂ cup chopped parsley
Salt and freshly ground black pepper
250 ml/8 fl oz/1 cup dry white wine
1.2 litres/2 pts/5 cups boiling water
450 g/1 lb/2 cups arborio or other risotto rice
Lemon wedges

Heat the oil in a large flameproof casserole (Dutch oven). Add the garlic clove and the onion and fry (sauté) gently for 2 minutes. Add the seafood, the parsley, a little salt and pepper, the wine and 250 ml/8 fl oz/1 cup of the water. Bring to the boil, reduce the heat and simmer gently for about 6 minutes or until the liquid has evaporated. Remove the garlic clove. Stir in the rice and cook for 1 minute. Add a quarter of the remaining water and simmer, stirring until it has been absorbed. Repeat the process until the rice is just tender (about 15–20 minutes). Remove from the heat, taste and re-season if necessary. Serve garnished with lemon wedges.

Black Risotto with Squid

Serves 4
750 g/1¹/₂ lb squid
30 ml/2 tbsp olive oil
1 garlic clove
1 small onion, finely chopped
Salt and freshly ground black pepper
375 ml/13 fl oz/1¹/₂ cups dry white wine
450 g/1 lb/2 cups arborio or other risotto rice
900 ml/1¹/₂ pts/3³/₄ cups boiling water
15 g/¹/₂ oz/1 tbsp unsalted (sweet) butter
100 g/4 oz/1 cup freshly grated Parmesan cheese

Ask the fishmonger to clean the squid for you, reserving the ink sacs. Empty the ink sacs into a bowl. Wash the squid well, pat dry and slice the bodies into rings and cut the tentacles into short lengths. Heat the oil in a large flameproof casserole (Dutch oven). Add the garlic clove and the onion and fry (sauté) for 3 minutes until golden. Remove the garlic and discard. Add the squid to the pan and fry for 2 minutes, stirring. Season with salt and pepper, add the wine and simmer very gently for about 20 minutes until the squid is tender. Add the rice and stir for 1 minute. Stir in a quarter of the water and simmer, stirring occasionally until it has been absorbed. Add the ink and some more water and simmer, stirring until absorbed. Repeat this process until the rice is just tender (about 15-20 minutes). Remove from the heat and stir in the butter and cheese. Serve straight away.

Scallop Stir-fry

Serves 4
225 g/8 oz/1 cup long-grain rice
8 spring onions (scallions), cut into diagonal pieces
225 g/8 oz/2 cups bean sprouts
2 carrots, cut into matchsticks
1 celery stick, cut into matchsticks
60 ml/4 tbsp sunflower oil
16 queen scallops
15 ml/1 tbsp dry sherry
1.5 ml/¹/₄ tsp grated fresh root ginger
10 ml/2 tsp light soy sauce
Juice of 1 lime
Salt and freshly ground black pepper

Cook the rice in plenty of boiling salted water until just tender. Drain, rinse with boiling water, drain again and cover with a clean cloth. Keep hot. Meanwhile, stir-fry the spring onions, bean sprouts, carrot and celery in 45 ml/3 tbsp of the sunflower oil in a wok or large frying pan (skillet) for 3 minutes. Push to one side. Add the remaining oil, heat, then add the scallops and stir-fry for 2 minutes. Add the sherry, ginger, soy sauce, lime juice and a little salt and pepper and cook, stirring, for 1 minute. Spoon the rice into small bowls. Top with the scallops and vegetables and serve straight away.

At Home Seafood Thermidor

Serves 6
2 celery sticks, chopped
1 bunch of spring onions (scallions), chopped
1 small green (bell) pepper, chopped
100 g/4 oz/¹/₂ cup butter
30 ml/2 tbsp plain (all-purpose) flour
250 ml/8 fl oz/1 cup single (light) cream
60 ml/4 tbsp white wine
1 bay leaf
1 small can pimientos, drained and chopped
50 g/2 oz strong Cheddar cheese, grated
A good pinch of cayenne
5 ml/1 tsp Worcestershire sauce
170 g/6 oz/1 can crabmeat
170 g/6 oz/1 can prawns (shrimp), drained
250 g/9 oz/1 can mussels, drained
185 g/6¹/₂ oz/1 can tuna, drained
Salt and freshly ground black pepper
50 g/2 oz/1 cup breadcrumbs
350 g/12 oz/1¹/₂ cups long-grain rice
5 ml/1 tsp turmeric
Chopped parsley

Fry (sauté) the celery, spring onions and green pepper in half the butter for 3 minutes, stirring until softened but not browned. Blend in the flour and cook for 1 minute. Stir in the cream, wine and bay leaf. Bring to the boil and simmer for 2 minutes until thickened, stirring all the time. Stir in the pimientos, cheese, cayenne, Worcestershire sauce and the seafood. Season to taste. Remove the bay leaf and turn the mixture into an ovenproof dish. Sprinkle with the breadcrumbs and dot with the remaining butter. Bake at 160°C/325°F/gas mark 3 for 40 minutes or until the top is golden brown. Meanwhile, cook the rice in plenty of boiling water to which the turmeric has been added for 10 minutes or until just tender. Drain and fluff up with a fork. Sprinkle with the parsley and serve with the seafood.

Chinese Fried Rice

Serves 4-6
30 ml/2 tbsp oil
¹/₂ bunch of spring onions (scallions), chopped
100 g/4 oz mushrooms, chopped
1 small red (bell) pepper, chopped
1 small green (bell) pepper, chopped
450 g/1 lb/4 cups cooked long-grain rice
100 g/4 oz/1 cup peeled prawns (shrimp)
100 g/4 oz/1 cup cooked ham, diced
2.5 ml/¹/₂ tsp ground ginger
1.5 ml/¹/₄ tsp cayenne
Salt

Heat the oil in a large frying pan (skillet) or wok. Add the onions, mushrooms and peppers. Fry (sauté) for 2 minutes, stirring. Add the rice and fry, stirring for 3 minutes. Add the remaining ingredients and cook for about 4 minutes, stirring until piping hot.

No-mess Kipper Kedgeree

Serves 3-4

200 g/7 oz/1 packet boil-in-the-bag
  kippers
100 g/4 oz/¹/₂ cup long-grain rice
50 g/2 oz/¹/₂ cup frozen peas
2-3 eggs scrubbed under the cold tap
60 ml/4 tbsp mayonnaise
30 ml/2 tbsp chopped parsley
A good pinch of nutmeg
Salt and freshly ground black
  pepper

Bring a large pan of water to the boil. Add the kippers in their bag, the rice, peas and eggs in their shells. Cook for 10 minutes. Lift out the eggs and continue cooking the fish and rice for a further 5 minutes. Meanwhile, plunge the eggs into cold water, then shell and roughly chop them. Lift the bag of fish out of the pan. Drain the rice and peas and return to the pan. Open the bag of fish and drain off any liquid into the rice. Flake the fish, discarding any skin and bones. Add to the rice with the mayonnaise, parsley, nutmeg and a little salt and pepper. Toss gently, fold in the eggs and serve hot.

No-mess Cod and Parsley Kedgeree

Serves 3-4

Prepare as for No-mess Kipper Kedgeree but substitute boil-in-the-bag cod in parsley sauce for the kippers.

Smoky Supper

Serves 4

225 g/8 oz/1 cup long-grain rice
1 onion, finely chopped
30 ml/2 tbsp olive oil
1 garlic clove, crushed
200 g/7 oz/1 small carton low-fat
  soft cheese
Milk
105 g/4¹/₄ oz/1 small can smoked
  mussels
Lemon juice
Salt and freshly ground black
  pepper
Chopped parsley

Cook the rice in plenty of boiling salted water until tender. Drain, rinse with boiling water and drain again. Meanwhile, fry (sauté) the onion in the oil for 1 minute. Add the garlic and fry for a further minute. Stir in the cheese until melted and thin to a smooth sauce with milk. Add the mussels and lemon juice and seasoning to taste. Pile the rice on to serving plates. Spoon the sauce into the centre and sprinkle with the parsley.

Cream Cheese Kedgeree

Serves 4

450 g/1 lb golden cutlets, or other yellow smoked fish
Milk
100 g/4 oz/¹/₂ cup long-grain rice
225 g/8 oz green beans, cut into short lengths
175 g/6 oz/³/₄ cup cream cheese
Grated rind and juice of 1 lemon
1.5 ml/¹/₄ tsp cayenne
Freshly ground black pepper
2 tomatoes, chopped
1 green (bell) pepper, chopped
5 cm/2 in piece cucumber, chopped

Poach the fish in just enough milk to cover for about 8-10 minutes until tender. Drain, reserving the milk. Remove the skin and flake the fish. Meanwhile, cook the rice in plenty of boiling salted water for 10-12 minutes until just tender. Add the beans half-way through cooking. Drain. Stir in the fish. Blend the cream cheese with 90 ml/6 tbsp of the fish milk. Add to the rice and stir in gently. Season with the lemon rind, cayenne and black pepper to taste. Pile on to a warm serving dish. Drizzle with the lemon juice. Mix together the tomato, pepper and cucumber and pile on top.

Prawn Fried Rice

Serves 4

225 g/8 oz/1 cup long-grain rice
100 g/4 oz/1 cup frozen peas
1 small onion, finely chopped
30 ml/2 tbsp olive oil
Salt and freshly ground black pepper
225 g/8 oz/2 cups peeled prawns (shrimp)
Soy sauce

Cook the rice in plenty of boiling salted water until tender. Add the peas after 5 minutes cooking time. Drain really well. Fry (sauté) the onion in the oil in a large frying pan (skillet) or in a wok. Add the rice and stir until the rice glistens with the oil and is turning golden. Add a little salt and pepper and the prawns. Heat through, stirring. Serve piping hot sprinkled with soy sauce.

Tuna Fried Rice

Serves 4

Prepare as for Prawn Fried Rice but fry (sauté) a chopped green (bell) pepper with the onion and substitute 185 g/6 ¹/₂ oz/ 1 small can drained tuna for the prawns (shrimp).

Sardine Fried Rice

Serves 4

Prepare as for Prawn Fried Rice but substitute ¹/₂ bunch of spring onions (scallions) for the onion and 120g/4¹/₂ oz/1 small can sardines in oil, drained and roughly cut up, for the prawns. Sprinkle with Worcestershire sauce instead of soy before serving.

Anchovy and Olive Fried Rice

Serves 4

Prepare as for Prawn Fried Rice but add a chopped red (bell) pepper with the onion. Chop a 50 g/2 oz/1 small can anchovies and add in place of the prawns (shrimp) with 2 hard-boiled (hard-cooked) eggs, chopped and 50 g/2 oz/⅓ cup sliced, stuffed olives.

Tuna-stuffed Pittas

Serves 4

100 g/4 oz/½ cup long-grain rice
½ bunch of spring onions
(scallions), chopped
185 g/6½ oz/1 small can tuna,
drained
90 ml/6 tbsp mayonnaise
10 ml/2 tsp lemon juice
5 ml/1 tsp dried mint
Salt and freshly ground black
pepper
4 sesame pitta breads

Cook the rice in plenty of boiling salted water until tender. Drain and mix with the spring onions, tuna, mayonnaise, lemon juice and mint. Season to taste. Cut the pittas in half and split open gently to form pockets. Fill with the tuna mixture. Wrap each in foil and place on a baking sheet. Bake in the oven at 200°C/400°F/gas mark 6 for 10-15 minutes until piping hot. Serve straight away.

Prawn and Avocado-stuffed Pittas

Serves 4

Prepare as for Tuna-stuffed Pittas but substitute 1 ripe avocado, finely diced and tossed in lemon juice, for the spring onions (scallions), prawns (shrimp) for the tuna and snipped chives for the mint. Use wholemeal pittas instead of sesame ones.

Cheesey Tuna Rice

Serves 4

225 g/8 oz/1 cup long-grain rice
185 g/6½ oz/1 small can tuna,
drained
200 g/7 oz/1 small can sweetcorn
(corn), drained
100 g/4 oz/½ cup cottage cheese
30 ml/2 tbsp chopped parsley
Salt and freshly ground black
pepper
75 g/3 oz Cheddar cheese, grated
2 tomatoes, sliced

Cook the rice in plenty of boiling salted water until tender. Drain, rinse with boiling water and drain again. Return to the saucepan and add the tuna, sweetcorn, cottage cheese and parsley. Stir well over a gentle heat and season with salt and pepper. Spoon into a flameproof dish. Cover with the Cheddar cheese and arrange the tomatoes around. Place under a hot grill (broiler) until the cheese melts and bubbles. Serve straight away.

Salmon and Asparagus Rice

Serves 4

Prepare as for Cheesy Tuna Rice but substitute a can of pink salmon, skinned and boned, for the tuna. Add a 300 g/11 oz/1 small can asparagus spears, drained and cut into short lengths, in place of the corn.

Sardine and Tomato Rice

Serves 4

Prepare as for Cheesy Tuna Rice but substitute mashed sardines for the tuna and 200 g/7 oz/1 small can chopped tomatoes with herbs for the corn.

Prawn and Fennel Pilau

Serves 4

225 g/8 oz/1 cup long-grain rice
298 g/10¹/₂ oz/1 can condensed beef consommé
400 g/14 oz/1 large can chopped tomatoes
1 bay leaf
1 head of Florence fennel, chopped, reserving the green fronds
30 ml/2 tbsp tomato purée (paste)
Salt and freshly ground black pepper
5 ml/1 tsp caster (superfine) sugar
2.5 ml/¹/₂ tsp paprika
175 g/6 oz/1¹/₂ cups peeled prawns (shrimp)
50 g/2 oz Cheddar cheese, grated

Place the rice in a saucepan. Make the consomme up to 450 ml/³/₄ pt/2 cups with water. Add to the pan, bring to the boil, reduce the heat, cover and simmer gently for 8 minutes. Add the remaining ingredients except the prawns and cheese. Simmer gently for 10 minutes or until the rice and fennel are tender and the liquid is nearly absorbed. Stir in the prawns, heat through and turn into a flameproof dish. Sprinkle with the cheese and brown under a hot grill (broiler).

Saucy Prawn and Tuna Pot

Serves 4

50 g/2 oz/¼ cup butter
1 large onion, chopped
225 g/8 oz/1 cup long-grain rice
600 ml/1 pt/2½ cups vegetable or
 fish stock
100 g/4 oz/1 cup frozen peas
185 g/6½ oz/1 small can tuna,
 drained
100 g/4 oz/1 cup peeled prawns
 (shrimp)
200 g/7 oz/1 small can Mexican
 sweetcorn (corn with bell peppers)
15 ml/1 tbsp lemon juice
Salt and freshly ground black
 pepper
25 g/1 oz/¼ cup plain (all-purpose)
 flour
300 ml/½ pt/1¼ cups milk
30 ml/2 tbsp chopped parsley

Melt half the butter in a flameproof casserole (Dutch oven). Add the onion and fry (sauté) for 3 minutes, stirring. Stir in the rice and cook for 2 minutes, stirring. Add the stock and peas, bring to the boil, cover and simmer for 15 minutes. Add the tuna, prawns, sweetcorn (including any juice), lemon juice and a little salt and pepper. Stir gently then re-cover and cook for a further 5-10 minutes until the rice is tender and has absorbed all the liquid. Meanwhile, melt the remaining butter and whisk in the flour and milk. Bring to the boil and cook for 2 minutes, whisking all the time. Stir in the parsley and seasoning to taste. Spoon the rice on to serving plates and pour a little of the sauce over.

Acapulco Prawns

Serves 4

225 g/8 oz/1 cup wild rice mix
15 ml/1 tbsp chilli oil (optional)
750 g/1½ lb/6 cups whole raw
 prawns
100 g/4 oz/½ cup butter
60 ml/4 tbsp groundnut (peanut) oil
6 garlic cloves, finely chopped
1 green chilli, seeded and chopped
Grated rind and juice of 1 lime
Salt and freshly ground black
 pepper
Chopped parsley

Cook the rice mix according to the packet directions. Drain, return to the pan and add the chilli oil, if using. Toss gently. Meanwhile, peel the prawns, leaving the tails attached. Rinse and remove the black thread down the backs. Place in a single layer in a shallow ovenproof dish. Heat the butter and oil in a frying pan (skillet). Add the garlic, chilli, lime rind and juice and fry (sauté) for 1 minute. Pour over the prawns. Bake in the oven at 200°C/400°F/gas mark 6 for 8-10 minutes until the prawns are just cooked and sizzling. Season to taste. Pile the rice on to serving plates. Top with the prawns in their spicy butter and sprinkle with the parsley.

Mexican Monkfish

Serves 4

Prepare as for Acapulco Prawns but substitute monkfish cut into chunks for the prawns and bake for 15 minutes or until the fish is just tender but not dry.

Crab Pilaf

Serves 4

25 g/1 oz/2 tbsp butter
1 onion, chopped
225 g/8 oz/1 cup long-grain rice
600 ml/1 pt/2¹/₂ cups fish stock
100 g/4 oz French (green) beans, cut
    into short lengths
2 × 170 g/2 × 6 oz/2 small cans
    crabmeat
200 g/7 oz/1 small can pimientos,
    drained and chopped
Salt and freshly ground black
    pepper
2.5 ml/¹/₂ tsp grated nutmeg
Lemon wedges
Chopped parsley

Melt the butter in a flameproof casserole
(Dutch oven). Add the onion and fry
(sauté) for 3 minutes until softened and
slightly browned. Add the rice and cook,
stirring, for 1 minute. Add the stock and
beans, bring to the boil, cover, reduce the
heat and simmer for 15 minutes. Stir in the
crab with its juice, the pimientos, a little
salt and pepper and the nutmeg. Re-cover
and cook gently for a further 5 minutes or
until the rice is tender and has absorbed all
the liquid. Fluff up with a fork and garnish
with lemon wedges and parsley.

Mussel Pilaf

Serves 4

Prepare as for Crab Pilaf but substitute
drained canned mussels for the crab.

Salmon Steaks and Saffron Rice

Serves 4

225 g/8 oz/1 cup long-grain rice
600 ml/1 pt/2¹/₂ cups chicken or fish
    stock
1 large bay leaf
2 whole cloves
5 ml/1 tsp saffron powder
Salt and freshly ground black
    pepper
4 salmon steaks
30 ml/2 tbsp butter, melted
15 ml/1 tbsp chopped parsley
10 ml/2 tsp chopped tarragon

Put the rice, stock, bay leaf, cloves and saffron in a saucepan with a little salt and
pepper. Bring to the boil, stir well, cover,
reduce the heat and simmer for 15 minutes.
Leave undisturbed for 10 minutes, then
remove the lid and fluff up with a fork, discarding the bay leaf and cloves.
Meanwhile, place the salmon steaks on foil
on a grill (broiler) rack. Brush with some
of the melted butter and add a little of the
herbs. Add a good grinding of pepper but
no salt. Grill (broil) for 2-3 minutes.
Carefully turn over, brush with the remaining butter, add a little more of the herbs
(reserving some for garnish) and a little
more pepper. Grill until the fish is tender
and just cooked through. Spoon the rice on
to serving plates and top each with a steak.
Spoon any cooking juices and any remaining melted butter over and sprinkle with
the remaining herbs.

Mexican Cod Balls with Tomato Sauce

Serves 4

60 ml/4 tbsp olive oil
2 small onions
2 × 400 g/2 × 14 oz/2 large cans chopped tomatoes
1 bouquet garni sachet
A pinch of salt and freshly ground black pepper
A pinch of sugar
30 ml/2 tbsp white wine vinegar
1 slice white bread, crusts removed
750 g/1½ lb cod fillet, skinned
30 ml/2 tbsp tomato purée (paste)
2.5 ml/½ tsp chilli powder
1 garlic clove
15 ml/1 tbsp parsley
2 eggs, beaten
1 green (bell) pepper, cut into thin strips
225 g/8 oz/1 cup long-grain rice
100 g/4 oz/⅔ cup stoned (pitted) black olives, chopped

Heat the oil in a saucepan. Finely chop one of the onions and add to the pan. Fry (sauté) for 2 minutes. Add the tomatoes, bouquet garni sachet and seasoning and bring to the boil. Simmer uncovered for 10 minutes until pulpy. Meanwhile, pour the vinegar over the bread. Place the fish, the remaining onion, quartered, the tomato purée, chilli powder, garlic and parsley in a blender or food processor. Add the soaked bread and run the machine until the mixture is finely minced. Mix with enough of the egg to bind. Shape into golfball-sized balls. Add the green pepper to the sauce, then drop in the fish balls. Simmer gently for 20 minutes. Meanwhile, cook the rice in plenty of boiling salted water. Stir in the chopped olives. Pile the rice on to warm serving dishes and top with the fish balls and sauce.

Mixed Fish Pot

Serves 4-6

1 onion, finely chopped
2 leeks, chopped
1 head of celeriac (celery root), chopped
25 g/1 oz/2 tbsp butter
400 g/14 oz/1 large can chopped tomatoes
1 bouquet garni sachet
Grated rind and juice of ½ lemon
600 ml/1 pt/2½ cups fish or chicken stock
100 g/4 oz/½ cup long-grain rice
225 g/8 oz cod fillet, skinned and cubed
225 g/8 oz mackerel fillet, skinned and cubed
225 g/8 oz trout fillet, skinned and cubed
Salt and freshly ground black pepper
Chopped parsley

Cook the onion, leek and celeriac in the butter for 2 minutes, stirring. Add the tomatoes, bouquet garni sachet, lemon rind and juice and stock and simmer for 10 minutes. Add the rice and cook for a further 5 minutes. Stir in the mixed fish and season well. Cover and simmer for 10 minutes until the fish, rice and vegetables are tender. Discard the bouquet garni sachet. Ladle into bowls and sprinkle with the parsley before serving.

Eastern Fish and Coconut Pilaf

Serves 6

750 g/1½ lb white fish fillet, cut into
  chunks
30 ml/2 tbsp plain (all-purpose) flour
5 ml/1 tsp ground coriander
  (cilantro)
5 ml/1 tsp ground cumin
15 ml/1 tbsp garam masala
1.5 ml/¼ tsp chilli powder
5 ml/1 tsp turmeric
1.5 ml/¼ tsp ground ginger
Salt and freshly ground black pepper
60 ml/4 tbsp oil
2 onions, finely chopped
450 g/1 lb/2 cups basmati rice
Boiling water
45 ml/3 tbsp desiccated (shredded)
  coconut
15 ml/1 tbsp lemon juice
A few coriander (cilantro) leaves
Lemon wedges

Place the fish in a bowl. Mix the flour with
the spices and a little salt and pepper and
use to coat the fish. Heat half the oil in a
flameproof casserole (Dutch oven). Add
the fish and fry (sauté) for 2 minutes until
lightly golden. Remove from the pan with
a draining spoon. Heat the remaining oil.
Add the onion and fry for 3 minutes, stirring. Add the rice and fry for 1 minute,
stirring. Return the fish to the pan. Just
cover with boiling water, add the coconut
and lemon juice. Cover with a lid, reduce
the heat and simmer gently for 20 minutes
until the rice is tender and has absorbed the
liquid, adding a little more water as necessary during cooking. Serve straight from
the pan, garnished with coriander leaves
and lemon wedges.

Seafood Curry with Saffron Rice

Serves 4

350 g/12 oz white fish fillet, cut into
  chunks
300 ml/½ pt/1¼ cups water
Salt and freshly ground black
  pepper
1 bay leaf
25 g/1 oz/2 tbsp butter
1 onion, thinly sliced
1 green (bell) pepper, thinly sliced
25 g/1 oz/¼ cup plain (all-purpose)
  flour
30 ml/2 tbsp curry paste
450 ml/¾ pt/2 cups apple juice
45 ml/3 tbsp sultanas (golden
  raisins)
1 eating (dessert) apple, chopped
100 g/4 oz/1 cup peeled prawns
  (shrimp)
1 quantity Saffron Rice with
  Peppers (page 225)
30 ml/2 tbsp desiccated coconut

Poach the fish in the water with a little salt
and pepper and the bay leaf for 5-8 minutes until it flakes easily with a fork. Drain.
Meanwhile, melt the butter in a pan. Add
the onion and pepper and fry (sauté) for 4
minutes until soft and lightly golden. Add
the flour and curry paste and cook for 1
minute. Remove from the heat and gradually blend in the apple juice. Return to the
heat, bring to the boil and simmer for 2
minutes. Add the fish, sultanas, apple, and
prawns and simmer for 5 minutes. Season
to taste. Meanwhile, prepare the saffron
rice. Spoon the fish curry over and sprinkle
with the coconut before serving.

Haddock Cakes with Bacon

Serves 6

450 g/1 lb smoked haddock fillet,
skinned and finely chopped
350 g/12 oz/1¹/₂ cups mashed potato
100 g/4 oz/1 cup cooked long-grain
rice
5 ml/1 tsp anchovy essence (extract)
Grated rind and juice of ¹/₂ lemon
Freshly ground black pepper
A pinch of grated nutmeg
1 egg, beaten
A little plain (all-purpose) flour
6 rashers (slices) streaky bacon,
rinded
10 ml/2 tsp sunflower oil
Passata (sieved tomatoes)

Mix the fish with the potato, rice, anchovy essence, lemon rind and juice, a good grinding of pepper and the nutmeg. Mix with the egg to bind. With well-floured hands, shape the mixture into 6 finger shapes. Wrap each in a rasher of bacon. Lay in a lightly oiled roasting tin (pan) and brush with a little more oil. Bake in the oven at 190°C/375°F/gas mark 5 for 30 minutes, turning once half-way through cooking, until golden brown and cooked through. Serve hot with hot passata.

Cod Cakes with Pancetta

Serves 4

Prepare as for Haddock Cakes with Bacon but substitue white cod for the smoked haddock, and wrap in slices of pancetta instead of streaky bacon.

Oriental Salmon Patties

Serves 4

225 g/8 oz/1 small can pineapple
rings
200 g/7 oz/1 small can pink salmon,
drained
100 g/4 oz/1 cup cooked long-grain
rice
2.5 cm/1 in piece cucumber, grated
¹/₂ small red (bell) pepper, finely
chopped
10 ml/2 tsp mayonnaise
Salt and freshly ground black
pepper
A pinch of cayenne
1 egg, beaten
50 g/2 oz/1¹/₂ cup dried breadcrumbs
Fish stock
30 ml/2 tbsp tomato purée (paste)
15 ml/1 tbsp light brown sugar
10 ml/2 tsp malt vinegar
15 ml/1 tbsp cornflour (cornstarch)
15 ml/1 tbsp water
Oil for shallow-frying

Drain the pineapple, reserving the juice, and chop finely. Flake the fish, discarding the skin and any bones. Mix with the rice, pineapple, cucumber, red pepper and mayonnaise. Season with salt and pepper to taste and the cayenne. Add the egg to bind and shape into round cakes. Coat in the breadcrumbs. Make the pineapple juice up to 300 ml/¹/₂ pt/1¹/₄ cups with fish stock. Place in a pan with the tomato purée, sugar and vinegar. Blend the cornflour with the water and stir in. Bring to the boil and simmer for 1 minute, stirring. Shallow-fry the patties in the hot oil for 4-5 minutes, turning once, until golden brown on both sides and cooked through. Drain on kitchen paper and serve hot with the sauce.

Chinese Tuna Cakes

Serves 4

Prepare as for Oriental Salmon Patties but substitute drained tuna fish for the salmon and use yellow (bell) pepper instead of the red.

Crispy Crab Fritters

Serves 4

100 g/4 oz/1 cup plain (all-purpose) flour
10 ml/2 tsp curry powder
Salt and freshly ground black pepper
2 eggs
200 ml/7 fl oz/scant 1 cup milk
225 g/8 oz crab sticks, chopped
30 ml/2 tbsp chopped parsley
50 g/2 oz/¹/₂ cup cooked long-grain rice
Oil for shallow-frying
Watercress
Lime wedges

Sift the flour and curry powder into a bowl. Add a little salt and pepper. Make a well in the centre. Add the eggs and milk and beat well until smooth. Stir in the crab sticks, parsley and rice. Heat about 1 cm/¹/₂ in of oil in a large frying pan (skillet). Fry (sauté) spoonfuls of the mixture until golden underneath. Carefully turn over and brown the other side. Drain on kitchen paper and keep hot while cooking the remainder. Serve the fritters hot, garnished with the watercress and lime wedges.

Crab Tettrazzini

Serves 4

100 g/4 oz any short ribbon noodles
20 g/³/₄ oz/3 tbsp plain (all-purpose) flour
20 g/³/₄ oz/1¹/₂ tbsp butter
150 ml/¹/₄ pt/²/₃ cup chicken stock
150 ml/¹/₄ pt/²/₃ cup single (light) cream
Salt and freshly ground black pepper
A pinch of nutmeg
175 g/6 oz/1 small can crabmeat
295 g/10¹/₂ oz/1 can asparagus spears, drained
120 ml/4 fl oz/¹/₂ cup soured (dairy sour) cream
50 g/2 oz/¹/₂ cup grated Parmesan cheese

Cook the pasta according to the packet directions. Drain. Meanwhile, blend the flour with the butter and stock in a saucepan. Stir in the cream. Bring to the boil and cook for 2 minutes, stirring. Season to taste with salt, pepper and nutmeg. Stir in the crabmeat. Butter a shallow ovenproof dish. Lay the asparagus spears in the base of the dish. Mix the cooked noodles with the soured cream and a little salt and pepper. Spoon over the asparagus. Sprinkle with some of the Parmesan cheese. Spoon the crab in sauce over and sprinkle with more Parmesan. Bake at 180°C/350°F/gas mark 4 for about 30 minutes until golden and bubbling.

Nashville Baked Seasoned Trout

Serves 4

175 g/6 oz/³/₄ cup brown rice
50 g/2 oz/¹/₂ cup pine nuts
100 g/4 oz/2 cups button
  mushrooms, chopped
4 stoned (pitted) black olives,
  chopped
5 ml/1 tsp lime juice
Salt and freshly ground black
  pepper
5 ml/1 tsp paprika
1.5 ml/¹/₄ tsp cayenne
4 trout, cleaned
Olive oil
Lime wedges

Cook the rice for about 40 minutes in plenty of boiling salted water until tender. Drain well. Mix with the pine nuts, mushrooms, olives, lime juice, a little salt and pepper, the paprika and cayenne. Use to stuff the trout then lay in an oiled roasting tin (pan). Brush with oil, cover with foil and bake at 180°C/350°F/gas mark 4 for 20-25 minutes until cooked through. Serve garnished with lime wedges.

Southern States Shrimp

Serves 4

225 g/8 oz/1 cup long-grain rice
50 g/2 oz/¹/₄ cup butter
30 ml/2 tbsp corn oil
2 onions, chopped
1 garlic clove, crushed
2 celery sticks, chopped
15 ml/1 tbsp plain (all-purpose) flour
2 × 14 oz/2 × 400 g/2 large cans
  chopped tomatoes
1 bay leaf
1.5 ml/¹/₄ tsp dried thyme
1 red chilli, seeded and chopped
100 g/4 oz mushrooms, chopped
200 g/7 oz/1 small can pimientos,
  drained and diced
450 g/1 lb/4 cups raw peeled prawns
  (shrimp)
Salt and freshly ground black
  pepper

Cook the rice in plenty of boiling salted water until tender. Drain, rinse with boiling water, drain again and return to the pan. Cook over a gentle heat for 1 minute to dry out then stir in the butter and fluff up with a fork. Meanwhile, heat the oil in a saucepan. Add the onion, garlic and the celery and fry (sauté) for 3 minutes, stirring until golden. Add the flour and cook for 1 minute. Stir in the tomatoes, bay leaf, thyme, chilli, mushrooms and pimientos and simmer for 10 minutes, stirring occasionally. Remove the black veins from the prawns and add to the sauce half-way through cooking. Season to taste. Serve hot with the buttered rice.

New Orleans Seafood Gumbo

Serves 6

25 g/1 oz/ 2 tbsp butter
175 g/6 oz okra, cut into
  1 cm/¹/₂ in pieces
1 bunch of spring onions (scallions),
  chopped
1 garlic clove, crushed
1 small green (bell) pepper, diced
15 ml/1 tbsp plain (all-purpose) flour
120 ml/4 fl oz/¹/₂ cup passata (sieved
  tomatoes)
30 ml/2 tbsp tomato purée (paste)
450 ml/³/₄ pt/2 cups chicken stock
1 bay leaf
15 ml/1 tbsp chopped parsley
Salt and freshly ground black
  pepper
1.5 ml/¹/₄ tsp chilli powder
6-12 oysters
225 g/8 oz/2 cups peeled prawns
  (shrimp)
225 g/8 oz/2 cups crabmeat
350 g/12 oz/1¹/₂ cups long-grain rice

Melt the butter in a large pan. Add the okra, spring onions, garlic and green pepper and fry (sauté) for 3 minutes until softened. Stir in the flour and cook for 1 minute. Blend in the passata, tomato purée and stock. Add the seasonings and simmer very gently for 1¹/₂ hours. Carefully remove the oysters from their shells, reserving the juice. Add to the pan with the prawns and crab. Simmer for a further 20 minutes until thick and a rich colour and discard the bay leaf. Meanwhile, cook the rice in plenty of boiling salted water until tender. Drain, rinse with boiling water and drain again. Fluff up with a fork. Spoon the rice into large bowls and spoon the gumbo on top.

American Shrimp with Almonds

Serves 6

120 ml/4 fl oz/¹/₂ cup sunflower oil
1 large green (bell) pepper, diced
1 large onion, chopped
4 celery sticks, chopped, including
  the leaves
120 ml/4 fl oz/¹/₂ cup ready-prepared
  hot chilli sauce
75 g/3 oz/¹/₂ cup raisins
2.5 ml/¹/₂ tsp dried thyme
Salt and freshly ground black pepper
2.5 ml/¹/₂ tsp curry paste
1 bay leaf
400 g/14 oz/1 large can chopped
  tomatoes
100 g/4 oz/1 cup toasted, blanched
  almonds
750 g/1¹/₂ lb/6 cups peeled prawns
  (shrimp)
350g/12 oz/1¹/₂ cups long-grain rice
50 g/2 oz/¹/₄ cup butter
1 bunch of spring onions (scallions),
  chopped

Heat the oil in a large frying pan (skillet). Add the pepper, onion and celery. Fry (sauté) for 2 minutes until softened but not browned. Add the chilli sauce, raisins, thyme, a little salt and pepper, the curry paste, bay leaf and tomatoes. Simmer very gently for 1 hour. Stir in the almonds and prawns and heat through. Meanwhile, cook the rice in plenty of boiling salted water until tender. Drain, rinse with boiling water and drain again. Melt the butter in the rice saucepan. Add the spring onions and fry for 2 minutes until slightly softened. Add the rice and toss well. Pile on to a serving dish and make a large nest. Spoon the prawn and almond mixture in the centre and serve hot.

Prawn Risotto

Serves 4

20 raw, unpeeled prawns
*750 ml/1¼ pts/3 cups hot fish or
chicken stock*
45 ml/3 tbsp olive oil
1 onion, finely chopped
*450 g/1 lb/2 cups arborio or other
risotto rice*
450 ml/¾ pt/2 cups dry white wine
*25 g/1 oz/2 tbsp unsalted (sweet)
butter*
*Salt and freshly ground black
pepper*
*100 g/4 oz/1 cup freshly grated
Parmesan cheese*

Cook the prawns in the stock for 3 minutes. Remove with a draining spoon, cool slightly, then peel and remove the black thread down their backs. Heat the oil in a flameproof casserole (Dutch oven). Add the onion and fry (sauté) for 2 minutes, stirring. Stir in the rice and cook for 1 minute. Add 2 ladlefuls of the hot stock and simmer until it has been absorbed. Repeat until all the stock is used. Stir in the prawns and wine. Simmer for about 5 minutes until the wine is absorbed. Remove from the heat, stir in the butter, a little salt and pepper and the cheese. Serve straight away.

Rice with King Prawn Sauce

Serves 4-6

*12 whole king prawns (jumbo
shrimp)*
*25 g/1 oz/2 tbsp unsalted (sweet)
butter*
30 ml/2 tbsp olive oil
1 onion, finely chopped
1 celery stick, finely chopped
1 large carrot, finely chopped
120 ml/4 fl oz/½ cup brandy
250 ml/8 fl oz/1 cup dry white wine
*Salt and freshly ground black
pepper*
*1.2 litres/2 pts/5 cups chicken or fish
stock*
*450 g/1 lb/2 cups arborio or other
risotto rice*
Lemon twists

Shell and de-vein the prawns, leaving the tails on. Heat half the butter with the oil in a saucepan. Add the onion, celery and carrot and fry (sauté) for 3 minutes, stirring. Add the brandy, wine and prawns. Season with salt and pepper and simmer very gently for 15 minutes until slightly thickened. Meanwhile, bring the stock to the boil. Add the rice and simmer for 15-20 mintues until the rice is tender and has absorbed the liquid. Stir in the remaining butter then spread the rice on a hot serving dish. Spoon the prawn sauce on top and serve straight away, garnished with lemon twists.

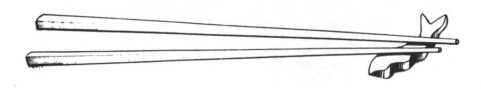

Coriander Mackerel with Rice

Serves 6

6 large mackerel fillets, cut into
  wide strips
1-2 eggs, beaten
100 g/4 oz/2 cups breadcrumbs
15 ml/1 tbsp chopped coriander
  (cilantro)
Corn oil
50 g/2 oz/¹/₄ cup butter
45 ml/3 tbsp pine nuts
450 g/1 lb/2 cups long-grain rice
1 litre/1³/₄ pts/4¹/₄ cups boiling water
Salt and freshly ground black
  pepper
5 ml/1 tsp saffron powder
Coriander leaves
Lemon wedges

Dip the mackerel strips in beaten egg then in the breadcrumbs mixed with the coriander. Chill while preparing the rice. Heat 120 ml/4 fl oz/¹/₂ cup of corn oil in a saucepan with the butter. Add the pine nuts and fry (sauté) until brown. Remove from the pan with a draining spoon and drain on kitchen paper. Add the rice to the oil and butter and fry for 1 minute. Stir in the boiling water, a little salt and pepper and the saffron. Bring to the boil, reduce the heat, cover and simmer for 20 minutes or until the rice is tender and has absorbed the liquid. Fluff up with a fork. Meanwhile, shallow-fry the mackerel strips in corn oil until crisp and golden. Remove from the pan with a draining spoon. Pile the rice on to a serving dish. Top with the fish, then drizzle any oil left in the pan over the top. Garnish with the coriander leaves and lemon wedges.

Plaice Goujons with Turnip, Orange and Basil

Serves 4

225 g/8 oz/1 cup long-grain rice
450 ml/³/₄ pt/2 cups chicken stock
1 orange, rind grated and reserved,
  then segmented
1 onion, finely chopped
15 g/¹/₂ oz/1 tbsp butter
1 turnip, cut into thin matchsticks
30 ml/2 tbsp orange juice
450 g/1 lb ready-crumbed plaice
  goujons
6 basil leaves, torn into small pieces

Wash the rice well. Drain and place in a pan with the stock and orange rind. Bring to the boil, cover, reduce the heat and cook gently for 20 minutes until the stock is absorbed and the rice is tender. Meanwhile, fry (sauté) the onion in the butter for 2 minutes until soft but not brown. Add the turnip and cook for 1 minute. Add the orange juice, cover and simmer gently for 3-4 minutes until the turnip is almost tender but still has 'bite'. Grill (broil) the goujons, turning once. Spoon the orange rice on to serving plates. Arrange the goujons to one side. Garnish with a little pile of turnip, scattered with the basil leaves at one side of the plates and the orange segments.

Scotch Lobster

Serves 2-4

225 g/8 oz/1 cup wild rice mix
75 g/3 oz/¹/₃ cup unsalted (sweet)
butter
1 good-sized cooked lobster
60 ml/4 tbsp Scotch whisky
150 ml/¹/₄ pt/²/₃ cup double (heavy)
cream
Salt and freshly ground black
pepper

Cook the rice according to the packet directions. Drain, rinse with boiling water, drain again and return to the pan. Add 25 g/1 oz/2 tbsp of the butter and toss over a gentle heat. Pile on to warm serving plates. Meanwhile, remove all the meat from the lobster and cut into chunks. Melt the remaining butter in a frying pan (skillet). Add the lobster and cook gently for 2 minutes, stirring. Add the whisky and ignite. Shake the pan until the flames subside. Add the cream, a little salt and a good grinding of pepper. Bubble rapidly for 2 minutes until reduced by half. Spoon over the rice and serve straight away.

Chirashizushi
(Japanese Fish with Rice)

Serves 6

2 dried shiitake mushrooms
250 ml/8 fl oz/1 cup warm water
450 g/1 lb/2 cups short-grain rice
600 ml/1 pt/2¹/₂ cups cold water
45 ml/3 tbsp white wine or rice
vinegar
60 ml/3 tbsp caster (superfine) sugar
2.5 ml/¹/₂ tsp salt
30 ml/2 tbsp soy sauce
50 g/2 oz canned bamboo shoots,
chopped
1 small carrot, finely chopped
90 ml/6 tbsp dashi or ordinary fish
stock
25 g/1 oz/¹/₄ cup frozen peas
5 ml/1 tsp groundnut (peanut) oil
1 size 1 egg, beaten
75 g/3 oz/³/₄ cup peeled prawns
(shrimp)
¹/₂ sheet nori (dried seaweed) or 50 g/
2 oz spring greens (spring cabbage),
shredded and deep-fried until crisp

Soak the mushrooms in the warm water for 30 minutes. Meanwhile, rinse the rice in several changes of cold water. Drain and place in a saucepan with the measured cold water. Bring to the boil, cover, reduce the heat and cook gently for 15-20 minutes. Turn off the heat and leave undisturbed for 10 minutes. Mix the vinegar, half the sugar and the salt together. When the rice is cooked add this mixture and fluff up with a fork. Cut off the stems from the mushrooms and discard, slice the caps and place with half the soaking water in a saucepan. Bring to the boil, add the remaining sugar and simmer for 3 minutes. Stir in half the soy sauce. Simmer until nearly all the liquid has evaporated and the mushrooms are tender. Add to the rice. In a separate pan, simmer the bamboo shoots and carrots in the remaining mushroom soaking water with the fish stock and remaining soy sauce for 15 minutes. Add the peas for the last 5 minutes. Drain off any excess stock. Add the vegetables to the rice. Brush a frying pan (skillet) with the oil. Add the egg, sprinkle with salt and cook gently until set but not brown. Slide out of the pan and cut into fine shreds. Toss the vegetables into the rice. Pile on to a serving plate. Top with the shredded egg and the prawns and finally the shredded *nori* or fried greens. Serve warm.

Cheesey Prawns on Rice

Serves 4
225 g/8 oz/2 cups peeled prawns (shrimp)
298 g/10¹/₂ oz/1 can condensed mushroom soup
15 ml/1 tbsp tomato ketchup (catsup)
50 g/2 oz/1 cup breadcrumbs
100 g/4 oz Cheddar cheese, grated
225 g/8 oz/1 cup long-grain rice
225 g/8 oz broccoli, cut into tiny florets
50 g/2 oz/¹/₂ cup toasted flaked almonds

Mix the prawns with the soup, ketchup, half the breadcrumbs and half the cheese in a shallow ovenproof serving dish. Sprinkle with the remaining breadcrumbs and cheese. Bake at 200°C/400°F/gas mark 6 for 20-25 minutes until golden and bubbling. Meanwhile, cook the rice in plenty of boiling salted water for 10 minutes. Add the broccoli for the last 6 minutes of cooking. Drain and mix in the almonds. Serve the rice mixture topped with the prawns.

Prawns in Garlic Butter with Basil Rice

Serves 4
225 g/8 oz/1 cup long-grain rice
50 g/2 oz/¹/₂ cup button mushrooms, chopped
15 ml/1 tbsp olive oil
15 ml/1 tbsp chopped basil
350 g/12 oz/1¹/₂ cups unsalted (sweet) butter
2 garlic cloves, crushed
150 ml/¹/₄ pt/²/₃ cup dry white wine
30 ml/2 tbsp chopped parsley
Salt and freshly ground black pepper
1 small onion, chopped
24 peeled king prawns (jumbo shrimp)
50 g/2 oz/1 cup breadcrumbs

Cook the rice in plenty of boiling salted water until just tender. Drain, rinse with boiling water, drain again and return to the pan. Meanwhile, fry (sauté) the mushrooms in the oil for about 3 minutes until tender. Add to the cooked rice with the basil and toss thoroughly. Turn into a serving dish. Meanwhile, purée the butter, garlic, wine, parsley, a little salt and pepper and the onion in a blender or food processor. Spread half this mixture in the base of a shallow ovenproof dish. Top with the prawns then the remaining butter mixture. Sprinkle with the breadcrumbs and bake at 200°C/400°F/gas mark 6 for 15 minutes until golden and bubbling. Serve hot with the basil rice.

Tiger Prawns with Cinnamon Rice

Serves 4

225 g/8 oz/1 cup long-grain rice
5 cm/2 in piece cinnamon stick
30 ml/2 tbsp sunflower oil
1 garlic clove, chopped
2 leeks, sliced
3 tomatoes, skinned and chopped
60 ml/4 tbsp tomato purée (paste)
600 ml/1 pt/2¹/₂ cups fish or chicken stock
750 g/1¹/₂ lb/6 cups raw peeled tiger prawns (jumbo shrimp)
Salt and freshly ground black pepper
30 ml/2 tbsp chopped parsley
Ground cinnamon

Cook the rice in plenty of boiling salted water with the cinnamon stick for 10 minutes or until just tender. Drain. Meanwhile heat the oil in a pan, add the garlic and leek and fry (sauté) for 4 minutes, stirring. Add the tomatoes and cook for a further 3 minutes. Add the tomato purée and stock, bring to the boil, reduce the heat and boil rapidly for 30 minutes or until reduced and thickened. Add the prawns and cook gently for a further 5-8 minutes until cooked. Season to taste. Add the parsley to the rice, spoon on to serving plates and form into a nest on each plate. Dust with the cinnamon. Spoon the prawn mixture into the centre of each and serve straight away.

Arabian Sayadieh

Serves 4-6

750 g/1¹/₂ lb white fish fillets, skinned and cubed
Grated rind and juice of 1 lemon
Salt and freshly ground black pepper
30 ml/2 tbsp plain (all-purpose) flour
120 ml/4 fl oz/¹/₂ cup corn oil
1 onion, chopped
225 g/8 oz/1 cup long-grain rice
450 ml/³/₄ pt/2 cups fish stock
2.5 ml/¹/₂ tsp ground cumin
A pinch of saffron powder
50 g/2 oz/¹/₂ cup toasted pine nuts

Put the fish in a glass bowl. Add the lemon rind and juice and season with salt. Leave to stand for 30 minutes. Drain and pat dry on kitchen paper. Season the flour with a little salt and pepper and use to coat the fish. Heat the oil in a frying pan (skillet) and fry (sauté) the fish until lightly golden. Remove from the pan with a draining spoon and drain on kitchen paper. Add the onion to the pan and fry until golden. Put the fish and onion in a flameproof casserole (Dutch oven). Add the rice, stock, cumin and saffron. Bring to the boil and simmer for 10 minutes until the rice has absorbed nearly all the liquid. Then reduce the heat to as low as possible, cover and simmer very gently for about 10 minutes until the rice is tender. Leave undisturbed for 5 minutes then turn out on to a serving dish and sprinkle with the pine nuts.

Tandoori Fish with Tomato Rice

Serves 4

450 g/1 lb white fish fillet, cut into 4
    equal pieces
150 ml/¼ pt/⅔ cup plain yoghurt
15 ml/1 tbsp lemon juice
5 ml/1 tsp ground cumin
5 ml/1 tsp ground coriander
    (cilantro)
2.5 ml/½ tsp chilli powder
2.5 ml/½ tsp turmeric
Salt
175 g/6 oz/¾ cup basmati rice
400 g/14 oz/1 large can chopped
    tomatoes
300 ml/½ pt/1¼ cups water
15 ml/1 tbsp chopped coriander
    (cilantro)
Lemon wedges
A few coriander leaves

Lay the fish in a shallow ovenproof dish in a single layer. Mix the yoghurt, lemon juice, spices and a good pinch of salt together and pour over the fish to coat completely. Leave to marinate for up to 3 hours if possible. Cook in the oven at 180°C/350°F/gas mark 4 for 20 minutes, basting occasionally. Meanwhile, put the rice in a pan with the tomatoes and water. Bring to the boil, cover, reduce the heat and simmer for 20 minutes until the rice is tender and has absorbed the liquid. Stir in the chopped coriander. Pile the rice on to warm serving plates. Top with the fish and any juices and garnish with lemon wedges and coriander leaves.

Prawn Biryani

Serves 6

450 g/1 lb/2 cups basmati rice
45 ml/3 tbsp sunflower oil
2 onions, thinly sliced
600 ml/1 pt/2½ cups canned coconut
    milk
300 ml/½ pt/1¼ cups chicken stock
10 curry leaves
2 green chillies, seeded and chopped
450 g/1 lb/4 cups peeled prawns
    (shrimp)
Salt and freshly ground black
    pepper

Soak the rice in cold water for 30 minutes. Drain well. Heat the oil in a saucepan and fry (sauté) the onion for 3 minutes until softened and golden. Add the coconut milk and the stock. Stir, then add the drained rice, curry leaves and chillies. Bring to the boil, reduce the heat, cover tightly and cook over a gentle heat for 20 minutes. Quickly stir in the prawns and re-cover. Cook for a further 5 minutes or until the rice is tender and has absorbed all the liquid. Fluff up with a fork and season to taste. Serve straight away.

Fish Pot

Serves 4

600 ml/1 pt/ 2¹/₂ cups fish stock
5 ml/1 tsp anchovy essence (extract)
100 g/4 oz/1 cup conchiglie
2 carrots, diced
100 g/4 oz green beans, cut into
short lengths
350 g/12 oz white fish fillet, skinned
and cut into chunks
400 g/14 oz/1 large can chopped
tomatoes with herbs
Salt and freshly ground black pepper

Put the stock in a saucepan with the anchovy essence, pasta and carrot. Bring to the boil and simmer for 10 minutes. Add the remaining ingredients and cook for 5-6 minutes or until the pasta, vegetables and fish are tender. Taste and re-season if necessary. Serve with lots of crusty bread.

Oriental Seafood Hot-pot

Serves 6

3 plaice fillets, skinned and cut into
strips
4 mackerel fillets, skinned and cut
into strips
6 peeled king prawns (jumbo shrimp)
6 scallops, sliced
4 small squid, cut into rings
1.2 litres/2 pts/5 cups chicken stock
5 ml/1 tsp chopped fresh root ginger
4 spring onions (scallions), chopped
50 g/2 oz/¹/₂ cup cellophane noodles,
soaked in warm water for 5
minutes
450 g/1 lb/4 cups shredded spring
greens (spring cabbage)
Hoisin sauce

Place all the seafood and the stock, ginger and spring onions in a large flameproof casserole (Dutch oven). Bring to the boil, reduce the heat, cover and simmer for 5 minutes. Add the remaining ingredients except the hoisin sauce and simmer for 5-10 minutes until the fish and cabbage are tender. Stir in a little hoisin sauce to taste and serve ladled into warm bowls.

Orient Express

Serves 6

100 g/4 oz/1 slab Chinese egg
noodles
2 × 185 g/2 × 6¹/₂ oz/2 small cans
tuna, drained
298 g/10¹/₂ oz/1 can cream of
mushroom soup
60 ml/4 tbsp water
15 ml/1 tbsp soy sauce
2 celery sticks, chopped
100 g/4 oz/1 cup cashew nuts
4 spring onions (scallions), chopped
100 g/4 oz/2 cups button
mushrooms, quartered

Cook the noodles according to the packet directions. Drain. Mix with all the remaining ingredients in an ovenproof dish. Bake at 190°C/375°F/gas mark 5 for about 40 minutes until golden and bubbling.

Pasta with Tuna and Pesto

Serves 4

350 g/12 oz/3 cups rotelli
225 g/8 oz/2 cups frozen peas
185 g/6½ oz/1 small can tuna,
* drained*
1 quantity Pesto Sauce (page 60)
15 ml/1 tbsp olive oil
A few basil leaves

Cook the pasta according to the packet directions, adding the peas for the last 5 minutes cooking time. Drain, rinse with boiling water and drain again. Return to the pan. Stir in the tuna and pesto and toss over a gentle heat. Pile on to serving plates and drizzle with the olive oil. Serve garnished with basil leaves.

Bucatini Tonnata

Serves 4-6

450 g/1 lb bucatini
25 g/1 oz/2 tbsp butter
1 onion, finely chopped
2 garlic cloves, crushed
30 ml/2 tbsp olive oil
250 ml/8 fl oz/1 cup fish or chicken
* stock*
45 ml/3 tbsp dry vermouth
185 g/6½ oz/1 small can tuna,
* drained*
Salt and freshly ground black
* pepper*
30 ml/2 tbsp snipped chives

Cook the bucatini according to the packet directions, drain, return to the saucepan and toss in the butter. Meanwhile, fry (sauté) the onion and garlic in the oil for 3 minutes until soft but not brown. Add the stock and vermouth, bring to the boil and boil rapidly until reduced by half. Stir in the tuna, a little salt and lots of pepper. Add to the pasta and toss gently. Serve sprinkled with the chives.

Quick Herby Tuna Pasta

Serves 4

225 g/8 oz/2 cups rigatoni
185 g/6½ oz/1 small can tuna in oil
30 ml/2 tbsp olive oil
15 ml/1 tbsp lemon juice
15 ml/1 tbsp chopped parsley
15 ml/1 tbsp chopped marjoram
Salt and freshly ground black
* pepper*
Grated Parmesan cheese

Cook the rigatoni according to the packet directions. Drain and return to the saucepan. Add the contents of can of tuna (do not drain first). Add the olive oil, lemon juice, herbs, a little salt and lots of pepper. Toss over a gentle heat until well combined and hot through. Serve straight away with the Parmesan.

Midweek Macaroni Munch

Serves 4

225 g/8 oz/2 cups short-cut
  macaroni
1 onion, finely chopped
50 g/2 oz/¹/₄ cup butter
50 g/2 oz/¹/₄ cup plain (all-purpose)
  flour
600 ml/1 pt/2¹/₂ cups milk
1 bay leaf
5 ml/1 tsp made mustard
Salt and freshly ground black
  pepper
75 g/3 oz Gouda cheese, grated
185 g/6¹/₂ oz/1 small can tuna,
  drained
4 hard boiled (hard-cooked) eggs,
  sliced
12 stuffed olives, sliced

Cook the pasta according to the packet directions, drain. Meanwhile, fry (sauté) the onion in the butter for 3 minutes until soft and lightly golden. Stir in the flour then blend in the milk until smooth. Add the bay leaf, bring to the boil and cook for about 2 minutes, stirring all the time, until thickened. Remove the bay leaf. Stir in the mustard and season to taste. Stir in the macaroni then add a third of the cheese and all the remaining ingredients. Taste and re-season, if necessary. Pile into an ovenproof dish. Top with the remaining cheese and bake in the oven at 200°C/400°F/gas mark 6 for about 25 minutes until bubbling and golden.

Tuna Gnocchi

Serves 4

600 ml/1 pt/2¹/₂ cups milk
7.5 ml/1¹/₂ tsp salt
Freshly ground black pepper
1 bay leaf
1.5 ml/¹/₄ tsp grated nutmeg
150 g/5 oz/scant 1 cup semolina
  (cream of wheat)
2 eggs
100 g/4 oz Cheddar cheese, grated
185 g/6¹/₂ oz/1 small can tuna,
  drained
298 g/10¹/₂ oz/1 can condensed
  cream of mushroom soup
30 ml/2 tbsp melted butter

To make the gnocchi, put the milk, salt, a little pepper, the bay leaf, nutmeg and semolina in a saucepan. Bring to the boil and cook for 10 minutes, stirring, until really thick. Discard the bay leaf. Beat in the eggs with 75 g/3 oz/³/₄ cup of the cheese. Turn on to a well- greased baking sheet and smooth out with a wet knife to a square about 2 cm/³/₄ in thick. Leave to cool then chill until set. Meanwhile, mix the tuna with the soup in a 1.2 litre/2 pt/5 cup ovenproof dish. Cut the gnocchi into 3 cm/1¹/₂ in squares and arrange on top of the tuna. Brush with the melted butter and sprinkle with the remaining cheese. Bake at 200°C/400°F/gas mark 6 for 30 minutes until golden.

Tuscan Tuna with Beans

Serves 6

250 ml/8 fl oz/1 cup olive oil
100 ml/3¹/₂ fl oz/6¹/₂ tbsp lemon juice
2 garlic cloves, crushed
2 × 425 g/2 × 15 oz/2 large cans
  cannellini beans, drained
30 ml/2 tbsp chopped parsley
185 g/6¹/₂ oz/1 small can tuna,
  drained
Salt and freshly ground black
  pepper
225 g/8 oz/2 cups short-cut
  macaroni
A few black olives
Snipped chives

Mix the oil, lemon juice, garlic, beans and parsley together in a saucepan. Cook for 5 minutes, stirring occasionally until hot through. Gently fold in the tuna and a little salt and pepper and heat through, taking care to keep the tuna in chunks. Meanwhile, cook the macaroni according to the packet directions, drain. Add to the sauce, toss gently and serve garnished with the black olives and chives.

Tuna and Sweetcorn Family Favourite

Serves 4

1 quantity Basic Macaroni Cheese
  (page 296)
185 g/6¹/₂ oz/1 small can tuna,
  drained
200 g/7 oz/1 small can sweetcorn
  (corn), drained
15 ml/1 tbsp chopped parsley
Salt and freshly ground black
  pepper
Garlic croûtons

Make up the Basic Macaroni Cheese. Add the remaining ingredients except the croûtons and heat through, stirring until piping hot. Spoon on to serving plates and garnish with the croûtons before serving.

Tuna and Tomato Temptation

Serves 4

1 garlic clove, crushed
150 ml/¹/₄ pt/²/₃ cup chicken stock
200 g/7 oz/1 small can chopped
  tomatoes
15 ml/1 tbsp tomato purée (paste)
30 ml/2 tbsp snipped chives
45 ml/3 tbsp dry vermouth
185 g/6¹/₂ oz/1 small can tuna,
  drained
10 ml/2 tsp cornflour (cornstarch)
15 ml/1 tbsp water
Salt and freshly ground black
  pepper
15 ml/1 tbsp olive oil
350 g/12 oz any ribbon noodles
30 ml/2 tbsp single (light) cream

Place the garlic, stock, tomatoes, tomato purée, chives and vermouth in a saucepan. Bring to the boil, reduce the heat and simmer for 5 minutes or until reduced by half. Add the tuna and heat through, stirring. Blend the cornflour with the water. Add to the sauce, bring to the boil and simmer for 1 minute, stirring. Season to taste and stir in the olive oil. Meanwhile, cook the pasta according to the packet directions. Drain and toss in the cream. Add a good grinding of black pepper and pile on to warm plates. Spoon the tuna sauce on top and serve straight away.

Fishy Pasta Grill

Serves 4

225 g/8 oz/2 cups pasta shapes
215 g/7¹/₂ oz/1 can pilchards in
  tomato sauce, mashed
30 ml/2 tbsp olive oil
30 ml/2 tbsp snipped chives
A squeeze of lemon juice
60 ml/4 tbsp passata (sieved
  tomatoes)
Salt and freshly ground black
  pepper
75 g/3 oz Cheddar cheese, grated
2 tomatoes, sliced

Cook the pasta according to the packet directions, drain and return to the saucepan. Add the remaining ingredients except the cheese and sliced tomatoes. Toss over a gentle heat until well combined and hot through. Season to taste. Add a little more passata to moisten if necessary. Turn into a flameproof dish. Cover with the cheese and garnish with the tomato slices. Grill (broil) until the cheese melts and bubbles. Serve straight away.

Spaghetti alla Vongole

Serves 4-6

1 quantity Spaghetti Al Pomodoro
(page 257)
2 × 295 g/2 × 10¹/₂ oz/2 cans baby
clams, drained
1 lemon, sliced

Prepare the tomato sauce as in Spaghetti
Al Pomodoro. Add the clams and heat
through. Cook the spaghetti according to
the packet directions. Drain. Spoon on to
serving plates, top with the clam sauce and
add twists of lemon to garnish.

Spaghettini alla Vongole Blanco

Serves 4-6

40 g/1¹/₂ oz/3 tbsp butter
15 ml/1 tbsp olive oil
3 garlic cloves, crushed
100 ml/3¹/₂ fl oz/6¹/₂ tbsp dry white
wine
2 × 295 g/2 × 10¹/₂ oz/2 cans baby clams
Freshly ground black pepper
350 g/12 oz spaghettini
Chopped parsley

Melt the butter with the oil in a saucepan.
Add the garlic and cook gently for 2 minutes until lightly golden but not too brown.
Add the wine, bring to the boil and simmer
for 2 minutes until slightly reduced. Drain
the clams, reserving the juice. Add the
clams and 45 ml/3 tbsp of their juice to the
saucepan. Heat through gently until piping
hot, add a good grinding of pepper.
Meanwhile, cook the spaghettini according
to the packet directions. Drain, and pile on
to warm plates. Spoon the sauce over and
sprinkle with the parsley before serving.

Fusilli with Clams and Bacon

Serves 4

1 bunch of spring onions (scallions),
chopped
1 carrot, finely diced
150 ml/¹/₄ pt/²/₃ cup olive oil
2 garlic cloves, crushed
4 streaky bacon rashers (slices),
finely diced
2 × 295 g/2 × 10¹/₂ oz/2 cans baby
clams, drained
A pinch of cayenne
10 ml/2 tsp chopped thyme
Freshly ground black pepper
350 g/12 oz fusilli
Chopped parsley

Fry (sauté) the onions and carrot in 60 ml/4
tbsp of the oil for 3 minutes until softened
but not browned. Add the garlic and bacon
and continue cooking for a further 3 minutes, stirring. Add the remaining oil with
the clams, cayenne, thyme and a good
grinding of pepper. Heat through gently,
stirring, until piping hot. Meanwhile, cook
the fusilli according to the packet directions. Drain. Add the sauce and toss well.
Garnish with parsley and serve.

187

Conchiglie con Cozze

Serves 4

1 kg/2¹/₄ lb mussels in their shells
2 garlic cloves, chopped
15 ml/1 tbsp olive oil
450 g/1 lb tomatoes, skinned, seeded
  and chopped
15 ml/1 tbsp chopped parsley
15 ml/1 tbsp chopped basil
75 ml/5 tbsp dry white wine
225 g/8 oz/2 cups conchiglie
Salt and freshly ground black
  pepper
Lemon juice

Scrub the mussels, pull off the beards and discard any shells that are broken, or open and won't close when sharply tapped. Fry (sauté) the garlic gently in the oil for 1 minute. Add the tomatoes and herbs and bring just to the boil then reduce the heat and cook very gently. Meanwhile, put the mussels in a large pan with the wine. Cover and cook over a moderate heat, shaking the pan for 3-4 minutes until the mussels have opened, discarding any that have not. When cooked, strain the liquid into the tomato mixture and continue simmering until pulpy (about 20 minutes in all). Remove the mussels from their shells. Cook the conchiglie according to the packet directions. Drain and turn into a warm serving dish. Stir the mussels into the tomato sauce and season to taste with salt, pepper and lemon juice. Spoon over the pasta and serve hot.

Fiery Mussels

Serves 4

30 ml/2 tbsp olive oil
1 onion, finely chopped
1 garlic clove, crushed
1-2 red chillies, seeded and chopped
2 canned pimiento caps, chopped
400 g/14 oz/1 large can chopped
  tomatoes
15 ml/1 tbsp tomato purée (paste)
250 g/9 oz/1 small can mussels in
  brine, drained
Salt and freshly ground black
  pepper
350 g/12 oz spaghettini

Heat the oil in a saucepan. Add the onion and garlic and cook gently for 2 minutes until softened but not browned. Add the chillies, pimientos, tomatoes and tomato purée. Bring to the boil, reduce the heat and simmer gently for 10 minutes until pulpy. Stir in the mussels. Season to taste and heat through gently until piping hot. Meanwhile, cook the spaghettini according to the packet directions. Drain and pile on to warm plates. Spoon the sauce over and serve straight away.

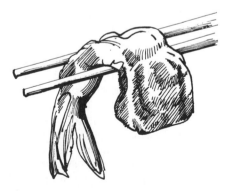

Vermicelli Marina

Serves 4-6

2 kg/4¹/₂ lb mussels in their shells
120 ml/4 fl oz/1 cup olive oil
3 garlic cloves, crushed
150 ml/¹/₄ pt/²/₃ cup chicken stock
450 g/1 lb vermicelli
15 ml/1 tbsp brandy
Salt and freshly ground black
  pepper
30 ml/2 tbsp chopped parsley

Scrub the mussels, remove the beards and discard any shells that are damaged, or open and won't close when sharply tapped. Heat 45 ml/3 tbsp of the oil in a large pan. Add the garlic and fry (sauté) gently until golden. Add the mussels and chicken stock. Cover and cook gently, shaking the pan for 3-4 minutes or until the mussels open. Discard any that don't. Drain, reserving the liquid. Carefully remove the mussels from their shells and return to the liquid. Meanwhile, cook the vermicelli according to the packet directions. Drain and return to the saucepan. Add the mussels in their liquid and the brandy. Season to taste, add the parsley and toss well before serving.

Prawn and Artichoke Adventure

Serves 4

45 ml/3 tbsp olive oil
1 onion, finely chopped
45 ml/3 tbsp dry white vermouth
425 g/15 oz/1 large can artichoke
  hearts, drained and chopped
100 g/4 oz/1 cup peeled prawns
  (shrimp)
6 stoned (pitted) green olives, halved
Freshly ground black pepper
225 g/8 oz/2 cups farfalle
Snipped chives
25 g/1 oz/2 tbsp Danish lumpfish roe

Heat the oil in a saucepan. Add the onion and fry (sauté) gently for 3 minutes until softened but not browned. Add the vermouth, bring to the boil and simmer for 1 minute. Add the artichokes, prawns, olives and a good grinding of pepper. Heat through, stirring gently until piping hot. Meanwhile, cook the farfalle according to the packet directions, drain. Add the chives and the sauce and toss well. Spoon on to serving plates and top each with a spoonful of lumpfish roe.

Cidered Prawns with Lumachi

Serves 4-6

50 g/2 oz/¹/₄ cup butter or margarine
1 bunch of spring onions (scallions), chopped
2 courgettes (zucchini), sliced
450 ml/³/₄ pt/2 cups fish stock
150 ml/¹/₄ pt/²/₃ cup dry cider
30 ml/2 tbsp cornflour (cornstarch)
225 g/8 oz/2 cups peeled prawns (shrimp)
Salt and freshly ground black pepper
150 ml/¹/₄ pt/²/₃ cup single (light) cream
15 ml/1 tbsp chopped parsley
225g/8 oz/2 cups lumachi

Melt the butter or margarine in a saucepan. Add the spring onions and courgettes and fry (sauté) gently for 2 minutes. Cover and cook for 5 minutes until softened but not browned, stirring occasionally. Add the stock and bring to the boil. Simmer for 2 minutes. Blend the cider with the cornflour and stir into the mixture. Bring to the boil and simmer for 1 minute, stirring all the time. Stir in the prawns, a little salt and pepper, the cream and parsley. Heat through gently, until piping hot. Meanwhile, cook the pasta according to the packet directions. Drain. Add to the sauce, toss gently and serve straight away.

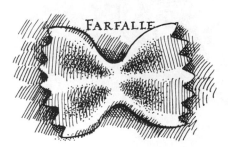

FARFALLE

Speciality Crab Conchiglie

Serves 4-6

Use the recipe for Cidered Prawns with Lumachi but substitute diced crabsticks for the prawns, a fruity German white wine for the cider, and conchiglie for the lumachi.

Chinese-style Prawns with Cucumber

Serves 4

1 cucumber, diced
50 g/2 oz/¹/₄ cup butter
175 g/6 oz/3 cups button mushrooms, sliced
15 ml/1 tbsp plain (all-purpose) flour
150 ml/¹/₄ pt/²/₃ cup chicken stock
15 ml/1 tbsp medium-dry sherry
5 ml/1 tsp grated fresh root ginger
90 ml/6 tbsp single (light) cream
175 g/6 oz/1¹/₂ cups peeled prawns (shrimp)
Salt and freshly ground black pepper
250 g/9 oz/1 packet Chinese wheat or egg noodles

Boil the cucumber in lightly salted water for 3 minutes. Drain, rinse with cold water and drain again. Melt the butter in the same saucepan. Add the mushrooms and cook for 2 minutes, stirring. Add the cucumber, cover and cook for a further 3 minutes. Stir in the flour then the stock, sherry, ginger and cream. Bring to the boil and cook for 2 minutes, stirring. Add the prawns, heat through until piping hot and season to taste. Meanwhile, cook the noodles according to the packet directions. Drain and pile into warm bowls. Spoon the prawn mixture over and serve.

Prawn and Cucumber Lu Mein

Serves 4

Use the recipe for Chinese-style Prawns with Cucumber but omit the flour. Instead of wheat or egg noodles add 250 g/9 oz/ 1 packet of soaked cellophane noodles with the stock, sherry and ginger. Do not add the cream at this stage. Simmer the noodles until cooked, adding a little more stock if necessary. Then add the cream and prawns, heat through and season to taste.

Quick Curried Prawn and Pasta Supper

Serves 4

225 g/8 oz/2 cups pasta shapes
298 g/10¹/₂ oz/1 can condensed
  cream of chicken soup
15 ml/1 tbsp curry paste
225 g/8 oz/2 cups peeled prawns
  (shrimp)
15 ml/1 tbsp chopped coriander
  (cilantro) or parsley
50 g/2 oz/1 cup breadcrumbs
15 g/¹/₂ oz/1 tbsp butter, melted

Cook the pasta according to the packet directions. Drain. Mix with the remaining ingredients except the breadcrumbs and butter. Heat gently, stirring until piping hot and well mixed. Turn into a flameproof dish. Mix the crumbs with the butter and sprinkle over. Place under a hot grill (broiler) until crisp and golden. Serve straight away.

Cod Ragoût

Serves 4-6

1 onion, chopped
1 garlic clove, crushed
15 ml/1 tbsp olive oil
100 g/4 oz/2 cups button
  mushrooms, sliced
400 g/14 oz/1 large can chopped
  tomatoes
15 ml/1 tbsp tomato purée (paste)
50 g/2 oz/¹/₂ cup frozen peas
15 ml/1 tbsp chopped basil
Salt and freshly ground black
  pepper
450 g/1 lb cod fillet, skinned and
  cubed
350 g/12 oz pappardelle
A few basil leaves
50 g/2 oz Cheddar cheese, grated

Fry (sauté) the onion and garlic in the oil for 2 minutes until softened but not browned. Add the remaining ingredients except the cod, pasta, basil for garnish and the cheese. Bring to the boil, reduce the heat and simmer for 10 minutes until pulpy. Add the fish and cook for a further 5 minutes, stirring gently occasionally until the fish is cooked. Meanwhile, cook the pappardelle according to the packet directions. Drain. Pile on to a warm serving dish, spoon the cod ragoût over, garnish with basil leaves and serve with the cheese.

Lasagne Di Mare

Serves 4

1 onion, finely chopped
1 garlic clove, crushed
100 g/4 oz mushrooms, finely
 chopped
400 g/14 oz/1 large can chopped
 tomatoes
15 ml/1 tbsp tomato purée (paste)
2.5 ml/¹/₂ tsp dried oregano
450 g/1 lb cod fillet, skinned and
 cubed
Salt and freshly ground black pepper
50 g/2 oz/¹/₂ cup plain (all-purpose)
 flour
50 g/2 oz/¹/₄ cup butter
600 ml/1 pt/2¹/₂ cups milk
100 g/4 oz Cheddar cheese, grated
8 sheets no-need-to-precook lasagne

Put the onion, garlic, mushrooms, tomatoes, tomato purée and oregano in a saucepan. Bring to the boil, reduce the heat and simmer for 15 minutes until pulpy. Stir in the fish and cook for a further 5 minutes. Season to taste. Meanwhile, blend the flour, butter and a little of the milk in a saucepan. Stir in the remaining milk. Bring to the boil and cook for 2 minutes, stirring until thickened. Season to taste and add half the cheese. Spoon a thin layer of the cheese sauce in the base of a 2.25 litres/4 pts/10 cups ovenproof dish. Cover with a layer of lasagne, breaking it to fit. Cover with a third of the fish sauce, then a little more cheese sauce. Repeat the layers twice more, making sure you have plenty of cheese sauce for the top. Sprinkle with the remaining cheese and bake at 190°C/375°F/gas mark 5 for about 35-40 minutes until the pasta feels tender when a knife is inserted down through the centre.

Quick Conchiglie Cod Casserole

Serves 4

175 g/6 oz/1¹/₂ cups conchiglie
15 g/¹/₂ oz/1 tbsp butter, for greasing
450 g/1 lb cod fillet, skinned and
 diced
300 ml/¹/₂ pt/1¹/₄ cups milk
425 g/15 oz/1 large can crab bisque
Salt and freshly ground black
 pepper
30 ml/2 tbsp chopped parsley

Put the dry pasta in the base of a well-buttered casserole (Dutch oven). Put the fish in a layer over the top. Blend the remaining ingredients together and pour over. Cover and bake in the oven at 180°C/350°F/gas mark 4 for about 50 minutes until the pasta is cooked.

Portuguese Fishermen's Friend

Serves 4

450 g/1 lb salt cod, soaked in cold
  water overnight
15 ml/1 tbsp lemon juice
50 g/2 oz/¹/₂ cup plain (all-purpose)
  flour
Oil for shallow frying
15 ml/1 tbsp olive oil
1 garlic clove, crushed
1 onion, chopped
400 g/14 oz/1 large can chopped
  tomatoes
15 ml/1 tbsp tomato purée (paste)
5 ml/1 tsp caster (superfine) sugar
12 stuffed green olives
6 cocktail gherkins (cornichons),
  halved lengthways
10 ml/2 tsp capers
225 g/8 oz/2 cups zite
15 ml/1 tbsp chopped parsley

Drain the cod. Place in a saucepan and
cover with cold water. Add the lemon
juice. Bring to the boil, part-cover and boil
for 5 minutes. Drain and repeat until the
fish is tender. Remove the skin and any
bones and break the fish into bite-sized
pieces. Dust with the flour. Shallow-fry
until golden brown. Drain on kitchen
paper. Meanwhile, heat the olive oil in a
saucepan. Fry (sauté) the garlic and onion
for 3 minutes until soft but not brown. Add
the tomatoes, tomato purée and sugar.
Bring to the boil, reduce the heat and simmer for 10 minutes until pulpy. Stir in the
cod, olives, gherkins and capers. Simmer
gently for 3 minutes. Meanwhile, cook the
zite according to the packet directions.
Drain and spoon on to a warmed serving
dish. Spoon the sauce over and sprinkle
with the parsley. Serve piping hot.

Country Cod Bake

Serves 6

300 ml/¹/₂ pt/1¹/₄ cups fish or
  vegetable stock
60 ml/4 tbsp tomato ketchup
  (catsup)
30 ml/2 tbsp mayonnaise
350 g/12 oz/3 cups frozen mixed
  country vegetables
Salt and freshly ground black
  pepper
450 ml/1 lb cod fillet, skinned and
  cubed
2.5 ml/¹/₂ tsp dried mixed herbs
350 g/12 oz fettuccine
75 g/3 oz Cheddar cheese, grated

Mix the stock, ketchup and mayonnaise
together in a saucepan. Add the vegetables
and a little seasoning, cover and simmer
for 10 minutes or until tender. Add the fish
and herbs and simmer for 5 minutes.
Meanwhile, cook the pasta according to
the packet directions. Drain and turn into a
flameproof dish. Spoon the sauce over. Top
with the cheese and place under a hot grill
(broiler) until the cheese melts, bubbles
and is turning golden.

Delicate Cod Pie

Serves 4
225 g/8 oz/2 cups farfalle
450 g/1 lb cod fillet, skinned and
  cubed
450 ml/³/₄ pt/2 cups milk
25 g/1 oz/¹/₄ cup plain (all-purpose)
  flour
25 g/1 oz/2 tbsp butter
Salt and freshly ground black
  pepper
2 hard boiled (hard-cooked) eggs,
  roughly chopped
30 ml/2 tbsp chopped parsley
150 ml/¹/₄ pt/²/₃ cup single (light)
  cream
2 eggs, beaten
50 g/2 oz Cheddar cheese, grated

Cook the pasta according to the packet directions. Drain. Meanwhile, cook the cod in the milk for about 5 minutes until just tender. Drain, reserving the milk. Whisk the flour into a little of the milk. Add the remaining milk and butter and bring to the boil, whisking all the time until thickened. Season to taste. Gently fold in the pasta, fish, hard-boiled eggs and parsley. Turn into an ovenproof dish. Whisk the cream and eggs together with a little salt and pepper. Pour over and sprinkle on the cheese. Bake at 190°C/375°F/gas mark 5 for about 25 minutes or until the top is set and golden. Serve hot.

Special Crab Ravioli

Serves 4
225 g/8 oz/2 cups plain (all-purpose)
  flour
1.5 ml/¹/₄ tsp salt
2 size 1 eggs, beaten
75 g/3 oz/¹/₃ cup butter
2 × 170 g/2 × 6 oz/2 small cans
  crabmeat
15 ml/1 tbsp mayonnaise
20 ml/4 tsp lemon juice
Cayenne
Salt and freshly ground black
  pepper
1 size 4 egg, beaten
Flour for dusting
150 ml/¹/₄ pt/²/₃ cup milk
20 ml/4 tsp cornflour (cornstarch)
300 ml/¹/₂ pt/1¹/₄ cups single (light)
  cream
15 ml/1 tbsp tomato purée (paste)
Freshly grated Parmesan cheese

Sift the flour and salt into a bowl. Make a well in the centre and add the size 1 eggs. Melt half the butter and add to the bowl. Mix well to form a firm dough, adding a little cold water if necessary. Knead gently on a lightly floured surface until shiny and elastic. Wrap in a polythene bag and leave to rest for at least 30 minutes. Meanwhile, mix the crabmeat with the mayonnaise, 5 ml/1 tsp of the lemon juice and cayenne and salt and pepper to taste. Roll out the dough on a floured surface as thinly as possible to a large square. Spoon the crab mixture at 4 cm/1¹/₂ in intervals across half the dough. Brush between the filling with beaten egg. Fold over the other half of the dough and press down between each pile of filling. Using a pastry wheel or sharp knife, cut between the filling piles to make little cushions. Dust with flour and leave to rest while making the sauce. Blend the milk and cornflour in a saucepan. Add the cream and tomato purée and bring to the boil, stirring all the time. Add the remaining lemon juice and cayenne, salt and pepper to taste. Drop the ravioli, one after the other, into a large pan of boiling, lightly salted water. When they are all in the pan, cook for about 7 minutes until just tender. Remove from the pan with a draining spoon and transfer to a warm serving dish. Spoon the hot sauce over and dust with the Parmesan before serving.

Salmon Fish Cakes

Serves 4
200 g/7 oz/1 small can pink salmon
5 ml/1 tsp anchovy essence (extract)
100 g/4 oz/¹/₂ cup mashed potato
100 g/4 oz/1 cup cooked long-grain
  rice
15 ml/1 tbsp snipped chives
15 ml/1 tbsp chopped parsley
2 eggs, beaten
Salt and freshly ground black
  pepper
30 ml/2 tbsp plain (all-purpose) flour
50 g/2 oz/1 cup breadcrumbs
Oil for shallow-frying
Lemon wedges

Drain and flake the salmon, removing the skin and bones. Mix the fish with the anchovy essence, potato, rice and herbs. Add enough beaten egg to bind the mixture. Season lightly and mix again. Shape into round cakes with floured hands. Coat in the remaining egg then the breadcrumbs. Shallow-fry in hot oil until golden brown on both sides. Drain on kitchen paper and garnish with the lemon wedges.

Spinach Cod Bake

Serves 4
175 g/6 oz/³/₄ cup brown rice
1 onion, finely chopped
1 celery stick, chopped
50 g/2 oz/¹/₄ cup butter
450 g/1 lb/2 cups frozen chopped
  spinach
Salt and freshly ground black
  pepper
A pinch of grated nutmeg
4 cod fillets
60 ml/4 tbsp boiling water
1 fish stock cube
300 ml/¹/₂ pt/1¹/₄ cups single (light)
  cream
100 g/4 oz Leerdammer or
  Emmental (Swiss) cheese, grated

Cook the rice according to the packet directions. Drain and place in a buttered ovenproof dish. Meanwhile, fry (sauté) the onion and celery in the butter for 3 minutes, stirring. Add the spinach and cook, stirring, for 4 minutes. Season to taste with the salt, pepper and nutmeg. Spoon over the rice. Top with the fish fillets. Blend the water with the crumbled stock cube and mix with the cream. Pour over and sprinkle with the cheese. Bake at 180°C/350°F/gas mark 4 for about 30 minutes until cooked through and the top is golden and bubbling.

Friday Plaice with Buttery Rice

Serves 4
225 g/8 oz/1 cup long-grain rice
100 g/4 oz/¹/₂ cup unsalted (sweet) butter
30 ml/2 tbsp single (light) cream
4 plaice fillets
A little seasoned flour
Lemon juice
Chopped parsley

Cook the rice in plenty of boiling salted water until just tender. Drain and rinse with boiling water, drain again. Return to the pan, add 50 g/2 oz/¹/₄ cup of the butter and the cream and toss gently until well combined. Spoon into a warmed shallow serving dish. Meanwhile, coat the plaice in the seasoned flour. Fry (sauté) the plaice fillets in half the remaining butter until golden and cooked through. Lay on top of the rice. Melt the remaining butter and fry until nut brown. Add the lemon juice and parsley and spoon over the fish. Serve straight away.

Smokies Supper

Serves 4
1 onion, chopped
50 g/2 oz/¹/₄ cup butter
225 g/8 oz Cheddar cheese, grated
275 g/10 oz smoked trout fillets, skinned and diced
4 large tomatoes, skinned, seeded and chopped
225 g/8 oz/2 cups cooked long-grain rice
2.5 ml/¹/₂ tsp dried mixed herbs
Juice of 1 lemon
Salt and freshly ground black pepper

Fry (sauté) the onion in the butter for 2 minutes, stirring. Mix with half the cheese and all the remaining ingredients. Pack into 4 individual ovenproof dishes and sprinkle with the remaining cheese. Bake at 200°C/400°F/gas mark 6 for about 20 minutes until bubbling and golden on top.

Ray in Black Butter with Wild Rice

Serves 4
225 g/8 oz/1 cup wild rice mix
15 ml/1 tbsp chopped parsley
2 large ray wings
120 ml/4 fl oz/¹/₂ cup white wine vinegar
2 garlic cloves, crushed
1 bunch of spring onions (scallions), finely chopped
100 g/4 oz/¹/₂ cup butter
30 ml/2 tbsp capers

Cook the rice mix according to the packet directions. Drain and stir in the parsley. Meanwhile, wipe the fish with kitchen paper. Heat the vinegar, garlic and spring onions in a large frying pan (skillet). Add the fish, cover and cook for 10 minutes, turning two or three times until cooked through. Remove from the pan, reserving the juices. Scrape off the thin membrane covering the wings. Scrape the flesh into a bowl and keep warm. Melt the butter in a clean pan and heat until a nutty brown (do not burn). Add the fish-cooking juices and boil rapidly for 30 seconds. Return the fish to the pan, toss quickly and serve spooned next to the wild rice mix on a warm serving dish. Scatter a few capers over for garnish.

Bacon-stuffed Grey Mullet

Serves 4
4 grey mullet, cleaned and scaled
8 rashers (slices) smoked streaky bacon, rinded and finely chopped or minced (ground)
15 ml/1 tbsp chopped sage
50 g/2 oz/¹/₂ cup cooked long-grain rice
Salt and freshly ground black pepper
50 g/2 oz/¹/₄ cup butter
150 ml/¹/₄ pt/²/₃ cup dry white wine
120 ml/4 fl oz/¹/₂ cup single (light) cream

Wipe the fish inside and out with kitchen paper. Make several slashes on each side of the fish. Mix the bacon and sage together. Use half to spread in the slits. Mix the remainder with the rice and season well with salt and pepper. Pack into the body cavities of the fish and lay them in a baking dish, well greased with the butter. Pour over the wine. Cover with foil and bake at 200°C/400°F/gas mark 6 for 15 minutes. Remove the foil and bake for a further 15 minutes. Pour over the cream and cook for a further 5 minutes. Serve straight away.

Grilled Mackerel with Gooseberries and Ginger Rice

Serves 4

225 g/8 oz/1 cup Thai fragrant rice
450 ml/³/₄ pt/2 cups boiling water
10 ml/2 tsp grated fresh root ginger
Salt and freshly ground black pepper
4 mackerel fillets
50 g/2 oz/¹/₄ cup butter
450 g/1 lb/4 cups gooseberries, topped and tailed
45 ml/3 tbsp water
Sugar to taste
15 ml/1 tbsp chopped parsley
5 ml/1 tsp lemon juice

Wash the rice well, drain and place in a pan. Add the boiling water, ginger and a little salt and pepper. Bring to the boil again, cover tightly, reduce the heat to as low as possible and cook for 20 minutes. Turn off the heat and leave undisturbed for 5 minutes. Meanwhile, fry (sauté) the mackerel fillets in the butter for about 5 minutes, turning once, until cooked through. Cook the gooseberries in the water until they pop. Stir in sugar to taste. Purée in a blender or food processor and pass through a sieve. Fluff up the ginger rice with a fork. Pile on to serving plates. Lay a mackerel fillet on each. Add the parsley and lemon juice to the butter in the pan. Spoon over the fish. Serve with the gooseberry purée on the side.

Brandied Crab Crisp

Serves 4-6

25 g/1 oz/¹/₄ cup plain (all-purpose) flour
25 g/1 oz/2 tbsp butter
300 ml/¹/₂ pt/1¹/₄ cups milk
30 ml/2 tbsp single (light) cream
50 g/2 oz Cheddar cheese, grated
5 ml/1 tsp Dijon mustard
2.5 ml/¹/₂ tsp dried thyme
Salt and freshly ground black pepper
15 ml/1 tbsp brandy
2 × 170 g/2 × 6 oz/2 small cans crabmeat
225 g/8 oz/2 cups farfalle
50 g/2 oz/1 cup breadcrumbs
15 g/¹/₂ oz/1 tbsp butter, melted

Whisk the flour, butter, and milk together in a saucepan until the flour is blended in. Bring to the boil and cook for 2 minutes, stirring all the time. Stir in the cream, cheese, mustard and thyme. Season with a little salt and pepper. Add the brandy and the contents of the cans of crabmeat, including the juice. Stir in gently. Heat through until piping hot. Taste and re-season if necessary. Meanwhile, cook the pasta according to the packet directions, drain. Turn half the pasta into a flameproof dish. Add half the sauce. Repeat the layers. Mix the breadcrumbs with the butter. Sprinkle over and place under a hot grill (broiler) until crisp and golden on top.

Crab Creation

Serves 4

225 g/8 oz green tagliatelle (verdi)
225 g/8 oz crab sticks, diced
425 g/15 oz/1 large can crab bisque
Salt and freshly ground black
    pepper
30 ml/2 tbsp single (light) cream
30 ml/2 tbsp chopped parsley
Lemon juice
Lemon twists

Cook the pasta according to the packet directions. Drain and return to the pan. In a separate pan, put the crab sticks, soup, a little salt and pepper, the cream and parsley and heat through gently, stirring. Spike with lemon juice to taste. Add to the cooked pasta and toss gently. Pile on to serving plates and serve hot, garnished with a lemon twist on each plate.

Queen Scallop and Bacon Tagliatelle

Serves 4-6

2 small leeks, sliced
25 g/1 oz/2 tbsp butter
90 ml/6 tbsp fish stock
3 rashers (slices) streaky bacon,
    rinded and diced
175 g/6 oz/1½ cups queen scallops
50 g/2 oz/¼ cup fromage frais
Salt and freshly ground black
    pepper
350 g/12 oz green tagliatelle (verdi)
Chopped parsley

Fry (sauté) the leeks in half the butter for 2 minutes until softened but not browned. Add the stock, cover and simmer gently for 5 minutes until tender. Purée in a blender or food processor then return to the saucepan. Meanwhile, dry-fry the bacon until the fat runs. Add the scallops and cook quickly, tossing for 2 minutes until cooked through. Stir the fromage frais into the leek purée. Add the bacon and scallops and stir in gently. Season to taste and heat through until piping hot. Meanwhile, cook the tagliatelle according to the packet directions. Pile on to warm serving plates, spoon the scallop mixture over and sprinkle with the parsley before serving.

Tagliatelle alla Rustica

Serves 4

2 garlic cloves, crushed
90 ml/6 tbsp olive oil
50 g/2 oz/1 small can anchovies,
    chopped, reserving the oil
5 ml/1 tsp dried oregano
45 ml/3 tbsp roughly chopped
    parsley
Salt and freshly ground black
    pepper
225 g/8 oz tagliatelle, preferably
    fresh (page 10)
Thin slivers of fresh Parmesan
    cheese

Fry (sauté) the garlic in the oil until golden brown. Remove from the heat and add the anchovies in their oil. Return to the heat and cook gently, stirring, until the anchovies form a paste. Stir in the oregano, parsley, a very little salt and lots of black pepper. Meanwhile, cook the tagliatelle (see page 10 if fresh, or according to the packet directions). Drain and return to the pan. Add the sauce, toss well and serve garnished with the Parmesan.

Squid and Radicchio Euphoria

Serves 4
450 g/1 lb baby squid
60 ml/4 tbsp olive oil
2 garlic cloves, crushed
1 red onion, chopped
¹/₂ green (bell) pepper, chopped
Salt and freshly ground black pepper
30 ml/2 tbsp lemon juice
1 small head of radicchio
30 ml/2 tbsp chopped parsley
225 g/8 oz any ribbon noodles

Clean the squid, slice into rings and chop the tentacles. Heat the oil in a large frying pan (skillet) and fry (sauté) the garlic, onion and pepper for 3 minutes, stirring until softened but not browned. Add the squid, season well with salt and pepper and add the lemon juice. Stir-fry for 1 minute then cover and cook gently for 5 minutes. Separate the radicchio into leaves and then tear into bite-sized pieces. Add to the pan and cook, stirring for 2 minutes until slightly wilted. Sprinkle with half the parsley and heat through for a further minute. Meanwhile, cook the noodles according to the packet directions. Drain and return to the pan. Add the sauce, toss quickly over a gentle heat and serve garnished with the remaining parsley.

Smoked Haddock Macaroni Cheese

Serves 4
225 g/8 oz smoked haddock fillet
450 ml/³/₄ pt/2 cups milk
1 bay leaf
50 g/2 oz/¹/₄ cup butter
100 g/4 oz/2 cups button mushrooms, sliced
25 g/1 oz/¹/₄ cup plain (all-purpose) flour
100 g/4 oz Cheddar cheese, grated
Salt and white pepper
225 g/8 oz/2 cups elbow macaroni
Passata (sieved tomatoes)

Poach the fish in the milk with the bay leaf added for about 5 minutes until it flakes easily with a fork. Drain, reserving the milk. Discard the skin and any bones from the fish and break into bite-sized pieces. Melt the butter in the saucepan and add the mushrooms. Cook gently, stirring for 1 minute. Add the flour and cook for a further 1 minute. Remove from the heat, gradually blend in the reserved milk, discarding the bay leaf. Return to the heat, bring to the boil and cook for 2 minutes, stirring. Stir in 75g/3 oz/³/₄ cup of the cheese and season to taste. Gently fold in the fish and reheat until piping hot. Meanwhile, cook the macaroni according to the packet directions. Drain. Fold gently into the fish mixture and turn into a flameproof dish. Top with the remaining cheese and place under a hot grill (broiler) to brown. Serve straight away with warm passata handed separately.

Macaroni Cheese Brunch

Serves 4-6

Prepare as for Smoked Haddock Macaroni Cheese but substitute kipper fillets for the haddock and 3 quartered hard-boiled (hard-cooked) eggs for the mushrooms. Omit the passata, if preferred.

Golden Creamy Cannelloni

Serves 4-6

450g/1 lb smoked haddock fillet
600 ml/1 pt/2¹/₂ cups milk
1 bouquet garni sachet
90 ml/6 tbsp double (heavy) cream
Salt and freshly ground black pepper
15 ml/1 tbsp chopped parsley
40 g/1¹/₂ oz/3 tbsp butter
25 g/1 oz/¹/₄ cup plain (all-purpose) flour
100 g/4 oz Leerdammer or Gruyère (Swiss) cheese, grated
12 cannelloni tubes
350 g/12 oz/1 large can sweetcorn (corn), drained

Poach the haddock in the milk with the bouquet garni added, until it flakes easily with a fork, about 8 minutes. Drain, reserving the milk. Discard the bouquet garni. Remove any skin and bones from the fish and mash well. Stir in the cream, season with salt and pepper and add the parsley. Melt 25 g/1 oz/2 tbsp of the butter in a saucepan. Blend in the flour, then the reserved milk. Bring to the boil and cook for 2 minutes, stirring. Season to taste and stir in half the cheese. Cook the cannelloni tubes, if necessary, according to the packet directions. Put the fish mixture in a piping bag and pipe it or spoon it into the tubes. Butter an ovenproof dish with the remaining butter. Spread the corn in the base of the dish. Spoon a little of the cheese sauce over. Lay the cannelloni on top and cover with the remaining cheese sauce. Sprinkle with the remaining cheese and bake in the oven at 190°C/375°F/gas mark 5 for about 35 minutes until golden and bubbling and the cannelloni is cooked through.

Smoked Salmon and Broccoli Centrepiece

Serves 6

225 g/8 oz broccoli, cut into tiny florets
100 g/4 oz/1 cup smoked salmon, cut into small pieces
300 ml/¹/₂ pt/1¹/₄ cups crème fraîche
15 ml/1 tbsp chopped dill (dill weed)
2 hard-boiled (hard-cooked) eggs, roughly chopped
Salt and freshly ground black pepper
225 g/8 oz red tagliatelle (al pomodoro)
A little butter
Dill sprigs

Steam the broccoli or boil in a little salted water until just tender. Drain and return to the pan. Add the remaining ingredients except the pasta, butter and dill sprigs and heat through gently, stirring lightly until piping hot. Meanwhile, cook the pasta according to the packet directions. Drain and return to the pan. Toss in a little butter and pile on to warm plates. Spoon the sauce over and garnish with small sprigs of dill.

Fresh Salmon and Pimiento Wheels

Serves 4

225 g/8 oz fresh salmon fillet,
   skinned and cut into thin strips
Grated rind and juice of ¹/₂ lemon
90 ml/6 tbsp olive oil
8 spring onions (scallions), chopped
400 g/14 oz/1 large can pimientos,
   drained and chopped
15 ml/1 tbsp chopped basil
Salt and freshly ground black
   pepper
225 g/8 oz/2 cups wholewheat ruote
50 g/2 oz/1 cup breadcrumbs
15 g/¹/₂ oz/1 tbsp butter

Put the salmon in a dish with the lemon rind and juice and leave to marinate while preparing the rest of the sauce. Heat 60 ml/4 tbsp of the oil in a saucepan and fry (sauté) the spring onions for about 3 minutes until softened but not browned. Add the pimientos and toss in the oil for 2 minutes. Add the salmon with any juices and cook gently for 2 minutes until just cooked - do not overcook. Add the basil and remaining oil and season well with salt and pepper. Heat through until piping hot. Meanwhile, cook the pasta according to the packet directions. Drain and return to the pan. Add the hot sauce, toss well. Meanwhile, fry the breadcrumbs in the butter until golden. Pile the pasta on to warm plates and sprinkle with the buttered crumbs.

Simple Salmon Supper

Serves 4

25 g/1 oz/¹/₄ cup plain (all-purpose)
   flour
300 ml/¹/₂ pt/1¹/₄ cups milk
25 g/1 oz/2 tbsp butter
200 g/7 oz/1 small can pink or red
   salmon
A few drops of anchovy essence
   (extract)
Salt and freshly ground black
   pepper
225 g/8 oz/2 cups short-cut
   macaroni
100 g/4 oz Cheddar cheese, grated
Lemon wedges

Whisk the flour with the milk in a saucepan until smooth. Add the butter. Bring to the boil and cook for 2 minutes, stirring. Discard the skin and any bones from the fish. Stir into the sauce with the juice. Add a few drops of anchovy essence and salt and pepper to taste. Meanwhile, cook the macaroni according to the packet directions. Drain and stir into the fish sauce. Turn into a flameproof dish. Sprinkle the cheese over and brown under a hot grill (broiler). Garnish with lemon wedges before serving.

Smoked Haddock Carbonara

Serves 4

450 g/1 lb smoked haddock fillet
350 g/12 oz spaghetti
4 rashers (slices) streaky bacon,
  rinded and diced
25 g/1 oz/2 tbsp butter
30 ml/2 tbsp chopped parsley
Freshly ground black pepper
3 eggs, beaten
Grated Parmesan cheese

Poach the fish in water for 8 minutes until it flakes easily with a fork. Drain, remove the skin and flake the fish. Meanwhile, cook the spaghetti according to the packet directions. Drain. Fry (sauté) the bacon in the butter in the spaghetti pan for 2 minutes, stirring. Return the spaghetti and add the fish, parsley and a good grinding of black pepper. Add the eggs and cook over a gentle heat, stirring until just beginning to scramble but still creamy. Remove from the heat, quickly spoon on to plates and top with the Parmesan cheese.

Prawn Carbonara

Serves 4

Prepare as for Smoked Haddock Carbonara but substitute 225 g/8 oz/2 cups peeled prawns (shrimp) for the haddock and add 225 g/8 oz/4 cups sliced button mushrooms.

Tagliatelle Royale

Serves 6

450 g/1 lb green tagliatelle (verdi)
200 ml/7 fl oz/scant 1 cup double
  (heavy) cream
75 g/3 oz/¹⁄₃ cup cream cheese with
  chives
Grated rind and juice of ¹⁄₂ lemon
5 ml/1 tsp anchovy essence (extract)
5 ml/1 tsp tomato purée (paste)
225 g/8 oz smoked salmon pieces,
  chopped
Freshly ground black pepper
15 ml/1 tbsp chopped dill (dill weed)
Gherkin (cornichon) fans

Cook the pasta according to the packet directions. Drain. Meanwhile, heat the cream with the cheese, stirring until smooth. Add the lemon rind and juice, anchovy essence, tomato purée, salmon, lots of black pepper and the dill. Heat gently for 3 minutes. Add the pasta, toss gently then pile on to warm serving plates and garnish each with a gherkin fan.

Neapolitan Halibut

Serves 4

1 onion, finely chopped
1 garlic clove, crushed
45 ml/3 tbsp olive oil
400 g/14 oz/1 large can chopped
    tomatoes
15 ml/1 tbsp tomato purée (paste)
5 ml/1 tsp capers, chopped
4 gherkins (cornichons), chopped
Salt and freshly ground black
    pepper
225 g/8 oz tagliatelle
15 g/¹/₂ oz/1 tbsp unsalted (sweet)
    butter
30 ml/2 tbsp plain (all-purpose) flour
4 halibut steaks
Oil for deep-frying
8 black olives
4 lemon wedges

Fry (sauté) the onion and garlic in the oil for 2 minutes until soft but not brown. Add the tomatoes, tomato purée, capers and gherkins. Bring to the boil, reduce the heat and simmer for 5 minutes until pulpy. Season to taste. Meanwhile, cook the pasta according to the packet directions. Drain, rinse with boiling water, drain again and return to the pan. Add the butter and toss well. Season the flour with a little salt and pepper and use to coat the fish. Deep-fry in hot oil for 3 minutes or until cooked through and golden. Drain on kitchen paper. Spoon the noodles on to a large serving dish. Lay the fish on top and spoon the sauce over. Garnish with the olives and lemon wedges before serving.

Saucy Salmon and Mushroom Pasta

Serves 4

225 g/8 oz/2 cups farfalle
298 g/10¹/₂ oz/1 can condensed
    cream of mushroom soup
200 g/7 oz/1 small can pink salmon,
    skinned and boned
150 ml/¹/₄ pt/²/₃ cup single (light)
    cream
15 ml/1 tbsp chopped parsley
Salt and freshly ground black
    pepper
Grated rind and juice of ¹/₂ lemon
Lemon slices

Cook the pasta according to the packet directions. Drain. Pour the soup into the pasta pan. Heat gently until smooth. Stir in the fish, cream, parsley, a little salt and pepper and the lemon rind and juice. Heat through, stirring occasionally until bubbling. Add the pasta and heat through again. Pile on to plates and garnish with the lemon slices.

Saucy Tuna and Celery Pasta

Serves 4

Prepare as for Saucy Salmon and Mushroom Pasta but substitute tuna for the salmon, use celery soup instead of mushroom, and add 15 ml/1 tbsp finely chopped celery before heating through, which will remain crunchy.

Wild Mushroom and Anchovy Bake

Serves 4

25 g/1 oz/¹/₄ cup dried ceps
Hot water
50 g/2 oz/1 small can anchovies,
    drained
A little milk
350 g/12 oz/3 cups rigatoni
50 g/2 oz/¹/₄ cup unsalted (sweet)
    butter
100 g/4 oz field mushrooms, peeled
    and sliced
1 shallot, finely chopped
25 g/1 oz/¹/₄ cup plain (all-purpose)
    flour
300 ml/¹/₂ pt/1¹/₄ cups milk
1 bay leaf
Salt and freshly ground black
    pepper
150 ml/¹/₄ pt/²/₃ cup single (light)
    cream
30 ml/2 tbsp snipped chives
50 g/2 oz/¹/₂ cup grated Parmesan
    cheese
50 g/2 oz Cheddar cheese, grated
Parsley sprigs

Soak the ceps in hot water for up to 1 hour until soft. Soak the anchovies in a little milk to remove the saltiness. Cook the pasta according to the packet directions, drain. Drain the ceps, coarsely chop. Melt half the butter in a pan. Add the ceps, field mushrooms and shallot and fry (sauté), stirring for 2 minutes. Stir in the remaining butter then add the flour. Blend in the measured amount of milk and add the bay leaf. Bring to the boil and cook, stirring, for 2 minutes. Drain and chop the anchovies and add to the sauce. Stir in the pasta, a little salt and pepper, the cream and the chives. Discard the bay leaf. Pour into an oven-proof serving dish and sprinkle with the two cheeses. Bake at 180°C/350°F/gas mark 4 for 30 minutes until the top is golden and bubbling. Garnish with the parsley sprigs.

Springtime Red Caviare Spaghettini

Serves 4

750 g/1¹/₂ lb mangetout (snow peas),
    topped and tailed
15 ml/1 tbsp olive oil
25 g/1 oz/2 tbsp unsalted (sweet)
    butter
250 ml/8 fl oz/1 cup crème fraîche
Salt and freshly ground black
    pepper
350 g/12 oz spaghettini
225 g/8 oz/2 large jars red Danish
    lumpfish roe
Grated rind of ¹/₂ lemon
Snipped chives

Fry (sauté) the mangetout in the oil and butter for 5 minutes, stirring until softened. Stir in the crème fraîche and season to taste. Meanwhile, cook the spaghettini according to the packet directions. Drain and return to the saucepan. Stir the lumpfish roe and lemon rind into the sauce then add to the spaghettini and toss over a gentle heat until piping hot. Pile on to serving plates and sprinkle with snipped chives before serving.

Springtime Prawn Perfection

Serves 4

Prepare as for Springtime Red Caviare Spaghettini but use 225 g/8 oz/2 cups of peeled prawns (shrimp) instead of the lumpfish roe.

English Seaside Pasta

Serves 2-4

175 g/6 oz any ribbon noodles
225 g/8 oz/2 cups small whole shrimps
4 spring onions (scallions), finely
chopped
25 g/1 oz/¹/₂ cup fresh breadcrumbs
75 ml/5 tbsp olive oil
1 handful of rocket or lamb's tongue
lettuce, shredded
Salt and freshly ground black pepper
60 ml/4 tbsp cider

Cook the pasta according to the packet directions. Drain. Remove the heads and tails from the shrimps. Fry (sauté) the spring onions and breadcrumbs in half the oil for 3 minutes, stirring until the bread is golden. Stir in the rocket or lettuce and cook for 1 minute. In a separate pan, fry the shrimps in the remaining oil for 2 minutes. Add the cider and cook for 1 minute. Add all the ingredients to the pasta, toss well and serve straight away.

Spiced Pasta Oceana

Serves 4-6

25 g/1 oz/2 tbsp butter
1 onion, finely chopped
400 g/14 oz/1 large can chopped
tomatoes
2.5 ml/¹/₂ tsp dried mixed herbs
1 green chilli, seeded and chopped
450 g/1 lb tagliatelle
225 g/8 oz/2 cups peeled prawns
(shrimp)
125 g/4¹/₂ oz/1 small jar mussels in
tomato sauce
50 g/2 oz/1 small can anchovies,
drained and chopped
Salt and freshly ground black pepper
Chopped coriander (cilantro)

Melt the butter in a large pan. Add the onion and fry (sauté) for 3 minutes, stirring until lightly golden. Add the tomatoes, herbs and chilli. Simmer gently for 10 minutes until pulpy. Meanwhile, cook the tagliatelle according to the packet directions. Drain. Stir the prawns, mussels and anchovies into the sauce and season to taste. Pile the pasta on to warm serving plates and spoon the sauce over. Sprinkle with the coriander before serving.

Bubbling Seafood Pasta

Serves 4 or 5

225 g/8 oz/2 cups conchiglie
175 g/6 oz cod fillet, skinned and diced
250 g/9 oz/1 small can mussels in
brine, drained
175 g/6 oz/1¹/₂ cups peeled prawns
(shrimp)
15 ml/1 tbsp chopped dill (dill weed)
10 ml/2 tsp cornflour (cornstarch)
375 ml/13 fl oz/1¹/₂ cups single (light)
cream
Salt and freshly ground black pepper
Grated rind and juice of 1 lime
25 g/1 oz/2 tbsp butter
50 g/2 oz/1 cup breadcrumbs

Cook the pasta according to the packet directions. Drain. Meanwhile, cook the cod in a little water for about 5 minutes until just tender. Drain. Mix with the mussels and prawns. Add the dill and cornflour and toss to coat evenly. Stir in the cream, a little salt and pepper and the lime rind and juice. Stir in the pasta and turn into an ovenproof dish. Melt the butter and stir in the breadcrumbs. Sprinkle liberally over the dish and bake at 190°C/375°F/gas mark 5 for 25-30 minutes until golden and bubbling. Serve straight from the oven.

Creamy Prawn Pasta

Serves 4

1 onion, finely chopped
1 garlic clove, crushed
25 g/1 oz/2 tbsp butter
15 g/¹/₂ oz/2 tbsp plain flour
150 ml/¹/₄ pt/²/₃ cup milk
1 bay leaf
300 ml/¹/₂ pt/1¹/₄ cups single (light)
* cream*
30 ml/2 tbsp chopped parsley
Grated rind and juice of ¹/₂ lemon
5 ml/1 tsp anchovy essence (extract)
350 g/12 oz/3 cups peeled prawns
* (shrimp)*
225 g/8 oz/2 cups lumachi

Fry (sauté) the onion and garlic in the butter for 2 minutes, stirring. Blend in the flour and cook for 1 minute. Stir in the milk, bay leaf and cream. Bring to the boil and cook for 2 minutes, stirring. Add the parsley, lemon rind and juice, the anchovy essence and prawns and simmer gently for 10 minutes. Meanwhile, cook the pasta according to the packet directions. Drain. Add to the prawn sauce, discard the bay leaf and serve hot.

Portuguese Pappardelle

Serves 4

1 onion, finely chopped
1 garlic clove, crushed
30 ml/2 tbsp olive oil
200 g/7 oz/1 small can pimientos,
* drained and chopped*
400 g/14 oz/1 large can chopped
* tomatoes*
120 g/5 oz/1 small can sardines,
* roughly chopped*
50 g/2 oz/¹/₂ cup pine nuts
15 ml/1 tbsp chopped parsley
Salt and freshly ground black
* pepper*
350 g/12 oz pappardelle
Grated rind of 1 lemon

Fry (sauté) the onion and garlic in the oil for 2 minutes, stirring. Add the pimientos and tomatoes and simmer gently for 5 minutes. Add the sardines, pine nuts and parsley and simmer for a further 10 minutes. Season to taste. Meanwhile, cook the pappardelle according to the packet directions. Drain and rinse with boiling water. Drain again and pile on to serving plates. Spoon the sardine sauce over and sprinkle with the lemon rind.

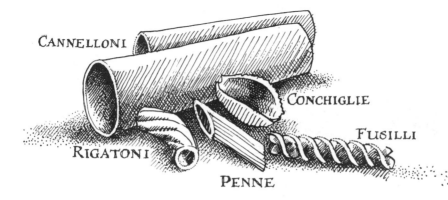

CANNELLONI

CONCHIGLIE

FUSILLI

RIGATONI

PENNE

Spaghettini with Anchovies and Fennel

Serves 6

1 onion, finely chopped
1 garlic clove, crushed
45 ml/3 tbsp olive oil
50 g/2 oz/1 small can anchovies,
  drained, reserving the oil and
  chopped
30 ml/2 tbsp finely chopped Florence
  fennel
15 ml/1 tbsp snipped chives
15 ml/1 tbsp chopped parsley
400 g/14 oz/1 large can chopped
  tomatoes
2.5 ml/¹/₂ tsp caster (superfine) sugar
Freshly ground black pepper
450 g/1 lb spaghettini
A few green fennel fronds

Fry (sauté) the onion and garlic in the oil for 2 minutes, stirring. Add the anchovies, fennel, herbs, tomatoes, sugar and lots of pepper. Bring to the boil, reduce the heat and simmer gently for 15 minutes until pulpy and the fennel is tender. Meanwhile, cook the pasta according to the packet directions. Drain and return to the pan. Add the anchovy sauce and toss well. Pile on to warm plates, drizzle a little of the anchovy oil over and garnish with a few fennel fronds.

Tangy Tuna Fettuccine

Serves 6

45 ml/3 tbsp olive oil
3 garlic cloves, crushed
2 × 400 g/2 × 14 oz/2 large cans
  chopped tomatoes
30 ml/2 tbsp tomato purée (paste)
5 ml/1 tsp dried oregano
5 ml/1 tsp dried basil
5 ml/1 tsp dried thyme
5 ml/1 tsp caster (superpfine) sugar
2 × 185 g/2 × 6¹/₂ oz/2 small cans
  tuna, drained
100 g/4 oz/²/₃ cup stoned (pitted)
  green olives, sliced
450 g/1 lb fettuccine

Heat the oil in a saucepan. Add the garlic and fry (sauté) for 1 minute. Add the tomatoes, tomato purée, herbs and sugar. Simmer gently for 10 minutes until pulpy. Stir in the tuna and olives and simmer for 5 minutes. Meanwhile, cook the fettuccine according to the packet directions. Drain and pile on to serving plates. Top with the sauce and serve straight away.

Seafood Sensation

Serves 6

45 ml/3 tbsp olive oil
3 shallots, finely chopped
3 garlic cloves, crushed
1 yellow (bell) pepper, diced
1 green (bell) pepper, diced
375 ml/13 fl oz/1½ cups fish stock
2 × 400 g/2 × 14 oz/2 large cans
  chopped tomatoes
30 ml/3 tbsp tomato purée (paste)
5 ml/1 tsp caster (superfine) sugar
10 ml/2 tsp fennel seeds
1 bouquet garni sachet
175 g/6 oz monkfish, diced
175 g/6 oz/1½ cups queen scallops
175 g/6 oz/1½ cups peeled king
  prawns (jumbo shrimp)
Salt and freshly ground black
  pepper
450 g/1 lb linguini
Lemon wedges

Heat the oil in a pan. Add the shallots and garlic and fry (sauté) for 2 minutes, stirring. Add the peppers and fry for a further 1 minute. Add the stock, bring to the boil and boil rapidly for about 5 minutes until reduced by half. Add the tomatoes, tomato purée, sugar, fennel seeds and bouquet garni. Boil fairly rapidly for about 10 minutes until thick and pulpy. Add the seafood and cook for about 5 minutes until tender. Discard the bouquet garni and season to taste. Meanwhile, cook the linguini according to the packet directions. Drain and pile on to serving plates. Spoon the sauce over and serve straight away with lemon wedges.

Pasta Da Vinci

Serves 6

1 onion, finely chopped
30 ml/2 tbsp olive oil
400 g/14 oz/1 large can chopped
  tomatoes
45 ml/3 tbsp capers, chopped
175 g/6 oz/1 cup stoned (pitted)
  black olives, roughly chopped
2 × 50 g/2 × 2 oz/2 small cans
  anchovies, drained and chopped
185 g/6½ oz/1 small can tuna,
  drained
2.5 ml/½ tsp cayenne
Freshly ground black pepper
450 g/1 lb spaghettini
Chopped parsley

Fry (sauté) the onion in the oil for 2 minutes until softened but not browned. Add all the remaining ingredients except the pasta and parsley. Simmer uncovered for about 20 minutes until pulpy. Meanwhile, cook the spaghettini according to the packet directions. Drain, transfer to serving plates and spoon the sauce over. Sprinkle with the parsley before serving.

Canadian Vermicelli

Serves 4

175 g/6 oz/1¹/₂ cups smoked salmon
pieces, roughly chopped
150 ml/¹/₄ pt/²/₃ cup olive oil
2 garlic cloves, crushed
15 ml/1 tbsp capers, chopped
25 g/1 oz/¹/₄ cup chopped dill (dill
weed)
Salt and freshly ground black
pepper
25 g/1 oz/¹/₄ cup freshly grated
Parmesan cheese
350 g/12 oz vermicelli
60 ml/4 tbsp soured (dairy sour)
cream
1 small red onion, finely chopped

Blend the smoked salmon, oil, garlic,
capers, dill, a pinch of salt and a good
grinding of pepper in a bowl. Add the
cheese. Cook the vermicelli according to
the packet directions. Drain and return to
the pan. Add the salmon mixture and toss
over a gentle heat for 2-3 minutes until
piping hot. Season to taste. Pile on to warm
serving plates and top each with a spoonful
of soured cream and a little chopped onion.

Marinated Salmon with Fettuccine

Serves 4

225 g/8 oz salmon tail, skinned and
boned
1 large onion, finely chopped
30 ml/2 tbsp chopped parsley
8 basil leaves, torn into pieces
120 ml/4 fl oz/¹/₂ cup olive oil
l lemon
3 red (bell) peppers, cut into thin
strips
6 spring onions (scallions), chopped
225 g/8 oz fettuccine
Salt and freshly ground black
pepper
50 g/2 oz/1 cup toasted fresh
breadcrumbs

Cut the salmon into thin strips. Place in a
dish with the onion, parsley, basil and 90
ml/6 tbsp of the oil. Add the juice of half
the lemon and leave to marinate. Heat the
remaining oil in a frying pan (skillet). Add
the peppers and spring onions and fry
(sauté) for 3 minutes. Add the salmon mixture and continue to cook for a further 2
minutes, stirring until the fish is just
cooked. Meanwhile, cook the pasta
according to the packet directions. Drain,
rinse with boiling water, drain again and
return to the pan. Add the fish mixture and
toss well. Season to taste and add a little
more lemon juice if liked. Pile on to serving plates and garnish with the breadcrumbs.

Tagliatelle Cheri

Serves 4

225 g/8 oz tagliatelle
60 ml/4 tbsp olive oil
3 garlic cloves, crushed
2.5 ml/¹⁄₂ tsp chilli powder
10 ml/2 tsp chopped oregano
10 ml/2 tsp chopped basil
450 g/1 lb/4 cups raw peeled prawns
(shrimp), de-veined
350 g/12 oz/3 cups cherry tomatoes,
quartered
Salt and freshly ground black
pepper
25 g/1 oz/¹⁄₄ cup freshly grated
Parmesan cheese
A few fresh basil leaves
Thinly pared rind of 1 lemon, cut
into thin shreds

Cook the pasta in plenty of boiling salted water until tender. Drain, rinse with boiling water, drain again and return to the pan. Meanwhile, heat the oil in a large frying pan (skillet). Add the garlic, chilli, herbs and prawns and cook, stirring for 2 minutes. Add the tomatoes and a little salt and pepper and cook for a further 2 minutes. Add to the pasta and toss well. Sprinkle with the cheese, pile on to serving plates and garnish with a few torn basil leaves and shreds of lemon rind.

Linguini with Crab Butter

Serves 4-6

350 g/12 oz linguini
225 g/8 oz/2 cups crabmeat
175 g/6 oz/³⁄₄ cup unsalted (sweet)
butter
30 ml/2 tbsp lemon juice
30 ml/2 tbsp snipped chives
Salt and freshly ground black
pepper
Chopped flatleaf parsley
Lemon twists

Cook the linguini according to the packet directions. Drain and return to the saucepan. Meanwhile, purée the remaining ingredients except the parsley and lemon twists in a blender or food processor. Add to the hot pasta and toss over a gentle heat until well mixed. Pile on to serving plates and garnish with the parsley and lemon twists.

Spaghetti with Creamy Cockles

Serves 4-6

225 g/8 oz/2 cups cockles (not preserved in vinegar)
100 g/4 oz/¹/₂ cup unsalted (sweet) butter
4 garlic cloves, crushed
2 small onions, finely chopped
250 ml/8 fl oz/1 cup dry white wine
750 ml/1¹/₄ pts/3 cups crème fraîche
350 g/12 oz spaghetti
45 ml/3 tbsp chopped parsley
Salt and freshly ground white pepper

Wash the cockles thoroughly in several changes of water. Melt the butter in a large pan. Add the garlic and onion and fry (sauté) for 2 minutes until softened but not browned. Stir in the wine and boil rapidly for 5 minutes or until reduced by half. Add the crème fraîche and simmer for about 10-15 minutes until thick and well reduced. Meanwhile, cook the spaghetti according to the packet directions. Drain, rinse with boiling water and drain again. Stir the cockles into the sauce and simmer for 2 minutes. Add the parsley and season to taste. Pile the pasta on to serving plates and spoon the creamy sauce over.

Golden Mussel Dream

Serves 4

50 g/2 oz/¹/₄ cup unsalted (sweet) butter
3 small onions, finely chopped
600 ml/1 pt/2¹/₂ cups double (heavy) cream
15 ml/1 tbsp brandy
5 ml/1 tsp saffron powder
150 ml/¹/₄ pt/²/₃ cup strong fish stock
250 g/9 oz/1 small can mussels in brine, drained
Salt and freshly ground black pepper
350 g/12 oz capellini
Snipped chives

Melt the butter in a pan. Add the onions and fry (sauté) for 3 minutes until slightly golden. Add the cream, brandy, saffron and stock and bring to the boil. Simmer over a moderate heat until thickened and reduced by half. Stir in the mussels and a little salt and pepper. Meanwhile, cook the pasta according to the packet directions. Add to the sauce and toss gently. Pile on to serving plates and garnish with chives.

Valentine's Special

Serves 2

*25 g/1 oz/2 tbsp unsalted (sweet)
butter
2 shallots, finely chopped
250 ml/8 fl oz/1 cup dry champagne
100 g/4 oz/1 cup shelled oysters
(about 1 dozen with shells)
250 ml/8 fl oz/1 cup double (heavy)
cream
Salt and freshly ground black
pepper
175 g/6 oz vermicelli
Chopped parsley*

Melt the butter in a large frying pan (skillet). Add the shallots and fry (sauté) for 2 minutes until softened but not browned. Add the champagne and oysters. Simmer very gently for 3 minutes then remove the oysters with a draining spoon. Boil the cooking liquid for 5 minutes until reduced by half, then add the cream and boil rapidly for 10 minutes until reduced and thick. Return the oysters to the sauce and season to taste. Meanwhile, cook the vermicelli according to the packet directions. Drain, rinse with boiling water and drain again. Spoon on to warm serving plates, top with the sauce and garnish with a little parsley.

Antipasto Pasta

Serves 4-6

*6 red (bell) peppers
250 ml/8 fl oz/1 cup olive oil
4 garlic cloves, crushed
6 × 50 g/6 × 2 oz/6 small cans
anchovies, drained
350 g/12 oz/3 cups rotelli
1 bunch of parsley, chopped
Freshly ground black pepper
Thin slivers of fresh Parmesan
cheese*

Grill (broil) the peppers, turning occasionally until the skins are black. Rub off in a tea-towel (dish cloth). Cut into strips, discarding the cores. Heat the oil and fry (sauté) the garlic for 1 minute. Add the peppers and anchovies and heat, stirring, for 2-3 minutes. Meanwhile, cook the pasta according to the packet directions. Drain and return to the pan. Add the anchovy mixture to the pasta and throw in the parsley. Toss well and pile on to serving plates. Add a good grinding of pepper to each and scatter over some Parmesan slivers.

213

Vegetable Dishes

The glorious colours and flavours of vegetables with rice and pasta often make ideal main meals in their own right or dishes which can be served as starters or accompaniments to fish or meat (when they'll serve more people). The combinations are endless and the results always rewarding.

Caribbean Rice and Peas

Serves 6

225 g/8 oz/1¹/₃ cups dried red kidney beans, soaked overnight
600 ml/1 pt/2¹/₂ cups canned coconut milk
900 ml/1¹/₂ pts/3³/₄ cups water
Salt and freshly ground black pepper
1 red chilli, seeded and chopped
30 ml/2 tbsp chopped spring onion (scallion)
450 g/1 lb/2 cups long-grain rice
15 ml/1 tbsp chopped thyme

Drain the beans and place in a large pan with the coconut milk and water. Bring to the boil and boil rapidly for 10 minutes. Reduce the heat and simmer, part-covered, for about 1 hour or until the beans are tender. Add the remaining ingredients except the thyme. Bring to the boil, reduce the heat, cover and simmer for about 20 minutes or until the rice is tender. Drain off any excess liquid. Stir in the thyme and serve hot.

Asian Rice with Peas

Serves 6

75 ml/5 tbsp corn oil
2 small onions, finely sliced
2 whole cloves
5 ml/1 tsp cumin seeds
2.5 cm/1 in piece cinnamon stick
900 ml/1¹/₂ pts/3³/₄ cups water
100 g/4 oz/1 cup frozen peas
5 ml/1 tsp salt
450 g/1 lb/2 cups basmati rice, soaked and drained

Heat the oil in a large pan. Add the onions and fry quickly for about 4 minutes until browned. Add the remaining ingredients except the rice and bring to the boil. Stir in the rice, bring to the boil again, reduce the heat and simmer gently for about 15-20 minutes until the rice is tender and all the water has been absorbed. Cover tightly, turn off the heat and leave to stand for 5 minutes until the rice is fluffy. Fork through and serve at once.

Risotto with Peas

Serves 6

30 ml/2 tbsp olive oil
1 small onion, finely chopped
175 g/6 oz/1¹/₂ cups shelled peas
    (fresh or frozen)
1 tomato, skinned and chopped
450 g/1 lb/2 cups arborio or other
    risotto rice
1.2 litres/2 pints/5 cups hot chicken
    stock
Salt and freshly ground black
    pepper
25 g/1 oz/2 tbsp unsalted (sweet)
    butter
100 g/4 oz/1 cup grated Parmesan
    cheese

Heat the oil in a flameproof casserole
(Dutch oven). Add the onion and fry
(sauté) for 2 minutes. Stir in the peas,
tomato and rice and stir for 1 minute. Add
250 ml/8 fl oz/1 cup of the stock and bring
to the boil. Simmer until the stock is
absorbed. Continue adding stock, a little at
a time, until the rice is just tender and
creamy. Season to taste and stir in the butter. Serve straight away with the cheese
handed separately.

No-fuss Italian Rice and Peas

Serves 4-6

450 g/1 lb/2 cups arborio or other
    risotto rice
30 ml/2 tbsp olive oil
50 g/2 oz/¹/₄ cup butter
1 onion, finely chopped
275 g/10 oz/2¹/₂ cups fresh shelled,
    frozen or drained canned peas
250 ml/8 fl oz/1 cup beef or chicken
    stock
Salt and freshly ground black
    pepper

Cook the rice in plenty of boiling salted
water for 18 minutes until just tender.
Drain thoroughly. Meanwhile, heat the oil
and half the butter in a large frying pan
(skillet). Fry (sauté) the onion for 2 minutes until golden. Add the peas and cook
for 1 minute, stirring. Add the stock and
simmer for 4 minutes. Season with salt and
pepper. Stir in the rice and the remaining
butter, mix well, then turn into a serving
dish.

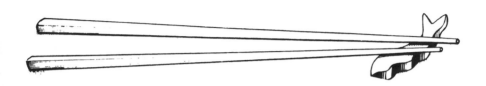

Riso con Peperone Rosso e Piselli

Serves 6
350 g/12 oz/1¹/₂ cups arborio or other risotto rice
1 red (bell) pepper, cut into thin strips
1 small onion, finely chopped
45 ml/3 tbsp olive oil
275 g/10 oz/2¹/₂ cups fresh shelled, frozen or drained canned peas
Salt and freshly ground black pepper

Cook the rice in plenty of boiling salted water for about 18 minutes until just tender. Drain thoroughly. Spoon on to a hot serving dish. Meanwhile, fry (sauté) the pepper and onion in the oil for 3 minutes, stirring. Add the peas and cook for a further 4 minutes. Spoon over the rice, season well and serve immediately.

Armenian Rice with Nuts

Serves 4
225 g/8 oz/1 cup long-grain rice
30 ml/2 tbsp raisins
100 g/4 oz/¹/₂ cup butter
450 ml/³/₄ pt/2 cups chicken stock
Salt and freshly ground black pepper
30 ml/2 tbsp pine nuts
30 ml/2 tbsp shelled pistachio nuts
30 ml/2 tbsp slivered almonds
30 ml/2 tbsp olive oil

Wash the rice in several changes of cold water. Drain well. Soak the raisins in boiling water for 10 minutes. Melt the butter in a saucepan. Add the rice and cook gently for 2 minutes. Add the stock, bring to the boil, season with salt and pepper, reduce the heat, cover and simmer for about 20 minutes until the rice is tender and has absorbed all the liquid. Meanwhile fry (sauté) the nuts in the olive oil until lightly golden. Drain the raisins and add to the cooked rice with the nuts and their oil. Cover with a clean cloth, replace the lid and leave to steam for 5 minutes. Fluff up with a fork and serve.

Riso Tricolore

Serves 4-6
350 g/12 oz/1¹/₂ cups arborio or other risotto rice
1 red (bell) pepper, cut into thin strips
40 g/1¹/₂ oz/3 tbsp unsalted (sweet) butter
30 ml/2 tbsp chopped pistachios
100 g/4 oz/1 cup chopped parsley

Cook the rice in plenty of boiling salted water for about 18 minutes until just tender. Drain thoroughly and return to the saucepan. Meanwhile, fry (sauté) the pepper in half the butter for 1 minute until slightly softened. Add to the rice with the nuts, parsley and remaining butter. Toss over a gentle heat until thoroughly combined. Serve straight away.

Turkish Pilaf

Serves 6

50 g/2 oz/¹/₄ cup butter
1 small onion, finely chopped
1 large garlic clove, chopped
275 g/10 oz/1¹/₄ cups long-grain rice
600 ml/1 pt/2¹/₂ cups chicken stock
5 ml/1 tsp caraway seeds
A little salt

Melt the butter in a saucepan. Add the onion and garlic and fry (sauté) for 2 minutes to soften slightly. Add the rice and fry for a further 2 minutes. Stir in the stock, caraway seeds and a little salt. Bring to the boil, reduce the heat, cover and simmer gently for 20 minutes or until the rice has absorbed the water. Remove from the heat, fluff up with a fork, then cover with a clean cloth and leave for 30 minutes before serving.

Cypriot Rice Pilaff with Spinach

Serves 4

450 g/1 lb spinach, well washed
750 ml/1¹/₄ pts/3 cups water
30 ml/2 tbsp corn oil
1 onion, finely chopped
Salt
225 g/8 oz/1 cup long-grain rice
Plain yoghurt

Put the spinach in a pan with the water, oil, onion and a little salt. Cook gently until the spinach is tender, about 10 minutes. Strain, reserving the liquid and finely chop the spinach. Make the liquid up to 450 ml/ ³/₄ pt/2 cups with water. Bring to the boil and add the rice. Simmer gently until the liquid is absorbed and the rice is tender.

Stir in the spinach, then remove from the heat, cover with a cloth and leave to stand for 5 minutes. Serve with yoghurt spooned over.

Stuffed Courgette Flowers

Serves 4-6

2 bunches of courgette (zucchini)
blossoms (about 24)
2 onions, finely chopped
150 ml/¹/₄ pt/²/₃ cup olive oil
15 ml/1 tbsp chopped mint
15 ml/1 tbsp chopped parsley
100 g/4 oz/¹/₂ cup long-grain rice
15 ml/1 tbsp currants (optional)
Salt and freshly ground black
pepper

Wash the flowers and gently pat dry on kitchen paper. Fry (sauté) the onion in 15 ml/1 tbsp of the oil until soft but not brown. Stir in the herbs, rice and currants, if using. Season well. Fill the flowers with the mixture and fold over the petals. Pack into a heavy-based pan. Drizzle the remaining oil over and add enough water to just cover. Bring to the boil, reduce the heat, cover and simmer very gently for about 40 minutes until rice is tender. Serve hot.

Dosas

Serves 6

350 g/12 oz/1¹/₂ cups long-grain rice
75 g/3 oz/¹/₂ cup split green lentils
2.5 ml/¹/₂ tsp fenugreek seeds
7.5 ml/1¹/₂ tsp salt
Oil for shallow-frying
Coconut chutney

Put the rice and lentils in a bowl with the fenugreek seeds. Cover with water and leave to soak for 5 hours. Purée in a blender or food processor to a smooth batter. Stir in the salt, cover tightly and leave in a warm place overnight. Heat 2.5 ml/¹/₂ tsp oil in a heavy-based frying pan (skillet). Add 2-3 spoonfuls of the batter and spread it over the base using circular movements. Add a little more oil to the pan and cook until the dosa is browning at the edges. Flip over and brown the other side. Remove from the pan and keep warm in a clean cloth while making the remaining dosas. Serve warm with coconut chutney.

Middle Eastern Mujadarra

Serves 6

350 g/12 oz/2 cups whole green
lentils, soaked
225 g/8 oz/1 cup long-grain rice
3 garlic cloves, crushed
2 onions, finely chopped
120 ml/4 fl oz/¹/₂ cup olive oil
750 ml/1¹/₄ pts/3 cups vegetable
stock or water
2.5 ml/¹/₂ tsp cumin seeds
Salt and freshly ground black
pepper
150 ml/¹/₄ pt/²/₃ cup plain yoghurt
¹/₂ cucumber, chopped
5ml/1 tsp dried mint

Drain the lentils and place in a pan with enough water to cover. Bring to the boil and simmer for about 1 hour or until tender. Meanwhile, soak the rice for 30 minutes in warm water. Drain. Fry (sauté) the garlic and onion in the oil for 3 minutes until soft and lightly golden. Add the drained rice and oil and onion mixture to the lentils. Add the stock or water and the coarsely crushed cumin seeds. Season lightly. Bring to the boil, reduce the heat, cover and simmer gently for about 15 minutes until the rice is tender and has absorbed all the water. Add more boiling water if the rice is drying out too quickly. Mix the yoghurt with the cucumber, mint and a little salt and pepper. Serve the rice mixture with the yoghurt mixture.

Italian New Year's Eve Rice

Serves 4-6

120 ml/4 fl oz/¹/₂ cup olive oil
1 small onion, finely chopped
350 g/12 oz/2 cups split lentils,
    soaked
750 ml/1¹/₄ pts/3 cups water
Salt and freshly ground black
    pepper
350 g/12 oz/1¹/₂ cups arborio or
    other risotto rice

Heat 60 ml/4 tbsp of the oil in a large pan. Fry (sauté) the onion gently for 2 minutes, stirring until softened but not browned. Drain the lentils and add with the water. Season with salt and pepper. Bring to the boil, reduce the heat, cover and simmer gently until the lentils are tender, adding more water if necessary. Meanwhile, cook the rice in plenty of boiling salted water for 18 minutes until just tender. Drain thoroughly. Pile the rice and lentils in two separate mounds on small serving plates. Drizzle the remaining olive oil over and serve very hot

Lentil Rice and Mushroom Rissoles

Serves 4-6

100 g/4 oz/²/₃ cup brown or green
    lentils, washed well
100 g/4 oz/¹/₂ cup brown rice
1 onion, finely chopped
100 g/4 oz/2 cups mushrooms, finely
    chopped
45 ml/3 tbsp olive oil
5 ml/1 tsp dried basil
2.5 ml/¹/₂ tsp chilli powder
Salt and freshly ground black
    pepper
75 g/3 oz/1¹/₂ cups breadcrumbs
1 egg, beaten
Oil for shallow-frying
Tomato sauce (see Spaghetti al
    Pomodoro page 257) or a jar of
    passata, heated through
Plain yoghurt

Put the lentils and rice in a saucepan and cover with water. Bring to the boil, reduce the heat and simmer for about 1 hour or until pulpy, adding a little more water if necessary to prevent sticking. If there is any liquid left when they are tender, boil rapidly until it evaporates. Meanwhile, fry (sauté) the onion and mushrooms in the olive oil for 2 minutes, stirring. Stir in the cooked lentils and rice, basil, chilli powder, a little salt and lots of pepper. Mix in the breadcrumbs and egg to bind. Shape into 16 round 'cakes' using floured hands. Fry in hot oil until golden brown on each side. Drain on kitchen paper and serve hot with tomato sauce or hot passata and a swirl of yoghurt.

Arroz Blanco

Serves 4-6
1 onion, finely chopped
30 ml/2 tbsp sunflower oil
225 g/8 oz/1 cup long-grain rice
¹/₂ red (bell) pepper, cut into thin
  strips
450 ml/³/₄ pt/2 cups boiling water
Salt

Fry (sauté) the onion in the oil until soft but not brown. Stir in the rice and the pepper and cook for 2 minutes. Stir in the boiling water and a little salt. Bring to the boil again, reduce the heat, cover and simmer gently for about 15 minutes until the rice is tender and has absorbed the liquid. Fluff up with a fork and serve hot with chicken or meat dishes.

Saffron Pilau

Serves 4
350 g/12 oz/1¹/₂ cups basmati rice
100 g/4 oz/¹/₂ cup butter
250 ml/8 fl oz/1 cup plain yoghurt
¹/₂ cinnamon stick, broken into
  small pieces
2 cardamom pods, split at one side
6 cloves
30 ml/2 tbsp currants
15 ml/1 tbsp chopped pistachio nuts
15 ml/1 tbsp chopped cashew nuts
15 ml/1 tbsp caster (superfine) sugar
10 ml/2 tsp salt
15 ml/1 tbsp ground cumin
500 ml/18 fl oz/2¹/₄ cups boiling
  water
15 ml/1 tbsp saffron powder

Wash and drain the rice thoroughly. Place in a casserole (Dutch oven) with the remaining ingredients and mix well.

Cover tightly and cook in the oven at 200°C/400°F/gas mark 6 for 10 minutes. Reduce the heat to 150°C/300°F/gas mark 2 and cook for a further 40 minutes or until the rice is tender and has absorbed all the liquid. Fluff up with a fork and serve hot.

Mexican Rice

Serves 4
25 g/1 oz/2 tbsp butter
2 garlic cloves, crushed
1 red (bell) pepper, chopped
1 green (bell) pepper, diced
1 onion, finely chopped
225 g/8 oz/1 cup long-grain rice
4 tomatoes, skinned, seeded and
  chopped
450 ml/³/₄ pt/2 cups vegetable stock
  or water
Salt and freshly ground black
  pepper
12 stuffed olives

Melt the butter. Stir in the garlic, peppers and onion and fry (sauté) for 2 minutes. Add the rice and fry, stirring, until turning golden. Stir in the tomatoes, stock or water and a little salt and pepper. Bring to the boil, reduce the heat and simmer uncovered over as low a heat as possible until the liquid is absorbed and the rice is tender. Fluff up with a fork. Pile into a serving dish and garnish with the olives.

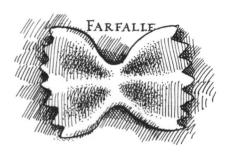

FARFALLE

Scented Pea Pilau

Serves 6
350 g/12 oz/1¹/₂ cups basmati rice
50 g/2 oz/¹/₄ cup butter
1 garlic clove, crushed
225 g/8 oz/2 cups frozen peas
2 bay leaves
5 ml/1 tsp ground cardamom
750 ml/1¹/₄ pts/3 cups water
15 ml/1 tbsp salt
150 ml/¹/₄ pt/²/₃ cup plain yoghurt

Wash and drain the rice. Heat the butter in a flameproof casserole (Dutch oven) and fry (sauté) the garlic, rice, peas, bay leaves and cardamom gently for 5 minutes over a moderate heat. Add the water and salt. Bring to the boil, cover and cook in the oven at 150°C/300°F/gas mark 2 for 40 minutes or until the rice is tender and has absorbed all the liquid. Remove the bay leaves, fluff up with a fork and serve with a little yoghurt spooned over.

Indian Spiced Rice

Serves 6
450 g/1 lb/2 cups basmati rice
900 ml/1¹/₂ pts/4 cups chicken or
  vegetable stock
60 ml/4 tbsp sunflower oil
2 cardamom pods, lightly crushed
2.5 cm/1 in piece cinnamon stick
5 whole cloves
5 ml/1 tsp black peppercorns
5 ml/1 tsp cumin seeds
5 ml/1 tsp black mustard seeds
5 ml/1 tsp salt

Wash the rice then leave it to soak for 30 minutes in the stock. Heat the oil in a nonstick saucepan. Add the spices and fry (sauté) for 1 minute until the mustard seeds begin to pop. Add the rice and stock and season with salt. Bring to the boil, reduce the heat to as low as possible, cover tightly with a lid (or foil and a lid if it is not tight fitting) and cook for 25 minutes without uncovering. Remove the lid, fluff up with a fork and serve straight away.

South American Okra Pilaf

Serves 4
4 streaky bacon rashers (slices),
  rinded
225 g/8 oz okra, thickly sliced
600 ml/1 pt/2¹/₂ cups water
5 ml/1 tsp salt
Freshly ground black pepper
225 g/8 oz/1 cup long-grain rice

Fry (sauté) the bacon in a large frying pan (skillet) until crisp. Remove and crumble the bacon and reserve. Fry the okra in the bacon fat, stirring over a moderate heat for about 5 minutes or until golden. Add the water and remaining ingredients. Stir well and bring to the boil. Cover, reduce the heat and simmer gently for 20 minutes or until the rice is tender and has absorbed all the liquid. Stir lightly then sprinkle with the bacon and serve straight from the pan.

Rice with Garlic and Pecans

Serves 4-6

225 g/8 oz/1 cup long-grain rice·
2 chicken stock cubes
1 lemon, halved
30 ml/2 tbsp chopped parsley
2 garlic cloves
25 g/1 oz/¹/₄ cup shelled pecans
50 g/2 oz/¹/₂ cup grated Parmesan
  cheese
45 ml/3 tbsp olive oil
Salt and freshly ground black
  pepper

Cook the rice in plenty of boiling salted water to which the stock cubes and lemon have been added until tender. Drain, and discard the lemon. Return to the saucepan. Meanwhile, pound or purée in a blender the parsley, garlic and nuts. Work in the cheese, then the oil a little at a time until a smooth paste is formed. Tip into the hot rice and toss gently with two forks. Season to taste. When glistening and well mixed, pile into a warm serving dish and serve as an accompaniment to meat casseroles.

Curried Fried Rice with Leeks

Serves 6

225 g/8 oz/1 cup brown basmati rice
Salt
1 kg/2¹/₄ lb leeks, sliced
50 g/2 oz/¹/₄ cup unsalted (sweet)
  butter
5 ml/1 tsp curry powder
Freshly ground black pepper
25 g/1 oz/¹/₄ cup toasted flaked
  almonds

Cook the rice in plenty of boiling salted water for about 25 minutes or until tender. Drain, rinse with boiling water and drain again. Cook the leeks in boiling, lightly salted water for 5 minutes, drain. Melt the butter in a large frying pan (skillet) and fry (sauté) the leeks for 8-10 minutes until cooked and lightly golden. Add the cooked rice and toss over a gentle heat. Sprinkle over the curry powder and lots of black pepper. Toss over the heat for 4 minutes until well blended and piping hot. Serve sprinkled with the almonds.

Pyrenees Rice

Serves 4

175 g/6 oz/³/₄ cup long-grain rice
1 onion, thinly sliced
1 green (bell) pepper, cut into thin
  strips
25 g/1 oz/2 tbsp unsalted (sweet) butter
400g/14 oz/1 large can chopped
  tomatoes
Salt and freshly ground black pepper
5 ml/1 tsp light brown sugar
l bay leaf
8 stuffed olives, sliced
50 g/2 oz/¹/₂ cup grated Parmesan
  cheese

Cook the rice in plenty of boiling salted water for 8 minutes until almost tender, drain. Meanwhile fry (sauté) the onion and pepper in the butter in a large saucepan for 2 minutes. Cover and cook gently for 5 minutes until soft. Stir in the tomatoes, a little salt and pepper, the sugar and bay leaf. Bring to the boil. Stir in the rice, reduce the heat and simmer for 15 minutes, stirring frequently, until all the tomato juice has been absorbed and the rice is tender. Discard the bay leaf, stir in the olives and fluff up with a fork. Serve sprinkled with the Parmesan cheese.

Tomato Rice with Basil

Serves 4

1 red (bell) pepper, quartered
1 yellow (bell) pepper, quartered
Olive oil
1 small onion, finely chopped
450 g/1 lb ripe tomatoes, skinned,
*   seeded and chopped*
225 g/8 oz/1 cup arborio or other
*   risotto rice*
900 ml/1¹/₂ pts/3³/₄ cups vegetable
*   stock*
1 small onion, finely chopped
225 g/8 oz/1 cup arborio or other
*   risotto rice*
6 basil leaves, chopped
60 ml/4 tbsp freshly grated
*   Parmesan cheese*

Lay the peppers, shiny side up, in a roasting tin (pan), lined with foil. Drizzle with olive oil and bake at 180°C/350°F/gas mark 4 for about 12 minutes until softening. Cool slightly then peel off the outer skins. Heat 60 ml/4 tbsp olive oil in a flameproof casserole (Dutch oven). Add the onion and fry (sauté) for 2 minutes. Stir in the tomatoes and rice and cook for 1 minute. Add 250 ml/8 fl oz/1 cup of the stock. Bring to the boil and simmer until it is absorbed. Add more stock and continue until the rice is just tender (about 15 minutes). Stir in the basil leaves, pile on to a serving dish and lay the roasted peppers on top. Serve with the Parmesan cheese.

White Rice with Tomato Sauce

Serves 4-6

30 ml/2 tbsp olive oil
1 onion, finely chopped
1 carrot, finely chopped
2 × 400 g/2 × 14 oz/2 large cans
*   chopped tomatoes*
Salt and freshly ground black
*   pepper*
2.5 ml/¹/₂ tsp dried oregano
350 g/12 oz/1¹/₂ cups arborio or
*   other risotto rice*

Heat the oil in a frying pan (skillet). Add the onion and carrot and fry (sauté) for 2 minutes, stirring. Add the tomatoes and season with salt and pepper. Stir in the oregano. Simmer for about 15 minutes until pulpy and the oil floats to the surface. Meanwhile, cook the rice in plenty of boiling salted water for 18 minutes. Drain thoroughly. Spoon on to warm serving plates and spoon the hot sauce over. Serve straight away.

Asparagus Arborio

Serves 4

45 ml/3 tbsp olive oil
1 onion, finely chopped
350 g/12 oz/1¹/₂ cups arborio or
  other risotto rice
900 ml/1¹/₂ pts/3³/₄ cups chicken
  stock
1 bunch of asparagus, trimmed and
  cut into 2.5 cm/1 in pieces
40 g/1¹/₂ oz/3 tbsp unsalted (sweet)
  butter
Salt and freshly ground black
  pepper
Freshly grated Parmesan cheese

Heat the oil in a flameproof casserole (Dutch oven). Add the onion and fry (sauté) for 2 minutes. Stir in the rice and cook for 1 minute. Add 2 ladlefuls of the stock, bring to the boil and simmer until it is absorbed. Add more stock and continue to cook in the same way. After 10 minutes, add the asparagus and the remaining stock. Simmer for 10 minutes until the rice is creamy and the asparagus is tender. Stir in the butter and season to taste. Pile on to a serving dish and dust with Parmesan cheese before serving.

Green Sweet Spiced Rice

Serves 6

350 g/12 oz/1¹/₂ cups arborio or
  other risotto rice
450 g/1 lb spinach
30 ml/2 tbsp olive oil
40 g/1¹/₂ oz/3 tbsp unsalted (sweet)
  butter
1 large garlic clove
Salt and freshly ground black
  pepper
1.5 ml/¹/₄ tsp ground nutmeg
1.5 ml/¹/₄ tsp ground mace
45 ml/3 tbsp freshly grated
  Parmesan cheese

Cook the rice in plenty of boiling salted water for 18 minutes until just tender. Drain thoroughly and return to the saucepan. Meanwhile, wash the spinach in several changes of cold water. Chop and cook in a saucepan with no extra water for 3 minutes. Drain. Heat the oil and half the butter in a large pan. Add the garlic and lightly cooked spinach and fry (sauté), stirring for 4 minutes. Remove and discard the garlic. Stir the remaining butter into the hot rice and add the spinach, a little salt and pepper and the spices. Toss gently and serve sprinkled with the Parmesan.

Saffron Rice with Peppers

Serves 6

1 large green (bell) pepper
1 large red (bell) pepper
1 large yellow (bell) pepper
1 onion, finely chopped
60 ml/4 tbsp olive oil
450 g/1 lb/2 cups arborio or other
  risotto rice
1.2 litres/2 pts/5 cups hot chicken
  stock
1.5 ml/¹/₄ tsp saffron powder
Salt and freshly ground black
  pepper

Spear a pepper on a skewer and hold over a gas flame, turning until blackened and charred. Repeat with the remaining peppers. Or grill (broil), turning in the same way. Rub off the charred skins in a clean tea towel (dish cloth). Halve, remove the seeds and cut into thin strips. Fry (sauté) the onion in the oil for 2 minutes in a flameproof casserole (Dutch oven). Stir in the rice and cook for 1 minute. Add the peppers and 250 ml/8 fl oz/1 cup of the stock. Stir in the saffron. Bring to the boil and simmer until the stock has been absorbed. Continue adding stock until the rice is tender and creamy (about 15-20 minutes). Season to taste and serve hot.

Country-style Vegetable Risotto

Serves 4-6

45 ml/3 tbsp olive oil
1 onion, finely chopped
1 carrot, finely chopped
2 celery sticks, finely chopped
3 courgettes (zucchini), finely
  chopped
225 g/8 oz/2 cups shelled fresh or
  frozen peas
450 g/1 lb/2 cups arborio or other
  risotto rice
1.2 litres/2 pts/5 cups hot vegetable
  or chicken stock
25 g/1 oz/2 tbsp unsalted (sweet)
  butter
100 g/4 oz/1 cup freshly grated
  Parmesan cheese

Heat the oil in a flameproof casserole (Dutch oven). Add the prepared vegetables and fry (sauté), stirring, for 2 minutes. Add the rice and cook for 1 minute. Gradually add the stock, a little at a time, simmering in between until it is absorbed, and the rice is just tender but still has some texture (about 15 minutes). Remove from the heat and stir in the butter and cheese. Serve straight away.

Crafty Stuffed Cabbage Leaves

Serves 4

8 large outer cabbage leaves
430 g/15¹/₂ oz/1 large can ratatouille
60 ml/4 tbsp cooked long-grain rice
300 ml/¹/₂ pt/1¹/₄ cups vegetable stock
45 ml/3 tbsp passata (sieved tomatoes)
Salt and freshly ground black pepper
Grated Cheddar cheese

Cut away the thick central base stalk from the leaves. Plunge the leaves in a pan of boiling water and cook for 3-4 minutes to soften. Drain, rinse with cold water and drain again. Mix the ratatouille with the rice. Pat the leaves dry on kitchen paper. Lay them upside-down on a board. Overlap the two points where the stalk was. Put a good spoonful of the filling on top. Fold in the sides, then roll up. Pack in a single layer in a flameproof casserole (Dutch oven). Mix the stock with the passata and pour over. Season with salt and pepper, then bring to the boil. Reduce the heat, cover and simmer for 20 minutes or until the cabbage is tender. Sprinkle with the cheese before serving.

Stuffed Rainbow Peppers

Serves 4

1 each of red, green, orange and yellow (bell) peppers, even-sized
1 onion, finely chopped
30 ml/1 tbsp sunflower oil
50 g/2 oz mushrooms, chopped
2 rashers (slices) sweetcure streaky bacon, rinded and diced
200 g/7 oz/1³/₄ cups chicken livers, trimmed and chopped
175 g/6 oz/1¹/₂ cups cooked long-grain rice
5 ml/1 tsp dried oregano
Salt and freshly ground black pepper
1 size 4 egg, beaten
75 ml/3 oz Cheddar cheese, grated
300 ml/¹/₂ pt/1¹/₄ cups passata (sieved tomatoes)

Cut the peppers in halves lengthways and remove the stalks and seeds. Plunge in boiling water for 3 minutes. Drain, rinse with cold water and drain again. Arrange in a single layer in a baking tin (pan). Fry (sauté) the onion in the oil for 2 minutes, stirring. Add the mushrooms and bacon and fry for a further 2 minutes, stirring. Add the chicken livers and cook quickly, stirring, for 1 minute. Remove from the heat. Stir in the rice, half the oregano, some salt and pepper and the egg to bind. Spoon into the peppers and sprinkle with the cheese. Pour 45 ml/3 tbsp of cold water around the peppers. Cover with foil and bake in the oven at 180°C/350°F/gas mark 4 for 35-40 minutes until tender. Meanwhile, heat the passata with the remaining oregano and a little salt and pepper. When ready to serve, spoon a pool of passata on to 4 serving plates and place two halves of peppers of different colours in the centre. Serve hot.

Monday Munch Tomatoes

Serves 6

12 large ripe tomatoes
1 onion, finely chopped
50 g/2 oz/¼ cup butter
100 g/4 oz/1 cup minced (ground)
    cooked beef, pork or lamb
100 g/4 oz/1 cup cooked long-grain
    rice
50 g/2 oz/½ cup cooked or frozen
    peas
45 ml/3 tbsp leftover gravy
10 ml/2 tsp Worcestershire sauce
2.5 ml/½ tsp dried mixed herbs
Salt and freshly ground pepper
75 g/3 oz Cheddar cheese, grated
30 ml/2 tbsp breadcrumbs or
    crushed cornflakes

Cut a slice off the top of each tomato, scoop out the seeds and discard. Chop the tomato-top slices. Fry (sauté) the onion in half the butter for 2 minutes until softened. Stir in the chopped tomato, meat, rice, peas, gravy, Worcestershire sauce, herbs and a little salt and pepper. Pack into the tomatoes. Grease a shallow ovenproof dish with the remaining butter and arrange the tomatoes in it. Mix the cheese and breadcrumbs together and sprinkle liberally over. Bake uncovered in the oven at 190°C/375°F/gas mark 5 for about 20 minutes until golden and piping hot.

Spiced Mushroom Pilaf

Serves 4

1 large onion, finely chopped
1 garlic clove, crushed
30 ml/2 tbsp olive oil
2.5 cm/1 in piece fresh root ginger,
    grated
5 ml/1 tsp garam masala
225 g/8 oz/2 cups basmati rice
400 ml/14 fl oz/1¾ cups vegetable
    stock
175 g/6 oz/3 cups button
    mushrooms, sliced
50 g/2 oz/⅓ cup sultanas (golden
    raisins)
30 ml/2 tbsp chopped coriander
    (cilantro)
Salt and freshly ground black
    pepper

Fry (sauté) the onion and garlic in the oil for 5 minutes, stirring until a rich golden brown (be careful not to burn them). Stir in the ginger, garam masala and the rice and cook, stirring for 1 minute. Stir in the stock and add the mushrooms and sultanas. Bring to the boil, reduce the heat, cover tightly with a lid and cook over the gentlest heat for 20 minutes. Turn off the heat and leave undisturbed for 5 minutes. Remove the lid, fork in half the coriander and a little salt and pepper to taste and serve hot, garnished with the remaining coriander.

Risotto con Funghi Porcini

Serves 4-6

40 g/1¹/₂ oz/³/₄ cup dried porcini
mushrooms
45 ml/3 tbsp olive oil
1 onion, finely chopped
450 g/1 lb/2 cups arborio or other
risotto rice
1.2 litres/2 pts/5 cups hot chicken
stock
30 ml/2 tbsp unsalted (sweet) butter
45 ml/3 tbsp freshly grated
Parmesan cheese
Salt and freshly ground black
pepper

Soak the mushrooms in boiling water for at least 30 minutes. Drain and rinse thoroughly. Squeeze dry and cut into neat pieces. Heat the oil in a flameproof casserole (Dutch oven). Add the onion and fry (sauté) for 2 minutes. Stir in the rice and cook for 1 minute. Add 250 ml/8 fl oz/ 1 cup of the stock, bring to the boil and simmer until the stock is absorbed. Repeat twice more. Add the mushrooms and continue adding stock until the rice is just tender and creamy (15 -20 minutes). Remove from the heat, stir in the butter and cheese and season to taste.

Californian Rice for Chicken

Serves 4

1 onion, finely chopped
25 g/1 oz/2 tbsp butter
175 g/6 oz/³/₄ cup long-grain rice
40 g/1¹/₂ oz/¹/₄ cup stoned (pitted)
raisins (not seedless ones)
450 ml/³/₄ pt/2 cups chicken stock
Salt and freshly ground black
pepper
50 g/2 oz/¹/₂ cup roasted, unsalted
peanuts
Chopped coriander (cilantro)

Fry (sauté) the onion in the butter in a large frying pan (skillet) for 2 minutes until soft but not brown. Stir in the rice, raisins, stock and a little salt and pepper. Bring to the boil, reduce the heat, cover and simmer gently for 15-20 minutes until the rice is tender and has absorbed all the liquid. Stir in the peanuts and fluff up with a fork. Sprinkle with coriander and serve hot straight from the pan with roast or grilled chicken.

Piquant Broccoli Casserole

Serves 6

350 g/12 oz/1¹/₂ cups long-grain rice
350 g/12 oz broccoli, cut into florets
1 onion, finely chopped
2 celery sticks, finely chopped
1 small green (bell) pepper, finely chopped
25 g/1 oz/2 tbsp butter
298 g/10¹/₂ oz/1 can condensed cream of mushroom soup
100 g/4 oz/¹/₂ cup Cheddar cheese spread
Salt and freshly ground black pepper
Tabasco sauce
50 g/2 oz Cheddar cheese, grated

Cook the rice in plenty of boiling salted water for 15 minutes until just tender. Add the broccoli half-way through cooking. Drain, rinse with boiling water and drain again. Turn into a casserole (Dutch oven). Mix together the remaining ingredients except the grated cheese and pour over. Sprinkle with the grated cheese and bake at 180°C/350°F/gas mark 4 for about 30 minutes until piping hot and golden brown.

Risotto alla Milanese

Serves 4

30 ml/2 tbsp olive oil
1 small onion, finely chopped
450 g/1 lb/2 cups arborio or other risotto rice
1.5 ml/¹/₄ tsp saffron powder
1.2 litres/2 pts/5 cups hot chicken stock
Salt and freshly ground black pepper
30 ml/2 tbsp unsalted (sweet) butter
60 ml/4 tbsp freshly grated Parmesan cheese

Heat the oil in a flameproof casserole (Dutch oven). Add the onion and fry (sauté) for 3 minutes until soft and lightly golden. Stir in the rice and cook for 1 minute. Add the saffron and 250 ml/8 fl oz/1 cup of the stock. Bring to the boil, stirring. Reduce the heat and simmer until the stock is absorbed then add another portion of stock. Continue in this way until the rice is just tender (15-20 minutes), using as much of the stock as necessary. Season to taste. Stir in the butter and Parmesan cheese and serve straight away.

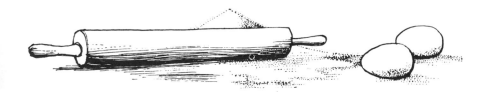

Crispy Vegetable Rolls

Makes 24

100 g/4 oz/1 cup Brussels sprouts,
  shredded
1 onion, finely chopped
1 large carrot, grated
1 celery stick, finely chopped
50 g/2 oz/¹⁄₂ cup cooked long-grain
  rice
30 ml/2 tbsp soy sauce
5 ml/1 tsp light brown sugar
15 ml/1 tbsp sherry
1.5 ml/¹⁄₄ tsp ground ginger
Salt and freshly ground black
  pepper
375 g/13 oz frozen ready-rolled puff
  pastry sheet, thawed
Beaten egg
Oil for deep-frying

Mix the vegetables and rice in a bowl. Add
the soy sauce, sugar, sherry, ginger and a
little salt and pepper and mix well. Cut the
pastry into 24 equal pieces by cutting in
half lengthways, then each half into 12
'squares'. Mix the filling well again and
divide it among the centres of the squares.
Brush the edges with egg. Fold in the
sides, then roll up to form small sausage
shapes. Deep-fry in hot oil, a few at a time,
until golden and crisp. Drain on kitchen
paper and serve hot.

Stuffed Cucumber Boats

Serves 6

3 large cucumbers
175 g/6 oz/³⁄₄ cup long-grain rice
1 onion, finely chopped
100 g/4 oz/¹⁄₂ cup butter
225 g/8 oz/4 cups button
  mushrooms, thinly sliced
4 slices Westphalian ham, chopped
6 stoned (pitted) black olives,
  chopped
2.5 ml/¹⁄₂ tsp dried oregano
2 eggs, beaten
Salt and freshly ground black
  pepper
15 ml/1 tbsp chopped parsley
Grated Fontina or Cheddar cheese

Cut the cucumbers in halves crossways
then each half in half lengthways. Scoop
out the seeds and discard. Boil the cucumber 'boats' in salted water for 10 minutes.
Drain and keep warm. Meanwhile, cook
the rice in plenty of boiling salted water for
10 minutes or until tender. Drain, rinse
with boiling water and drain again. Fry
(sauté) the onion in half the butter for 2
minutes until softened but not browned.
Add the mushrooms, ham and olives and
cook, stirring, for 2 minutes. Stir in the
rice, the oregano and half the remaining
butter. Heat through. Heat the remaining
butter in a large frying pan (skillet) and
make an omelette with the eggs, seasoned
lightly with salt and pepper. Chop up and
add to the rice. Spoon the rice mixture into
the boats then arrange them in a starburst
pattern on a large serving plate. Pile any
remaining mixture into the centre. Sprinkle
with the parsley and serve straight away
with the grated cheese handed separately.

Mexican White Rice with Onion

Serves 4

45 ml/3 tbsp corn oil
2 large onions, sliced
2 garlic cloves, crushed
350 g/12 oz/1¹/₂ cups long-grain rice
750 ml/1¹/₄ pts/3 cups chicken stock
1 green chilli, seeded and chopped
Salt and freshly ground black
    pepper
15 ml/1 tbsp chopped parsley

Heat the oil in a pan. Add the onions and garlic and fry (sauté) for 4 minutes until lightly golden, stirring all the time. Add the rice and fry for a further 1 minute. Stir in the stock with the chilli and seasoning to taste. Bring to the boil, reduce the heat, cover and simmer gently for 20 minutes. Turn off the heat and leave undisturbed for 5 minutes. Remove the lid, fluff up with a fork and serve hot garnished with the parsley.

Mexican Guacamole Rice

Serves 4

Prepare as for Mexican White Rice with Onion but add 2 ripe avocados, diced and tossed in the grated rind and juice of 1 lime, just before serving.

Curried Spring Onion Rice

Serves 4

25 g/1 oz/2 tbsp butter
1 bunch of spring onions (scallions),
    chopped
1 small onion, chopped
10 ml/2 tsp curry powder
5 ml/1 tsp paprika
225 g/8 oz/1 cup basmati rice
450 ml/³/₄ pt/2 cups vegetable stock
Salt and freshly ground black
    pepper

Melt the butter in a flameproof casserole (Dutch oven). Add the spring onions and onion and fry (sauté) for 4 minutes, stirring until lightly golden. Add the remaining ingredients. Bring to the boil, cover tightly, reduce the heat and cook gently, stirring occasionally for 25-30 minutes. Fluff up with a fork and serve.

Fruity Curried Rice

Serves 4

Prepare as for Curried Spring Onion Rice but add 100 g/4 oz/²/₃ cup chopped dried fruit salad before cooking.

231

Indian Saffron Pilau Rice

Serves 4

350 g/12 oz/1¹/₂ cups basmati rice
100 g/4 oz/¹/₂ cup unsalted (sweet)
  butter, melted
250 ml/8 fl oz/1 cup plain yoghurt
4 small pieces cinnamon stick
2 cardamoms, split along one side
4 whole cloves
30 ml/2 tbsp sultanas (golden
  raisins)
15 ml/1 tbsp chopped pistachio nuts
15 ml/1 tbsp chopped almonds
15 ml/1 tbsp caster (superfine) sugar
10 ml/2 tsp salt
15 ml/1 tbsp ground cumin
500 ml/18 fl oz/2¹/₄ cups water
15 ml/1 tbsp saffron powder

Wash and drain the rice thoroughly. Place in a saucepan with all the remaining ingredients. Stir well. Cover and cook in the oven at 200°C/400°F/gas mark 6 for 10 minutes. Reduce the heat to 150°C/300°F/gas mark 2 and cook for a further 40 minutes or until the rice is tender and has absorbed all the liquid. Fluff up with a fork and serve.

Yellow Spicy Rice

Serves 4

Prepare as for Indian Saffron Pilau Rice but add a small green chilli, seeded and chopped, to the rice mixture and substitute turmeric for the saffron.

Vegetable Curry with Sultana Rice

Serves 4

50 g/2 oz/¹/₄ cup butter
2 onions, chopped
15 ml/1 tbsp curry paste
15 ml/1 tbsp tomato purée (paste)
15 ml/1 tbsp mango chutney
5 ml/1 tsp lemon juice
2 × 425 g/2 × 15 oz/2 large cans
  cream of vegetable soup
1 kg/2¹/₄ lb/5 cups frozen mixed
  vegetables
225 g/8 oz/1 cup basmati rice
15 ml/1 tbsp flaked almonds
50 g/2 oz/¹/₃ cup sultanas (golden
  raisins)
4 hard-boiled (hard-cooked) eggs,
  quartered

Melt half the butter in a saucepan. Add half the onion and fry (sauté) for 3 minutes, stirring. Add the curry paste and fry for 1 minute. Stir in the tomato purée, chutney, lemon juice, cans of soup and the vegetables. Cover and simmer gently for 10-15 minutes or until the vegetables are tender. Meanwhile, cook the rice in plenty of boiling salted water until just tender. Drain, rinse with boiling water and drain again. Melt the remaining butter in the rice saucepan. Stir in the remaining onion and fry for 3 minutes until golden. Add the nuts and sultanas and fry for 1 minute. Stir in the rice, toss well, garnish with the hard-boiled egg and serve with the curry.

Country Brown Rice Casserole

Serves 4
600 ml/1 pt/2¹/₂ cups vegetable stock
225 g/8 oz/1 cup brown rice
1 onion, chopped
225 g/8 oz/4 cups button mushrooms, quartered
425 g/15 oz/1 large can flageolet beans, drained
350g/12 oz/1 large can Mexican sweetcorn (corn with bell peppers), drained
Salt and freshly ground black pepper
298 g/10¹/₂ oz/1 can condensed cream of mushroom soup
278 g/10 oz/1 can asparagus, drained
100 g/4 oz Cheddar cheese, grated

Bring the stock to the boil in a flameproof casserole (Dutch oven). Add the rice and onion, stir then cover and simmer for 15 minutes. Stir in the mushrooms and cook for a further 5 minutes. Stir in the flageolets, sweetcorn and a little salt and pepper. Spoon the soup on top, arrange the asparagus spears attractively over and sprinkle with the cheese. Grill (broil) until the cheese is bubbling and turning golden brown.

Indian Baked Pea Pilau

Serves 4
350g/12 oz/1¹/₂ cups basmati rice
50 g/2 oz/¹/₄ cup butter
225 g/8 oz/2 cups frozen peas
2 bay leaves
2.5 ml/¹/₂ tsp ground cardamom
750 ml/1¹/₄ pts/3 cups water
5ml/1 tsp salt

Wash and drain the rice thoroughly. Melt the butter in a flameproof casserole (Dutch oven) and fry (sauté) the rice, peas, bay leaves and cardamom for 4 minutes, stirring. Add the water and salt and bring to the boil. Cover and cook in the oven at 150°C/300°F/gas mark 2 for 40 minutes or until the rice is tender and has absorbed the liquid. Fluff up with a fork and serve.

Bean and Mushroom Pilau

Serves 4
Prepare as for Indian Baked Pea Pilau, but substitute green beans, cut into short lengths, for the peas and add 50 g/2 oz/ 1 cup sliced mushrooms.

Baked Spiced Aubergine and Mushroom Rice

Serves 4

1 large aubergine (eggplant), finely
   diced
Salt
100 g/4 oz/¹/₂ cup butter
1 small onion, sliced
50 g/2 oz mushrooms, sliced
350 g/12 oz/1¹/₂ cups basmati rice
4 bay leaves
2 small pieces cinnamon stick
750 ml/1¹/₄ pts/3 cups water
15 ml/1 tbsp salt

Put the aubergine in a colander, sprinkle
with salt and leave to stand for 30 minutes.
Rinse and dry on kitchen paper. Melt the
butter in a large flameproof casserole
(Dutch oven). Add the onion, aubergine
and mushrooms and fry (sauté), stirring,
for 5 minutes. Stir in the rice and fry for a
further 1 minute. Add 1 bay leaf, the cinnamon sticks, water and salt. Stir well and
bring to the boil. Cover and bake in the
oven at 150°C/300°F/gas mark 2 for 40
minutes or until the rice is tender and has
absorbed the liquid. Fluff up with a fork,
discard the bay leaf and cinnamon sticks
and serve garnished with the remaining
bay leaves.

Baked Spiced Courgette and Pepper Rice

Serves 4

Prepare as for Baked Spiced Aubergine
and Mushroom Rice, but substitute 2 large
courgettes (zucchini) for the aubergine (no
need to salt before cooking) and 1 diced
red (bell) pepper for the mushrooms.

Cheesey Stuffed Aubergines

Serves 4

100 g/4 oz/¹/₂ cup long-grain rice
2 large aubergines (eggplants),
   halved lengthways
1 onion, chopped
1 garlic clove, crushed
30 ml/2 tbsp olive oil
400 g/14 oz/1 large can chopped
   tomatoes
5 ml/1 tsp ground cinnamon
30 ml/2 tbsp chopped parsley
Salt and freshly ground black
   pepper
100 g/4 oz Cheddar cheese, grated

Cook the rice in plenty of boiling salted
water until tender. Drain, rinse with cold
water and drain again. Meanwhile, scoop
out most of the flesh from the aubergines
and cut into dice. Boil the cubes and the
aubergine shells in salted water for 5 minutes. Drain, rinse with cold water and drain
again. Lay the aubergine shells in a
greased baking tin (pan). Fry (sauté) the
onion and garlic in the oil for 2 minutes.
Stir in the tomatoes, rice and aubergine
dice and simmer for 5 minutes or until the
rice has absorbed most of the liquid.
Season with the cinnamon, parsley and a
little salt and pepper. Pile into the
aubergine skins. Sprinkle with the cheese
and bake at 180°C/350°F/gas mark 4 for
20 minutes or until tender and the tops are
golden brown.

Saucy Quorn-stuffed Peppers

Serves 4

175 g/6 oz/³/₄ cup long-grain rice
4 green (bell) peppers
50 g/2 oz/¹/₄ cup butter
1 bunch of spring onions (scallions),
  chopped
175 g/6 oz/1¹/₂ cups minced (ground)
  quorn
60 ml/4 tbsp tomato ketchup
  (catsup)
5 ml/1 tsp dried basil
Salt and freshly ground black pepper
25 g/1 oz/¹/₄ cup plain (all-purpose)
  flour
300 ml/¹/₂ pt/1¹/₄ cups milk
100 g/4 oz Cheddar cheese, grated

Cook the rice in plenty of boiling salted water for about 10 minutes until just tender. Drain, rinse with cold water and drain again. Cut the tops off the peppers, remove and discard the seeds, and blanch for 5 minutes in boiling water. Drain, rinse with cold water and drain again. Melt half the butter in a frying pan (skillet). Add the spring onions and fry (sauté) for 3 minutes, stirring. Add the quorn and fry for a further 2 minutes, stirring. Stir in the tomato ketchup, basil and the rice. Season to taste. Pack into the peppers and stand in a baking dish. Melt the remaining butter and whisk in the flour and milk until smooth. Bring to the boil and cook for 2 minutes, stirring all the time. Stir in 75g/3 oz/³/₄ cup of the cheese and season to taste. Pour over the peppers and sprinkle the tops with the remaining grated cheese. Bake in the oven at 180°C/350°F/gas mark 4 for 30-40 minutes until tender and golden on top. Serve hot.

Saucy Ham-stuffed Peppers

Serves 4

Prepare as for Saucy Quorn-stuffed Peppers, but substitute finely chopped or minced (ground) ham for the quorn and add 5 ml/1 tsp Dijon mustard to the mixture.

English Vegetable Risotto

Serves 4

30 ml/2 tbsp sunflower oil
1 large onion, sliced
225 g/8 oz/1 cup long-grain rice
750 ml/1¹/₄ pts/3 cups vegetable
  stock
450 g/1 lb/4 cups frozen mixed
  vegetables
1 red (bell) pepper, chopped
45 ml/3 tbsp Worcestershire sauce
Salt and freshly ground black
  pepper
Grated cheese

Heat the oil in a saucepan. Add the onion and fry (sauté) gently for 3 minutes. Add the rice and cook, stirring, for a further 1 minute. Add 600 ml/1 pt/2¹/₂ cups of the stock and bring to the boil. Simmer gently for 15 minutes or until the liquid is absorbed. Stir in the remaining ingredients except the cheese, including the rest of the stock, and simmer for a further 10 minutes or until the liquid is absorbed and the rice and vegetables are tender. Serve hot with grated cheese sprinkled over.

Vegetable Biryani

Serves 6

450 g/1 lb/2 cups basmati rice
1 litre/1³/₄ pts/4¹/₄ cups water
60 ml/4 tbsp corn oil
2.5 ml/¹/₂ tsp ground cardamom
2.5 cm/1 in piece cinnamon stick
4 whole cloves
5 ml/1 tsp black peppercorns,
* coarsely crushed*
3 onions, sliced
10 ml/2 tsp ground ginger
350 g/12 oz/3 cups chopped mixed
* vegetables*
2 vegetable stock cubes
Salt

Wash the rice in several changes of water, then soak in the measured water for 30 minutes. Heat the oil in a flameproof casserole (Dutch oven) and fry (sauté) the cardamom, cinnamon, cloves and peppercorns for 3 minutes, stirring. Add the onions and ginger and fry for a further 4 minutes until golden. Stir in the vegetables and cook for 1 minute, stirring, until coated in oil. Add the rice and soaking water, the crumbled stock cubes and a little salt. Bring to the boil, cover tightly with a lid (or use foil then the lid) and cook over the gentlest heat for 20 minutes. Turn off the heat and leave undisturbed for 5 minutes. Fluff up with a fork and serve.

Mixed Pulse Supper

Serves 4

225 g/8 oz/1 cup brown rice
1 garlic clove, crushed
1 onion, finely chopped
30 ml/2 tbsp olive oil
230 g/15¹/₂ oz/1 large can mixed
* pulses, drained*
2.5 ml/¹/₂ tsp dried oregano
100 g/4 oz Cheddar cheese, grated
2 tomatoes, sliced

Cook the rice according to the packet directions (or see page 12). Drain. Meanwhile, fry (sauté) the garlic and onion in the oil for 4 minutes until a rich golden brown, stirring. Stir in the pulses, oregano and rice and heat through, stirring. Pile into a flameproof dish, top with the cheese and garnish with the sliced tomatoes. Grill (broil) until the top is golden and bubbling. Serve hot.

Saucy Bean Supper

Serves 4

Prepare as for Mixed Pulse Supper, but top the rice and pulse mixture with a can of condensed cream of tomato soup before adding the grated cheese. Bake in the oven for 30 minutes at 190°C/375°F/gas mark 5 instead of under the grill (broiler).

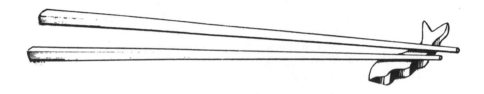

Baked Stuffed Courgettes

Serves 4

50 g/2 oz/1¼ cup long-grain rice
8 large courgettes (zucchini)
1 large onion, chopped
15 g/½ oz/1 tbsp butter
200 g/7 oz/1 small can sweetcorn (corn), drained
100 g/4 oz Gruyère (Swiss) cheese, grated
8 stoned (pitted) green olives, chopped
1 egg, beaten
Salt and freshly ground black pepper
2.5 ml/½ tsp dried thyme

Cook the rice in plenty of boiling salted water until tender. Drain, rinse with cold water and drain again. Cut the courgettes in half lengthwise and scoop out the seeds. Fry (sauté) the onion in the butter for 2 minutes, stirring. Add the rice, corn, half the cheese, the olives and egg. Stir in a little salt and pepper and the dried thyme. Spoon into the courgettes, lay in a lightly greased baking tin (pan), and sprinkle with the remaining cheese. Bake at 180°C/350°F/gas mark 4 for about 40 minutes or until the courgettes are tender and the tops are golden brown.

Baked Corn with Bacon and Mushroom Rice

Serves 4

1 onion, finely chopped
30 ml/2 tbsp olive oil
75 g/3 oz/⅓ cup butter
6 rashers (slices) streaky bacon, rinded and diced
50 g/2 oz/1 cup button mushrooms, sliced
175 g/6 oz/¾ cup long-grain rice
450 ml/¾ pt/2 cups vegetable stock
4 corn cobs, husks and silks removed
5 ml/1 tsp dried mixed herbs
Salt and freshly ground black pepper

Fry (sauté) the onion in the oil and 15 g/½ oz/1 tbsp of the butter in a flameproof casserole (Dutch oven) for 3 minutes until lightly golden. Add the bacon and mushrooms and fry for a further 2 minutes, stirring. Stir in the rice and cook for 1 minute. Add the stock, bring to the boil and simmer for 5 minutes. Stir, cover with a lid and place in the oven at 180°C/350°F/gas mark 4. Cook for 20 minutes or until the rice is tender and has absorbed all the liquid. Meanwhile, lay the corn cobs on squares of foil. Mash the remaining butter with the herbs and a little salt and pepper. Spread over the corn and wrap in the foil. Place on a baking sheet and bake on the top shelf above the rice for 15 minutes or until tender. Fluff up the rice, spoon on to serving plates and lay a cob with its herby butter on top of each.

Buttered Rice with Barbecue Beans

Serves 4

225 g/8 oz/1 cup long-grain rice
25 g/1 oz/2 tbsp unsalted (sweet)
  butter
30 ml/2 tbsp chopped parsley
30 ml/2 tbsp olive oil
1 onion, finely chopped
1 garlic clove, crushed
15 ml/1 tbsp tomato purée (paste)
15 ml/1 tbsp brown table sauce
15 ml/1 tbsp tomato ketchup
  (catsup)
1.5 ml/¹/₄ tsp made mustard
A few drops of Tabasco sauce
15 ml/1 tbsp golden (light corn)
  syrup
2 × 425 g/2 × 15 oz/2 large cans
  cannellini beans, drained
Tomato and cucumber slices

Cook the rice in plenty of boiling salted water until just tender. Drain, rinse with boiling water, drain again and return to the pan. Add the butter and parsley, toss well and keep hot. Meanwhile, heat the oil in a saucepan. Fry (sauté) the onion and garlic for 3 minutes until soft and lightly golden. Add the tomato purée, brown sauce, ketchup, mustard, Tabasco and the syrup. Heat gently, stirring until well blended. Stir in the beans and simmer gently for 10 minutes. Pile on to a bed of the buttered rice and garnish with tomato and cucumber slices.

Quick Rice with Barbecued Beans

Serves 4

225 g/8 oz/1 cup long-grain rice
25 g/1 oz/2 tbsp butter
30 ml/2 tbsp chopped parsley or
  coriander (cilantro)
2 × 400 g/2 × 14 oz/2 large cans
  barbecue baked beans
75 g/3 oz Cheddar cheese, grated

Cook the rice in plenty of boiling salted water until tender. Drain, rinse with boiling water, drain again and mix with the butter and parsley and pile on a serving dish. Heat the beans in a saucepan. Pile on to the rice and serve topped with the cheese.

Mushroom and Olive Brown Rice Risotto

Serves 4

1 large onion, thinly sliced
75 g/3 oz/¹/₃ cup butter
225 g/8 oz/1 cup brown rice
150 ml/¹/₄ pt/²/₃ cup dry white wine
600 ml/1 pt/2¹/₂ cups vegetable stock
225 g/8 oz/4 cups button
* mushrooms, sliced*
8 stoned (pitted) green olives, sliced
Salt and freshly ground black
* pepper*
15 ml/1 tbsp chopped basil
50 g/2 oz/¹/₂ cup grated Parmesan
* cheese*

Fry (sauté) the onion in the butter for 2 minutes. Stir in the rice and continue cooking over a gentle heat for 10 minutes, stirring occasionally. Stir in the wine, bring to the boil and simmer until it has been absorbed. Add a third of the stock, the mushrooms and olives and simmer gently until all the liquid has been absorbed. Repeat until all the stock is used and the rice is tender but 'nutty'. Season to taste, stir in the basil and half the cheese. Pile on to a serving dish and sprinkle the remaining cheese over.

Mixed Vegetable Curry with Tandoori Rice

Serves 6

225 g/8 oz/1 cup basmati rice
15 g/¹/₂ oz/1 tbsp unsalted (sweet)
* butter*
5-10 ml/1-2 tsp tandoori powder
3 potatoes, diced
3 carrots, diced
¹/₂ small swede, finely diced
100 g/4 oz green beans, cut into
* short lengths*
100 g/4 oz/1 cup frozen peas
30 ml/2 tbsp sunflower oil
1 large onion, chopped
15 ml/1 tbsp curry powder
Vegetable stock
¹/₂ block creamed coconut
15 ml/1 tbsp chopped coriander
* (cilantro)*
15 ml/1 tbsp tomato purée (paste)
10 ml/2 tsp mango chutney
Salt and freshly ground black pepper
Lemon wedges

Cook the rice by the absorption method (see Basmati Rice, page 12). Stir in the butter and tandoori powder. Meanwhile, boil the potato, carrot, swede, beans and peas for 4 minutes. Drain. Heat the oil in a large pan. Add the onion and fry (sauté) for 2 minutes. Add the par-boiled vegetables and cook, stirring for a further 2 minutes. Stir in the curry powder and cook for 1 minute. Add enough vegetable stock to cover, then break up the coconut and stir in with the coriander, tomato purée, mango chutney and a little salt and pepper. Bring to the boil, cover, reduce the heat and simmer for 15 minutes until tender and bathed in a rich sauce, stirring frequently. Taste and re-season if necessary. Pile the rice on to serving plates and spoon the curry over. Garnish with lemon wedges.

Monday Naan Rolls

Serves 4

100 g/4 oz/1 cup cooked long-grain rice
225 g/8 oz/2 cups diced cooked leftover vegetables
Gravy from the Sunday joint or vegetable stock
15 ml/1 tbsp curry paste
15 ml/1 tbsp tomato purée (paste)
Salt and freshly ground black pepper
15 ml/1 tbsp chopped coriander (cilantro) (optional)
4 pieces naan bread
Plain yoghurt
Desiccated (shredded) coconut

Mix the rice with the vegetables in a saucepan. Add enough gravy to moisten and stir in the curry paste and tomato purée. Season to taste and add the coriander, if using. Bring to the boil, stirring. Meanwhile, warm the naan bread. Spread the vegetable mixture over, add a little yoghurt and a sprinkling of coconut. Roll up and serve immediately.

Turkish Tomatoes

Serves 4

175 g/6 oz/³/₄ cup long-grain rice
50 g/2 oz/¹/₄ cup butter
450 g/1 lb tomatoes, skinned and chopped
2.5 ml/¹/₂ tsp caster (superfine) sugar
300 ml/¹/₂ pt/1¹/₄ cups thick plain yoghurt
Salt and freshly ground black pepper
30 ml/2 tbsp chopped mint
50 g/2 oz/¹/₂ cup pine nuts

Cook the rice in plenty of boiling salted water for 10 minutes until just tender. Drain, rinse with boiling water and drain again. Place in a warm serving dish. Melt the butter in a large pan. Add the tomatoes and cook gently, stirring for 3 minutes until soft but still with some texture. Stir in the sugar, yoghurt, a little salt and pepper and the mint and heat through. Meanwhile, dry-fry the nuts in a frying pan (skillet) until brown all over. Spoon the tomato mixture over the rice and sprinkle with the pine nuts. Serve warm.

Vegetable Kebabs with Hollandaise

Serves 4

2 courgettes (zucchini), cut into
  short lengths
8 cherry tomatoes
8 button (pearl) onions
8 button mushrooms
1 green (bell) pepper, diced
15 ml/1 tbsp olive oil
15 ml/1 tbsp cider vinegar
15 ml/1 tbsp chopped basil
Salt and freshly ground black
  pepper
225 g/8 oz/1 cup wild rice mix
2 eggs
30 ml/2 tbsp lemon juice
A pinch of cayenne
100 g/4 oz/½ cup butter, melted

Place all the vegetables in a shallow dish. Drizzle with the oil and vinegar and sprinkle on the basil and a little salt and pepper. Toss well and leave to marinate for 30 minutes. Thread on to skewers. Grill (broil) for 5-8 minutes, brushing with the marinade and turning once or twice. Meanwhile, cook the rice according to the packet directions. Drain, rinse with boiling water and drain again. Whisk the eggs in a small pan with the lemon juice and cayenne. Gradually whisk in the melted butter and cook, whisking all the time, over a gentle heat until thick. Do NOT allow to boil. Arrange the kebabs on a bed of rice and serve with the Hollandaise sauce.

German-style Kebabs

Serves 4

Prepare as for Vegetable Kebabs with Hollandaise, but thread pieces of vegetarian sausage on to the skewers in place of the mushrooms. Add 5 ml/1 tsp of German mustard to the eggs in the Hollandaise sauce.

French Peas with Rice

Serves 6

175 g/6 oz/¾ cup long-grain rice
50 g/2 oz/¼ cup butter
1 bunch of spring onions (scallions),
  chopped
1 little gem lettuce, shredded
5 ml/1 tsp caster (superfine) sugar
450 g/1 lb/4 cups frozen minted
  garden peas
Salt and freshly ground black
  pepper

Cook the rice in plenty of boiling salted water until tender. Drain, rinse with boiling water and drain again. Meanwhile, melt the butter in a pan. Add the spring onions and fry (sauté) for 2 minutes. Add the remaining ingredients and simmer gently for 10 minutes. Stir into the rice and serve hot

Italian Peas with Tomatoes and Rice

Serves 4

Prepare as for French Peas with Rice but substitute 1 head of radicchio for the little gem lettuce and add 6 quartered cherry tomatoes just before serving.

Spiced Beans and Rice

Serves 6

45 ml/3 tbsp sunflower oil
1 onion, thinly sliced
5 ml/1 tsp grated fresh root ginger
1.5 ml/¹/₄ tsp grated nutmeg
1 red chilli, seeded and chopped
175 g/6 oz/³/₄ cup basmati rice
450 g/1 lb dwarf beans, cut into
  short lengths
375 ml/13 fl oz/1¹/₂ cups chicken
  stock
Salt and freshly ground black pepper
Chopped coriander (cilantro)

Heat the oil in a flameproof casserole (Dutch oven). Add the onion and fry (sauté) for 2 minutes, stirring. Add the ginger, nutmeg, chilli and rice and stir for 1 minute. Add the beans and stock and season to taste. Bring to the boil, reduce the heat, cover and simmer over the gentlest heat for 20 minutes. Turn off the heat, leave for 5 minutes, then fluff up with a fork and serve hot garnished with coriander.

Lebanese Rice with Vermicelli

Serves 6

225 g/8 oz/1 cup long-grain rice
75 g/3 oz/¹/₃ cup butter
100 g/4 oz vermicelli, broken into
  small pieces
500 ml/17 fl oz/2¹/₄ cups chicken
  stock
Salt and freshly ground black pepper
1.5 ml/¹/₄ tsp allspice

Soak the rice for 30 minutes. Drain well. Melt the butter and fry (sauté) the vermicelli until golden brown, stirring all the

time. Stir in the rice and cook for 1 minute. Add the stock, a little salt and pepper and the allspice. Bring to the boil, reduce the heat, cover and simmer for 20 minutes until the rice and pasta are cooked and have absorbed all the stock. Press a clean cloth on top, re-cover and leave undisturbed for 10 minutes. Fluff up with a fork before serving.

Fettucci with Roasted Vegetables

Serves 4-6

2 courgettes (zucchini), cut into chunks
1 red onion, quartered
1 small aubergine (eggplant), cut
  into chunks
1 yellow (bell) pepper, quartered
1 green (bell) pepper, quartered
1 red (bell) pepper, quartered
Olive oil
10 ml/2 tsp dried oregano
Salt and freshly ground black pepper
350 g/12 oz fettucci
2 vegetable stock cubes
225 g/8 oz Mozzarella cheese, sliced
A few torn basil leaves

Place the prepared vegetables in a roasting tin (pan) and drizzle with olive oil. Sprinkle the oregano over and season well with salt and lots of black pepper. Roast in the oven at 190°C/375°F/gas mark 5 for about 30 minutes or until tender and turning golden on top. Toss a couple of times during cooking. Meanwhile, cook the fettucci in plenty of boiling water with the stock cubes added until just tender. Drain and turn into a flameproof dish. Spoon over the roasted vegetables and all the juices. Top with the cheese and place under a hot grill (broiler) until the cheese melts and bubbles. Serve straight away, sprinkled with the basil.

Spaghettini with Aubergines and Olives

Serves 4-6
1 large aubergine (eggpant), thickly
  sliced then cut into strips
Salt
30 ml/2 tbsp plain (all-purpose) flour
Freshly ground black pepper
120 ml/4 fl oz/¹/₂ cup olive oil
350 g/12 oz spaghettini
12 stoned (pitted) black olives,
  halved

Place the aubergine strips in a colander and sprinkle liberally with salt. Leave to drain for 30 minutes. Rinse well with cold water and pat dry on kitchen paper. Season the flour with a little salt and pepper and use to coat the aubergine strips. Heat half the oil in a large frying pan (skillet) and fry (sauté) the aubergine strips until crisp and golden. Meanwhile, cook the spaghettini according to the packet directions. Drain and return to the saucepan. Pour over the remaining oil and toss well. Add the aubergines and olives and lots of black pepper. Toss well over a gentle heat, then serve straight away.

Greek-style Aubergine Pie

Serves 6
175 g/6 oz/1¹/₂ cups elbow macaroni
  or rigatoni
1 large aubergine, sliced
350 g/12 oz shortcrust pastry (basic
  pie crust)
40 g/1¹/₂ oz/¹/₃ cup plain (all-purpose)
  flour
40 g/1¹/₂ oz/3 tbsp butter
300 ml/¹/₂ pt/1¹/₄ cups milk
150 ml/¹/₄ pt/²/₃ cup plain yoghurt
Salt and freshly ground black pepper
75 g/3 oz Cheddar cheese, grated
425 g/15¹/₂ oz/1 large can black-eyed
  beans, drained
50 g/2 oz Feta cheese, crumbled
6 black olives

Cook the pasta according to the packet directions. Drain. Boil the aubergine in salted water for 3-4 minutes until just tender. Drain. Roll out the pastry and use to line a shallow rectangular ovenproof dish or deep Swiss (jelly) roll tin (pan). Prick the base with a fork and crimp the edges between finger and thumb. Put the flour, butter, milk and yoghurt in a saucepan. Whisk until the flour is blended, then bring to the boil, whisking all the time, until thickened and smooth. Season to taste and stir in 50 g/ 2 oz/¹/₂ cup of the Cheddar cheese and the black-eyed beans. Stir in the pasta and spoon the mixture into the pastry-lined dish. Lay the aubergine slices on top then sprinkle with the remaining Cheddar and the Feta cheese. Decorate with the olives. Place on a baking sheet and bake in the oven at 190°C/375°F/gas mark 5 for 35-40 minutes until golden brown and bubbling. Cover loosely with foil if over-browning during cooking.

Egyptian Koushari

Serves 6

450 g/2 oz/1½ cup short-cut macaroni
45 ml/3 tbsp sunflower oil
4 large onions, sliced into rings
225 g/8 oz/1 cup long-grain rice
75 g/3 oz/1½ cup red lentils
450 ml/¾ pt/2 cups water
Salt and freshly ground black
*   pepper*
120 ml/4 fl oz/1½ cup passata (sieved
*   tomatoes)*
15 ml/1 tbsp tomato purée (paste)
45 ml/3 tbsp water
1 garlic clove, crushed
Tabasco sauce

Cook the macaroni according to the packet directions, drain. Meanwhile, heat the oil in a large pan and fry (sauté) the onions until golden brown. Remove from the pan with a draining spoon and drain on kitchen paper. Stir the rice and lentils into the oil in the pan. Cook, stirring, for 1 minute. Add the water and a little salt and pepper. Bring to the boil, reduce the heat, cover and simmer very gently for about 20 minutes until the rice and lentils are cooked. Stir in the cooked macaroni and heat through. Meanwhile, heat the passata in a pan with the tomato purée, blended with the water, and the garlic. Heat through and add Tabasco to taste. Pile the rice, lentils and pasta mixture on to a serving dish, spoon the sauce over and scatter the onions on top.

Ricotta and Spinach Lasagne

Serves 4

1 small onion, finely chopped
1 garlic clove, crushed
30 ml/2 tbsp olive oil
225 g/8 oz frozen leaf spinach
5 ml/1 tsp dried oregano
Salt and freshly ground black
*   pepper*
A pinch of grated nutmeg
100 g/4 oz Cheddar cheese, grated
350 g/12 oz/1½ cups Ricotta cheese
A knob of butter for greasing
6-8 sheets no-need-to-precook
*   lasagne*
150 ml/¼ pt/⅔ cup single (light)
*   cream*
1 egg
A little grated Parmesan cheese

Fry (sauté) the onion and garlic in half the oil for 2 minutes, stirring. Add the spinach and cook until thawed. Stir in the oregano, salt and pepper and the nutmeg. Boil rapidly until all the moisture has evaporated. Remove from the heat and cool slightly. Stir half the Cheddar into the Ricotta and stir into the spinach mixture. Put a thin layer of the spinach mixture into the base of a greased ovenproof dish. Top with a layer of lasagne. Continue layering, finishing with a layer of pasta. Beat the cream and egg together with a little salt and pepper. Stir in the remaining Cheddar. Spoon on top of the pasta and sprinkle with Parmesan. Cook in a moderately hot oven at 190°C/375°F/gas mark 5 for about 35-40 minutes until the pasta is cooked through and the top is golden brown.

Cannellini Cannelloni

Serves 4

8 cannelloni tubes
450 g/1 lb spinach
430 g/15½ oz/l large can cannellini
  beans, drained
25 g/1 oz/2 tbsp butter
1 garlic clove, crushed
25 g/1 oz/¼ cup plain (all-purpose)
  flour
200 ml/7 fl oz/scant 1 cup milk
2.5 ml/½ tsp dried mixed herbs
5 ml/1 tsp yeast extract (optional)
Salt and freshly ground black
  pepper
400 g/14 oz/1 large can chopped
  tomatoes
15 ml/1 tbsp tomato purée (paste)
50 g/2 oz Cheddar cheese, grated
50 g/2 oz/½ cup grated Parmesan
  cheese

Cook the cannelloni in plenty of boiling
salted water for about 15 minutes until tender. Drain, rinse with cold water and drain
again. (If you use no-need-to-precook
tubes omit this step.) Wash the spinach in
several changes of water, then cook without water in a non-stick, covered pan for 5
minutes until tender. Drain and finely
chop. Mash the cannellini beans and mix
with the spinach. Melt the butter in a
saucepan. Stir in the garlic and cook for 30
seconds only. Blend in the flour and milk,
bring to the boil and cook for 2 minutes,
stirring until thickened. Stir in the spinach
and bean mixture and season with the
herbs, yeast extract, if using, and salt and
pepper to taste. For ease, use a piping bag
fitted with a large plain tube (tip) and pipe
the stuffing mixture into the cannelloni
tubes, or spoon it in. Arrange in a greased
ovenproof dish. Blend the tomatoes with
the tomato purée and a little salt and pepper. Spoon over the tubes and sprinkle with
the cheeses. Bake in the oven at
180°C/350°F/gas mark 4 for 30 minutes or
until piping hot, cooked through and gold-
en on top.

Note: if using no-need-to-precook tubes,
add 30 ml/2 tbsp water to the tomato mixture and cook for 35-40 minutes.

Indonesian Tofu with Mushrooms

Serves 4

30 ml/2 tbsp peanut butter
15 ml/1 tbsp clear honey
75 ml/5 tbsp soy sauce
1 red chilli, seeded and sliced
15 ml/1 tbsp red wine vinegar
250 ml/8 fl oz/1 cup tomato juice
285 g/10 oz/1 packet tofu, cubed
175 g/6 oz flat mushrooms, sliced
30 ml/2 tbsp sunflower oil
2 red (bell) peppers, diced
175 g/6 oz/1½ cups bean sprouts
15 ml/1 tbsp roughly chopped
  coriander (cilantro) leaves
225 g/8 oz Chinese egg noodles

Mix the peanut butter with the honey, soy
sauce, chilli, vinegar and tomato juice in a
saucepan. Heat gently, stirring until melted. Remove from the heat, stir in the tofu
and mushrooms and leave to marinate for
at least 30 minutes. Heat the oil in a large
frying pan (skillet). Fry (sauté) the peppers
for 2 minutes. Add the bean sprouts,
coriander and tofu mixture. Cook, stirring,
over a high heat for 4 minutes. Meanwhile,
cook the noodles according to the packet
directions. Pile the noodles on to the sides
of 4 serving plates and spoon the tofu mixture beside them. Serve straight away.

Cashew MacBurgers

Serves 4

75 g/3 oz/³/₄ cup short-cut macaroni
50 g/2 oz/¹/₂ cup wholemeal flour
50 ml/2 fl oz/3¹/₂ tbsp sunflower oil
300 ml/¹/₂ pt/1¹/₄ cups vegetable stock
2.5 ml/¹/₂ tsp yeast extract
5 ml/1 tsp tomato purée (paste)
75 g/3 oz/³/₄ cup salted cashew nuts,
chopped
1 egg, beaten
100 g/4 oz/2 cups fresh wholemeal
breadcrumbs
Oil for shallow-frying
Tomato relish

Cook the macaroni according to the packet directions. Drain, rinse with cold water and drain again. Blend the flour and sunflower oil in a saucepan. Stir in the stock then bring to the boil, stirring. Cook for 2 minutes, stirring all the time until thick and smooth. Stir in the yeast extract, tomato purée, nuts and macaroni. When cool enough to handle, shape into 8 balls and flatten into rounds. Coat in egg then breadcrumbs and shallow-fry until golden brown on both sides. Drain on kitchen paper and serve with tomato relish.

Spicy Vegetable and Noodle Pancakes

Serves 4

100 g/4 oz/1 cup plain (all-purpose)
flour
A pinch of salt
1 egg, beaten
300 ml/¹/₂ pt/1¹/₄ cups milk
6 spring onions (scallions), chopped
30 ml/2 tbsp olive oil
1 courgette (zucchini), sliced
50 g/2 oz/1 cup button mushrooms,
sliced
100 g/4 oz/1 cup broad (lima) beans
1 green chilli, seeded and chopped
10 ml/2 tsp ground cumin
Freshly ground black pepper
400 g/14 oz/1 large can chopped
tomatoes
15 ml/1 tbsp tomato purée (paste)
100 g/4 oz quick-cook egg noodles
A little oil for frying
75 g/3 oz Cheddar cheese, grated

Sift the flour and salt into a bowl. Make a well in the centre and add the egg and half the milk. Gradually work in the flour and beat until smooth. Stir in the remaining milk. Leave to stand while making the filling. Fry (sauté) the spring onions in the oil for 1 minute. Add the courgette and mushrooms and fry for 3 minutes, stirring. Stir in the beans, chilli, cumin and a little salt and pepper and fry for 1 minute. Add the tomatoes and tomato purée and simmer for 15 minutes until thick and pulpy. Meanwhile, cook the noodles according to the packet directions. Drain and stir into the vegetable mixture. Heat a little oil in a frying pan (skillet). Add enough of the batter to swirl over base of the pan. Cook until golden underneath then flip over and brown the other side. Slide out of the pan and keep warm while making 7 more pancakes. Grease a flameproof dish. Divide the filling among the pancakes and roll up. Place in the dish and cover with the cheese. Place under a hot grill (broiler) to brown.

Chilli Bean Lasagne

Serves 4-6

1 onion, chopped
1 garlic clove, crushed
100 g/4 oz mushrooms, sliced
1 small red (bell) pepper, chopped
30 ml/2 tbsp olive oil
400 g/14 oz/1 large can chopped
*   tomatoes*
1 red chilli, seeded and chopped
5 ml/1 tsp ground cumin
5 ml/1 tsp dried oregano
Salt and freshly ground black
*   pepper*
2 × 425 g/2 × 15 oz/2 large cans red
*   kidney beans, drained*
6 sheets no-need-to-precook lasagne
*   verdi*
225 g/8 oz/1 cup curd (smooth
*   cottage) cheese*
150 ml/¹/₄ pt/²/₃ cup plain yoghurt
75 g/3 oz Cheddar cheese, grated
A few black olives, stoned (pitted)
*   and chopped*

Fry (sauté) the onion, garlic, mushrooms and pepper in the oil for 2 minutes, stirring. Add the tomatoes, chilli, cumin, oregano and some salt and pepper. Bring to the boil, reduce the heat and simmer for 10 minutes. Stir in the kidney beans. Put a thin layer of the bean mixture in the base of a 1.5 litre/2¹/₂ pts/6 cups shallow ovenproof dish. Cover with a layer of lasagne sheets. Top with half the remaining bean mixture. Mix the curd cheese and yoghurt together and spread half of it over the bean mixture. Repeat the layers. Sprinkle with the grated cheese and bake in the oven at 190°C/375°F/gas mark 5 for about 40 minutes or until golden brown and the lasagne feels soft when a knife is inserted down through the centre. Sprinkle the olives on top and serve hot.

247

Farmhouse Vegetable Lasagne

Serves 4-6

75 g/3 oz/¹/₃ cup butter
3 leeks, sliced
3 celery sticks, chopped
1 parsnip, finely diced
2 carrots, finely diced
400 g/14 oz/1 large can chopped
  tomatoes with herbs
15 ml/1 tbsp tomato purée (paste)
10 ml/2 tsp Worcestershire sauce
50 g/2 oz/1 cup button mushrooms,
  sliced
Salt and freshly ground black
  pepper
5 ml/1 tsp clear honey
20 g/³/₄ oz/3 tbsp plain (all-purpose)
  flour
150 ml/¹/₄ pt/²/₃ cup milk
150 ml/¹/₄ pt/²/₃ cup single (light)
  cream
2.5 ml/¹/₂ tsp dried mixed herbs
100 g/4 oz/¹/₂ cup cottage cheese
  with chives
6-8 sheets no-need-to-precook
  lasagne verdi
75 g/3 oz Cheddar cheese, grated

Melt 25 g/1 oz/2 tbsp of the butter and fry (sauté) the prepared vegetables, stirring, for 4 minutes until slightly softened and turning golden. Stir in the tomatoes, tomato purée, Worcestershire sauce, mushrooms, a little salt and pepper and the honey. Bring to the boil, reduce the heat and simmer gently for 20 minutes until the vegetables are tender and the mixture has formed a thick sauce. Meanwhile, whisk the flour with a little of the milk in a saucepan. Stir in the remaining milk and the cream and add the remaining butter and the herbs. Bring to the boil and cook for 2 minutes, whisking all the time until thickened and smooth. Season to taste. Put a thin layer of the vegetable mixture in the base of a greased, shallow, ovenproof dish. Top with a layer of lasagne sheets. Spoon over half the vegetable mixture, then half the cottage cheese, then a layer of lasagne sheets. Repeat the layers, then spoon the white sauce over. Sprinkle with the Cheddar cheese and bake at 190°C/375°F/gas mark 5 for 35-40 minutes until golden brown and the lasagne feels tender when a knife is inserted down through the centre.

Tagliatelle with Walnuts and Broccoli

Serves 4-6

225 g/8 oz green tagliatelle (verdi)
175 g/6 oz broccoli, cut into tiny
  florets
120 ml/4 fl oz/¹/₂ cup mayonnaise
120 ml/4 fl oz/¹/₂ cup fromage frais
25 g/1 oz/¹/₄ cup coarsely chopped
  walnuts
5 ml/1 tsp Dijon mustard
Salt and freshly ground black
  pepper

Cook the tagliatelle in plenty of boiling salted water for 10 minutes or until just tender. Add the broccoli for the last 4 minutes of cooking time. Drain and return to the pan. Mix the mayonnaise with the fromage frais, walnuts and mustard. Add to the pan with a little salt and lots of black pepper. Toss lightly over a gentle heat and serve straight away.

Beany Pasta Bake

Serves 4-6

225g/8 oz/2 cups wholewheat ruote
25 g/1 oz/¹/₄ cup plain (all-purpose)
flour
300 ml/¹/₂ pt/1¹/₄ cups milk
50 g/2 oz/¹/₄ cup butter
100 g/4 oz Cheddar cheese, grated
Salt and freshly ground black pepper
2 × 425 g/2 × 15 oz/2 large cans
baked beans in tomato sauce
50 g/2 oz/1 cup button mushrooms,
thinly sliced

Cook the pasta according to the packet directions, drain. Meanwhile, whisk the flour with a little of the milk in a saucepan. Stir in the remaining milk and add half the butter. Bring to the boil and cook for 2 minutes, whisking all the time. Stir in half the cheese and season to taste. Put a layer of half the pasta in an ovenproof dish, well-greased with the remaining butter. Spoon one of the cans of beans over and sprinkle with half the mushrooms. Repeat the layers. Top with the cheese sauce and sprinkle with the remaining cheese. Bake in the oven at 200°C/400°F/gas mark 6 for about 25 minutes until bubbling and the top is golden brown.

Vegetable Fritters Tartare

Serves 4

50 g/2 oz/¹/₂ cup elbow macaroni
100 g/4 oz/1 cup frozen mixed
vegetables
100 g/4 oz/1 cup plain (all-purpose)
flour
A pinch of salt
15 g/¹/₂ oz/1 tbsp olive oil
150 ml/¹/₄ pt/²/₃ cup water
2.5 ml/¹/₂ tsp dried mixed herbs
150 ml/¹/₄ pt/²/₃ cup mayonnaise
30 ml/2 tbsp chopped capers
2.5 cm/1 in piece cucumber, finely
chopped
15 ml/1 tbsp chopped pursley
1 egg white
Oil for deep-frying

Cook the pasta according to the packet directions, adding the mixed vegetables for last 5 minutes cooking time. Drain, rinse with cold water and drain again. Meanwhile, mix the flour and salt in a bowl. Add the olive oil and beat in the water to form a smooth batter. Stir in the herbs. To make the tartare sauce, mix the mayonnaise with the capers, cucumber and parsley in a small bowl. Stir the pasta and vegetables into the batter. Whisk the egg white until stiff and fold into the batter with a metal spoon. Heat the oil to 190°C/375°F or until a cube of day-old bread browns in 30 seconds. Drop spoonfuls of the mixture into the hot oil and deep-fry until crisp and lightly golden. Do not over-cook or the pasta will go hard. Drain on kitchen paper and serve hot with the tartare sauce.

Pasta Surprise

Serves 4

225 g/8 oz/2 cups rigatoni
300 ml/¹/₂ pt/1¹/₄ cups passata (sieved tomatoes)
198 g/7 oz/1 small can sweetcorn (corn)
2.5 ml/¹/₂ tsp dried oregano
225 g/8 oz frozen chopped spinach
25 g/1 oz/¹/₄ cup plain (all-purpose) flour
300 ml/¹/₂ pt/1¹/₄ cups milk
25 g/1 oz/2 tbsp butter
100 g/4 oz Cheddar cheese, grated
Salt and freshly ground black pepper

Cook the pasta in plenty of boiling salted water, according to the packet directions, drain and return to the pan. Stir in the passata, sweetcorn and oregano and heat through. Meanwhile, cook the spinach according to the packet directions. Drain. Whisk the flour with the milk in a saucepan. Add the butter and bring to the boil, whisking all the time. Stir in half the cheese and season to taste. Put half the pasta in a 1.5 litre/2¹/₂ pt/6 cup ovenproof dish. Top with the spinach then the rest of the pasta. Pour the sauce over. Sprinkle with the remaining cheese and grill (broil) for about 5 minutes until bubbling and golden brown.

Kaleidoscope Pasta

Serves 4

225g/8 oz/1¹/₃ cups red lentils
400 g/14 oz/1 large can chopped tomatoes
200 g/7 oz/1 small can pimientos, drained and chopped
5 ml/1 tsp dried mixed herbs
15 ml/1 tbsp tomato purée (paste)
5 ml/1 tsp caster (superfine) sugar
Tabasco sauce
Salt and freshly ground black pepper
15 ml/1 tbsp chopped parsley
225 g/8 oz/2 cups multicoloured pasta shapes (mista)
Olive oil
15 ml/1 tbsp grated Parmesan cheese
15 ml/1 tbsp grated red Leicester cheese
15 ml/1 tbsp grated Mozzarella cheese

Boil the lentils in salted water for 10 minutes, drain and return to the saucepan. Add the tomatoes, pimiento, herbs, purée, sugar and a good sprinkling of Tabasco. Bring to the boil and simmer for 10 minutes until pulpy. Season to taste and stir in the parsley. Meanwhile, cook the pasta according to the packet directions. Drain and return to the saucepan. Drizzle with a little olive oil and toss. Add the lentil sauce, toss well and turn into a large flameproof dish. Sprinkle the three cheeses over and flash under a hot grill until melted and bubbling. Serve straight away.

Russian-style Lentil Warmer

Serves 4-6
1 onion, grated
1 small swede, grated
50 g/2 oz/¹/₄ cup butter
2 large cooked beetroot (red beets), grated
100 g/4 oz/²/₃ cup red lentils
750 ml/1¹/₄ pts/3 cups vegetable stock
15 ml/1 tbsp red wine vinegar
2.5 ml/¹/₂ tsp dried tarragon
Salt and freshly ground black pepper
225 g/8 oz/2 cups wholewheat ruote
150 ml/¹/₄ pt/²/₃ cup soured (dairy sour) cream
Grated mature Cheddar cheese

Fry (sauté) the onion and swede in the butter for 2 minutes, stirring. Add the remaining ingredients, except the pasta, soured cream and Cheddar, seasoning well with salt and pepper. Bring to the boil, reduce the heat and simmer uncovered for 30 minutes until the vegetables are cooked through. Meanwhile, cook the ruote according to the packet directions. Drain and add to the cooked lentil mixture. Simmer gently for 5 minutes, stirring. Pile on to warm serving plates. Top each with a spoonful of soured cream and serve with grated Cheddar.

Simple Chick Pea Goulash

Serves 4
1 onion, chopped
1 garlic clove, crushed
1 carrot, finely diced
45 ml/3 tbsp olive oil
15 ml/1 tbsp paprika
430 g/15¹/₂ oz/1 large can chick peas (garbanzos)
60 ml/4 tbsp passata (sieved tomatoes)
15 ml/1 tbsp tomato purée (paste)
2.5 ml/¹/₂ tsp dried mixed herbs
Salt and freshly ground black pepper
50 g/2 oz/¹/₂ cup frozen peas
225 g/8 oz any ribbon noodles
150 ml/¹/₄ pt/²/₃ cup soured (dairy sour) cream
A few caraway and sesame seeds

Fry (sauté) the onion, garlic and carrot in the oil for 2 minutes until softened but not browned. Add the paprika and fry for 1 minute, stirring. Add the contents of the can of chick peas (including the liquid) and the remaining ingredients except the pasta, soured cream and caraway and sesame seeds. Bring to the boil, reduce the heat and simmer gently for about 10 minutes until thickened. Meanwhile, cook the noodles according to the packet directions. Drain. Pile on to serving dishes. Spoon the goulash over and garnish with the soured cream and a sprinkling of caraway and sesame seeds.

Special Chick Pea Goulash

Serves 4-6

Prepare as for Simple Chick Pea Goulash but add a diced green (bell) pepper and a diced courgette (zucchini) with the carrot. Cook a handful of cut green beans with the noodles. Toss in olive oil seasoned with a little paprika before serving with the goulash, garnished as before.

Greek Mushroom Lunch

Serves 6

1 onion, chopped
90 ml/6 tbsp olive oil
300 ml/¹/₂ pt/1¹/₄ cups dry white wine
Salt and freshly ground black pepper
1 bouquet garni sachet
1 garlic clove, crushed
200 g/7 oz/1 small can chopped tomatoes
350 g/12 oz/6 cups button mushrooms, quartered
225 g/8 oz/2 cups short-cut macaroni
Chopped parsley

Fry (sauté) the onion in two-thirds of the oil for 3 minutes until softened but not browned. Add the remaining ingredients except the macaroni and parsley. Bring to the boil, reduce the heat and simmer for about 15 minutes until the mushrooms are cooked and the liquid is reduced and thickened. Remove the bouquet garni sachet, taste and re-season if necessary. Meanwhile cook the macaroni according to the packet directions. Drain. Add to the mushrooms and mix well. Pile into warm bowls and sprinkle with the parsley.

Snow-capped Aubergine Mountain

Serves 4

1 small aubergine (eggplant), diced
Salt
45 ml/3 tbsp olive oil
1 garlic glove, crushed
430 g/15¹/₂ oz/1 large can red kidney beans, drained
30 ml/2 tbsp tomato purée (paste)
1 sun-dried tomato, chopped
150 ml/¹/₄ pt/²/₃ cup vegetable stock
Freshly ground black pepper
15 ml/1 tbsp chopped basil
225 g/8 oz spaghetti
100 g/4 oz/¹/₂ cup Mascarpone cheese
A few basil sprigs

Sprinkle the aubergine with salt in a colander and leave for 30 minutes. Rinse thoroughly in cold water and pat dry with kitchen paper. Heat the oil in a saucepan, add the garlic and aubergine and fry (sauté), stirring for 5 minutes. Add the remaining ingredients, except the basil, spaghetti and cheese. Bring to the boil, reduce the heat and simmer gently for 15 minutes until the sauce is reduced and slightly thickened. Stir in the chopped basil. Meanwhile, cook the spaghetti according to the packet directions. Drain and pile on to warm serving plates. Spoon the aubergine sauce over and top each with a good spoonful of Mascarpone cheese. Garnish with basil sprigs and serve straight away.

Mediterranean Extravaganza

Serves 4
1 large aubergine (eggplant), diced
Salt
Olive oil
1 red onion, thinly sliced
1 garlic clove, crushed
1 yellow (bell) pepper, cut into thin
strips
2 ripe tomatoes, skinned, seeded and
chopped
A dash of anchovy essence (extract)
2.5 ml/¹/₂ tsp dried oregano
Freshly ground black pepper
150 ml/¹/₄ pt/²/₃ cup dry white wine
225 g/8 oz olive-flecked or plain
spaghetti
A few black or green olives

Place the aubergine in a colander, sprinkle with salt and leave for 30 minutes. Drain, rinse with cold water and pat dry with kitchen paper. Heat 45 ml/3 tbsp of the oil in a saucepan, add the aubergine and fry (sauté) until golden brown and tender, stirring. Remove from the pan and reserve. Add a further 15 ml/1 tbsp of oil and fry the onion and garlic for 2 minutes until slightly softened. Add the pepper, tomatoes, anchovy essence, oregano and a good grinding of pepper. Return the aubergine to the pan, cover and simmer gently for 10 minutes or until pulpy, stirring occasionally. Add the wine and simmer uncovered for about 5 minutes until well reduced. Taste and re-season if necessary. Cook the spaghetti according to the packet directions. Drain and toss in a little olive oil. Pile on to a warm serving dish, spoon the sauce over and scatter with a few olives before serving.

Devilled Mushroom Munch

Serves 4
1 onion, finely chopped
30 ml/2 tbsp olive oil
350 g/12 oz/6 cups button
mushrooms, quartered
2 tomatoes, skinned and chopped
30 ml/2 tbsp Worcestershire sauce
30 ml/2 tbsp tomato ketchup
(catsup)
4 drops of Tabasco sauce
225 g/8 oz spaghetti with
mushrooms or plain
15 ml/¹/₂ oz/1 tbsp butter
Crumbled Wensleydale or
Caerphilly cheese

Fry (sauté) the onion in the oil for 2 minutes until softened but not browned. Add the mushrooms and tomatoes and cook, stirring for 2 minutes. Add the remaining ingredients except the pasta, butter and cheese and cook gently for about 5 minutes until the mushrooms are cooked but not too soft. Meanwhile, cook the spaghetti according to the packet directions. Drain, add the butter and toss. Pile on to warm plates, spoon the mushrooms over and sprinkle with crumbled cheese.

Creamed Chanterelle Pasta

Serves 4

100 g/4 oz streaky bacon, rinded and diced
25 g/1 oz/2 tbsp butter
2 large onions, halved and sliced
450 g/1 lb chanterelles, halved
150 ml/¹/₄ pt/²/₃ cup dry white wine
150 ml/¹/₄ pt/²/₃ cup chicken stock
30 ml/2 tbsp soy sauce
Freshly ground black pepper
15 ml/1 tbsp cornflour (cornstarch)
120 ml/4 fl oz/¹/₂ cup single (light) cream
30 ml/2 tbsp chopped coriander (cilantro)
225 g/8 oz/2 cups rotelli

Fry (sauté) the bacon in the butter for 2 minutes, stirring. Add the onion and cook, stirring, for 2 minutes until softened. Add the chanterelles, wine, stock, soy sauce and a good grinding of pepper. Stir well, then bring to the boil. Reduce the heat and simmer for 10 minutes. Blend the cornflour with the cream. Stir into the mixture, bring to the boil and cook, stirring, for 2 minutes. Add half the coriander. Meanwhile, cook the rotelli according to the packet directions. Drain and turn into a warmed serving dish. Spoon the chanterelle cream over and garnish with the remaining coriander.

Quick Creamy Corn and Vegetable Lunch

Serves 4

300 g/11 oz/1 can creamed corn
200 g/7 oz/1 small can diced mixed vegetables, drained
50 g/2 oz Cheddar cheese, grated
2.5 ml/¹/₂ tsp dried mixed herbs
Freshly ground black pepper
A little milk
225 g/8 oz/1 cup farfalle
A little crisp, crumbled bacon

Empty the corn into a saucepan. Stir in the vegetables, cheese, herbs and a good grinding of pepper. Heat through, stirring all the time until piping hot. Thin slightly with a little milk if liked. Meanwhile, cook the pasta according to the packet directions, drain. Add to the corn mixture, toss well and serve with the bacon.

Sweet Potato and Cucumber Grill

Serves 4

1 large sweet potato, finely diced
1 cucumber, diced
150 ml/¹/₄ pt/²/₃ cup dry white wine
300 ml/¹/₂ pt/1¹/₄ cups milk
25 g/1 oz/¹/₄ cup plain (all-purpose)
  flour
40 g/1¹/₂ oz/3 tbsp butter
100 g/4 oz Cheddar cheese, grated
Salt and freshly ground black
  pepper
5 ml/1 tsp Dijon mustard
225 g/8 oz/1 cup wholewheat
  rigatoni
50 g/2 oz/1 cup breadcrumbs

Cook the sweet potato in boiling water until just tender, about 5 minutes depending on the size of the dice. Drain. Simmer the cucumber in the wine for 6-8 minutes until just tender. Lift out the cucumber with a draining spoon and add to the potatoes. Whisk the milk and flour together until smooth. Stir into the wine with two-thirds of the butter and bring to the boil, stirring. Simmer for 2 minutes. Stir in three-quarters of the cheese and season to taste with salt, pepper and the mustard. Gently stir in the sweet potatoes and cucumber and heat through until piping hot. Meanwhile, cook the pasta according to the packet directions, drain. Turn half into a flameproof dish. Spoon half the sweet potato mixture over. Add the remaining pasta, then the remaining sauce. Mix the remaining cheese with the breadcrumbs. Sprinkle over and dot with the remaining butter. Grill (broil) until the top is golden. Serve hot.

Ratatouille with Tagliatelle

Serves 4-6

45 ml/3 tbsp olive oil
1 small aubergine (eggplant), diced
3 courgettes (zucchini), sliced
1 onion, chopped
1 green (bell) pepper, diced
4 tomatoes, chopped
Salt and freshly ground black
  pepper
15 ml/1 tbsp tomato purée (paste)
30 ml/2 tbsp red wine
15 ml/1 tbsp chopped basil
350 g/12 oz tagliatelle
15 g/¹/₂ oz/1 tbsp butter
Grated Parmesan cheese

Put the oil in a large saucepan. Add all the vegetables. Cook, stirring, for about 5 minutes until they are beginning to soften. Add a little salt and pepper and the tomato purée blended with the wine. Cover and simmer gently, stirring occasionally for about 15 minutes until the vegetables are just tender. Stir in the basil. Meanwhile, cook the tagliatelle according to the packet directions. Drain and toss in the butter. Pile on to warmed serving plates. Spoon the ratatouille over and top with grated Parmesan cheese.

Rigatoni with Green Asparagus Hollandaise

Serves 4-6

450 g/1 lb asparagus
1 bunch of watercress
30 ml/2 tbsp chopped parsley
2 eggs
30 ml/2 tbsp lemon juice
100 g/4 oz/¹/₂ cup butter, melted
1.5 ml/¹/₄ tsp caster (superfine) sugar
Salt and white pepper
225 g/8 oz/2 cups rigatoni
Cayenne

Trim the asparagus stalks and tie the spears in a bundle. Stand the bundle in a pan of boiling, lightly salted water. Cover with a lid or foil and cook for 10 minutes. Turn off the heat and leave for 5 minutes. Drain. Cut the spears into short lengths. Meanwhile, trim off the watercress stalks and chop the leaves, reserving a few small sprigs for garnish. Mix with the parsley. Whisk the eggs in a saucepan with the lemon juice. Gradually whisk in the melted butter. Cook, whisking all the time, over a gentle heat until thickened. Do NOT allow to boil or the mixture will curdle. Season with the sugar and a little salt and pepper. Add the asparagus and allow to heat through very gently. Meanwhile, cook the rigatoni according to the packet directions. Drain. Add the asparagus sauce and toss lightly. Pile on to warm plates and sprinkle with cayenne. Garnish with the reserved watercress sprigs.

Mediterranean Courgettes

Serves 4

90 ml/6 tbsp olive oil
1 onion, chopped
1 garlic clove, crushed
6 courgettes (zucchini), sliced
4 ripe tomatoes, skinned, seeded and
  chopped
15 ml/1 tbsp tomato purée (paste)
5 ml/1 tsp caster (superfine) sugar
Salt and freshly ground black
  pepper
12 black olives, halved
350 g/12 oz linguini
Grated Parmesan cheese

Heat two-thirds of the oil in a large saucepan. Add the onion and fry (sauté) for 3 minutes until softened but not browned. Add the garlic, the courgettes and tomatoes and cook, stirring for 3 minutes until the courgettes are slightly softened. Add the tomato purée, sugar, a little salt and pepper and half the olives. Cover and simmer gently for 15 minutes. Meanwhile, cook the linguini according to the packet directions. Drain and pile on a serving dish. Spoon the courgette mixture over. Drizzle with the remaining olive oil and scatter the remaining olives over. Serve with grated Parmesan cheese.

Spaghetti al Pomodoro (Smooth Version)

Serves 4-6
45 ml/3 tbsp olive oil
2 garlic cloves, crushed
1 large onion, finely chopped
1 carrot, finely diced
1 celery stick, finely chopped (optional)
500 ml/17 fl oz/2¼ cups passata (sieved tomatoes)
5 ml/1 tsp caster (superfine) sugar
15 ml/1 tbsp chopped basil
Salt and freshly ground black pepper
350 g/12 oz spaghetti
Grated Parmesan cheese

Heat the oil in a saucepan. Add the garlic, onion, carrot and celery, if using, and cook gently, stirring for 3 minutes until the onion is softened but not browned. Add the passata and sugar, cover and simmer gently for 30 minutes. Stir in the basil and season to taste with salt and lots of pepper. Meanwhile, cook the spaghetti according to the packet directions. Drain. Pile on to a serving dish, spoon the sauce over and sprinkle with grated Parmesan cheese before serving.

Spaghetti al Pomodoro (Textured Version)

Serves 4-6
Prepare as for the smooth version but substitute 400 ml/14 oz/1 large can chopped tomatoes, 30 ml/2 tbsp tomato purée (paste) and 30 ml/2 tbsp white wine for the passata. Use chopped marjoram in place of the basil.

Spaghetti al Pomodoro con Funghi

Serves 4-6
1 quantity Spaghetti al Pomodoro (Smooth or Textured version)
100g/4 oz/2 cups button mushrooms, sliced
15 g/½ oz/1 tbsp unsalted (sweet) butter
Crisp-fried pancetta or streaky bacon, crumbled (optional)

Prepare the Spaghetti al Pomodoro. Fry (sauté) the mushrooms in the butter for 2-3 minutes until lightly golden and softened. Stir into the tomato sauce with the herbs. Garnish with the pancetta or streaky bacon, if liked.

Monday Veggie-out

Serves 4-6
1 quantity Spaghetti al Pomodoro (Smooth Version)
225 g/8 oz/2 cups diced cooked leftover vegetables (e.g. any combination of broccoli, carrots, potatoes, peas, beans)
Grated Cheddar cheese

Prepare the Spaghetti al Pomodoro. Add the vegetables half-way through simmering the tomato sauce. Pile on to the cooked spaghetti and sprinkle liberally with grated Cheddar cheese before serving.

Crunchy Cauliflower and Coriander Rigatoni

Serves 4

75 g/3 oz/¹⁄₃ cup butter
2 thick slices of bread, cubed
1 onion, chopped
1 garlic clove, crushed
5 ml/1 tsp ground cumin
2 courgettes (zucchini), diced
1 small cauliflower, cut into small florets
150 ml/¹⁄₄ pt/²⁄₃ cup double (heavy) cream
15 ml/1 tbsp chopped coriander
Salt and freshly ground black pepper
225g/8 oz/2 cups rigatoni

Melt 50 g/2 oz/¹⁄₄ cup of the butter in a frying pan (skillet) and fry (sauté) the bread cubes until crisp and golden. Drain on kitchen paper. Melt the remaining butter in a saucepan, add the onion and garlic and fry gently for 2 minutes. Add the cumin and fry for 1 minute. Add the courgettes, stir gently, then cover, reduce the heat and simmer for 5 minutes until the courgettes are just tender. Meanwhile, cook the cauliflower florets in boiling salted water for 4-5 minutes until just tender. Drain. Add the cauliflower to the courgette mixture. Stir in the cream, coriander and seasoning. Heat through. Meanwhile, cook the rigatoni according to the packet directions. Drain and return to the saucepan. Add the hot sauce and toss gently. Stir in the croûtons just before serving.

Spiced Carrot and Garlic Supreme

Serves 4

750 g/1¹⁄₂ lb carrots, chopped
30 ml/2 tbsp milk
40 g/1¹⁄₂ oz/3 tbsp butter
1 garlic clove, crushed
1.5 ml/¹⁄₄ tsp mixed (apple pie) spice
Salt and freshly ground black pepper
225 g/8 oz wholewheat spaghetti
Chopped parsley
50 g/2 oz Feta cheese, crumbled

Put the carrots in a saucepan with just enough water to cover them. Bring to the boil and cook for about 10 minutes until really tender. Drain, reserving the cooking liquid. Turn the carrots into a food processor or blender with the milk, butter and garlic. Run the machine until the mixture is smooth. Return to the saucepan. Add the mixed spice, salt and pepper to taste and enough of the cooking water to give a smooth purée. Heat through gently until piping hot. Meanwhile, cook the spaghetti according to the packet directions. Drain. Pile on to serving plates. Spoon the carrot purée over and garnish with the parsley and Feta cheese.

Milanese Spinach and Anchovy Pasta

Serves 4-6
50 g/2 oz/1 small can anchovy fillets
45 ml/3 tbsp milk
450 g/1 lb spinach
1 bunch of spring onions (scallions), chopped
45 ml/3 tbsp olive oil
25 g/1 oz/2 tbsp butter
150 ml/¹/₄ pt/²/₃ cup vegetable stock
1.5 ml/¹/₄ tsp freshly grated nutmeg
30 ml/2 tbsp crème fraîche
Freshly ground black pepper
350 g/12 oz spaghetti
25 g/1 oz Milano salami, thinly sliced and cut into strips
Grated Pecorino cheese

Soak the anchovies in the milk for 5 minutes, drain and chop. Well wash the spinach under running water. Place in a saucepan without extra water. Cover and cook gently for 4-5 minutes until really tender. Drain well then squeeze out any remaining moisture. Fry (sauté) the spring onions in the oil and butter for 5 minutes until soft. Add the anchovies and spinach and cook for a further 1 minute. Place in a blender or processor. Add the stock and run the machine until the mixture is smooth. Stir in the nutmeg and crème fraîche and season to taste with pepper. Return to the saucepan and heat through, stirring, until piping hot. Meanwhile, cook the spaghetti according to the packet directions. Drain. Pile on to a serving dish. Spoon the sauce over and top with the strips of salami. Serve with grated Pecorino cheese.

Welsh Leek and Cheese Supper

Serves 4
3 leeks, sliced
50 g/2 oz/¹/₄ cup butter
20 g/³/₄ oz/3 tbsp plain (all-purpose) flour
300 ml/¹/₂ pt/1¹/₄ cups milk
5 ml/1 tsp Dijon mustard
50 g/2 oz Cheddar cheese, grated
50 g/2 oz Caerphilly cheese, grated
Salt and freshly ground black pepper
225 g/8 oz/2 cups short-cut macaroni
Chopped parsley

Fry (sauté) the leeks in the butter for 2 minutes until they begin to soften. Reduce the heat, cover and cook gently for 10 minutes until tender. Stir in the flour and cook for 1 minute. Gradually blend in the milk. Bring to the boil and simmer for 2 minutes, stirring. Stir in the mustard, half the cheeses and salt and pepper to taste. Meanwhile, cook the macaroni according to the packet directions. Drain and add to the sauce. Mix well and turn into a flameproof dish. Top with the remaining cheeses mixed together, and grill (broil) until golden and bubbling. Garnish with parsley before serving.

Party Welsh Supper

Serves 4
Prepare as for Welsh Leek and Cheese Supper but add a diced green and red (bell) pepper to the leek when frying. Put half of the mixture in a flameproof dish. Top with a can of chopped tomatoes. Cover with the remaining leek and macaroni mixture and continue as above.

Belgian Pasta Speciality

Serves 4

225 g/8 oz/1 cup wholewheat penne
120 ml/4 fl oz/1½ cup olive oil
1 bunch of spring onions (scallions),
  chopped
2 heads chicory (Belgian endive)
200 g/7 oz/1 small can pimientos,
  drained and cut into thin strips
50 g/2 oz mushrooms, sliced
1 garlic clove, crushed
10 ml/2 tsp capers, chopped
Salt and freshly ground black
  pepper
75 g/3 oz Leerdammer or Emmental
  (Swiss) cheese, grated
Grated Parmesan cheese

Cook the pasta in plenty of boiling salted water until just tender. Drain. Meanwhile, heat half the oil in a saucepan. Add the onions and cook gently for 3 minutes, stirring. Cut out a cone-shaped core from the base of each head of chicory then shred the leaves. Add to the onions and toss for 1 minute. Add the remaining oil and all the ingredients except the cheeses and cook, stirring occasionally for about 5 minutes until the chicory is just tender. Mix in the pasta and toss well over a gentle heat. Add the Leerdammer or Emmental and toss again until just melting. Spoon on to plates and serve with grated Parmesan.

Glorious Creamy Green Pasta

Serves 4

350 g/12 oz green tagliarini (verdi)
225 g/8 oz/2 cups frozen peas
60 ml/4 tbsp olive oil
1 bunch of watercress, chopped
30 ml/2 tbsp chopped basil
120 ml/4 fl oz/1½ cup crème fraîche
Salt and freshly ground black
  pepper
Grated nutmeg

Cook the pasta according to the packet directions. Drain and return to the pan. Meanwhile, gently stew the peas in the olive oil in a covered saucepan for 4 minutes, stirring occasionally. Don't have the heat too high or you will fry (sauté) rather than stew them. Add the remaining ingredients with seasoning to taste, stir well and simmer for a further 2-3 minutes. Add to the tagliarini, toss well and serve hot.

Green Velvet Pasta

Serves 4

Prepare as for Glorious Creamy Green Pasta but substitute half the peas with broad (lima) beans and chopped marjoram for the basil. Add 30 ml/2 tbsp chopped parsley. When cooked, purée in a food processor or blender. Toss with the tagliarini and sprinkle with garlic croûtons before serving with grated Pecorino cheese.

Gnocchi Verdi

Serves 4-6
450 g/1 lb spinach
100 g/4 oz/¹/₂ cup butter
175 g/6 oz/³/₄ cup curd (smooth cottage) cheese
45 ml/3 tbsp plain flour
30 ml/2 tbsp double (heavy) cream
2 eggs, beaten
Salt and freshly ground black pepper
2.5 ml/¹/₂ tsp freshly grated nutmeg
100 g/4 oz/1 cup freshly grated Parmesan cheese
A little extra flour

Wash the spinach in several changes of water. Put in a saucepan with no extra water, cover and cook for 5 minutes. Drain, squeeze out all excess moisture then finely chop. Melt half the butter in a saucepan. Add the spinach and curd cheese and cook, stirring, for 3-4 minutes. Remove from the heat, stir in the flour, cream, eggs, some salt and pepper, the nutmeg and 25 g/1 oz/¹/₄ cup of the Parmesan cheese. Mix thoroughly, then turn the mixture into a large shallow dish and chill for 2 hours until firm. With floured hands, shape the gnocchi into small balls. Drop a few at a time into a pan of boiling water and cook until they puff up and rise to the surface. Remove with a draining spoon and arrange in a buttered flameproof dish. Melt the remaining butter and drizzle over the gnocchi. Sprinkle with the remaining cheese and grill (broil) until the top is golden brown. Serve straight away.

Potato Gnocchi

Serves 4
450 g/1 lb potatoes, cut into small pieces
Salt and freshly ground black pepper
1.5 ml/¹/₄ tsp freshly grated nutmeg
100 g/4 oz/1 cup plain (all-purpose) flour
1 egg, beaten
50 g/2 oz/¹/₄ cup butter, melted
75 g/3 oz/³/₄ cup freshly grated Parmesan cheese

Cook the potatoes in plenty of boiling salted water until tender. Drain and return to the pan for a few moments to dry out. Rub through a sieve or potato ricer into a bowl (do not blend in a processor or the mixture will go runny). Season well with salt and pepper, then mix in the nutmeg and flour. Stir in the egg and beat thoroughly until smooth. With floured hands, shape the mixture into 24 small balls. Drop into a large pan of boiling water, a few at a time, and cook for about 5 minutes or until they rise to the surface. Transfer with a draining spoon to a warm serving dish and keep warm. When all the gnocchi are cooked, drizzle with the melted butter and sprinkle with Parmesan cheese before serving.

Greek Courgette and Noodle Pannies

Serves 4

50 g/2 oz any ribbon noodles, broken
  into short lengths
2 courgettes (zucchini), grated
225 g/8 oz Feta cheese, crumbled
15 ml/1 tbsp chopped mint
Salt and freshly ground black
  pepper
45 ml/3 tbsp plain (all-purpose) flour
3 eggs, beaten
Olive oil for shallow-frying

Cook the noodles in plenty of boiling salted water until tender. Drain, rinse with cold water and drain again. Squeeze the courgettes to remove excess moisture then add to the noodles with the cheese, mint and a little salt and pepper. Stir in the flour then the eggs to form a thick batter. Heat 5 mm/¹/₄ in of oil in a large frying pan (skillet). Fry (sauté) large spoonfuls of the batter, a few at a time, until golden on the underside, turn over and cook until crisp and golden. Drain on kitchen paper and keep hot while cooking the remainder. Serve hot.

Aubergine Sandwiches

Serves 4

2 large aubergines (eggplants)
Salt
Olive oil
100 g/4 oz/¹/₂ cup Ricotta cheese
25 g/1 oz/¹/₄ cup grated Parmesan
  cheese
50 g/2 oz/¹/₄ cup unsalted (sweet)
  butter, softened
2 large tomatoes
15 ml/1 tbsp chopped basil
Salt and freshly ground black
  pepper
175 g/6 oz spaghetti
50 g/2 oz Mozzarella cheese, sliced
A few basil leaves

Cut 4 thick slices from the widest part of each aubergine (use the remainder for ratatouille, page 255). Sprinkle the slices with salt, place in a colander and leave for 30 minutes. Rinse, then pat dry on kitchen paper. Brush both sides with oil and grill (broil) for 2 minutes on each side until just tender. Meanwhile, mix the Ricotta with the Parmesan and work in the butter. Seed and chop one of the tomatoes and add to the mixture with the chopped basil and a little salt and pepper. Cook the spaghetti according to the packet directions. Drain and return to the pan. Add the butter mixture and toss over a gentle heat until well blended. Place 4 aubergine slices on oiled foil on a baking sheet. Top with the spaghetti mixture. Cover with the remaining aubergine slices then top with sliced Mozzarella, a slice of the remaining tomato and a good grinding of pepper. Bake in the oven at 230°C/450°F/gas mark 8 for 8-10 minutes until piping hot and the cheese has melted. Garnish with basil leaves and serve.

Aubergine Pesto Sandwiches

Serves 4

Prepare as for Aubergine Sandwiches but use 1 quantity of Pesto Sauce (page 60) and toss with 175 g/6 oz cooked green tagliatelle (verdi) instead of spaghetti.

Aubergine Tapenade Sandwiches

Serves 4

Prepare as for Aubergine Sandwiches but use the Tapenade recipe (page 59) and use 175 g/6 oz black spaghetti (flavoured with mushrooms) instead of plain and top the tomato garnished with half a stoned (pitted) black olive.

Peppery Spaghetti

Serves 6

450 g/1 lb spaghetti
2 red (bell) peppers
5 ml/1 tsp coarsely crushed black peppercorns
120 ml/4 fl oz/¹/₂ cup olive oil
1 red chilli, seeded and chopped
3 garlic cloves, crushed
30 ml/2 tbsp chopped parsley
15 ml/1 tbsp snipped chives
Salt

Cook the spaghetti according to the packet directions. Drain and return to the saucepan. Meanwhile, grill (broil) the peppers or hold over a gas flame on a fork, turning until the skins are blackened. Rub off the skins in a tea towel (dish cloth). Slice the peppers into thin strips, discarding the cores. Place in a saucepan with the peppercorns, oil, chilli and garlic and cook, stirring, for 3 minutes. Add to the spaghetti and toss well. Stir in the herbs and season with salt. Serve hot.

Vegetable Bolognese

Serves 4

50 g/2 oz/¹/₄ cup butter
2 garlic cloves, crushed
1 onion, finely chopped
225 g/8 oz/4 cups button mushrooms, sliced
100 g/4 oz/1 cup walnut halves
200 g/7 oz/1 small can chopped tomatoes
75 g/3 oz/¹/₂ cup tomato purée (paste)
2.5 ml/¹/₂ tsp dried oregano
Salt and freshly ground black pepper
100 g/4 oz/²/₃ cup stoned (pitted) black olives, halved
450 g/1 lb spaghetti
Grated Parmesan cheese

Melt the butter and fry (sauté) the garlic and onion for 2 minutes, stirring. Add the remaining ingredients except the spaghetti and cheese and simmer gently for 10-15 minutes. Taste and re-season if necessary. Meanwhile, cook the spaghetti according to the packet directions. Drain. Pile on to plates, top with the sauce and sprinkle with Parmesan cheese before serving.

Spicy Spinach Penne

Serves 4

175 g/6 oz/1¹/₂ cups penne
40 g/1¹/₂ oz/3 tbsp unsalted (sweet)
  butter
2.5 ml/¹/₂ tsp grated nutmeg
2 large onions, chopped
5 ml/1 tsp chilli powder
900 g/2 lb spinach, well washed and
  torn into pieces
Salt and freshly ground black
  pepper
150 ml/¹/₄ pt/²/₃ cup soured (dairy
  sour) cream

Cook the pasta according to the packet directions. Drain, rinse with boiling water, drain again and return to the pan. Add a third of the butter and the nutmeg. Toss well. Meanwhile, melt the remaining butter in a pan. Add the onions and fry (sauté) for 3 minutes, stirring until lightly golden. Stir in the chilli powder and cook for 1 minute. Add the spinach, cover and cook gently until tender, about 4-5 minutes, stirring from time to time. Season with salt and pepper. Pile on to the hot pasta and serve topped with soured cream.

Spicy Spring Greens and Tomato Rigatoni

Serves 4

Prepare as for Spicy Spinach Penne but substitute rigatoni for the penne, shredded spring greens (spring cabbage) for the spinach and cook for 10 minutes. Add 4 seeded, chopped tomatoes for the last 5 minutes cooking.

Tomato and Walnut Bake

Serves 4

100 g/4 oz/1 cup elbow macaroni
2 leeks, sliced
15 ml/1 tbsp olive oil
400 g/14 oz/1 large can chopped
  tomatoes
1 garlic clove, crushed
1 bay leaf
Salt and freshly ground black pepper
100 g/4 oz/1 cup walnuts, chopped
150 ml/¹/₄ pt/²/₃ cup plain yoghurt
2 eggs, beaten
75 g/3 oz Cheddar cheese, grated

Cook the macaroni according to the packet directions. Drain and rinse with boiling water. Meanwhile, fry (sauté) the leeks in the oil for 2 minutes to soften. Add the tomatoes, garlic, bay leaf and a little salt and pepper. Bring to the boil, reduce the heat and simmer until pulpy. Discard the bay leaf. Stir the macaroni into the sauce. Spoon half into a lightly greased ovenproof dish. Sprinkle the walnuts over then top with the remaining macaroni. Beat the yoghurt with the eggs and a little salt and pepper. Pour over and sprinkle with the cheese. Bake in the oven at 190°C/375°F/gas mark 5 for 30 minutes until the top is set and golden.

Tomato, Cashew and Chilli Bake

Serves 4

Prepare as for Tomato and Walnut Bake but substitute cashew nuts for the walnuts and add 1 red chilli, seeded and chopped, with the tomatoes.

Exotic Mushroom Medley

Serves 4

225 g/8 oz spaghetti
45 ml/3 tbsp olive oil
2 garlic cloves, finely chopped
225 g/8 oz oyster mushrooms,
  stemmed and coarsely chopped
100 g/4 oz shiitake mushrooms,
  stemmed and coarsely chopped
100 g/4 oz chanterelles, stemmed
  and coarsely chopped
Salt
5 ml/1 tsp coarsely crushed green
  peppercorns
60 ml/4 tbsp chicken stock
60 ml/4 tbsp dry Aqua Libra (or
  similar herbal drink)
Freshly grated Parmesan cheese

Cook the pasta according to the packet directions. Drain and return to the pan. Meanwhile, heat the oil in a large frying pan (skillet). Add the garlic, all the mushrooms, a little salt and the peppercorns. Cook, stirring, for 2 minutes. Add the stock and simmer for a further 1 minute. Add the Aqua Libra and simmer until reduced by half. Add to the pasta and toss well over a gentle heat until all the liquid is absorbed. Serve sprinkled with Parmesan.

Tagliatelle Primavera

Serves 4

350 g/12 oz green tagliatelle (verdi)
1 bunch of spring onions (scallions),
  cut into short lengths
2 carrots, cut into matchsticks
2 leeks, cut into matchsticks
50 g/2 oz mangetout (snow peas),
  topped and tailed
100 g/4 oz/1 cup asparagus tips
60 ml/4 tbsp dry vermouth
250 ml/8 fl oz/1 cup crème fraîche
Salt and freshly ground black
  pepper
10 ml/2 tsp chopped parsley
Paprika
Freshly grated Parmesan cheese

Cook the pasta according to the packet directions. Drain and return to the pan. Meanwhile, cook the prepared vegetables in boiling, salted water for 3 minutes. Drain. Boil the vermouth and crème fraîche for about 5 minutes until reduced by half. Add the blanched vegetables, season to taste and stir in the parsley Pour over the pasta and toss gently. Pile on to serving plates and sprinkle with paprika before serving with freshly grated Parmesan cheese.

265

Artichoke Pasta Pie

Serves 4

75 g/3 oz/³/₄ cup spaghetti, broken
 into short lengths
225 g/8 oz shortcrust pastry (basic
 pie crust)
400 g/14 oz/1 large can artichoke
 hearts, drained and quartered
100 g/4 oz Mozzarella cheese, grated
400 g/14 oz/1 large can chopped
 tomatoes, drained
40 g/1¹/₂ oz/¹/₃ cup grated Parmesan
 cheese
1 garlic clove, finely chopped
15 g/1 tbsp chopped parsley
15 ml/1 tbsp olive oil

Cook the spaghetti according to the packet
directions, drain, rinse with cold water and
drain again. Meanwhile, roll out the pastry
and use to line a 23 cm/9 in flan dish (pie
pan). Prick the base with a fork, then add
the cooked spaghetti and spread evenly.
Cover with the artichoke hearts then a
layer of Mozzarella. Top with the tomatoes, then the Parmesan cheese. Finally,
mix the garlic and parsley together, sprinkle over and drizzle with olive oil. Place on
a baking sheet and bake in the oven at
220°C/425°F/gas mark 7 for 25 minutes
until golden and cooked through.

Vegetable Speciality Pie

Serves 6

225 g/8 oz/2 cups elbow macaroni
15 ml/1 tbsp olive oil
1 small aubergine (eggplant), sliced
 and quartered
1 courgette (zucchini), sliced
1 green (bell) pepper, diced
1 leek, sliced
200 g/7 oz/1 small can Mexican
 sweetcorn (corn with bell peppers)
30 ml/2 tbsp snipped chives
5 ml/1 tsp dried oregano
15 ml/1 tbsp chopped parsley
250 g/8 fl oz/1 cup double (heavy) cream
2 eggs, beaten
75 g/3 oz Cheddar cheese, grated
225 g/8 oz puff pastry (paste)

Cook the pasta according to the packet
directions. Drain. Heat the oil and fry
(sauté) the aubergine, courgette, pepper and
leek for 3 minutes. Stir in the corn, herbs
and the macaroni. Whisk the cream with
the eggs. Pour all but 15 ml/1 tbsp into the
vegetable mixture. Stir in with the cheese.
Turn into a lightly buttered, ovenproof
rimmed dish. Roll out the pastry to 2 cm/
³/₄ in larger than the dish. Trim, then lay the
trimmings on the rim, dampened with
water. Brush the trimmings with water. Lay
the pastry on top, press well together to
seal, then knock up and flute with the back
of a knife. Make a hole in the centre to
allow steam to escape and brush with the
remaining egg and cream to glaze. Bake at
220°C/425°F/gas mark 7 for 15 minutes
then reduce the heat and cook at
180°C/350°F/gas mark 4 for a further 25
minutes or until the filling is set and the top
a rich golden brown. Cover loosely with
foil if over-browning.

Gingered Carrots and Cauliflower with Noodles

Serves 4
6 carrots, sliced diagonally
½ cauliflower, cut into tiny florets
½ bunch of spring onions (scallions),
cut into short diagonal lengths
1 garlic clove, crushed
30 ml/2 tbsp groundnut (peanut) oil
1.5 ml/¼ tsp chilli powder
15 ml/1 tbsp soy sauce
1 piece stem ginger in syrup,
chopped
10 ml/2 tsp of the ginger syrup
Salt and freshly ground black
pepper
250 g/9 oz/1 packet Chinese egg
noodles

Boil the carrots and cauliflower in salted water for 3 minutes. Drain. Fry (sauté) the spring onions and garlic in the oil in a large pan for 2 minutes, stirring. Stir in the carrots and cauliflower and cook for 1 minute, stirring. Add the remaining ingredients except the noodles and cook, stirring, for 4 minutes or until the vegetables are almost tender but still 'nutty'. Meanwhile, cook the noodles according to the packet directions. Add to the pan and toss with the vegetables. Serve hot.

Lemon and Ginger Broccoli and Parsnip Noodles

Serves 4
Prepare as for Gingered Carrots and Cauliflower with Noodles but substitute 3 parsnips for the carrots (halve lengthways before slicing), 225 g/8 oz broccoli for the cauliflower, and add the grated rind of a lemon to the mixture.

Pe-tsai Mein

Serves 4
1 Chinese leaves (stem lettuce),
thickly shredded
50 g/2 oz/¼ cup butter
150 ml/¼ pt/⅔ cup vegetable stock
1 bunch of spring onions (scallions),
cut into short lengths
1 garlic clove, crushed
4 ripe tomatoes, skinned and
chopped
15 ml/1 tbsp soy sauce
2 × 85 g/2 × 3½ oz/2 small packets
tomato-flavoured instant noodles

Stir-fry (sauté) the Chinese leaves in half the butter for 3 minutes until slightly softened. Add the stock, spring onions, garlic, tomatoes and soy sauce. Boil fairly rapidly until the Chinese leaves are just tender and bathed in sauce. Meanwhile, cook the noodles according to the packet directions. Pile on to serving plates and spoon the Chinese leaves over. Serve hot.

Conchiglie Chakchouka

Serves 4

275 g/6 oz/1¹/₂ cups multicoloured
  conchiglie
30 ml/2 tbsp olive oil
2 onions, sliced
1 green chilli, seeded and chopped
2 red (bell) peppers, sliced
2 green (bell) peppers, sliced
3 beefsteak tomatoes, skinned and
  chopped
15 ml/1 tbsp tomato purée (paste)
30 ml/2 tbsp hot water
Salt and freshly ground black
  pepper
4 eggs

Cook the pasta according to the packet
directions. Drain, rinse with boiling water
and drain again. Turn into 4 individual
ovenproof dishes. Meanwhile, heat the oil
and fry (sauté) the onions for 2 minutes
until soft but not brown. Add the chilli and
peppers and fry for a further 1 minute. Add
the tomatoes and tomato purée blended
with the hot water. Cover and simmer gently for 8 minutes. Season, then spoon over
the pasta. Make a hollow in the centre of
each and break an egg into it. Season again
and bake at 200°C/400°F/gas mark 6 for
about 15 minutes or until the eggs are set.

Tuoni e Lampo (Thunder and Lightning)

Serves 4

225 g/8 oz/2 cups spirali
1 onion, chopped
1 garlic clove, crushed
30 ml/2 tbsp olive oil
430 g/15¹/₂ oz/1 large can chick peas
  (garbanzos), drained
5 ml/1 tsp dried oregano
450 g/³/₄ pt/2 cups passata (sieved
  tomatoes)
30 ml/2 tbsp tomato purée (paste)
5 ml/1 tsp caster (superfine) sugar
Salt and freshly ground black
  pepper
10 ml/2 tsp chopped basil
75 g/3 oz/³/₄ cup grated Pecorino
  cheese
A few green stoned (pitted) olives,
  halved

Cook the pasta according to the packet
directions. Drain. Meanwhile, fry (sauté)
the onion and garlic in the oil for 3 minutes, stirring. Add the chick peas and
oregano and cook gently for a further 5
minutes. Add to the pasta and toss well.
Meanwhile, simmer the passata, tomato
purée, sugar and a little salt and pepper
gently for 10 minutes, stirring occasionally. Add the chopped basil and half the
cheese. Pile the pasta mixture on to warm
serving plates. Spoon the tomato sauce
over, sprinkle with the remaining Pecorino
cheese and garnish with the olives.

Thunderbolts

Serves 4

Prepare as for Tuoni e Lampo, but substitute a can of cannellini beans for the chick peas (garbanzos), and add a seeded and chopped red chilli.

Cheese and Tomato Cannelloni

Serves 4

2 × 400 g/2 × 14 oz/2 large cans chopped tomatoes
75 g/3 oz/1½ cups fresh breadcrumbs
100 g/4 oz Cheddar cheese, grated
15 ml/1 tbsp chopped basil
Salt and freshly ground black pepper
8 tubes no-need-to-precook cannelloni
2.5 ml/½ tsp dried mixed herbs

Drain one of the cans of tomatoes and mix with the breadcrumbs, half the cheese, the basil and a little salt and pepper. Spoon into the cannelloni tubes. Lay in a lightly greased ovenproof dish. Spoon the other can of tomatoes over, sprinkle with the mixed herbs, then the remaining grated cheese. Bake in the oven at 190°C/375°F/gas mark 5 for 35 minutes until the cannelloni is cooked through and the top is golden.

Market Garden Spaghetti Layer

Serves 4

350 g/12 oz spaghetti
2 garlic cloves, crushed
2 × 400 g/2 × 14 oz/2 large cans chopped tomatoes
2 sun-dried tomatoes, chopped
15 ml/1 tbsp chopped basil
5 ml/1 tsp caster (superfine) sugar
10 ml/2 tsp Tabasco sauce
Salt and freshly ground black pepper
100 g/4 oz Mozzarella cheese, sliced
225 g/8 oz Cheddar cheese, grated
50 g/2 oz/½ cup grated Parmesan cheese

Cook the spaghetti according to the packet directions, drain. Meanwhile, put the garlic, canned tomatoes and sun-dried tomatoes in a saucepan. Bring to the boil and cook for 5 minutes until fairly pulpy. Mix in the basil, sugar, Tabasco and a little salt and pepper to taste. Put half the spaghetti in a 20 cm/8 in square baking dish. Spoon over half the sauce, then add a layer of all the Mozzarella, then half the Cheddar and half the Parmesan. Top with the remaining spaghetti, pressing down firmly. Cover with the remaining sauce, then the remaining Cheddar and Parmesan. Bake in the oven at 200°C/400°F/gas mark 6 for 30 minutes until golden and bubbling.

Vermicelli with Tomatoes and Wine

Serves 2

30 ml/2 tbsp olive oil
4 garlic cloves, crushed
1 red onion, finely chopped
2 × 400 g/2 × 14 oz/2 large cans chopped tomatoes
325 ml/11 fl oz/1¹/₃ cups water
75 ml/5 tbsp dry white wine
50 g/2 oz/¹/₂ cup chopped basil
50 g/2 oz/¹/₂ cup chopped flatleaf parsley
5 ml/1 tsp caster (superfine) sugar
Salt and freshly ground black pepper
175 g/6 oz vermicelli
Freshly grated Parmesan cheese

Heat the oil in a flameproof casserole (Dutch oven). Add the garlic and onion and fry (sauté) for 2 minutes, stirring. Add all the remaining ingredients except the pasta and cheese. Bring to the boil, stirring. Add the pasta and simmer, stirring for 8 minutes until the pasta is cooked and bathed in sauce. Sprinkle with Parmesan and serve straight away.

Vermicelli with Mushrooms and Vermouth

Serves 2

Prepare as for Vermicelli with Tomatoes and Wine, but substitute dry white vermouth for the wine, and add 75 g/3 oz/1¹/₂ cups sliced mushrooms with the onions and garlic.

Vermicelli with Olives and Red Wine

Serves 2

Prepare as for Vermicelli with Tomatoes and Wine, but use red wine in place of white, and add 50 g/2 oz/¹/₃ cup each of halved stoned (pitted) green and halved stoned black olives with the tomatoes.

Wholewheat Spaghetti with Roasted Plum Tomatoes

Serves 4

1 kg/2¹/₄ lb ripe plum tomatoes, thickly sliced lengthways
3 garlic cloves, finely chopped
75 ml/5 tbsp olive oil
30 ml/2 tbsp chopped basil
5 ml/1 tsp caster (superfine) sugar
A few drops of Tabasco sauce
Salt and freshly ground black pepper
25 g/1 oz/¹/₄ cup freshly grated Parmesan cheese
350 g/12 oz wholewheat spaghetti
100 g/4 oz Mozzarella cheese, grated

Gently mix the tomatoes with the garlic, olive oil, basil, sugar, Tabasco, a little salt and pepper and the Parmesan cheese. Arrange the tomatoes in a single layer on a baking sheet. Bake for 30 minutes at 230°C/450°F/gas mark 8 until slightly charred at the edges. Meanwhile, cook the spaghetti according to the packet directions. Drain and return to the saucepan. Add the tomatoes, toss very gently, then serve topped with the Mozzarella and a good grinding of black pepper.

Garlicky Spaghetti with Tomatoes and Melting Cheese

Serves 4

2 onions, finely chopped
2 large garlic cloves, crushed
75 ml/5 tbsp olive oil
400 g/14 oz/1 large can chopped
tomatoes
2 sun-dried tomatoes in oil, chopped
with 5 ml/1 tsp of their oil
15 ml/1 tbsp tomato purée (paste)
2.5 ml/¹/₂ tsp caster (superfine) sugar
1 bay leaf
1 slice of lemon
Salt and freshly ground black
pepper
350 g/12 oz spaghetti
175 g/6 oz Mozzarella cheese, grated
50 g/2 oz/¹/₂ cup grated Pecorino
cheese

Fry (sauté) half of the onion with the garlic in 45 ml/3 tbsp of the olive oil for 3 minutes until softened and lightly golden. Remove from the heat and reserve. In a separate pan, heat the remaining oil and fry the remaining onion for 2 minutes until slightly softened. Add the canned and sundried tomatoes, their oil, the tomato purée, sugar, bay leaf and slice of lemon. Bring to the boil, reduce the heat and simmer gently for 15 minutes or until pulpy. Discard the bay leaf and lemon slice. Season to taste. Meanwhile, cook the spaghetti according to the packet directions. Drain and return to the pan. Add the onion and garlic in their oil and toss over a gentle heat until piping hot. Spoon into individual flameproof bowls. Top with the tomato sauce, then the Mozzarella. Flash under a hot grill (broiler) until the cheese melts. Serve sprinkled with a little grated Pecorino cheese.

Crumb-topped Broad Bean Casserole

Serves 4

175 g/8 oz/1¹/₂ cups elbow macaroni
450 g/1 lb/4 cups fresh, shelled or
frozen broad (lima) beans
4 hard-boiled (hard-cooked) eggs,
quartered
40 g/1¹/₂ oz/¹/₃ cup plain (all-purpose)
flour
450 ml/³/₄ pt/2 cups milk
50 g/2 oz/¹/₄ cup butter
1 bay leaf
50 g/2 oz/¹/₂ cup grated Parmesan
cheese
25 g/1 oz/¹/₂ cup breadcrumbs

Cook the pasta according to the packet directions. Drain, rinse with boiling water, drain again and place in a lightly greased ovenproof dish. Meanwhile, cook the beans in a little boiling, salted water until tender. Drain. Spoon half the beans over the pasta. Top with the eggs, then the remaining beans. Meanwhile, whisk the flour with a little of the milk in a saucepan until smooth. Stir in the remaining milk and add 40 g/1¹/₂ oz/3 tbsp of the butter and the bay leaf. Bring to the boil and cook for 2 minutes, whisking all the time. Season to taste and stir in 25 g/1 oz/¹/₄ cup of the Parmesan. Pour over the beans. Melt the remaining butter, stir in the breadcrumbs and remaining Parmesan. Sprinkle over the top and bake at 200°C/400°F/gas mark 6 for about 25 minutes or until golden and bubbling.

Runner Bean and Bacon Casserole

Serves 4

Prepare as for Crumb-topped Broad Bean Casserole, but substitute sliced runner beans for the broad (lima) beans and add 100 g/4 oz/1 cup crisp, crumbled bacon to the crumb topping.

Sicilian Pasta with Plenty

Serves 4

75 ml/5 tbsp olive oil
1 large onion, sliced
1 garlic clove, crushed
450 g/1 lb courgettes (zucchini), sliced
1 aubergine (eggplant), quartered and sliced
1 green (bell) pepper, sliced
100 g/4 oz/²/₃ cup stoned (pitted) black olives
25 g/1 oz/¹/₂ can anchovy fillets, chopped
5 ml/1 tsp chopped capers
10 ml/2 tsp chopped marjoram
15 ml/1 tbsp chopped parsley
450 g/1 lb pappardelle
Salt and freshly ground black pepper
50 g/2 oz/¹/₂ cup grated Parmesan cheese

Heat the oil in a large pan. Add the prepared vegetables and fry (sauté), stirring for 4 minutes. Add the olives, anchovies, capers and herbs. Reduce the heat, cover and cook gently for 15 minutes. Meanwhile, cook the pappardelle according to the packet directions. Drain and return to the pan. Add the vegetable mixture and toss well. Season to taste, then serve with the cheese sprinkled over.

Cheese, Egg, and Cream Based Dishes

The following recipes have cheese, egg or cream - or all three - as their main ingredient. Many are quite rich and are good served with a crisp mixed leaf salad and some warm crusty bread - perhaps ciabatta flavoured with olives, mushrooms or sun-dried tomatoes. Others make good accompaniments to plain grilled meat or fish.

Italian-style Savoury Rice Cake

Serves 4
450 ml/³/₄ pt/2 cups milk
Salt and freshly ground black pepper
225 g/8 oz/1 cup arborio or other risotto rice
25 g/1 oz/2 tbsp unsalted (sweet) butter
75 g/5 tbsp freshly grated Parmesan cheese
4 size 1 eggs, separated
Chopped parsley

Bring the milk to the boil with a pinch of salt and pepper. Add the rice, cover and simmer gently for 15 minutes or until the milk is absorbed and the rice is just tender. Remove from the heat and stir in half the butter, the cheese and the egg yolks. Mix thoroughly, taste and re-season. Use the remaining butter to grease a 1.5 litre/2¹/₂ pt/ 6 cup soufflé dish. Whisk the egg whites until stiff and fold into the rice with a metal spoon. Turn into the prepared dish and bake in the oven at 180°C/350°F/gas mark 4 for about 30 minutes until golden and just set. Loosen the edge of the cake and turn out on to a serving plate. Garnish with parsley and serve straight away.

Risotto Bianco

Serves 4-6
75 g/3 oz/¹/₃ cup unsalted (sweet) butter
15 ml/1 tbsp olive oil
1 onion, finely chopped
1 garlic clove, crushed
225 g/8 oz/1 cup arborio or other risotto rice
900 ml/1¹/₂ pts/3³/₄ cups hot chicken stock
Salt and freshly ground black pepper
100 g/4 oz/1 cup grated Pecorino cheese

Heat 50 g/2 oz/¹/₄ cup of the butter in a large saucepan with the oil. Add the onion and garlic and fry (saute) for 3 minutes until softened and lightly golden. Stir in the rice and cook, stirring, for 1 minute until glistening with the oil and butter. Add a third of the stock. Bring to the boil, reduce the heat, cover and simmer until the stock has been absorbed. Gradually stir in the remaining stock, bring to the boil, reduce the heat, re-cover and simmer gently for about 15 minutes until all the stock has been absorbed and the rice is creamy. Boil rapidly, if necessary, to evaporate any remaining stock. Season well with salt and lots of pepper. Spoon into a warm serving dish and sprinkle with the Pecorino cheese before serving.

Risotto Bianco di Napoli

Serves 4

Prepare as for Risotto Bianco but stir in 100 g/4 oz/1 cup grated Mozzarella cheese just before serving and garnish with green olives. Omit the Pecorino cheese if preferred.

Risotto al Forno

Serves 4

60 ml/4 tbsp olive oil
1 small onion, finely chopped
450 g/1 lb/2 cups arborio or other risotto rice
1.2 litres/2 pts/5 cups beef, veal or chicken stock
Salt and freshly ground black pepper
15 g/¹/₂ oz/1 tbsp unsalted (sweet) butter
1 quantity tomato sauce (see Spaghetti al Pomodoro, textured version, page 257)

Heat the oil in a flameproof casserole (Dutch oven). Add the onion and fry (sauté) for 2 minutes. Stir in the rice and cook for 1 minute. Stir in the stock, season well and bring to the boil. Cover tightly and bake in the oven at 180°C/350°F/gas mark 4 for 1 hour. Stir in the butter and re-season if necessary. Serve with the tomato sauce.

Milk Risotto

Serves 4

1.2 litres/2 pts/5 cups milk
450 g/1 lb/2 cups arborio or other risotto rice
5 ml/1 tsp salt
30 ml/2 tbsp unsalted (sweet) butter
50 g/2 oz/¹/₂ cup freshly grated Parmesan cheese

Put the milk in a heavy-based saucepan. Add the rice and salt. Bring to the boil, reduce the heat and simmer gently for 15-20 minutes until the rice is just tender and has absorbed the milk. Stir from time to time. Stir in the butter and cheese and serve straight away.

Rich and Creamy Risotto

Serves 4

15 g/¹/₂ oz/1 tbsp unsalted (sweet) butter
1 small onion, finely chopped
100 g/4 oz/1 cup pancetta or unsmoked streaky bacon, finely diced
450 g/1 lb/2 cups arborio or other risotto rice
1.2 litres/2 pts/5 cups hot chicken stock
120 ml/4 fl oz/¹/₂ cup double (heavy) cream
Salt and freshly ground black pepper
100 g/4 oz/1 cup freshly grated Parmesan cheese

Heat the butter in a flameproof casserole (Dutch oven). Add the onion and pancetta and fry (sauté) for 3 minutes until the onion is golden and the pancetta has lost its pink colour. Stir in the rice and cook for 1 minute. Blend in 2 ladlefuls of the stock and simmer until it has been absorbed. Repeat, adding a little stock at a time until the rice is just tender (about 15 to 20 minutes). Stir in the cream, season to taste and add the Parmesan. Serve straight away.

Risotto with Cheese, Garlic and Parsley

Serves 4
45 ml/3 tbsp olive oil
3 garlic cloves, finely chopped
450 g/1 lb/2 cups arborio or other risotto rice
1.2 litres/2 pts/5 cups hot chicken or vegetable stock
100 g/4 oz/1 cup chopped parsley
75 g/5 tbsp grated Parmesan cheese
Salt and freshly ground black pepper

Heat the oil in a heavy-based saucepan. Add the garlic and fry (sauté) gently for 1 minute. Stir in the rice and cook for 1 minute. Add 250 ml/8 fl oz/1 cup of the stock and simmer until it has been absorbed. Repeat the process until the rice is just tender and the risotto creamy. Stir in the parsley, cheese and salt and pepper to taste. Serve hot.

Risotto with Cheese and Mixed Herbs

Serves 4
Prepare as for Risotto with Cheese, Garlic and Parsley but use just 1 garlic clove and add 15 ml/1 tbsp each chopped thyme, oregano and basil with the parsley.

Creamed Baked Rice with Cheese

Serves 4-6
450 g/1 lb/2 cups arborio or other risotto rice
225 g/8 oz Fontina cheese, thinly sliced
25 g/1 oz/2 tbsp unsalted (sweet) butter
Salt and freshly ground black pepper
60 ml/4 tbsp double (heavy) cream
100 g/4 oz/1 cup grated Parmesan cheese

Cook the rice in plenty of boiling salted water for about 15 minutes until almost tender. Drain thoroughly. Spread half the rice in a shallow ovenproof dish. Cover with half the Fontina cheese, dot with butter and season lightly. Drizzle over half the cream. Repeat the layers and sprinkle with the Parmesan. Bake at 180°C/350°F/gas mark 4 for about 20 minutes until golden on top. Serve straight away

Riso Caldo al Pressemolo

Serves 6

450 g/1 lb/2 cups arborio or other
  risotto rice
15 g/¹/₂ oz/1 tbsp unsalted (sweet)
  butter
30 ml/2 tbsp olive oil
50 g/2 oz/¹/₂ cup chopped parsley
1 large garlic clove
100 g/4 oz/1 cup grated Parmesan
  cheese

Cook the rice in plenty of boiling salted water for 16-18 minutes until just tender. Drain thoroughly and turn into a hot serving dish. Meanwhile, heat the butter and oil in a large frying pan (skillet). Add the parsley and garlic and fry (sauté) for 2 minutes until the garlic begins to brown. Discard the garlic. Pour the sauce over the rice and toss well. Sprinkle the Parmesan cheese over and serve straight away.

Parmesan Rice with Basil

Serves 4

30 ml/2 tbsp olive oil
1 onion, finely chopped
225 g/8 oz/1 cup arborio or other
  risotto rice
600 ml/1 pt/2¹/₂ cups hot chicken or
  vegetable stock
50 g/2 oz/¹/₂ cup chopped basil
50 g/2 oz/¹/₂ cup chopped parsley
Salt and freshly ground black
  pepper
200 g/4 oz/1 cup freshly grated
  Parmesan cheese

Heat the oil in a large saucepan. Add the onion and fry (sauté) for 2 minutes. Stir in the rice and cook for 1 minute. Add 2 ladlefuls of the stock and simmer until it is absorbed. Repeat until the rice is tender and creamy (about 15-20 minutes). Stir in the herbs, some salt and pepper and half the cheese. Pile on to a warm serving dish and top with the remaining cheese.

Extra-fragrant Parmesan Rice

Serves 4

Prepare as for Parmesan Rice with Basil but add a large sprig of rosemary and a bay leaf to the rice while cooking. Discard before serving.

Riso Pecorino Romano

Serves 4

350 g/12 oz/1¹/₂ cups arborio or
  other risotto rice
6 basil leaves, finely chopped
75 ml/5 tbsp grated Pecorino cheese
30 ml/2 tbsp olive oil
Salt and freshly ground black
  pepper
3 tomatoes, cut in wedges
Parsley sprigs

Cook the rice in plenty of boiling salted water for 18 minutes. Drain well and return to the saucepan. Stir in the basil, cheese and oil. Season to taste. Press into a large mould (mold). Immediately turn out on to a hot serving plate, garnish with the tomatoes and parsley and serve straight away.

Gorgonzola Speciality

Serves 4-6

50 g/2 oz/¹/₄ cup unsalted (sweet)
  butter
175 g/6 oz Gorgonzola, crumbled
120 ml/4 fl oz/¹/₂ cup crème fraîche
120 ml/4 fl oz/¹/₂ cup white wine
Salt and freshly ground black
  pepper
350 g/12 oz/1¹/₂ cups arborio or
  other risotto rice
A few basil leaves

Melt the butter in a saucepan. Stir in the cheese until melted. Blend in the crème fraîche and wine. Heat for about 1¹/₂ minutes, stirring until thickened. Season lightly. Cook the rice in plenty of boiling, salted water until just tender, about 18 minutes. Drain and turn into a hot serving dish. Re-heat the sauce if necessary and drizzle over the rice. Garnish with basil leaves and serve very hot.

Dolcelatte and Watercress Mould

Serves 4-6

Prepare as for Gorgonzola Speciality but substitute Dolcelatte for the Gorgonzola. After cooking the rice, add 1 chopped bunch of watercress. Press the rice mixture into a hot mould (mold). Immediately turn out on to a serving dish and pour the sauce over.

Cheese Timbale

Serves 4

350 g/12 oz/1¹/₂ cups arborio or
  other risotto rice
40 g/1¹/₂ oz/3 tbsp unsalted (sweet)
  butter
60 ml/4 tbsp grated Parmesan
  cheese
175 g/6 oz Fontina cheese, thinly
  sliced
175 g/6 oz Gruyère (Swiss) cheese,
  thinly sliced
175 g/6 oz/ 1¹/₂ cups diced cooked
  ham
Watercress sprigs

Cook the rice in plenty of boiling salted water for 18 minutes. Drain thoroughly and return to the saucepan. Grease a large ring mould (mold) with a little of the butter, stir the remaining butter and the Parmesan into the rice. Spoon a third of the rice into the mould and press down well. Top with a third of the sliced cheeses and ham. Repeat the layers twice more until all the ingredients are used. Bake for 5-8 minutes at 180°C/350°F/gas mark 4 to melt the cheeses and heat the ham through. Loosen the edge of the mould and turn out on to a serving dish. Serve straight away, garnished with watercress in the centre.

The Rice of a Lifetime

Serves 4-6

*350 g/12 oz/1¹/₂ cups arborio or
other risotto rice
225 g/8 oz Mozzarella cheese, cubed
150 g/5 oz boiled ham, diced
2 size 1 egg yolks, lightly beaten
30 ml/2 tbsp freshly grated
Parmesan cheese
Salt and freshly ground black
pepper
Parsley sprigs*

Cook the rice in plenty of boiling salted water for 18 minutes. Drain thoroughly and return to the saucepan. Add the remaining ingredients except the parsley. Toss over a gentle heat until well combined. Pile on to serving plates, garnish with parsley and serve immediately.

Creamed Risotto with Lemon

Serves 4

*30 ml/2 tbsp unsalted (sweet) butter
350 g/12 oz/1¹/₂ cups arborio or
other risotto rice
Grated rind and juice of 1 lemon
1 litre/1³/₄ pts/4¹/₄ cups hot lamb
stock
15 ml/1 tbsp plain (all-purpose) flour
Salt and freshly ground black
pepper
75 ml/5 tbsp double (heavy) cream*

Melt half the butter in a heavy-based pan. Add the rice and cook, stirring, for 1 minute. Add the lemon rind to the stock. Add 2 ladlefuls of the stock and simmer until it has been absorbed. Repeat the process until the rice is just tender (about 15-20 minutes). Melt the remaining butter in a saucepan. Stir in the flour, then blend in the remaining stock. Bring to the boil and cook for 2 minutes until thickened. Season to taste and stir in the lemon juice and cream. Pile the rice into a warmed serving dish, pour the sauce over, stir lightly and serve.

Creamy Champagne Risotto

Serves 4

*25 g/1 oz/2 tbsp unsalted (sweet)
butter
1 small onion, finely chopped
450 g/1 lb/2 cups arborio or other
risotto rice
¹/₂ bottle dry champagne
750 ml/1¹/₄ pts/3 cups hot beef or
chicken stock
120 ml/4 fl oz/¹/₂ cup double (heavy)
cream
75 ml/5 tbsp freshly grated
Parmesan cheese
Salt*

Melt the butter in a flameproof casserole (Dutch oven). Add the onion and fry (sauté) for 2 minutes. Stir in the rice and cook for 1 minute. Add half the champagne, bring to the boil and simmer until it has been absorbed. Add a third of the stock and simmer until it is absorbed. Repeat the process with champagne and stock until the rice is just tender and creamy (about 15-20 minutes). Warm the cream in a small saucepan. When the rice is cooked, stir in the cream and cheese and season with salt. Serve straight away.

Cheese and Rice Cakes

Serves 4-6

225 g/8 oz/1 cup long-grain rice
30 ml/2 tbsp lemon juice
2 chicken stock cubes
100 g/4 oz Gruyère (Swiss) cheese, grated
25 g/1 oz/2 tbsp unsalted (sweet) butter
Salt and freshly ground black pepper
2 eggs
100 g/4 oz/2 cups white breadcrumbs
Oil for deep-frying
Tomato relish

Cook the rice in plenty of boiling water, to which the lemon juice and stock cubes have been added, for 10 minutes or until just tender. Drain. Transfer to a mixing bowl and stir in the cheese, butter, a little salt and lots of black pepper. Beat one of the eggs and stir in. Shape into small sausage shapes. Beat the second egg. Dip the rolls in breadcrumbs, then beaten egg, then in breadcrumbs again. Chill until firm. Deep-fry in hot oil a few at a time until crisp and golden brown. Drain on kitchen paper and serve with tomato relish.

Risotto al Gorgonzola

Serves 4

25 g/1 oz/2 tbsp unsalted (sweet) butter
30 ml/2 tbsp olive oil
1 small onion, finely chopped
450 g/1 lb/2 cups arborio or other risotto rice
1.2 litres/2 pts/5 cups hot beef or chicken stock
175 g/6 oz Gorgonzola cheese, crumbled
Salt and freshly ground black pepper
Grated Parmesan cheese (optional)

Heat the butter and oil in a flameproof casserole (Dutch oven). Add the onion and fry (sauté) for 2 minutes. Add the rice and cook for 1 minute. Stir in 250 ml/8 fl oz/1 cup of the hot stock. Bring to the boil and simmer until the stock is absorbed. Repeat until the rice is just tender and creamy (about 15-20 minutes). Stir in the Gorgonzola and cook gently for 2 minutes, stirring until the cheese has melted and blends with the rice. Season to taste and serve straight away with Parmesan cheese, if liked.

Risotto with Cheese and Wine

Serves 4

30 ml/2 tbsp olive oil
2 onions, finely chopped
450 g/1 lb/2 cups arborio or other
  risotto rice
1 litre/1³/₄ pts/4¹/₄ cups hot beef or
  chicken stock
250 ml/8 fl oz/1 cup Italian white
  wine
15 g/¹/₂ oz/1 tbsp unsalted (sweet)
  butter
60 ml/4 tbsp freshly grated
  Parmesan cheese
Salt and freshly ground black
  pepper

Heat the oil in a flameproof casserole
(Dutch oven). Add the onion and cook,
stirring for 2 minutes. Stir in the rice and
cook for 1 minute. Add 250 ml/8 fl oz/
1 cup of the stock, bring to the boil and
simmer until the stock is absorbed. Repeat
until the rice is just tender and the risotto
creamy (about 15-20 minutes). Add half
the wine after 10 minutes cooking. Stir in
the butter, the remaining wine and the
cheese. Taste and season if necessary.
Serve straight away.

White Wine Risotto with Truffles

Serves 4

1 quantity Risotto with Cheese and
  Wine
1 white truffle
50 g/2 oz/¹/₂ cup extra grated
  Parmesan cheese

Prepare the Risotto with Cheese and Wine.
Spoon on to hot serving plates and grate a
little truffle over each portion. Top with the
extra Parmesan cheese.

Tuscan Risotto with Raisins

Serves 4

45 ml/3 tbsp seedless (pitless) raisins
45 ml/3 tbsp olive oil
1 garlic clove
450 g/1 lb/2 cups arborio or other
  risotto rice
1.2 litres/2 pts/5 cups hot beef or
  chicken stock
50 g/2 oz/¹/₂ cup chopped parsley
Salt and freshly ground black
  pepper
50 g/2 oz/1 wedge of Parmesan
  cheese

Soak the raisins in boiling water for 30
minutes. Drain and pat dry in kitchen
paper. Heat the oil in a flameproof casserole (Dutch oven). Add the garlic and fry
(sauté) until golden, then discard. Add the
rice and cook for 1 minute. Stir in 250 ml/
8 fl oz/1 cup of the stock and simmer until
the stock is absorbed. Repeat twice more.
Stir in the raisins and continue adding
stock until the rice is just tender and the
risotto creamy (15-20 minutes). Stir in the
parsley and season with salt and pepper.
Shave off flakes of Parmesan with a potato
peeler and scatter over the surface.

Arancini Siciliani

Serves 6

225 g/8 oz/1 cup arborio or other
  risotto rice
50 g/2 oz/½ cup grated Parmesan
  cheese
2 size 4 eggs, beaten
300 ml/½ pt/1¼ cups passata (sieved
  tomatoes)
Salt and freshly ground black
  pepper
50 g/2 oz Mozzarella cheese, finely
  diced
50 g/2 oz/½ cup cooked ham, finely
  diced
50 g/2 oz/1 cup fresh breadcrumbs
Oil for deep-frying
15 ml/1 tbsp chopped basil
6 small basil sprigs

Cook the rice in plenty of boiling salted water for 15 minutes. Drain and leave until cold. Turn into a bowl and stir in the Parmesan cheese, eggs, 15 ml/1 tbsp of the passata and a little salt and pepper. Mix well. Put the cheese and ham in a separate bowl with another 15 ml/1 tbsp of the passata and season lightly. Divide the cold rice mixture into 12 portions. Using well-floured hands, shape each into a ball. Make a hollow in the centre and add a small spoonful of the cheese and ham mixture. Re-shape into a ball, adding a little more rice if necessary. Repeat with each portion of rice. Roll each thickly in the breadcrumbs. Chill if time. Deep-fry a few at a time until crisp and golden brown. Drain on kitchen paper. Meanwhile, warm the remaining passata with the chopped basil and a little salt and pepper. When all the arancini are cooked, spoon a little passata on to 6 serving plates. Place 2 arancini on each plate and top each with a basil sprig.

Suppli al Telefono

Serves 6

1 onion, finely chopped
50 g/2 oz/¼ cup butter
225 g/8 oz/1 cup arborio or other
  risotto rice
400 g/14 oz/1 large can tomato juice
150 ml/¼ pt/1¼ cups chicken stock
30 ml/2 tbsp grated Parmesan cheese
Salt and freshly ground black pepper
1.5 ml/¼ tsp cayenne
2 size 2 eggs, beaten
100 g/4 oz Mozzarella cheese, cut
  into 12 cubes
100 g/4 oz salami, finely chopped
75 g/3 oz/1½ cups fresh breadcrumbs
Oil for deep-frying

Fry (sauté) the onion in the butter for 2 minutes until softened and turning golden. Stir in the rice and cook for 1 minute. Stir in the tomato juice and stock. Bring to the boil, reduce the heat, cover and cook gently for 15-20 minutes until the rice is cooked and has absorbed all the liquid. If there is any left, boil rapidly for a few minutes, stirring all the time. Remove from the heat and stir in the Parmesan. Season with salt, pepper and the cayenne. Stir in the eggs, turn the mixture into a bowl, leave to cool, then chill until fairly firm. With floured hands, take a good spoonful of the mixture and flatten in the palm. Place a cube of cheese and a twelfth of the chopped salami in the centre. Top with another spoonful of rice and shape into a ball. Repeat with the remaining ingredients. Roll in the breadcrumbs. Chill again, if time. Deep-fry a few at a time in hot oil until crisp and golden. Drain on kitchen paper and serve straight away.

Note: When the balls are pulled apart the cheese should stretch into long threads, like telephone wires, hence the name.

Cottage Rice Casserole

Serves 6

350 g/12 oz/1½ cups long-grain rice
50 g/2 oz/¼ cup butter
1 large onion, finely chopped
450 ml/¾ pt/2 cups soured (dairy sour) cream
225 g/8 oz/1 cup cottage cheese
15 ml/1 tbsp snipped chives
Salt and freshly ground white pepper
2 green chillies, seeded and chopped
225 g/8 oz Cheddar cheese, grated

Cook the rice in plenty of boiling salted water for 10 minutes or until tender. Drain. Meanwhile, melt the butter in a pan and fry (sauté) the onion until soft but not brown. Stir into the cooked rice with the cream, cottage cheese, chives and a little salt and pepper. Spoon half this mixture into a buttered ovenproof dish. Sprinkle with half the chillies and half the grated cheese. Repeat the layers. Bake in the oven at 190°C/375°F/gas mark 5 for about 25 minutes or until the top is golden brown.

Savoury Eggy Rice

Serves 4

1 packet savoury rice with (bell) peppers
4 eggs
Garlic bread

Empty the rice into a large frying pan (skillet). Add water as directed on the packet. Bring to the boil, reduce the heat, cover and simmer for 15 minutes. Remove the lid and stir well. Make 4 wells in the rice mixture and break an egg into each. Cover and continue cooking over a gentle heat for 5 minutes or until the eggs are set to your liking. Serve straight from the pan with garlic bread.

Egg Fried Rice with Bacon

Serves 6

3 onions, thinly sliced
5 rashers (slices) streaky bacon, rinded and cut into thin strips
30 ml/2 tbsp sunflower oil
100 g/4 oz/1 cup frozen peas
50 g/2 oz /¼ cup unsalted (sweet) butter
4 eggs, beaten
Salt and freshly ground black pepper
350 g/12 oz/3 cups cooked long-grain rice

Fry (sauté) the onion and bacon in the oil for 2 minutes, stirring. In a separate pan, cook the peas in the butter for 2 minutes. Add the eggs to the bacon and onion and season lightly. Swirl the pan so the egg covers the base. Cook gently until the egg sets, then scramble lightly but don't break up the egg too much. Stir in the rice and peas and heat through, tossing gently so the rice grains stay separate. Serve straight away.

Eastern Rice with Egg

Serves 6
450 g/1 lb/2 cups basmati rice
750 ml/1¹/₄ pts/3 cups water
Salt
60 ml/4 tbsp sunflower oil
2 onions, thinly sliced
2.5 ml/¹/₂ tsp turmeric
1.5 ml/¹/₄ tsp chilli powder
8 hard-boiled (hard-cooked) eggs
30 ml/2 tbsp chopped coriander
  (cilantro)

Wash and drain the rice thoroughly. Place in a large heavy-based saucepan with the water and salt. Bring to the boil, reduce the heat, cover and simmer gently for 15 minutes or until the rice is almost tender and has absorbed all the liquid. Meanwhile, heat the oil in a separate pan. Add the onions and fry (sauté) for about 4 minutes, stirring until soft and golden. Stir in the turmeric and chilli powder and fry for 1 minute, stirring. Add the shelled whole eggs and cook, stirring gently for 3 minutes until the eggs are golden. Add the rice to the eggs with 15 ml/1 tbsp water. Cover tightly and cook very gently for 5 minutes until piping hot. Stir in the coriander and serve hot.

Ceylonese Rice

Serves 4
225 g/8 oz/1 cup long-grain rice
75 ml/5 tbsp groundnut (peanut) oil
3 leeks, sliced
1 green chilli, seeded and chopped
1 small onion, thinly sliced
4 size 1 eggs, beaten
Salt and freshly ground black
  pepper

Cook the rice in plenty of boiling salted water for 10 minutes or until just tender. Drain and rinse with boiling water. Meanwhile, heat the oil in a large frying pan (skillet) and fry (sauté) the leeks, chilli and onion until soft but not brown, about 5-8 minutes. Add the eggs and a little salt and pepper and fry, stirring until the eggs begin to scramble. Add the rice a spoonful at a time, stirring well. Pile on to a warm serving dish and serve hot.

Riso al' Uova

Serves 4
350 g/12 oz/1¹/₂ cups arborio or
  other risotto rice
2 size 1 egg yolks, lightly beaten
20 g/³/₄ oz/1¹/₂ tbsp unsalted (sweet)
  butter
Salt and freshly ground black
  pepper
50 g/2 oz/¹/₂ cup grated Parmesan
  cheese

Cook the rice in plenty of boiling salted
water for about 16-18 minutes until just
tender. Drain thoroughly. Return to the pan
over a gentle heat. Pour the egg yolks over
the rice and stir vigorously until well
mixed and set. Stir in the butter and season
with salt and pepper. Stir in the cheese and
serve straight away.

Arroz Poblano

Serves 6
350 g/12 oz/1¹/₂ cups long-grain rice
60 ml/4 tbsp groundnut (peanut) oil
2 green chillies, seeded and chopped
1 small onion, finely chopped
1 garlic clove, crushed
1.75 litres/3 pts/7¹/₂ cups chicken
  stock
Salt and freshly ground black
  pepper
100 g/4 oz Cheddar cheese, grated

Fry (sauté) the rice in the oil until golden,
stirring all the time. Add the chillies, onion
and garlic and cook for 1 minute. Stir in
the stock and a little salt and pepper. Bring
to the boil, reduce the heat, cover and cook
gently for about 20 minutes until the rice is
tender and has absorbed the liquid. Stir
occasionally and add a little more stock if
drying out too quickly. Pile into a flameproof serving dish, top with the cheese and
flash under a hot grill (broiler) until the
cheese melts. Serve straight away.

Egg Vindaloo Basmati

Serves 4
2 onions, finely chopped
30 ml/2 tbsp sunflower oil
10 ml/2 tsp curry powder
2.5 ml/¹/₂ tsp chilli powder
30 ml/2 tbsp plain (all-purpose) flour
150 ml/¹/₄ pt/²/₃ cup cider vinegar
450 ml/³/₄ pt/2 cups vegetable stock
1 bay leaf
1 small piece cinnamon stick
2.5 ml/¹/₂ tsp dried thyme
Salt and freshly ground black
  pepper
8 hard-boiled (hard-cooked) eggs
225 g/8 oz/1 cup basmati rice
5 ml/1 tsp garam masala
60 ml/ 4 tbsp desiccated (shredded)
  coconut
Plain yoghurt

Fry (sauté) the onion in the oil for 3 minutes until softened and lightly golden in a
saucepan. Add the curry and chilli powders
and fry for 1 minute. Stir in the flour and
cook for 2 minutes, stirring. Remove from
the heat and gradually blend in the vinegar
and stock. Return to the heat and bring to
the boil, stirring. Add the bay leaf, cinnamon stick and thyme and season to taste
with salt and pepper. Reduce the heat,

cover and simmer very gently for 45 minutes, stirring occasionally to prevent sticking. Remove the bay leaf and cinnamon. Halve the eggs and add to the sauce. Heat gently for 8-10 minutes. Meanwhile, cook the rice in plenty of boiling salted water for 10 minutes, drain and return to the pan. Sprinkle over the garam masala and half the coconut. Stir in lightly but evenly. Pile the rice on to warm serving plates. Spoon 4 halves of egg and sauce over each and garnish with a swirl of yoghurt and a dusting of the remaining coconut.

Eggy Wedges with Salsa

Serves 4
225 g/8 oz/1 cup long-grain rice
Salt and freshly ground black
*   pepper*
2 eggs, beaten
100 g/4 oz Mozzarella cheese, grated
2.5 ml/¹/₂ tsp dried oregano
1 jar Spicy Tomato Salsa

Cook the rice according to the packet directions. Drain, rinse with cold water and drain again thoroughly. Add a little salt and a good grinding of pepper. Mix with the eggs, cheese and oregano. Press into a lightly greased 23 cm/9 in round baking dish. Bake in the oven at 230°C/450°F/gas mark 8 for about 15 minutes or until set and golden brown. Leave to cool slightly, then cut into wedges and serve warm with the salsa.

Blue Cheese Wedges with Relish

Serves 4
Prepare as for Eggy Wedges with Salsa, but substitute 50 g/2 oz/¹/₂ cup crumbled blue cheese for half the Mozzarella, and serve with cucumber relish instead of salsa.

Indian Rice with Egg

Serves 4
450 g/1 lb/2 cups basmati rice
750 ml/1¹/₄ pts/ 3 cups chicken stock
Salt and freshly ground black
*   pepper*
60 ml/4 tbsp groundnut (peanut) oil
2 onions, sliced
1 garlic clove, crushed
10 ml/2 tsp chopped coriander
*   (cilantro)*
2.5 ml/¹/₂ tsp turmeric
1.5 ml/¹/₄ tsp chilli powder
8 hard-boiled (hard-cooked) eggs,
*   quartered*

Place the washed rice in a large pan with the stock and a little salt and pepper. Bring to the boil, reduce the heat, cover and simmer for 15 minutes until the rice is almost tender and has absorbed the liquid. Heat the oil in a separate pan and fry (sauté) the onions and the garlic for 2 minutes. Stir in the coriander, turmeric and chilli and cook for 1 minute. Add to the rice and stock and add 30 ml/2 tbsp water. Lay the eggs on top. Bring to the boil, cover with foil then a lid and cook over a gentle heat for 5 minutes. Leave undisturbed for 5 minutes then fluff up and serve.

Golden Egg and Onion Supper

Serves 4

225 g/8 oz/1 cup long-grain rice
5 ml/1 tsp turmeric
50g/2 oz/¼ cup butter
450 g/1 lb onions, thinly sliced
6 hard-boiled (hard-cooked) eggs, sliced
25 g/1 oz/¼ cup plain (all-purpose) flour
300 ml/½ pt/1¼ cups milk
5 ml/1 tsp made mustard
A pinch of cayenne
Salt and freshly ground black pepper
100 g/4 oz Cheddar cheese, grated

Cook the rice in plenty of boiling salted water to which the turmeric has been added. Drain well and turn into a lightly greased flameproof dish. Meanwhile, melt half the butter and fry (sauté) the onions until soft and lightly golden. Spoon over the rice and top with the eggs. Melt the remaining butter in the onion pan. Stir in the flour and cook for 1 minute. Remove from the heat and blend in the milk, mustard, cayenne and a little salt and pepper. Return to the heat, bring to the boil and cook for 2 minutes, stirring all the time. Stir in half the cheese and spoon over the eggs. Top with the remaining cheese and grill (broil) for 4 minutes until golden, bubbling and piping hot.

Golden Sausage Supper

Serves 4

Prepare as for Golden Egg and Onion Supper but add a layer of sliced grilled (broiled) pork sausages on top of the eggs before adding the sauce.

Dutch Rice Layer

Serves 4

100 g/4 oz/½ cup long-grain rice
25 g/1 oz/2 tbsp butter
2 onions, finely chopped
225 g/8 oz Gouda cheese, grated
4 tomatoes, sliced
30 ml/2 tbsp crushed cornflakes

Cook the rice in plenty of boiling salted water until just tender. Drain, rinse with boiling water and drain again. Meanwhile, melt half the butter in a frying pan (skillet) and fry (sauté) the onions for 3 minutes until lightly golden. Use the remaining butter to grease an ovenproof serving dish. Add the rice, then top with half the cheese. Add a layer of onion, then tomato, then top with the remaining cheese. Sprinkle the cornflakes on top. Bake in the oven at 190°C/375°F/gas mark 5 for 30 minutes or until golden and bubbling.

Dutch Bean and Rice Layer

Serves 4

Prepare as for Dutch Rice Layer, but substitute 400 g/14 oz/1 large can baked beans in tomato sauce for the sliced tomatoes, and use Edam cheese instead of Gouda.

White Rice Pilaf

Serves 4

50 g/2 oz/¹/₄ cup unsalted (sweet) butter
225 g/8 oz/1 cup long-grain rice
600 ml/1 pt/2¹/₂ cups chicken stock
Salt and freshly ground black pepper
15 ml/1 tbsp chopped coriander (cilantro)
15 ml/1 tbsp chopped flatleaf parsley
300 ml/¹/₂ pt/1¹/₄ cups plain yoghurt

Melt the butter in a flameproof casserole (Dutch oven). Add the rice and cook for 1 minute, stirring. Stir in the stock and a little salt and pepper, bring to the boil, cover and simmer gently for 15 minutes until the rice is tender and has absorbed all the liquid. Remove the lid and boil rapidly if necessary until any remaining liquid has evaporated. Stir in half the herbs and season again to taste. Serve hot, with the yoghurt spooned over and sprinkle with the remaining herbs.

Brown Rice Pilaf

Serves 4

Prepare as for White Rice Pilaf but use brown rice and cook for 25 minutes before removing the lids.

Minted Egg Pilaf

Serves 4

225 g/8 oz/1 cup Thai fragrant rice or basmati rice
450 ml/³/₄ pt/2 cups boiling water
5 ml/1 tsp salt
2 eggs, beaten
Grated rind and juice of ¹/₂ lemon
15 ml/1 tbsp chopped mint
50 g/2 oz/¹/₂ cup grated Parmesan cheese

Place the rice in a pan with the water and salt. Bring to the boil, cover, reduce the heat and cook very gently for 15-20 minutes or until the rice is tender and has absorbed all the liquid, adding a little more water after 15 minutes if dry and still not quite tender. Stir in the eggs, lemon rind and juice, mint and half the cheese. Toss over a gentle heat until lightly scrambled but still creamy. Serve straight away, sprinkled with the remaining cheese.

Anchovy Eggs with Tagliarini

Serves 4

300 ml/¹/₂ pts/1¹/₄ cups milk
25 g/1 oz/¹/₄ cup plain (all-purpose) flour
75 g/3 oz/¹/₃ cup unsalted (sweet) butter
Salt and freshly ground black pepper
75g/3 oz/³/₄ cup grated Parmesan cheese
8 hard-boiled (hard-cooked) eggs
30 ml/2 tbsp anchovy essence (extract)
100 ml/3¹/₄ fl oz/6¹/₂ tbsp double (heavy) cream
350 g/12 oz/3 cups tagliarini
10 ml/2 tsp capers, chopped
15 ml/1 tbsp chopped parsley

Blend a little of the milk with the flour in a saucepan. Stir in the remaining milk and add 25 g/1 oz/2 tbsp of the butter. Bring to the boil and cook for 2 minutes, stirring all the time. Season with salt and pepper and stir in the cheese. Halve the eggs and rub the yolks through a sieve (strainer). Beat in half the remaining butter, the anchovy essence and the cream. Season to taste. Pipe or spoon the mixture into the egg whites and place in a large ovenproof dish. Cover with foil and heat through in the oven at 150°C/300°F/gas mark 2 for about 10 minutes. Meanwhile cook the tagliarini according to the packet directions. Drain and return to the saucepan. Add the remaining butter in small flakes, a good grinding of pepper, the capers and parsley and toss well. Pile on to serving plates and put 4 halves of egg to one side of each serving.

Watercress and Egg Pasta

Serves 4

1 bunch of watercress
30 ml/2 tbsp chopped parsley
30 ml/2 tbsp lemon juice
6 eggs
100 g/4 oz/¹/₂ cup butter, melted
Salt and freshly ground black pepper
225 g/8 oz/2 cups penne
Cayenne

Chop the watercress, discarding the feathery stalks. Mix with the parsley. Whisk all but 5 ml/1 tsp of the lemon juice with 2 of the eggs in a saucepan. Gradually whisk in the melted butter and cook, whisking over a very gentle heat until thickened. Do NOT boil or the mixture will scramble. Stir in the watercress and parsley and season to taste. Cook the penne according to the packet directions, drain. Divide among 4 individual serving dishes. Meanwhile, poach the eggs in a pan of gently simmering water to which the remaining lemon juice has been added. Remove with a draining spoon and place on top of the pasta. Spoon the warm Hollandaise sauce over and flash under a hot grill (broiler) to glaze. Serve straight away, dusted with a little cayenne.

Tortellini with Piquant Sunflower Sauce

Serves 4

2 garlic cloves, crushed
45 ml/3 tbsp chopped parsley
25 g/1 oz/¹/₄ cup grated Parmesan
 cheese
30 ml/2 tbsp sunflower seeds
30 ml/2 tbsp capers
Salt and freshly ground black
 pepper
120 ml/4 fl oz/¹/₂ cup sunflower oil
250 g/9 oz/1 packet tortellini stuffed
 with cheese and spinach
15 ml/1 tbsp olive oil

Purée or pound the garlic, parsley, cheese, sunflower seeds and capers until the mixture forms a paste. Season well. Gradually beat in the sunflower oil until the paste glistens. Cook the tortellini according to the packet directions. Drain and return to the pan. Add the sauce and toss well over a gentle heat. Serve immediately, drizzled with the olive oil.

Pasta Soufflé Sensation

Serves 4

Butter for greasing
425 g/15 oz/1 can pasta in tomato
 sauce
298 g/10¹/₂ oz/1 large can condensed
 cream of celery soup
75 g/3 oz Cheddar cheese, grated
4 eggs, separated
Freshly ground black pepper

Butter a 20 cm/8 in round soufflé dish. Empty the contents of the can of pasta into the dish. Put the soup in a bowl. Whisk in the cheese and egg yolks and season with pepper. Whisk the egg whites until stiff and fold into the soup mixture with a metal spoon. Turn into the soufflé dish and bake in the hot oven at 200°C/400°F/gas mark 6 for about 25-30 minutes until well risen and golden. Serve straight away.

Gloucester Macaroni

Serves 4

225 g/8 oz/2 cups short-cut
 macaroni
450ml/³/₄ pt/2 cups milk
25 g/1 oz/¹/₄ cup plain (all-purpose)
 flour
50 g/2 oz/¹/₄ cup butter
175 g/6 oz double Gloucester cheese,
 grated
400 g/14 oz/1 large can chopped
 tomatoes, drained
100 g/4 oz/1 cup cooked ham, diced
Salt and freshly ground black
 pepper
45 ml/3 tbsp crushed cornflakes

Cook the macaroni according to the packet directions. Drain. Meanwhile, blend a little of the milk in a saucepan with the flour. Add the remaining milk and half the butter. Bring to the boil and cook for 2 minutes, stirring all the time. Stir in 100 g/ 4 oz/1 cup of the cheese, the tomatoes, ham and a little salt and pepper. Turn into a shallow ovenproof dish. Mix the remaining cheese with the cornflakes and sprinkle over. Dot with the remaining butter and bake in the oven at 200°C/400°F/gas mark 6 for about 20 minutes or until bubbling and golden brown.

Nouille Fraiches au Buerre

Serves 4

225 g/8 oz fresh tagliatelle
50 g/2 oz/¹/₄ cup unsalted (sweet) butter
Freshly ground black pepper
50 g/2 oz/¹/₃ cup freshly grated Parmesan

Cook the pasta in boiling salted water for about 4 minutes until just tender. Drain. Melt the butter in the saucepan. Add the noodles and lots of pepper and toss well with two forks over a gentle heat. Pile on to a serving dish and top with the cheese before serving.

Tarragon Peppered Tagliatelle

Serves 4

225 g/8 oz tagliatelle
25 g/1 oz/2 tbsp butter
1 small onion, finely chopped
30 ml/2 tbsp chopped tarragon
30 ml/2 tbsp white wine vinegar
30 ml/2 tbsp dry white wine
150 g/5 oz/²/₃ cup soft cheese with black pepper
150 ml/¹/₄ pt/²/₃ cup single (light) cream
2 pastrami slices, cut in thin strips
A few tarragon sprigs

Cook the tagliatelle according to the packet directions. Drain and return to the pan. Meanwhile, melt the butter in a saucepan. Add the onion and cook gently for 2 minutes until softened but not browned. Add the chopped tarragon, vinegar and wine and boil rapidly until well reduced and thickened. Stir in the cheese and cream and heat through gently for 2-3 minutes. Add to the pasta and toss lightly. Pile on to serving plates and garnish with the pastrami and a few tarragon sprigs.

Four-cheese Melting Moment

Serves 4

225 g/8 oz green tagliarini (verdi)
25 g/1 oz/¹/₄ cup plain (all-purpose) flour
600 ml/1 pt/2¹/₂ cups milk
25 g/1 oz/2 tbsp butter
1 bay leaf
50 g/2 oz Emmental (Swiss) cheese, grated
50 g/2 oz Fontina cheese, grated
50 g/2 oz Mozzarella cheese, grated
50 g/2 oz/¹/₂ cup grated Pecorino cheese
Salt and freshly ground black pepper
A few basil leaves

Cook the pasta according to the packet directions, drain. Meanwhile, whisk the flour and milk together in a saucepan until smooth. Add the butter and bay leaf and bring to the boil, whisking all the time until thickened and smooth. Simmer for 2 minutes, stirring. Remove the bay leaf. Stir in the cheeses and a little seasoning. Heat through until melted. Add to the cooked tagliarini and toss well. Serve with a good grinding of black pepper and torn basil leaves scattered over.

Spaghetti with Ricotta and Broccoli

Serves 4-6
450 g/1 lb broccoli, cut into tiny
    florets
75 g/3 oz/¹/₃ cup butter
175 g/6 oz/³/₄ cup Ricotta cheese
50 g/2 oz/¹/₂ cup grated Parmesan
    cheese
60 ml/4 tbsp chopped parsley
1.5 ml/¹/₄ tsp cayenne
Salt and freshly ground black
    pepper
350 g/12 oz spaghetti

Steam the broccoli or boil in lightly salted water until just tender. Drain. Melt all but 15 g/¹/₂ oz/1 tbsp of the butter in a saucepan. Add the cheeses and parsley and heat through, stirring. Add the broccoli and heat through. Season to taste with the cayenne and a little salt and pepper. Meanwhile, cook the spaghetti according to the packet directions. Drain and toss in the remaining butter. Pile on to warm plates and top with the sauce.

Spaghettini with Ricotta and Asparagus

Serves 4
Prepare as for Spaghetti with Ricotta and Broccoli, but substitute spaghettini for the spaghetti, and asparagus for the broccoli. Trim the stalks, lay in a steamer and steam for about 10 minutes until tender. Cut into short lengths.

Continental Welsh Rarebit

Serves 4
225 g/8 oz/2 cups short-cut
    macaroni
350 g/12 oz Cheddar cheese, grated
10 ml/2 tsp made mustard
60 ml/4 tbsp light ale
A little milk
15 g/¹/₂ oz/1 tbsp butter
50 g/2 oz/1 cup fresh breadcrumbs
A few snipped chives

Cook the macaroni according to the packet directions. Drain. Meanwhile, put the cheese, mustard and beer in a saucepan and heat through, stirring until the cheese has melted and the mixture is well blended. Add a little milk if the mixture seems too sticky. Add the macaroni and mix well. Melt the butter and fry (sauté) the breadcrumbs until golden. Spoon the pasta on to warm plates and top with the breadcrumbs and a few snipped chives.

Italian Buck Rarebit

Serves 4
Prepare as for Continental Welsh Rarebit, but substitute cider or white wine for the beer, and top each serving with a poached egg before garnishing.

Dolcelatte Dream

Serves 4

2 celery sticks, finely chopped
25 g/1 oz/2 tbsp butter
100 g/4 oz Dolcelatte, diced
50 g/2 oz/¹/₄ cup medium-fat soft
cheese
90 ml/6 tbsp single (light) cream
Freshly ground black pepper
15 ml/1 tbsp chopped parsley
350 g/12 oz tagliatelle

Put the celery and butter in a double saucepan or in a bowl over a pan of gently simmering water. Cover and cook gently for about 8 minutes or until softened. Add the cheeses and cook, stirring until smooth and melted. Stir in the cream. Add plenty of pepper and stir well. Stir in the parsley. Meanwhile, cook the tagliatelle according to the packet directions. Drain. Add to the sauce, toss well and serve straight away.

Garlic and Herb Quickie

Serves 4

225 g/8 oz/2 cups multicoloured
penne
15 ml/1 tbsp cornflour (cornstarch)
300 ml/¹/₂ pt/1¹/₄ cups milk
15 g/¹/₂ oz/1 tbsp butter
80 g/3¹/₂ oz/ scant ¹/₂ cup garlic and
herb cheese
Salt and freshly ground black
pepper
Snipped chives

Cook the pasta according to the packet directions. Drain. Whisk the cornflour with a little of the milk in a saucepan. Stir in the remaining milk and add the butter. Bring to the boil, stirring until thickened. Add the cheese and stir over a gentle heat until smooth. Season with salt and pepper. Add the pasta, toss well and serve garnished with the chives.

Goatherd Mountain Special

Serves 4

350 g/12 oz spaghettini
120 ml/4 fl oz/¹/₂ cup olive oil
2 garlic cloves, crushed
4 ripe tomatoes, diced
Salt and freshly ground black
pepper
50 g/2 oz/¹/₂ cup basil leaves, torn
into small pieces
50 g/2 oz goat's cheese, roughly
crumbled
A few black olives

Cook the spaghettini according to the packet directions. Drain. Meanwhile, heat the oil in a saucepan. Add the garlic and cook gently for 1 minute. Add the tomatoes and a little salt and pepper and cook gently for 1-2 minutes, stirring, until heated through but the tomatoes still hold their shape. Add the basil leaves and toss gently. Add the spaghettini and toss well. At the last minute, add the cheese, toss again and serve immediately with a few olives scattered over.

Piquant Goat's Cheese and Radicchio Farfalle

Serves 4

25 g/8 oz/2 cups farfalle
25 g/1 oz/2 tbsp butter
2 garlic cloves, finely chopped
1 small raddichio, coarsely shredded
Salt
5 ml/1 tsp pickled green peppercorns
250 ml/8 fl oz/1 cup double (heavy) cream
50 g/2 oz goat's cheese, crumbled
Freshly ground black or green pepper

Cook the pasta according to the packet directions. Drain. Meanwhile, melt the butter in a saucepan. Add the garlic and radicchio, toss then cover and cook gently for 4 minutes. Season lightly with salt and add the peppercorns. In a separate pan, heat the cream. Add half the cheese and whisk until smooth. Stir in the radicchio mixture. Add to the farfalle with the remaining cheese. Toss quickly and serve garnished with a good grinding of black or green pepper.

Rich Gorgonzola and Walnut Wheels

Serves 4

225 g/8 oz/2 cups wholewheat ruote
2 garlic cloves, finely chopped
25 g/1 oz/2 tbsp butter
225 g/8 oz Gorgonzola, crumbled
50 g/2 oz/¹/₂ cup walnuts, chopped
Salt and freshly ground black pepper
30 ml/2 tbsp milk or single (light) cream
30 ml/2 tbsp freshly grated Parmesan cheese
Chopped parsley

Cook the pasta according to the packet directions, drain. Meanwhile, cook the garlic gently in the butter for 1 minute. Add the remaining ingredients except the parsley and heat through gently until melted and well combined. Do not boil. Add to the pasta and toss well. Pile on to serving plates and garnish with parsley.

293

Greek-style Gourmet

Serves 4

350 g/12 oz spaghetti
90 ml/6 tbsp olive oil
2 garlic cloves, chopped
4 spring onions (scallions), chopped
5 ml/1 tsp dried oregano
1 large beefsteak tomato, diced
Freshly ground black pepper
75 g/3 oz/¹/₂ cup Greek black olives
30 ml/2 tbsp freshly grated Parmesan cheese
100 g/4 oz chilled Feta cheese, crumbled

Cook the spaghetti according to the packet directions. Drain and return to the pan. Meanwhile, heat two-thirds of the oil in a saucepan. Add the garlic and spring onions and soften for 1 minute. Add the oregano, tomato and a good grinding of pepper and cook gently for 1-2 minutes until hot but the tomatoes still hold their shape. Add the remaining ingredients except the rest of the olive oil and toss lightly over a gentle heat to combine. Quickly add the remaining olive oil to the spaghetti, toss gently and pile on to serving plates. Spoon the Feta mixture over and serve straight away.

Austrian Schinkenfleckerl

Serves 4

10 ml/2 tsp olive oil
30 ml/2 tbsp dried breadcrumbs
225 g/8 oz/2 cups short-cut macaroni
1 small onion, finely chopped
50 g/2 oz/¹/₄ cup butter
250 ml/8 fl oz/1 cup soured (dairy sour) cream
2 eggs
225 g/8 oz kaiserfleisch or lean-cooked ham, finely diced
50 g/2 oz Emmental (Swiss) cheese, grated
Salt and freshly ground black pepper
3 tomatoes, halved
6 open mushrooms
A little extra olive oil

Grease a 15 cm/6 in round, deep cake tin (pan) with the oil and coat with the breadcrumbs. Cook the macaroni according to the packet directions. Drain, rinse with cold water and turn into a large bowl. Fry (sauté) the onion in the butter gently for 3 minutes until soft but not brown. Stir the onions and butter into the pasta. Whisk the cream and eggs together. Add to the pasta with the ham and cheese. Mix well and season to taste. Spoon into the prepared tin and level the surface. Stand in a roasting tin (pan) with enough cold water to come a third of the way up the tin. Bake in the oven at 200°C/400°F/gas mark 6 for 30 minutes or until set and the top is golden brown. Remove from the baking tin and allow to cool for 5 minutes. Meanwhile grill (broil) the tomatoes and mushrooms, brushed with a little olive oil, if liked. Turn the schinkenfleckerl out on to a serving dish and garnish with the tomatoes and mushrooms before serving cut in wedges.

Middle-Eastern Cottage Cheese Pasta

Serves 4-6
900 g/2 lb/4 cups cottage cheese
50 g/2 oz/¹/₂ cup caraway seeds
50 g/2 oz/¹/₂ cup poppy seeds
Freshly ground black pepper
350 g/12 oz pappardelle
15 g/¹/₂ oz/1 tbsp butter
Coarse sea salt
Paprika

Mix together the cottage cheese, seeds and a good grinding of pepper. Place in a bowl over a pan of hot water (or a double saucepan) and warm gently but do not allow to boil. Meanwhile, cook the pappardelle according to the packet directions. Drain and toss in the butter. Pile on to a serving dish. Top with the cheese mixture and sprinkle with coarse sea salt and paprika before serving.

Tortellini with Fresh Parmesan and Avocado Cream

Serves 4
290 g/9 oz/1 packet tortellini stuffed with mushrooms
175 ml/6 fl oz/³/₄ cup double (heavy) cream
1 ripe avocado, peeled and stoned (pitted)
75 g/5 tbsp freshly grated Parmesan cheese
30 ml/2 tbsp lemon juice
Salt and freshly ground black pepper
Tiny watercress sprigs

Cook the tortellini according to the packet directions. Drain and keep hot. Meanwhile, place the cream in a saucepan and heat gently but do not boil. Purée the avocado in a blender or food processor with the cheese and lemon juice. Or mash well with a fork then beat until smooth. Stir into the hot cream and season well. Heat gently for a further 2-3 minutes. Add to the hot tortellini, toss well and serve straight away garnished with a few watercress sprigs.

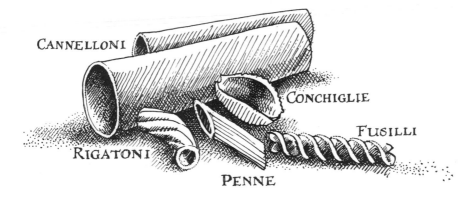

CANNELLONI

CONCHIGLIE

FUSILLI

RIGATONI

PENNE

Tocco di Nocci con Cappelletti

Serves 4

250 g/9 oz/1 packet cappelletti
stuffed with cheese and spinach
225 g/8 oz/2 cups walnut pieces
Thick slice of white bread, crusts
removed
75 ml/5 tbsp milk
1 garlic clove, crushed
Salt and freshly ground black
pepper
45 ml/3 tbsp olive oil
100 g/4 oz/¹/₂ cup Mascarpone
cheese

Cook the cappelletti according to the packet directions, drain. Place the nuts in boiling water for 2 minutes. Drain and rub off the skins in a clean tea towel. Soak the bread in the milk. Grind the nuts to a fine powder in a blender or food processor. Squeeze out the bread and add to the nuts with the garlic and a little salt and pepper. Run the machine until the mixture is smooth. With the machine running, add the oil in a thin stream and then finally add the cheese. Add to the cappelletti and toss well over a gentle heat. Serve straight away.

Alpine Fresh Pasta

Serves 4

350g/12 oz fresh tagliarini
90 ml/6 tbsp olive oil
1 red (bell) pepper, chopped
1 green (bell) pepper, chopped
4 spring onions (scallions), chopped
100 g/4 oz/1 cup pine nuts, roughly
crushed
450 g/1 lb/2 cups cottage cheese
Salt and freshly ground black
pepper
Lemon twists
Cress

Cook the tagliarini (see page 10 or according to the packet directions). Heat two-thirds of the oil in a saucepan. Add the peppers and onion and cook gently for 2 minutes. Add the remaining ingredients except the rest of the olive oil, the lemon twists and cress, and cook gently until hot through, stirring all the time. Toss the tagliarini in the remaining olive oil. Divide between serving plates. Spoon the cheese mixture over and garnish each with a lemon twist and a little cress.

Basic Macaroni Cheese

Serves 4

225 g/8 oz/2 cups short-cut
macaroni
20 g/³/₄ oz/3 tbsp plain (all-purpose)
flour
300 ml/¹/₂ pt/1¹/₄ cups milk
20 g/³/₄ oz/1¹/₂ tbsp butter
1 bay leaf
5 ml/1 tsp made English or Dijon
mustard
75 g/3 oz Cheddar cheese, grated
Salt and freshly ground black pepper
Extra grated cheese

Cook the macaroni according to the packet directions. Drain. Whisk the flour with a little of the milk in a saucepan until smooth. Whisk in the remaining milk and add the butter and bay leaf. Bring to the boil and boil for 2 minutes, stirring all the time. Stir in the mustard and cheese and season to taste with salt and pepper. Discard the bay leaf. Add to the pasta and stir well. Turn into a flameproof dish, top with a little extra grated cheese and grill (broil) until golden and bubbling.

Special Macaroni Cheese

Serves 4

Prepare as for Basic Macaroni Cheese but add 50 g/2 oz/1 cup sliced mushrooms and 1 diced green (bell) pepper, both fried (sautéed) in a little butter, and 50 g/2 oz/¹/₂ cup diced cooked ham (optional), to the sauce with the cooked pasta. Arrange sliced tomatoes round the top with the extra cheese before grilling (broiling).

Italian Lunchtime Fettuccine

Serves 4

450 g/1 lb/4 cups fettuccine
100 g/4 oz/¹/₂ cup unsalted (sweet) butter
300 ml/¹/₂ pt/1¹/₄ cups double (heavy) cream
Salt and freshly ground black pepper

Cook the fettuccine according to the packet directions. Drain and return to the saucepan. Cut the butter into flakes and add to the pan with the cream. Stir over a gentle heat until well coated. Season thoroughly with a little salt and lots of black pepper. Serve with crusty bread and a bowl of green olives.

Fettuccine with Jalopeno Pepper Cream

Serves 4-6

120 ml/4 fl oz/¹/₂ cup white wine vinegar
2.5 ml/¹/₂ tsp salt
1 small onion, finely chopped
1 jalopeno pepper, seeded and chopped
600 ml/1 pt/2¹/₂ cups double (heavy) cream
30 ml/2 tbsp chopped coriander (cilantro)
350 g/12 oz fettuccine

Put the vinegar, salt, onion and jalopeno pepper in a saucepan. Bring to the boil and boil rapidly for about 5 minutes until the mixture is reduced by half. Add the cream, bring to the boil and boil rapidly for about 15 minutes until the mixture is well reduced and thickened. Add half the coriander and stir well. Meanwhile, cook the pasta according to the packet directions. Drain. Add the cream sauce, toss well and sprinkle with the remaining coriander before serving.

Salsa Alfredo (for fresh pasta)

Serves 4
350 g/12 oz any fresh pasta
450 ml/³/₄ pt/2 cups double (heavy) cream
50 g/2 oz/¹/₄ cup butter
175 g/6 oz/1¹/₂ cups freshly grated Parmesan cheese
Freshly ground black pepper
A little crisp, crumbled bacon (optional)

Cook the fresh pasta (see page 10 or according to the packet directions). Drain. Meanwhile, bring the cream and butter to the boil in a saucepan. Reduce the heat and simmer for 1 minute. Add half the cheese and some pepper and whisk until smooth. Add to the pasta with the remaining cheese and toss over a gentle heat. Pile on to warm plates add a good grinding of pepper and serve topped with crumbled bacon, if liked.

Spaghetti Carbonara

Serves 4
350 g/12 oz spaghetti
100 g/4 oz unsmoked streaky bacon, finely diced
75 g/3 oz/¹/₃ cup butter
5 eggs
30 ml/2 tbsp chopped parsley
Salt and freshly ground black pepper
50 g/2 oz/¹/₂ cup grated Parmesan cheese

Cook the spaghetti according to the packet directions. Drain and return to the saucepan. Meanwhile, fry (sauté) the bacon in the butter until browned. Beat the eggs with the parsley, a little salt, lots of pepper and the cheese. Add the hot bacon and its fat to the spaghetti and toss. Add the egg mixture and stir and toss until the mixture is creamy and piping hot. Do not allow to scramble completely. Serve immediately.

Wraysbury Carbonara

Serves 2-3
225 g/8 oz spaghetti
60 ml/4 tbsp olive oil
4 rashers (slices) streaky bacon, rinded and diced
1 onion, finely chopped
1 garlic clove, crushed
Salt and freshly ground black pepper
2 eggs
60 ml/4 tbsp milk
30 ml/2 tbsp chopped parsley
Grated Parmesan cheese

Cook the spaghetti according to the packet directions. Drain and return to the pan. Meanwhile, heat the oil in a small saucepan. Add the bacon, onion and garlic and fry (sauté) for 1 minute, stirring. Add a little salt and a good grinding of pepper, cover and cook over a gentle heat until the pasta is cooked. Add the mixture to the spaghetti and toss well. Beat the eggs with the milk and add to the pan with half the parsley. Stir and toss over a gentle heat until lightly scrambled but still very creamy. Spoon on to warm plates, garnish with the parsley and lots of grated Parmesan cheese.

Tagliatelle alla Panna

Serves 4

350 g/12 oz green tagliatelle (verdi)
40 g/1½ oz/3 tbsp butter
75 ml/5 tbsp double (heavy) cream
100 g/4 oz cooked ham, cut into thin
  strips
Salt and freshly ground black
  pepper
Freshly grated nutmeg
Grated Parmesan cheese

Cook the tagliatelle according to the packet directions, drain and return to the pan. Add the butter, cream, ham, a sprinkling of salt, a good grinding of pepper and lots of nutmeg and toss over a gentle heat until piping hot and well mixed. Serve garnished with lots of grated Parmesan cheese.

High Society Pasta

Serves 4-6

350 g/12 oz bucatini
15 g/½ oz/1 tbsp butter
4 eggs, beaten
150 ml/¼ pt/⅔ cup single (light)
  cream
100 g/4 oz/1 cup smoked salmon, cut
  into tiny strips
Freshly ground pepper
A little red Danish lumpfish roe
  (optional)
Chopped parsley

Cook the bucatini according to the packet directions. Drain. Melt the butter in a saucepan. Add the eggs and cream and whisk lightly. Stir over a gentle heat until just beginning to scramble but still quite runny. Stir in the salmon and good grinding of black pepper. Immediately add the bucatini and toss gently over a low heat until just scrambled but still creamy. Pile on to hot plates and top with a little lumpfish roe, if liked, and a sprinkling of chopped parsley.

Penne Piperade

Serves 4

100 g/4 oz/1 cup penne
15 ml/1 tbsp olive oil
15 g/½ oz/1 tbsp butter
2 onions, sliced
2 green (bell) peppers, sliced
4 large tomatoes, quartered
1 garlic clove, crushed
4 eggs, beaten
Salt and freshly ground black
  pepper

Cook the penne according to the packet directions. Drain. Meanwhile heat the oil and butter in a large frying pan (skillet). Add the onions, peppers, tomatoes and garlic and stir-fry for 5 minutes until soft and lightly golden. Add the pasta, the eggs, a little salt and lots of pepper. Cook, lifting and stirring gently until the mixture has set. Serve straight from the pan.

Savoury Egg Pasta

Serves 4

225 g/8 oz/2 cups wholewheat pasta
  shapes
30 ml/2 tbsp olive oil
1 onion, chopped
1 garlic clove, crushed
225 g/8 oz/2 cups spring greens
  (spring cabbage), shredded
400 g/14 oz/1 large can chopped
  tomatoes
15 ml/1 tbsp chopped sun-dried
  tomato
2.5 ml/¹/₂ tsp dried mixed herbs
Salt and freshly ground black
  pepper
2 hard-boiled (hard-cooked) eggs,
  chopped
50 g/2 oz/1 cup fresh breadcrumbs
50 g/2 oz/¹/₂ cup grated red Leicester
  cheese
15 g/¹/₂ oz/1 tbsp butter

Cook the pasta according to the packet directions. Drain. Meanwhile, heat the oil in a large saucepan. Add the onion and garlic and cook for 2 minutes until softened but not browned. Add the greens and cook for 1 minute until beginning to wilt. Add the canned tomatoes, the sun-dried tomato, herbs, a little salt and lots of pepper. Cover and cook gently for 5 minutes. Stir in the pasta and eggs. Turn into a 1.2 litre/2 pt/5 cup ovenproof dish. Mix the breadcrumbs and cheese together and sprinkle over. Dot with butter and bake in the oven at 190°C/375°F/gas mark 5 for about 20 minutes until the top is golden brown and the mixture is piping hot.

Cheese Gnocchi

Serves 4

600 ml/1 pt/2¹/₂ cups milk
1 onion
2 whole cloves
1 bay leaf
100 g/4 oz/²/₃ cup semolina (cream of
  wheat)
175 g/6 oz Cheddar cheese, grated
30 ml/2 tbsp chopped parsley
Salt and freshly ground black
  pepper
Tabasco sauce
1 egg, beaten
100 g/4 oz/1 cup dried breadcrumbs
Oil for deep-frying

Put the milk in a saucepan. Stud the onion with the cloves and place in the milk with the bay leaf. Bring to the boil, remove from the heat and leave to infuse for 15 minutes. Strain and return to the saucepan. Blend in the semolina. Bring to the boil, stirring all the time, and cook for about 5 minutes until thick, stirring all the time. Remove from the heat and stir in the cheese and parsley. Season well with salt and pepper and a few drops of Tabasco. Spread the mixture on to a wetted cold dinner plate to make a round and chill for 2 hours. Cut into wedges, dip in the beaten egg then the breadcrumbs and deep-fry in hot oil until crisp and golden. Drain on kitchen paper and serve hot.

Spaghetti all'Uova

Serves 4-6
450 g/1 lb spaghetti
225 g/8 oz/1 cup unsalted (sweet)
butter
75 g/3 oz/³/₄ cup grated Pecorino
cheese
6 eggs, beaten
Salt and freshly ground black
pepper

Cook the spaghetti according to the packet directions. Drain in a colander. Cut half the butter into small pieces and place in the same saucepan. Return the spaghetti to the saucepan. Sprinkle with half the cheese, add the eggs, a little salt and lots of pepper. Toss over a very gentle heat until thoroughly blended and the eggs have just set. Turn into warm serving bowls, dot with flakes of the remaining butter and sprinkle with the remaining cheese.

Gnocchi alla Romana

Serves 6
900 ml/1¹/₂ pts/3³/₄ cups milk
1 sprig of rosemary
225 g/8 oz/1¹/₃ cups semolina (cream
of wheat)
100 g/4 oz/¹/₂ cup unsalted (sweet)
butter
175 g/6 oz/1¹/₂ cups freshly grated
Parmesan cheese
Salt and freshly ground black
pepper
3 size 1 eggs, beaten
Freshly grated nutmeg

Put the milk in a saucepan with the rosemary. Bring to the boil, remove from the heat and leave to infuse for 15 minutes. Remove the rosemary. Stir in the semolina, bring to the boil and cook for 5 minutes, stirring all the time. Remove from the heat and stir in half the butter and 100g/4 oz/ 1 cup of the cheese. Season well with salt and pepper. Gradually beat the eggs into the mixture. Turn into a greased shallow baking tin (pan) and chill for 2 hours until firm. Cut into squares, then roll into walnut-sized balls with lightly floured hands. Use a little of the remaining butter to grease an ovenproof dish. Arrange the gnocchi in a single layer in the dish. Sprinkle with a little more salt and pepper and some grated nutmeg. Melt the remaining butter and drizzle over the surface. Sprinkle with the remaining cheese and bake at 180°C/350°F/gas mark 4 for about 40 minutes until golden brown. Serve straight away.

Creamy Fettuccine with Nutmeg

Serves 4
350 g/12 oz fettuccine
50 g/2 oz/¹/₄ cup unsalted (sweet)
butter
150 ml/¹/₄ pt/²/₃ cup double (heavy)
cream
2.5 ml/¹/₂ tsp freshly grated nutmeg
Freshly ground black pepper
75 g/3 oz/³/₄ cup freshly grated
Parmesan cheese
30 ml/2 tbsp snipped chives

Cook the pasta according to the packet directions. Drain. In the same pan, melt the butter, add the cream and simmer for 3 minutes. Stir in the seasonings and cheese. Add the pasta, toss well and serve garnished with the chives.

Creamy Fettuccine with Fire

Serves 4

Prepare as for Creamy Fettuccine with Nutmeg, but substitute a red jalopeno pepper, seeded and chopped, for the nutmeg, and sprinkle with chopped red (bell) pepper instead of chives.

Buttered Tagliatelle with Toasted Sesame Seeds

Serves 4

350 g/12 oz tagliatelle
50 g/2 oz/¹/₂ cup sesame seeds
100 g/4 oz/¹/₂ cup unsalted (sweet) butter
Salt and freshly ground black pepper
50 g/2 oz/¹/₂ cup grated Pecorino cheese

Cook the tagliatelle according to the packet directions. Drain and return to the pan. Meanwhile, dry-fry the sesame seeds until golden. Add to the pasta with the butter cut into small pieces. Toss over a gentle heat until the butter melts. Season with a little salt and lots of pepper. Toss again and sprinkle with the cheese before serving.

Toasted Hazelnut Tagliatelle

Serves 4

Prepare as for Buttered Tagliatelle with Toasted Sesame Seeds, but substitute chopped hazelnuts for the sesame seeds and toast them in the same way. Add 15 ml/1 tbsp chopped parsley with the butter, and sprinkle with grated Mozzarella instead of Pecorino cheese.

Buttered Tagliatelle with Mixed Seeds

Serves 4

Prepare as for Buttered Tagliatelle with Toasted Sesame Seeds, but use only 15 ml/1 tbsp sesame seeds and add 15 ml/1 tbsp each of poppy, black and white mustard and caraway seeds. Instead of dry-frying them, melt the butter first and fry (sauté) the seeds until they begin to pop.

Buttered Tagliatelle with Pine Nuts and Sunflower Seeds

Serves 4

Prepare as for Buttered Tagliatelle with Mixed Seeds, but substitute 25 g/1 oz/ ¹/₄ cup pine nuts and 25 g/1 oz/¹/₄ cup sunflower seeds for the mixed seeds. Fry (sauté) in the butter until the pine nuts are golden.

Spaghettini Crisps

Serves 6
225 g/8 oz spaghettini
Oil for deep-frying
2.5 ml/¹/₂ tsp cayenne
10 ml/2 tsp salt
60 ml/4 tbsp grated Parmesan
  cheese

Cook the pasta according to the packet directions, drain thoroughly and cut into short lengths. Heat the oil to 180°C/350°F and deep-fry the spaghettini a batch at a time until crisp and golden (do not cook too much at one go). Sprinkle each batch with the cayenne mixed with salt, and then with some Parmesan cheese. Pile into a bowl and serve with drinks.

Crispy Buttered Noodles

Serves 4
225 g/8 oz any ribbon noodles
50 g/2 oz/¹/₄ cup unsalted (sweet)
  butter
50 g/2 oz/1 cup fresh breadcrumbs
30 ml/2 tbsp chopped parsley
50 g/2 oz/¹/₂ cup thinly shaved fresh
  Parmesan

Cook the pasta according to the packet directions. Drain, rinse with boiling water, drain again and return to the pan. Meanwhile, melt the butter and fry (sauté) the breadcrumbs until crisp and golden. Add to the noodles with the parsley and toss well. Serve straight away, topped with the Parmesan shavings.

Crisp Garlic and Herb Buttered Noodles

Serves 4
Prepare as for Crispy Buttered Noodles, but add 5 ml/1 tsp dried mixed herbs and 5 ml/1 tsp garlic salt to the breadrumbs.

Bucatini with Italian Melted Cheese

Serves 4
350 g/12 oz bucatini
60 ml/6 tbsp olive oil
1 onion, finely chopped
2 garlic cloves, chopped
75 g/3 oz Mozzarella cheese, cubed
50 g/2 oz/¹/₂ cup freshly grated
  Parmesan cheese
Salt and freshly ground black
  pepper

Cook the pasta according to the packet directions. Drain and return to the pan. Meanwhile, heat the oil and fry (sauté) the onion and garlic gently for 5 minutes until very soft and lightly golden. Add to the bucatini with the cheeses and toss well until the Mozzarella begins to melt. Season with salt and pepper and serve straight away.

Bucatini with Swiss Melted Cheese

Serves 4

Prepare as for Bucatini with Italian Melted Cheese, but substitute Gruyère (Swiss) cheese for the Mozzarella, and sprinkle in 10 ml/2 tsp kirsch when adding the cheese.

Tagliatelle with Fried Mozzarella

Serves 4

225 g/8 oz tagliatelle
60 ml/4 tbsp olive oil
175 g/6 oz Mozzarella cheese, cut into 4 thick slices
30 ml/2 tbsp chopped basil
Juice of ¹/₂ lemon
Salt and freshly ground black pepper

Cook the pasta according to the packet directions. Drain, divide between 4 warm plates and keep warm. Heat the oil in a large heavy frying pan (skillet). Add the Mozzarella and fry (sauté), moving the slices so they don't stick, until the bases are browned. Turn over quickly and brown the other sides. Quickly transfer to the pasta, spoon the oil over, sprinkle with the basil and lemon juice and season with salt and lots of pepper. Serve immediately.

Tagliatelle with Fried Camembert and Cranberry Sauce

Serves 4

Prepare as for Tagliatelle with Fried Mozzarella, but use individual wedges of Camembert. Garnish with parsley instead of basil, and top with a spoonful of cranberry sauce instead of the lemon juice.

Tagliatelle Verdi con Ricotta

Serves 4

350 g/12 oz green tagliatelle (verdi)
225 g/8 oz/1 cup unsalted (sweet) butter
1 kg/2¹/₄ lb/4¹/₂ cups Ricotta cheese
Salt and freshly ground black pepper
Paprika

Cook the pasta according to the packet directions. Drain and return to the pan. Add the butter in small flakes and toss until melted. Spoon the Ricotta over and season well with salt and pepper. Toss, pile on to plates and sprinkle with paprika before serving.

Tagliatelle with Cottage Cheese and Chives

Serves 4

Prepare as for Tagliatelle Verdi con Ricotta, but substitute cottage cheese and chives for the Ricotta.

Fettucci with Goat's Cheese and Chives

Serves 4

350 g/12 oz fettucci
15 g/¹/₂ oz/1 tbsp unsalted (sweet)
    butter
3 garlic cloves, crushed
250 ml/8 fl oz/1 cup crème fraîche
225 g/8 oz goat's cheese, crumbled
Salt and freshly ground black
    pepper
60 ml/4 tbsp snipped chives

Cook the pasta according to the packet directions. Drain and return to the pan. Melt the butter in a saucepan. Add the garlic and fry (sauté) very gently for 2 minutes but do not allow to brown. Add the crème fraîche and increase the heat slightly. Stir in the cheese and stir until it has melted. Season to taste and add half the chives. Pour over the pasta, toss gently and serve garnished with the remaining chives.

Italian Farmhouse Pasta

Serves 4

Prepare as for Spicy Farmhouse Pasta but substitute pancetta for the streaky bacon and Provalone cheese for the Cheddar. Use Dijon mustard in place of English.

Spicy Farmhouse Pasta

Serves 6

350 g/12 oz/3 cups rigatoni
30 ml/2 tbsp unsalted (sweet) butter
450 g/1 lb sweetcure streaky bacon,
    rinded and diced
750 ml/1¹/₄ pts/3 cups double (heavy)
    cream
750 g/1¹/₂ lb farmhouse Cheddar,
    grated
5 ml/1 tsp made English mustard
A few drops of Tabasco sauce
Salt and freshly ground black
    pepper

Cook the pasta according to the packet directions, drain. Meanwhile, melt the butter in a large pan. Add the bacon and fry (sauté) for 4-5 minutes until crisp. Drain on kitchen paper. Add the cream to the butter and bacon fat. Bring to the boil, stirring. Add the cheese and stir until it has melted and thickened the sauce. Stir in the mustard and Tabasco sauce. Season to taste. Pile the pasta on to warm plates. Spoon the sauce over and sprinkle liberally with the bacon.

Seductive Cream and Calvados Ribbons

Serves 4-6

40 g/1¹/₂ oz/³/₄ cup dried porcini mushrooms
375 ml/13 fl oz/1¹/₂ cups calvados or brandy
75 g/3 oz/¹/₃ cup unsalted (sweet) butter
4 garlic cloves, finely chopped
4 shallots, finely chopped
750 ml/1¹/₄ pts/3 cups double (heavy) cream
Salt and freshly ground black pepper
350 g/12 oz linguini
45 ml/3 tbsp chopped flatleaf parsley

Wash the mushrooms well. Place in a bowl with the calvados. Leave to soak for 10 minutes. Drain, reserving the calvados, and roughly chop the mushrooms. Melt the butter in a large pan. Add the garlic and shallots and fry (sauté) for 3 minutes until soft but not brown. Add the mushrooms and fry for a further 1 minute. Add the reserved calvados, ignite and shake the pan until the flames subside. Add the cream and boil for about 20 minutes until the sauce is thick and reduced by half. Season to taste. Meanwhile, cook the linguini according to the packet directions. Drain. Add to the sauce, toss, then pile on to warm plates and sprinkle with the parsley before serving.

Egg and Macaroni Florentine

Serves 4

1 quantity Basic Macaroni Cheese (page 296)
350 g/12 oz/3 cups chopped frozen spinach
4 hard-boiled (hard-cooked) eggs, quartered
Paprika

Cook the macaroni and cheese sauce as for Basic Macaroni Cheese, but do not mix together. Cook the spinach according to the packet directions. Drain thoroughly and place in the base of an ovenproof dish. Cover with the macaroni, then the eggs. Spoon the cheese sauce over, sprinkle with paprika and bake in the oven at 190°C/375°F/gas mark 5 for 25-30 minutes until bubbling and golden.

Rosy Eggs with Macaroni

Serves 4

Prepare as for Egg and Macaroni Florentine, but substitute 400 g/14 oz/ 1 large can chopped tomatoes with herbs for the spinach.

Macaroni Cheese Omelette

Serves 4

100 g/4 oz/1 cup elbow macaroni
1 bunch of spring onions (scallions),
finely chopped
50 g/2 oz/¹/₄ cup butter
4 eggs
30 ml/2 tbsp milk
15 ml/1 tbsp Worcestershire sauce
100 g/4 oz Cheddar cheese, grated
Salt and freshly ground black
pepper
2 tomatoes, sliced

Cook the pasta according to the packet directions, drain. Meanwhile, fry (sauté) the spring onions in the butter for 4 minutes until soft and golden brown. Beat the eggs with the milk, Worcestershire sauce and half the cheese. Season and stir in the macaroni. Pour over the onions and cook, lifting and stirring, until the base is golden and set. Lay the slices of tomato on top and sprinkle with the remaining cheese. Place under the grill (broiler) until bubbling, golden brown and the egg is set. Serve cut into wedges.

Tuna and Caper Pasta Omelette

Serves 4

100 g/4 oz/1 cup soup pasta
Chicken stock
185 g/6¹/₂ oz/1 small can tuna,
drained
10 ml/2 tbsp capers, chopped
15 ml/1 tbsp snipped chives
4 eggs
30 ml/2 tbsp milk
Salt and freshly ground black
pepper
25 g/1 oz/2 tbsp butter

Put the pasta in a saucepan. Add enough stock to cover. Bring to the boil and simmer until tender, topping up with stock or water if necessary. Drain off any remaining liquid. Mix with the tuna, capers and chives. Beat the eggs with the milk. Stir in the fish mixture and season lightly. Melt the butter in a large frying pan (skillet). Add the fish and egg mixture and cook, lifting and stirring, until the base is set and golden. Place the pan under a hot grill (broiler) until the top is golden and the egg is set. Serve cut into wedges.

Salmon and Cucumber Wedges

Serves 4

Prepare as for Tuna and Caper Pasta Omelette, but substitute canned salmon for the tuna, discarding any skin and bones. Substitute 15 ml/1 tbsp chopped cucumber for the capers, and add a squeeze of lemon juice. Serve each wedge with a spoonful of mayonnaise.

Mozzarella Omelette

Serves 4

225 g/8 oz green tagliatelle (verdi)
6 eggs
25 g/1 oz/¹/₄ cup grated Parmesan
* cheese*
30 ml/2 tbsp cold water
15 ml/1 tbsp chopped parsley
Salt and freshly ground black
* pepper*
15 ml/1 tbsp olive oil
15 g/¹/₂ oz/1 tbsp unsalted (sweet)
* butter*
175 g/6 oz Mozzarella cheese, sliced
60 ml/4 tbsp passata (sieved
* tomatoes)*
2.5 ml/¹/₂ tsp dried basil

Cook the pasta according to the packet directions. Drain, rinse with cold water, drain again and chop roughly. Beat the eggs with the cheese, water, parsley and a little salt and pepper. Stir in the pasta. Heat the oil and butter in a large frying pan (skillet). Add the egg mixture and cook gently for 2 minutes, lifting and stirring gently, until the underside is setting and turning golden. Add the cheese slices, cover with foil or a lid and cook for about 5 minutes until the egg is set and the cheese melted. Meanwhile, heat the passata with the basil and a little salt and pepper. Fold the omelette over, cut into 4 wedges and serve with the passata spooned over.

Swiss Omelette

Serves 4

Prepare as for Mozzarella Omelette, but substitute Emmental (Swiss) cheese for the Mozzarella, and flavour the passata with tarragon instead of basil.

Prawn Foo Yung with Noodles

Serves 4

100 g/4 oz Chinese egg noodles
2 spring onions (scallions), chopped
30 ml/2 tbsp sunflower oil
5 ml/1 tsp grated fresh root ginger
175 g/6 oz/1¹/₂ cups peeled prawns
* (shrimp)*
4 eggs
15 ml/1 tbsp water
15 ml/1 tbsp dry sherry
30 ml/2 tbsp soy sauce
5 ml/1 tsp caster (superfine) sugar
Shredded lettuce
1 green (bell) pepper, halved and
* thinly sliced*

Cook the noodles according to the packet directions. Drain. Fry (sauté) the spring onions in the oil for 3 minutes, stirring until softened. Add the ginger, prawns and noodles and stir for 1 minute. Beat the eggs with the water, sherry, soy sauce and sugar. Pour into the pan and cook over a moderate heat, lifting and stirring, until the base is set and golden. Place the pan under a hot grill (broiler) until the egg is set and the top is golden brown. Place some shredded lettuce and green pepper on 4 serving plates. Cut the omelette into quarters and place on top of the salad.

Salad Days

Pasta and rice are both wonderful bases for a myriad of salads. The recipes all make great starters too, in smaller portions of course, and are also ideal for buffets and picnics.

Dutch Rice Ring

Serves 4

175 g/6 oz/³/₄ cup long-grain rice
100 g/4 oz/1 cup frozen diced mixed
    vegetables
30 ml/2 tbsp olive oil
15 ml/1 tbsp white wine vinegar
Salt and freshly ground black
    pepper
A pinch of grated nutmeg
2 ripe pears, diced
175 g/6 oz Edam cheese, diced
1 head of Florence fennel, chopped,
    reserving the green fronds
45 ml/3 tbsp plain yoghurt
15 ml/1 tbsp snipped chives

Cook the rice and mixed vegetables in plenty of boiling salted water for 10 minutes. Drain, rinse with cold water and drain again. Whisk the oil, vinegar, a little salt and pepper and the nutmeg together and pour over the rice. Toss well. Spoon the mixture into an oiled 1.5 litre/2½ pt/6 cup ring mould (mold). Press down well, and chill while preparing the filling. Mix the pears, cheese, fennel and yoghurt with a little salt and pepper and the chives. Turn out the rice ring on to a serving plate. Spoon the cheese filling into the middle and garnish with the fennel fronds.

Minted Brown Rice Ring

Serves 6

225 g/8 oz/1 cup brown rice
50 g/2 oz/½ cup frozen peas
3 ripe tomatoes, seeded and diced
30 ml/2 tbsp currants
50 g/2 oz/½ cup pine nuts
25 g/1 oz/¼ cup toasted flaked
    almonds
30 ml/2 tbsp sunflower oil
15 ml/1 tbsp white wine vinegar
Salt and freshly ground black
    pepper
5 ml/1 tsp caster (superfine) sugar
15 ml/1 tbsp chopped mint
1 bunch of watercress

Cook the rice according to the packet directions or see page 12. Add the peas for the last 5 minutes of cooking. Drain, rinse with cold water and drain again. Add the tomatoes, currants, pine nuts and almonds and mix well. Whisk the oil and vinegar with a little salt, plenty of pepper, the sugar and mint. Pour over the rice mixture and toss well. Pack into a 1.5 litre/2½ pt/6 cup ring mould (mold). Chill. When ready to serve, turn out onto a serving dish and garnish with the watercress in the centre.

Party Rice Salad

Serves 10

275 g/10 oz/1¼ cups long-grain rice
100 g/4 oz/1 cup frozen peas
50 g/2 oz/⅓ cup sultanas (golden
    raisins)
25 g/1 oz/¼ cup toasted flaked
    almonds
4 celery sticks, chopped
45 ml/3 tbsp olive oil
15 ml/1 tbsp white wine vinegar
A pinch of salt
A pinch of caster (superfine) sugar
2.5 ml/½ tsp made English mustard
Freshly ground black pepper

Cook the rice in plenty of boiling salted
water for 10 minutes, adding the peas half-
way through cooking. Drain, rinse with
cold water and drain again. Mix with the
sultanas, nuts and celery in a large salad
bowl. Blend the remaining ingredients
together with a good grinding of black
pepper. Pour over the salad and toss well.

Greek Mushroom Salad

Serves 6

1 onion, chopped
90 ml/6 tbsp olive oil
300 ml/½ pt/1¼ cups dry white wine
Salt and freshly ground black
    pepper
1 bouquet garni sachet
1 garlic clove, crushed
200 g/7 oz/1 small can chopped
    tomatoes
350 g/12 oz/6 cups button
    mushrooms, quartered
225 g/8 oz/1 cup long-grain rice
Chopped parsley

Fry (sauté) the onion in two-thirds of the
oil for 3 minutes until softened but not
browned. Add the remaining ingredients
except the rice and parsley. Bring to the
boil, reduce the heat and simmer for about
15 minutes until the mushrooms are
cooked and the liquid is reduced and thickened. Remove the bouquet garni sachet,
taste and re-season if necessary. Leave to
cool, then chill. Meanwhile, cook the rice
in plenty of boiling salted water until just
tender. Drain, rinse with cold water and
drain again. Make nests of the rice on serving plates. Spoon the chilled mushrooms in
the centre and sprinkle with the chopped
parsley.

Apple Harvest Salad

Serves 4

225 g/8 oz/1 cup long-grain rice
1 large green eating (dessert) apple ,
    diced
Juice of 2 lemons
6 pecan halves, roughly chopped
100 g/4 oz Fontina cheese, diced
175 g/6 oz/1¼ cups cooked ham,
    diced
45 ml/3 tbsp olive oil
15 ml/1 tbsp Worcestershire sauce
Salt and freshly ground black
    pepper

Cook the rice in plenty of boiling salted
water until just tender. Drain, rinse with
cold water and drain again. Place in a large
salad bowl. Toss the apple in a little of the
lemon juice to prevent browning. Add to
the rice with the nuts, cheese and ham and
toss gently. Whisk the olive oil, the
remaining lemon juice and the
Worcestershire sauce together with a little
salt and pepper and pour over the salad.
Toss gently until completely coated then
serve.

Californian Fruit and Rice for Pork

Serves 6
425 g/15 oz/1 large can crushed
  pineapple, drained, reserving the
  juice
300 g/11 oz/1 small can mandarin
  oranges, drained, reserving the
  juice
1 packet lemon jelly (jello)
2 carrots, grated
50 g/2 oz/¹/₃ cup seedless (pitless)
  raisins
2 spring onions (scallions), finely
  chopped
225 g/8 oz/2 cups cooked long-grain
  rice
Cos (romaine) lettuce leaves

Put the juice from the pineapple and man-
darins in a measuring jug. Use to dissolve
the jelly according to the packet directions,
adding water if necessary. Mix the pineapple, mandarin oranges, carrots, raisins and
spring onions together in a large jelly
mould (mold). Pour over half the jelly and
leave to set. Mix the remaining jelly with
the cooked rice. Spoon over the set fruit
and chill again until set. Dip briefly in hot
water. Turn out on to a serving dish and
garnish with the lettuce leaves. Serve with
grilled (broiled) pork chops or spare ribs.

Beetroot Layer

Serves 6
4 cooked beetroot (red beet), sliced
1 bunch of spring onions (scallions),
  chopped
100 g/4 oz/1 cup cooked long-grain
  rice
30 ml/2 tbsp gherkins (cornichons),
  sliced
50 g/2 oz/¹/₂ cup walnuts, chopped
45 ml/3 tbsp French dressing (or 2
  parts oil to 1 part vinegar and a
  little salt, pepper and sugar)

Layer the beetroot, onions, rice, gherkins
and walnuts in a glass serving dish. Spoon
the dressing over and chill for at least 30
minutes before serving.

Curried Lamb Salad

Serves 4
225g/8 oz/1 cup long-grain rice
50 g/2 oz/¹/₂ cup frozen peas
25 g/1 oz/¹/₆ cup currants
15 ml/1 tbsp toasted flaked almonds
60 ml/4 tbsp mayonnaise
15 ml/1 tbsp mild curry paste
30 ml/2 tbsp curried fruit chutney
5 ml/1 tsp lemon juice
225 g/8 oz/2 cups cold cooked lamb,
  diced
425 g/15 oz/1 large can haricot
  (navy) beans, drained
2 tomatoes, cut into wedges

Cook the rice in plenty of boiling salted
water for 10 minutes or until just tender.
Add the peas after 5 minutes cooking.
Drain, rinse with cold water and drain
again. Stir in the currants and nuts and
spoon the mixture into a border on a large
serving plate. Mix the mayonnaise with the
curry paste and chutney. Stir in the lemon
juice. Fold in the lamb and beans and pile
the mixture into the centre of the rice.
Garnish with the tomato wedges before
serving.

Sausage Salad Supreme

Serves 4-6

100 g/4 oz/1¹/₂ cup wild rice mix
4 slices white bread, cubed
45 ml/3 tbsp oil
8 thick sausages, cooked and sliced
325 g/11¹/₂ oz/1 large can Mexican
  sweetcorn (corn with bell
  peppers), drained
430 g/15¹/₂ oz/1 large can butter
  beans, drained
¹/₂ cucumber, diced
1 bunch of radishes, trimmed and
  quartered
1 garlic clove, crushed
150 ml/¹/₄ pt/²/₃ cup thick plain
  yoghurt
30 ml/2 tbsp snipped chives

Cook the rice according to the packet directions. Drain, rinse with cold water and drain again. Fry (sauté) the bread in the oil until golden. Drain on kitchen paper. Mix the rice with the sausages, corn, butter beans, cucumber and radishes. Mix the garlic with the yoghurt and chives. Just before serving, stir the fried bread into the salad, divide between serving plates and top each with a spoonful of the dressing.

Chilled Tomato and Cardamom Rice

Serves 4

15 ml/1 tbsp sunflower oil
6 cardamom pods, split
5 ml/1 tsp cumin seeds
225 g/8 oz/1 cup basmati rice
45 ml/3 tbsp tomato juice
15 ml/1 tbsp tomato purée (paste)
1.5 ml/¹/₄ tsp salt

Grated rind and juice of 1 orange
4 tomatoes, cut into wedges
1 orange, cut into small wedges

Heat the oil in a pan. Add the cardamom and cumin and fry (sauté), stirring, until the seeds pop. Stir in the rice, tomato juice, purée, salt and orange rind and juice. Pour over enough water to cover by 2.5 cm/1 in. Bring to the boil, reduce the heat, cover and simmer gently for 20 minutes or until the rice is tender and has absorbed all the liquid. Cool then chill. Pile on to a serving dish and garnish with tomato and orange wedges before serving.

Warm Carrot, Courgette and Wild Rice Salad

Serves 6

100 g/4 oz/1¹/₂ cup wild rice or wild
  rice mix
225 g/8 oz/2 cups grated carrots
225 g/8 oz/2 cups grated courgettes
  (zucchini)
90 ml/6 tbsp sunflower oil
30 ml/2 tbsp mustard seeds
30 ml/2 tbsp lemon juice

Cook the wild rice according to the packet directions. Drain, rinse with cold water and drain again. Place in a bowl and add the carrots and courgettes. Heat the oil in a frying pan (skillet). Add the mustard seeds and fry (sauté) quickly until they begin to pop. Stir in the lemon juice, pour over the salad, toss quickly and serve straight away.

Fragrant Stuffed Tomatoes

Serves 4

8 tomatoes
1 small onion, finely chopped
25 g/1 oz/2 tbsp butter
50 g/2 oz/¹/₄ cup brown rice
150 ml/¹/₄ pt/²/₃ cup vegetable stock
Salt and freshly ground black
  pepper
15 g/¹/₂ oz/2 tbsp chopped pistachio
  nuts
15 ml/1 tbsp currants
2 rosemary sprigs

Cut a slice off the rounded ends of the tomatoes and reserve for lids. Scoop out the seeds and reserve. Fry (sauté) the onion in the butter for 2 minutes, until softened but not browned. Stir in the rice, stock and a little salt and pepper. Bring to the boil, reduce the heat, cover and simmer gently for 30 minutes. Stir in the nuts, currants and rosemary and cook for a further 15 minutes or until the rice is really tender and has absorbed all the liquid. Remove the rosemary, taste and re-season if necessary. Stir in the tomato seeds. Pack into the tomatoes, replace the lids and chill until ready to serve.

Picnic Paella

Serves 6

1 onion, finely chopped
1 garlic clove, crushed
30 ml/2 tbsp olive oil
1 small red (bell) pepper, diced
1 small green (bell) pepper, diced
100 g/4 oz pork fillet, diced
1 chicken breast, diced
225 g/8 oz/1 cup long-grain rice
600 ml/1 pt/2¹/₂ cups chicken stock
5ml/1 tsp saffron powder or
  turmeric
250 g/9 oz/1 small can mussels in
  brine
100 g/4 oz/1 cup peeled prawns
  (shrimp)
50 g/2 oz/¹/₂ cup frozen peas
Salt and freshly ground black
  pepper
6 whole prawns (shrimp)
Cucumber slices

Fry (sauté) the onion and garlic in the oil for 2 minutes until soft but not brown. Add the peppers and fry for a further 2 minutes. Stir in the pork and chicken and fry, stirring, for 3 minutes. Stir in the rice. Add the stock and saffron or turmeric, bring to the boil, reduce the heat, cover and simmer for 15 minutes. Stir in the contents of the can of mussels, the peeled prawns and the peas and season with salt and pepper. Re-cover and cook for 5 minutes. Remove the lid and continue cooking until the rice is tender and has absorbed all the liquid. Spoon into a lightly oiled 1.2 litre/2 pt/5 cup pudding basin. Leave to cool then chill for at least 2 hours. Turn out on to a serving plate and garnish with the whole prawns and cucumber slices.

Salmon and Rice Picnic Lunch

Serves 4

225 g/8 oz/1 cup long-grain rice
200 g/7 oz/1 small can red salmon
5 cm/2 in piece cucumber, diced
4 cherry tomatoes, quartered
2 hard-boiled (hard-cooked) eggs, quartered
30 ml/2 tbsp olive oil
15 ml/1 tbsp lemon juice
Salt and freshly ground black pepper

Cook the rice in plenty of boiling salted water until just tender. Drain, rinse with cold water and drain again. Place in a bowl. Drain the salmon, discard any skin and bone and break the flesh into pieces. Add to the rice with the remaining ingredients. Toss gently until combined but try to keep the fish in neat pieces. Serve chilled.

American-style Hot Chicken Salad

Serves 6

175 g/6 oz/³/₄ cup long-grain rice
450 g/1 lb cooked chicken, cut into pieces
¹/₂ bunch of spring onions (scallions), finely chopped
1 canned pimiento, chopped
275 g/10 oz/1 can cream of chicken soup
275 g/10 oz/1 can cream of mushroom soup
100 ml/3 fl oz/6¹/₂ tbsp mayonnaise
Salt and freshly ground black pepper
2 celery sticks, chopped
1 carrot, grated
50 g/2 oz/¹/₂ cup toasted flaked almonds
50 g/2 oz/¹/₂ cup grated Cheddar cheese
50 g/2 oz/2 cups cornflakes

Cook the rice in plenty of boiling salted water until tender. Drain. Mix with the remaining ingredients except the cornflakes. Turn into a large ovenproof dish. Crush the cornflakes on top and bake at 180°C/350°F/gas mark 4 for 30 minutes.

Hawaii Chicken

Serves 4

300 g/11 oz/1 small can pineapple chunks, drained
175 g/6 oz/1¹/₂ cups cooked long-grain rice
175 g/6 oz/1¹/₂ cups cooked chicken, diced
198 g/7 oz/1 small can Mexican sweetcorn (corn with bell peppers), drained
30 ml/2 tbsp mayonnaise
Lettuce leaves
Tomato wedges

Mix all the ingredients except the lettuce leaves and tomato wedges in a bowl. Fold in gently until well combined. Pile on to a bed of lettuce and garnish with tomato wedges before serving.

Continental Tuna and Vegetable Salad

Serves 4
225 g/8 oz/1 cup arborio or other
    risotto rice
45 ml/3 tbsp olive oil
Juice of 3 lemons
185 g/6¹/₂ oz/1 small can tuna,
    drained
1 yellow (bell) pepper, diced
2 tomatoes, diced
3 hard-boiled (hard-cooked) eggs,
    cut into chunks
175 g/6 oz Gruyère (Swiss) cheese,
    cubed
60 ml/4 tbsp chopped parsley
4 basil leaves, finely chopped
Salt and freshly ground black
    pepper
A few stoned (pitted) green olives

Cook the rice in plenty of boiling salted water for 15-20 minutes until just tender but still with some texture. Drain, rinse with cold water and drain again. Place in a bowl and drizzle with the oil and lemon juice. Add the remaining ingredients except the olives. Toss lightly. Pack into a large mould (mold) and chill for 1 hour. Turn out on to a serving plate and garnish with the olives, cut into quarters.

Umbrian Tuna Pea Salad

Serves 4
225 g/8 oz/1 cup arborio or long-
    grain rice
A good sprig of mint
225 g/8 oz/2 cups frozen peas
185 g/6¹/₂ oz/1 small can tuna,
    drained and flaked
3 stoned (pitted) green olives, finely
    chopped
60 ml/4 tbsp olive oil
Juice of 2 lemons
Salt and freshly ground black
    pepper
Lettuce leaves
2 hard-boiled (hard-cooked) eggs,
    sliced

Cook the rice in plenty of boiling salted water with the mint added for 15 minutes or until just tender. Add the peas for the last 5 minutes cooking time. Drain, rinse with cold water and drain again. Remove the mint. Place the rice and peas in a bowl. Add the tuna, olives, oil and lemon juice. Season well, then toss. Press into a mould (mold) and chill for at least an hour, then turn out on to a bed of lettuce. Alternatively, simply pile on to the lettuce. Garnish with the sliced egg and serve.

Lebanese-style Cucumber and Rice Salad

Serves 4-6
225 g/8 oz/1 cup long-grain rice
1 cucumber, grated
150 ml/¹/₄ pt/²/₃ cup thick plain
  yoghurt
10 ml/2 tsp dried mint
Salt and freshly ground black
  pepper

Cook the rice in plenty of boiling salted water until just tender. Drain, rinse with cold water and drain again. Grate the cucumber and squeeze out the excess moisture. Add to the rice and mix thoroughly. Spoon on to a serving dish. Mix the yoghurt with the mint and season with salt and lots of black pepper. Spoon over the rice and cucumber and chill until ready to serve.

English Country Prawn Salad

Serves 4-6
350 g/12 oz/1¹/₂ cups long-grain rice
225 g/8 oz/2 cups peeled prawns
  (shrimp)
1 cucumber, thinly sliced
2 hard-boiled (hard-cooked) eggs,
  sliced
2 tomatoes, halved, seeded and cut
  into chunks
45 ml/3 tbsp olive oil
Juice of 2 lemons
Salt and freshly ground black
  pepper
Lettuce leaves

Cook the rice in plenty of boiling salted water until tender. Drain, rinse with cold water and drain again. Place in a large bowl and gently mix in all the remaining ingredients except the lettuce. Turn into a large, lightly oiled pudding basin and press down firmly. Chill for at least 1 hour. Loosen the edge, then turn out on to a bed of lettuce and serve. Alternatively, simply toss gently in a salad bowl and serve with the lettuce.

Ligurian Prawn Salad

Serves 4-6
350 g/12 oz/1¹/₂ cups arborio or
  other risotto rice
350 g/12 oz/3 cups peeled prawns
  (shrimp)
225 g/8 oz/2 cups shelled fresh
  young peas
90 ml/6 tbsp olive oil
50 g/2 oz/¹/₂ cup chopped parsley
Salt and freshly ground black
  pepper
Lemon wedges

Cook the rice in plenty of boiling salted water for 15-20 minutes until just tender but still with texture. Drain, rinse with cold water and drain again. Place in a bowl and gently mix in the prawns, peas, oil and parsley. Season well and toss lightly. Garnish with lemon wedges before serving.

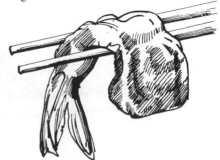

No-fuss Curried Chicken Mayonnaise

Serves 4
1 packet savoury rice with mushrooms
½ cooked chicken
45 ml/3 tbsp mayonnaise
20 ml/4 tsp mango chutney
10 ml/2 tsp curry paste
Paprika
Bite-sized popadoms

Cook the rice according to the packet directions. Drain, spoon into a ring on a large serving plate and leave until cold. Pick all the meat off the chicken and cut into bite-sized pieces. Mix the mayonnaise with the chutney and curry paste. Fold in the chicken and pile into the centre of the cold rice. Sprinkle with paprika and serve with the popadoms.

Chicken and Vegetable Cassata

Serves 4-6
350 g/12 oz/1½ cups arborio or other risotto rice
225 g/8 oz/2 cups shelled fresh young peas, cooked if preferred
100 g/4 oz/1 cup cooked chicken, shredded
3 thick slices ham, cut into thin strips
4 stoned (pitted) black olives, chopped
4 basil leaves, chopped
75 ml/5 tbsp olive oil
30 ml/2 tbsp balsamic vinegar
Salt and freshly ground black pepper
Lettuce leaves

3 hard-boiled (hard-cooked) eggs, cut into wedges

Cook the rice in plenty of boiling salted water for 15-20 minutes until just tender but still with some texture. Drain, rinse with cold water and drain again. Place in a large bowl and add the remaining ingredients except the lettuce and eggs. Mix gently, then pack into a large, lightly oiled pudding basin. Press down well, then chill for at least 1 hour. Loosen the edge then turn out on to a bed of lettuce and garnish with wedges of hard-boiled egg.

Saffron Rice Salad

Serves 4
225 g/8 oz/1 cup long-grain rice
225 g/8 oz/2 cups frozen peas
2 carrots, roughly chopped
2 courgettes (zucchini), roughly chopped
1.5 ml/¼ tsp saffron powder
25 ml/1½ tbsp olive oil
Salt and freshly ground black pepper
250 ml/8 fl oz/1 cup mayonnaise
Fresh basil leaves

Cook the rice in plenty of boiling salted water for 12 minutes. Add the peas, carrots and courgettes half-way through cooking. Drain, rinse with cold water and drain again. Stir in the saffron and olive oil and season to taste. Pack into a lightly oiled ring mould (mold). Chill for at least 1 hour. Turn out on to a serving plate. Spoon the mayonnaise into the centre and scatter with torn basil leaves.

Economical Curried Rice and Cheese Salad

Serves 4
225 g/8 oz/1 cup long-grain rice
400 g/14 oz/1 large can baked beans
  in tomato sauce
10 ml/2 tsp curry powder
15 ml/1 tbsp salad cream
30 ml/2 tbsp sultanas (golden
  raisins)
100 g/4 oz Cheddar cheese, cubed
Lettuce leaves
Chopped parsley

Cook the rice in plenty of boiling salted water until tender. Drain, rinse with cold water and drain again. Place in a bowl. Add the beans, curry powder, salad cream, sultanas and cheese. Toss well. Pile on a bed of lettuce and serve garnished with parsley.

Warm Brown Rice and Nut Salad

Serves 4
225 g/8 oz/1 cup brown rice
750 ml/1¹/₄ pts/3 cups chicken stock
1 onion, chopped
3 celery sticks, chopped
1 garlic clove, crushed
1 green (bell) pepper, chopped
30 ml/2 tbsp olive oil
Salt and freshly ground black
  pepper
225 g/8 oz/2 cups mixed nuts,
  roughly chopped
A squeeze of lemon juice

Cook the rice in the stock for about 45 minutes or until tender and the stock is absorbed, stirring occasionally. Remove from the heat, turn into a serving dish and leave to cool slightly while preparing the dressing. Fry (sauté) the onion, celery, garlic and pepper in the oil for just 1 minute until slightly softened. Add to the rice with a little salt and pepper and the nuts and toss well. Add a good squeeze of lemon juice and serve warm.

Salami and Rice Salad with Spinach

Serves 4
225 g/8 oz/1 cup long-grain rice
50 g/2 oz salami, cut into small thin
  strips
50 g/2 oz/¹/₂ cup fresh shelled peas
30 ml/2 tbsp olive oil
15 ml/1 tbsp white wine vinegar
Salt and freshly ground black
  pepper
100 g/4 oz young spinach leaves

Cook the rice according to the packet directions. Drain, rinse with cold water, drain again. Mix with the salami and peas. Whisk the oil, vinegar and a little salt and pepper together and pour over. Toss well. Pile on a bed of spinach leaves and chill, if time, before serving.

Piedmont-style Rice Salad

Serves 4

225 g/8 oz/1 cup arborio or other risotto rice
45 ml/3 tbsp olive oil
12 cooked asparagus tips
225 g/8 oz/4 cups button mushrooms, sliced
2 celery sticks, chopped
2 hard-boiled (hard-cooked) eggs
15 ml/1 tbsp Dijon mustard
Juice of 1 lemon
15 ml/1 tbsp double (heavy) cream
15 ml/1 tbsp Marsala or medium sherry
Salt and freshly ground black pepper
1 white truffle

Cook the rice in plenty of boiling salted water for 15-20 minutes until just tender but still with some texture. Drain, rinse with cold water and drain again. Toss in half the oil. Add the asparagus, mushrooms and celery. Remove the yolks from the whites of the eggs. Chop the whites and add to the rice. Mash the yolks with the mustard, lemon juice, cream, Marsala and a little salt and pepper. Whisk in the remaining oil to form a creamy dressing. Pour over the rice and toss gently. Pile into a serving bowl and grate the truffle over the top.

Mushroom and Artichoke Salad

Serves 4-6

350 g/12 oz/1½ cups long-grain rice
400 g/14 oz/1 large can artichoke hearts, drained
6 open mushrooms, sliced
30 ml/2 tbsp olive oil
45 ml/3 tbsp dry white wine
45 ml/3 tbsp chopped parsley
6 rashers (slices) streaky bacon, rinded and diced
250 ml/8 fl oz/1 cup mayonnaise
Lettuce leaves

Cook the rice in plenty of boiling salted water for 12 minutes until tender. Drain, rinse with cold water and drain again. Meanwhile, rinse the artichokes, pat dry on kitchen paper and cut into bite-sized pieces. Fry (sauté) with the mushrooms in the oil for 3 minutes until golden. Add the wine and cook until most of the wine has evaporated. Stir in the parsley and leave to cool. Dry-fry the bacon until crisp. Drain on kitchen paper. Fold the cooled artichoke mixture and the mayonnaise into the rice. Pile on to a bed of lettuce and sprinkle with the crisp bacon before serving.

319

Curried Artichoke Salad

Serves 6
225 g/8 oz/1 cup long-grain rice
600 ml/1 pt/2¹/₂ cups vegetable stock
400 g/14 oz/1 large can artichoke
  hearts, drained and quartered
250 ml/8 fl oz/1 cup mayonnaise
15 ml/1 tbsp curry paste
Crisp lettuce leaves
50 g/2 oz/¹/₂ cup toasted flaked
  almonds

Cook the rice in the stock and simmer for about 15 minutes until tender and the stock has been absorbed. Remove from the heat, turn into a bowl and leave to cool. When cold, add the artichoke hearts. Blend the mayonnaise with the curry paste, then stir into the rice. Pile on to a bed of lettuce and scatter the nuts over.

Insalata al Fresco

Serves 4
225 g/8 oz/1 cup arborio or other
  risotto rice
1 onion, thinly sliced into rings
45 ml/3 tbsp olive oil
30 ml/2 tbsp balsamic vinegar
5 ml/1 tsp caster (superfine) sugar
3 stoned (pitted) black olives,
  chopped
Salt and freshly ground black
  pepper
3 tomatoes, skinned, seeded and
  roughly chopped
4 mint leaves, chopped

Cook the rice in plenty of boiling salted water for 15-20 minutes until just cooked but still with texture. Drain, rinse with cold water and drain again. Turn into a bowl. Meanwhile, cook the onion in the oil gently for 3 minutes until softened. Stir in the vinegar, sugar, olives and some salt and pepper and simmer very gently for 5 minutes. Pour the hot onion mixture over the rice, add the tomatoes and mint. Toss and serve straight away.

Bittersweet Rice Salad

Serves 4-6
350 g/12 oz/1¹/₂ cups long-grain rice
75 ml/5 tbsp olive oil
2 large onions, finely chopped
45 ml/3 tbsp balsamic vinegar
15 ml/1 tbsp caster (superfine) sugar
Salt and freshly ground black
  pepper
2 tomatoes, skinned, seeded and
  roughly chopped
2 heads chicory (Belgian endive)
Mint leaves

Cook the rice in plenty of boiling salted water for 12 minutes. Drain, rinse with cold water and drain again. Meanwhile, heat the oil in a frying pan (skillet) and fry (sauté) the onion for 3 minutes until softened. Stir in the vinegar, sugar, salt and pepper to taste. Stir in the tomatoes. Add this mixture to the cool rice and fold in gently. Cut out the cores in a cone shape from the chicory. Shred the leaves and arrange on a serving plate. Pile the rice mixture on top and garnish with a few mint leaves.

Mediterranean Rice and Bean Salad

Serves 4

225 g/8 oz/1 cup long-grain rice
225 g/8 oz/2 cups very thin green
  beans, cut into short lengths
6 black olives in oil (not brine),
  stoned (pitted) and chopped
45 ml/3 tbsp olive oil (use a little
  from the olives if liked)
30 ml/2 tbsp balsamic vinegar

Cook the rice with the beans in plenty of boiling, salted water for about 10-12 minutes until just tender. Drain, rinse with cold water and drain again. Turn into a bowl. Add the remaining ingredients and toss well but lightly. Serve at room temperature.

Russian Rice Salad

Serves 4

225 g/8 oz/1 cup long-grain rice
275 g/10 oz can diced mixed
  vegetables, drained
Mayonnaise
Salt and freshly ground black
  pepper
Lettuce leaves

Cook the rice in plenty of boiling salted water until just tender. Drain, rinse with cold water and drain again. Place in a bowl and mix in the vegetables. Moisten with mayonnaise and season to taste. Pile on to a bed of lettuce. Serve with cold meat.

Rooted Rice Medley

Serves 4

225 g/8 oz/1 cup long-grain rice
15-30 ml/1-2 tbsp mayonnaise
1 large carrot, grated
1 parsnip, grated
$^1/_2$ small swede, grated
30 ml/2 tbsp olive oil
15 ml/1 tbsp lemon juice
30 ml/2 tbsp caraway seeds
Salt and freshly ground black
  pepper
12 black grapes, halved and seeded
  (pitted)

Cook the rice in plenty of boiling salted water until just tender. Drain, rinse with cold water and drain again. Mix with enough mayonnaise just to moisten. Spoon into a ring on a large round plate (or press into a large oiled ring mould (mold), then turn out on to the plate). Mix the grated vegetables with the oil, lemon juice to taste, the caraway seeds and some salt and pepper. Toss well and spoon into the centre of the rice. Garnish all round the edge with the grapes.

Three Bean and Rice Salad

Serves 6

225 g/8 oz/1 cup brown rice
425 g/15 oz/1 large can each of red
 kidney, flageolet and cannellini
 beans, drained
1 green (bell) pepper, cut into thin
 rings
1 small onion, cut into thin rings
45 ml/3 tbsp olive oil
15 ml/1 tbsp red wine vinegar
15 ml/1 tbsp snipped chives
Salt and freshly ground black
 pepper

Cook the rice (see page 12 or according to
the packet directions). Drain, rinse with
cold water and drain again. Mix with all
the remaining ingredients and toss well.

Scallop and Bacon Kebab Salad

Serves 6

175 g/6 oz/³/₄ cup wild rice mix
24 queen scallops
6 rashers (slices) streaky bacon
15 g/¹/₂ oz/1 tbsp butter
30 ml/2 tbsp olive oil
5 ml/1 tsp balsamic vinegar
10 ml/2 tsp white wine vinegar
A pinch of caster (superfine) sugar
Salt and freshly ground black
 pepper
225 g/8 oz mixed salad leaves
1 ripe avocado, sliced and tossed in
 lemon juice
A pinch of cayenne

Cook the rice according to the packet
directions. Drain, rinse with cold water and
drain again. Wrap each of the scallops in a
quarter of a rasher of bacon. Arrange 3 on
each of 8 wooden cocktail sticks (toothpicks). Fry (sauté) in the butter and 15
ml/1 tbsp of the oil for about 4 minutes
until golden brown and cooked through,
turning occasionally. Remove from the pan
and keep warm. Stir the remaining oil into
the pan with the vinegars, sugar, salt and
pepper. Heat through, stirring. Arrange the
salad leaves on serving plates with a small
mound of the rice in the centre. Lay 2
kebabs on each and spoon the hot dressing
over. Garnish with avocado slices, dusted
with cayenne.

Pisa Pepper Rice

Serves 4

225 g/8 oz/1 cup arborio or other
 risotto rice
2 hard-boiled (hard-cooked) eggs,
 roughly chopped
1 potato, boiled and diced
1 red (bell) pepper, diced
8 stoned (pitted) green olives,
 roughly chopped
75 ml/5 tbsp Ricotta cheese
45 ml/3 tbsp olive oil
15 ml/1 tbsp red wine vinegar
Salt and freshly ground black
 pepper

Cook the rice in plenty of boiling salted
water for 15-20 minutes until just tender
but still with some texture. Drain, rinse
with cold water and drain again. Fold in all
the remaining ingredients gently with a
metal spoon. Serve chilled.

Cottage Cornucopia

Serves 4

225 g/8 oz/1 cup long-grain rice
45 ml/3 tbsp olive oil
15 ml/1 tbsp lemon juice
Salt and freshly ground black
*   pepper*
Mixed lettuce leaves
225 g/8 oz/1 cup cottage cheese with
*   chives*
300 g/11 oz can pineapple chunks,
*   drained*
100 g/4 oz/1 cup cooked ham, diced
4 tomatoes, seeded and diced
2 satsumas, peeled and segmented
¹/₄ cucumber, diced
1 red (bell) pepper, diced
45 ml/3 tbsp mayonnaise
15 ml/1 tbsp milk
Paprika
8 radishes, left whole or cut into
*   roses if liked*

Cook the rice in plenty of boiling salted water until tender. Drain, rinse with cold water and drain again. Mix with the oil, lemon juice and a little salt and pepper. Press into a ring mould (mold), then turn out on to a bed of lettuce. Mix the cottage cheese with the pineapple, ham, tomatoes, satsumas, cucumber and pepper. Blend the mayonnaise with the milk and a little salt and pepper. Add to the cheese mixture and toss lightly. Pile in the centre and sprinkle with paprika. Garnish with the radishes before serving.

Curried Egg and Pepper Salad

Serves 4

175 g/6 oz/³/₄ cup basmati rice
15 ml/1 tbsp currants
30 ml/2 tbsp chopped walnuts
15 ml/1 tbsp sunflower oil
15 ml/1 tbsp walnut oil
10 ml/2 tsp white wine vinegar
Salt and freshly ground black
*   pepper*
8 hard-boiled (hard-cooked) eggs,
*   halved*
2 green (bell) peppers, sliced into
*   rings*
1 red (bell) pepper, sliced into rings
1 yellow (bell) pepper, sliced into
*   rings*
60 ml/4 tbsp mayonnaise
30 ml/2 tbsp plain yoghurt
15 ml/1 tbsp curry paste
A little milk
A good pinch of caster (superfine)
*   sugar*
Coriander (cilantro) leaves

Cook the rice in plenty of boiling salted water. Drain, rinse with cold water and drain again. Mix with the currants, walnuts, sunflower and walnut oils and the vinegar. Season to taste and mix well. Pile on to a serving plate and make into a large nest. Arrange the eggs, rounded sides up, in the centre. Scatter the pepper rings attractively all around. Blend the mayonnaise with the yoghurt and curry paste. Thin, if necessary, with a little milk and stir in the sugar and salt and pepper to taste. Spoon over the eggs, garnish with coriander leaves and chill before serving.

Spiced Lamb's Tongue and Apple Salad

Serves 4

100 g/4 oz/1½ cup long-grain rice
1 small green (bell) pepper, diced
30 ml/2 tbsp sultanas (golden raisins)
1 red-skinned eating (dessert) apple, diced but unpeeled
Lemon juice
75 ml/5 tbsp mayonnaise
10 ml/2 tsp curry paste
2.5 ml/½ tsp Dijon mustard
Mango chutney
8 slices pressed lamb's tongue
Watercress sprigs

Cook the rice in plenty of boiling salted water until tender. Drain, rinse with cold water and drain again. Place in a bowl and add the pepper and sultanas. Mix the apple with a little lemon juice to prevent browning and add to the bowl. Blend the mayonnaise with the curry paste and mustard. Add to the rice mixture, toss and pile on a serving plate. Spread a little mango chutney on each slice of tongue. Roll up and arrange on top of the rice. Chill, then garnish with sprigs of watercress before serving.

Spiced Ham and Pear Salad

Serves 4

Prepare as for Spiced Lamb's Tongue and Apple Salad, but substitute ham for the tongue, and under-ripe pears for the apple. Spread the ham with peach chutney instead of mango.

Prawn and Mushroom Salad with Wild Rice

Serves 4

175 g/6 oz/¾ cup wild rice mix
5 ml/1 tsp dried tarragon
45 ml/3 tbsp olive oil
15 ml/1 tbsp white wine vinegar
Salt and freshly ground black pepper
150 ml/¼ pt/⅔ cup crème fraîche
Lemon juice
2.5 ml/½ tsp caster (superfine) sugar
A few drops of Tabasco sauce
225 g/8 oz/4 cups button mushrooms, sliced
225 g/8 oz/2 cups peeled prawns (shrimp)
Lemon wedges
Parsley sprigs

Cook the wild rice mix according to the packet directions. Drain, rinse with cold water and drain again. Whisk the tarragon with the oil, vinegar and a little salt and pepper. Add to the rice and toss well. Pile on to a serving dish and make a well in the centre. Blend the crème fraîche with lemon juice to taste. Stir in the sugar, a few drops of Tabasco sauce and a little salt and pepper. Fold in the mushrooms and prawns. Pile on to the rice mixture and garnish with lemon wedges and a few parsley sprigs.

Chicken and Corn Salad with Wild Rice

Serves 4

Prepare as for Prawn and Mushroom Salad with Wild Rice, but substitute chicken for the prawns and 200g/7 oz/1 small can sweetcorn (corn) for the mushrooms.

Avocados with Ham and Asparagus

Serves 4

75 g/3 oz/1¹/₃ cup Thai fragrant rice
2 large, ripe avocados, halved and stoned (pitted)
15 ml/1 tbsp lemon juice
100 g/4 oz/1 cup cooked ham, diced
275 g/10 oz/1 small can asparagus tips, chopped
4 stuffed olives, sliced
15 g/1 tbsp snipped chives
45 ml/3 tbsp olive oil
A pinch of caster (superfine) sugar
Salt and freshly ground black pepper
2.5 ml/¹/₂ tsp wholegrain mustard

Cook the rice in plenty of boiling salted water until tender. Drain, rinse with cold water and drain again. Place in a bowl. Scoop out the avocado flesh, keeping the skin intact, and cut into small dice. Mix with the lemon juice to prevent browning. Add the remaining ingredients and mix well. Pile back into the avocado skins and serve chilled.

Valencian Salad

Serves 4

175 g/6 oz/³/₄ cup long-grain rice
2 oranges, peeled, sliced and cut into quarters
1 onion, sliced and separated into rings
200 g/7 oz/1 small can pimientos, drained and cut into thin strips
12 stuffed green olives, sliced
100 g/4 oz/1 cup chorizo sausage, thinly sliced
60 ml/4 tbsp olive oil
1 garlic clove, crushed
15 ml/1 tbsp chopped parsley
15 ml/1 tbsp white wine vinegar
5 ml/1 tsp clear honey
Salt and freshly ground black pepper
Lettuce leaves

Cook the rice in plenty of boiling salted water until just tender. Drain, rinse with cold water and drain again. Place in a bowl with the oranges, onion, pimientos, half the olives and the chorizo. Blend the oil with the garlic, parsley, vinegar, honey and a little salt and pepper. Pour over the salad and toss well. Pile on to a bed of lettuce and scatter the remaining sliced olives over. Add a good grinding of black pepper before serving.

Chilli Bean Salad

Serves 4

175 g/6 oz/³/₄ cup long-grain rice
225 g/8 oz/1 cup cottage cheese with chives
¹/₄ iceberg lettuce, shredded
2 × 425 g/2 × 15 oz/2 large cans red kidney beans, drained and rinsed
1 green (bell) pepper, diced
1 small onion, sliced and separated into rings
2 celery sticks, chopped
1 green chilli, seeded and chopped
45 ml/3 tbsp olive oil
15 ml/1 tbsp red wine vinegar
2.5 ml/¹/₂ tsp ground cumin
2.5 ml/¹/₂ tsp dried oregano
Salt and freshly ground black pepper
50 g/2 oz Cheddar cheese, grated

Cook the rice in plenty of boiling salted water until just tender. Drain, rinse with cold water and drain again. Mix with the cottage cheese and spoon in a large ring on a bed of lettuce on a flat serving dish. Mix the beans with the pepper, onion, celery and chilli. Blend the oil with the vinegar, cumin, oregano, a little salt and a good grinding of pepper. Pour over the beans and toss well. Spoon into the centre of the rice. Spoon the grated cheese in a ring between the rice and beans. Chill before serving.

Spinach and Walnut Dream

Serves 4

175 g/6 oz/³/₄ cup Thai fragrant rice
1 large avocado, halved and stoned (pitted)
Lemon juice
100 g/4 oz young spinach leaves, torn
2 spring onions (scallions), finely chopped
50 g/2 oz/¹/₂ cup walnuts, roughly chopped
30 ml/2 tbsp walnut oil
15 ml/1 tbsp olive oil
A pinch of caster (superfine) sugar
Salt and freshly ground black pepper
50 g/2 oz Wensleydale cheese, cubed

Cook the rice in plenty of boiling salted water until just tender. Drain, rinse with cold water and drain again. Peel the avocado, dice and toss in lemon juice to prevent browning. Place in a bowl with the spinach, rice, spring onions and walnuts. Whisk the oils with 15 ml/1 tbsp of lemon juice, the sugar and a little salt and pepper. Pour over the salad and toss gently. Pile into a serving bowl and scatter the cheese over.

Oak-leaf and Pine Nut Dream

Serves 4

Prepare as for Spinach and Walnut Dream, but substitute oak-leaf lettuce for the spinach, and toasted pine nuts for the walnuts. Use Ricotta cheese instead of Wensleydale.

Cheese and Peanut Pick-me-up

Serves 4-6

100 g/4 oz/¹/₂ cup long-grain rice
50 g/2 oz/1 small packet peanuts and raisins
4 tomatoes, chopped
5 cm/2 in piece cucumber, chopped
100 g/4 oz Cheddar cheese, diced
200 g/7 oz/1 small can Mexican sweetcorn (corn with bell peppers)
30 ml/2 tbsp olive oil
15 ml/1 tbsp white wine vinegar
Salt and freshly ground black pepper
1.5 ml/¹/₄ tsp dried mixed herbs

Cook the rice in plenty of boiling salted water until just tender. Drain, rinse with cold water and drain again. Mix with all the remaining ingredients and toss gently but thoroughly. Pile into bowls and eat with a fork.

Blue Cheese Bite

Serves 4

Prepare as for Cheese and Peanut Pick-me-up, but substitute coarsely chopped mixed nuts and raisins for the peanuts and raisins, and use Cambazola or other soft blue cheese in place of Cheddar.

Stir-fry Brown Rice Salad

Serves 4

100 g/4 oz/¹/₂ cup brown rice
450g/1 lb/1 large packet prepared fresh stir-fry vegetables, well rinsed and drained
200 g/7 oz/1 small can pineapple pieces, drained, reserving the juice
30 ml/2 tbsp soy sauce
15 ml/1 tbsp Worcestershire sauce
30 ml/2 tbsp olive oil
Salt and freshly ground black pepper

Cook the rice according to the packet directions (or see page 12). Drain, rinse with cold water and drain again. Place in a bowl with the vegetables and pineapple pieces. Whisk 30 ml/2 tbsp of the reserved pineapple juice with the soy and Worcestershire sauces, the oil and a little salt and pepper. Pour over the salad and toss well before serving.

Chicken and Prawn Brown Rice Stir-fry

Serves 4

Prepare as for Stir-fry Brown Rice Salad, but add 175 g/6 oz/1½ cups diced, cooked chicken and 100 g/4 oz/1 cup peeled prawns (shrimp) to the mixture.

Canny Stir-fry Rice Salad

Serves 4

225 g/8 oz/1 small can apricots
225 g/8 oz/1 cup long-grain rice
425 g/15 oz/1 large can stir-fry
* vegetables, drained, rinsed and*
* drained again*
45 ml/3 tbsp light soy sauce
30 ml/2 tbsp sunflower oil
Toasted sesame seeds

Drain the apricots, reserving the juice, and chop roughly. Cook the rice in plenty of boiling salted water until tender. Drain, rinse with cold water and drain again. Place in a bowl and add the vegetables and apricots. Mix 30 ml/2 tbsp of the apricot juice with the soy sauce and oil. Add to the bowl and toss gently. Garnish with the sesame seeds.

Canny Duck Stir-fry Rice Salad

Serves 4

Prepare as for Canny Stir-fry Rice Salad, but add 1 cooked, sliced duck breast to the mixture and add 10 ml/2 tsp of hoisin sauce to the dressing.

Roll-mop Rigatoni

Serves 4-6

175 g/6 oz/1½ cups rigatoni
4 rollmops
¼ cucumber, diced
30 ml/2 tbsp mayonnaise
30 ml/2 tbsp plain yoghurt
15 ml/1 tbsp chopped dill (dill weed)
Salt and freshly ground black
* pepper*
Lettuce leaves

Cook the pasta according to the packet directions. Drain, rinse with cold water and drain again. Cut the rollmops into thin slices, using a sharp knife. Place in a bowl with the pasta and cucumber. Mix the mayonnaise, yoghurt and dill together with a little salt and lots of pepper. Add to the pasta and rollmops and toss gently. Pile on to a bed of lettuce leaves to serve.

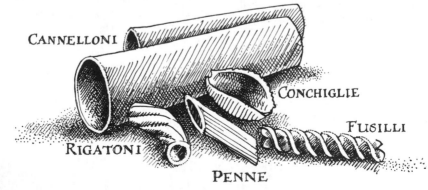

CANNELLONI

CONCHIGLIE

FUSILLI

RIGATONI

PENNE

Crunchy Ham and Pasta Medley

Serves 4

15 g/½ oz/2 tbsp plain (all-purpose) flour
250 ml/8 fl oz/ 1 cup milk
15 g/½ oz/1 tbsp butter
Salt and freshly ground black pepper
150 ml/¼ pt/⅔ cup mayonnaise
5 ml/1 tsp Dijon mustard
100 g/4 oz/1 cup farfalle, cooked
100 g/4 oz/1 cup cooked ham, diced
4 celery sticks, sliced
1 red (bell) pepper, diced
1 green (bell) pepper, diced
225 g/8 oz/1 small can water chestnuts, drained
100 g/4 oz Emmental (Swiss) cheese, cubed
1 spring onion (scallion), finely chopped

Blend the flour and milk in a saucepan. Add the butter and bring to the boil, stirring until thickened. Simmer for 2 minutes, then remove from the heat and season to taste. Leave to cool. When cold, stir in the mayonnaise and mustard. Fold in all the remaining ingredients except the spring onion and pile into a serving dish. Sprinkle the spring onion over and serve cold.

Warm Spinach and Bacon Pasta

Serves 6

175 g/6 oz/1½ cups farfalle
6 streaky bacon rashers (slices), rinded and diced
225 g/8 oz young spinach leaves
25 g/1 oz/⅙ cup seedless (pitless) raisins
50 g/2 oz/½ cup walnut pieces
60 ml/4 tbsp walnut oil (or half walnut and half sunflower oil)
30 ml/2 tbsp cider vinegar
2.5 ml/½ tsp caster (superfine) sugar
5 ml/1 tsp wholegrain mustard
Salt and freshly ground black pepper

Cook the pasta according to the packet directions. Drain and rinse with cold water, drain again. Place in a bowl. Dry-fry the bacon until crisp. Remove from the pan with a draining spoon and add to the pasta. Wash the spinach in several changes of cold water. Pat dry on kitchen paper then tear into small pieces and add to the pasta with the raisins and walnuts. Blend the remaining ingredients into the bacon fat in the pan with a little salt and lots of pepper. Bring to the boil, stirring, and pour over the salad. Toss well and serve straight away.

Herby Mixed Salad

Serves 6

100 g/4 oz/1 cup zite or rigatoni
50 g/2 oz/1 cup button mushrooms,
sliced
2 small courgettes (zucchini), sliced
1 bunch of spring onions (scallions),
sliced
12 black olives
45 ml/3 tbsp olive oil
15 ml/1 tbsp tarragon vinegar
15 ml/1 tbsp chopped tarragon
Salt and freshly ground black
pepper
¹/₂ curly endive (frissé lettuce)
50 g/2 oz Feta cheese, crumbled

Cook the pasta according to the packet directions. Drain, rinse with cold water and drain again. Place in a bowl with the mushrooms, courgettes, spring onions and olives. Mix the oil, vinegar, tarragon and a little salt and pepper together. Pour over the salad and toss well. Pile on to a bed of curly endive and sprinkle the Feta cheese over.

Tangy Watercress and Orange Salad

Serves 4

75 g/6 oz/1¹/₂ cups conchiglie
2 bunches of watercress
2 oranges
20 ml/4 tsp snipped chives
45 ml/3 tbsp olive oil
15 ml/1 tbsp lemon juice
Grated rind of ¹/₂ lemon
10 ml/2 tsp clear honey
2.5 ml/¹/₂ tsp Dijon mustard
Salt and freshly ground black
pepper

Cook the pasta in plenty of boiling salted water according to the packet directions. Drain, rinse with cold water and drain again. Place in a serving bowl. Trim the watercress and separate into small sprigs. Add to the bowl. Holding the oranges over the bowl, pare off all the rind and pith and separate them into segments. Add to the bowl and squeeze over any juice left in the membranes. Add the chives. Mix the oil, lemon juice, lemon rind, honey, mustard and a little salt and pepper until thoroughly blended. Pour over the salad and toss well before serving.

Stilton and Walnut Salad

Serves 4

225 g/8 oz/2 cups pasta shapes
50 g/2 oz Stilton cheese, crumbled
150 ml/¹/₄ pt/²/₃ cup plain yoghurt
A good pinch each of mustard
 powder, caster (superfine) sugar,
 salt and pepper
50 g/2 oz/¹/₂ cup chopped walnuts
Mixed lettuce leaves
Chopped parsley

Cook the pasta according to the packet directions. Drain, rinse with cold water and drain again. Mash the cheese with the yoghurt. Add the mustard, sugar, salt and pepper and mix again. Fold in the walnuts. Pile the pasta on to a bed of mixed lettuce leaves. Spoon the dressing over, garnish with parsley and serve chilled.

Chow Mein Salad

Serves 6

100 g/4 oz/1 cup Chinese egg
 noodles
100 g/4 oz mangetout (snow peas)
175 g/6 oz/1¹/₂ cups bean sprouts
1 red (bell) pepper, sliced
100 g/4 oz/2 cups button
 mushrooms, sliced
¹/₂ bunch of spring onions
 (scallions), chopped
100 g/4 oz/1 cup peeled prawns
 (shrimp)
1 little gem lettuce, shredded
45 ml/3 tbsp sunflower oil
15 ml/1 tbsp sesame oil
30 ml/2 tbsp lemon juice
2.5 cm/1 in piece fresh root ginger,
 grated
30 ml/2 tbsp sesame seeds

Cook the noodles according to the packet directions. Drain, rinse with cold water, drain again and place in a bowl. Top and tail the mangetout and break in half. Place in the bowl with the bean sprouts, pepper, mushrooms, spring onions, prawns and lettuce. Whisk the remaining ingredients together and pour over the salad. Toss well and serve.

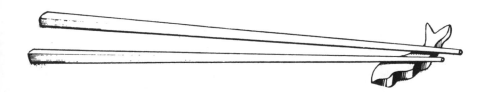

Stuffed Eggs with Pasta and Green Vinaigrette

Serves 4

175 g/6 oz/1¹/₂ cups ruote
45 ml/3 tbsp olive oil
15 ml/1 tbsp white wine vinegar
Salt and freshly ground black
  pepper
15 ml/1 tbsp chopped parsley
1 small bunch of watercress,
  chopped
4 hard-boiled (hard-cooked) eggs
15 ml/1 tbsp mayonnaise
100 g/4 oz/1 cup peeled prawns
  (shrimp)
A few drops of anchovy essence
  (extract)

Cook the pasta according to the packet directions. Drain, rinse with cold water and drain again. Mix with the oil, vinegar, a little salt and pepper, the parsley and watercress and toss well. Chill. Halve the eggs and scoop out the yolks into a bowl. Mash with the mayonnaise. Reserve 8 prawns for garnish, chop the remainder and add to the egg yolk mixture. Season to taste with the anchovy essence and a little salt and pepper. Pile back into the egg whites. Spoon the pasta mixture on to a serving dish. Arrange the eggs on top and garnish each with a reserved prawn.

Lemony Mushroom Salad

Serves 4

175 g/6 oz/1¹/₂ cups penne
225 g/8 oz/4 cups small button
  mushrooms, halved
30 ml/2 tbsp mayonnaise
30 ml/2 tbsp thick plain yoghurt
Grated rind and juice of ¹/₂ lemon
15 ml/1 tbsp chopped parsley
100 g/4 oz young spinach leaves
Garlic croûtons

Cook the pasta according to the packet directions. Drain, rinse with cold water and drain again. Place in a bowl with the mushrooms. Mix the mayonnaise with the yoghurt. Stir in the lemon rind and juice and half the parsley. Season to taste. Spoon over the pasta mixture and toss. Pile on to a bed of spinach leaves and garnish with garlic croûtons and the remaining parsley.

Caribbean Pasta Salad

Serves 6

100 g/4 oz/1 cup conchiglie
1 oak-leaf lettuce
½ small iceberg lettuce
4 celery sticks, chopped
4 carrots, grated
225 g/8 oz/1 small can pineapple
* chunks, drained*
75 g/3 oz/1½ cup stoned (pitted)
* dates, chopped*
45 ml/3 tbsp mayonnaise
Finely grated rind and juice of 1
* lime*
90 ml/6 tbsp sunflower oil
Salt and freshly ground black
* pepper*
50 g/2 oz/1½ cup walnut halves,
* chopped*

Cook the pasta according to the packet directions. Drain, rinse with cold water and drain again. Line a salad bowl with the lettuce leaves. Mix together all the remaining ingredients except the walnuts and toss lightly. Pile on to the bed of lettuce and sprinkle with the walnuts before serving.

Chinese Prawn and Bean Sprout Salad

Serves 4

100 g/4 oz/1 cup cooked Chinese egg
* noodles*
175 g/6 oz/1½ cups peeled prawns
* (shrimp)*
100 g/4 oz/1 cup bean sprouts
45 ml/3 tbsp sunflower oil
15 ml/1 tbsp sherry vinegar
15 ml/1 tbsp light soy sauce
A pinch of ground ginger
1 red (bell) pepper, cut into thin
* strips*
2.5 cm/1 in piece cucumber, cut into
* thin strips*
4 spring onions (scallions), chopped

Mix all the ingredients together in a bowl. Toss well and chill before serving.

Oriental Green Bean and Peanut Salad

Serves 4-6

250 g/9 oz/1 packet soba or Chinese
* egg noodles*
225 g/8 oz/2 cups thin green beans,
* cut into short lengths*
90 ml/6 tbsp peanut butter
30 ml/2 tbsp caster (superfine)
* sugar)*
150 ml/¼ pt/⅔ cup dashi or
* vegetable stock*
30 ml/2 tbsp soy sauce

Cook the noodles according to the packet directions. Drain, rinse with cold water and drain again. Boil the beans in salted water for 5 minutes until just tender. Drain, rinse with cold water and drain again. Blend the peanut butter, sugar, stock and soy sauce together in a bowl. Add the beans and noodles. Toss well and serve straight away.

333

Summer TV Supper

Serves 4
225 g/8 oz/2 cups ruote
4 tomatoes, chopped
¹/₄ cucumber, diced
175 g/6 oz Cheddar cheese, cubed
350 g/12 oz/1 large can sweetcorn
    (corn), drained
45 ml/3 tbsp olive oil
15 ml/1 tbsp lemon juice
5 ml/1 tsp Dijon mustard
Salt and freshly ground black
    pepper

Cook the pasta according to the packet directions. Drain, rinse with cold water and drain again. Put in a bowl and add the tomatoes, cucumber, cheese and corn. Mix gently. Whisk the remaining ingredients together and pour over. Toss lightly. Serve in bowls.

Pasta Niçoise

Serves 4
225 g/8 oz/2 cups rigatoni
225 g/8 oz/2 cups French (green)
    beans, cut into short lengths
2 hard-boiled (hard-cooked) eggs,
    roughly chopped
1 small onion, sliced into rings
4 tomatoes, roughly diced
185 g/6¹/₂ oz/1 small can tuna,
    drained
50 g/2 oz/1 small can anchovies,
    drained and cut into thin slivers
90 ml/6 tbsp olive oil
30 ml/2 tbsp red wine vinegar
Salt and freshly ground black
    pepper
Cos (romaine) lettuce leaves
A few black olives

Cook the pasta according to the packet directions. Add the beans for the last 5 minutes. Drain, rinse with cold water and drain again. Place in a bowl with the remaining ingredients except the lettuce and olives and season lightly with salt and lots of black pepper. Toss very gently so as not to break up the tuna too much. Pile on to a bed of lettuce and scatter a few black olives over.

Bacon, Egg and Pasta Salad

Serves 4
175 g/6 oz/1¹/₂ cups rigatoni
6 rashers (slices) streaky bacon,
    rinded and diced
3 eggs
25 g/1 oz/2 tbsp butter
15 ml/1 tbsp single (light) cream
Salt and freshly ground black
    pepper
1 little gem lettuce
15 ml/1 tbsp olive oil
10 ml/2 tsp lemon juice

Cook the pasta according to the packet directions. Drain, rinse with cold water and drain again. Dry-fry the bacon until crisp. Drain on kitchen paper. Beat the eggs and scramble with the butter until creamy and only lightly set. Do not overcook. Remove from the heat and stir in the cream to prevent the eggs cooking further. Add to the pasta with the bacon, a little salt and a good grinding of pepper. Toss lightly. Toss the lettuce leaves in the oil and lemon juice. Arrange on plates and pile the egg and pasta mixture on top. Serve straight away.

Mozzarella and Cherry Tomato Vinaigrette

Serves 4
225 g/8 oz/2 cups lumachi
225 g/8 oz Mozzarella cheese, diced
350 g/12 oz/3 cups cherry tomatoes,
*   quartered*
16 torn fresh basil leaves
120 ml/4 fl oz/¹/₂ cup olive oil
30 ml/2 tbsp red wine vinegar
Freshly ground black pepper
Coarse sea salt

Cook the pasta according to packet directions. Drain, rinse with cold water and drain again. Put all the ingredients, including lots of black pepper in a bowl. Toss lightly and chill for 30 minutes. Serve sprinkled with a little coarse sea salt.

Mexican Avocado Salad

Serves 4
350 g/12 oz green tagliatelle (verdi)
75 ml/5 tbsp olive oil
2 ripe avocados, peeled and stoned
*   (pitted)*
30 ml/2 tbsp lemon juice
30 ml/2 tbsp Worcestershire sauce
5 ml/1 tsp grated onion
2.5 ml/¹/₂ tsp chilli powder
Salt and freshly ground black
*   pepper*
5 cm/2 in piece cucumber, chopped
2 tomatoes, seeded and chopped
1 red (bell) pepper, chopped
Snipped chives
Tortilla chips

Cook the pasta according to the packet directions. Drain, rinse with cold water and drain again. Add 15 ml/1 tbsp of the olive oil and toss well. Mash the avocados in a bowl with the lemon juice. Beat in the Worcestershire sauce, the onion and the chilli powder. Beat in the remaining oil a little at a time to form a mayonnaise-type mixture. Season to taste with salt and lots of pepper. Fold in the cucumber, tomatoes and pepper. Spoon the pasta on to serving plates. Top with the avocado mixture, sprinkle with chives and serve with tortilla chips.

Curried Chicken Pasta Salad

Serves 4
225 g/8 oz/2 cups spiralli
60 ml/4 tbsp mayonnaise
30 ml/2 tbsp curried peach chutney
2 dried peaches, chopped
10 ml/2 tsp curry paste
175 g/6 oz/1¹/₂ cups chopped cooked
*   chicken*
Lettuce leaves
Lemon wedges

Cook the pasta according to the packet directions. Drain, rinse with cold water and drain again. Blend the mayonnaise in a bowl with the chutney, peaches and curry paste. Fold in the chicken and pasta and chill until ready to serve on a bed of lettuce, garnished with lemon wedges.

Sunny Tuna Salad

Serves 4
175g/6 oz/1¹/₂ cups conchiglie
185 g/6¹/₂ oz/1 small can tuna in oil
30 ml/2 tbsp chopped parsley
200 g/7 oz/1 small can sweetcorn
 (corn), drained
30 ml/2 tbsp olive oil
15 ml/1 tbsp lemon juice
¹/₂ bunch of spring onion (scallions),
 chopped
Lettuce leaves

Cook the pasta according to the packet directions. Drain, rinse with cold water and drain again. Mix with the remaining ingredients except the lettuce. Toss gently and pile on to lettuce leaves for serving.

Nutty Apricot Cooler

Serves 4
175 g/6 oz/1¹/₂ cups ruote
100 g/4 oz/²/₃ cup ready-to-eat dried
 apricots, quartered
50 g/2 oz/¹/₂ cup pine nuts
12 stoned (pitted) black olives,
 halved
1 cucumber, diced
150 ml/¹/₄ pt/²/₃ cup soured (dairy
 sour) cream
Grated rind and juice of 1 lime
15 ml/1 tbsp clear honey
Salt and freshly ground black
 pepper
15 ml/1 tbsp snipped chives
Curly endive (frissé lettuce) leaves
Cayenne

Cook the pasta according to the packet directions. Drain, rinse with cold water, drain again and place in a bowl. Add the apricots, pine nuts, olives and cucumber.

Blend the cream with the lime rind and juice, the honey, a little salt and pepper and the chives. Mix well, then pour over the salad and toss well. Chill for at least 1 hour to allow the flavours to develop, then pile on to a bed of curly endive and sprinkle with cayenne before serving.

Prawn Cocktail Pasta

Serves 4
225 g/8 oz/2 cups short-cut
 macaroni
150 ml/¹/₄ pt/²/₃ cup mayonnaise
15 ml/1 tbsp tomato ketchup
 (catsup)
15 ml/1 tbsp single (light) cream
10 ml/2 tsp horseradish cream
A dash of Worcestershire sauce
6 stuffed olives, chopped
1 hard-boiled (hard-cooked) egg,
 chopped
1 green (bell) pepper, chopped
175 g/6 oz/1¹/₂ cups peeled prawns
 (shrimp)
Shredded lettuce
Paprika
Lemon wedges

Cook the pasta according to the packet directions. Drain, rinse with cold water and drain again. Mix the mayonnaise with the tomato ketchup, cream and horseradish in a large bowl. Add all the remaining ingredients except the lettuce, paprika and lemon wedges and toss well but lightly. Chill until ready to serve. Pile on to a bed of lettuce and garnish with a little paprika and lemon wedges.

Warm Crunchy Fried Bread and Herb Salad

Serves 4

225 g/8 oz/2 cups spiralli
225 g/8 oz/4 cups fresh wholemeal
*   breadcrumbs*
12 cherry tomatoes, chopped
15 ml/1 tbsp chopped thyme
15 ml/1 tbsp chopped basil
15 ml/1 tbsp chopped parsley
Salt and freshly ground black
*   pepper*
120 ml/4 fl oz/¹⁄₂ cup olive oil
3 garlic cloves, crushed
Freshly grated Parmesan cheese

Cook the pasta according to the packet directions. Drain, rinse with boiling water and drain in a colander while preparing the salad. Dry-fry the breadcrumbs in a large frying pan (skillet), tossing all the time, until crisp but not burnt. Mix the tomatoes, herbs, a little salt and lots of pepper in a bowl. Heat the oil in a frying pan, add the breadcrumbs and garlic and fry (sauté) until golden brown. Add to the bowl and toss well. Add to the warm spiralli, toss quickly and serve straight away with Parmesan cheese.

Blushing Beetroot Bite

Serves 4

100 g/4 oz/1 cup pasta shapes
300 g/11 oz/1 small can mandarin
*   oranges in natural juice*
4 cooked baby beetroot (red beet),
*   diced*
100 g/4 oz Wensleydale cheese, diced
75 g/3 oz/¹⁄₃ cup curd (smooth
*   cottage) cheese*
15 ml/1 tbsp red wine vinegar
15 ml/1 tbsp cashew nut (or smooth
*   peanut) butter*
Salt and freshly ground black
*   pepper*
30 ml/2 tbsp chopped spring onion
*   (scallion)*
A few roasted cashew nuts or
*   peanuts*

Cook the pasta according to the packet directions. Drain, rinse with cold water and drain again and place in a bowl. Drain the oranges, reserving the juice. Add the fruit to the pasta with the beetroot and the Wensleydale cheese. Blend the curd cheese with 30 ml/2 tbsp of the reserved mandarin juice, the vinegar and cashew nut butter. Season to taste. Add to the pasta with the spring onions and toss well. Pile into individual glass dishes and garnish with a few roasted nuts. Chill before serving.

Rosy Melon and Pasta Salad

Serves 4

100 g/4 oz/1 cup red conchiglie (al pomodoro)
2 pink-fleshed cantaloupe melons, halved and seeded
225 g/8 oz/2 cups peeled prawns (shrimp)
1 small red (bell) pepper, diced
300 ml/¹/₂ pt/1¹/₄ cups mayonnaise
15 ml/1 tbsp tomato ketchup (catsup)
5 ml/1 tsp curry powder
Paprika
Lettuce leaves

Cook the pasta according to the packet directions. Drain, rinse with cold water and drain again. Scoop out the melon flesh with a baller or cut it into cubes. Place in a bowl with the pasta, prawns and red pepper. Blend the mayonnaise with the tomato ketchup and curry powder. Add to the melon mixture and toss lightly. Pile back in the melon skins and sprinkle with paprika before serving on a bed of lettuce.

Cherries Jubilee Salad

Serves 4

175 g/6 oz/1¹/₂ cups conchiglie
50 g/2 oz/¹/₂ cup frozen peas
175 g/6 oz/1¹/₂ cups diced cooked duck
225 g/8 oz/1¹/₂ cups red cherries, halved and stoned (pitted)
30 ml/2 tbsp mayonnaise
30 ml/2 tbsp plain yoghurt
Grated rind and juice of ¹/₂ orange
A pinch of cayenne
Salt and freshly ground black pepper
Lollo rosso lettuce
50 g/2 oz/¹/₂ cup toasted flaked almonds

Cook the pasta according to the packet directions, adding the peas for the last 5 minutes cooking. Drain, rinse with cold water and drain again. Place in a bowl and add the duck and cherries. Blend the mayonnaise with the yoghurt, orange juice, cayenne and salt and pepper to taste. Add to the salad and toss gently. Pile on to a bed of lollo rosso leaves and sprinkle with the almonds. Chill before serving.

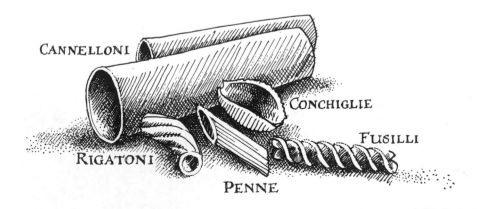

CANNELLONI
CONCHIGLIE
FUSILLI
RIGATONI
PENNE

Warm Mexican Salsa Salad

Serves 2 or 4
2 garlic cloves
1 small red onion, quartered
450 g/1 lb ripe tomatoes
25 g/1 oz/¹/₄ cup pickled chillies
5 ml/1 tsp dried oregano
50 g/2 oz/¹/₂ cup chopped coriander
   (cilantro) leaves
2.5 ml/¹/₂ tsp salt
Freshly ground black pepper
60 ml/4 tbsp olive oil
225 g/8 oz spaghetti
Tortilla chips
Freshly grated Parmesan cheese

Place the garlic and onion in a food processor and chop briefly. Add the tomatoes and
chillies and chop fairly finely but still with
lots of texture. Turn the mixture into a
sieve (strainer) over a bowl and allow to
drain for 5 minutes. Pour away the liquid,
add the tomato mixture then stir in the
herbs, salt, pepper and oil. Meanwhile,
cook the spaghetti according to the packet
directions. Drain, add to the salsa and toss
well. Pile on to serving plates, surround
with tortilla chips and sprinkle with grated
Parmesan.

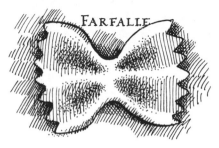

FARFALLE

Warm Mexican Salsa Salad with Avocado and Pineapple

Serves 4
Prepare as for Warm Mexican Salsa Salad,
but add 2 slices of chopped fresh pineapple and 1 large, ripe sliced avocado to
the tomato salsa.

Swiss Chef's Salad

Serves 4
175 g/6 oz/1¹/₂ cups penne
225 g/8 oz cooked ham, cut into thin
   strips
50 g/2 oz/1 cup button mushrooms,
   sliced
3 cherry tomatoes, quartered
100 g/4 oz young spinach leaves,
   torn in pieces
15 ml/1 tbsp chopped marjoram
45 ml/3 tbsp olive oil
15 ml/1 tbsp red wine vinegar
Salt and freshly ground black
   pepper
100 g/4 oz Gruyère (Swiss) cheese,
   cut into thin strips
3 hard-boiled (hard-cooked) eggs,
   quartered

Cook the penne according to the packet
directions. Drain, rinse with cold water and
drain again. Place in a bowl and add all the
ingredients except the cheese and eggs,
seasoning well with salt and pepper. Toss
gently but thoroughly, pile into bowls and
top with the cheese strips. Arrange the
eggs around the edge.

Winter Wonderland

Serves 6

175 g/6 oz/1¹/₂ cups multicoloured
 tagliatelle, broken into short
 lengths
¹/₂ small white cabbage, shredded
2 carrots, coarsely grated
5 ml/1 tsp grated onion
1 red-skinned eating (dessert) apple,
 unpeeled and chopped
2 celery sticks, sliced
30 ml/2 tbsp chopped walnuts
30 ml/2 tbsp seedless (pitless) raisins
1 small can evaporated milk
15 ml/1 tbsp light brown sugar
Salt and freshly ground black
 pepper
5 ml/1 tsp made mustard
White wine vinegar

Cook the pasta according to the packet directions. Drain, rinse with cold water and drain again. Place in a bowl with the cabbage, carrot, onion, apple, celery, walnuts and raisins. Whisk the evaporated milk with the sugar, some salt and pepper and the mustard. Whisk in vinegar to taste. Pour over the salad and toss well.

Cauliflower and Blue Cheese Euphoria

Serves 4

1 small cauliflower, cut into tiny
 florets
175 g/6 oz/1¹/₂ cups cappelletti
 stuffed with cheese
2 slices wholemeal bread, crusts
 removed, cubed
Oil for shallow-frying
1 garlic clove
100 g/4 oz blue Brie or other soft
 blue cheese, cubed
1 bunch of watercress, trimmed
60 ml/4 tbsp olive oil
20 ml/4 tsp white wine vinegar
5 ml/1 tsp chopped oregano
2.5 ml/¹/₂ tsp caster (superfine) sugar
2.5 ml/¹/₂ tsp Dijon mustard
Salt and freshly ground black
 pepper

Cook the cauliflower in boiling salted water for 3-4 minutes until almost tender but still with bite. Drain, rinse with cold water and drain again. Cook the cappelletti according to the packet directions. Drain, rinse with cold water and drain again. Mix together in a bowl. Meanwhile, fry (sauté) the bread cubes in the oil with the garlic clove added until the bread is crisp and golden. Drain on kitchen paper and discard the garlic. Add the cheese to the cauliflower mixture with the watercress sprigs. Blend the remaining ingredients together and pour over the salad. Toss well, add the croutons, toss again and serve straight away.

Broccoli and Camembert Combination

Serves 4

Prepare as for Cauliflower and Blue Cheese Euphoria, but substitute 225 g/ 8 oz broccoli for the cauliflower and Camembert for the blue cheese.

Curried Cheese and Mushrooms Salad

Serves 6

225 g/8 oz/2 cups zite
60 ml/4 tbsp olive oil
20 ml/4 tsp white wine vinegar
10 ml/2 tsp curry powder
20 ml/4 tsp tomato purée (paste)
5 ml/1 tsp light brown sugar
A squeeze of lemon juice
Salt and freshly ground black
 pepper
½ bunch of spring onions
 (scallions), cut into short lengths
225 g/8 oz/4 cups button
 mushrooms, thickly sliced
100 g/4 oz Cheddar cheese, diced
Chopped parsley

Cook the pasta according to the packet directions. Drain, rinse with cold water and drain again. Whisk the oil, vinegar, curry powder, tomato purée, sugar and lemon juice together with a little salt and pepper. Pour over the pasta and toss well. Add the spring onions, mushrooms and cheese and toss again. Pile on to a serving dish and garnish with the parsley.

Scandinavian Herring Munch

Serves 4

100 g/4 oz/1 cup conchiglie
2 red eating (dessert) apples, diced
Grated rind and juice of ½ lemon
225 g/8 oz cold new potatoes, diced
50 g/2 oz/⅓ cup seedless (pitless) red
 grapes, halved
4 rollmop herrings, sliced
150 ml/¼ pt/⅔ cup thick plain
 yoghurt
Salt and freshly ground black
 pepper
30 ml/2 tbsp snipped chives

Cook the pasta according to the packet directions. Drain, rinse with cold water and drain again. Toss the apples in the lemon juice and mix with the potatoes, lemon rind, grapes and herrings. Add the yoghurt, a little salt and a good grinding of pepper. Toss gently, then chill until ready to serve garnished with snipped chives.

Date and Walnut Delight

Serves 4

175 g/6 oz/1¹/₂ cups ruote
100 g/4 oz/²/₃ cup fresh dates, stoned
  (pitted) and diced
2 celery sticks, sliced
1 carrot, grated
1 red and 1 green eating (dessert)
  apple, chopped
Lemon juice
50 g/2 oz/¹/₂ cup walnuts, coarsely
  chopped
2 heads chicory (Belgian endive)
150 ml/¹/₄ pt/²/₃ cup plain yoghurt
15 ml/1 tbsp clear honey
Salt and freshly ground black
  pepper
75 g/3 oz Feta cheese, crumbled

Cook the pasta according to the packet directions. Drain, rinse with cold water and drain again. Mix with the dates, celery and carrot. Toss the apples in lemon juice and add with the walnuts. Cut a cone-shaped core out of the bases of the chicory, then separate into leaves. Arrange on a serving plate. Blend the yoghurt with the honey, a little salt and pepper and lemon juice to taste. Pour over the salad and toss well. Pile on to the chicory and sprinkle the Feta cheese over.

Greek Fig and Pine Nut Salad

Serves 4

Prepare as for Date and Walnut Delight, but substitute sliced fresh ripe figs for the dates, and toasted pine nuts for the walnuts.

Danish Salami Supper

Serves 4

175 g/6 oz/1¹/₂ cups lumachi
1 green (bell) pepper, diced
1 small onion, sliced and separated
  into rings
200 g/7 oz/1 small can sweetcorn
  (corn), drained
Salt and freshly ground black
  pepper
60 ml/4 tbsp mayonnaise
30 ml/2 tbsp soured (dairy sour)
  cream
1 little gem lettuce
100 g/4 oz pink Danish salami
  slices, halved

Cook the pasta according to the packet directions. Drain, rinse with cold water and drain again. Place in a bowl with the pepper, onion, corn, a little salt and a good grinding of pepper. Blend the mayonnaise with the soured cream and add to the bowl. Toss together, taste and re-season if necessary. Pile on to a bed of lettuce leaves. Fold the halved salami slices into cornet shapes and arrange all round the salad. Serve straight away.

Italian Salami Supper

Serves 4

Prepare as for Danish Salami Supper, but substitute Milano salami for the Danish variety, and drained canned peas for the corn.

Copenhagen Chicken

Serves 6

225 g/8 oz/2 cups lumachi
350 g/12 oz/3 cups cooked chicken, diced
2 hard-boiled (hard-cooked) eggs, quartered
2 dill pickled cucumbers (dill pickles), sliced
10 ml/2 tsp capers, chopped
6 olives, stuffed with anchovies, sliced
75 ml/5 tbsp mayonnaise
75 ml/5 tbsp soured (dairy sour) cream
Salt and freshly ground black pepper
Shredded lettuce
Chopped parsley
1 red onion, sliced into rings

Cook the pasta according to the packet directions. Drain, rinse with cold water and drain again. Place in a bowl with the chicken, eggs, pickles, capers and olives. Blend the mayonnaise with the soured cream and spoon over. Season lightly and toss gently. Pile on to the lettuce and garnish with the parsley and onion rings.

Turkey Temptation

Serves 4

225 g/8 oz/2 cups rotelli
225 g/8 oz/2 cups cooked turkey, diced
2 celery sticks, chopped
1 green (bell) pepper, diced
¹/₂ small onion, sliced and separated into rings
1 large carrot, grated
200 g/7 oz/1 small can sweetcorn (corn), drained
30 ml/2 tbsp olive oil
Lemon juice
Salt and freshly ground black pepper
Lettuce leaves
45 ml/3 tbsp mayonnaise
15 ml/1 tbsp cranberry sauce
Chopped parsley

Cook the pasta according to the packet directions. Drain, rinse with cold water and drain again. Place in a bowl with the turkey, celery, pepper, onion, carrot and sweetcorn. Toss in the olive oil and lemon juice to taste. Season well. Pile on to lettuce leaves on individual plates. Mix the mayonnaise with the cranberry and spike with lemon juice to taste. Season with a little salt and lots of pepper. Put a spoonful of the dressing on top of each salad and serve garnished with parsley.

Berlin Beauty

Serves 4

175 g/6 oz/1¹/₂ cups tortellini with cheese and spinach
400 g/14 oz/1 large can frankfurters, drained and cut into short lengths
¹/₂ bunch spring onions (scallions), chopped
1 red eating (dessert) apple, unpeeled and diced
5 ml/1 tsp lemon juice
60 ml/4 tbsp mayonnaise
60 ml/4 tbsp soured (dairy sour) cream
Salt and freshly ground black pepper
¹/₂ small white cabbage, shredded
1 bunch of watercress, trimmed
30 ml/2 tbsp olive oil
10 ml/2 tsp white wine vinegar
Caraway seeds

Cook the pasta according to the packet directions. Drain, rinse with cold water and drain again. Place in a bowl with the frankfurters, spring onion and apple, tossed in the lemon juice. Blend the mayonnaise with the soured cream and a little salt and pepper. Pour over the salad and toss gently. Mix the cabbage with the watercress sprigs, oil, vinegar and a little salt and pepper. Toss well and pile on a serving plate. Spoon the frankfurter mixture on top and sprinkle with a few caraway seeds.

London Lovely

Serves 4

Prepare as for Berlin Beauty, but substitute cold grilled pork chipolatas for the frankfurters. Add a pinch of mustard powder to the mayonnaise, and garnish with chopped parsley instead of caraway seeds.

Chinese Pastravaganza

Serves 6

225 g/8 oz tagliatelle, broken into short lengths
225 g/8 oz/1 small can pineapple chunks in natural juice, drained, reserving the juice
2 tomatoes, quartered
5 cm/2 in piece cucumber, cut into matchsticks
1 carrot, cut into matchsticks
1 small green (bell) pepper, cut into thin strips
100 g/4 oz/1 cup bean sprouts
2 celery sticks, cut into thin strips
4 spring onions (scallions), cut into short lengths
90 ml/6 tbsp sunflower oil
30 ml/2 tbsp reserved pineapple juice
15 ml/1 tbsp soy sauce
2.5 ml/¹/₂ tsp grated fresh root ginger (or 1.5 ml/¹/₄ tsp ground ginger)
Salt and freshly ground black pepper

Cook the pasta according to the packet directions. Drain, rinse with cold water and drain again. Place in a bowl with the pineapple, tomatoes and all the prepared vegetables. Whisk the remaining ingredients together and pour over. Toss well, pile on to a serving dish and chill before serving.

Courgette and Sun-dried Tomato Twists

Serves 4

6 courgettes (zucchini), thinly sliced
60 ml/4 tbsp olive oil
400 g/14 oz/1 large can chopped
    tomatoes
1 garlic clove, crushed
3 sun-dried tomatoes, finely chopped
30 ml/2 tbsp red wine
Salt and freshly ground black
    pepper
A pinch of caster (superfine) sugar
2.5 ml/^{1}/$_2$ tsp dried basil
175 g/6 oz/1^1/$_2$ cups rotelli
Chopped parsley

Fry (sauté) the courgettes in the olive oil for 3 minutes. Add the tomatoes, garlic, sun-dried tomatoes, wine, a little salt and pepper, the sugar and basil. Bring to the boil, reduce the heat and simmer for 15-20 minutes until the courgettes are cooked and bathed in the sauce. Leave to cool, then chill. Meanwhile, cook the pasta according to the packet directions. Drain, rinse with cold water and drain again. Add to the courgette mixture, toss well and serve garnished with parsley.

Aubergine Twists

Serves 4

Prepare as for Courgette and Sun-dried Tomato Twists, but substitute 2 small aubergines for the courgettes (zucchini), and use dried oregano instead of basil.

Hot Spaghetti with Summer Tomato Sauce

Serves 4

3 garlic cloves, crushed
Grated rind and juice of 1 orange
1 kg/2^1/$_4$ lb tomatoes, skinned,
    seeded and roughly chopped
50 g/2 oz/^{1}/$_2$ cup torn basil leaves
2.5 ml/^{1}/$_2$ tsp dried thyme
1.5 ml/^{1}/$_4$ tsp cayenne
25 g/1 oz/^{1}/$_4$ cup freshly grated
    Parmesan cheese
90 ml/6 tbsp olive oil
Salt and freshly ground black
    pepper
350 g/12 oz wholewheat spaghetti

Mix all the ingredients except the pasta in a large bowl. Chill for several hours to allow the flavours to develop. When ready to serve, cook the spaghetti according to the packet directions. Drain, rinse with boiling water and drain again. Return to the saucepan. Add the cold sauce, toss well and serve straight away with a good grinding of black pepper on each serving.

Neapolitan Courgettes

Serves 4

175 g/6 oz/1¹/₂ cups conchiglie
4 courgettes (zucchini), thinly sliced
50 g/2 oz/1 cup button mushrooms,
  sliced
90 ml/6 tbsp olive oil
30 ml/2 tbsp red wine vinegar
2.5 ml/¹/₂ tsp dried tarragon
1 small onion, finely chopped
Salt and freshly ground black
  pepper
6 cherry tomatoes, quartered
8 black olives
Chopped parsley

Cook the pasta according to the packet directions. Drain, rinse with cold water and drain again. Mix with the courgettes and mushrooms. Blend the oil, vinegar, tarragon and onion with a little salt and pepper. Pour over the salad, toss well and leave to marinate for at least 1 hour. Add the tomatoes and olives, toss lightly and serve sprinkled with parsley.

Chinese Curried Pasta Salad

Serves 4

350 g/12 oz vermicelli, broken into 3
  pieces
60 ml/4 tbsp olive oil
2 garlic cloves, crushed
1.5 ml/¹/₄ tsp chilli powder
30 ml/2 tbsp curry powder
30 ml/2 tbsp oyster sauce
450 g/1 lb/4 cups peeled prawns
  (shrimp)
Grated rind and juice of 1 lime
1 red (bell) pepper, cut into thin
  strips
4 spring onions (scallions), shredded
50 g/2 oz/¹/₂ cup torn basil leaves
5 ml/1 tsp caster (superfine) sugar
Salt and freshly ground black
  pepper

Cook the pasta in plenty of boiling salted water until tender. Drain, rinse with cold water and drain again. Heat the oil in a frying pan (skillet). Add the garlic, chilli and curry powder and fry (sauté) for 1 minute. Remove from the heat and stir in the oyster sauce. Add to the cold pasta and toss well. Add all the remaining ingredients. Toss well again and chill until ready to serve.

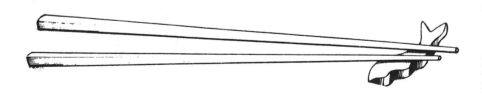

Mosaic Pasta Salad

Serves 4

350g/12 oz/3 cups conchiglie
90 ml/6 tbsp mayonnaise
A little milk
350g/12 oz/1 large can baby corn
  cobs, drained
200 g/7 oz/1 small can pimientos,
  shredded
225 g/8 oz Mortadella sausage, diced
12 stuffed olives, sliced
5 cm/2 in piece cucumber, cut into
  short sticks
Salt and freshly ground black
  pepper
50 g/2 oz/1 small can anchovies,
  drained

Cook the pasta according to the packet directions. Drain, rinse with cold water and drain again. Mix the mayonnaise with a little milk to thin slightly. Add all the remaining ingredients, except 8 slices of the olives and the anchovies and toss well, adding seasoning to taste. Pile into a serving bowl and garnish with a lattice of anchovies and the reserved olive slices.

Crunchy Italian Salad

Serves 4

100 g/4 oz/1 cup wholewheat ruote
2 thick slices white bread, crusts
  removed, diced
90 ml/6 tbsp olive oil
1 garlic clove
1 bunch spring onions (scallions),
  cut into short lengths
1/4 iceberg lettuce, torn into pieces
50 g/2 oz/1 cup button mushrooms,
  sliced
100 g/4 oz/1 cup prosciutto, diced
1 green (bell) pepper, diced
50 g/2 oz/1 small can anchovies,
  drained
15 ml/1 tbsp lemon juice
30 ml/2 tbsp Worcestershire sauce
Salt and freshly ground black
  pepper
6 cherry tomatoes, halved
25 g/1 oz/1/4 cup shaved fresh
  Parmesan cheese
A few black olives

Cook the pasta according to the packet directions. Drain, rinse with cold water and drain again. Place in a bowl. Fry (sauté) the bread cubes in 30 ml/2 tbsp of the oil until crisp and golden. Drain on kitchen paper. Rub a salad bowl with the garlic clove and discard. Add the spring onions to the pasta with the lettuce, mushrooms, prosciutto and green pepper and toss gently. Chop the anchovies. Blend the remaining oil with the lemon juice, Worcestershire sauce, a little salt and pepper and the anchovies. Pour over the salad and toss well. Add the fried bread, toss again, and serve immediately, garnished with the tomatoes halves, the Parmesan and olives.

Creamy Macaroni with Mushrooms

Serves 6

225 g/8 oz/1 cup elbow macaroni
350 g/12 oz/6 cups button
mushrooms, sliced
45 ml/3 tbsp lemon juice
30 ml/2 tbsp olive oil
1 garlic clove, crushed
150 ml/¹/₄ pt/²/₃ cup thick plain
yoghurt
150 ml/¹/₄ pt/²/₃ cup mayonnaise
15 ml/1 tbsp chopped chervil
A few fennel seeds

Cook the pasta according to the packet directions. Drain, rinse with cold water and drain again. Place in a bowl with the mushrooms. Whisk together the remaining ingredients except the fennel seeds and add to the salad. Toss well, sprinkle with fennel seeds and chill for at least 1 hour to allow the flavour to develop.

Creamy Macaroni with Olives and Tomatoes

Serves 4

Prepare as for Creamy Macaroni with Mushrooms, but substitute 100 g/4 oz/²/₃ cup stoned (pitted) mixed black and green olives, halved, and 225 g/8 oz/2 cups quartered, cherry tomatoes for the mushrooms.

Caesar Salad with Pasta

Serves 4

100 g/4 oz/1 cup lumachi
30 ml/2 tbsp garlic and herb cheese
60 ml/4 tbsp olive oil
Lemon juice
40 g/1¹/₂ oz/3 tbsp butter
1 egg, beaten
4 slices French bread, cubed
1 garlic clove
50 g/2 oz/1 small can anchovy fillets,
chopped
50 g/2 oz/¹/₂ cup grated Parmesan
cheese
¹/₂ cos (romaine) lettuce, torn into
pieces

Cook the pasta according to the packet directions. Drain, rinse with cold water and drain again. Place in a salad bowl. Blend the garlic and herb cheese with the oil, a little at a time until smooth. Add lemon juice to taste. Melt a third of the butter in a small pan. Add the egg and scramble lightly but keep creamy. Remove from the heat and immediately plunge the base of the pan in cold water to prevent further cooking. Melt the remaining butter in a frying pan (skillet). Add the bread cubes and garlic and fry (sauté) until the bread is golden. Discard the garlic and drain the bread on kitchen paper. Add everything to the pasta and toss gently but thoroughly. Serve immediately.

Canny Summer Pasta

Serves 4-6

425 g/15 oz/1 large can pasta shapes
in tomato sauce
60 ml/4 tbsp sunflower oil
30 ml/2 tbsp white wine vinegar
2.5 ml/¹/₂ tsp dried tarragon
2.5 ml/¹/₂ tsp caster (superfine) sugar
Salt and freshly ground black
pepper
2 celery sticks, chopped
¹/₂ bunch spring onions (scallions),
chopped
50 g/2 oz/1 small packet peanuts
and raisins
1 green (bell) pepper, diced
5 cm/2 in piece cucumber, diced
1 little gem lettuce
Ready-made herb or garlic croûtons
2 hard-boiled (hard-cooked) eggs,
quartered

Empty the pasta shapes into a saucepan.
Whisk together the oil, vinegar, tarragon,
sugar and a little salt and pepper. Add 30
ml/3 tbsp to the pasta and simmer, stirring
until the dressing is absorbed. Leave to
cool. Add the celery, spring onions,
peanuts and raisins, pepper and cucumber.
Add the remaining dressing and toss well.
Pile on to a bed of torn lettuce leaves and
garnish with croûtons and the hard-boiled
eggs.

Hot and Cold Desserts

If all you can think of is good old traditional rice pudding then think again. Delicious though this is, there are many more exciting hot and cold sweets to tempt even the most discerning palate.

Old English Rice Pudding

Serves 4

15 g/¹/₂ oz/1 tbsp butter
40 g/1¹/₂ oz/3 tbsp short-grain (pudding) rice
25 g/1 oz/2 tbsp granulated sugar
600 ml/1 pt/2¹/₂ cups full-cream milk
15 ml/1 tbsp rose water

Grease a 900 ml/1¹/₂ pt/3³/₄ cup ovenproof dish with the butter. Add the remaining ingredients and stir well. Bake in the oven at 160°C/325°F/gas mark 3 for 2 hours. Serve warm.

Tutti Frutti Rice

Serves 6

50 g/2 oz/¹/₄ cup butter
100 g/4 oz/¹/₂ cup short-grain (pudding) rice
Grated rind of 1 lemon
50 g/2 oz/¹/₆ cup golden (light corn) syrup
300 ml/¹/₂ pt/1¹/₄ cups milk
300 ml/¹/₂ pt/1¹/₄ cups single (light) cream
1 egg
25 g/1 oz/¹/₆ cup sultanas (golden raisins)
25 g/1 oz/2 tbsp mixed (candied) peel
25 g/1 oz/2 tbsp chopped glacé (candied) cherries
25 g/1 oz/2 tbsp chopped angelica
Freshly grated nutmeg

Liberally grease a 1.2 litre/2 pt/5 cup oven-proof dish with half the butter. Put the rice in the dish with the lemon rind. Spoon over the syrup. Whisk the milk, cream and egg together and strain over. Stir in the fruits, peel and angelica and grate some nutmeg over. Dot with the remaining butter and bake in the oven at 160°C/325°F/gas mark 3 for 2 hours.

Everyday Rice Pudding

Serves 4-6

600 ml/1 pt/2¹/₂ cups milk
30 ml/2 tbsp dried milk (non-fat milk) powder (optional)
75 g/3 oz/¹/₃ cup short-grain (pudding) rice
25 g/1 oz/2 tbsp granulated sugar
A few drops of vanilla essence (extract)
Grated nutmeg
A knob of butter

Mix the milk, milk powder (if using), rice, sugar and vanilla in a 1.2 litre/2 pt/5 cup ovenproof dish. Sprinkle with nutmeg and dot with butter. Bake at 160°C/325°F/gas mark 3 for 2 hours until golden on top and creamy underneath.

Winter Fruit Salad Pudding

Serves 6
175 g/6 oz/1 cup dried fruit salad,
  soaked
75 g/3 oz/¹/₃ cup short-grain
  (pudding) rice
600 ml/1 pt/2¹/₂ cups milk
40 g/1¹/₂ oz/3 tbsp granulated sugar
2 eggs, beaten
Grated nutmeg
15 ml/1 tbsp medium dry sherry

Stew the fruit salad according to the packet directions. Drain, reserving any juice. Meanwhile, put the rice and milk in a saucepan and bring to the boil. Half-cover and simmer gently for about 45 minutes, stirring occasionally, until soft and creamy. Stir in the sugar. Cool slightly, then stir in the fruit salad and eggs. Turn into a lightly greased ovenproof dish. Sprinkle with nutmeg and bake at 190°C/375°F/gas mark 5 for about 20 minutes until golden brown. Serve with any reserved fruit salad juice laced with the sherry.

Warm Blueberry Rice

Serves 4
120 ml/4 fl oz/¹/₂ cup water
100 g/4 oz/¹/₂ cup short-grain
  (pudding) rice
3 eggs, beaten
100 g/4 oz/¹/₂ cup light brown sugar
5 ml/1 tsp vanilla essence (extract)
A pinch of salt
75 g/3 oz/¹/₂ cup raisins
600 ml/1 pt/2¹/₂ cups full-cream milk
225 g/8 oz/2 cups blueberries
Granulated sugar

Bring the water to the boil. Stir in the rice, bring to the boil again, then remove from the heat and leave to stand for 5 minutes. Drain. Beat the eggs, sugar, vanilla and salt together. Blend in the raisins, milk and rice and turn into an ovenproof dish. Stand the dish in a roasting tin (pan) of hot water. Bake in the oven at 180°C/350°F/gas mark 4 for 1¹/₄ hours or until the rice is cooked and set firm. Remove from the oven and allow to cool for 15 minutes. Meanwhile, put the blueberries in a pan with 30 ml/ 2 tbsp water and a little sugar. Heat gently until the juice runs, then cover and simmer for about 5 minutes until the fruit is tender. Purée in a blender or food processor or pass through a sieve. Taste and add more sugar if liked. Serve the rice cut into pieces with the sauce poured over.

Baked Banana Rice Cake

Serves 4-6
1.2 litres/2 pts/5 cups milk
350 g/12 oz/1¹/₂ cups arborio or
other risotto rice
2 large ripe bananas, mashed well
2 size 1 eggs, separated
20 g/³/₄ oz/1¹/₂ tbsp unsalted (sweet)
butter

Bring the milk to the boil, add the rice, reduce the heat, cover and simmer gently for 15-20 minutes, stirring occasionally, until the rice is just tender and has absorbed the milk. Remove from the heat and stir in the bananas, eggs yolks and butter until well blended. Beat well. Whisk the egg whites until stiff and fold into the rice mixture with a metal spoon. Turn into a buttered large soufflé dish. Bake for 30 minutes at 180°C/350°F/gas mark 4 until just set and golden on top. If liked, cool slightly, then loosen the edge and turn out on to a warm serving plate. Serve warm.

Toffee Cocktail Rice

Serves 4
430g/15¹/₂ oz/1 large can creamed
rice pudding
430 g/15¹/₂ oz/1 large can fruit
cocktail, drained, reserving the
juice
60 ml/4 tbsp light brown sugar
10 ml/2 tsp arrowroot
10 ml/2 tsp lemon juice

Mix the rice and fruit in a saucepan and heat through, then turn into 4 individual flameproof dishes. Or place directly in microwave-safe flameproof dishes and heat in the microwave, stirring occasionally. Sprinkle the tops liberally with the sugar to cover completely. Place under a hot grill (broiler) until bubbling and melted. Blend the arrowroot with the lemon juice in a saucepan. Stir in the reserved juice and bring to the boil, stirring until thickened. Pour into a jug and serve with the toffee rice.

Princess of Puddings

Serves 6
50 g/2 oz/1 cup white bread, crusts
removed and diced
300 ml/¹/₂ pt/1¹/₄ cups milk
25 g/1 oz/2 tbsp unsalted (sweet)
butter
2 size 4 eggs, separated
Grated rind of 1 lemon
75 g/3 oz/¹/₃ cup caster (superfine)
sugar
60 ml/4 tbsp apricot jam (conserve)
430 g/15¹/₂ oz/1 large can creamed
rice

Put the bread in a large buttered baking dish. Warm the milk and butter until the fat melts. Beat in the egg yolks, lemon rind and 25 g/1 oz/2 tbsp of the sugar. Pour over the bread and bake in the oven at 180°C/350°F/gas mark 4 for 15-20 minutes or until set. Remove from the oven and spread the jam over. Top with the creamed rice. Whisk the egg whites until stiff and fold in the remaining sugar with a metal spoon. Pile on top of the rice to cover completely and return to the oven for a further 10 minutes or until golden. Serve warm.

Italian Rice Cakes

Serves 6

150 g/5 oz/²/₃ cup arborio rice
300 ml/¹/₂ pt/1¹/₄ cups milk
A pinch of salt
100 g/4 oz/¹/₂ cup caster (superfine)
  sugar
40 g/1¹/₂ oz/3 tbsp butter
1 lemon
65 g/2¹/₂ oz/good ¹/₂ cup plain (all-
  purpose) flour
3 eggs, separated
30 ml/2 tbsp rum or amaretti liqueur
Oil for deep-frying
10 ml/2 tsp ground cinnamon

Cook the rice in plenty of boiling water for 7 minutes. Drain, rinse with cold water, drain again and return to the pan with the milk. Bring to the boil, reduce the heat, cover and simmer for 10 minutes or until the milk has been absorbed. Remove from the heat and stir in the salt, 15 ml/1 tbsp of the sugar and the butter. Grate the rind from the lemon and add to the rice (reserve the fruit for serving). Leave to cool for 15 minutes, then stir in the flour and beat in the egg yolks and rum or liqueur. Whisk the egg whites until stiff and fold into the mixture with a metal spoon. Deep-fry spoonfuls of the mixture, a few at a time, until crisp and lightly golden. Drain on kitchen paper. Mix the remaining sugar with the cinnamon. Sprinkle over the rice cakes and serve with the lemon cut in wedges.

Frittelle di Riso

Serves 4-6

900 ml/1¹/₂ pts/3³/₄ cups milk
A pinch of salt
225 g/8 oz/1 cup arborio or other
  risotto rice
2 size 1 eggs
15 ml/1 tbsp plain (all-purpose) flour
Grated rind of 1 orange and 1
  lemon, reserving the fruit
Granulated sugar
Oil for shallow-frying
100 g/4 oz/¹/₂ cup icing
  (confectioners') sugar

Place the milk in a saucepan with a pinch of salt. Bring to the boil, add the rice, cover and simmer gently for 15-20 minutes, stirring occasionally until the rice is cooked and creamy, adding a little more milk if necessary. Remove from the heat and beat in the eggs, flour, orange and lemon rinds. Sweeten to taste with sugar. Heat the oil in a heavy frying pan (skillet). Drop spoonfuls of the mixture into the oil and fry (sauté) for about 4 minutes until the bases are golden. Turn over and brown the other sides. Drain on kitchen paper. Keep warm in a low oven while cooking the remainder. Sprinkle with sifted icing sugar and serve with the orange and lemon, cut into wedges, to squeeze over.

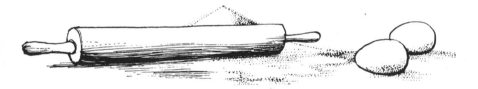

Quick Rhubarb and Rice Charlotte

Serves 6

25 g/1 oz/2 tbsp butter, melted
4 slices of buttered bread
430 g/15¹/₂ oz/1 large can creamed
  rice
10 ml/2 tsp cornflour (cornstarch)
567 g/ 1¹/₄ lb/ l large can rhubarb
25 g/1 oz/2 tbsp light brown sugar

Liberally grease a 1.2 litre/2 pt/5 cup ovenproof dish with half the butter. Line the dish with 2¹/₂ slices of the buttered bread. Spoon the rice into the dish and level the surface. Blend the cornflour with a little of the rhubarb juice in a saucepan. Add the remaining juice and bring to the boil, stirring. Stir in the rhubarb pieces and spoon over the rice. Cut the remaining buttered bread into small cubes and scatter over the rhubarb. Drizzle with the remaining melted butter and sprinkle with the sugar. Bake at 200°C/400°F/ gas mark 6 for about 40 minutes until the top is crisp and golden.

Creamed Rice Brulée

Serves 6

75 g/3 oz/¹/₃ cup short-grain
  (pudding) rice
600 ml/1 pt/2¹/₂ cups milk
30 ml/2 tbsp caster (superfine) sugar
300 ml/¹/₂ pt/1¹/₄ cups double (heavy)
  cream
4 egg yolks
2.5 ml/¹/₂ tsp vanilla essence
  (extract)
60 ml/4 tbsp demerara sugar

Simmer the rice in the milk for 30 minutes until the rice is soft. Stir in the sugar. Turn into a greased shallow ovenproof dish and leave to cool. Heat the cream in a saucepan but do not boil. Whisk in the egg yolks and vanilla essence. Pour over the rice. Stand the dish in a baking tin (pan) with enough hot water to come half-way up the sides of the dish. Bake at 150°C/300°F/gas mark 2 for 1¹/₂ hours or until the custard has set. Cool, then chill. Just before serving, sprinkle the top liberally with the demerara sugar. Place under a hot grill (broiler) until the sugar melts and caramelises. Serve straight away.

Lenten Pie

Serves 6-8

175 g/6 oz/1¹/₂ cups plain (all-
purpose) flour
A pinch of salt
75 g/3 oz/¹/₃ cup margarine
45 ml/3 tbsp cold water (approx.)
300 ml/¹/₂ pt/1¹/₄ cups milk
25 g/1 oz/¹/₄ cup ground rice
50 g/2 oz/¹/₄ cup butter
50 g/2 oz/¹/₄ cup caster (superfine)
sugar
2 eggs, beaten
Grated rind and juice of 1 lemon
25 g/1 oz/¹/₆ cup currants
Freshly grated nutmeg

Sift the flour and salt into a bowl. Add the
margarine and rub in with the fingertips
until the mixture resembles fine breadcrumbs. Mix with enough cold water to
form a firm dough. Knead gently on a
lightly floured surface. Roll out and use to
line a 23 cm/9 in flan dish (pie pan). Prick
the base with a fork. Put the milk in a
saucepan. Stir in the ground rice, bring to
the boil and cook for 2 minutes, stirring.
Leave to cool. Cream the butter and sugar
until light and fluffy. Beat in the eggs, a little at a time, beating well after each addition. Beat in the lemon rind and juice and
the cooled rice mixture. Turn into the pastry case and scatter the currants and some
grated nutmeg over. Place on a baking
sheet and bake in the oven at 190°C/
375°F/gas mark 5 for about 35 minutes
until set and turning golden. Serve warm.

Hot Lime Meringue Pudding

Serves 4

45 ml/3 tbsp short-grain (pudding)
rice
600 ml/1 pt/2¹/₂ cups milk
90 ml/6 tbsp caster (superfine) sugar
2 eggs, separated
Grated rind and juice of 1 large or 2
small limes
15 g/¹/₂ oz/1 tbsp butter

Put the rice in a saucepan with the milk.
Bring to the boil, stirring, and simmer for
30 minutes or until the rice is tender and
creamy. Whisk in 30 ml/2 tbsp of the sugar
and the egg yolks. Stir in the lime rind and
juice and turn into a baking dish greased
with the butter. Whisk the egg whites until
stiff. Fold in half the remaining sugar and
whisk again until stiff and glossy. Fold in
the remaining sugar and pile on top of the
rice. Bake at 180°C/350°F/gas mark 4 for
15 minutes or until the meringue is turing
a pale golden brown. Serve hot.

Hot Banana and Jam Rice

Serves 4

45 ml/3 tbsp short-grain (pudding) rice
600 ml/1 pt/2¹/₂ cups milk
90 ml/6 tbsp caster (superfine) sugar
15 g/¹/₂ oz/1 tbsp butter
2 eggs, separated
4 ripe bananas
10 ml/2 tsp lemon juice
60 ml/4 tbsp seedless raspberry jam (clear conserve)
15 ml/1 tbsp water

Put the rice in a pan with the milk. Bring to the boil and simmer, stirring occasionally, for 30 minutes or until creamy and tender. Stir in 30 ml/2 tbsp of the sugar, the butter and the egg yolks. Turn into a lightly buttered ovenproof serving dish. Mash the bananas with the lemon juice until pulpy. Spread gently over the rice. Whisk the egg whites until stiff. Add half the remaining sugar and whisk until stiff and glossy. Fold in the remaining sugar with a metal spoon. Pile on the bananas and bake in the oven at 180°C/350°F/gas mark 4 for about 15 minutes or until the meringue is turning golden. Meanwhile, melt the jam in a saucepan with the water. Pour into a jug. Serve the banana meringue with the jam sauce poured over.

Chocolate Rice Pudding

Serves 4

45 ml/3 tbsp round-grain (pudding) rice
30 ml/2 tbsp granulated sugar
45 ml/3 tbsp cocoa (unsweetened chocolate) powder
60 ml/4 tbsp boiling water
600 ml/1 pt/2¹/₂ cups milk
A few drops of vanilla essence (extract)

Put the rice in an ovenproof dish with the sugar. Blend the cocoa with the water. Stir in the milk then pour on to the rice and add the vanilla essence. Stir well again, then bake in the oven at 160°C/325°F/gas mark 3 for 2 hours or until creamy and the rice is tender, stirring twice during the first hour of cooking.

Super Sinful Chocolate Rice Pudding

Serves 4

Prepare as for Chocolate Rice Pudding, but put a layer of 45 ml/3 tbsp chocolate and hazelnut spread in the base of the dish. Cook the rice, sugar, and cocoa blended with water in the milk on the hob for 15 minutes, stirring frequently, then pour over the chocolate spread and bake in the oven for about 1³/₄ hours, without stirring. Serve with whipped cream.

Quick Chocolate Rice

Serves 2-3

*430g/15¹/₂ oz/1 large can creamed
rice pudding
45 ml/3 tbsp drinking (sweetened)
chocolate powder
Chocolate finger biscuits (crackers)*

Heat the rice and 30 ml/2 tbsp of the drinking chocolate in a saucepan, stirring. Spoon into small bowls and serve sprinkled with the remaining chocolate powder and a chocolate finger in each serving.

Quick Mocha Rice

Serves 2-3

Make as for Quick Chocolate Rice, but substitute 5 ml/1 tsp of the chocolate powder with instant coffee powder. Serve with 2 chocolate coffee matchsticks in each serving.

Caribbean Rice

Serves 4

*430g/15¹/₂ oz/1 large can creamed
rice pudding
30 ml/2 tbsp grated plain (semi-
sweet) chocolate
2 bananas, halved, then halved
again lengthways
25 g/1 oz/2 tbsp butter
30 ml/2 tbsp rum
30 ml/2 tbsp dark brown sugar*

Put the rice in a saucepan with the chocolate. Heat through gently until the rice is marbled with melted chocolate. Don't over-stir. Meanwhile fry (sauté) the bananas in the butter for 2 minutes until just softening. Push to one side and stir in

the rum and sugar. Heat through until the sugar melts. Spoon the rice into serving bowls, add 2 pieces of banana to each and spoon the sauce over. Serve straight away.

Coffee and Walnut Rice Pudding

Serves 4

*45 ml/3 tbsp pudding (short-grain)
rice
30 ml/2 tbsp light brown sugar
600 ml/1 pt/2¹/₂ cups milk
15 ml/1 tbsp instant coffee powder
50 g/2 oz/¹/₂ cup chopped walnuts
Clotted cream*

Mix the rice with the sugar, milk and coffee powder in an ovenproof dish. Stir in the walnuts. Bake at 160°C/325°F/gas mark 3 for 2 hours or until the rice is tender and creamy, stirring twice during the first hour. Serve with clotted cream.

Almond Strawberry Rice

Serves 4
225 g/8 oz/2 cups strawberries, sliced
15 ml/1 tbsp kirsch
15 ml/1 tbsp caster (superfine) sugar
230 g/15¹/₂ oz/1 large can creamed rice
A few drops of almond essence (extract)
150 ml/¹/₄ pt/²/₃ cup double (heavy) cream
25 g/1 oz/¹/₄ cup toasted flaked almonds

Place the strawberries in a pan with the kirsch and sugar. Cover and stew gently for 3 minutes. Turn into an ovenproof dish. Mix the rice with the almond essence. Spoon over. Pour over the cream and bake at 190°C/375°F/gas mark 5 until the top is golden brown. Sprinkle with the almonds and serve warm.

Vanilla Rice Soufflé with Lemon Sauce

Serves 4
30 ml/2 tbsp ground rice
30 ml/2 tbsp caster (superfine) sugar
300 ml/¹/₂ pt/1¹/₄ cups milk
3 eggs, separated
5 ml/1 tsp vanilla essence (extract)
60 ml/4 tbsp lemon curd
15 ml/1 tbsp lemon juice

Blend the rice with the sugar and a little of the milk in a saucepan. Stir in the remaining milk. Bring to the boil and cook for 5 minutes, stirring all the time, until thick. Remove from the heat and whisk in the egg yolks and vanilla. Whisk the egg whites until stiff and fold in with a metal spoon. Turn into a 15 cm/6 in soufflé dish and bake in the oven at 190°C/375°F/gas mark 5 for about 30 minutes until risen and golden. Meanwhile, heat the lemon curd with the lemon juice and add enough water to form a smooth pouring sauce. Serve the hot soufflé straight from the oven with the sauce.

Chocolate Rice Soufflé with Cherry Sauce

Serves 4
Prepare as for Vanilla Rice Soufflé with Lemon Sauce, but add 30 ml/2 tbsp of cocoa (unsweetened chocolate) powder to the rice and sugar mixture before adding the remaining milk. Substitute cherry jam for the lemon curd and omit the lemon juice.

Macaroni Fruit Cobbler

Serves 4-6
425 g/15 oz/1 large can macaroni pudding
375 g/13¹/₂ oz/1 large can apple and raspberry pie filling
5 plain scones, split and buttered
25 g/1 oz/2 tbsp light brown sugar

Empty the can of macaroni pudding into a saucepan. Add the fruit pie filling and heat gently, folding the two together until hot. Spoon into a 1.2 litre/2 pt/5 cup flameproof serving dish. (Or heat in the dish in the microwave.) Arrange the scones, buttered sides up, around the edge of the dish. Sprinkle the sugar over the scones and grill (broil) for about 4 minutes until the top is golden. Serve straight away.

Lemon Meringue Surprise

Serves 4

*100 g/4 oz/1 cup conchiglietti or
    other soup pasta*
450 ml/³/₄ pt/2 cups milk
1 small can evaporated milk
5 ml/1 tsp ground cinnamon
*150 g/5 oz/²/₃ cup caster (superfine)
    sugar*
1 packet lemon meringue pie filling
300 ml/¹/₂ pt/1¹/₄ cups water
2 eggs, separated

Put the pasta in a saucepan with the milk,
evaporated milk and cinnamon. Bring to
the boil, stirring. Reduce the heat, cover
and simmer gently for about 15 minutes or
until the pasta is soft and the milk is
creamy. Stir in 25 g/1 oz/2 tbsp of the
sugar and turn the mixture into an ovenproof dish. Make up the pie filling according to the packet directions with the water
and both egg yolks. Spoon over the pasta.
Whisk the egg whites until stiff and gradually whisk in the remaining sugar until stiff
and glossy. Pile on top of the lemon mixture and bake at 180°C/350°F/gas mark 4
for about 15 minutes until the top is just
turning golden. Serve hot.

Dutch Macaroni Cream

Serves 6

*1 litre/1³/₄ pts/4¹/₄ cups full-cream
    milk*
150 g/5 oz/1¹/₄ cups short-cut macaroni
Grated rind of ¹/₂ lemon
75 g/3 oz/¹/₂ cup seedless (pitless) raisins
75 g/3 oz/¹/₃ cup granulated sugar
40 g/1¹/₂ oz/3 tbsp butter
50 g/2 oz/1 cup cake crumbs

Bring the milk to the boil in a saucepan.
Add the macaroni, lemon rind and raisins.
Bring to the boil, reduce the heat, cover
and simmer for 40 minutes. Stir in half the
sugar and butter. Turn into an ovenproof
dish. Melt the remaining butter and stir in
the cake crumbs and the remaining sugar.
Sprinkle over the macaroni and bake in a
hot oven at 200°C/400°F/gas mark 6 for
about 15 minutes until golden on top.

Almond Zarda from Pakistan

Serves 4-6

175 g/6 oz/³/₄ cup butter
6 cardamom pods, split open
*225 g/8 oz vermicelli, broken into
    small pieces*
*225 g/8 oz/1 cup caster (superfine)
    sugar*
*A few drops of orange food
    colouring*
450 ml/³/₄ pt/2 cups water
50 g/2 oz/¹/₂ cup blanched almonds
Strips of silver paper or foil

Melt the butter in a saucepan. Add the
cardamom pods and fry (sauté) for 1
minute. Add the vermicelli and fry until
golden but not too brown. Stir in the sugar,
food colouring and water and bring to the
boil. Simmer, stirring, until the water evaporates and the vermicelli is tender. Cover,
turn off the heat and leave to stand for 10
minutes to allow the flavour to develop.
Pile on to a serving dish. Decorate with the
almonds and thin strips of silver paper laid
over attractively before serving.

Lemony Butterscotch Bows

Serves 4

450 ml/³/₄ pt/2 cups milk
75 g/3 oz/³/₄ cup farfalle
Grated rind and juice of 2 lemons
40 g/1¹/₂ oz/3 tbsp caster (superfine) sugar
50 g/2 oz/¹/₄ cup butter
75 g/3 oz/¹/₃ cup light brown sugar
20 ml/4 tsp cornflour (cornstarch)
30 ml/2 tbsp water

Put the milk, pasta and lemon rind in a saucepan. Bring to the boil, stirring, reduce the heat, cover and simmer for 15-20 minutes, stirring occasionally until the pasta is soft and the milk creamy. Stir in the caster sugar and turn into an ovenproof dish. Meanwhile, make the lemon juice up to 200 ml/7 fl oz/scant 1 cup with water. Bring to the boil. In a separate pan heat the butter and brown sugar until melted and bubbling. Pour in the hot lemon juice and stir until dissolved. Blend the cornflour with the water. Add to the pan, bring to the boil and cook for 1 minute, stirring until thickened and clear. Pour over the pasta and bake at 190°C/375°F/gas mark 5 for 20 minutes. Serve hot.

Pasta Puffs with Raspberry Coulis

Serves 4-6

300 g/11 oz/1 small can raspberries in natural juice
30 ml/2 tbsp icing (confectioners') sugar, sifted
100 g/4 oz/¹/₂ cup butter
300 ml/¹/₂ pt/1¹/₄ cups water
150 g/5 oz/1¹/₄ cups plain (all-purpose) flour, sifted
3 eggs, separated
75 g/3 oz/1¹/₂ cups cooked short-cut macaroni
Oil for deep-frying
A little caster (superfine) sugar

Purée the raspberries and their juice in a blender or food processor, then pass through a sieve into a small serving bowl. Stir in the icing sugar. Place the butter in a saucepan with the water and heat until the butter melts, then bring to the boil. Add the flour all in one go and beat with a wooden spoon until the mixture leaves the sides of the pan clean. Remove from the heat and beat for a further 1 minute. Beat in the egg yolks. Whisk the egg whites until stiff and fold into the mixture with a metal spoon. Fold in the macaroni. Heat the oil until a cube of day-old bread browns in 30 seconds. Fry spoonfuls of the mixture, a few at a time, until crisp and golden. Drain on kitchen paper, then dust with caster sugar. Pile on to a plate with the bowl of sauce in the middle. Serve straight away.

Apple and Mincemeat Meringue Layer

Serves 6
100 g/4 oz/1 cup tagliatelle
Butter for greasing
2 large cooking (tart) apples, thinly
* sliced*
225 g/8 oz/1 cup mincemeat
2 eggs, separated
430 g/15½ oz/1 large can custard
100 g/4 oz/½ cup caster (superfine)
* sugar*

Cook the tagliatelle in plenty of boiling water until tender. Drain. Place half in the base of a 1.5 litre/2½ pt/6 cup clear oven-proof dish well greased with the butter. Press down well. Top with half the apple slices. Spread half the mincemeat over. Beat the egg yolks into the custard. Pour half over the mincemeat. Repeat the layers. Cover with foil and bake in the oven at 180°C/350°F/gas mark 4 for 15 minutes. Meanwhile, whisk the egg whites until stiff. Whisk in half the sugar until stiff and glossy. Fold in the remaining sugar. Remove the foil and pile the meringue on top of the pudding. Return to the oven for 15 minutes until lightly golden. Serve straight away.

Greek-style Noodle Dessert

Serves 4
225 g/8 oz ribbon noodles, broken
* into short lengths*
50 g/2 oz/¼ cup butter
15 ml/1 tbsp sesame seeds
30 ml/2 tbsp seedless (pitless) raisins
45 ml/3 tbsp clear honey
2.5 ml/½ tsp rose water
2.5 ml/1½ tsp ground cinnamon
150 ml/¼ pt/⅔ cup Greek-style plain
* yoghurt*

Cook the pasta according to the packet directions. Drain and rinse with boiling water, drain again and return to the saucepan. Heat the butter in a frying pan (skillet). Add the sesame seeds and fry (sauté) until golden brown but do not allow to burn. Stir in the raisins, honey, rose water and cinnamon and mix well. Pour over the noodles, toss well, pile into bowls and serve topped with a spoonful of Greek yoghurt.

Cherry Choc Noodles

Serves 4

*225 g/8 oz/2 cups ribbon noodles
  broken into short lengths*
50 g/2 oz/¹/₄ cup butter
50 g/2 oz/¹/₄ cup light brown sugar
*45 ml/3 tbsp cocoa (unsweetened
  chocolate) powder*
15 ml/1 tbsp brandy
*425 g/15 oz/1 large can stoned
  (pitted) black cherries, drained,
  reserving the juice*
10 ml/2 tsp arrowroot
Toasted flaked almonds

Cook the pasta according to the packet directions. Drain, rinse with boiling water and drain again. In the same pan, melt the butter and stir in the sugar and cocoa powder. Cook, stirring until the sugar has dissolved. Stir in the brandy. In a separate pan, blend a little of the cherry juice with the arrowroot, stir in the remaining juice and bring to the boil, stirring until thickened. Stir in the cherries. Add the noodles to the chocolate mixture and toss well. Pile on to serving plates and spoon the hot cherries over. Sprinkle with the almonds and serve straight away.

Candy Fruit Farfalle

Serves 4

900 g/1¹/₂ pts/3 cups milk
175 g/6 oz/1¹/₂ cups farfalle
50 g/2 oz/¹/₃ cup sultanas (golden raisins)
*50 g/2 oz/¹/₂ cup multicoloured glacé
  (candied) cherries, quartered*
25 g/1 oz/2 tbsp light brown sugar
*50 g/2 oz/¹/₂ cup toasted hazelnuts,
  roughly chopped*
1.5 ml/¹/₄ tsp grated nutmeg
60 ml/4 tbsp double (heavy) cream

Bring the milk to the boil in a large saucepan. Add the pasta, sultanas, cherries and sugar and simmer for about 10 minutes until tender. Stir in the nuts and nutmeg. Spoon into serving bowls and drizzle with cream before serving.

Marshmallow Moment

Serves 4

225 g/8 oz/2 cups farfalle
100 g/4 oz/¹/₂ cup butter
30 ml/2 tbsp light brown sugar
175 g/6 oz/1¹/₂ cups marshmallows
1 small can evaporated milk
5 ml/1 tsp rose water
Crystallised (candied) rose petals

Cook the pasta according to the packet directions. Drain, rinse with boiling water and drain again. Melt the butter in the same pan. Stir in the sugar, marshmallows and evaporated milk and cook gently, stirring until melted. Stir in thr rose water. Add the noodles, toss and pile on to serving plates. Scatter a few crystallized rose petals over just before serving.

Blackcurrant Macaroni Meringue

Serves 4

430 g/15¹/₂ oz/1 large can creamed
*   macaroni pudding*
2 eggs, separated
300 g/11 oz/1 small can
*   blackcurrants in syrup*
5 ml/1 tsp cornflour (cornstarch)
60 ml/4 tbsp caster (superfine) sugar

Spoon the macaroni into an ovenproof dish. Whisk in the egg yolks until well blended. Blend a little of the blackcurrant juice with the cornflour in a saucepan. Stir in the remaining juice, bring to the boil and cook for 1 minute, stirring. Add the black-currants, then spoon the thickened fruit over the macaroni. Whisk the egg whites until stiff. Whisk in half the sugar and whisk again until stiff and glossy. Fold in the remaining sugar. Pile on to the black-currants and bake at 200°C/400°F/gas mark 6 for 8-10 minutes until the top is crisp and golden. Serve straight away.

Apricot Rice Ring

Serves 4

175 g/6 oz/³/₄ cup long-grain rice
600 ml/1 pt/2¹/₂ cups apple juice
1 small piece cinnamon stick
15 g/¹/₂ oz/1 tbsp powdered gelatine
425 g/15 oz/1 large can apricots
3 glacé (candied) cherries, halved
450 ml/³/₄ pt/2 cups apricot yoghurt

Put the rice in a saucepan with the apple juice and cinnamon. Bring to the boil, cover and cook over a very gentle heat for 15 minutes or until the rice has absorbed all the juice and is tender. Remove the piece of cinnamon. Stir in the gelatine until completely dissolved. Drain the can of apricots and reserve the juice. Place half a glacé cherry, cut side down, in the cavity of 6 apricot halves and arrange them, rounded sides up at intervals around the base of a lightly oiled 1.2 litre/2 pt/5 cup ring mould (mold). Stir the yoghurt into the rice mixture and spoon into the ring. Chill until set (about 2 hours). Turn out on to a serving plate, chop the remaining apricots and place in the centre.

Zuppa di Inglese

Serves 6

4 eggs
50 g/2 oz/1¼ cup caster (superfine)
  sugar
30 ml/2 tbsp rice flour
900 ml/1½ pts/3¾ cups milk
Grated rind and juice of 1 orange
50 g/2 oz/½ cup plain (semi-sweet)
  chocolate
1 slab plain cake, thinly sliced
60 ml/4 tbsp medium dry sherry, or
  half sherry and half kirsch
Grated chocolate

Whisk together the eggs and sugar in a saucepan. Blend the rice flour with a little of the milk. Stir in the remaining milk and add to the saucepan with the orange rind. Bring to the boil slowly over a gentle heat, stirring all the time until thickened. Do not boil rapidly or the mixture will curdle. Pour half the custard into a separate bowl. Melt the chocolate in a bowl in the microwave or over a pan of hot water and stir into the saucepan of custard. Put a layer of one-third of the cake in the base of a round glass serving dish. Mix the orange juice and sherry together and drizzle a third over the cake. Spoon over a third of the plain custard then a third of the chocolate custard. Repeat these layers, finishing with a layer of chocolate custard. Cover and chill for several hours until set. Sprinkle with grated chocolate before serving.

Banana and Rhubarb Condé

Serves 4-6

450 g/1 lb pink forced rhubarb,
  trimmed and cut into 2.5 cm/1 in
  lengths
175 g/6 oz/¾ cup caster (superfine)
  sugar
Grated rind and juice of 1 orange
450 g/1 lb bananas (unpeeled weight)
430 g/15½ oz/1 large can creamed
  rice

Place the rhubarb in a casserole (Dutch oven) with the sugar and orange juice. Stir well, then cover and cook in the oven at 160°C/325°F/gas mark 3 for 35 minutes. Remove from the oven and leave to cool. Slice the bananas thinly and place half in 1 large or 4-6 individual glass dishes. Mix the orange rind with the rice and spoon half over the bananas. Spoon half of the cool rhubarb over. Repeat the layers. Chill until ready to serve.

Trauttmansdorff

Austrian Fruit Rice Dessert
Serves 4-6

450 ml/¾ pt/2 cups milk
100 g/4 oz/½ cup short-grain
  (pudding) rice
A pinch of salt
Grated rind and juice of 1 lemon
45 ml/3 tbsp caster (superfine) sugar
1 sachet of powdered gelatine
450 g/1 lb/1 large can fruit cocktail
  in natural juice
250 ml/8 fl oz/1 cup whipping cream,
  whipped

Put the milk in a saucepan with the rice, salt and lemon rind. Bring to the boil, reduce the heat and simmer gently for 30 minutes or until the rice is really tender and creamy. Stir in the sugar and leave to cool. Soften the gelatine in the lemon juice, then stand in a pan of hot water or microwave to dissolve completely. Strain off the juice from the can of fruit. Add 250 ml/8 fl oz/1 cup to the gelatine and stir well. Stir into the cold rice with the drained fruit. Fold in the whipped cream. Turn into a lightly oiled mould (mold) and chill until set. Loosen the edges, dip the mould in hot water, then turn out on to a serving dish and serve cold.

Rice and Citrus Mallow

Serves 4-6
1 small orange
1 lemon
1 lime
75 g/3 oz/⅓ cup short-grain (pudding) rice
900 ml/1½ pts/3¼ cups milk
45 ml/3 tbsp granulated sugar
14 white marshmallows
45 ml/3 tbsp double (heavy) cream

Pare the rind thinly from the fruits. Cut into thin strips and boil in water for 5 minutes. Drain, rinse with cold water and drain again. Squeeze the juice from the fruits. Put the rice, milk and sugar in a saucepan. Bring to the boil, reduce the heat and simmer gently for 30 minutes or until the rice is really tender, stirring occasionally. Stir in the marshmallows, then the fruit juices and cream. Spoon into individual glass dishes and sprinkle with the fruit rinds. Chill until ready to serve.

Riz à l'Impératrice

Serves 5-6
100 g/4 oz/½ cup long-grain rice
250 ml/8 fl oz/1 cup milk
A pinch of salt
2.5 ml/½ tsp vanilla essence (extract)
10 ml/2 tsp powdered gelatine
30 ml/2 tbsp water
50 g/2 oz/¼ cup caster (superfine) sugar
2 egg yolks
300 ml/½ pt/1¼ cups single (light) cream
50 g/2 oz/⅓ cup crystallized (candied) fruits
30 ml/2 tbsp kirsch
300 ml/½ pt/1¼ cups whipping cream
Glacé (candied) cherries
Angelica leaves

Cook the rice in the milk with the salt for about 30 minutes until tender, stirring occasionally. Stir in the vanilla essence. Soften the gelatine in the water then stir into the hot rice, stirring until completely dissolved. Meanwhile, whisk the sugar, egg yolks and single cream together. Cook in a bowl over a pan of hot water (or use a double saucepan), stirring continuously until the mixture coats the back of a spoon. Stir into the rice mixture and leave until just beginning to set. Meanwhile, soak the fruits in the kirsch. Whip the whipping cream. When the rice mixture is on the point of setting, fold in the fruits in kirsch and the cream. Turn into a wetted mould (mold) and chill until set. Turn out and decorate with the glacé cherries and angelica before serving.

M'hal'labeeyeh

Serves 4
15 ml/1 tbsp cornflour (cornstarch)
15 g/¹/₂ oz/2 tbsp ground rice
600 ml/1 pt/2¹/₂ cups milk
100 g/4 oz/¹/₂ cup sugar
5 ml/1 tsp orange flower water
Crystallized (candied) orange slices

Blend the cornflour and rice to a paste with a little of the milk in a heavy-based saucepan. Stir in the remaining milk and the sugar. Bring to the boil, reduce the heat and simmer until the mixture thickens and coats the back of a spoon, stirring all the time. Remove from the heat and stir in the orange flower water. Pour into individual dishes, leave to cool, then chill for several hours. Decorate with crystallized orange slices before serving.

Golden Gate Roulade

Serves 6
4 eggs, separated
100 g/4 oz/¹/₂ cup caster (superfine)
  sugar
100 g/4 oz/1 cup grated carrot
50 g/2 oz/¹/₂ cup chopped hazelnuts
100 g/4 oz/1 cup plain (all-purpose)
  flour
2.5 ml/¹/₂ tsp mixed (apple pie) spice
A little sifted icing (confectioners')
  sugar
150 g/5 oz/1 small can creamed rice
  pudding
225 g/8 oz/1 cup fromage frais

Grease and line an 18 × 28 cm/7 × 11 in Swiss (jelly) roll tin (pan) with greased greaseproof (waxed) paper. Whisk the egg yolks and caster sugar together until thick and pale. Fold in the carrot and hazelnuts.

Sift the flour and mixed spice and fold in with a metal spoon. Whisk the egg whites until stiff and fold in with a metal spoon. Turn into the prepared tin and bake at 190°C/375°F/gas mark 5 for 25 minutes or until the centre springs back when lightly pressed with a finger. Turn out on to a sheet of greaseproof paper dusted with icing sugar. Remove the cooking paper and roll up with the sugared paper. Carefully transfer to a wire rack and leave to cool. When cold, carefully unroll and remove the sugared paper. Mix the rice with the fromage frais, spread over the surface then re-roll. Chill until ready to serve.

Lime Zinger

Serves 4
1 tablet lime jelly (jello)
Boiling water
430 g/15¹/₂ oz/l large can creamed
  rice pudding

Break up the jelly tablet in a measuring jug. Make up to 300 ml/¹/₂ pt/1¹/₄ cups with boiling water. Stir until dissolved. Empty the rice into a bowl. Stir in 150 ml/¹/₄ pt/²/₃ cup of the jelly. Stir well. Turn into a 600 ml/1 pt/2¹/₂ cups wetted mould (mold) and chill until set. Chill the remaining jelly in the jug also. When set, turn the rice mould out on to a serving plate. Chop the remaining lime jelly and spoon around the outside to decorate.

Creamy Apple Mousse

Serves 6

15 ml/1 tbsp powdered gelatine
Juice of 1 lemon
600 ml/1 pt/2¹/₂ cups sweetened
  apple purée (sauce)
2 eggs, separated
430 g/15¹/₂ oz/1 large can creamed
  rice
A little whipped cream
Ratafias

Put the gelatine in a cup with the lemon juice, stir well, then stand in a pan of hot water and stir until dissolved, or dissolve in the microwave but do not allow to boil. Stir the dissolved gelatine into the apple purée and beat in the egg yolks. Fold in the rice. Whisk the egg whites until stiff and fold in with a metal spoon. Turn the mixture into a glass dish and chill until set. Pipe the whipped cream around the top and decorate with ratafias before serving.

Elizabethan Chilled Rice Pudding

Serves 6

100 g/4 oz/¹/₂ cup round-grain
  (pudding) rice
750 ml/1¹/₄ pts/3 cups milk
120 ml/4 fl oz/¹/₂ cup double (heavy)
  cream
2 egg yolks
100 g/4 oz/¹/₂ cup light brown sugar
A pinch of salt
A pinch of white pepper
1.5 ml/¹/₄ tsp ground cloves
1.5 ml/¹/₄ tsp ground mace
50 g/2 oz/¹/₃ cup currants
50 g/2 oz/¹/₃ cup stoned (pitted)
  dates, chopped
25 g/1 oz/2 tbsp unsalted (sweet)
  butter

Mix the rice and milk in a large, heavy saucepan. Bring to the boil, reduce the heat, cover and simmer gently for 30 minutes or until the rice is tender and creamy. Blend in the remaining ingredients, bring to the boil, reduce the heat and cook very gently for 10 minutes, stirring occasionally. Turn into a glass dish, leave to cool, then chill before serving.

Italian Summer Rice

Serves 4-6

450 ml/³/₄ pt/2 cups milk
350 g/12 oz/1¹/₂ cups arborio or other risotto rice
60 ml/4 tbsp caster (superfine) sugar
15 g/¹/₂ oz/1 tbsp unsalted (sweet) butter
1 eating (dessert) apple, cut into chunks
1 firm but ripe banana, cut into chunks
225 g/8 oz/2 cups strawberries, hulled and cut into bite-sized pieces
Juice of 2 lemons

Place the milk in a saucepan and bring to the boil. Add the rice, reduce the heat, cover and simmer for 15-20 minutes until just tender, stirring occasionally and adding a little more milk if necessary as the mixture will be very thick. Meanwhile, place 15 ml/1 tbsp of the sugar in a small pan with 45 ml/3 tbsp water. Bring to the boil and cook until golden. Pour into a large, deep ring mould (mold) and tilt to coat the base. When the rice is cooked, remove from the heat and stir in the butter and remaining sugar. Spoon into the mould and smooth the surface. Place in a roasting tin (pan) containing enough boiling water to come half-way up the sides of the mould. Bake at 180°C/350°F/gas mark 4 for about 20 minutes or until golden on top. Remove from the oven, cool then chill. Meanwhile, mix the prepared fruits with the lemon juice. Chill. Loosen the edge of the rice ring with a sharp knife, then turn out on to a serving plate. Spoon the fruit into the centre and serve.

Black Forest Sundae

Serves 4

410 g/14¹/₂ oz/1 large can cherry pie filling
430 g/15¹/₂ oz/1 large can chocolate rice pudding
100 g/4 oz/1 small can cream
Grated chocolate

Layer the cherry pie filling with the chocolate rice in 4 sundae dishes. Drain off the whey from the can of cream. Stir well, then pipe or spoon a swirl of cream over the top of each dessert. Sprinkle with chocolate and chill before serving.

Rhubarb and Rice Fool

Serves 4

225 g/8 oz rhubarb
25 g/1 oz/2 tbsp butter
50 g/2 oz/¹/₄ cup caster (superfine) sugar
2.5 ml/¹/₂ tsp ground cinnamon
430 g/15¹/₂ oz/1 large can creamed rice pudding
150 ml/¹/₄ pt/²/₃ cup thick plain yoghurt

Chop the rhubarb and place in a saucepan with the butter, sugar and cinnamon. Cover and cook gently for abut 10 minutes or until pulpy. Beat well and leave to cool. Stir in the rice and yoghurt. Turn into 4 sundae dishes and chill.

Melon and Rice Delight

Serves 4

350 g/12 oz/1¹/₂ cups arborio or
other risotto rice
450 ml/³/₄ pt/2 cups milk
45 ml/3 tbsp caster (superfine) sugar
15 ml/1 tbsp cinnamon
2 ripe cantaloupe melons

Cook the rice in boiling water for 10 minutes. Drain and rinse with cold water.
Drain again. Bring the milk to the boil, add
the rice and simmer for 8 minutes until
tender. Remove from the heat and leave to
cool. When cold, stir in the sugar and cinnamon. Cut the melons in half, scoop out
the seeds and discard. Scoop out the flesh
in bite-sized pieces, or use a melon baller.
Place the shells on a plate. Stir the melon
flesh into the rice. Pile into the shells and
chill before serving.

Strawberry Rice Quickie

Serves 4

415 g/14¹/₂ oz/1 large can strawberry
pie filling
430 g/15¹/₂ oz/1 large can creamed
rice pudding
100 g/4 oz/1 small can cream
A few angelica leaves
A few glacé (candied) cherries

Spoon half the pie filling into 4 sundae
glasses. Top with half the rice. Repeat the
layers. Drain off the whey from the can of
cream, stir well, then pipe or swirl on top.
Decorate with angelica leaves and halved
cherries. Chill until ready to serve.

Stuffed Peaches

Serves 6

900 ml/1¹/₂ pts/3³/₄ cups milk
350 g/12 oz/1¹/₂ cups arborio or
other risotto rice
2 size 1 egg yolks
30 ml/2 tbsp granulated sugar
6 yellow peaches
15 g/¹/₂ oz/1 tbsp unsalted (sweet)
butter
15 ml/1 tbsp icing (confectioners')
sugar

Put 450 ml/³/₄ pt/2 cups of the milk in a
saucepan and bring to the boil. Add the
rice, reduce the heat, cover and simmer
gently for 15-20 minutes until just tender,
but still with some texture, stirring occasionally. Leave to cool. Meanwhile, put the
remaining milk in a separate pan. Heat
gently. Whisk the yolks and sugar in a
bowl. Add a little of the warm milk, whisk
well, then return to the pan of milk. Stir
over a gentle heat until the mixture thickens and coats the back of a spoon. Do NOT
boil. Leave to cool. Halve the peaches and
remove the stones (pits). Scoop out most
of the pulp, leaving a thin wall. Place the
shells in a shallow baking dish, greased
with the butter, in a single layer. Mix the
rice with the custard. Chop the scooped-
out peach flesh and mix in. Spoon into the
peach shells and sprinkle with the icing
sugar. Bake at 180°C/350°F/gas mark 4 for
about 20 minutes until the tops are golden.
Serve immediately, or cool, then chill.

Italian Surprise

Serves 4
350 g/12 oz/1¹/₂ cups arborio or
other risotto rice
75 g/3 oz/¹/₂ cup seedless (pitless)
raisins
45 ml/3 tbsp rum
250 ml/8 fl oz/1 cup double (heavy)
cream
1 size 1 egg, beaten
225 g/8 oz/1 cup Ricotta cheese
100 g/4 oz/1 cup grated Parmesan
cheese

Cook the rice in plenty of boiling water for
18 minutes. Drain, rinse with cold water,
drain again and leave to cool. Meanwhile,
put the raisins in a bowl with the rum and
leave to soak. Whip the cream until stiff.
Stir the egg, raisins and rum, the Ricotta
and Parmesan into the rice. Lastly, fold in
the cream. Spoon into a glass dish, level
the surface and chill before serving.

Tyrolean Dessert

Serves 6
65 g/2¹/₂ oz/good ¹/₄ cup short-grain
(pudding) rice
600 ml/1 pt/2¹/₂ cups milk
40 g/1¹/₂ oz/3 tbsp granulated sugar
10 ml/2 tsp powdered gelatine
1 green eating (dessert) apple
Lemon juice
225 g/8 oz/2 cups strawberries,
hulled and quartered
150 ml/¹/₄ pt/²/₃ cup double (heavy)
cream, whipped
15 ml/1 tbsp icing (confectioners')
sugar

Put the rice and milk in a saucepan. Bring
to the boil, reduce the heat and simmer for
30 minutes, stirring occasionally until the
rice is tender and the mixture is creamy.
Stir in the sugar and gelatine, stiring until
both are completely dissolved. Core and
dice the apple and toss in lemon juice. Mix
the apple with half the strawberries. Fold
into the rice, then fold in the cream. Turn
into a 900 ml/1¹/₂ pt/3³/₄ cup wetted mould
(mold) and chill until set. Meanwhile,
purée the remaining strawberries with the
icing sugar. Turn the rice mould out on to
a serving plate, spoon the sauce around
and serve cold.

Riz Bil-Halib

Serves 4
100 g/4 oz/¹/₂ cup short-grain
(pudding) rice
450 ml/³/₄ pt/2 cups water
375 ml/13 fl oz/1¹/₂ cups full-cream
milk
100 g/4 oz/¹/₂ cup granulated sugar
10 ml/2 tsp rose water
A few crystallized (candied) rose
petals (optional)

Wash the rice thoroughly in several
changes of cold water. Place in a saucepan
and add the water. Bring to the boil and
simmer for 20 minutes. Stir in the milk,
sugar and rose water and simmer, stirring
until thick and creamy and the rice is tender. Cool slightly, then pour into individual
dishes. Leave until cold, then chill before
serving decorated with crystallised rose
petals, if liked.

Strawberry Ratafia Sundae

Serves 4

350 g/12 oz/3 cups strawberries
100 g/4 oz/1 cup ratafias, crushed
230 g/15¹/₂ oz/1 large can creamed rice
Grated rind and juice of 1 orange
25 g/1 oz/2 tbsp caster (superfine) sugar
150 ml/¹/₄ pt/²/₃ cup double (heavy) cream

Reserve 4 of the strawberries for decoration and hull and slice the rest. Mix with the ratafias, rice and the orange rind. Turn into 4 large sundae dishes. Whisk the orange juice, sugar and cream until thick. Spoon on top and decorate each with a strawberry.

Raspberry and Maple Syrup Surprise

Serves 6

175 g/6 oz/¹/₂ cup maple syrup
50 g/2 oz pecan nuts, chopped
350 g/12 oz/3 cups raspberries
430 g/15¹/₂ oz/l large can creamed rice pudding

Put 30 ml/2 tbsp of the syrup in a bowl Divide the remainder between 6 sundae glasses. Sprinkle on the pecan nuts. Add 275 g/10 oz/2¹/₂ cups of the raspberries to the bowl and crush with the syrup. Fold in the rice pudding and divide between the sundae glasses. Decorate with the remaining raspberries and chill until ready to serve.

Peach Rice Ring

Serves 6

15 g/¹/₂ oz/1 tbsp powdered gelatine
60 ml/4 tbsp water
2 × 430 g/2 × 15 oz/2 large cans creamed rice pudding
5 ml/1 tsp vanilla essence (extract)
425 g/15 oz/1 large can peach slices, drained
150 ml/¹/₄ pt/²/₃ cup whipped cream
Glacé (candied) cherries
Angelica leaves

Dissolve the gelatine in the water in a bowl over a pan of hot water or in the microwave (do not allow to boil). Stir into the rice with the vanilla essence. Turn into a wetted ring mould (mold) and chill until set. Turn out on to a serving plate. Fill the centre with the peach halves, arranged attractively. Decorate with whipped cream, glacé cherries and angelica leaves.

Italian Cassata Rice

Serves 4

50 g/2 oz/¹/₃ cup currants
30 ml/2 tbsp Amaretti liqueur
425 g/15 oz/1 large can creamed rice
150 ml/¹/₄ pt/²/₃ cup plain yoghurt
50 g/2 oz/¹/₂ cup multicoloured glacé
  (candied) cherries, chopped
50 g/2 oz/¹/₂ cup toasted chopped
  nuts
15 g/¹/₂ oz/1 tbsp powdered gelatine
60 ml/4 tbsp water
300 g/11 oz/1 small can raspberries
  in natural juice
Icing (confectioners') sugar

Soak the currants in the liqueur for 30 minutes. Mix with the rice, yoghurt, cherries and nuts. Dissolve the gelatine in the water in a bowl over a pan of hot water or in the microwave (do not allow to boil). Stir into the rice, mixing well. Turn into 4 individual wetted moulds (molds) and chill until set. Sieve the raspberries and sweeten to taste with sifted icing sugar. Spoon on to serving plates and carefully turn out a cassata on to each.

Paphos Pleasure

Serves 4

230 g/15¹/₂ oz/1 large can creamed
  rice, chilled
2.5 ml/¹/₂ tsp ground cinnamon
30 ml/2 tbsp sultanas (golden
  raisins)
50 g/2 oz/¹/₂ cup halva, crushed
150 ml/¹/₄ pt/²/₃ cup Greek-style plain
  yoghurt
20 ml/4 tsp clear honey

Mix the rice with the cinnamon, sultanas and halva. Spoon into serving dishes, top with the yoghurt and a little swirl of honey. Serve straight away.

Vitality Pudding

Serves 4

100 g/4 oz/1 cup cold cooked brown
  rice
50 g/2 oz/¹/₃ cup sultanas (golden
  raisins)
50 g/2 oz/¹/₂ cup chopped nuts
300 ml/¹/₂ pt/1¹/₄ cups thick plain
  yoghurt
2 bananas, sliced
1 red eating (dessert) apple, diced
Lemon juice
Clear honey

Mix the rice with the sultanas, nuts and yoghurt. Toss the banana and apple in lemon juice to prevent browning. Add to the yoghurt mixture and fold in gently. Pile into wine goblets and drizzle thickly with the honey. Serve chilled.

Scandinavian Apple Rice

Serves 4-6

100 g/4 oz/¹/₂ cup brown rice
750 g/1¹/₂ lb cooking (tart) apples,
  sliced
45 ml/3 tbsp water
75 g/3 oz/¹/₃ cup butter
75 g/3 oz/¹/₃ cup light brown sugar
2.5 ml/¹/₂ tsp ground cinnamon
50 g/2 oz/1 cup cake crumbs
150 ml/¹/₄ pt/²/₃ cup double (heavy)
  cream
45 ml/3 tbsp redcurrant jelly (clear
  conserve)

Cook the rice according to the packet directions. Drain. Meanwhile, put the apples in a pan with the water and stew gently until pulpy. Beat in half the butter and sugar. Mix the remaining butter and sugar into the rice with the cinnamon and cook over a gentle heat until absorbed. Layer the apple and rice mixture in a glass serving dish. Top with a layer of cake crumbs and leave to cool. Whip the cream and spread over. Melt the redcurrant jelly and drizzle attractively all over the top. Chill until ready to serve.

Poached Pears on Rice

Serves 4
50 g/2 oz/¹/₄ cup short-grain (pudding) rice
600 ml/1 pt/2¹/₂ cups milk
45 ml/3 tbsp caster (superfine) sugar
15 g/¹/₂ oz/1 tbsp butter
4 pears, peeled, halved and cored
300 ml/¹/₂ pt/1¹/₄ cups apple juice
2.5 cm/1 in piece cinnamon stick
45 ml/3 tbsp light brown sugar
Crème fraîche
Chopped toasted nuts

Cook the rice in the milk for about 30 minutes until tender and creamy, stirring occasionally. Stir in the caster sugar and butter and leave to cool. Meanwhile, place the pears in a saucepan with the apple juice, cinnamon and light brown sugar. Cover and simmer gently for about 10 minutes until the pears are tender. Leave to cool in the syrup. Spoon the cold rice into glass dishes. Lay 2 pear halves on top of each and spoon a little of the syrup over. Put a dollop of crème fraîche on top and sprinkle with chopped nuts.

Gingered Pear Condé

Serves 4
Prepare as for Poached Pears on Rice. When the rice is cooked and the sugar and butter added, turn the mixture into a wetted mould (mold) and leave to set. Quarter instead of halve the pears. Poach in the same way but add 2 chopped pieces of stem ginger in syrup to the poaching liquid instead of cinnamon. Turn the mould out into a large serving dish and spoon the pears with their syrup around. Serve decorated with whipped cream instead of crème fraîche.

Chocolate Mousse Layer

Serves 6
175 g/6 oz/1¹/₂ cups plain (semi-sweet) chocolate, broken into pieces
3 size 1 eggs, separated
15 ml/1 tbsp rum or brandy
430 g/15¹/₂ oz/1 large can chocolate rice pudding
Whipped cream
A little grated chocolate

Melt the chocolate in a bowl over a pan of hot water or in the microwave. Stir in the egg yolks and brandy or rum. Whisk the egg whites until stiff and fold into the chocolate with a metal spoon. Layer the rice and chocolate mousse in sundae glasses. Chill until set. Decorate with whipped cream and a little grated chocolate.

Chocolate Banana Layer

Serves 6

Prepare as for Chocolate Mousse Layer, but substitute banana-flavoured rice pudding for the chocolate, and add a layer of sliced banana tossed in lemon juice in the centre.

Vanilla Fluff

Serves 4

30 ml/2 tbsp ground rice
A pinch of salt
600 ml/1 pt/2¹/₂ cups milk
2 eggs, separated
30 ml/2 tbsp caster (superfine) sugar
15 g/¹/₂ oz/1 tbsp butter
5 ml/1 tsp vanilla essence (extract)
Whipped cream (optional)

Put the rice with the salt and milk in a saucepan. Whisk in the egg yolks. Bring to the boil and cook for 5 minutes or until thickened and smooth. Stir in the sugar, butter and vanilla essence. Cool slightly. Whisk the egg whites until stiff and fold in with a metal spoon. Turn into 4 individual dishes and chill until set. Decorate with whipped cream, if liked, before serving.

Chocolate Fluff

Serves 4

Prepare as for Vanilla Fluff, but add 45 ml/3 tbsp cocoa (unsweetened chocolate) powder blended with 60 ml/4 tbsp boiling water to the cooked rice mixture.

Chocolate and Peppermint Fluff

Serves 4

Prepare as for Chocolate Fluff, but after cooking the rice mixture divide the mixture in half. Add half the chocolate flavouring to one half of the mixture and add a few drops of green food colouring and a few drops of peppermint essence (extract) to the remainder. Fold half the whisked egg whites into each mixture and spoon in layers in glass sundae dishes. Top each with a halved After Eight mint stuck in at a jaunty angle.

Chocolate Orange Fluff

Serves 4

Prepare as for Chocolate Peppermint Fluff, but instead of green colouring and peppermint essence (extract) add the grated rind of an orange and a few drops of orange food colouring to the plain mixture. Whisk the orange juice with 150 ml/¹/₄ pt/²/₃ cup of double (heavy) cream and swirl on top.

Tutti Frutti Fluff

Serves 4

Prepare as for Vanilla Fluff, but add 15 ml/1 tbsp each of chopped glacé (candied) cherries, chopped angelica, chopped mixed (candied) peel and chopped seedless (pitless) raisins to the mixture and flavour with the grated rind of 1 lemon.

Butterscotch Fluff

Serves 4

Prepare as for Vanilla Fluff, but melt the butter with 100 g/4 oz/¹/₂ cup dark brown sugar and a squeeze of lemon juice until dissolved then stir into the cooked rice and continue as before, omitting the caster (superfine) sugar.

Apricot Smoothie

Serves 4
410 g/14¹/₂ oz/1 large can apricots in natural juice
45 ml/3 tbsp ground rice
30 ml/2 tbsp caster (superfine) sugar
15 g/¹/₂ oz/1 tbsp butter
Crème fraîche
Chopped pistachio nuts

Purée the apricots with their juice in a blender or food processor. Make up to 600 ml/1 pt/2¹/₂ cups with water. Place in a saucepan and stir in the rice. Bring to the boil and simmer for 5 minutes, stirring, until thick. Sweeten to taste with the sugar and stir in the butter. Pour into individual glass dishes and chill until set. Top with crème fraîche and chopped pistachio nuts.

Raspberry Smoothie

Serves 4
Prepare as for Apricot Smoothie, but substitute a can of raspberries for the apricots. After puréeing, pass through a sieve (strainer) to remove the seeds. Top with Greek yoghurt flavoured with honey and decorate with chopped hazelnuts.

Blackcurrant Smoothie

Serves 4
Prepare as for Apricot Smoothie, but substitute a can of blackcurrants for the apricots. Top with whipped cream and decorate with crushed gingernut biscuits (cookies).

Rockley Beach Pudding

Serves 4
75 g/3 oz/³/₄ cup short-cut macaroni
425 g/15 oz/1 large can custard
30 ml/2 tbsp rum
2 bananas
5 ml/1 tsp lemon juice
150 ml/¹/₄ pt/²/₃ cup whipped cream
2 gingernut biscuits (cookies), crushed

Cook the macaroni in plenty of boiling water for 15 minutes until really soft. Drain, rinse with cold water and drain again. Mix with the custard and rum. Slice the bananas and toss in the lemon juice to prevent browning. Spoon into 4 sundae glasses. Top with the custard mixture. Spread the whipped cream over. Chill, if time, and top with the gingernuts just before serving.

Greek-style Green Fig Spinners

Serves 4
75 g/3 oz/³/₄ cup ruote
425 g/15 oz/1 large can green figs in syrup
5 ml/1 tsp cornflour (cornstarch)
300 ml/¹/₂ pt/1¹/₄ cups Greek-style plain yoghurt
Clear honey

Cook the pasta in plenty of boiling water for about 15 minutes until really soft. Drain, rinse with cold water and drain again. Meanwhile, drain the figs, reserving the juice. Blend a little of the juice with the cornflour in a saucepan. Stir in the remaining juice. Bring to the boil and cook for 1 minute, stirring. Leave to cool. Roughly chop the figs and add to the pasta with the fig juice sauce. Mix well. Divide between 4 individual dishes and top with yoghurt. Top the yoghurt with a swirl of honey and chill before serving.

More Than a Quick Trifle

Serves 6-8
4 trifle sponges
425 g/15 oz/l large can strawberries
30 ml/2 tbsp sherry
430 g/15 oz/l large can macaroni pudding
430 ml/15 oz/1 large can custard
Grated chocolate

Break up the sponges in a glass dish. Spoon the strawberries over with their juice and drizzle with the sherry. Spoon the macaroni pudding over, then top with the custard. Scatter grated chocolate over and chill until ready to serve.

Chocolate Rum 'n' Conchiglietti Mousse

Serves 6-8
50 g/2 oz/¹/₂ cup conchiglietti
175 g/6 oz/1¹/₂ cups plain (semi-sweet) chocolate
5 eggs, separated
5 ml/1 tsp instant coffee
30 ml/2 tbsp rum
300 ml/¹/₂ pt/1¹/₄ cups double (heavy) cream
Grated chocolate

Cook the pasta in boiling water for about 10 minutes until really tender. Drain, rinse with cold water and drain again. Melt the chocolate in a bowl over a pan of hot water, or in the microwave. Cool slightly, then beat in the egg yolks. Dissolve the coffee in the rum and stir into the chocolate. Whisk the egg whites until stiff and then the cream until peaking. Fold the cream into the chocolate mixture with the pasta shapes. Finally, fold in the egg whites. Turn into a serving dish. Chill until set, then decorate with grated chocolate.

Maraschino Macaroni

Serves 4
225 g/8 oz cooking (tart) apples, sliced
15 ml/1 tbsp water
15 g/¹/₂ oz/1 tbsp butter
Granulated sugar
1 small jar maraschino cherries
150 ml/¹/₄ pt/²/₃ cup double (heavy) cream
430 g/15¹/₂ oz/1 large can creamed macaroni pudding
Toasted flaked almonds

Cook the apples with the water and butter until pulpy. Beat well and sweeten to taste. Leave to cool. Halve the cherries, reserving the syrup. Mix the cherries with the apple. Whip the cream with 45 ml/3 tbsp of the maraschino syrup until peaking. Layer the macaroni pudding, apple and cream in glass sundae dishes, finishing with a layer of cream. Top with flaked almonds and chill until ready to serve.

Macaroni Cocktail Brulée

Serves 6
410 g/14¹/₂ oz/1 large can fruit
  cocktail, drained
430 g/15¹/₂ oz/1 large can creamed
  macaroni pudding
Dark brown sugar

Put the fruit cocktail in a shallow, flame-proof serving dish. Top with the macaroni pudding. Sprinkle liberally with the sugar to cover the top completely. Place under a hot grill (broiler) until the sugar melts and caramelizes. Chill until ready to serve.

Crunchy Orange Sundae

Serves 4
4 oranges, peeled and segmented
60 ml/4 tbsp sweet sherry
150 ml/¹/₄ pt/²/₃ cup double (heavy)
  cream
430 g/15¹/₂ oz/1 large can creamed
  macaroni pudding
A few drops of vanilla essence
  (extract)
4 meringues, crushed
Grated chocolate

Place the oranges in 4 sundae dishes. Spoon the sherry over. Whip the cream until softly peaking. Fold in the macaroni and flavour to taste with vanilla. Stir in the meringue and spoon on to the oranges. Top with grated chocolate and chill until ready to serve.

Lemon Cheese Pots

Serves 6
175 g/6 oz/1¹/₂ cups soup pasta
Grated rind and juice of 1 large
  lemon
200 g/7 oz/1 carton low-fat soft
  cheese
Caster (superfine) sugar
150 ml/¹/₄ pt/²/₃ cup double (heavy)
  cream
Crystallized (candied) lemon slices

Cook the pasta in plenty of boiling water until tender. Drain, rinse with cold water and drain again. Beat the lemon rind and juice with the cheese and sugar to taste until smooth. Whip the cream until lightly peaking and fold in with the pasta. Spoon into ramekin dishes (custard cups) and chill until set. Decorate with crystallized lemon slices.

Italian Peach Melba

Serves 6

1.2 litres/2 pts/5 cups milk
100 g/4 oz/1 cup conchiglietti or
other soup pasta
25 g/1 oz/¹/₄ cup cornflour
(cornstarch)
Caster (superfine) sugar
150 ml/¹/₄ pt/²/₃ cup double (heavy)
cream
30 ml/2 tbsp peach or amaretti
liqueur
300 g/11 oz/1 small can raspberries
in natural juice
30 ml/2 tbsp icing (confectioners')
sugar
6 canned white peach halves
6 scoops raspberry ripple ice cream

Put 90 ml/6 tbsp of the milk in a small
bowl. Pour the remainder in a saucepan.
Bring to the boil and add the pasta. Cook
for 15 minutes, stirring from time to time,
until the pasta is tender. Blend the cornflour with the reserved milk. Stir into the
pasta and cook, stirring for 2 minutes.
Sweeten to taste with caster sugar. Leave
to cool. Whip the cream with the liqueur
until lightly peaking, fold into the pasta
and divide between 6 dessert dishes. Pass
the raspberries through a sieve (strainer)
and stir in the sifted icing sugar. Put a
peach half, cut-side up, on top of the pasta
mixture. Add a scoop of the ice cream,
then drizzle the raspberry sauce over and
serve straight away.

Breads, Biscuits and Cakes

Ground rice and rice flour have long been favourites for improving the texture of many biscuits and cakes but you may not have thought of using cooked rice or pasta before. Here is an exciting array of recipes to revolutionise your baking.

Honeycombed Rice Bread

Makes 1 large loaf
75 g/3 oz/¹/₃ cup arborio or other risotto rice
500 ml/17 fl oz/2¹/₂ cups hand-hot water
15 g/¹/₂ oz/1 tbsp fresh yeast
30 ml/2 tbsp warm water
550 g/1¹/₂ lb/6 cups strong plain (bread) flour
15 ml/1 tbsp salt
A little extra flour
Butter for greasing

Put the rice in a saucepan with 250 ml/8 fl oz/1 cup of the hand-hot water. Bring to the boil, cover, reduce the heat and simmer very gently for about 25 minutes until the rice has absorbed all the liquid and bubble holes appear on the surface. Meanwhile, cream the yeast with the warm water. When the rice is cooked, stir in the flour, salt, creamed yeast and remaining hand-hot water. Mix to form a rather wet dough Cover with oiled polythene and leave in a warm place to rise for 1-1¹/₂ hours until doubled in size. Dust the top with flour, then knock back. Turn into a well-buttered large loaf tin (pan). Cover with the oiled polythene and leave until the dough rises above the top of the tin. Bake at 230°C/450°F/gas mark 8 for 15 minutes, then reduce the heat to 200°C/400°F/gas mark 6 and cook for a further 15 minutes. Turn out of the tin and return to the oven for a further 15 minutes to crisp and brown the crust. Cool on a wire rack.

Tangy Rice Tea Bread

Makes 2 loaves
100 g/4 oz/¹/₂ cup long-grain rice
300 ml/¹/₂ pt/1¹/₄ cups pure orange juice
400 g/14 oz/1³/₄ cups caster (superfine) sugar
2 eggs, beaten
Grated rind and juice of 1 orange
50 g/2 oz/¹/₄ cup butter, melted
225 g/8 oz/2 cups plain (all-purpose) flour
175 g/6 oz/1¹/₂ cups wholemeal flour
10 ml/2 tsp baking powder
5 ml/1 tsp bicarbonate of soda (baking soda)
5 ml/1 tsp salt
50 g/2 oz/¹/₂ cup chopped walnuts
50 g/2 oz/¹/₃ cup sultanas (golden raisins)
50 g/2 oz/¹/₄ cup icing (confectioners') sugar
Butter for spreading (optional)

Cook the rice in plenty of boiling salted water for about 15 minutes until tender. Drain, rinse with cold water and drain again. Meanwhile, mix the pure orange juice, sugar, eggs, all but 2.5 ml/¹/₂ tsp of the orange rind (reserve the rest and the

379

juice for the icing) and the melted butter in a mixing bowl. Sift the flours, baking powder, bicarbonate of soda and salt over the top, then tip in the bran remaining in the sieve. Fold in using a metal spoon. Fold in the cold rice, the nuts and sultanas. Turn into two 450 g/1 lb greased loaf tins (pans). Bake at 180°C/350°F/gas mark 4 for about 1 hour or until risen and golden and a skewer inserted in the centres comes out clean. Leave to cool in the tins for 10 minutes, then turn out on to a wire rack to cool. Blend the icing sugar with enough of the reserved orange juice and rind to form a smooth paste. Drizzle over the loaves and leave to set. Served sliced, with butter if liked.

Scottish Shortbread

Makes 2 × 20 cm/8 in shortbread
225 g/8 oz/1 cup butter
175 g/6 oz/³/₄ cup caster (superfine) sugar
400 g/14 oz/3¹/₂ cups plain (all-purpose) flour
50 g/2 oz/¹/₂ cup rice flour
5 ml/1 tsp baking powder

Cream the butter and sugar together until light and fluffy. Sift the flour, rice flour and baking powder together and knead into the mixture to form a smooth dough. Divide the mixture in half. Mark a 20 cm/8 in round on 2 sheets of baking parchment placed on baking sheets. Flatten the dough into the rounds. Pinch the edges between finger and thumb and prick all over with a fork. Bake at 160°C/325°F/gas mark 3 for about 40 minutes until a pale golden brown. Leave to cool for 10 minutes, then mark into eighths with the back of a knife and leave to cool completely. Store in an airtight tin.

Lemon Butter Biscuits

Makes about 20
100 g/4 oz/1 cup ground rice
100g/4 oz/1 cup plain (all-purpose) flour
75 g/3 oz/¹/₃ cup caster (superfine) sugar
A pinch of salt
2.5 ml/¹/₂ tsp baking powder
100 g/4 oz/¹/₂ cup butter
Grated rind of 1 lemon
1 egg, beaten

Mix the ground rice, flour, sugar, salt and baking powder together in a bowl. Rub in the butter until the mixture resembles fine breadcrumbs. Stir in the lemon rind and mix with enough of the egg to form a firm dough. Knead gently, then roll out on a floured surface and cut into shapes with a biscuit cutter. Place on a greased baking sheet and bake at 180°C/350°F/gas mark 4 for 30 minutes. Cool slightly then transfer to a wire rack to cool completely.

Almond Macaroons

Makes 10-20

Rice paper
100 g/4 oz/$1\frac{1}{2}$ cup caster (superfine)
  sugar
50 g/2 oz/$1\frac{1}{2}$ cup ground almonds
5 ml/1 tsp ground rice
A few drops of almond essence
  (extract)
1 size 1 egg white
Halved blanched almonds

Line a baking sheet with rice paper. Mix all the ingredients except the blanched almonds together to form a stiff paste. Beat well, then place spoonfuls of the mixture a little apart on the rice paper. Top each with a halved almond and bake for 25 minutes at 160°C/325°F/gas mark 3. Leave to cool on the baking sheet, then cut round each macaroon with scissors.

Hazelnut Dreams

Makes 12-18

3 egg whites
175 g/6 oz/$\frac{3}{4}$ cup caster (superfine)
  sugar
25 g/1 oz/2 tbsp ground rice
150 g/5 oz/$1\frac{1}{4}$ cups ground
  hazelnuts

Whisk the egg whites until stiff. In a separate bowl, mix the sugar, ground rice and hazelnuts together and fold in with a metal spoon. Spread to about 2 cm/$\frac{3}{4}$ in thick on a piece of non-stick baking parchment on a baking sheet. Bake at 180°C/350°F/gas mark 4 for 15-20 minutes until golden and crisp. Cut into squares, turn over carefully and dry off in the oven, turned down to 140°C/275°F/gas mark 1 for 15 minutes.

Jelly Centres

Makes about 12

50 g/2 oz/$\frac{1}{4}$ cup butter
50 g/2 oz/$\frac{1}{4}$ cup caster (superfine)
  sugar
100 g/4 oz/1 cup plain (all-purpose)
  flour
1 egg, separated
1.5 ml/$\frac{1}{4}$ tsp baking powder
50 g/2 oz/$\frac{1}{2}$ cup ground almonds
15 g/$\frac{1}{2}$ oz/1 tbsp ground rice
A few drops of almond essence
  (extract)
Chopped almonds
Seedless raspberry jam (clear
  conserve)

Cream the butter and half the sugar until light and fluffy. Add a little of the flour and the egg yolk and beat in well. Sift the remaining flour and the baking powder over the mixture. Work into the mixture until it forms a dough. Knead gently, then roll out and cut into rounds using a plain biscuit cutter. Transfer to a baking sheet. Mix the remaining sugar with the ground almonds, rice, essence and enough of the egg white to form a stiff paste. Beat well, then pipe a ring on top of each biscuit using a piping bag fitted with a large plain or star tube (tip). Sprinkle with the chopped nuts. Bake at 160°C/325°F/gas mark 3 for about 25 minutes or until golden. Transfer to a wire rack to cool. Spoon a little raspberry jam into the centre of each before serving.

Rice Cookies

Makes about 24
(depending on the size)
175 g/6 oz/¹/₂ cup clear honey
225 g/8 oz/1 cup granulated sugar
60 ml/4 tbsp water
350 g/12 oz/1 box puffed rice
  breakfast cereal
100 g/4 oz/1 cup roasted peanuts

Put the honey, sugar and water in a saucepan. Heat through until the sugar has completely melted. Leave to cool for 5 minutes then stir in the rice cereal and peanuts. Roll into balls, place in paper cases and leave until cool and set.

Chocolate Toffette

Makes about 225 g/8 oz
50 g/2 oz/¹/₄ cup butter
30 ml/2 tbsp golden (light corn)
  syrup
30 ml/2 tbsp cocoa (unsweetened
  chocolate) powder
60 ml/4 tbsp caster (superfine) sugar
50 g/2 oz/¹/₂ cup ground rice

Melt the butter and syrup in a saucepan. Stir in the cocoa and sugar until dissolved then stir in the ground rice. Bring gently to the boil, reduce the heat and bubble gently for 5 minutes, stirring all the time. Turn into a 20 cm/8 in square shallow tin (pan) lined with non-stick baking parchment. Cool slightly, then mark into squares with the back of a knife. Leave until completely cold, then lift out of the tin and cut into squares with a heavy knife. Store in an airtight container.

Brown Rice and Sunflower Bites

Makes 12-15
75 g/3 oz/³/₄ cup cooked brown rice
50 g/2 oz/¹/₂ cup sunflower seeds
25 g/1 oz/¹/₄ cup sesame seeds
40 g/1¹/₂ oz/¹/₄ cup seedless (pitless)
  raisins
40 g/1¹/₂ oz/¹/₄ cup glacé (candied)
  cherries, quartered
25 g/1 oz/2 tbsp dark brown sugar
15 ml/1 tbsp clear honey
75 g/3 oz/¹/₃ cup butter
5 ml/1 tsp lemon juice

Mix together the rice, seeds and fruit. Melt the sugar, honey, butter and lemon juice in a saucepan. Stir into the rice mixture and mix well. Divide the mixture between 12-15 paper cases on a baking sheet and bake at 200°C/400°F/gas mark 6 for 15 minutes. Cool on a wire rack and store in an airtight tin.

Spiced Rice and Muesli Cookies

Makes about 24
75 g/3 oz/³/₄ cup cooked brown rice
50 g/2 oz/¹/₂ cup muesli
75 g/3 oz/³/₄ cup wholemeal flour
2.5 ml/¹/₂ tsp salt
2.5 ml/¹/₂ tsp bicarbonate of soda (baking soda)
5 ml/1 tsp mixed (apple pie) spice
50 g/2 oz/¹/₆ cup clear honey
75 g/3 oz/¹/₃ cup butter or margarine

Mix together the rice, muesli, flour, salt, bicarbonate of soda and spice. Cream the butter and honey until soft. Beat into the rice mixture. Shape the mixture into walnut-sized balls and place well apart on greased baking sheets. Flatten slightly then bake at 190°C/375°F/gas mark 5 for 15 minutes or until golden brown. Leave to cool for 10 minutes then transfer to a wire rack to cook completely. Store in an airtight tin.

Grantham Gingerbreads

Makes 12
225 g/8 oz/2 cups plain (all-purpose) flour
2.5 ml/¹/₂ tsp ground mace
10 ml/2 tsp ground ginger
75 g/3 oz/¹/₃ cup butter
175 g/6 oz/³/₄ cup caster (superfine) sugar
1 size 4 egg, beaten
15 ml/1 tbsp lemon juice
30 ml/2 tbsp ground rice

Sift the flour and spices into a bowl. Rub in the butter, then stir in the sugar. Mix with the egg and lemon juice to form a firm dough. Knead gently. Dust a work surface liberally with the ground rice. Roll out the dough to about 1 cm/¹/₂ in thick. Cut into rounds with a large biscuit cutter. Transfer to greased baking sheets and bake for 20 minutes at 180°C/350°F/gas mark 4 until firm to the touch. Cool slightly, then transfer to a wire rack to cool completely.

Chocolate-topped Chocolate Chip Fingers

Makes 16
175 g/6 oz/³/₄ cup butter
75 g/3 oz/¹/₃ cup caster (superfine) sugar
175 g/6 oz/1¹/₂ cups plain (all-purpose) flour
50 g/2 oz/¹/₂ cup ground rice
75 g/3 oz/¹/₂ cup chocolate chips
100 g/4 oz/1 cup plain (semi-sweet) chocolate, melted

Cream the butter with the sugar until light and fluffy. Work in the flour and ground rice. Knead in the chocolate chips. Press into a Swiss (jelly) roll tin (pan) and prick with a fork. Bake at 160°C/325°F/gas mark 3 for 35-40 minutes until lightly golden. Cool slightly, then mark into fingers deeply with the back of a knife. Leave until cold. Spread the melted chocolate over and leave to set. Cut into fingers and store in an airtight tin.

Coconut and Chocolate Cakes

Makes 12

100 g/4 oz shortcrust pastry (basic
   pie crust)
50 g/2 oz/¹/₄ cup butter
50 g/2 oz/¹/₄ cup caster (superfine)
   sugar
1 egg, beaten
25 g/1 oz/2 tbsp rice flour
50 g/2 oz/¹/₂ cup desiccated
   (shredded) coconut
1.5 ml/¹/₄ tsp baking powder
Chocolate spread

Roll out the pastry and use to line the sections of a tartlet tin (patty pan). Cream the butter and sugar together. Beat in the egg and rice flour, then stir in the coconut and baking powder. Put a small spoonful of chocolate spread in the base of each pastry case. Spoon the coconut mixture over and bake for 15 minutes at 200°C/400°F/gas mark 6 until risen and golden. Cool in the tins for 5 minutes then transfer to a wire rack to cool completely.

Rice Crispy Cakes

Makes 25-30

50 g/2 oz/¹/₄ cup butter
30 ml/2 tbsp golden (light corn)
   syrup
50 g/2 oz/¹/₂ cup drinking (sweetened)
   chocolate powder
90 g/3¹/₂ oz/scant 2 cups puffed rice
   breakfast cereal

Melt the butter and syrup in a saucepan. Remove from the heat. Stir in the chocolate powder and cereal. Spoon into paper cake cases and chill until set.

Shakespeare's Fine Cakes

Makes about 24

175 g/6 oz/³/₄ cup unsalted (sweet)
   butter
100 g/4 oz/¹/₂ cup caster (superfine)
   sugar
1 egg, separated
175 g/6 oz/1¹/₂ cups plain (all-
   purpose) flour
25 g/1 oz/¹/₄ cup ground rice
2.5 ml/¹/₂ tsp ground cloves
1.5 ml/¹/₄ tsp ground mace
1.5 ml/¹/₄ tsp saffron powder

Cream the butter and sugar until light and fluffy. Beat in the egg yolk. Sift the flour, ground rice, cloves, mace and saffron together. Add to the creamed mixture and work with a wooden spoon until the mixture forms a ball. Press into a greased 23 cm/9 in square shallow baking tin (pan) or a Swiss (jelly) roll tin (pan). Brush with the lightly beaten egg white. Bake at 160°C/325°F/gas mark 3 for about 45 minutes or until firm to the touch. Cool slightly, then cut into squares and transfer to a wire rack to cool completely.

Scented Macaroon Cakes

Makes 12

*100 g/4 oz shortcrust pastry (basic
  pie crust)*
Lime marmalade
2 egg whites
*50 g/2 oz/¹/₄ cup caster (superfine)
  sugar*
25 g/1 oz/¹/₄ cup ground almonds
10 ml/2 tsp ground rice
5 ml/1 tsp orange flower water

Roll out the pastry and use to line the sections of a tartlet tin (patty pan). Put a small spoonful of marmalade into each pastry case. Whisk the egg whites until stiff. Whisk in the sugar until stiff and glossy. Fold in the almonds, rice and orange flower water. Spoon into the cases, covering the marmalade completely. Bake at 180°C/350°F/gas mark 4 for 30 minutes until risen and golden brown.

Arabian Rawanee

*225 g/8 oz/1 cup caster (superfine)
  sugar*
250 ml/8 fl oz/1 cup water
2.5 ml/¹/₂ tsp lemon juice
6 eggs
*A few drops of vanilla essence
  (extract)*
75 g/3 oz/³/₄ cup rice flour
2.5 ml/¹/₂ tsp baking powder

Heat the sugar, water and lemon juice in a pan, stirring until the sugar has dissolved. Simmer very gently for about 10 minutes until the syrup is thick but do not allow to colour. Leave to cool. Beat the eggs with an electric whisk for 5 minutes. Add the remaining ingredients and beat gently for at least 5 minutes. Turn into a non-stick 15 cm/6 in deep, round cake tin (or line with baking parchment if necessary). Bake at 150°C/300°F/gas mark 2 for 30 minutes until set. Do not open the door during cooking. Leave to cool in the tin, then cut into small shapes and drizzle with the syrup before lifting out and serving.

Portuguese Coconut Cake

4 eggs, separated
*450 g/1 lb/2 cups caster (superfine)
  sugar*
*450 g/1 lb/4 cups desiccated
  (shredded) coconut*
100 g/4 oz/1 cup rice flour
50 ml/2 fl oz/3¹/₂ tbsp rose water
1.5 ml/¹/₄ tsp ground cardamom
1.5 ml/¹/₄ tsp ground cinnamon
A pinch of ground cloves
A pinch of ground mace
25 g/1 oz/¹/₄ cup slivered almonds

Put the egg yolks in a bowl with the sugar and beat well. Stir in the coconut, then fold in the flour. Stir in the rose water and spices. Whisk the egg whites until stiff and fold into the mixture with a metal spoon. Pour into a greased baking tin (pan) and sprinkle the almonds over the top. Bake at 180°C/350°F/gas mark 4 for about 50 minutes or until a skewer inserted in the centre comes out clean. Leave to cool in the tin for 10 minutes, then cut into squares.

Angel's Food Cake

4 egg whites
2.5 ml/¹/₂ tsp cream of tartar
A few drops of vanilla essence
(extract)
150 g/5 oz/²/₃ cup caster (superfine)
sugar
50 g/2 oz/¹/₂ cup plain (all-purpose)
flour
15 g/¹/₂ oz/1 tbsp rice flour
A pinch of salt
A little vanilla-flavoured glacé icing

Dust a plain ring mould (mold) with flour (do not grease). Whisk the egg whites until frothy. Whisk in the cream of tartar and vanilla essence until stiff. Sift the sugar, flours and salt together twice. Fold a little at a time into the egg whites, using a metal spoon. Turn into the ring mould. Level the surface and bake at 160°C/325°F/gas mark 3 for about 30 minutes until firm. Leave the cake to cool in the tin. Loosen the edge, turn out and spoon a little glace icing over before serving.

Almond Rice Cake

225 g/8 oz/1 cup butter or margarine
225 g/8 oz/1 cup caster (superfine)
sugar
3 eggs, beaten
100 g/4 oz/1 cup plain (all-purpose)
flour
75 g/3 oz/³/₄ cup self-raising (self-
rising) flour
75 g/3 oz/³/₄ cup ground rice
2.5 ml/¹/₂ tsp almond essence (extract)

Beat the fat and sugar together until light and fluffy. Beat in the egg a little at a time. Sift the flours together and fold in with the ground rice and almond essence. Turn into

a greased and lined 20 cm/8 in round cake tin (pan) and bake at 150°C/300°F/gas mark 2 for 1¹/₄ hours or until firm to the touch. Cool in the tin for 10 minutes, then turn out on to a wire rack to cool completely.

Lemon Rice Square Cake

100 g/4 oz/¹/₂ cup butter
100 g/4 oz/¹/₂ cup caster (superfine)
sugar
2 eggs
100 g/4 oz/1 cup plain (all-purpose)
flour
50 g/2 oz/¹/₂ cup ground rice
2.5 ml/¹/₂ tsp baking powder
Grated rind and juice of 1 lemon
100 g/4 oz/¹/₂ cup icing
(confectioners') sugar, sifted

Cream the butter and sugar together until light and fluffy. Beat in the eggs one at a time, beating well after each addition. Mix the flour, rice and baking powder together with the lemon rind. Fold into the mixture with a metal spoon. Turn into a greased and lined 18 cm/7 in square cake tin (pan). Bake in the oven at 180°C/350°F/gas mark 4 for about 1 hour or until the centre springs back when lightly pressed. Cool slightly, then turn out, remove the paper and leave to cool on a wire rack. Make a smooth icing with a little of the lemon juice and the icing sugar. Spoon over the cake and leave to set.

Torta di Riso al Grand Marnier

1.5 litres/2¹/₂ pts/6 cups milk
A pinch of salt
350 g/12 oz/1¹/₂ cups arborio or
  other risotto rice
Grated rind of 1 lemon
60 ml/4 tbsp caster (superfine) sugar
3 size 1 eggs
25 g/1 oz/2 tbsp unsalted (sweet)
  butter
1 size 1 egg yolk
30 ml/2 tbsp chopped mixed
  (candied) peel
225 g/8 oz/2 cups toasted slivered
  almonds
45 ml/3 tbsp Grand Marnier
30 ml/2 tbsp dried breadcrumbs

Place the milk and salt in a heavy pan. Bring to the boil, add the rice and lemon rind, reduce the heat, cover and simmer for 18 minutes, stirring occasionally. Remove from the heat. Stir in the sugar, the whole eggs and butter and leave to cool. When just warm, beat in the egg yolk, peel, nuts and liqueur. Turn into a buttered 20 cm/ 8 in cake tin (pan), coated in the breadcrumbs. Smooth the surface and bake at 150°C/300°F/gas mark 2 for 45 minutes or until golden and a skewer inserted in the centre comes out clean. Leave to cool in the tin, turn out and serve just warm.

Cointreau Torte

Butter for greasing
25 ml/1¹/₂ tbsp breadcrumbs
1.5 litres/2¹/₂ pts/6 cups milk
A pinch of salt
350 g/12 oz/1¹/₂ cups short-grain
  (pudding) rice
Grated rind of 1 orange
60 ml/4 tbsp caster (superfine) sugar
3 size 1 eggs
25 g/1 oz/2 tbsp unsalted (sweet)
  butter
1 egg yolk
30 ml/2 tbsp chopped mixed
  (candied) peel
225 g/8 oz/2 cups toasted slivered
  almonds
45 ml/3 tbsp Cointreau

Grease a 20 cm/8 in square baking tin (pan) and dust with the breadcrumbs. Put the milk and salt in a saucepan and bring to the boil. Add the rice and orange rind, reduce the heat and simmer gently for 20 minutes or until the rice is just cooked but not too soft. Remove from the heat. Stir in the sugar, whole eggs and butter and when blended, leave to cool. When just warm, stir in the egg yolk, peel, almonds and liqueur. Turn into the prepared tin and level the surface. Bake at 150°C/300°F/gas mark 2 for 45 minutes or until golden and a skewer inserted in the centre comes out clean. Remove from the oven, leave to cool and serve cut into squares.

Cheese and Tomato Rolls

Makes 12
400 g/14 oz/3¹/₂ cups plain (all-purpose) flour
50 g/2 oz/¹/₂ cup rice flour
45 ml/3 tbsp baking powder
10 ml/2 tsp salt
5 ml/1 tsp mustard powder
5 ml/1 tsp cayenne
450 g/1 lb Cheddar cheese, grated
120 ml/4 fl oz/¹/₂ cup tomato relish
2 size 1 eggs, beaten
300 ml/¹/₂ pt/1¹/₄ cups milk
Butter

Sift the flour with the rice flour, baking powder, salt, mustard and cayenne. Stir in three-quarters of the cheese. Add the tomato relish, the eggs and enough milk to form a soft but not sticky dough. Knead gently on a lightly floured surface and shape into 12 rolls. Place on a lightly greased baking sheet brush with any remaining milk and sprinkle with the remaining cheese. Bake in the oven at 220°C/425°F/gas mark 7 for 20 minutes or until risen and golden brown. Serve warm with butter.

Country Griddle Cakes

Makes about 12
25 g/1 oz/2 tbsp butter, melted
100 g/4 oz/¹/₂ cup cottage cheese with chives
2 eggs, beaten
40 g/1¹/₂ oz/¹/₃ cup plain (all-purpose) flour
15 g/¹/₂ oz/2 tbsp rice flour
5 ml/1 tsp baking powder
15 ml/1 tbsp milk
Sunflower oil

Mix the butter with the cheese and beat in the remaining ingredients except the oil to form a thick batter. Heat a little oil in a frying pan (skillet). Drain off the excess. Fry (sauté) spoonfuls of the mixture in the pan until the undersides are golden. Turn over with a palette knife and cook the other sides. Wrap in a clean napkin while cooking the remainder. Serve hot.

Maple Dropped Scones

Makes about 30
200 g/7 oz/1³/₄ cups self-raising (self-rising) flour
25 g/1 oz/¹/₄ cup rice flour
10 ml/2 tsp baking powder
25 g/1 oz/2 tbsp caster (superfine) sugar
A pinch of salt
15 ml/1 tbsp maple syrup
1 egg, beaten
200 ml/7 fl oz/scant 1 cup milk
Sunflower oil
50 g/2 oz/¹/₄ cup butter, softened
15 ml/1 tbsp finely chopped walnuts or pecans

Sift the flour, rice flour, baking powder, sugar and salt together. Make a well in the centre. Add the maple syrup, egg and half the milk. Beat well until smooth, then stir in the remaining milk to form a thick batter. Heat a little oil in a large frying pan (skillet). Pour off the excess. Drop spoonfuls of the batter into the pan and cook until the undersides are golden. Flip over with a palette knife and cook the other sides. Keep warm in a clean napkin while cooking the remainder. Mash the butter with the nuts. Spread a little on each warm scone and serve.

Black Treacle and Ginger Scones

Makes 10

400 g/14 oz/3½ cups plain (all-purpose) flour
50 g/2 oz/½ cup rice flour
5 ml/1 tsp bicarbonate of soda
2.5 ml/½ tsp cream of tartar
10 ml/2 tsp ground ginger
2.5 ml/½ tsp salt
10 ml/2 tsp caster (superfine) sugar
50 g/2 oz/¼ cup butter
30 ml/2 tbsp black treacle (molasses)
300 ml/½ pt/1¼ cups milk
Butter and gooseberry jam
(conserve) (optional)

Sift all the dry ingredients together. Rub in the butter. Stir in the treacle and enough milk to form a soft but not sticky dough. Knead gently on a lightly floured surface and cut into 10 rounds, using a 7.5 cm/3 in fluted cutter. Place on a lightly greased baking sheet. Brush with any remaining milk to glaze and bake in the oven at 220°C/425°F/gas mark 7 for about 15 minutes until well risen and the bases sound hollow when tapped. Serve warm split and buttered and topped with gooseberry jam, if liked.

Yoghurt Scones

Makes 10

200 g/7 oz/1¾ cups plain (all-purpose) flour
25 g/1 oz/¼ cup rice flour
10 ml/2 tsp baking powder
A pinch of salt
15 ml/1 tbsp caster (superfine) sugar
50 g/2 oz/½ cup butter
150 ml/½ pt/⅔ cup plain yoghurt
Clotted cream
Strawberry jam (conserve)

Sift the flour, rice flour, baking powder, salt and sugar into a bowl. Add the butter and rub in with the fingertips until the mixture resembles breadcrumbs. Stir in the yoghurt to form a soft but not sticky dough. Flatten with the hand on a floured surface to about 2 cm/¾ in thick. Cut into 10 rounds using a 5 cm/2 in cutter. Place on a greased baking sheet and bake at 200°C/400°F/gas mark 6 for about 15 minutes until risen and golden and the bases sound hollow when tapped. Serve warm with cream and jam.

Fruity Chocolate Crisp Gateau

150 g/5 oz/²/₃ cup butter
30 ml/2 tbsp golden (light corn) syrup
175 g/6 oz/1¹/₂ cups digestive biscuits (Graham crackers), crushed
50 g/2 oz/2 cups puffed rice breakfast cereal
30 ml/2 tbsp sultanas (golden raisins)
25 g/1 oz/¹/₄ cup glacé (candied) cherries, chopped
25 g/1 oz/¹/₄ cup angelica, chopped
225 g/8 oz/2 cups chocolate dots
30 ml/2 tbsp water
175 g/6 oz/³/₄ cup icing (confectioners') sugar, sifted

Melt 100 g/4 oz/¹/₂ cup of the butter in a saucepan with the syrup. Remove from the heat and stir in the biscuits, rice cereal, sultanas, cherries, angelica and three-quarters of the chocolate dots. Mix well and press into a greased 450 g/1 lb loaf tin, lined with non-stick baking parchment. Chill until firm. Melt the remaining butter and chocolate in a saucepan with the water. Stir in the icing sugar until smooth. Remove the cake from the tin and carefully cut in halves lengthways. Sandwich together with a little of the icing. Place on a serving plate and spread the remaining icing over. Decorate with a fork and chill until ready to serve.

No-bake Chestnut Slice

225 g/8 oz/2 cups plain (semi-sweet) chocolate, broken into pieces
100 g/4 oz/¹/₂ cup butter, softened
100 g/4 oz/¹/₂ cup caster (superfine) sugar
450 g/16 oz/1 large can unsweetened chestnut purée
25 g/1 oz/¹/₄ cup rice flour
A few drops of vanilla essence (extract)
150 ml/¹/₄ pt/²/₃ cup whipping cream
Grated chocolate

Melt the chocolate in a bowl over a pan of hot water or in the microwave. Cream the butter and sugar until light and fluffy. Beat in the purée, melted chocolate, rice flour and a few drops of vanilla essence. Turn into a greased 450 g/1 lb loaf tin, lined with non-stick baking parchment. Chill until firm. Turn out on to a serving plate and remove the paper. Decorate with whipped cream and grated chocolate before serving.

Chocolate Coconut Crunchies

Makes about 12
100 g/4 oz/1 cup plain (semi-sweet) chocolate, broken into pieces
30 ml/2 tbsp milk
30 ml/2 tbsp golden (light corn) syrup
100 g/4 oz/4 cups puffed rice breakfast cereal
50 g/2 oz/¹/₂ cup desiccated (shredded) coconut
Paper cake cases (cupcake papers)

Melt the chocolate, milk and syrup in a saucepan. Remove from the heat and stir in the rice cereal and coconut. Put spoonfuls into the cake cases and leave to set.

White Chocolate and Raisin Crunchies

Makes about 12

Prepare as for Chocolate Coconut Crunchies but use white chocolate instead of plain (semi-sweet), 175 g/6 oz/6 cups rice cereal and substitute 50 g/2 oz/¹/₃ cup seedless (pitless) raisins, roughly chopped, for the coconut.

Pasta Ribbon Cake

*300 g/11 oz/2³/₄ cups plain (all-
  purpose) flour*
50 g/2 oz/¹/₄ cup butter, melted
3 size 1 eggs, beaten
A pinch of salt
Oil or butter for greasing
Flour for dusting
225 g/8 oz/2 cups chopped almonds
*200 g/7 oz/scant 1 cup caster
  (superfine) sugar*
Grated rind and juice of 1 lemon
90 ml/6 tbsp kirsch

Sift the flour into a bowl. Make a well in the centre and pour in the butter, eggs and salt. Knead together with the fingers to form a soft dough. Roll out thinly and cut into narrow ribbons. Cover with a clean tea towel (dish cloth). Grease a 23 cm/9 in cake tin (pan) and dust with a little flour. Mix the chopped almonds with the sugar and lemon rind. Arrange a layer of the pasta ribbons in the base of the tin. Sprinkle with a little of the almond mixture and drizzle with a little of the liqueur. Continue layering, ending with a layer of pasta. Cover with buttered greaseproof (waxed) paper and bake at 180°C/350°F/gas mark 4 for 1 hour. Carefully loosen the edges and turn out on to a serving plate. Serve warm or cold.

Pasta Coconut Bites

Serves 8

900 ml/1¹/₂ pts/3³/₄ cups water
225 g/8 oz/2 cups soup pasta shapes
225 g/8 oz/1 cup dark brown sugar
2.5 ml/¹/₂ tsp salt
*100 g/4 oz/1 cup sweetened
  desiccated (shredded) coconut*
*A few drops each of green and pink
  food colouring*
Paper cake cases (cupcake papers)

Bring the water to the boil, add the pasta, sugar and salt and simmer for about 15 minutes until the pasta is soft and the mixture is thick. Turn into a shallow greased tin (pan) and leave to cool. Colour half the coconut green and half pink. Take spoonfuls of the mixture, roll into balls, then roll half of the balls in the green coconut, the other in pink, to coat completely. Place in paper cases to serve as cakes for tea or as sweetmeats with after-dinner coffee.

Leftover Luxuries for the Connoisseur

Quite often when you cook rice or pasta plain, you do too much and wonder what to do with the remainder. Invariably it isn't enough for another meal on its own, so here are some clever quickies.

Simple Soups

Radical Tomato and Orange Soup

Mix a large can of cream of tomato soup with a 250 ml/8 fl oz/1 cup of pure orange juice. Add 30 ml/2 tbsp of cold cooked long-grain rice and serve hot or cold.

Minted Pea Soup Surprise

Purée a large can of minted garden peas and stir in 300 ml/¹/₂ pt/1¹/₄ cups of milk. Season well with salt and freshly ground black pepper and stir in 30-45 ml/2-3 tbsp of cooked long-grain rice. Heat through and serve with croûtons.

Oxtail Extra

Heat a large can of oxtail soup with 30 ml/2 tbsp of port or medium dry sherry. Stir in 45 ml/3 tbsp of cooked brown rice and serve.

Consommé with Peas and Rice

Heat a can of condensed consommé with 2 cans of water and 30 ml/2 tbsp of red wine. Stir in 30 ml/2 tbsp of cooked peas and 30 ml/2 tbsp of cooked long-grain rice.

Crab Bisque Special

Heat a can of crab bisque. Stir in a can of dressed crab and 150 ml/¹/₄ pt/²/₃ cup of single (light) cream. Add 15 ml/1 tbsp of brandy and 30 ml/2 tbsp of cooked long-grain rice.

Mushroom and Wild Rice Wonder

Heat a large can of cream of mushroom soup. Meanwhile fry (sauté) 3-4 sliced button mushrooms in a little butter until just cooked. Stir into the soup. Ladle into soup bowls and top each with a small spoonful of Mascarpone cheese, or a swirl of single (light) cream, and a spoonful of wild rice.

Asparagus Extra

Heat a large can of asparagus soup. Add a small can of cut asparagus, including the liquid. Gently stir in 45 ml/3 tbsp of cooked brown rice. Top each portion with a swirl of single (light) cream.

Pretend Minestrone

Heat a large can of vegetable soup. Add a small can of chopped tomatoes, 2.5 ml/ ½ tsp of dried oregano and 30 ml/2 tbsp of cooked macaroni or chopped spaghetti. Serve with grated Parmesan cheese.

Curried Dhal Soup

Heat a large can of pease-pudding. Thin down to taste with chicken or beef stock. Stir in 10 ml/2 tsp of toasted onion flakes and 15 ml/1 tbsp of curry paste. Stir in 30 ml/2 tbsp of cooked long-grain rice and sweeten, if liked, with a little mango chutney.

Quick Chicken Noodle Soup

Mix 600 ml/1 pt/2½ cups of boiling water with 2 chicken stock cubes. Add chopped cooked vermicelli and a little chopped parsley and serve.

Quick Cheese and Onion Soup

Make up a packet of onion sauce mix according to the packet directions. Thin down with stock or milk. Stir in a good handful of grated strong Cheddar cheese and add 30 ml/2 tbsp of cooked pasta shapes.

Ravioli Soup (a storecupboard standby)

Mix a good 15 ml/1 tbsp of yeast extract with 600 ml/1 pt/2½ cups of boiling water. Stir in a large can of ravioli in tomato sauce and heat through. Serve with grated cheese to sprinkle over.

Sneaky Nibbles and Starters

Stuffed Pepper Rings

Mash smooth liver pâté with a little butter, some cooked long-grain rice and some snipped chives. Cut off the tops and remove the seeds from (bell) peppers. Pack the mixture inside and chill. Cut into slices and serve.

Tuna Cheese Slices

Mash a can of drained tuna with the same weight of low-fat soft cheese. Stir in 45 ml/3 tbsp of cooked long-grain rice and season with lemon juice, some chopped parsley and a little salt and pepper. Shape into a roll on greaseproof (waxed) paper. Roll up and chill. Cut into slices and serve on plates, garnished with a little salad.

Stuffed Salad Bits

Mix 45 ml/3 tbsp of cooked brown rice with 15 ml/1 tbsp of currants and 15 ml/ 1 tbsp of pine nuts. Moisten with French dressing and use to fill hollowed-out chunks of cucumber or ripe tomatoes.

Cheesey Fruit Rolls

Put a small carton of low-fat cheese with chives in a bowl. Work in a little cooked long-grain rice and stir in a small can of drained mandarin oranges. Spread on square slices of ham, cut in half. Roll up and secure with cocktail sticks (toothpicks).

Salami Curls

Mix a small carton of low-fat soft cheese with a little cooked long-grain rice. Add a chopped canned pimiento and moisten with a little milk if too stiff. Spread on slices of salami, roll up and secure with cocktail sticks (toothpicks).

Party Patties

Mix any finely chopped cold cooked left-over vegetables with any cold cooked rice. Add Worcestershire sauce, salt and pepper to taste and enough beaten egg to bind. Shape into small flat cakes. Dust with flour and fry (sauté) in a little olive oil until crisp and golden. Serve on their own or with a yoghurt and mint dip.

Prawn and Coleslaw Canapés

Mix a small carton of coleslaw with enough cold cooked rice to absorb the dressing. Add a few prawns. Pile into small ready-made pastry shells and serve topped with a slice of stuffed olive.

Prawn-stuffed Lettuce

Mix a drained can of prawns with a little cooked long-grain rice and moisten with mayonnaise. Season to taste. Spoon a little on to round lettuce leaves. Fold in the sides and roll up.

Curried Rice Balls

Mix a little low-fat soft cheese with curry paste and a dash of tomato purée (paste) to taste. Work in enough cold cooked rice to form a stiff mixture. Roll into balls and chill.

Cheese Footballs

Finely grate a little strong Cheddar cheese. Mix with a dash of single (light) cream and some snipped chives. Work in some cold cooked rice, then shape into small balls. Chill.

Cheese 'n' Tomato Wild Rice Balls

Mash a small carton of low-fat soft cheese with 1 sachet of instant tomato soup. Roll in cooked wild rice and chill.

Garlic and Herb Bites

Mash garlic and herb soft cheese with a little milk to give a smooth piping consistency. Pipe the mixture into cooked rigatoni or penne, using a piping bag fitted with a fairly small plain tube (tip). Dip one end of the tubes in mayonnaise, yoghurt or cream, then in finely chopped parsley or paprika.

Hot Stuff

As Garlic and Herb Bites, but substitute soft cheese with black pepper for the garlic and herb cheese.

Liver Sausage Lovelies

As Garlic and Herb Bites, but substitute liver sausage mashed with a little single (light) cream for the cheese.

Pâté-stuffed Mushrooms

Mash some smooth liver pâté with garlic with some cooked long-grain rice. Add a little chopped parsley. Peel some flat mushrooms. Remove and chop the stems and add to the stuffing. Press the stuffing on to the black gills. Lay in a roasting tin (pan) and season with salt and a good grinding of pepper. Pour a little white wine mixed with water around. Cover with foil and bake at 190°C/375°F/gas mark 5 for about 15-20 minutes until the mushrooms are tender. Transfer to warm serving plates. Boil the juices rapidly until well reduced. Spoon over and serve hot.

Blue Cheese Pears

Mash some blue Stilton cheese with cold cooked long-grain rice and moisten with mayonnaise to make a stiffish paste. Pile on to drained canned pear halves and arrange on a bed of lettuce.

Conchiglie Olives

Put a stuffed olive into each conchiglie shell. Spear on cocktail sticks (toothpicks) and serve with a hot chilli salsa.

Smoked Mussel Maruzze

Put a smoked mussel inside each cooked pasta shell. Spear on cocktail sticks and serve with a horseradish-flavoured mayonnaise as a dip.

Tortellini with Bacon

Wrap half a stretched bacon rasher round a piece of cooked tortellini. Bake in a moderately hot oven for about 15 minutes or grill (broil), turning once until the bacon is cooked. Serve speared on cocktail sticks (toothpicks).

Salty Crunchies

Deep-fry cooked pasta shapes in hot oil until crisp and golden. Drain on kitchen paper. Toss in either plain, onion or garlic salt. For those who like their nibbles hot, mix the salt with a little chilli powder and a pinch of mixed (apple-pie) spice.

Spaghetti Nests

Take small handfuls of cold cooked spaghetti. Shape into nests. Lower into hot oil and deep-fry until golden and crisp. Drain on kitchen paper. Fill with diced Mozzarella and chopped cherry tomatoes, sprinkle lightly with olive oil and a good grinding of black pepper, and top with a few torn basil leaves.

Sausage Satay

Thread cooked cocktail sausages and cooked rigatoni alternately on to wooden skewers or cocktail sticks (toothpicks). Serve with commercial peanut satay sauce or make your own by mixing crunchy peanut butter with canned coconut milk to a dipping consistency. Stir in chilli powder, lemon juice and sugar to taste. Serve the sauce hot or cold.

Special Baked Eggs

Put a few cooked pasta shapes in the base of buttered ramekins (custard cups). Top with a little passata (sieved tomatoes) and a little chopped basil (or a pinch of dried will do). Break an egg over each. Top with a spoonful of single (light) cream and a little salt and pepper. Bake for 20-25 minutes until the eggs are cooked to your liking.

Canapés on Rice Cakes

Snack-sized rice cakes are the ideal vehicle for a variety of nibbles to have with drinks or as part of a finger buffet. Spread them lightly with butter before adding the toppings to prevent them going soggy.

Spicy Avocado Cream

Mash a small ripe avocado with a little lemon juice until smooth. Add 30 ml/ 2 tbsp of mayonnaise, 5 ml/1 tsp of Worcestershire sauce, a few drops of Tabasco sauce (to taste) and a little salt and pepper. Spoon on to the cakes and garnish with tiny wedges of cherry tomato and a sprinkling of snipped chives.

Cream Cheese and Caviare

Spread the cakes with a little cream or low-fat soft cheese and top each with 2.5 ml/ ½ tsp of Danish lumpfish roe.

Scrambled Egg and Smoked Salmon

Scramble an egg with a knob of butter and 10 ml/2 tsp of single (light) cream. Season with salt and pepper. Spoon on to the cakes and top with a tiny curl of smoked salmon.

Hard-boiled Egg and Anchovy

Slice hard-boiled (hard-cooked) eggs, lay a slice on each rice cake, and top with a rosette of mayonnaise and a curl of canned anchovy fillet.

Taramasalata Tickle

Pipe or spoon a swirl of taramasalata (cods' roe pâté) on each cake and top with a dusting of paprika and a piece of pickled chilli.

Hummus with Olives

Swirl hummous (chick pea (garbanzo) pâté) on the cakes and top each with half a stoned (pitted) black olive and a dusting of cayenne.

Garlic and Herb Cheese with Bacon

Pipe or swirl garlic and herb soft cheese on the cakes. Top with tiny grilled or fried (sautéed) bacon curls.

Minted Cucumber Cooler

Grate cucumber, squeeze out the excess moisture and dry on kitchen paper. Mix with low-fat soft cheese and a little thick plain yoghurt. Add chopped mint, salt and pepper to taste. Spoon on to the rice cakes and top each with a tiny sprig of mint and a quarter slice of cucumber.

Fromage Frais and Strawberry

Pipe or swirl fromage frais on the cakes. Halve small strawberries, trying to keep half a green hull on each. Make several slits from the point to the green hull. Gently open out and place on the cheese.

Sardine and Gherkin

Mash drained sardines with a little low-fat soft cheese. Add a pinch of cayenne and spike with lemon juice. Spoon on to the cakes. Make several slits lengthways in cocktail gherkins (cornichons), not quite through the stalk end. Gently open out to a fan and place on top of the sardine mixture.

Pâté with Peppers

Mash smooth liver pâté with a little softened butter or low-fat soft cheese to form a soft paste. Add a little chopped red (bell) pepper and the green part of spring onion (scallion). Cut small diamonds from the remaining pepper and slices from the white part of the onion. Swirl the pâté mixture on the cakes and top each with a diamond of pepper and a slice of onion.

Prawn Cocktail

Chop peeled prawns (shrimp) and bind with a little mayonnaise. Stir in just enough tomato ketchup (catsup) to colour the mixture pink and add a few drops of Worcestershire sauce. Season lightly. Put a tiny curl of lettuce on each rice cake. Top with a spoonful of the prawn mixture and garnish with a whole peeled prawn and a tiny parsley sprig.

Ploughman's Special

Mix grated red Leicester or Cheddar cheese with a little softened butter and pickle to taste. Pile the mixture on to the cakes. Top each with a cocktail onion and a tiny wedge of cherry tomato.

Cottage Ham and Pineapple

Cut out rounds of ham the same size as the cakes using a biscuit cutter. Place on the cakes and top with a small spoonful of cottage cheese with pineapple.

Cheesey Pepper and Mandarin

Mash some low-fat or cream cheese with a little chopped green (bell) pepper. Spread on the cakes and top each with a drained canned mandarin.

Curried Chicken

Finely chop cooked chicken and bind with mayonnaise and a little curry paste to taste. Spoon on to the rice cakes and top each with a tiny triangular piece of sliced lemon and a piece of coriander (cilantro) leaf.

Chicken Tropicana

Mix 45 ml/3 tbsp of cold cooked rice with 6 chopped apricots, 15 ml/1 tbsp of desiccated (shredded) coconut and 1 small mashed banana. Season well with salt and freshly ground black pepper and 15 ml/ 1 tbsp of chopped parsley. Make a slit along the top of 4 chicken breasts. Spoon in the stuffing, sew up or secure with cocktail sticks. Brush with oil or butter and grill (broil) or fry (sauté) until golden and cooked through. Deglaze the juices in the pan with a little chicken stock and spoon over.

Herby Rice Parcels

Mix 60 ml/4 tbsp of cold cooked brown rice with 30 ml/2 tbsp of mixed chopped herbs. Add a crushed garlic clove, if liked. Season well and add a beaten size 4 egg. Use to stuff chicken breasts and cook as for Chicken Tropicana.

Lemony Rice Chicken

Mix 60 ml/4 tbsp of cold cooked wild rice mix with the grated rind and juice of 1 lemon, 15 ml/1 tbsp of chopped parsley, a crushed garlic clove and some salt and pepper. Add a beaten size 4 egg and continue as for Chicken Tropicana.

Pizza Pasta Chicken

Mix 45 ml/3 tbsp of chopped cooked pasta with 45 ml/3 tbsp of grated Mozzarella and 15 ml/1 tbsp of grated Parmesan. Add 2 chopped tomatoes and 2.5 ml/^{1}/$_2$ tsp of dried oregano. Mix together. Season, then stuff the chicken and cook as for Chicken Tropicana.

Tuna-stuffed Chicken

Mix 45 ml/3 tbsp of chopped cooked pasta with 95 g/3^1/$_2$ oz/1 small can of drained tuna. Moisten with mayonnaise and a little lemon juice. Season, then stuff the chicken and cook as for Chicken Tropicana.

Minted Pea Lamb

Mix 60 ml/4 tbsp of cooked long-grain rice with 50 g/2 oz/^{1}/$_2$ cup of cooked peas and 5 ml/1 tsp of dried mint. Season with salt and pepper and add a little beaten egg to bind. Spread over a boned breast of lamb. Roll up and secure. Season with pepper. Weigh the joint then roast at 190°C/ 375°F/gas mark 5 for 20 minutes per 450 g/1 lb plus 20 minutes over. Leave to stand for 10 minutes before carving into thick slices. Use the pan juices to make gravy.

Redcurrant Rice Regalia

Mix 60 ml/4 tbsp of cooked brown rice with 25 g/1 oz of chopped mushrooms, 15 ml/1 tbsp of redcurrant jelly (clear conserve), 15 ml/1 tbsp of port and a good pinch of mixed herbs. Spread over a boned breast of lamb. Roll up and continue as for Minted Pea Lamb.

Eastern Stuffed Lamb

Mix 60 ml/4 tbsp of cooked basmati rice with 5 ml/1 tsp of curry powder, 2.5 ml/ ^{1}/$_2$ tsp of garam masala, 10 ml/2 tsp of mango chutney, 10 ml/2 tsp of currants and 30 ml/2 tbsp of cooked chopped carrots. Moisten with a little plain yoghurt if necessary. Spread over a boned breast of lamb. Roll up and continue as for Minted Pea

Lamb. If liked, rub the outer skin with a little garam masala too.

Paprika Stuffed Lamb

Mix 60 ml/4 tbsp of chopped cooked pasta with 1 chopped canned pimiento, 15 ml/ 1 tbsp of paprika, 15 ml/1 tbsp of tomato ketchup (catsup), 2.5 ml/½ tsp of dried mixed herbs and 1 finely chopped stick of celery. Spread over a boned breast of lamb. Roll up and continue as for Minted Pea Lamb, rubbing the outer skin with a little more paprika. Stir a little single (light) cream into the gravy.

Garlic and Rosemary Lamb

Mix 60 ml/4 tbsp of chopped cooked pasta with 50 g/2 oz/¼ cup of softened butter, 5 ml/1 tsp of crushed dried rosemary and a crushed garlic clove. Work in 100 g/4 oz/ 2 cups of finely chopped mushrooms and season well. Spread over a boned breast of lamb. Roll up and continue as for Minted Pea Lamb. Deglaze the pan juices to serve over the lamb.

Pyrenees Pork

Shred 4 slices of salami with 45 ml/3 tbsp of cooked rice, a chopped tomato and 4 sliced stoned (pitted) black olives. Add a good grinding of black pepper and a little salt. Toss in olive oil until hot. Meanwhile, fry (sauté) 4 pork chops in a little butter. Transfer to serving plates and pile the rice mixture on top. Deglaze the pan juices with a little stock, season and pour over.

Pork Fillet with Apricots

Mix 45 ml/3 tbsp of cooked rice with 6-8 chopped ready-to-eat dried apricots, 10 ml/2 tsp of pine nuts and 15 ml/1 tbsp of chopped chives. Moisten with a little orange juice. Season well. Make a slit down the length of a 450 g/1 lb piece of pork fillet. Spoon in the stuffing. Tie up securely. Melt a little butter and olive oil in a heavy frying pan (skillet). Brown the meat quickly all over. Reduce the heat, cover and cook gently for about 40 minutes until tender and cooked through. Carve into thick slices and serve with a sauce made from the pan juices, a little stock and a splash of apricot liqueur, brandy or kirsch and thickened with cornflour (cornstarch) if necessary.

Pasta and Orange-stuffed Vegetables

Mix 60 ml/4 tbsp of chopped cooked pasta with a peeled, chopped orange, a handful of chopped walnuts and a handful of chopped parsley. Season well and use to stuff halved, seeded courgettes (zucchini), halved, seeded (bell) peppers or slices of marrow (squash). Place in a roasting tin (pan) with 2.5 cm/1 in of water. Sprinkle liberally with grated cheese, cover with foil and bake for about 30 minutes at 190°C/375°F/gas mark 5 until tender.

Tomato Birds

Mix skinned, seeded, chopped tomatoes with chopped cooked pasta. Add a few shredded basil leaves, a good squeeze of tomato purée (paste), a pinch of caster (superfine) sugar and lots of salt and pepper. Beat to flatten chicken or turkey breasts, veal escalopes, or pieces of pork fillet. Spread with the stuffing, roll up and secure with cocktail sticks (toothpicks). Brown in butter in a flameproof casserole (Dutch oven). Pour over a little stock and cook in the oven for about 40 minutes at 190°C/375°F/gas mark 5 until cooked through and tender.

Pork and Rice Balls

Mince (grind) cooked leftover pork, with a small onion and a few sage leaves. Mix with an equal quantity of cooked rice. Season well and add enough beaten egg to bind. Shape into balls with well-floured hands and shallow-fry in hot oil until golden all over. Serve with hot passata (sieved tomatoes).

Ham Wellington

Cut a 450 g/1 lb/1 large round can of cooked ham into 3 or 4 slices, discarding the jelly. Mix a little cold cooked rice with some canned chopped pineapple and a chopped tomato. Add 2.5 ml/½ tsp of dried mixed herbs. Roll out a packet of puff pastry (paste) and cut into 4 squares. Put a slice of ham on each and top with the rice mixture. Brush the edges with water. Wrap the pastry over to form parcels. Place sealed sides down on a dampened baking sheet. Decorate with any pastry trimmings. Brush with milk, beaten egg, cream or yoghurt. Bake in a hot oven at 200°C/400°F/gas mark 6 for about 15 minutes until the pastry is puffed and golden. Serve with redcurrant jelly (clear conserve) melted in a little orange juice and a dash of port or sherry.

Quick Coulibiacs

Mix a little cold cooked rice with a small can of drained salmon, a few cooked peas, a chopped hard-boiled (hard-cooked) egg, some salt and pepper and a pinch of nutmeg. Moisten with cream or yoghurt. Spoon into the centres of squares of puff pastry (paste). Dampen the edges, then fold over to form parcels. Invert on a dampened baking sheet. Make several slashes in the pastry. Brush and bake as for Ham Wellington.

Risotto al Salto

Coat the base of a non-stick frying pan (skillet) with a little olive oil. Press a thin, even layer of any leftover risotto into the pan over a gentle heat. Cook slowly until the base is golden brown and crusty. Loosen, then flip over like a pancake and continue cooking until the other side is golden and crisp. Slide on to a warm serving plate and serve cut into wedges.

Curry Puffs

Mix a can of chicken or meat curry with enough cooked rice to form a stiffish mixture. Divide between squares of puff pastry (paste). Brush the edges with water then fold over to form triangles. Knock up the edges and crimp between a finger and thumb. Transfer to a dampened baking sheet. Brush with a little beaten egg or milk and cook in the oven at 200°C/400°F/gas mark 6 until puffy and golden brown. Serve hot or cold.

Curried Veggie Bites

Mix a can of curried beans with enough cooked long-grain rice to absorb the tomato sauce. Roll out puff pastry (paste) and cut into squares. Put a spoonful of the mixture in the centre of each. Brush the edges with milk or beaten egg. Fold over to form triangles and knock up the edges. Brush with milk or beaten egg, transfer to a dampened baking sheet and bake at

200°C/400°F/gas mark 6 for about 15 minutes or until puffy and golden brown.

Celery au Gratin

Put a layer of leftover cooked pasta in the base of an ovenproof dish. Cover with canned celery hearts. Top with cheese sauce (a packet mix is fine) and sprinkle with buttered breadcrumbs. Bake at 190°C/375°F/gas mark 5 for about 25 minutes until turning golden on top.

Lasagnette

Use up the last couple of sheets of broken lasagne in a packet. Break into small bits. Layer with a large can of ratatouille in an ovenproof dish. Top with grated Cheddar cheese and bake at 190°C/375°F/gas mark 5 for about 30 minutes until the pasta is tender and the top is golden brown.

Store-cupboard Stir-fry

Heat a little oil in a large frying pan (skillet) or wok. Add a drained can of stir-fry vegetables, any leftover cooked spaghetti, ribbon noodles or other strands of pasta, chopped cooked chicken, turkey, pork or canned or frozen prawns. Toss over a moderate heat and add a little ground ginger, light brown sugar, a dash of sherry and soy sauce to taste. Toss until piping hot and serve straight away.

Monday Spring Rolls

Chop or shred any leftover cooked vegetables from the Sunday roast. Add a little chopped meat if liked and any cooked strands of pasta (quantity doesn't matter at all). Season with garlic salt and sprinkle with soy sauce. Add a pinch of ground ginger, if liked. Spoon on to squares of filo or thinly rolled puff pastry (paste). Dampen the edges, fold in the sides, then roll up. Deep-fry in hot oil until crisp and golden. Drain on kitchen paper.

Emerald Island Bake

Mix a large can of Irish stew with a little cold cooked pasta. Place half in an ovenproof dish. Top with a layer of thawed frozen chopped spinach, then the remaining stew mixture. Top with buttered breadcrumbs and bake at 190°C/375°F/gas mark 5 for 30 minutes.

Index

404